Studies in Adolescence

A Book of Readings in Adolescent Development

THIRD EDITION

SELECTED AND EDITED BY

Robert E. Grinder

Arizona State University

Macmillan Publishing Co., Inc.
New York

Collier Macmillan Publishers
London

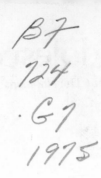

MACMILLAN PUBLISHING CO., INC.
866 THIRD AVENUE, NEW YORK, NEW YORK 10022

COLLIER-MACMILLAN CANADA, LTD.

Library of Congress Cataloging in Publication Data

Grinder, Robert E.   ed.
    Studies in adolescence.

    Includes bibliographical references and index.
    1. Adolescence—Addresses, essays, lectures.
I. Title.
BF724.G7   1975   155.5'08   74–11750
ISBN 0–02–347300–2

Printing: 1 2 3 4 5 6 7 8   Year: 5 6 7 8 9 0

Preface

THIS volume marks the third edition of *Studies in Adolescence*. Earlier versions published in 1963 and 1969 introduced students to a series of exploratory investigations concerning the nature of adolescence. The present volume brings together current, substantive studies; it is comprised of theoretical discussions and empirical tests of propositions and hypotheses, which provide a basis for deriving predictions of adolescent behavior in contemporary society. In addition to contributing to an understanding of adolescence, the selected papers also are highly provocative and stimulating treatises that raise many questions. During the past decade research has burgeoned independently and more vigorously than ever in several disciplines—anthropology, education, medicine, psychology, social work, and sociology. An interdisciplinary approach is necessary to draw together the insights from these diverse sources. *Studies in Adolescence* aims to meet this requirement; 5 of its 44 selections were prepared especially for this edition. The other 39 articles have been compiled from 28 journals, only 5 of which are primarily psychological in orientation.

Two basic assumptions furnish the rationale for the selection of papers that have been included in all three volumes of *Studies in Adolescence*. First, it is assumed that with the advent of adolescence, persons and institutions of society-at-large become increasingly important as agents of socialization as parents and family diminish in status and influence. Second, it is

v

assumed that the adolescent must extinguish many childhood habits and roles as he or she simultaneously masters several new patterns of behavior, which are appropriate not only for one's sex and age but also for apprenticeship of the adult positions that one will eventually occupy. Hence, a study of development during adolescence necessitates an analysis of the specific developmental, sociocultural, familial, peer, school, and workplace issues affecting the socialization process.

Too frequently it is assumed that an understanding of adolescence derives from knowledge of youth's consciousness, on the grounds that personal factors—aspirations, attitudes, beliefs, dispositions—are the primary determinants of whether adolescents will eventually sustain themselves as adults —in terms of intimate and persistent social relationships, vocational and economic responsibilities, and religious and philosophical convictions. The significance of youth's consciousness cannot be underestimated; however, to gain a comprehensive understanding of personality development during adolescence, it is also necessary to study the interaction between youth and social institutions—peer-group, familial, educational, economic, and political.

Events have so altered society during the past decade that studies in adolescence often are out of date before they can be disseminated; a book of readings in 1975 must be timely, offering insight not only on contemporary adolescence but also on the directions that socialization may take in the next year or two. When agrarianism and simple technology dominated life, social institutions served youth in much the same manner year after year. In 1963, when the first edition of this volume appeared, the country looked to be at the threshold of unprecedented prosperity. Career opportunities were bountiful, the civil rights movement was beginning, and sexual expression was still bound to traditional mores. When the second edition was published in 1969, the drug scene, countercultures, political marches, school boycotts, underground newspapers, and sexual openness were commonplace. The outlook on drugs, sexual behavior, and youth-culture life-styles is more sophisticated today, and much of the idealism reflected in political activism has yielded to preoccupation with vocational and career issues. Changes in relations between social institutions and adolescence have been swift, and to keep pace with them, the 1975 revision of *Studies in Adolescence* includes only six articles from the 1969 edition and none from the 1963.

This edition emphasizes trends in the study of adolescence that have emerged since the 1969 volume. The new patterns of adolescents' participation in the labor force and the changes needed in educational practices to facilitate their entry into productive work are treated in detail. The cultural biases that affect adolescent girls' socialization are being scrutinized, and such important topics as sex-role stereotyping in high schools, vocational preferences, and career mobility are reviewed. High-school curricula, educators' attitudes toward dissent, and teachers' perceptions of students' characteristics have undergone striking alterations during the past few years, and seven of the papers included illustrate the effectiveness with which present-day high schools function as agents of instruction and learning. The youth culture has risen in significance and discussion of slang, dating, the Jesus Movement, and protest music highlight its prominence. Recent changes in sexual orientation are documented in analyses of sources of sexual knowledge, processes of sexual decision-making, and attitudes toward sexual expression and marriage. Represented in the text, too, are studies of ancillary youth-culture activities and problems—drugs, smoking, alcohol, automobile driving, and delinquency.

Studies in Adolescence also strongly emphasizes traditional areas of research on adolescent development. Sex-role identification, parental power structure, parent–peer cross-pressures, and moral development are stressed. Two papers dealing with formal operations and egocentrism in adolescent cognitive behavior augment the major review of socialization. Although new investigations supplant many of the papers representing traditional areas in the first edition, the new ones are often direct outgrowths of the studies that they replaced, e.g., historical analyses, initiation rites, and physical development.

Studies in Adolescence collates the scholarship of nearly 70 researchers, and I am grateful to them and to their publishers for permitting me to reprint their materials here. A footnote included on the introductory page of each article formally acknowledges their contribution. In the preparation of the manuscript, I was aided immensely by Frances A. Brown, whose keen attention to detail improved every phase of its production. I am indebted, too, to C. Rayfield Haynes, for his invaluable editorial suggestions, and to LaVina Hegle, whose secretarial assistance greatly expedited the book's development. I am very much pleased that I may express my appreciation to them here.

Robert E. Grinder

Contents

ix

Part 3   Schools as Agents of Social Change, Instruction, and Learning *127*

Adolescence and Society

Events in adolescence accelerated during the past decade at crescendo tempo. Adolescents rode the vanguard of social and ideological unrest from the hippie commune to the Jesus Movement, the civil rights protests to anti-war demonstrations, and the panty raids to the student boycotts. Parents, relatives, neighbors, teachers, and employers saw many familiar pathways to adulthood abandoned for strange and bewildering lifestyles. The four papers in Part 1 of Studies in Adolescence *offer perspective on why adolescence has become an extraordinary phenomenon. The first selection places adolescence in a context of social change and explores circumstances in which youth are likely to question adult values. The second describes both theoretical assumptions behind earlier "scientific" investigations of adolescent behavior and pitfalls of drawing conclusions about adolescence from unsubstantiated premises. The third selection questions the credibility of traditional patterns of socialization and calls for a reorganization of educational systems to include contributions from economic institutions. The fourth draws from anthropological literature to discuss implications of adolescent initiation rites.*

Studies in Adolescence is introduced by a discussion of the historical conditions in the United States that led to the prolonging of the years of childhood, and consequently "the invention or discovery" of adolescence. According to Bakan, as a result of urban-industrial pressures, adolescence became the period of time between the initiation of physical growth changes and "the ages specified by law for compulsory education, employment, and criminal procedure." He places the major economic, social, and political movements of the nineteenth century in the context of humanitarian concerns and argues that recognition of the interplay of these forces may help us understand the expectations of society toward adolescents. Bakan also observes that adults, because they are oriented toward conventional ethics of achievement and status, tend to believe that an adolescent who does what he is "supposed to do" will eventually realize success, status, income, and power. He notes, nonetheless, that for many youth this "profoundly pervasive metaphor of appropriate behavior in adolescence as a form of capital investment for the realization of returns in the future necessarily falters in cogency as the likelihood of such returns declines."

G. Stanley Hall's concept of adolescence, described in the second paper within the context of nineteenth-century genetic psychology, was the first thorough integration of the literature from the philosophical and natural sciences into psychology. The Lamarckian evolutionary viewpoint and the theory of recapitulation led Hall to regard the adolescent period as the moment for uplifting mankind to superanthropoid status and to view assumptions about "nature-is-right," catharsis, superiority of physical over cognitive growth, and nascent periods as forming basic developmental principles. For all his genius, enthusiasm, and energy, however, Hall's efforts to establish recapitulation theory as the all-explanatory principle of psychological development aborted early in the twentieth century. The anonymity into which he has fallen, as a consequence, has rendered Hall's assumptions about adolescence relatively inaccessible and misunderstood.

The third paper contrasts youth's transition to adulthood in pre- and post-industrial America. Coleman analyzes changes in occupational learning opportunities in the school, family, and workplace. A steady decline of work-roles in the family and a decrease in the availability of jobs has fostered on the school a difficult burden in training youth for nonintellectual, experiential skills. Coleman holds that the conventionally organized schools are "destined to fail as educational institutions in areas other than teaching of intellectual skills," and calls, not for additional vocational schools, but for a radical redesign of economic institutions in order to provide "not only for productive efficiency, but for learning efficiency as well." He argues persuasively that educational reform efforts must recognize that "schooling" (formal, planned training in intellectual or cognitive matters) should augment training in vocational and citizenship skills. Coleman acknowledges that enormous transformations in industry would have to occur and new standards of educational performance would have to be devised, but the outcome, he believes, would yield a comprehensive program of socialization, strong public service commitments from economic institutions, less reliance on intellectual criteria in school testing programs, and, because educational workplaces would be distributed everywhere, greater racial integration.

In many preliterate societies a phenomenon occurs at adolescence that must seem strange to citizens of literate, western societies. Generally labeled the "initiation rite," it provides a formal, institutionalized procedure for inducting youth into adulthood. Sometimes in western societies—as in club, fraternity, or sorority initiations—an event occurs that marks a specific aspect of the adolescent's transition to adulthood, but such an event is likely to convey less significance in an industrial society than in a preliterate society where role expectations often are clearly anticipated. It is noteworthy that members of societies who practice initiation rites are usually only vaguely aware of why the rite transpires. Anthropologists have long been fascinated by initiation rites and the relationship of them to socialization. In the fourth paper, Brown summarizes some current explanations and suggests a variety of ways in which the rites may affect adolescents.

David Bakan

Adolescence in America:
From Idea to Social Fact

In the following paper, Bakan advances the idea that adolescence was added as a second stage of childhood in the later nineteenth and early twentieth centuries as a consequence of specific social changes in compulsory education, child labor legislation, and juvenile justice. He traces the significance of these changes to the rise of adolescence as a social fact and raises serious questions about the extent to which the adult society possesses credibility in the eyes of youth.

Instructional Objectives
To note early references to adolescence as a specific period in the lifecycle.
To identify the post-Civil War events—labor shortages, laws to protect property rights, and changes in morality—leading to the rise of adolescence.
To consider reasons for compulsory education.
To review reasons for the development of child labor legislation.
To describe the discrepancy between adult justice and juvenile justice.
To note the alternatives open to youth when the perquisites of adult status appear unattainable.

THE IDEA OF ADOLESCENCE

OFTEN a technical term is invented in order to create a social condition and a social fact; such has been true with respect to the term "adolescence." The idea of adolescence as an intermediary period in life starting at puberty and extending to some period in the lifecycle unmarked by any conspicuous physical change but socially defined as "manhood" or "womanhood" is the product of modern times. The *Oxford English Dictionary* traces the term to the fifteenth century. Prior to that, if we follow the thought of Philip Aries,[1] the notion of childhood hardly existed, let alone the idea of the prolongation of childhood beyond puberty, as the term adolescence suggests.

FROM *Daedalus*, © (1971), 979–995. Journal of the American Academy of Arts and Sciences, Boston, Mass. *Twelve to Sixteen: Early Adolescence.* Reprinted by permission of the author and the publisher.
[1] P. Aries, *Centuries of Childhood* (New York: Knopf, 1962).

3

Meaningful ascription of serious role characteristics for this period of life occurs, perhaps for the first time, in Rousseau's *Émile,* in which he characterized the period of adolescence as being beyond the earlier period of weakness of childhood and as a second birth. "We are born, so to speak, twice over; born into existence, and born into life; born a human being and born a man." [2] His aim was explicitly to prolong childhood, including the condition of innocence, as long as possible.

Although *Émile* has had considerable influence since its publication, the conversion of the idea of adolescence into a commonly accepted social reality was largely associated with modern urban-industrial life. Rousseau may have *invented* adolescence, as maintained by Musgrove,[3] but the notion as it is commonly understood in contemporary thought did not prevail prior to the last two decades of the nineteenth century and was "on the whole an American discovery." [4] The idea received an important stamp of reality from G. Stanley Hall in his monumental two-volume work on *Adolescence,* which he proudly presented to the reader as "essentially the author's first book" in 1904.[5] In point of fact he had introduced the idea as a special stage of development earlier.[6] In *Adolescence* he complained that we in America, because of our history, "have had neither childhood nor youth, but have lost touch with these stages of life because we lack a normal developmental history. . . . Our immigrants have often passed the best years of youth or leave it behind when they reach our shores, and their memories of it are in other lands. No country is so precociously old for its years." [7] The giving of social reality to adolescence would, as it were, youthen the nation.

By reviewing some of the history, I will attempt to show in this essay that the invention or discovery of adolescence in America was largely in response to the social changes that accompanied America's development in the latter half of the nineteenth and the early twentieth century, and that the principal reason was to prolong the years of childhood. Adolescence was added to childhood as a second childhood in order to fulfill the aims of the new urban-industrial society which developed so rapidly following the Civil War.

HISTORICAL BACKGROUND

From the days of the early settlement of America to the second half of the nineteenth century, America suffered a chronic labor shortage. It sought to

[2] Jean Jacques Rousseau, *Émile,* trans. Barbara Foxley (New York: Dutton, 1966; originally published 1762), pp. 128, 172.

[3] F. Musgrove, *Youth and the Social Order* (Bloomington, Ind.: Indiana University Press, 1964). Musgrove titles one of his chapters "The Invention of the Adolescent," pp. 33–57.

[4] John Demos and Virginia Demos, "Adolescence in Historical Perspective," *Journal of Marriage and the Family,* 31 (1969), 632–638, 632.

[5] G. Stanley Hall, *Adolescence: Its Psychology and Its Relations to Physiology, Anthropology, Sociology, Sex, Crime, Religion, and Education* (New York: D. Appleton and Company, 1904).

[6] G. Stanley Hall, "The Moral and Religious Training of Children," *Princeton Review* (January 1882), pp. 26–48.

[7] Hall, *Adolescence,* p. xvi.

overcome this labor shortage through slavery, the encouragement of immigration, and industrialization. The incompatibility of slavery and industrialization plagued America during much of its early history, and that incompatibility remained until the Civil War, the Emancipation Proclamation, and the Thirteenth Amendment resolved it in favor of industrialization. But with the development of urban-industrial society, the nation became possessed of new contradictions characteristic of modern technological society, most serious among them the presence of a large number of persons who were mature by historical standards but immature in the new context.

The country changed dramatically during the second half of the nineteenth century. In 1880 the railroad network was completely integrated; there was no longer a frontier; the number of cities that had populations of more than 8,000 almost doubled in the decade from 1880 to 1890. By the year 1900 more than a third of the population was living in cities and more than half the population of the North Atlantic area lived in cities of more than 8,000 persons. In 1890 more than a third of the American population were people of foreign parentage. The question of property was becoming increasingly salient, as testified to by the proliferation of criminal laws designed to protect property rights—a not unimportant fact when we consider the question of juvenile delinquency, because most juvenile crimes are crimes against property, such as burglary, larceny, robbery, and auto theft.

The low level of "morality" of the new occupants of the burgeoning cities was a matter of frequent comment. Drinking, sexual immorality, vagrancy, and crime were not only intrinsically threatening to orderliness, but were also particularly distressing influences on the young. The rapid breeding, the continuing threat of "street Arabs," evoked a strong cry that the state intercede in restraining and training the young. In an address before the American Social Science Association in 1875, the influential Mary Carpenter said that if the parents of the young fail in their duty, then the whole society suffers; it was therefore the duty of the state to intercede and "stand *in loco parentis* and do its duty to the child and to society, by seeing that he is properly brought up." [8] Not the least of the dangers was the presence of un-American ideas and ideologies brought by the new immigrants, which were considered threatening to the basic fiber of American life. Even private education, as compared with public education, was regarded as a threat, the fear being that the children would not be sufficiently socialized and "Americanized." The Ku Klux Klan, for example, took a firm stand against private education.

As a result of these conditions, three major social movements developed, all of which conspired to make a social fact out of adolescence: compulsory (and characteristically public) education, child labor legislation, and special legal procedures for "juveniles." By the explicit citation of a precise chronological age, the legislation associated with these three areas essentially removed the vagueness of all previous ideas of the time at which adolescence terminates. Thus adolescence became the period of time between pubes-

[8] As cited in Grace Abbot, ed., *The Child and the State* (Chicago: University of Chicago Press, 1938), II, 372.

cence, a concrete biological occurrence, and the ages specified by law for compulsory education, employment, and criminal procedure.

There is no doubt that these movements were strongly motivated, at least on the conscious level, by humanitarian considerations. The rhetoric in defense of these three types of law was always cast in terms of the benefit and the saving quality that they would have for the young. The presumption that the various child welfare laws were principally created for the benefit of youth must, however, be confronted with the fact that there has been only a small degree of legal attention to the serious problem of child abuse in our society. The so-called "battered child" was not discovered until the late 1940's and early 1950's, and to this day appropriate protective and social support legislation is still quite negligible in contrast to the magnitude of the problem and the frequency of cases of cruelty to children.[9] The confluence of humanitarian considerations with the major economic, social, and political forces in the society needs to be clearly recognized. Indeed, the recognition of these underlying forces may help us to understand some of the failures to fulfill humanitarian aims and the disabilities which currently prevail with respect to that period of life that we call adolescence.

COMPULSORY EDUCATION

In the late nineteenth century, public compulsory education for children between six and eighteen, characteristically to age sixteen, was introduced widely in the United States. English common law had given parents virtually complete control over the education of the child, a principle prevalent in colonial America and throughout most of our early history. However, the general legal position later became that: "The primary function of the public school . . . is not to confer benefits upon the individual as such." Rather "the school exists as a state institution because the very existence of civil society demands it. The education of youth is a matter of such vital importance to the democratic state and to the public weal that the state may do much, may go very far indeed, by way of limiting the control of the parent over the education of his child." [10]

In the case of a father who had violated the compulsory attendance law, the court stated in its opinion:

> The course of study to be pursued in the public schools of our state is prescribed either by statute or by the school authorities in pursuance thereof. These schools include not only elementary schools, but high schools as well

[9] See M. G. Paulsen, "The Law and Abused Children," in R. E. Helfer and C. H. Kempe, *The Battered Child* (Chicago: University of Chicago Press, 1968), pp. 175–207; and D. Bakan, *Slaughter of the Innocents: A Study of the Battered Child Phenomenon* (San Francisco: Jossey-Bass, 1971; Toronto: Canadian Broadcasting Corp., 1971).

[10] Newton Edwards, *The Courts and the Public Schools: The Legal Basis of School Organization and Administration*, rev. ed. (Chicago: University of Chicago Press, 1955), p. 24.

. . . A parent, therefore, is not at liberty to exercise a choice in that regard, but, where not exempt for some lawful reason, must send his child to the school where instruction is provided suitable to its attainments as the school authorities may determine.[11]

It has been held that even a competent parent may not engage in domestic education on the following grounds:

We have no doubt many parents are capable of instructing their own children, but to permit such parents to withdraw their children from the public schools without permission from the superintendent of schools, and to instruct them at home, would be to disrupt our common school system and destroy its value to the state.[12]

At the same time the school authorities have been granted virtually complete discretionary powers with respect to suspension, expulsion, and punishment.[13] Such power rests in the hands of school authorities even in cases where the pupil has violated no rules. In one case, for example, a pupil was expelled for general misbehavior. In holding that the board of education had power to expel the pupil, the court said:

It matters not whether rules have been announced by either the directors or teachers. If the conduct of the pupil is such as reasonably to satisfy such school officers that the presence of that pupil is detrimental to the interests of the school, then the power of expulsion is conferred.[14]

Thus, it has turned out that the power of the state in America is such that it can, through its officials, not only compel school attendance, but also bar a pupil access to educational resources. Certainly there have been numerous legislative acts and court actions which would qualify particular cases. However, the total thrust of the various steps that have been taken since the middle of the nineteenth century has been in the direction of increasing the power of the state rather than protecting the rights of young people and their parents.

At the same time as the legal power of school authorities over pupils and their parents has been great, the schools have been derelict in the teaching of law—instruction which some regard as essential for people living in a democracy. In a society that is heavily dependent for its functioning on law, it is important that an appreciation of law, how it works, and its limits be taught in the public schools. One critic of this aspect of American education, in

[11] *Miller v. State*, 77 Ind. App. 611, 134 N. E. 209, as cited by Edwards, *The Courts and the Public Schools*, p. 524.

[12] *State v. Counort*, 69 Wash. 361, 124 Pac. 910, 41 L.R.A. (N.S.) 95, as cited by Edwards, *The Courts and the Public Schools*, p. 522.

[13] Edwards, *The Courts and the Public Schools*, pp. 601ff.

[14] *State v. Hamilton*, 42 Mo. App. 24, as cited by Edwards, *The Courts and the Public Schools*, p. 603.

discussing the matter of education on due process, indicates that it is taught as though it applies only to criminals and that it fails to reflect itself in procedural fairness in school disciplinary matters. The idea of freedom of the press is characteristically not brought to bear in connection with school newspapers. "One of the difficult problems," he laconically comments, "is whether [proposed] law courses will be permitted to ventilate these issues, given the anxiety about them." [15]

Although from time to time there have been steps to increase the knowledge of law among educators, the emphasis has been on the kind of legal knowledge that an educator might require to deal with relationships of the school to outside institutions and individuals rather than on teaching law to students. One article along these lines, for example, deals with the legal structure of education, pupil personnel policies, control of pupil conduct, staff personnel policies, curricula, and liability. Illustrations are that: physical education coordinators should be expert in the law of liability for pupil injuries; guidance teachers should be familiar with compulsory education laws and their enforcement; curriculum coordinators should understand the legal position of parents in relation to school studies and activities; business administrators should understand contract law; personnel administrators should understand the legal aspects of employing and discharging teachers; and teachers of the history or philosophy of education should be acquainted with the relevant judicial opinions.[16]

CHILD LABOR

The movement to restrict child labor in the United States also provided a definition of the termination of adolescence. Though there is a considerable amount of variation from state to state, the laws with respect to employment give specific minimum ages for definitions of maturity of different kinds: eighteen, minimum age for work in "hazardous occupations"; under eighteen, eight-hour day and forty-hour week; under eighteen, employment certificate required; under sixteen, limited hours of night work; sixteen, minimum age for factory work and employment during school hours; fourteen, minimum age for work outside of school hours. These are fairly typical laws governing age and employment.

The regulation of child labor has been one of the most controversial issues in this country since the nineteenth century. The harm to children from work in factories has been stridently declaimed. On the other hand, the virtues of work, the harm associated with idleness, and even the economic discriminatory effect of such legislation have also been consistently indicated. As an

---

[15] Alex Elson, "General Education in Law for Non-Lawyers," in The American Assembly, Columbia University, *Law in a Changing America* (Englewood Cliffs, N.J.: Prentice-Hall, 1968), pp. 183–191, 189.

[16] E. E. Reutter, Jr., "Essentials of School Law for Educators," in Harold J. Carter, ed., *Intellectual Foundations of American Education* (New York: Pitman Publishing Corporation, 1965), pp. 216–225.

example, Senator Alexander Wiley, in questioning the representative of the American Federation of Labor before a Senate subcommittee to investigate juvenile delinquency said: "To me when I see the youth of this country in idleness, walking the streets of the cities, [I feel] we are meeting a challenge to our common sense because we know idleness breeds not only crime but everything else." [17] There have been repeated charges that the legal regulation of child labor is partly responsible for the widespread unemployment among young people, particularly Negroes.[18]

Adolescents in the labor force were a common occurrence throughout American history. In 1832 about 40 per cent of the factory workers in New England were children. Starting a few years after the Civil War the major historical trend of a chronic labor shortage began to reverse itself, with ever-increasing evidences of labor surplus. With the changes in the kinds of work needed in the growing cities in the second half of the nineteenth century, an increasing proportion of females sought gainful employment. Indeed, the possibility of a close relationship between the various movements in connection with "child saving" and female employment has been seriously suggested.[19] Labor began to organize. The Knights of Labor, the precursor of the American Federation of Labor, was founded in 1869. In 1885 it had a membership of 100,000; a year later it could boast a membership of 730,000. Virtually from its founding, the Knights of Labor began its campaign for the prohibition of child labor. In spite of its efforts, child labor increased. The participation rate of youth between the ages of ten and fifteen in the labor force increased until 1900 and then began to decline. Indeed, in the decade which ended in 1900, the number of child laborers in the canneries, glass industry, mines, and so forth in the South tripled. The effort to control the labor supply in the United States was evident also in legislation to restrict immigration. In 1882 the Chinese Exclusion Act, barring immigration of Chinese laborers, was passed and was followed by other laws which severely restricted immigration.

Among employers there was a polarization. On the one hand there were certainly those employers who were in favor of having access to the cheap labor of young people and new immigrants; on the other hand the nature of industrial requirements was changing rapidly in favor of more skilled, and

---

[17] *Juvenile Delinquency: Hearings before the Subcommitte to Investigate Juvenile Delinquency,* Senate, 1955 (New York: Greenwood Press, 1968), p. 86.

[18] See, for example, the effort to counter these charges by H. M. Haisch of the U.S. Department of Labor: H. M. Haisch, "Do Child Labor Laws Prevent Youth Employment?" *Journal of Negro Education,* 33 (1964), 182–185.

[19] "Although child saving had important symbolic functions for preserving the prestige of middle-class women in a rapidly changing society, it also had considerable instrumental significance for legitimizing new career openings for women. The new role of social worker combined elements of an old and partly fictitious role—defender of family life—and elements of a new role—social servant. Social work and philanthropy were thus an affirmation of cherished values and an instrumentality for women's emancipation." Anthony M. Platt, *The Child Savers: The Invention of Delinquency* (Chicago: University of Chicago Press, 1969), p. 98.

especially more reliable, workers. One of the most serious interferences with the reliability of labor was alcohol, and the prohibition movement grew simultaneously with the efforts to remove young people from the labor market and to restrict immigration. The prohibition movement gained increasing support from industrial leaders, "who were not unaware of the economic implications of the trade in intoxicants." [20]

The belief, common during the early part of the nineteenth century, that the children of the poor should work and that education of the children of the poor was filled with social danger tended to decline in the course of the century. The enlightened leaders of industry, taking ever longer views of history, recognized the dependence of industry on the existence of a reasonably educated labor force, educated not only with respect to knowledge and skill, but also with respect to bureaucratic subordination and reliable work habits.[21] At the same time, organized labor sought not only reforms in the conditions of child labor, but also education for their own children, to increase the likelihood of vertical social mobility. The continuing interest of both industry and labor in the education of the young is evidenced by the clear agreement on this on the part of both the National Association of Manufacturers and organized labor.[22]

One of the classic conflicts in connection with child labor was that between the textile manufacturers of the North and those in the South. The northern manufacturers charged that the South had a competitive advantage from its greater use of young workers.[23] Among the factors that eventually led to a resolution of the conflict was the later discovery, resulting in part from the changed nature of manufacture and experience of some restrictive legislation, that, as the *Textile World Journal* in 1918 put it: "The labor of children under fourteen years of age is not only inefficient in itself, but tends to lower the efficiency of all departments in which they are employed; also children of fourteen to sixteen years, worked on a short time basis, are scarcely less efficient and have a disorganizing effect in the departments where they are utilized. Because of these facts, and entirely apart from humanitarian considerations, large numbers of southern mills will not re-employ children of these ages." [24]

JUVENILE DELINQUENCY

Quite analogous to the "invention of adolescence," as Musgrove put it, was the "invention of delinquency," as Anthony M. Platt puts it in his book on

---

[20] John Allen Krout, *The Origins of Prohibition* (New York: Russell and Russell, 1967), p. 302.

[21] For an analysis of relations between education and industry see John Galbraith, *The New Industrial State* (Boston: Houghton Mifflin, 1967).

[22] See Charles R. Sligh, Jr., "Views on Curriculum," *Harvard Educational Review*, 4 (1957), 239–245; Walter P. Reuther, "What the Public Schools Should Teach," *Harvard Educational Review*, 4 (1957), 246–250.

[23] Stephen B. Wood, *Constitutional Politics in the Progressive Era: Child Labor and the Law* (Chicago: University of Chicago Press, 1968), p. 9.

[24] Cited by Wood, *Constitutional Politics*, p. 172.

the history of the notion of delinquency in the United States.[25] The humane motivation associated with the development of the notion of the juvenile delinquent was the desire to remove young people from the rigidities and inexorabilities associated with criminal justice and to allow wider discretionary powers to authorities in dealing with juveniles. The new legal apparatus was intended to separate young offenders from older offenders, and to provide corrective rather than punitive treatment. The first Juvenile Court Act was passed by the Illinois legislature in 1899 and brought together for single consideration cases of dependency, neglect, and delinquency. The hearings under the act were to be informal, the records were to be confidential, the young people were to be detained separately from adults. The aims were to be investigation and prescription rather than the determination of guilt or innocence. Lawyers were to be unnecessary. The definition of the "juvenile delinquent" in the various laws which multiplied after the model legislation in Illinois now vary for the upper limit from sixteen to twenty-one. The United States Children's Bureau had recommended nineteen, and this has been followed in about two-thirds of the states.[26]

Although the juvenile acts tended to free the courts from the obligation of imposing punishments associated with the criminal codes, they also had the effect of suspending the fundamental principle of legality, that one may not be punished for an offense unless a definite law in effect at the time when the act in question was committed has been broken. Considerations of due process were not obligatory. Guilt did not have to be established beyond a reasonable doubt. Among the acts reported under the heading of juvenile delinquency may be found the following: immoral conduct around schools, association with vicious or immoral persons, patronizing public pool rooms, wandering about railroad yards, truancy, incorrigibility, absenting self from home without consent, smoking cigarettes in public places, begging or receiving alms (or in street for purpose of).[27] As Harvey Baker of the Boston juvenile court put it in 1910:

> The court does not confine its attention to just the particular offense which brought the child to its notice. For example, a boy who comes to court for such a trifle as failing to wear his badge when selling papers may be held on probation for months because of difficulties at school; and a boy who comes in for playing on the street may . . . be committed to a reform school because he is found to have habits of loafing, stealing or gambling which can not be corrected outside.[28]

Questions have been raised as to whether the procedures of such courts adequately protect the rights of young offenders and whether they are con-

[25] Anthony M. Platt, *The Child Savers: The Invention of Delinquency* (Chicago: University of Chicago Press, 1969).

[26] Robert W. Winslow, ed., *Juvenile Delinquency in a Free Society: Selections from the President's Commission on Law Enforcement and Administration of Justice* (Belmont, Calif.: Dickenson Publishing Company, 1968), pp. 119–120.

[27] Winslow, *Juvenile Delinquency*, pp. 166–167.

[28] Cited in Platt, *The Child Savers*, p. 142.

sistent with constitutional rights.[29] In some states corrective legislation has been attempted by providing for legal defense of persons who come under the jurisdiction of the juvenile courts. However, the evidence is that this is not common. Indeed, treatment by officials tends to be more kindly toward young persons who admit guilt and indicate that they will mend their ways than toward those who are defensive or those whose parents are defensive.[30] The failure of the juvenile court to achieve its avowed objectives is notorious.

Suggestions that the aim of the juvenile court is to introduce a middle-class child-rearing orientation to the courtroom are apparent in the opinion of Judge Ben Lindsey of Denver, one of the pioneers in the juvenile court movement, and in the findings of Melvin L. Kohn. In an introduction to a book called *Winning the Boy* by Lilburn Merrill, Lindsey stressed the importance of "character," rather than the act itself.

> You have not really a safe citizen until there comes into the boy's heart the desire to do right because it is right . . . I ask the boy why he will not steal again and he invariably replies, "Because I will get in jail." He is afraid of jail; he is not afraid to do wrong . . . Conscience is the moral director; without it character is impossible, and character is the greatest need, for it means that the pure in heart shall see and know and act the truth, as surely as they shall see God.[31]

Kohn has been able to show, on the basis of comparative data which he has collected, that there are differences in corrective actions between working-class and middle-class parents. Working-class parents tend to punish the external consequences of an action, as contrasted with middle-class parents who tend to punish on the basis of intention, rather than the action itself.[32] The latter mode is clearly suggested in Judge Lindsey's comment. Thus one way of interpreting the development of juvenile delinquency practices is as an effort to bring middle-class child-rearing practices into play, even when they involved the suspension of the principle of legality.

The legal disability of those who come under the juvenile laws is not limited to a small minority of youth in our society. "Statutes often define juvenile delinquency so broadly as to make virtually all youngsters delinquent . . . Rough estimates by the Children's Bureau, supported by independent studies, indicate that one in every nine youths—one in every six male youths—will be referred to juvenile court in connection with a delinquent

[29] See Lewis Mayer, *The American Legal System* (New York: Harper and Row, 1964), pp. 146–149.

[30] Winslow, *Juvenile Delinquency*, pp. 140, 150.

[31] Cited in Bernard Wishy, *The Child and the Republic: The Dawn of Modern American Child Nurture* (Philadelphia: University of Pennsylvania Press, 1968), p. 134.

[32] M. L. Kohn, "Social Class and Parent-Child Relationships: An Interpretation," *American Journal of Sociology*, 68 (1963), 471–480; M. L. Kohn, "Social Class and the Exercise of Parental Authority," *American Sociological Review*, 24 (1959), 352–366; M. L. Kohn, *Class and Conformity: A Study in Values* (Homewood, Ill.: Dorsey Press, 1969).

act (excluding traffic offenses) before his 18th birthday." [33] As soon as the young person gains what may be called the animal sufficiency that comes with puberty, and may enter public places without an attendant, he becomes subject to extraordinary powers of the state until the legal definition of his maturity comes into being. This power of the state differs dramatically from the power of the state over adults in our society. The great discrepancy between adult justice and juvenile justice and the legal vulnerability of juveniles has been one of the major factors associated with the conversion of the idea of adolescence into the social fact of adolescence.

THE STUDY OF ADOLESCENCE

Starting with the work of G. Stanley Hall, adolescence became the subject of a considerable amount of investigation. There can be no doubt about the value of such investigation—indeed, this may be attested to by the essays in this volume. Nonetheless, this body of literature articulated with the cultural forces in the society at large. Although the intention of people like Hall to draw attention to an extremely important age period significant to the history of civilization generally, and the United States in particular, and thereby to create greater concern with proper development at that stage, was meritorious, there was another effect which needs to be pointed out. By stressing, for example, the presumptive emotional instability and unformed nature of people of that age—the work of Margaret Mead and others suggests that such phenomena of adolescence may be extrinsic rather than intrinsic [34]— Hall and others tended to put a gloss of psychopathology on this age period. Since it has long been a principle in our society that persons regarded as psychologically pathological are to be relieved of rights,[35] the effect of this literature has been to serve the general disability of persons under legal ages. In this way, the workers in the field of adolescence have tended to conspire, certainly unwittingly, with some of the forces depriving adolescents of their rights.

THE PROMISE

A major factor which has sustained the social fact of adolescence in our society has been the belief, so pervasive in our success-oriented culture, in "the promise." The promise is that if a young person does all the things he is "supposed to do" during his adolescence, he will then realize success, status, income, power, and so forth in his adulthood.

A study by Arthur L. Stinchcombe [36] may help us to understand the opera-

---

[33] Winslow, *Juvenile Delinquency*, p. 2.
[34] Margaret Mead, *Coming of Age in Samoa* (New York: W. Morrow and Co., 1928).
[35] See Thomas S. Szasz, *Law, Liberty and Psychiatry* (New York: Macmillan, 1963).
[36] Arthur L. Stinchcombe, *Rebellion in a High School* (Chicago: Quadrangle Books, 1964).

tion of the promise. He studied the attitudes, behavior, and perceptions of the labor market among high school students, and found a direct and dramatic relationship between the images of the future that the students have and their rebellious attitudes and behavior. His data bear out the hypothesis "that high school rebellion, and expressive alienation, are most common among students who do not see themselves as gaining an increment in future status from conformity in high school." [37] In elaborating on the dynamics of the hypothesis, he writes: "When a student realizes that he does not achieve status increment from improved current performance, current performance loses meaning. The student becomes hedonistic because he does not visualize achievement of long-run goals through current self-restraint. He reacts negatively to a conformity that offers nothing concrete. He claims autonomy from adults because their authority does not promise him a satisfactory future." [38] Stinchcombe's hypothesis is derived from considerations of the legitimacy of bureaucratic authority as developed by Max Weber. Among the interesting derivations Stinchcombe makes from the hypothesis is an explanation of the difference between the sexes in various categories of expressive alienation. Girls are less likely to be rebellious because they perceive at least the possibility of marriage as a viable "career." He points out that the relatively high delinquency rate among Negroes is associated with the perception of the employment discrimination against Negro adult males.

As the credibility of the promise declines, the willingness of young people to accept the varieties of disabilities of adolescence equally declines. The profoundly pervasive metaphor of appropriate behavior in adolescence as a form of capital investment for the realization of returns in the future necessarily falters in cogency as the likelihood of such returns declines. The problems of order in the schools, juvenile delinquency, and other forms of expressive alienation cannot readily be solved by making small changes in the schools, Stinchcombe says.[39] It would appear that the schools cannot promise much because the society cannot promise much.

A study by William Westley and Frederick Elkin [40] of young people in an upper-class suburb of Montreal in 1951 attempted to explode the notion of the adolescent period as being one of storm and stress, nonconformity, gang formation, struggle for emancipation, and the like. The data collected in that place and time indicated considerably greater harmony and positive social adjustment by conventional standards than one might expect. However, the characterization of these young people would clearly indicate that they expected that the promise would be fulfilled. The typical youth in the study

[37] Ibid., p. 49; see especially chaps. 3 and 4, pp. 49–102, titled "The Labor Market and Rebellion I; II."

[38] Ibid., pp. 5–6.

[39] Ibid., passim.

[40] William A. Westley and Frederick Elkin, "The Protective Environment and Adolescent Socialization," in Martin Gold and Elizabeth Douvan, eds., *Adolescent Development: Readings in Research and Theory* (Boston: Allyn and Bacon, 1969), pp. 158–164; reprinted from *Social Forces*, 35 (1957), 243–249.

"internalizes aspirations for a professional or business career; he learns the expected patterns of language and breeding; he learns to resolve disputes by peaceable means; he learns to defer many immediate gratifications for the sake of future gains." [41]

The major question in our society today is whether, for youth of *all* social classes, the promise has continued credibility. Unemployment among manual workers is increasingly patent. The public service advertisements directed at potential drop-outs to remain in school in order to get better jobs later are met with increasing cynicism. [42] The poor acceptance rates of college students into the labor market predicted in the early sixties [43] are rapidly materializing. Even for scientists with Ph.D.'s the possibilities for employment are extremely dismal. [44] And few young people are ignorant of the fact that a career in "free enterprise" is virtually impossible without access to capital. [45] The idyllic vision of Erik Erikson that adolescence "can be viewed as a *psychosocial moratorium* during which the individual through free role experimentation may find a niche in some section of his society, a niche which is firmly defined and yet seems to be uniquely made for him," [46] must increasingly be viewed cynically if that niche in life is contingent upon an appropriate niche in the labor force.

[41] Ibid., p. 158.

[42] See, for example, the stress on the employment advantages of school in the *National Stay-in-School Campaign Handbook for Communities* (Washington, D.C.: Government Printing Office, 1957). The campaign was sponsored jointly by the Department of Labor, Department of Health, Education and Welfare, and Department of Defense.

[43] J. Folger and C. Nam, "Trends in Education in Relation to the Occupational Structure," *Sociology of Education*, 38 (1964), 19–33; R. Havighurst and B. Neugarten, *Society and Education*, 2d ed. (Boston: Allyn and Bacon, 1962).

[44] Allan Cartter, "Scientific Manpower for 1970–1985," *Science*, 172 (1971), 132–140.

[45] Such has been the case at least since 1885 when Andrew Carnegie, the great exponent of the idea that any able and energetic young man could "rise to the top," told a group of students that "There is no doubt that it is becoming harder and harder as business gravitates more and more to immense concerns for a young man without capital to get a start for himself." Cited in H. J. Perkinson, *The Imperfect Panacea: American Faith in Education, 1865–1965* (New York: Random House, 1968), p. 120. Ironically, one of the few spheres in which "free enterprise," with relatively little capital and high returns on investment, is still possible is in the illegal merchandising of drugs.

[46] Erik H. Erikson, "The Problem of Ego Identity," in Gold and Douvan, *Adolescent Development*, p. 19; reprinted from *Identity and the Life Cycle* (New York: International Universities Press, 1959).

Robert E. Grinder

The Concept of Adolescence
in the Genetic Psychology
of G. Stanley Hall

No other psychologist has written more about adolescence than G. Stanley Hall. His famed two-volume treatise on adolescence was actually an encyclopedia. His interest ranged on the one hand from embryology to education and religion, and on the other, from gynecology to counseling techniques. Hall's nineteenth-century integration of Lamarckianism and recapitulation theory led to the first science of human development, and excerpts from Hall's Adolescence *are used in the selection below to illustrate how he fashioned a strikingly unusual interpretation of the adolescent years.*

Instructional Objectives
To describe nineteenth-century genetic psychology in the context of early theories of evolution.
To describe five basic principles of human development implicit in Hall's genetic psychology—superanthropoidism, nature-is-right, catharsis, primacy of physical growth, and racapitulatory growth.
To illustrate Hall's concept of physical development.
To illustrate Hall's view of cognitive growth.
To illustrate Hall's understanding of social development as revealed in his discussions of religiosity and delinquency.

G. STANLEY HALL is the father of child study in America. Social scientists working in developmental psychology are indebted more to Hall than to any other person for the initial momentum, organization, and eminence of the discipline. His illustrious accomplishments included earning the first U.S. Ph.D. in psychology, founding the American Psychological Association, establishing the *Pedagogical Seminary*, the first journalistic outlet for research investigations on child and adolescent development, and publishing some 340 papers, articles, and books. Lecturer at Harvard, professor at Johns

FROM *Child Development*, XL (1969), 355–369. Reprinted by permission of the Society for Research in Child Development.

Hopkins, and president-professor of Clark University from its inception until his retirement, Hall launched child-study associations in at least seven states and attracted impressively able graduate students, such as Arnold Gesell, Henry L. Goddard, and Lewis M. Terman. He pioneered the questionnaire method in an era before controlled surveys and experimental procedures in the social sciences were anticipated, collated massive quantities of research data, and reported them in *Adolescence* (1904), an enormously comprehensive two-volume treatise of 1,373 pages, which for decades has been the starting point of discussions on adolescent development.

But for all his genius, enthusiasm, and energy, Hall's pronouncements are casualties of scientific advance. He was first to be at the threshold of twentieth-century developmental psychology, but he turned his back on the future, preferring instead an outlook that expired with the nineteenth century. He stood alone among leading psychologists in the degree to which he applied antiquated principles of evolutionary theory to adolescent development. Hall dreamed of the honors that would accrue to a "Darwin of the mind"[1] and saw himself as the psychologist who could construct the history of the psyche from the lowly amoeba to man. Possession of such knowledge, he believed, would unlock the complexities of human development, accelerate evolutionary processes, and even reveal the purpose and destiny of life itself. His views on adolescent physical, cognitive, and social development are comprehensible only in the context of his imposing aspirations. With this perspective, his interpretations provide a major source of insight into both how he and his students conceptualized adolescent development and how their successors fashioned contemporary theories. The following discussion of Halls' concept of adolescence is preceded, therefore, by brief descriptions of both the essential features of genetic psychology and the basic principles Hall employed in his science of human development.

GENETIC PSYCHOLOGY

Charles Darwin, in *The Origin of Species* (1859), was first to muster sufficient evidence to sustain a theory of species mutability. His case for evolution rested initially on the notion of natural selection, the belief that plants and animals possessing superior qualities for adaptation would survive and, by chance variation, endow certain of their offspring with superior qualities, which, by continued chance variation, might then be passed on to progeny. Friends in geology, however, pointed out to Darwin that life on earth simply had not existed long enough for evolution to have occurred solely through random, miniscule variations derived from natural selection. In countering their arguments Darwin felt compelled to endorse Jean Lamarck's theory of acquired characters.[2] A half-century earlier Lamarck had advanced the no-

---

[1] G. S. Hall, *Life and Confessions of a Psychologist* (New York: Appleton, 1924), p. 360.

[2] R. E. Grinder, *A History of Genetic Psychology* (New York: Wiley, 1967).

tion that new habits and behaviors—acquired over time as adaptations to such events as climatic changes, migration, and geological upheaval—foist special shapes on organs and that these new structures, in turn, are inherited by offspring. Lamarck's viewpoint was at first unconvincing to fellow scientists. If certain species had indeed perished, what led some to survive and others to perish? Darwin's stress on survival of the fittest helped explain species mutability, but controversy raged among nineteenth-century scientists over the relative hereditary influences of natural selection and acquired characters.

Two major schools of thought emerged, one insisting that hereditary changes occurred solely from the natural selection of mysterious chance variations, wholly immune to environmental pressures, and another holding that hereditary changes resulted from structural modifications brought about by adaptation. The first view bound evolution to blind and senseless forces; the second generated boundless optimism, suggesting that the course of evolution could be both accelerated and governed through wise and rational exercise of willpower. The conflict subsided with the discovery of genes and chromosomes and the reformulation of hereditary theory in 1900 as based on Gregor Mendel's papers of 1865 on the hybridization of the sweet pea. Mendel's data revealed that hereditary changes occurred in large rather than imperceptibly small variations, reconciled the timing of mutability to the evidence of geologic time, and routed the Lamarckians, who never seemed able to demonstrate satisfactorily that experiences accumulated in one generation could be passed on to the next.

Darwin and other nineteenth-century scientists, however, vigorously incorporated Lamarckianism into the theory of evolution to complement the concept of natural selection. Mendel had published his views in a relatively obscure journal 6 years after *The Origin of Species* appeared, but Darwin and his cohort, in one of the strangest episodes in the annals of science, remained oblivious to them. The extent to which Mendel's startling revelations on heredity actually were obscured is unknown, but certainly few persons were prepared for the unnerving, mechanistic implications of his findings. The perennial fear and anguish reverberated in philosopher Le Conte's [3] distress: "To many, both skeptics and Christians, evolution seems to be synonymous with blank materialism, and therefore cuts up by the roots every form of religion by denying the existence of God and the fact of immortality." The naturalistic implications of evolution were so unpalatable to those who had long seen purpose in nature that to have compounded the fare with Mendelism would have been a bitter pill indeed. The only plausible antidote in those early, heady years was Lamarckianism.

The predicament of succumbing to mechanism was averted at the outset of the evolutionary era by the advent of the theory of recapitulation. The name of the individual who deserves credit for being the first to allude to the

[3] J. Le Conte, *Evolution: Its Nature, Its Evidence, and Its Relation to Religious Thought* (New York: Appleton, 1908), p. 284.

idea that each individual retraces the historical record of his species development (phylogeny) in his own growth (ontogeny) is irrecoverable. Aristotle and Rousseau both spoke of a connection between the emergence of species and the growth of individuals. Lorenz Oken, in *Natur Philosphie* (1805), was among the first naturalist-philosophers to formulate the belief as a law; and, among Darwin's strongest supporters, Ernst Haeckel and Herbert Spencer believed that they possessed evidence showing recapitulatory stages among embryos and lower forms of life. Suddenly it seemed that all the missing links in the evolution of living species might eventually be reconstructed by recourse to paleontology and comparative anthropology. More significantly, the rationale for the mighty processes of evolution and development was shown to have been endowed with meaning and purpose from the very beginning. Applied to organic growth, the law of recapitulation professed to explain how a teleological force or perfecting principle might act within natural necessity for ordained purposes. The grand design of evolution visà-vis recapitulation, augmented by the concepts of natural selection and acquired characters, demonstrated that the development of man was at once natural and divine, involving, during the recapitulatory period at least, a fixed sequence of growth patterns, the violation of which would be profane.

THE FIRST SCIENCE OF HUMAN DEVELOPMENT

G. Stanley Hall possessed ingenuous faith in Lamarckianism and the theory of recapitulation. The massive support derived from the natural sciences seemed incontrovertible, and in his grasp these viewpoints became more dogmas than testable hypotheses. He sought doggedly to strengthen the taxonomic links between the history of the human race and individual development and to learn, thereby, when to induce the new acquired characters and thus advance evolution. Hall's solicitude to maintain perfectly the relationship decreed by nature between phylogeny and ontogeny—to prevent both recapitulatory acceleration and reversion—was overridden only by his impatience to discover the optimal developmental moment at which to introduce new hereditary characters. These recapitulatory and Lamarckian assumptions led him implicitly to five basic principles that subsequently became the bedrock of his science of human development.

First and foremost was Hall's belief that "adolescence is . . . the only point of departure for the superanthropoid that man is to become." [4] When should new characters be introduced in ontogeny in order to insure phyletic or species advance? Paleontological observations of lower animal forms suggested that, while acquired characters might develop at any stage, they must appear at adolescence, at which time recapitulation ceases, if evolutionary advance rather than aberration is to occur. Earlier speculation by Rousseau, who had recognized that moral and intellectual traits appeared

[4] G. S. Hall, *Adolescence* (2 vols.; New York: Appleton, 1904), II, 94.

first at adolescence, corroborated the scientific evidence. One early twentieth-century educator proclaimed that "the child is naturally, successively animal, anthropoid, half-barbarian, and then civilized." [5] G. Stanley Hall agreed: "The influence of the environment in producing acquired characters transmissible by heredity is greatest in the soma during adolescence. At any rate, for those prophetic souls interested in the future of our race and desirous of advancing it, the field of adolescence is the quarry in which they must seek to find both goals and means. If such a higher stage is ever added to our race, it will not be by increments at any later plateau of adult life, but it will come by increased development at the adolescent stage, which is the bud of promise for the race." [6]

Second, Hall believed in the principle that "nature-is-right." In postulating that individual growth is a retracing of the steps of species evolution, the recapitulation theorists held that human development must conform to a repetition of the ancestral record until adolescence, a time when evolutionary momentum subsided. It followed that the heavy hand of nature should be prevented from disrupting the foreordained intent of each child's genetic heritage. Nothing must impede ontogenetic preparation for the acquisition of acquired characters during adolescence. "No stage to which nature impels, should by human artifice be either hastened or prolonged, let the magic order be disturbed. . . . Human efforts should be to let the forces of development do their perfect work." [7]

The notion that nature had preprogrammed recapitulation was strongly complemented by a third principle, catharsis. If the intrinsically determined sequence of growth changes in an individual necessitates a rehearsal of racial evolution, each succeeding stage then becomes a vital link in the developmental chain. Every stage of growth, therefore, should be permitted full expression, full living out, since each serves as a stimulus to the one that follows. Should environmental pressures suppress a given stage, the course of development might become arrested or retarded. Indeed, by the converse of the law of acquired characters, traits thus lost might signify the onset of regressive evolution for progeny. Catharsis insulated the "nature-is-right" principle from the objection that many propensities, including avarice, disobedience, and aggression, were hardly right. It required that an uncivilized trait characteristic of early racial history should be exercised in childhood to prevent its occurrence in adult years. By allowing children, for example, to express cruelty in mild forms of passion, by kicking the dog or twisting a sibling's arm, they would be rendered immune to expressions of cruelty in adolescence and adulthood. Fortunately for the safety of children, Hall wavered between insisting on the necessity of direct versus vicarious cathartic expression: "I incline to think that many children would

[5] J. M. Tyler, *Growth and Education* (Boston: Houghton Mifflin, 1907), p. 53.

[6] Hall, *Adolescence*, I, 50.

[7] E. G. Thorndike, *The Original Nature of Man* (New York: Columbia University Press, 1913), pp. 271–272.

be better and not worse for reading, providing it can be done in tender years, stories like those of Captain Kidd, Jack Sheppard, Dick Turpin, and other gory tales . . . on the principle of the Aristotelian catharsis to arouse betimes the higher faculties which develop later, and whose function it is to deplete the bad centers and suppress or inhibit their activity." [8]

Fourth, Hall esteemed physical growth to be of more critical developmental significance than cognitive growth. Study of the evolution of animal forms had revealed that complex intellectual behavior had appeared fairly late in phylogenetic history. "Conscious thought, neotics, intellect, reason, are popular and provisional terms for the last or neopsychic stages." [9] Childhood represented on the recapitulatory scale "the age of maturity in some remote, perhaps pigmoid, stage of human evolution." [10] Alfred R. Wallace, an English biologist who with Darwin coauthored the first paper on natural selection, suggested that the emergence of the human species had been preceded by occasions when natural selection worked on intellectual rather than on physical processes. Wallace had hypothesized that eventually evolution reached the state at which intellectual variations were of more adaptive value than physical changes, and, therefore, the transition from the apelike to the human condition was associated chiefly with changes in the mind and central nervous system. Hall agreed completely.

Fifth, G. Stanley Hall viewed the principle of the recapitulatory stage and its corollary, the nascent period, as the proper bases for deriving developmental norms. His concept of the nascent period appears to be a historical antecedent of contemporary interpretations of critical periods; for example, "any period of life when rapid organization is taking place is a critical period." [11] Hall envisaged the sequential, invariant patterns inherent in development as a parade of distinct anthropoid forms, each of which represented a steplike progression in the corresponding history of evolution. A child or adolescent persisted as if on a growth plateau while passing through one of its ancestral forms but accelerated at saltatory rates while migrating between stages. The plateau stages interested Hall, for they provided the norms needed to evaluate developmental progress, but the periods of transition, which he identified as "nascent," intrigued him. Recapitulatory momentum peaked at these times, and hereditary energy now facilitated the growth transition more effectively than the most propitious environment ever could. Hall and his students posed for themselves, therefore, the problem of finding precisely every clue to these wellsprings of developmental energy. Unadulterated recapitulation, nonetheless, was to be sustained. To augment certain growth propensities too soon might induce precocity in one part or stage, overwhelming other upcoming nascent stages and perhaps even contributing

[8] Hall, *Adolescence*, I, 408.
[9] Ibid., II, 450.
[10] Ibid., I, ix–x.
[11] J. P. Scott, *Early Experience and the Organization of Behavior* (Belmont, Calif.: Brooks/Cole, 1968), p. 69.

to their permanent arrest. To ignore inhibiting influences, on the other hand, might suppress nascent periods entirely.

The urgency with which Hall felt compelled to identify stages and nascent periods apparently constrained whatever doubts he may have entertained regarding the problem of defining them explicitly. He acknowledged, for example, that nascency failed to appear during recapitulation of remote ancestral stages: "The early stages of growth are telescoped into each other almost indistinguishably, so that phylogenetically, the embryo lives a thousand years in a day, and the higher the species, the more rapid relatively is the transit through the lower stages." [12] However, Hall failed to distinguish between two distinct meanings of nascency. On occasion, he insisted that the growth of each "part" of the body must be analyzed for clues to its particular nascent period. [13] Here he assumed that every identifiable part of the human body, including such components as the heart, liver, lungs, nose, and ears, attained their nascent moments at different times. But Hall also frequently asserted that, with all body and psychic parts taken collectively, children and adolescents must be observed to establish nascent benchmarks.

The Concept of Adolescence

G. Stanley Hall's concept of adolescence followed consistently from the basic principles of genetic psychology. He saw adolescents as infirm, hapless creatures. Recapitulatory instincts, so important in childhood, yielded in adolescence to societal pressures; Hall's attention therefore focused on the twin tasks of interpreting and suggesting changes in these new influences. A new, propitious environment for acquired characters would be of little avail, however, if parents and educators failed in their child-rearing practices to adhere faithfully to the "nature-is-right" and catharsis principles. Consequently, in *Adolescence*, Hall emphasized strongly that the child, so much older racially, was father of the adolescent, and that, to bring the adolescent to maturity, nascent periods at every stage of development must be carefully nurtured. Hall's exhortations and concerns are expressed cogently in the following excerpts from his views on adolescent physical, cognitive, and social development.

Physical Growth

In genetic psychology growth curves represented graphic records of racial history and the most important source of clues to nascent periods. Slow growth periods signified retardation in evolution; fast growth periods, acceleration. The great spurt accompanying adolescence held special hereditary significance. G. Stanley Hall was equally interested in every physical part of the body, for each possessed uniquely a racial history, nascent period, and, presumably, growth potential through acquired characters. "The law

---

[12] Hall, *Adolescence*, I, 3.
[13] Ibid., I, 35.

of nascent periods, or the age curve of growth of each organ or faculty, is one of the first desiderata of genetic psychology; how to apply it, by what means and to what degree to stimulate each part in its stage of most and least rapid growth, and how to apportion training of mind and body between developing the powers that excel to a degree of specialized culture that corresponds to their hereditary possibilities, or educating the weakest parts and powers in order to improve proportion and symmetry, is one of the chief problems of individual pedagogy." [14]

Hall encountered insurmountable problems in attempting to distinguish parts and organs of the body, but he managed, nonetheless, to establish five facts of growth: (*a*) The parts of the body grow in unequal ratios; otherwise, the infant would become a monster adult with an enormous head, short legs and arms, thick belly, and elongated trunk. (*b*) The parts grow rhythmically; that is, rapid increments alternate with slow. The development of each is represented by curves, "which differ greatly one from the other in the same person and also differ in different individuals in whom the summative measures of gross height and weight may coincide." [15] (*c*) The parts reach their maximum size at a different age, may continue to grow well into old age, and have their youth, maturity, and old age. The different periods neither coincide among parts nor with the body as a whole. (*d*) Every higher animal is composed of organs phyletically old and new, whose order of development may change as a consequence of their relative importance to the species. The heart, for example, develops before the blood vessels, a fact which suggested a reversal in the phylogenetic order. (*e*) Earlier stages of growth, because they are phyletically older and telescoped together during rapid-growth periods, are less susceptible to environmental influence.

Hall carefully articulated his belief that recapitulatory impulses weakened in adolescence and that during this period youth was especially vulnerable to environmental pressures, both physically and emotionally:

> Young children grow despite great hardships, but later adolescence is more de-
> pendent upon favoring conditions in the environment, disturbances of which
> more readily cause arrest and prevent maturity. Not only is the range of variation
> in growth now increased, but there is far greater liability to reversion. As we
> advance to the later stages of adolescence, all these liabilities are greatly in-
> creased, as is the predisposition to sickness. The young pubescent, achieving his
> growth in the realm of fundamental qualities, dimensions, and functions, comes
> up to adult size at eighteen relatively limp and inept, like an insect that has just
> accomplished its last molt, and is therefore far more in the need of protection,
> physical care, moral and intellectual guidance; . . . this last great wave of
> growth throws the child up onto the shores of manhood or womanhood relatively
> helpless as from a second birth.[16]

[14] Ibid., I, 128.
[15] Ibid., I, 53.
[16] Ibid., I, 47–48.

In Hall's judgment, exercise of every part of the body was absolutely essential. "We inherit tendencies of muscular coordination that have been of great racial utility." [17] "The best exercise for the young should thus be more directed to develop the basal powers old to the race than those peculiar to the individual. . . . Hereditary momenta really determine, too, the order in which nerve centers come into function." [18]

Hall never shirked from offering recapitulatory explanations of observable growth phenomena. Consider, for example, his interpretation of the relatively slow rate of growth that occurs in late childhood:

> The period of retardation represents a relative balance between assimilation and expenditure and, what is far more important, between fundamental growth of the large bones and muscles and the accessory development of the smaller and more peripheral parts and functions. Indeed, the boy of ten or eleven is tolerably well adjusted to the environment of savage life in a warm country where he could readily live independently of his parents, discharging all the functions necessary to his personal life, but lacking only the reproductive function. . . . We shall later also see in how many of his ways he resembles the savage and how each furnishes the key for understanding both the good and bad points in the other's character. All this suggests on the recapitulation theory some long stationary period during which life had been pretty fully unfolded. . . . This arrest may even suggest the age of senescence in some post-simian stage of ancestry. This short pause would thus be the present echo of a long phyletic stage when for many generations our prehuman forebearers were pigmoid adults, leading short lives and dying at or before the pubic growth increment now occurs. . . . Not only this, but hard conditions, like homelessness, imperfect food and health, and now sexual precocity develop strong tendencies to revert to or to remain in this stage. . . . Thus man, adult in years and stature, is constantly prone to drop to this lower level, development above which becomes a little more precarious than the preceding stages had been. The latter periods of growth are different and more insecure because newer and more unstable.[19]

Hall also offered two major explanations of why girls exceed boys in physical stature in the early phases of the adolescent growth spurt. Perhaps, he said, the human female had been prematurely impregnated in consequence of hyperactive sex passions of the human male. After civilized characteristics were acquired, males were less able to exploit their interests, and girls grew again at the normal rate. "Part of the sudden and early increment in girls is a trace of ancient but now deferred maternity due originally to premature male aggression." [20] But then, the larger size of the girls might be a result of natural selection augmented by acquired characters. Hall argued that the female instincts of "reserve and coyness" develop earlier than sexual desire which "normally develops progressively to a maximum

[17] Ibid., I, 206.
[18] Ibid., I, 207.
[19] Ibid., I, 44–45.
[20] Ibid., I, 42.

during years of greatest fertility." [21] The larger, more vigorous girls, therefore, would have been able to resist fertilization; even in an age of animal violence they would have been able to preserve their chastity, and thus pass on their strength to their progeny.

Cognitive Growth

Hall reasoned that conscious thought and cognition were latecomers in evolutionary history. "Muscles are in a most intimate and peculiar sense the organs of the will. They have built all the roads, cities, and machines in the world, written all the books, spoken all the words, and, in fact, done everything that man has accomplished with matter." [22] By virtue of its recency, the "psyche" he believed to be "a quantum and direction of vital energy, the processes of which most need exploration and description, ordering and directing." [23]

Hall assigned to adolescent intellect a crucial role in his scheme to raise mankind to superanthropoid status, but regarded environmental stimulation toward creativity and originality and other modes of enriching children's experiences as detrimental. "Staring, experimenting with sensation, surprise, active observation, the passion to touch, handle, taste everything" were behaviors associated with "the lust to know." "The question mania which may become a neurosis at about the earliest school age, anxiety to know the origin of life that is suppressed to stealthiness at about the same age when it really grows more intense; baffling theological queries, interest in death and in theological questions, in the *how* of mechanical processes that often motivates what seems destructiveness, desire to travel, the conquests of timidity by curiosity" lead to such problems as truancy and running away from home.[24] "All these expressions of a pure desire for knowledge are phenomena of the crepuscular dawn that precedes the sunrise of reason in adolescence." [25]

Hall's recapitulatory framework led him to conclude that parents and educators must respond differently to children's and adolescents' cognitive growth. The "only duty of young children is implicit obedience." [26] Children should express cathartically their boorish impulses, drill and exercise their minds, but avoid explanations and thinking. As difficult as inhibiting children's curiosity would be, harnessing the adolescents' blossoming intellect, checking precocity, preventing arrest, and simultaneously nurturing, guiding, and sustaining the budding powers seemed almost insuperable. Hall describes the difficult developmental transition in cognition as follows:

The chief mental training from about eight to twelve is arbitrary memorization, drill, habituation, with only limited appeal to the understanding. After the criti-

[21] Ibid., I, 43.
[22] Ibid., I, 131.
[23] Ibid., II, 69.
[24] Ibid., II, 450.
[25] Ibid.
[26] Ibid., II, 451.

cal transition age of six or seven, when the brain has achieved its adult size and weight and teething has reduced the chewing surface to its least extent, begins an unique stage of life marked by reduced growth and increased activity and power to resist both disease and fatigue, which, . . . suggest what was, in some just post-simian age of our race, its period of maturity. . . . The hand is never so near the brain. Most of the content of the mind has entered it through the senses, and the eye- and ear-gates should be opened at their widest. Authority should now take precedence of reason. Children comprehend much and very rapidly if we can only refrain from explaining, but this slows down intuition, intends to make casuists and prigs and to enfeeble the ultimate vigor of reason. . . . Boys of this age are now not very affectionate. . . . He should have fought, whipped and been whipped, used language offensive to the prude and prim precisian, been in some scrapes, had something to do with bad, if more with good associates, and been exposed to and already recovering from as many forms of ethical mumps and measles as, by having in mild form now he can be rendered immune to later when they become far more dangerous. . . . Something is amiss with the lad of ten who is very good, studious, industrious, thoughtful, altruistic, quiet, polite, respectful, obedient, gentlemanly, orderly, always in good toilet, docile to reason, who turns away from stories that reek with gore, prefers adult companionship to that of his mates, refuses all low associates, speaks standard English, or is pious and deeply in love with religious services as the typical maiden teacher. . . . Such a boy is either undervitalized and anemic and precocious by nature, a repressed, over-trained, conventionalized manikin, a hypocrite, as some can become under pressure thus early in life, or else, a genius of some kind with a little of all these.

But with the teens all this begins to be changed and many of these precepts must be gradually reversed. . . . The drill methods of the preceding period must be slowly relaxed and new appeals made to freedom and interest. We can no longer coerce a break, but must lead and inspire if we would avoid arrest. Individuality must have a longer tether. . . . There is nothing in the environment to which the adolescent nature does not keenly respond. . . . Plasticity is at its maximum. . . . The mind at times grows in leaps and bounds . . .[27]

Youth has a passion for callow ratiocination. . . . Reason is just coming to seem a universal solvent, and he would everywhere substitute the mediate for the immediate, and subordinate intuition to understanding. . . . The tender intellect sometimes crepitates and grows dizzy in the orgy and flux and loses its orientation and may waste powers in unifying the irreconcilable, in elaborating distinctions that have no existence, or giving the best arguments to the worst cause, and a kind of reasoning mania is easily possible.[28]

Hall's account of cognitive unfolding is largely discredited today. Behavioral scientists are no longer fettered by considerations of the primacy of physical growth, "nature-is-right," and catharsis. They insist that children neither fight to be rendered immune to "ethical mumps and measles" nor withdraw from intellectual stimulation. In contrast to Hall's views, "reasoning manias" are seen as less likely to occur during adolescence, when earlier

[27] Ibid., II, 451–454.
[28] Ibid., II, 533.

social experiences provide bases for cognitive learning. In one important respect, however, Hall accords well with a contemporary viewpoint. Piaget [29] and Kohlberg,[30] for example, look to changes in cognition as the *sine qua non* of the capacity to make moral judgments. In essence, both theorists see a morality of cooperation as following a morality of constraint. The latter, founded on adult authority and unilateral respect, leads children to equate "good" with obedience and duty, to focus on literal rather than abstract aspects of rules, and to evaluate actions by their conformity to rules rather than by the motives that prompted the actions. Eventually, moral autonomy and cooperation supplant constraint through mechanisms thought to be largely hereditary. Children attain the capacity to comprehend belief as hypotheses requiring verification, to manipulate logical relations rationally and consciously, to structure for themselves rather than to accept "laws" obediently, and to conceive rules as subject to modification and adaptation in terms of the intent and purpose of other individuals. Hall's account of children's moral development is strikingly similar to that of Piaget and Kohlberg. In the following excerpt Hall describes a research investigation involving the judgments of both boys and girls from 6 to 16. The youths were asked what should be done with a girl who, in seeking to please her mother, beautified the parlor chairs with a new box of paints.

> Most of the younger children whip the girl, but from fourteen on the number declines very rapidly. Few of the young children suggest explaining why it was wrong, while at twelve, one hundred and eighty-one, and at sixteen, seven hundred and fifty-one, would explain. The motive of the younger children in punishment is revenge; with the older ones that of preventing a repetition of the act comes in; and higher and later comes the purpose of reform. With age comes also a marked distinction between the act and its motive and a sense of the girl's ignorance. Only the older children would suggest extracting a promise not to offend again. Thus, with puberty comes a change of view-point from judging actions by results to judging by motives, and only the older ones see that wrong can be done if there are no bad consequences. There is also a great development of the quality of mercy with increased years.[31]

Social Development

The recapitulation theory convinced Hall that every person was born twice, once as an individual and again, in adolescence, as a member of the human race. Children were always self-centered, selfish, and aggressive, but adolescents could be altruistic and self-sacrificing. He recognized that hereditary impulses pushing toward a rebirth often failed to ascend and that in adolescence selfish actions might conquer altruistic inclinations permanently. To facilitate the new birth, or process of socialization, Hall aimed to find

[29] J. Piaget, *The Moral Judgment of the Child* (Glencoe, Ill.: Free Press, 1948).

[30] L. Kohlberg, "Moral Development and Identification," in H. W. Stevenson, ed., *The Yearbook of the National Society for the Study of Education*, 1963, LXII, Part I.

[31] Hall, *Adolescence*, II, 393–394.

the nascent periods of all the social instincts and hence maximize the salutary effects of intrinsic motivation.

Hall commenced his search for social instincts with the assumption that the oldest racial instinct is sexuality—possession and reproduction. From this common denominator the fundamental instincts of love and religiosity were distinguished. He described the genetic concept of love, for example, as a series of stages starting with a basic, animal-like, selfish love, rising to friendship, romantic love, marital love, love of children, love of community, race, and, eventually, love for a deity. To prove that love and religious instincts were derivations of the same underlying impulse, Hall observed that young people in love were prone to consider the building of houses in which they might live, to think, talk, and write about death, and to be exceedingly responsive to nature; likewise, religious persons have through the ages been preoccupied with building houses in which their gods could live and be worshipped, with death and immortality, and with nature as a source of religious inspiration.[32]

The degree to which the higher-order social instincts, those specific manifestations of love and religion which apparently resided in the conscience, were attributed to heredity is evident in Hall's thought: "Conscience . . . awakens with a longing hunger and thirst for righteousness, prompts to highest aspiration and resolve. Benevolence and love to all persons and all being is fresh from its original source, . . . so that for brief periods youth and maidens sometimes seem too good for this earth." Unfortunately, the necessity of cathartic expression, of fulfilling the barbaric aspects of the recapitulatory sequence precisely, led to the probability that social development, too, would be marked by turbulent and inconsistent behavior.

> The forces of sin and those of virtue never struggle so hotly for possession of the youthful soul. As statistics show, the age of most frequent conversions to true religion is precisely the years of the largest percentage of first commitments to houses of detention for crime. . . . It seems a law of psychic development, that more or less evil must be done to unloose the higher powers of constraint and to practice them until they can keep down the baser instincts. The religious struggles of this age bear abundant evidence to the violence of these storms and counter-currents of which the human soul is now the arena. Temptations hitherto unknown to sins hitherto impossible bring redeeming agencies also new into action, and while the juvenile offender and the debauchee is arrested in his development and remains through life under the power of evil, growth is benign, and those who achieve normal maturity domesticate their baser instincts into the service of goodness.[33]

Childhood was readily interpreted within the context of recapitulation. The spontaneous activities of children were regarded as rehearsals of activi-

[32] Ibid., II, 95–132.
[33] Ibid., II, 83.

ties corresponding to racial stages. When they climbed trees, they were reliving the stage of racial arboreal existence; and when wandering and camping engrossed them, they relived the nomadic stage.[34] The basis of sex typing, masculinity and femininity, also was differentiated early in the history of the race: "We have in the Christian doctrine of love, and of the spermatic *logos,* in the platonic stages of eroticism in the symposium, abundant evidence that the race has had a sexual consciousness." [35]

As hereditary propensities waned at the end of recapitulation, parents and other socializing agents suddenly became nature's surrogates in serving the ends of evolution. They must now foster and nurture the new but natural self-consciousness, bringing adolescents to new choices and new experiences and continuing their hereditary momentum toward superanthropoid status. Hereditary impulses toward sex-role identity, however, were scant aid to adolescents, whose racial instincts were weak and ineffectual. What might happen to them should they fall prey to an unfavorable social environment? Alienation, delinquency, and degenerate evolution would be propagated:

Alienation in youth is serious because so often hereditary. Moral insanity, which sometimes precedes and sometimes comes out at puberty, is characterized by incapacity for education, distaste for family life, marked peculiarities of character, extreme cleverness in certain directions, bad sexuality and criminality. The more passionate and instinctive men are, the more they resemble children in these respects and the more egotistic they are.[36]

. . . normal children often pass through stages of passionate cruelty, laziness, lying and thievery. . . . Their vanity, slang, obscenity, contagious imitativeness, their absence of moral sense, disregard of property, and violence to each other, constitute them criminals in all essential respects, lacking only the strength and insight to make their crime dangerous to the communities in which they live. We are told that to magnify the soul of the child before its more animal instincts are reduced to due proportion and controlled by conscience and reason, would give us the most truculent and menacing forms of criminality; just as to magnify all parts and organs of the infant's body in equal proportion would, as we have seen, produce deformity and monstrosity.[37]

Criminals are much like overgrown children—egotistic, foppish, impulsive, gluttonous, blind to the rights of others, and our passions tend to bring us to childish stages.[38]

The power of self-control is latent and undeveloped, and its necessity must be slowly learned. If he is degenerate or of a criminal type, or if his surroundings are unfavorable, the young criminal fails to acquire this power and falls a victim to the same appetites and impulses which all normal persons feel, but repress.

[34] Ibid., I, 202–204.
[35] Ibid., II, 99.
[36] Ibid., I, 330.
[37] Ibid., I, 334–335.
[38] Ibid., I, 338.

Perhaps the animal part of his nature is abnormally and congenitally disproportionate to the intellectual, so that there is no inner opposition to the gratification
of his desires.[39]

When the social organism is decaying, it does not readily and completely disappear, but drags a trail of *débris* from the past, and degenerate forms soon lose
the power to reacquire the conditions normal to their more perfect ancestors
. . . so that the degenerate condition is not attained by simply going backward
down the line of ascent, but is a new point of departure. . . .[40]

Hall studied socialization and the consequences of its failure not from
the viewpoint of identification and imitation but from that of recapitulation
theory. Parents and educators, he believed, should see that children realize
their nascent periods and ward away from them environmental enticements
that might promote precocity or arrest; in short, they should ease their
children's journey through the ancestral stages. But how long should the
parents stand aloof? How long should they refrain from exerting their own
modeling influence? How long should the acquisition of new acquired characters be held in abeyance? The answer depended on the accumulation of
acquired characters available to the adolescent. The son of a man who had
attained professional eminence would clearly have more critical experiences
to recapitulate than the son of an unskilled laborer. Hall agreed wholeheartedly with Redfield,[41] an early genetic psychologist: "If we could induce the
parents of each family to have one more child five years after they would
normally cease reproduction, the children so produced might do more for
the advancement of civilization and race progress than all the other children
put together."

Conclusion

The theory of recapitulation acquired the force of an incantation in the
hands of Hall. It was the first and thus far has been the last thorough
integration of the literature from the philosophical and natural sciences into
developmental psychology. His interest in linking ancestral evolution to
individual development gave impetus to taxonomic, normative, and descriptive activities that, although far removed in purposes from his intent, have
since accelerated in pediatrics, physical anthropology, and comparative
psychology.

Questions posed by recapitulation theorists regarding growth curves and
merits of psychical and physical traits in evolutionary progress are now
curios of a forgotten era. Lamarckianism has been largely discredited, and
the discrepancies in recapitulation have been shown to be as great as the
similarities. Hall attended to linkage between biological and psychological
forces during adolescence and provided a rationale for limited interest in

[39] Ibid., I, 339.
[40] Ibid., I, 336–337.
[41] C. F. Redfield, *Control of Heredity* (Chicago: Monarch, 1903), p. 267.

developmental events during infancy and childhood, a focus that contrasts sharply with contemporary practice in developmental psychology. He had overestimated the promise of adolescence and the insignificance of childhood. In his enthusiasm for catharsis as a purging mechanism, compounded by his fervor to harness the energy of nascent periods, he overlooked the degree to which childhood social experiences may resist extinction and subsequently influence adolescent development. Moreover, his belief that fostering intellectual and creative precocity might arrest and pervert other areas of development would be taken today as more misleading than quaint. Nonetheless, the massive quantity of facts and figures Hall wove into his interpretations provide invaluable perspective on the problems of adolescent development three-quarters of a century ago. His data offer a base from which to judge how much, or how little, progress has ensued.

James S. Coleman

How Do the Young Become Adults?[1]

In the following selection, Coleman traces the historical significance of the family, school, and workplace as agents in the occupational training of adolescents. He also observes a distinction between "formal schooling" and "informal education" and suggests that in contemporary society resources allocated to the former overshadow those assigned to the latter. Coleman argues cogently that, in order to return the two critical functions to proper balance, the process of socialization must be reorganized to include the "economic institutions of society."

Instructional Objectives
To review the circumstances that reduced opportunities for occupational learning in the family.
To note changes in the workplace that have lessened the availability of jobs and "experiential learning."

FROM *Review of Educational Research*, XLII (1972), 431–439. Reprinted by permission of the author and the American Educational Research Association.
  [1] This paper appeared before publication as a report of the Center for Social Organization of Schools, supported in part as a research and development center by funds from the United States Office of Education, Department of Health, Education, and Welfare. The opinions expressed in this publication do not necessarily reflect the position or policy of the Office of Education, and no official endorsement by the Office of Education should be inferred.

To observe how transformations in the high school have increased attention to intellectual skills.

To describe changes which are necessary in the American society to reorganize the economic institutions for learning efficiency.

To indicate the effect of a reorganized system of education on the social and racial integration of society.

I T IS important to ask, along with specific questions about how schools function, more general questions about the development from childhood through youth to adulthood. Only by continuing to ask these more general questions can we avoid waking up some day to find that educational institutions are finely tuned and efficiently designed to cope with the problems of an earlier day. Among the more general questions, we need to ask how it is that the young become adults, and what are the current and changing roles of the school, the family, and the workplace. I will reserve the school till last, because changes in the other two institutions proceed from other causes, without regard for their consequences for the young, while schools are explicitly designed with consequences for the young as their primary goal. Thus the family and the workplace—together with certain other aspects of society—form the environment within which the school functions.

CHANGES IN THE FAMILY

It is necessary only to give a quick overview of changes in the family's function in bringing children to adulthood, because those changes have been so great, and need only to be brought to attention. Classically, the family was the chief educational institution for the child, because he carried out most of his activities within it until he left it to form his own. That juncture in life was his transition to adult status—the transition to economic self-sufficiency and family head. The timing of this transition differed widely from place to place and from one economic setting to another. On an Irish farm, it may have been age 35 or even older. In an industrial city, it may have been 16 or even younger. But the transition to full adulthood has characteristically taken place when the former child married and either formed a new household or formed a sub-household within his parental family.

The family has gone through two major transitions that sharply limit its occupational training of the young. The first of these occurred when the father went out to work into a shop or an office, and thus began to carry out his major productive activities away from home behind the closed doors of an organization. The second occurred when the mother went out to work or otherwise stopped carrying out her major productive activities in the home.

Before the first transition, families contained the major productive activities of society. Thus the young learned not only the whole variety of things that one commonly associates with the family; they also learned their principal occupational skills and functions—if not in the family, then structurally close to it, in an apprentice relation.

For boys, this occupational learning within the family began to vanish as the father went out to work in a shop or an office. For girls, it continued longer, learning household work, cooking, sewing, child care from the mother, whose principal occupation that was. But by now in most families that second transition has taken place as well: the mother's principal occupation is no longer household work, for that work now occupies little of her time and attention. Either she goes out to work like her husband, or occupies herself in other activities which do not require the aid of her daughters. Even child care is minimal, as family sizes have declined. As an economist recently stated, "The home closes down during the day."

Thus the family as a source of occupational learning has declined as it lost its place as the central productive institution of society. But as both adults have come to carry out their central activities outside the home, they have removed other functions from the home and family as well. Friends are drawn from occupation, and adult cocktail parties have replaced neighborhood or extended family gatherings in the social life of the husband and wife. Less and less does the husband's and wife's social life take place in a setting that includes children. Some leisure activities are still carried out as a family, so I don't intend to overstate the case. But the point is that as these large occupational activities of adults moved out of the home, they took others with them, leaving it a less rich place in opportunities for learning for its younger members.

CHANGES IN THE WORKPLACE

Changes in the workplace, subsequent to its removal from the home into specialized economic institutions, have also affected the movement of the young into adulthood. The major changes have been away from small organizations to large ones; away from ad hoc informal hiring practices to formal procedures with formal credentials required of applicants; away from using children in secondary and service activities toward excluding them from workplaces under the guise of "protection;" away from jobs requiring low educational credentials toward jobs requiring more education; away from loosely organized occupational settings in which workers participated with varying schedules and varying amounts of time toward a rigidly-defined "full-time job" with a fixed schedule and fixed time commitment.

All of these trends (apart from some very minor and very recent movements in the other direction in a few of these dimensions) have led the workplace to become less available and less useful to the young until they enter it as full-time workers at the end of a longer and longer period of full-time schooling.[2]

These changes in the family and in occupational institutions have led both to become less useful as settings where the young can learn. In the family, the young remain, while the activities from which they could learn have moved out; in workplaces, the activities from which the young could learn remain, but the young themselves have been excluded. This exclusion places youth more on the fringes of society, outside its important institutions. If one is young, it is difficult to get a loan, to buy on credit, to rent an apartment, to have one's signature accepted for any of the many things that are commonplace for adults. The reason is simple: the young have no institutional base, they are a *lumpen* proletariat outside those institutions of society that are recognized by other institutions and give legitimacy to those persons who are within them.

Before turning to changes in the school, it is important to note one central aspect of the learning that occurred in home and workplaces, and still occurs, though to a sharply reduced extent. It is learning which is variously called "incidental learning" or "experiential learning." It is learning by acting and experiencing the consequences of that action. It is learning through occupying a role with responsibility for actions that affect others. It is learning that is recognized in colloquial parlance as taking place in "the school of hard knocks." It is not learning that proceeds in the way that learning typically takes place in the classroom, where the first step is cognitive understanding, and the last step—often omitted—is acting on that understanding.

Changes in the School

When the major educational functions were in the home, the school was an auxiliary and supplementary institution with two functions. First, for the small fraction of the population whose occupational destination was clerical or academic, it taught a large portion of the occupational skills: languages, mathematics, philosophy, history. Second, for the large majority, it taught the basic skills of reading, writing, and arithmetic. Then, as the changes in family and workplace took place, the school began to take on two additional functions: first, to provide occupational training for the increasing fraction of occupations ranging from engineering to journalism that seemed to require technical book learning; and second, to perform some of the educational

---

[2] There are some complications to these trends, and some statistics which appear to go in the opposite direction. For example, the labor force participation rates for persons aged 16–21 enrolled in school increased between 1960 and 1970, from 35 to 40 per cent for men and 25 to 36 per cent for women. But this change reflects an increase in school-going by those who in 1960 would have been only working. The proportion of persons aged 16 to 21 enrolled in school was much higher in 1970 than in 1960. This increase was largely due to a lack of full-time jobs in the labor force for a greatly-expanded age cohort. Thus for many, education became the full-time activity, and labor force participation was restricted to part-time or in-and-out work.

activities ranging from music appreciation to civics that were not occupational, but had been carried out to differing degrees and often with indifferent success in the family.

In addition to these explicit and positive functions, the school began to carry out an important but largely passive function as well: to house the young while the parents were off in their specialized adult activities outside the home. This is the function often derogatorily described as the "babysitting" function of the school. As women came more and more into the labor force, and desired to participate even more than they did, the demand for such babysitting agencies increased, extending downward in age to day-care centers for the very young. And as occupational opportunities for the young have lessened, the babysitting function has extended upward in age, with the universities, colleges, junior colleges, and community colleges acting as temporary holding stations on the way to adulthood.

This transformation of the schools in response to society has had a consequence that is important in considering the path to becoming adult. This is the massive enlargement of the *student* role of young persons, to fill the vacuum that the changes in the family and workplace created. The student role of young persons has become enlarged to the point where that role constitutes the major portion of their youth. But the student role is not a role of taking action and experiencing consequences. It is not a role in which one learns by hard knocks. It is a relatively passive role, always in preparation for action, but never acting. In attempting to provide the learning that had earlier taken place through experiential learning in the home and at the workplace, the school kept the same classroom mode of learning that was its hallmark: it not only moved the setting of those learning activities from outside the school to within; it changed the method from learning through experience as a responsible actor to learning through being taught as a student. There are some exceptions but the general pattern followed that of the classical school, in which a *teacher* was the medium through which learning was expected to take place. This replaced *action* as the medium through which learning had taken place in the family or the workplace. The student role, in which a person waits to be taught, became central to the young person's life.

The consequence of the expansion of the student role, and the action-poverty it implies for the young, has been an increased restiveness among the young. They are shielded from responsibility, and they become irresponsible; they are held in a dependent status, and they come to act as dependents; they are kept away from productive work, and they become unproductive. But even if we saw no signs of irresponsibility, stagnant dependency, and lack of productivity, the point would remain the same: the school, when it has tried to teach non-intellective things, does so in the only way it knows how, the way designed to teach intellective capabilities: through a teacher, transmitting cognitive skills and knowledge, in a classroom, to students.

Although the complex problems created by these changes cannot be solved easily, I believe it would be a step toward a solution if we began to conceive of matters a little differently. In particular, the problems become clearer if we wipe away the confusion between "schooling" and "education." Previously, it was natural that schooling could have been confused with education —for schooling was that part of the education of the young which took place formally, and thus had to be planned for and consciously provided. But the larger part of education took place outside the school. The child spent most of his time outside the school; school was a small portion of his existence. It taught him to read and write and work with numbers, but the most important parts of education it did not provide: learning about work, both the skills and the habits, learning how to function in society, learning how to be a father or mother, husband or wife, learning to take care of others and to take responsibility for others. Because these things were learned informally, through experience, or at least without formal organization, they could be disregarded, and "education" could come to be identified with "schooling."

But much of this other education evaporates as work takes place behind closed doors and as the family is reduced as a locus of important activities. "Schooling" meanwhile, continues to mean much the same thing that it did before, except extended in time: the learning of intellectual skills. Thus although schooling remains a small portion of education, it occupies an increasingly larger portion of a young person's time, while the remaining portion of his education is *not* well provided by ordinary, everyday, unplanned activities. Consequently, if an appropriate reform of education is to be made, it must begin with this fact: schooling is not all of education, and the other parts of education require just as much explicit planning and organization as does schooling.

Once this is recognized, then the way is paved for creation of a true educational system—not merely a system of schools, but a system of education that covers non-intellectual learning as well. If one were to go too quickly to a possible solution, or pattern for the future, he would see this as immediately leading toward a multi-track school system in which some young people concentrate on intellectual skills while others concentrate on "practical" or "mechanical" or "vocational" skills. But this pattern fails to recognize clearly the impact of the above separation of schooling and education: it is not only *some* young people who need the non-intellective portions of education, it is all. Thus it is not the *persons* who must be divided into different tracks to learn different skills; it is the *time* of *each* person that must be so divided. Further, the division is not merely a division between intellectual skills and vocational or practical skills. It is a division among a variety of skills, only some of which are intellectual or vocational. If I were asked to catalog the skills that should be learned in the educational system before age 18, I would certainly include all these:

1. Intellectual skills, the kinds of things that schooling at its best teaches.
2. Skills of some occupation that may be filled by a secondary school graduate,

so that every 18-year-old would be accredited in some occupation, whether he continued in school or not.

3. Decision-making skills: that is, those skills of making decisions in complex situations where consequences follow from the decisions.
4. General physical and mechanical skills: skills allowing the young person to deal with physical and mechanical problems he will confront outside work, in the home or elsewhere.
5. Bureaucratic and organizational skills: how to cope with a bureaucratic organization, as an employee, or a customer, or a client, or a manager, or an entrepreneur.
6. Skills in the care of dependent persons: skill in caring for children, old persons, and sick persons.
7. Emergency skills: how to act in an emergency, or an unfamiliar situation, in sufficient time to deal with the emergency.
8. Verbal communication skills in argumentation and debate.

This catalog of skills is certainly not all-inclusive, nor are all the skills listed on the same level of generality. They do, however, give a sense of the scope of what I believe must be explicitly included in education.

The next question becomes, "How is this all to be organized?" Or perhaps, "How do we change the schools to do all this?" But the second question puts the matter wrong. My principal point, and it is the central point of the educational pattern of the future that I envision, is that we do *not* attempt to have the schools do all this. Schools are prepared to do what they have done all along: teach young people intellectual things, both by giving them information and giving them intellectual tools, such as literacy, mathematics, and foreign languages. Schools are not prepared to teach these other skills—and the history of their attempts to change themselves so that they could do this shows only one thing: that these other activities—whether they are vocational education, driver training, consumer education, civics, home economics, or something else—have always played a secondary and subordinate role in schools, always in the shadow of academic performance. The mode of organization of schools, the fact that they are staffed by teachers who themselves have been measured by academic performance, the fact that they lead in a natural progression to more and more intellectually specialized institutions, the universities and then graduate schools—all this means that they are destined to fail as educational institutions in areas other than teaching of intellectual skills.

The pattern for the future, then, as I see it, is one in which the school comes to be reduced in importance and scope and time in the life of a young person from age 12 onward, with the explicit recognition that it is providing only a portion of education. This reduction would necessarily occur, because these other skills must be learned as well—many of them by experience and practice, some of them including a little admixture of teaching.

It then becomes necessary to ask just where these other skills would be learned. An immediate response, and an incorrect one, I believe, would be to attempt to design specialized institutions to teach these things, as vocational schools were designed to teach occupational skills—incorrect because if my arguments are correct, then these activities are best learned not by being taught but by being acted on. Thus it is necessary to ask where the action is. The answer is clear: it is in those specialized economic institutions of society into which first men, then women, went out from the family to work. It is in the occupational institutions of society. Women have learned this through the social-psychological poverty of home and neighborhood and have deserted the home for these workplaces.

Thus this education can appropriately take place only in the economic institutions of society—those organizations behind whose doors adults vanish while the child vanishes inside the walls of the school. Such education could not be hit-or-miss, merely placing a young person on the job or in an apprentice situation. It would be necessary to carefully lay out the skills that were necessary to learn, more carefully than I have done in the catalog of eight skills listed, and to organize the young person's experiences in such a way that he learns these skills. This would involve, of course, more than one institution outside the school. And it would require brilliance both in conception and in execution if it is to work well in early days. For it involves nothing less than a breaking open of the economic institutions of society, from factories to hospitals, a removing of the insulation that separates them from the young, and giving them an explicit role in the education of the young. How this would be done will differ from society to society: in the free enterprise capitalist economy of the U.S., it could probably best begin by providing the young with entitlements that could be redeemed by businesses and other enterprises that try to provide the appropriate learning experiences. In other countries, it might better be done in another way. But the end result would be similar—the young would be integrated into the economic activities of society from a very early age, *without* stopping their schooling, but merely by stopping the dilution of schooling that has occurred in recent years. The economic organizations of society would necessarily change, and change radically, to incorporate the young—not to become schools, but to become institutions in which work is designed not only for productive efficiency, but for learning efficiency as well. The revolution necessary in society is, if I am correct, a revolution within these occupational institutions—from General Motors to government agencies—from business offices to airports.

A reorganization of education in this way would require, if it is to be effective, standards of performance and criteria to be met in the areas other than intellectual, so that the credentials of a young person would be far broader than those implied by the various diplomas and degrees that have been carried over in modified form from an early period. Some of the credentials would be based on performance tests such as those used in industries and skilled crafts today. Others would be based on performance ratings by supervisors and on letters of recommendation. For developing other criteria, inventiveness and imagination would be necessary. But the essential point is that those skills must be just as explicitly evaluated and form just as much a portion of a young person's credentials as intellectual skills do today.

There are a number of important implications to this reorganization of the path toward adulthood. If we recognize that it requires an explicit breaking open of work organizations to incorporate the young, the most direct implication is an enormous transformation of these economic institutions. Their product would be not only goods and services to be marketed, but also learning, the latter paid from public funds as schools are today. They would become much more diversified institutions, no longer preserving the fiction that nothing but production occurs within them, but recognizing that much of adults' social lives, and most of their time expenditures, takes place within them, and expanding that recognition into explicit design of this experience.

A less direct implication of this reorganization of education is that it would reduce the relationship between educational performance and family educational background or social class. In schools, the pervasive power of testing on intellectual criteria—the only real criteria the school knows—exacerbates and emphasizes the inequalities of academic background that children bring with them to school. If education is appropriately defined to include these other equally important skills, then the artificially-heightened disparity between students from "advantaged" and "disadvantaged" backgrounds will be reduced—but only, of course, if these other activities are carried out in their natural habitat, rather than in the school, which constitutes an uncongenial setting for them.

Finally, a still less direct implication of this reorganization of education is related to the current controversy about school integration through balancing of the races or social classes in school. That controversy, which reflects a real problem where residential segregation is pronounced—as it is in all large urban areas—cannot be solved as long as education is identified with a school building containing classrooms and teachers. It can be solved if formal education takes place largely outside the schools and in economic institutions—for it is the economic institutions that of all those in society are the least segregated by race and in which racial integration produces least friction—because it occurs in a setting with work to be done in an organized, rather than anarchic, structure of interpersonal relations.

This effect of such a reorganized system of education in integrating the society racially is not an accidental one. It arises because this reorganization is not an ad hoc, makeshift patching up of outworn institutions. It is a reorganization that recognizes fundamental structural changes in society—the drying up of family functions and the specialization of economic activities—and asks where in such an emerging social structure is the appropriate locus for the young, if they are to have the opportunity for moving to adulthood. The answer is that the young belong where everyone else is, and where the action is: inside the economic institutions where the productive activities of society take place.

Judith K. Brown

Adolescent Initiation Rites: Recent Interpretations

Adolescent initiation rites may be of short or prolonged duration, laying stress upon external and outwardly impressive ceremonials. Although providing formal, institutionalized procedures for inducting youth into adulthood, citizens of societies that sponsor them are largely unaware of why the rites occur. In her paper, Brown surveys the anthropological literature, organizing the discussion in terms of three kinds of investigation —macro-studies, individual-centered studies, and micro-studies. She reviews a variety of hypotheses explored in these three types of study and suggests that their results allow for greater generality when they are viewed as complementary.

Instructional Objectives
To summarize explanations of initiation rites suggested by cross-cultural (macro-study) data.
To summarize explanations of initiation rites suggested by their effect on adolescents (individual-centered study).
To summarize explanations of initiation rites suggested by societal practices and beliefs (micro-study).

THERE is little agreement in our society as to when a young person should be considered adult. An adolescent may pay adult fares and admission charges for several years before he is licensed to drive a car and registered to vote. But his friends may still consider him too immature for marriage, a view he may not share. In many other societies, adulthood is conferred by means of an initiation ceremony and the initiated are adult by definition.

FROM paper prepared especially for this volume.

Even physical maturation may be believed to depend upon the supernatural forces invoked by the ritual.

Initiation rites vary greatly from society to society, but the following description of the initiation of girls among the Maroni River Caribs may serve as one illustration.[1] When a girl first menstruates, she is confined to a special part of the house for eight days. She remains in seclusion particularly to avoid the spirits of the river and of the forest. These would be offended by her condition and they would cause her to sicken and die. The girl is dressed in old clothes in order to be unattractive to the spirits, and her diet is restricted rather severely. During these eight days, she is expected to spin cotton to be used in making a hammock for a member of her family. At the end of her seclusion, an elderly couple noted for industry arrives at the home of the girl before sunrise. The girl is bathed. Then a small tuft of cotton is placed in the palm of her hand, and fire is set to it. She must move the cotton rapidly from hand to hand to avoid getting burned. This ritual is done because her hands must always be busy. Next her hand is placed in a bowl of large, biting ants. She must not show pain. The ants are to remind her always to be industrious like the ant. Were a lazy person to attend this part of the ceremony, the girl would also become lazy. The girl is then dressed, painted and adorned with jewelry. Guests arrive and there is drinking, dancing and singing. When she has washed her hands in grated manioc, she is free once more to move about the village, to take her daily bath in the river, and to work in the household.

Since we live in a "ritual-poor" society, such ceremonies appear exotic and difficult to explain. Richards has suggested that among the Bemba, the initiation of girls reflects the values and beliefs of the society. She writes:

> firstly, they [the rituals] are used to control what is uncontrollable by rational means . . . and that control is secured according to the people's belief either by supplication, the exact use of magic formulae or good behavior. Secondly, they are used to maintain and perpetuate systems of social relationship and structure of groups. They act as charters to maintain the power of those who already exercise it and express the moral rules on which the social structure depends. Lastly, they may provide the individual with spiritual experiences and represent the tribal philosophy or view of the world.[2]

Such a complex analysis is not undertaken by the Bemba themselves. Men view the rite as necessary to prepare girls for marriage. Women do not mention this but emphasize the need to transform the girls. They say the rite serves to teach the girl, to make her grow, and to "make her a woman as we are."[3]

[1] For a full account, see P. Kloos, "Female Initiation Among the Maroni River Caribs," *American Anthropologist*, LXXI (1969), 898–905; P. Kloos, *The Maroni River Caribs of Surinam* (Assen, The Netherlands: Van Gorcum, 1971), pp. 74–77.

[2] A. I. Richards, *Chisungu: A Girl's Initiation Ceremony Among the Bemba of Northern Rhodesia* (New York: Grove Press, 1956), pp. 152–153.

[3] Ibid., p. 121.

Because there are no analogous ceremonies in our society, the explanation of such phenomena has been a matter of heated controversy among anthropologists. Furthermore, there is a lack of consensus regarding the definition of initiation rites.[4] Disagreement also stems from differences in the scope and the methods of research.

The material to be presented here is limited to recent studies of initiation rites.[5] The summaries are necessarily brief, and interested readers are advised to consult original publications for additional information. Reconciliation of the various findings seems possible, provided the studies are viewed as complementary. In an effort to further such an interpretation, the research will be presented under three categories: first, macro-studies, which offer general explanations based on a worldwide overview; second, individual-centered studies, which investigate the effect of specific rituals on those who have been initiated; finally, micro-studies, which analyze the ceremonies of one society in relationship to its particular institutions.

MACRO-STUDIES

The first of the macro-studies was a publication by Whiting, Kluckhohn and Anthony,[6] which suggested not only why initiations for adolescent males are observed in certain societies, but also explained why such ceremonies are absent in others. In this study, and in those which follow, hypotheses were tested on a worldwide sample of societies which had been rated on relevant variables.

Whiting, Kluckhohn and Anthony suggest that initiation rites for adolescent males are a response to certain psychological conditions which in turn inhere in specific child-rearing practices. The authors suggest that long, exclusive mother-infant sleeping arrangements and an extended sex taboo after the birth of the child, observed by the infant's mother, create a particularly strong bond between the mother and her young son. These arrangements are typically terminated at weaning when the father replaces the child in the mother's bed. Resultant hostility toward the father exaggerates oedipal antagonisms. During adolescence, these hostilities and a strong attachment

[4] For example, the extensive genital mutilation of girls among the Egyptian Nubians, as described by Kennedy (J. G. Kennedy, "Circumcision and Excision in Egyptian Nubia," *Man*, V (1970), 175–191), does not conform to the definition of Kloos (op. cit.), since the operation is performed on small girls and not on adolescents. Kennedy, on the other hand, affirms that analysis should extend to all genital mutilations, regardless of the age of the initiate.

[5] For references to earlier studies, see: J. K. Brown, "A Cross-Cultural Study of Female Initiation Rites," *American Anthropologist*, LXV (1963), 837–853; J. K. Brown, "Female Initiation Rites: A Review of the Current Literature," in D. Rogers, ed., *Issues in Adolescent Psychology* (New York: Appleton-Century-Crofts, 1969), pp. 74–86; C. Harrington, "Sexual Differentiation in Socialization and Some Male Genital Mutilations," *American Anthropologist*, LXX (1968), 951–956.

[6] J. W. M. Whiting, R. Kluckhohn, and A. Anthony, "The Function of Male Initiation Ceremonies at Puberty," in E. Maccoby, T. M. Newcomb, and E. L. Hartley, eds., *Readings in Social Psychology* (New York: Henry Holt, 1958), pp. 359–370.

to the mother can have disruptive consequences. Therefore, at this point, the boy is subjected to rites which include severe hazing, tests of manliness, isolation from women, and a genital operation. An alternative solution is a change of residence for the son.

A subsequent paper by Burton and Whiting [7] also views these rites as a response to psychological conditions inherent in certain child-rearing practices. But analysis shifts to emphasis on conflict in sex identity. In infancy, long, exclusive mother-child sleeping arrangements foster a primary feminine sex identity. But the world of the household in patrilocal societies [8] is male dominated. As the child perceives this, he acquires a secondary male identification. The resulting sex identity conflict is resolved by the observance of initiation rites for boys. These "brainwash" the participants and establish a male identity.

In an acerbic article, Young [9] challenged Whiting's position by attacking the psychological nature of the explanation. He suggests that it is the presence of male peer groups practicing sex group solidarity that account for the presence of male initiation ceremonies (which he defines somewhat differently). Whiting's rejoinder states in part: "I would argue that both male solidarity and male initiation rites are a consequence of conflict in sex identity engendered in infancy and early childhood. . . ." [10]

A further challenge of Whiting's view concerning initiation was put forward by Cohen.[11] He suggests that initiation is but one of several customs that serve to make the child less dependent upon his nuclear family in those societies in which a larger kin group supplies the individual with emotional anchorage. "Extrusion" (making the child sleep away from his own family, in the home of relatives or in a youth house), brother-sister avoidance during the preadolescent years (a time during which Cohen feels the child is particularly vulnerable), and initiation at adolescence all serve this purpose.[12]

In part to answer his critics, and in part to further refine his original formulations, Whiting[13] published a subsequent paper on "circumcision rites." He noted that such ceremonies occur relatively more frequently in tropical

[7] R. V. Burton and J. W. M. Whiting, "The Absent Father and Cross-Sex Identity," *Merrill-Palmer Quarterly of Behavior and Development*, VII (1961), 85–95.

[8] Patrilocality refers to the practice of residing in or near the domestic unit of the husband's family after marriage.

[9] F. W. Young, "The Function of Male Initiation Ceremonies: a Cross-Cultural Test of an Alternative Hypothesis," *American Journal of Sociology*, LXVII (1962), 379–391.

[10] J. W. M. Whiting, "Comment," *American Journal of Sociology*, LXVII (1962), 392.

[11] Y. Cohen, *The Transition from Childhood to Adolescence: Cross-Cultural Studies of Initiation Ceremonies, Legal Systems, and Incest Taboos* (Chicago: Aldine Publishing Co., 1964).

[12] According to Cohen (Ibid.), these practices are typical of societies with legal systems characterized by "joint liability." In societies like our own, which practice "several liability," these pratices are absent and emotional anchorage remains in the nuclear family. For a criticism of Cohen's study, see Brown, "Female Initiation Rites," op. cit.

[13] J. W. M. Whiting, "Effects of Climate on Certain Cultural Practices," in W. Goodenough, ed., *Explorations in Cultural Anthropology* (New York: McGraw-Hill, 1964), pp. 511–544.

climates. Where winters are cold, infants typically have a cradle or sleeping bag of their own. On the other hand, mother-infant sleeping arrangements exclusive of the father are found in tropical climates. Further, the diet found in tropical areas, where the staple crop consists of low-protein roots and fruits, makes long nursing necessary. Because pregnancy appears to reduce the nutritional quality of the mother's milk, a prolonged postpartum sex taboo helps to insure the infant continued good nutrition. The long postpartum sex taboo in turn makes polygyny necessary and polygyny is particularly compatible with patrilocal residence. Such conditions are associated with the observance of male initiation rites. Tropical South America, however, fails to conform to Whiting's hypothesis. He suggests that abortion, which is widely practiced, is perhaps a functional equivalent of the long postpartum sex taboo.

The initiation of girls, although as prevalent as male initiation, has received far less consideration by anthropologists. A cross-cultural study of these ceremonies by Brown [14] has found statistically significant support for the following hypotheses. First, the rites are observed in societies in which the girl continues to live in the household of her parents after marriage. Initiation proclaims a status change in the girl, made necessary by the fact that she continues to reside in the same household since childhood. Second, the rites take place in those societies in which women make a considerable contribution to subsistence. It appears that the girl and the community must be assured that she will indeed be able to undertake her important role. Finally, those relatively rare rites that subject the girl to extreme pain (in some cases by a genital operation) appear also to be a response to a conflict in sex identity. These ceremonies are often related to similar painful rites for boys.

The explanations of initiation rites suggested by the macro-studies have generated a lively and prolonged debate among anthropologists. By specifying precisely both the conditions under which initiations are likely to occur and the circumstances under which they are likely to be absent, researchers are able to formulate testable hypotheses, which in turn, have led to highly reliable findings.

INDIVIDUAL-CENTERED STUDIES

The findings presented here are based on analyses derived from studies of individuals who have experienced initiation rites.

Recent research by Herzog [15] among the Kikuyu of Kenya was designed to measure changes in the self-concept of young men undergoing initiation. In earlier times male initiation among the Kikuyu was an elaborate annual cere-

[14] Brown, "A Cross-Cultural Study of Female Initiation Rites," op. cit.
[15] J. D. Herzog, "Initiation and Self-Image among Kikuyu Adolescents," paper presented at the meetings of the American Anthropological Association, San Diego, 1970.

mony involving circumcision, adoption by ritual parents, singing, dancing, being anointed with white earth, eating special foods, a symbolic race to a "sacred" fig tree, and eight days of seclusion from which the initiates emerged wearing long white cloths. After the ceremony, the young men served in a kind of local militia until marriage.

In the community near Nairobi where Herzog's study was conducted, circumcision now takes place in a nearby government dispensary. The operation is performed under local anesthetic and lasts a few minutes. The traditional eight days of seclusion are still observed. The initiation is often timed to coincide with the completion of primary school when the boy is about seventeen. Even today the ceremony is mandatory, and earns the young man respect and certain privileges such as staying out later at night. Adolescents feel their behavior improves as a result of the ceremony, and some report that it gives them added self-confidence.

With the help of his Kikuyu assistants, Herzog devised a questionnaire to "sample the boy's conception of himself" [16] by asking him for example to estimate his height and weight, how many miles he can run without stopping, and how much beer he can drink in one sitting. Initiates were questioned before the ceremony and then four months later. A group of boys who had been initiated the previous year (or even longer) were also questioned, as well as a group of boys postponing the ceremony for a year or more.

If the ceremony did indeed have an immediate, large-scale effect (the brainwashing suggested by Burton and Whiting), the scores of the initiates before and after the ceremony should have indicated dramatic change. This was not the case, however. Herzog states: "Thus, it seems that initiation does have a measurable impact on Kikuyu boys' self-image, which takes some time to appear (it is evident in twelve months . . .) after initiation." [17] Educational attainment is highly correlated with initiation due to the timing of the ceremonies. Herzog attempted to differentiate between the effect of school attainment and initiation on self-image. Because there were too few uninitiated boys who were attending high school, he was able to compare only the boys of the initiated group who were in elementary school with those who were attending high school. He found that "education predicts potency of self-concept with greater precision than initiation status." [18] Herzog concludes:

> Education . . . has a very strong impact on individuals' sense of selfhood. . . .
> Combining traditional initiation and modern schooling . . . [results in] a very
> powerful sequence of socialization experiences. . . . The hypothesized psycho-
> logical impact of the experience of initiation is unconfirmed by the present
> study.[19]

[16] Ibid., p. 3.
[17] Ibid., p. 6.
[18] Ibid., p. 7.
[19] Ibid.

The second study was conducted by Granzberg [20] among the Hopi of the American Southwest. Here no genital operation is performed at initiation, but there is painful hazing and seclusion. Granzberg investigated the possible "brainwashing effect" of the Hopi ceremonies. The boys who were studied were between the ages of eight and ten and were all attending the same day school. Tests were administered two months before initiation, immediately after initiation and two months after initiation. A group of boys postponing initiation were also tested. Because the purpose of initiation among the Hopi is to inhibit independence and aggression, these behaviors were studied by means of assigned tasks and by means of verbal and pictorial thematic apperception tests especially adapted for use with Hopi subjects. The first item was scored for the amount of time required for the child to ask for help. The projective tests were scored for dependent and aggressive responses. Results indicated that the initiated boys showed reduced aggression, and somewhat later also showed an increase in dependence. Granzberg concludes:

> This study, in demonstrating that Hopi initiation reduces the aggression of initiates and, in a delayed way, increases their dependence, supports the work of Hopi ethnographers and statements by the Hopi themselves . . . which detail the way disruptive aggression, impulsiveness, and independence in uninitiated children is eradicated by initiation and turned into compliance, conformity, and obedience. In so doing, these findings support Whiting's Freudian hypothesis that initiation rites serve to alter and "brainwash" disruptive behavior.[21]

Granzberg and Herzog's results seem to contradict each other on the brainwashing effect of initiation ceremonies. But the contradiction is more apparent than real. Herzog sought to investigate self-concept, and did so with a questionnaire. Granzberg was interested in dependent and aggressive behavior, which he examined by means of assigned tasks and projective tests. Herzog's subjects were older than the Hopi boys. Herzog also reports important changes in the nature of the Kikuyu rite in recent years. Granzberg does not report such changes for Hopi initiation. Kikuyu initiation involves circumcision; Hopi initiation does not. Although both studies deal with the effect of initiation on the individual, they are not fully comparable. It is therefore not surprising that they fail to agree on the immediate effect of initiation.

Micro-Studies

The studies to be reviewed in this section attempt to relate the initiation rites of a specific society to the practices, beliefs and values of that particular

[20] G. Granzberg, "Hopi Initiation Rites—A Case Study of the Validity of the Freudian Theory of Culture," *Journal of Social Psychology,* LXXXVII (1972), 189–195; G. Granzberg, "The Psychological Integration of Culture: A Cross-Cultural Study of Hopi Type Initiation Rites," *Journal of Social Psychology,* XC (1973), 3–7.
[21] Ibid., pp. 193–194.

society. Although broader interpretations are implied, findings apply only to one society.

Schwartz and Merten [22] have made an analysis of initiation into the high school sororities of a mid-western community. It is difficult to contain one's wrath at the implied cruelty and the obvious foolishness of the proceedings. The authors point out that this rite differs in many important respects from adolescent initiation in the non-western world. Schwartz and Merten's analysis suggests that expressive symbols are manipulated to transform individual identity in such a way as to enforce the ideology of the local status hierarchy.

Although there is ambiguity in the adolescent social system, certain statuses are recognized. Uppermost is the "socie," the "cool" attractive girl, whose appearance displays taste, and who behaves with social know-how. But there is also the "hoody" girl, whose appearance shows bad taste by implying a lack of sexual restraint, and a residual category of "other" girls who are nobodies. The initiation ritual reinforces this hierarchy rather than promoting social cohesion within the adolescent community. The individual initiate is given a new firmer identity as a socie, and is further set apart from the low-status hoody girls and the nondescript other girls. She is made to experience these undesirable identities in exaggerated form during the ritual, and emerges "forever cleansed of any possible latent impurities." [23] Schwartz and Merten write:

> By placing her in awkward situations, the ritual creates a sense of shame. It raises questions about the solidity of her personal identity and thereby opens her to the experience of radical reintegration of self. . . . the ritual induces identity diffusion, disrupts previous continuities in the perception of self, increases the initiate's emotional receptivity to the transition to the socie identity.[24]

A recent paper by Kennedy [25] concerning circumcision and excision in Egyptian Nubia describes a similar procedure. Here, in the initiation of boys, feminine wedding symbols are first attached to the small boy and then removed. Kennedy writes: ". . . the symbolism conveys a temporary assumption of female attributes in order that his maleness can be recognized and celebrated." [26]

Kennedy asserts that the rites he describes are not primarily concerned with identity and personality change, nor does the initiate embark on a transition or passage to a new status. Instead the ceremonies are an expression of the society's attitudes toward fertility, sexuality and gender perfection. According to Kennedy, their purpose is to convey "a sense of the mystery and importance of sex, a vivid fear of the evils of unchaste behaviour, the great

[22] G. Schwartz and D. Merten, "Social Identity and Expressive Symbols: The Meaning of an Initiation Ritual," *American Anthropologist*, LXX (1968), 1117–1131.

[23] Ibid., p. 1130.

[24] Ibid., p. 1129.

[25] Kennedy, op. cit.

[26] Ibid., p. 185.

responsibility of child rearing, and an intense awareness of his or her genitals."[27]

As in Egyptian Nubia, the Mae Enga of New Guinea segregate the sexes as much as possible. Meggitt's[28] study of Mae Enga male purification ceremonies emphasizes the relation of these rites to the relationship between the sexes in this society. Women are believed to be dangerous to men, particularly during menstruation and childbirth. Intercourse is viewed as depleting to men, though necessary for the propagation of the lineage. Because contact with women cannot be completely avoided, young men are repeatedly provided with magical protection through the observance of a periodic cleansing ritual. The ceremony strengthens them and makes them grow and become more handsome. According to Meggitt, the Mae Enga equate femininity not only with sexuality but also with peril because of their custom of seeking marriage partners among traditional enemies. He suggests that other New Guinea tribes which favor marriage among friendly groups will not make this association and will be less preoccupied with ritual purification from dangerous feminine influences.

The initiation rituals of the Ndembu of northwestern Zambia have been analyzed by Turner in several papers.[29] Only "Betwixt and Between: The Liminal Period in *Rites de Passage*" will be considered here. Following Van Gennep,[30] Turner identifies three stages in initiation: separation from the old, a transitional or liminal period and aggregation into the new. In this paper, Turner concerns himself with instruction and the use of symbolic themes in the liminal period of Ndembu male initiation.

According to Turner, the initiate, no longer a child and not yet a man, is a creature of paradox and ambiguity in the liminal state. Because his position in society is unclear, the initiate is considered polluting to those who are not magically protected. Though physically visible, the initiate has no social reality, therefore he is secluded or disguised. He is sexless or bisexual, because sex is an important structural principle among the Ndembu, and the initiate temporarily stands outside this structure. The symbols that are used

[27] Ibid., p. 184.

[28] M. J. Meggitt, "Male-Female Relationships in the Highlands of Australian New Guinea," *American Anthropologist*, LXVI (1964), Part 2, 204–224.

[29] V. Turner, "Betwixt and Between: The Liminal Period in *Rites de Passage*," in J. Helm, ed., *Symposium on New Approaches to the Study of Religion*, Proceedings of the 1964 Annual Spring Meeting of the American Ethnological Society (Seattle: University of Washington Press, 1964), pp. 4–20; "Colour Classification in Ndembu Ritual," in M. Banton, ed., *Anthropological Approaches to the Study of Religion* (London: Tavistock Publications, 1966), pp. 47–84; "*Mukanda:* The Rite of Circumcision," in V. Turner, ed., *The Forest of Symbols* (Ithaca: Cornell University Press, 1967), pp. 151–279; "Symbolization and Patterning in the Circumcision Rites of Two Bantu-Speaking African Societies," paper read at the meetings of the American Anthropological Association, Washington, 1967; "Symbols in African Ritual," *Science*, CLXXIX, No. 4078 (March 16, 1973), 1100–1105.

[30] A. Van Gennep, *Les Rites de Passage* (Paris: Libraire Critique Emile Nourry, 1909). According to Van Gennep, rites marking transition from category to category (e.g., infant, child, adult) in the course of the life cycle and other changes of status can all be subjected to a uniform analysis. Such rites contain three stages, as noted above.

in the ritual are both positive and negative, representing death and birth simultaneously.

Turner also analyzes the social structure which characterizes the liminal period: total authority for the elders (who represent society and tradition) and total equality among the initiates (who maintain a sense of brotherhood even after the rites). The initiates are put into a condition of extreme passivity and malleability, that they may receive the stamp of their instruction. Turner writes:

> The passivity of neophytes to their instructors, their malleability, which is increased by submission to ordeal, their reduction to a uniform condition, are signs of the process whereby they are ground down to be fashioned anew and endowed with additional powers to cope with their new station in life.[31]

In this condition they are ready to receive induction into the sacred mysteries. Often these take the form of sacred objects (such as masks and pottery emblems), which are readily identifiable but complex in their secret interpretation. The object is often formed disproportionately in order to provoke thought about its exaggerated features. The object may be monstrous, for in order to draw attention to the familiar, elements of reality are removed from their context. This helps the initiate to think abstractly about ordinary things, which he once took for granted. Finally there is the most sacred mystery in which the human body and its functions are likened to the universe or to the social order. Attributes of human physiology are used symbolically to communicate mystical knowledge. Turner refers to this mystery as the archetypal template, with which the neophyte will be stamped to impress upon him the basic assumptions of his culture. Turner writes:

> The central cluster of nonlogical *sacra* is then the symbolic template of the whole system of beliefs and values in a given culture, its archetypal paradigm and ultimate measure. Neophytes shown these are often told that they are in the presence of forms established from the beginning of things. . . . Thus the communication of *sacra* both teaches the neophytes how to think with some degree of abstraction about their cultural milieu and gives them ultimate standards of reference. At the same time it is believed to change their nature, transform them from one kind of human being into another.[32]

It is the most sacred objects and their interpretation that Turner hopes will be the subject of future cross-cultural research. Unfortunately few initiations have been described in sufficient detail to make such comparisons possible. Furthermore, not all initiations are as complex as those of the Ndembu. Nevertheless, Turner's analyses offer a number of insights which may inspire future investigations.[33]

[31] Turner, "Betwixt and Between," op. cit., p. 11.
[32] Ibid., p. 17.
[33] B. T. Grindal, " 'Washing Away the Hand': A Later Life Rite of Passage Among the Sisala of Northern Ghana," paper presented at the meetings of the Central States Anthropological Society, St. Louis, 1973.

Audrey Richards [34] has provided an analysis as rich as Turner's for the initiation of girls among the Bemba of what was formerly Northern Rhodesia. She describes very fully the actual ceremony she witnessed in 1931. She gives a detailed interpretation of the songs, the wall paintings, and pottery emblems which were made for the rite. Her analysis identifies the expressed purpose of the rite, its relation to tribal dogma and values, the unconscious tensions and conflicts that were expressed, and the rite's pragmatic effects.

Like Brown,[35] Richards notes the relationship of the ceremony to Bemba marital practices and to the important role of women in Bemba subsistence activities. It is not that the girls learn new skills, but rather that they acquire new attitudes toward their work. Certain observances are clearly tests of competence for the initiates. The duties of a wife, mother and breadwinner are all consecrated in the rite, expressing the coherence and full purpose of the lives of Bemba women.[36]

The description of the initiation of girls among the Maroni River Caribs with which this paper began, conforms to these formulations. Kloos writes:

> With the evident symbolism of industriousness in the Carib ritual in mind . . . it does not require much fantasy to assume a relationship between the existence of female initiation and the economic importance of women in Carib society.[37]

SUMMARY

Recent studies of initiation rites have offered a variety of hypotheses. Those suggested by macro-studies have indicated why initiation ceremonies for adolescents are observed only in some societies and not in others.

Macro-studies and individual-centered studies all worked with the same definitions and began with essentially similar assumptions. Micro-studies, on the other hand, take a number of different directions. Each is based on the particular circumstances found in one society.

The richly detailed analyses of the micro-studies will no doubt inspire the macro-studies of the future. By comparison the macro-studies appear overly simple. Yet this simplification is dictated by the need to make comparisons across cultures and culture areas. Although macro- and micro-studies vary in scope, in method and even in the definition of initiation, the research efforts can be viewed as complementary. This can best be demonstrated with the formulations concerning rites for girls. For example, Brown suggests, on the basis of cross-cultural evidence, that these ceremonies are related to the subsistence role of women. Both Kloos and Richards suggest the same inter-

[34] Richards, op. cit.
[35] Brown, "A Cross-Cultural Study of Female Initiation Rites," op. cit.
[36] For a reinterpretation of Richards' analysis, see: J. K. Brown, "The Recruitment of a Female Labor Force," paper presented at the meetings of the Central States Anthropological Society, St. Louis, 1973.
[37] Kloos, op. cit., p. 903.

pretation on the basis of the societies they studied. The findings of all three authors are made more plausible by the consensus.

CONCLUSION

What is the significance of research on initiation rites for the student of adolescence in our own society? Burton and Whiting [38] have shown that such research furthers an understanding of the father-absent household in our own society. Harrington [39] has demonstrated that the concept of sex identity conflict offers insight into errors in sex role behavior among American boys. Brown [40] has suggested the importance of female initiation rites in the recruitment of a female labor force. The absence of these ceremonies in our own society is diagnostic of our traditional view of the role of women, a view which is being seriously questioned.

Although our society is "youth oriented," we do not devote time and resources to celebrate the transition from childhood to adulthood. According to Turner, initiation rites reflect the society's beliefs and values. Perhaps one reason we do not celebrate such rites is the lack of consensus regarding what is sacred in a society as complex and varied as our own. Education may be a more powerful influence on the individual, as Herzog suggests. Yet the fact remains that for us, the assumption of adult status is vaguely defined and open to a variety of interpretations.

[38] Burton and Whiting, op. cit.
[39] C. Harrington, *Errors in Sex-Role Behavior in Teen-Age Boys* (New York: Teachers College Press, 1970).
[40] Brown, "Recruitment of a Female Labor Force," op. cit.

Toward Career and Work

Factors that influence how an adolescent arrives at a career commitment have changed over the years. Before the Industrial Revolution a son followed his father into farming or a trade, and a daughter followed her mother into the kitchen and nursery; there was little change from generation to generation, and even an illiterate adolescent could learn enough in the way of basic skills to do productive work. Although demand for sophisticated skills accelerated swiftly after the Industrial Revolution, there was still enough work for the unschooled. In recent years, however, mechanization, automation, and changes in living and working conditions have led to the elimination of many semi-skilled and unskilled jobs. The six papers in Part 2 reveal that the complexities inherent in contemporary occupational decision-making show few signs of abating. The first paper indicates changing age, sex, ethnic, and educational patterns of youth's participation in the labor force. The next three papers supplement Coleman's (Part 1) call for sweeping renovation in educational practices to facilitate adolescents' entry into productive work. The fifth and sixth papers describe the status of adolescent girls in the present-day world of vocational education and career mobility.

A special labor force report describes, in the first paper, how high-school graduates and dropouts fare in today's job market. Of the three million persons who graduated from high school in 1972, less than 50 per cent—the lowest proportion since 1968—entered college. The decline in college enrollments has occurred mainly among white youth, perhaps as a consequence of lessened pressure from military draft, disillusionment over job prospects, rising costs of tuition and other college expenses, and stronger desires to experiment in the workplace for a period between high school and college. Young's data also show that youth of Spanish origin, relative to whites and Blacks, comprise the highest proportion to drop out before graduation from high school. The statistics on the dropouts reveal that the proportion of Spanish-origin youth entering clerical or construction occupations is smallest; the proportion of Spanish-origin dropouts in farm work, on the other hand, is twice that for either white or Black adolescents.

Havighurst, Graham, and Eberly, in the second paper, point out that formal education has supplanted part-time work and marriage as society's mechanisms for preparing youth to enter adulthood. But these researchers contend that high school and college experiences are of little help to as many as 20 per cent to 30 per cent of youth between fifteen and twenty years-of-age. They agree with Coleman (see Part 1) on the necessity of an alternative "for the increasingly information-rich, action-poor world of the young" and they advocate "a program of national volunteer service." The researchers envisage a program that will enable young people to serve in locally directed and financed projects, which ideally, youth themselves will organize. Havighurst, Graham, and Eberly conceptualize volunteer public service as an answer to separatism between economic and educational institutions, and to illustrate the practicality of their proposal, describe a survey of occupational opportunities in three communities which shows how many jobs could be filled by youth.

Mincer explores, in the third selection, the economic bases of "some of the trends in family, school, and working life." He views education as "an investment in human capital," and after comparing current costs to such social returns as "informed and responsible citizenship, communication skills, lawful behavior, and standards of health," he concludes that "there is no evidence that the profitability of that investment has declined as numbers of students have grown." Nonetheless, Mincer observes that efficiency dictates consideration of different alternatives and outcomes. He also supplements positions expressed earlier in the text by Coleman and Havighurst et al.: "the progressively shrinking family, the increasingly abstract occupations, and the existing schooling which at best prepares for further schooling cannot simply be conjoined and revitalized for the education of the young." New experiments, he says, should be conducted in new institutional settings.

Rogers, in the fourth selection, specifies that participation by economic institutions is the key also to reform in secondary vocational education. He suggests more cooperative education and work-study programs, insisting that "there is no orderly or effective system of vocational training and supportive services for youth in America and none allowing for continuing interchange and movement between school and work." Rogers notes that national values lead us to emphasize college-bound studies and to insulate academic from vocational-technical training. Moreover, he identifies several barriers to youth employment: competition for jobs, employers' negative attitudes, child labor laws, and insurance requirements. A reform strategy, he says, should integrate occupational training programs with academic education and the economy.

Although the momentum of the civil rights and Women's Liberation Movements has opened new career opportunities for females, few adolescent girls today aspire to school superintendencies, high-level executive posts in business, or careers in professional sports. Harmon's analyses of adolescent girls' career preferences, in the fifth paper, show clearly how restrictively girls perceive opportunities available to them. Her report is based on the results of a questionnaire administered to nearly 1,200 female college freshmen. Each girl was asked to read a list including the names of 135 occupa-

tions and to indicate, retrospectively, which of them they had contemplated as careers earlier in their adolescence. The investigation covered popularity of each occupation, median age at which each occupation was initially considered, and persistency of various preferences. The findings revealed that the girls aspired to become housewives earliest and most persistently. The girls did express some interest in educational and social-service occupations; however, their preferences were restricted largely to occupations typically filled by women.

In the sixth paper, Shafer attempts to explain why adolescent girls possess strong cultural bias against choosing careers associated with leadership and responsibility. Although the proportion of women in the labor force has risen during the past thirty years from 25 per cent to 50 per cent, Shafer notes that "to a large extent girls and their parents and teachers are as yet uncertain about the opportunities that today have opened to women." Shafer analyzes carefully several factors that shape adolescent girls' attitude toward future career mobility—sex role identification, career models, regional considerations, school experiences, personality development, household responsibilities, employment practices, and legal barriers; however, she does not regard these as formidable obstacles to girls' career mobility. Adolescent girls will be persuaded to think about careers, Shafer believes, when (a) women are permitted to hold decision-making posts, enabling girls to identify with models performing professional roles, and (b) marriage, motherhood, and workplace phase together, enabling girls to fulfill meaningful, productive lifestyles.

Anne M. Young

The High School Class of 1972:
More at Work, Fewer in College

The Special Labor Force report reprinted below examines the status of youth in the 1972 job market. Young has classified data derived from the Bureau of Census by age, sex, and education. The data reveal that each year between 1968 and 1972 increasingly greater proportions of high-school graduates sought work and increasingly smaller proportions entered college. The data also show that youth of Spanish origin drop out of high school at higher rates than either whites or Blacks, and that most of these youth enter unskilled farmwork rather than clerical or service occupations. In her informative discussion, Young suggests several possible factors that might account for, respectively, why trends in enrollments in trade or business schools are presently downward, why youth drop out of high school, why fewer youth enter college today, and why the proportion of dropouts among youth of Spanish origin is so inordinately high.

Instructional Objectives
To describe the college enrollment and labor force status of 1972 high-school graduates.
To compare the employment status of white and Black 1972 high-school graduates and dropouts.
To describe the labor force status of high-school graduates and dropouts of Spanish origin.
To describe the occupations and industries employing high-school graduates and dropouts by age, sex, and ethnicity.

OF THE 3 million persons who were graduated from high school in 1972, only 49 per cent—the lowest proportion in 5 years—went on to college, and relatively more graduates than in recent years went to work.

FROM *Monthly Labor Review*, XCVI (1973), pp. 26–32. Reprinted by permission of the author and publisher.

However, a sizable number of graduates had not found jobs as of October 1972. And for those who did not make it through high school, unemployment was especially high.

Of the new graduates who did *not* go on to college, most, about 1.2 million, either held jobs or were looking for work in October.

In addition to the graduates, nearly three-fourths of a million youth left school before earning a diploma.

As part of the October 1972 survey of "school-age youth," [1] the Census Bureau obtained separate data on youth who identified themselves as Mexican-American, Chicano, Mexican (Mexicano), Puerto Rican, Cuban, or of "other Spanish origin." All these members of primarily Spanish-speaking minorities were then classified as "of Spanish origin."

A single year's data based on a sample survey should be interpreted with caution. Nevertheless, it is startling to find that, among all youth of Spanish origin aged 16 to 24, 1 in 3 was a school dropout, a much larger proportion than among all whites or Negroes.

GRADUATES AT WORK

Most 1972 high school graduates who did not go to college had entered the labor force by early fall. In October 1972, more than 90 per cent of the men and 75 per cent of the women were working or looking for work. Like those who went on to college, or who dropped out, these young people ranged in age from 16 to 24; the great majority were under 20. (See tables 1 and 2.)

The labor force participation rate for men did not change significantly over the year. With a lower proportion going on to college, more of the men were in the labor force. Most took blue-collar jobs, as is typical of young men entering the permanent labor force.

Among women graduates also, the number in the labor force increased, although the participation rate was not significantly different from that of a year earlier. Labor force participation was higher for single than for married women graduates, no doubt because of the latter's domestic responsibilities.

---

[1] This article is based on supplementary questions in the October 1972 Current Population Survey, conducted and tabulated for the Bureau of Labor Statistics by the Bureau of the Census. Data relate to persons 16 to 24 years of age in the civilian non-institutional population in the calendar week ending October 14, 1972. Estimates of the number of graduates may differ from figures published by the Office of Education, which are based on the total population and all age groups.

Since the estimates are based on a sample, they will, in all likelihood, differ to some extent from the figures that would have been obtained from a complete census. Sampling variability may be relatively large in cases where the numbers are small. Small estimates, or small differences between estimates, should be interpreted with caution.

The most recent report in this series was published in the *Monthly Labor Review*, May 1972, pp. 49–53, and reprinted with additional tabular data and explanatory notes as Special Labor Force Report 145.

Table 1 College Enrollment and Labor Force Status of 1972 High School Graduates,[1] October 1972 [Numbers in thousands]

Characteristic	Civilian Noninstitutional Population NUMBER	Civilian Noninstitutional Population PER CENT	Civilian Labor Force NUMBER	Civilian Labor Force AS PER CENT OF POPULATION	Civilian Labor Force EMPLOYED	UNEMPLOYED NUMBER	UNEMPLOYED AS PER CENT OF CIVILIAN LABOR FORCE	Not in Labor Force
All Persons								
Both sexes, total	2,961	100.0	1,788	60.4	1,543	245	13.7	1,173
Enrolled in college	1,457	49.2	551	37.8	488	63	11.4	906
Full time	1,366	46.1	477	34.9	416	61	12.8	889
Part time	91	3.1	74	81.3	72	2	(2)	17
Not enrolled in college	1,504	50.8	1,237	82.2	1,055	182	14.7	267
Men, total	1,420	100.0	921	64.9	809	112	12.8	499
Enrolled in college	749	52.7	309	41.3	272	37	12.0	440
Full time	706	49.7	273	38.7	237	36	13.2	433
Part time	43	3.0	36	(2)	35	1	(2)	7
Not enrolled in college	671	47.3	612	91.2	537	75	12.3	9
Women, total	1,541	100.0	867	56.3	734	133	15.3	674
Enrolled in college	708	45.9	242	34.2	216	26	10.7	466
Full time	660	42.8	204	30.9	179	25	12.3	456
Part time	48	3.1	38	(2)	37	1	(2)	10
Not enrolled in college	833	54.1	625	75.0	518	107	17.1	208
Single	675	43.8	536	79.4	449	87	16.2	139
Married, and other marital status [3]	158	10.3	89	56.3	69	20	22.5	69
White								
Both sexes, total	2,614	100.0	1,603	61.3	1,418	185	11.5	1,011
Enrolled in college	1,292	49.4	505	39.1	454	51	10.1	787
Not enrolled in college	1,322	50.6	1,098	83.1	964	134	12.2	224
Men, total	1,262	100.0	824	65.3	736	88	10.7	438
Enrolled in college	666	52.8	278	41.7	250	28	10.1	388
Not enrolled in college	596	47.2	546	91.6	486	60	11.0	50
Women, total	1,352	100.0	779	57.6	682	97	12.5	573
Enrolled in college	626	46.3	227	36.3	204	23	10.1	399
Not enrolled in college	726	53.7	552	76.0	478	74	13.4	174
Single	576	42.6	466	80.9	412	54	11.6	110
Married, and other marital status [3]	150	11.1	86	57.3	66	20	23.3	64
Negro and Other Races								
Both sexes, total	347	100.0	185	53.3	125	60	32.4	162
Enrolled in college	165	47.6	46	27.9	34	12	(2)	119
Not enrolled in college	182	52.4	139	76.4	91	48	34.5	43
Men, total	158	100.0	97	61.4	73	24	24.7	61
Enrolled in college	83	52.5	31	37.3	22	9	(2)	52
Not enrolled in college	75	47.5	66	88.0	51	15	(2)	9
Women, total	189	100.0	88	46.6	52	36	40.9	101
Enrolled in college	82	43.4	15	18.3	12	3	(2)	67
Not enrolled in college	107	56.6	73	68.2	40	33	(2)	34
Single	99	52.4	70	70.7	37	33	(2)	29
Married, and other marital status [3]	8	4.2	3	(2)	3	....	......	5

[1] 16 to 24 years old.
[2] Per cent not shown where base is less than 75,000.
[3] Includes widowed, divorced, and separated women.

NOTE: Figures for 1972 are not strictly comparable with data for earlier years because of the introduction of 1970 Census data into the estimation procedures. For example, the Census adjustment increased the number of 1972 graduates by about 40,000 and of all graduates 16 to 24 years old by about 175,000.

Also, the limits on employment imposed by the need to live in an area mutually convenient for husband and wife, and the difficulty of making hours of work fit a household schedule, probably restricted the availability of many married women for employment. Over half the women who were employed were in white-collar jobs, primarily as clerical workers.

About a third of all graduates not in college and not in the labor force were in special schools, such as trade schools or business colleges. There has been a downward trend in the enrollment of high school graduates in special schools since 1962, when more than half the graduates not in college and not in the labor force attended special schools. This trend may reflect the increasing opportunity for technical training in 2-year colleges whose students are counted as enrolled in "regular" school rather than a special school. Also, the development of company-sponsored "in-house" training programs provides some incentive to seek employment with business concerns which offer such programs, rather than remaining outside the labor force while obtaining training at a special school at one's own expense.

THE DROPOUTS

An estimated 730,000 persons 16 to 24 years old left elementary or high school during the year ended in October 1972. (See table 2.) An over-the-year increase of about 70,000 in the number quitting school brought the total back to the same level as in October 1970.

Among these dropouts, the labor force participation rate (per cent of population working or looking for work) for men (82 per cent) was substantially lower than that for out-of-school graduates (91 per cent); and the rates for both single and married women dropouts were much lower than for graduates. Unemployment rates for recent white dropouts were considerably higher than for recent white graduates who were no longer in school. Among Negro [2] youth, unemployment rates were about the same for high school graduates as for dropouts, and the rates have been persistently higher than for whites.

Many of the factors which may have influenced young persons to leave school, such as poor academic skills, discontent with programs offered, health problems, or trouble with authorities, were also likely to be a hindrance to employment. Their relative youth and inexperience—most were 16 or 17 years old—also tended to be obstacles in finding employment.

COLLEGE ENROLLMENT

The proportion of high school graduates enrolling in college soon after graduation has dropped sharply since the peak of 55 per cent in 1968. (See

[2] Data for all persons other than white represent Negroes, who constitute about 89 percent of all persons other than white in the United States.

Table 2   Employment Status of 1972 High School Graduates
Not Enrolled in College and Dropouts,[1] October 1972
[Numbers in thousands]

| | Civilian Noninstitutional Population | | Civilian Labor Force | | | | | Not in Labor Force | |
| | | | | | | UNEMPLOYED | | | |
Characteristic	NUMBER	PER CENT	NUMBER	AS PER CENT OF POPULATION	EMPLOYED	NUMBER	AS PER CENT OF CIVILIAN LABOR FORCE	TOTAL	IN SPECIAL SCHOOLS
1972 graduates not enrolled in college, total	1,504	100.0	1,237	82.2	1,055	182	14.7	267	87
Men	671	44.6	612	91.2	537	75	12.3	59	17
Women	833	55.4	625	75.0	518	107	17.1	208	70
Single	675	44.9	536	79.4	449	87	16.2	139	(2)
Married and other marital status [3]	158	10.5	89	56.3	69	20	22.5	69	(2)
White	1,322	87.9	1,098	83.1	964	134	12.2	224	76
Negro and other races	182	12.1	139	76.4	91	48	34.5	43	11
1971–72 school dropouts, [1] total	730	100.0	457	62.6	336	121	26.5	273	32
Men	371	50.8	305	82.2	234	71	23.3	66	14
Women	359	49.2	152	42.3	102	50	32.9	207	18
Single	202	27.7	111	55.0	75	36	32.4	91	17
Married and other marital status [3]	157	21.5	41	26.1	27	14	(4)	116	....
White	573	78.5	355	62.0	271	84	23.7	218	18
Negro and other races	157	21.5	102	65.0	65	37	36.3	55	11

[1] Persons who dropped out of elementary or high school between October 1971 and October 1972. In addition, 112,000 persons 14 and 15 years old dropped out of school.
[2] Not available.
[3] Includes widowed, divorced, and separated women.
[4] Per cent not shown where base is less than 75,000.

table 3.) The decline has been concentrated among men; their proportion going on to college in the year in which they graduate from high school fell sharply between 1968 and 1972, from 63 to 53 per cent. Among women going on to college, the proportion did not change significantly over this period. Despite the decrease in enrollment rates, the actual number going on to college—about 1.5 million—has changed little over these 4 years because population increases compensated for the drop in the rate.

The decrease in college enrollment has been entirely among white graduates, whose rate fell from 57 per cent in 1968 to 49 per cent in October 1972, a level about equal to that of 10 years earlier. On the other hand, the proportions of Negro graduates of 1972 who went on to college (48 per cent) was about the same as in 1968 but substantially higher than that 10 years earlier (34 per cent). As a result of these converging trends, there was no significant difference in the proportions of white and Negro graduates of 1972 enrolled in college in October. However, larger proportions of Negro youth drop out of junior high or high school; in October 1972, 21 per cent of all Negroes 16 to 24 had done so, compared to 14 per cent of the whites.

Table 3 Proportion of High School Graduates Enrolled in College in October of the Year of Graduation, 1962–72
[Per cent]

Graduation	Persons	Men	Women	White	Negro and Other Races
1962	49	55	43	51	34
1963	45	52	39	46	38
1964	48	57	41	49	39
1965	51	57	45	52	43
1966	50	59	43	52	32
1967	52	58	47	53	42
1968	55	63	49	57	46
1969	54	60	47	55	37
1970	52	55	49	52	48
1971	53	58	50	54	47
1972	49	53	46	49	48

What are the possible factors contributing to the decrease in college enrollment among white male youths? Undoubtedly, lessened pressure to go to college to avoid the draft is one. Another factor may be disillusionment over the prospects of obtaining a good job after graduation, in light of the increase in unemployment in recent years among new college graduates.[3] The rising costs of college tuition and other school-related expenses may be a bar to some youths. Still another influence may also have been the increasing number of young people who take time out between high school and college to work, travel, or otherwise try a change of pace. Several colleges have recognized the value of this interim for some high school seniors and will accept them for admission to college a year later.

The rising cost of higher education has been accompanied by a steady increase in the proportion of full-time college students in the labor force. This proportion among students entering college fresh from high school rose from 20 per cent in 1962 to 35 per cent in 1972, with most of the increase occurring before 1969. Even with the rise, however, the labor force participation rate for college students remained less than half that for part-time students and graduates not going on to college. The unemployment rate for men students was the same as that for those not in school, but among women the rate for students was much lower.

[3] See Vera C. Perrella, "Employment of recent college graduates," *Monthly Labor Review*, February 1973, pp. 41–50.

Median family income of these college freshmen was $13,260, compared to that of $10,470 for graduates not enrolled. Of particular interest is the very large difference in the family income of white and Negro freshmen. Whereas the median income for families of white students was $13,695, the median income for families of Negro students was $8,330. Seventy-five per cent of the whites came from families with an income of $10,000 or more, compared to 42 per cent of the Negroes. Only 5 per cent of the families of white students had incomes of $5,000 or less, compared to 32 per cent of the families of Negroes. Obviously, many of these students are in college through considerable financial sacrifice by their families, as well as with the help of scholarships, loans, and their own earnings. The decision on whether to go to college, while obviously dependent on financial support for the student, is also to some extent a matter of the accessibility of educational facilities— both physically and in terms of entrance standards—and on intangibles such as a graduate's motivation and a family's belief in the value of a college education.

While many students must work to meet college expenses, labor force participation by students is not necessarily directly related to family income. Although most Negro freshmen were from families with much lower income than those of white students, their labor force participation rate was 28 per cent compared with 39 per cent for the whites. The lower labor force rate among Negroes may be related to fewer job opportunities, possible discrimination in hiring, and the discouragement effect of high unemployment rates among all Negro youth.

Youth of Spanish Origin

Public awareness of the problems of persons classified as of Spanish origin [4] has grown in recent years as large-scale immigration and a high birth rate have led to a rapid growth in their population in the United States. Southwesterners of predominately Mexican descent constitute 60 per cent of all persons of Spanish origin in the United States, and an increasing number of immigrants from Puerto Rico and Latin America during the sixties contributed to concentrations of persons of Spanish origin in several Eastern cities (notably New York and Miami). Overall, persons of Spanish origin of all ages constituted about 4.5 per cent of the population in the United States in March 1972, and 5.5 per cent of youth 16 to 24 were of Spanish descent.[5]

The following analysis covers all out-of-school youth age 16 to 24, regardless of the year in which they finished school, rather than the latest year's

[4] Again, these were persons who identified themselves as Mexican-American, Chicano, Mexican (Mexicano), Puerto Rican, Cuban, or of "other Spanish origin." About 97 per cent were white and were also included in data published for "all white."

[5] See *Selected Characteristics of Persons and Families of Mexican, Puerto Rican, and Other Spanish Origin, Current Population Reports*, Series P–20, No. 224 (Bureau of the Census, 1971).

graduates and dropouts covered in the previous section. The total out-of-school population of Spanish origin age 16 to 24 years included 500,000 high school graduates and 600,000 who had left school before graduation. In addition to this 1.1 million no longer in school, there were 200,000 attending college or graduate school.

A much larger proportion of 16- to 24-year-olds of Spanish origin than of either whites or Negroes had dropped out before graduation from high school. As of 1972, the proportion of the youth population of Spanish origin who had dropped out of school was more than double that for all whites, as shown in the following tabulation:

	Spanish Origin	*All whites*	*Negro and Other Races*
Both sexes	34	14	21
Men	34	13	22
Women	35	14	21

The large proportion of dropouts among youth of Spanish origin reflects several socioeconomic factors. Some of these persons are recent immigrants to this country and had very limited educational opportunities in their native country. Also, many youth of Spanish origin face a language barrier which inhibits school attendance. Another reason for low educational attainment could be the fact that many may have had to drop out of school at an early age to help support themselves and other family members.

About 400,000 young high school graduates of Spanish origin were in the labor force in October 1973, equally divided between men and women. (See table 3.) The labor force rates for these persons were not significantly different from comparable groups of white and Negro graduates:

	Spanish Origin	*All Whites*	*Negro and Other Races*
Labor force participation rate:			
Men	95.7	95.5	91.6
Women	66.8	70.4	69.0
Unemployment rate:			
Men	10.1	7.2	12.8
Women	9.8	8.5	22.0

The tabulation above also shows that the unemployment rate for male graduates of Spanish origin was not statistically different from that for all whites or for Negro graduates. Among women, the rate for those of Spanish origin was about the same as for all whites and only half that for Negroes.

Table 4   Labor Force Status of High School Graduates of Spanish Origin [1] *Not in College, by Age and Sex, October 1972*
[Numbers in thousands]

	Both Sexes			*Men*	*Women*
Labor Force Status	TOTAL	16 TO 19 YEARS	20 TO 24 YEARS	16 TO 24 YEARS	16 TO 24 YEARS
Civilian noninstitutional population	514	108	406	207	307
Labor force	403	80	323	198	205
Labor force participation rate	78.4	74.1	79.6	95.7	66.8
Employed	363	71	292	178	185
Unemployed	40	9	31	20	20
Unemployment rate	9.9	11.2	9.6	10.1	9.8
Not in labor force	111	28	83	9	102

[1] These were persons who identified themselves as Mexican-American, Chicano, Mexican (Mexicano), Puerto Rican, Cuban, or of "other Spanish origin." About 97 per cent were white and were also included in data published for "all whites."

Over 250,000 men and 100,000 women dropouts of Spanish origin were in the labor force in October 1972. (See table 4.) The labor force rate for the men was somewhat higher than that for all whites and much higher than that for Negroes, but for women the rates were about the same:

	Spanish Origin	*All Whites*	*Negro and Other Races*
Labor force participation rate:			
Men	93.6	88.3	81.3
Women	34.0	38.6	41.7
Unemployment rate:			
Men	16.4	14.3	15.4
Women	14.3	17.6	34.3

In fact, the labor force rates of male graduates and dropouts of Spanish descent were about the same, whereas among whites as a group and Negroes, male dropouts had significantly lower labor force rates than graduates. With respect to unemployment, the rates for dropouts of Spanish origin were similar to those for white dropouts among men and women. However, the unemployment rate for women of Spanish origin was about half that for Negro women.

OCCUPATIONS AND INDUSTRIES

Employed youth of Spanish origin 16 to 24 years old were, generally, distributed among the various occupations and industries in October 1972 in about the same proportions as were their white and Negro contemporaries of equal educational attainment. (See table 5.) However, a much smaller proportion of Spanish origin than of white graduates were in professional and technical occupations, and a somewhat higher proportion of graduates of Spanish origin worked as operatives. Among the dropouts, lower proportions of youth of Spanish origin than of all whites were clerical workers or craftsmen, while the proportion who were farmworkers was double that of white dropouts.

Table 5   Labor Force Status of School Dropouts of Spanish Origin,[1]
by Age and Sex, October 1972
[Numbers in thousands]

Labor Force Status	Both Sexes			Men			Women		
	TOTAL	16 to 19	20 to 24	TOTAL	16 to 19	20 to 24	TOTAL	16 to 19	20 to 24
Civilian noninstitutional population	609	185	424	280	94	186	329	91	238
Labor force	374	117	257	262	84	178	112	33	79
Labor force participation rate	61.4	63.2	60.6	93.6	89.4	95.7	34.0	36.3	33.2
Employed	315	97	218	219	68	151	96	29	67
Unemployed	59	20	39	43	16	27	16	4	12
Unemployment rate	15.8	17.1	15.2	16.4	19.0	15.2	14.3	(2)	15.2
Not in labor force	235	68	167	18	10	8	217	58	159

[1] See footnote 1, table 4.
[2] Rates not computed where base is less than 75,000.

There were also some differences in occupational distribution between the Negro and Spanish origin minority groups. Relatively more Negro than Spanish origin graduates were in service occupations. Among dropouts, a lower proportion of youth of Spanish origin were in clerical occupations, at least in part because of the language problem. About one-fifth of both Spanish origin and Negro dropouts worked in laborer occupations but the majority of the Spanish origin laborers were on farms, while 8 out of 10 of the Negro laborers worked in construction and other nonagricultural industries. Although 84 per cent of the Spanish language population of all ages lived in metropolitan areas in 1970, many whose home base was in an urban area spent much of the year working in rural areas as migrant farmworkers.[6]

Table 6   Occupation and Industry of Employed High School Graduates and Dropouts, Age 16 to 24 Years, by Race or National Origin, October 1972
[Per cent distribution]

Occupation and Major Industry Group	Graduates [1]			Dropouts		
	ALL WHITES	SPANISH ORIGIN [2]	NEGRO AND OTHER RACES	ALL WHITES	SPANISH ORIGIN [2]	NEGRO AND OTHER RACES
Total employed: Number (thousands)	8,941	361	1,026	1,999	313	440
Occupation						
Total	100.0	100.0	100.0	100.0	100.0	100.0
White collar	51.7	45.2	41.0	13.1	7.7	11.1
Professional and technical workers	12.1	3.9	6.6	1.1	.6	.7
Managers and administrators, except farm	4.6	3.6	1.7	2.0	1.0	.5
Salesworkers	6.2	5.8	3.0	2.9	3.2	2.7
Clerical workers	28.8	31.9	29.6	7.1	2.9	7.3
Blue collar	35.4	41.8	40.5	65.8	59.7	58.9
Craftsmen and kindred workers	11.8	9.4	7.3	15.4	7.3	6.8
Operatives, except transport	13.6	19.4	20.7	31.5	37.4	25.2
Transport equipment operatives	3.1	3.0	3.4	5.4	5.7	8.6
Laborers, except farm	6.9	10.0	9.2	13.6	9.3	18.2
Service	10.7	10.8	17.1	15.3	19.8	25.5
Private household workers	.7	1.4	1.3	2.4	2.9	2.3
Other service workers	10.0	9.4	15.8	12.9	16.9	23.2
Farmworkers	2.2	2.2	1.4	5.9	12.8	4.5
Industry						
Total	100.0	100.0	100.0	100.0	100.0	100.0
Agriculture	2.6	2.8	1.5	7.1	14.0	5.5
Nonagricultural industries	97.4	97.2	98.5	92.9	86.0	94.5
Wage and salary workers	95.3	96.7	97.4	89.2	83.4	93.2
Mining	.7	.8	.4	.6	....	.2
Construction	6.8	6.6	5.6	13.6	4.5	10.2
Manufacturing	23.0	21.9	28.9	36.6	38.2	31.4
Durable goods	13.0	10.5	16.1	19.0	21.0	17.5
Nondurable goods	9.1	11.4	12.8	17.5	17.2	13.9
Transportation and public utilities	6.4	5.8	6.1	3.3	3.5	4.3
Wholesale and retail trade	22.7	24.7	16.9	20.6	19.1	17.8
Service	32.6	30.5	33.3	14.1	18.2	27.6
Private household	.8	1.4	1.5	2.4	3.5	3.0
Other services	31.8	29.1	30.8	11.7	14.6	24.6
Public administration	3.1	6.4	6.3	.6	....	1.6
Self-employed and unpaid family workers	2.1	.6	1.2	3.7	2.5	1.4

[1] Includes persons in the age group with 1 or more years of college.
[2] See footnote 1, table 4.

There were no significant differences between graduates of Spanish origin and all white graduates in the distribution of employment by industry. How-

[6] See "Spanish-Speaking Americans: Their Manpower Problems and Opportunities," *Manpower Report of the President*, March 1973, pp. 85–112.

ever, graduates of Spanish origin were somewhat less likely to be in manu-facturing industries than Negro graduates, especially in the durable goods sector. On the other hand, a larger proportion of the graduates of Spanish origin than of Negro graduates were in wholesale and retail trade.

Among dropouts, twice as high a proportion of Spanish origin youth were in agriculture as among whites as a group or Negroes, reflecting the propor-tions in farm occupations. However, a much smaller proportion of the dropouts of Spanish origin worked in the construction industry, reflecting the lower percentage who were craftsmen or nonfarm laborers. Dropouts of Spanish origin were as likely as white dropouts to be employed in service industries, but less likely than Negroes.

Robert J. Havighurst
Richard A. Graham
Donald Eberly

American Youth in the Mid-Seventies

Havighurst, Graham, and Eberly contend that basic changes are needed in American secondary education if adolescents are to realize enriching adult life-styles. These social scientists propose a national program of "action-learning" (volunteer public service) and present data drawn from three representative American communities that convinces them of the availability of opportunities for youth to achieve educational objectives through work-experience.

Instructional Objectives
To describe shifts over a ten-year period among proportions of youth, aged 16–21, who are out of school, unemployed and married.
To describe the occupational status of youth, aged 16–21.

FROM *The Bulletin of the National Association of Secondary School Principals*, LVI (1972), pp. 1–13. Reprinted by permission of the authors and the National Association of Secondary School Principals.

To describe the marital status of youth, by age, sex, and race.
To propose a program of action-learning for national volunteer service.
To review a survey of three American communities that illustrates favorable circumstances for action-learning programs.

W HAT it's like to be young in America changed drastically between 1960 and 1970. Opportunities for many young people growing up today are too limited. Jobs are not available, schooling seems pointless, military service is anathema, and early marriage is no solution.

Table 1   Changing Status of Youth: 1960-1970

| | | Percentages of Total | | |
		1960	1970	PERCENTAGE SHIFT OVER 10 YEARS
	Ages: 16–21			
Out of School	White male	40.4	38.0	− 6
	Non-White male	52.9	44.1	−17
	Non-White female	58.1	49.7	−14
	White female	52.0	45.3	−13
(as per cent	White male	9.9	12.0	+21
of labor	Non-White male	15.3	24.9	+63
force)	Non-White female	17.3	31.7	+83
Unemployed	White female	7.8	13.4	+72
Not in Labor	White male	42.1	38.4	− 9
Force	Non-White male	49.5	51.0	+ 3
	Non-White female	69.9	59.6	−15
	White female	61.8	50.6	−18
	Ages: 14–19			
Married	White male	3.1	2.8	−10
	Non-White male	4.3	1.6	−63
	Non-White female	12.1	8.7	−28
	White female	13.3	9.6	−28

Analysis of the census and labor statistics from 1960 to 1970 reveals that, while the numbers of teenagers increased by 30 per cent, unemployment rates in the 15- through 20-year-old age group increased even more—by

50 per cent. At the same time, teenage marriage rates decreased substantially —by 63 per cent for non-white males (Table 1).

TRENDS OF THE '60's CONTINUE

And the trends are persisting in the early 70's. Thus, teenage work and early marriage, traditional ways of taking adult responsibility in American society, are declining. Formal education has instead become the norm (Table 2). The number of young people remaining in school has increased, the sharpest rise occuring among 18- and 19-year-olds, a fact that is probably linked directly to the many new community colleges built during the last decade.

Table 2   Highest Educational Level Reached By Young People: 1971

	(Percentages)					
	Male			Female		
	TOTAL	WHITE	BLACK	TOTAL	WHITE	BLACK
High School Dropout	20	18	35	19	18	34
High School Graduate	26	24	40	38	37	48
College 1–3 years	30	32	14	24	25	10
College Graduate	25	26	11	19	20	8

SOURCE: U.S. Bureau of the Census. Series P-20. No. 224 March, 1972.

Leaving high school before graduation to go to work is now viewed as undesirable, though more than half of America's young people did just that as late as 1940. Formal schooling has almost totally preempted other, more traditional, routes to adulthood, but formal schooling is doing nothing for a large part of the population 15 through 20—they've dropped out—and it is not doing very well for another large group, those who stay on in school, graduate, but get little from it.

Almost 80 per cent *do* graduate from high school. Thirty per cent of the graduates get a paying job or become housewives; 5 per cent join the unemployed; and 45 per cent enter college, though less than half of them graduate four years later. As for the high school dropouts aged 15 through 20, about half take unskilled jobs or become housewives; the other half are unemployed most of the time.

Young college dropouts fare better. Most of them find work or keep house, and increasing numbers return later, either part-time or full-time, to complete their college degrees. Of those who graduate from college, most find work or go on to graduate school. But, since 1971, the number of unemployed college dropouts has increased markedly.

UNEMPLOYMENT LEVEL IS BLEAK

The peak level of unemployment for persons not in school now occurs at ages 18 and 19; it's roughly 16 or 17 per cent for males and a little more for females, with black youth having double the unemployment rate of whites (Table 3). The problem is particularly acute in large cities; in some metro areas of New York City, for example, almost half the young people 15 through 20 are out of school and unemployed. Nationwide, this unemployed, largely apathetic or alienated group of young people presents a major problem for itself and for society. Table 3 indicates that about one young person in seven is either unemployed and looking for work or is out of school, out of a job, and not looking for work.

Table 3   Labor Force Status of Persons Aged 16-21 in 1971

| | | *(Percentages)* | | | | | |
| | | MALES | | | FEMALES | | |
Age	16–17	18–19	20–21	16–17	18–19	20–21
In Military Service	1	9	18	—	—	—
Employed (Civilians)	37	50	53	28	44	52
At School, Not Working	44	24	15	49	25	13
Keeping House, Not Looking for Work	—	—	—	7	16	25
Unemployed, Looking for Work	9	9	8	7	9	6
Not at School, Not Looking for Work	8	6	4	9	5	3
Institutionalized, Unable to Work	1	2	2	—	1	1
Population (000s)	4030	3840	3440	3880	3750	3600
Unemployment Rates (%)						
White	17	14	11	17	14	10
Non-White	33	26	21	39	34	21

In addition to those who leave school or college and can't find jobs, there is another group of comparable size that remains in school but finds little pleasure or purpose in doing so. This group accepts the custodial care society provides through its educational institutions. Individuals in it, however, are dissatisfied with their lives and the society around them. Thus, for some 20 to 30 per cent of American youth aged 15 through 20, school and college is an unsatisfactory experience that does little to help them find directions for a full and useful life.

More and more young people who could make it through high school and college are electing not to. Some are members of a counter culture—a we'll-go-our-way, you-go-yours group; some, a more numerous category, are thought to represent a forerunner group, a group that seeks "the opportunity to change things rather than make out well within the current system." (This statement represented the views of 42 per cent of the 18 to 24-year-olds surveyed by Daniel Yankelovich in 1968.)

Until recently, society was thought to be doing better for young women than for young men. At the start of the last decade, half the young women in the United States were married by the age of 20 and had taken on what was viewed as an acceptable adult role. Very few young women were single, out of school, and unemployed. Now only 40 per cent (Table 4) are married at age 20, though it isn't yet clear whether young people are rejecting marriage generally or just early marriage. Increasing numbers of young women are looking for work and can't find it, and the changes now taking place in their values and life styles suggest that almost as many young women as young men are ill-served by the options presently available for education, employment, or family life.

Table 4   Marital Status of Young People, By Age, Sex, and Color: 1971

	(Per Cent Married)					
	Males			Females		
Age	WHITE	NON-WHITE	NUMBER (000)	WHITE	NON-WHITE	NUMBER (000)
14–17	0.7	0.5	8,126	2.7	2.5	7,898
18	4.5	3.8		17.4	12.0	
19	12.7	3.2		29.7	26.4	
20	20.6	10.9		42.7	37.3	
21	35.6	24.3		55.0	43.6	
22	43.2	29.8		67.4	56.2	
23	57.5	33.2		77.5	61.6	
24	68.6	54.1		80.7	65.9	
18–24	34.4	21.4	13,377	52.6	41.9	12,432

A PROPOSAL FOR THE MID-70's: ACTION-LEARNING

The existing combination of secondary schools, community colleges, job opportunities, military service, and early marriage has failed to meet the needs of several million young people. The indications are that it will do less well in the future and that some basic changes are needed in American secondary education, changes akin to those increasingly called for in American colleges and universities. For example, Alan Pifer, president of the Carnegie Corporation, has called for:

> the invention of viable alternatives for some young people, alternatives that are at least as productive to society, as useful to the individual, and no more costly than going to college. This is no small assignment. It means the investment of huge sums of money to create new jobs with the potential for useful learning and personal satisfaction to those who hold them. It means the invention and financing of new low-cost forms of national service. And perhaps it means some new ideas that no one has yet even thought of. (From the 1971 *Annual Report* of the Carnegie Corporation)

A greatly expanded opportunity for national service in programs such as the Peace Corps or VISTA or CCC work has been suggested again and again, often as a substitute for military service, a proposal based on the notion that it would be good for the nation and for its youth if every young person served his country for a year or two.

Programs of national service have been adopted by Israel, Iran, China, and other countries. A U.S. National Youth Service Foundation has been proposed by Senator Mark Hatfield and a National Service Agency by Representative Jonathan Bingham. Both proposals include features developed by the National Service Secretariat and endorsed by over 50 prominent Americans who advocate a program of national volunteer service that enables all young people to serve and learn for one to four years in locally-directed projects. Where possible, projects would be organized and directed by young people and would be locally financed. Participation would fulfill military service obligations, if any.

Other proposals have called for a compulsory, national program with domestic service accepted as an alternative to military service. Generally, the service program would be full-time, provide food and lodging, and enlist most young men and women between the ages of 19 and 21. It would be expensive—from $12 to $20 billion per year according to most estimates. But a voluntary army, if it comes into being, would make moot the question of whether national service should substitute for the draft, and there are other telling arguments against it. The Scranton Report on Campus Unrest recommended:

> First, national service projects, enlisting youth in a variety of civilian public service activities, should be tested. Whether in the form of pilot projects or a full-scale program, national service should be voluntary, and not, as some have proposed before this Commission and elsewhere, compulsory. (From the September 1970 Report of the Scranton Commission on Campus Unrest)

The Task Force on the Draft and National Service of the White House Conference on Youth agreed that compulsory service would be undesirable, that for some it would be evaded as was the draft, and that for others the effects of unwilling participation would be antithetical to the acquisition of habits and values associated with a self-directed life. Instead, the conference concluded that service and the learning that accompanies it should be so attractive an alternative to conventional schooling that young people would volunteer for it.

Whether, as Alan Pifer has suggested, huge sums of money will be needed to create new jobs or to finance a compulsory service program remains to be seen. The survey undertaken by the American Youth in the Mid-70's project indicates the contrary.

A SURVEY OF THREE CITIES

Three representative U.S. communities—the metropolitan central area of Portland, Ore., the part of the metropolitan fringe area of Washington, D.C., that includes Prince George's County, Md., and a non-metropolitan area, that of Sheboygan County, Wisc.—were surveyed in the spring of 1972 by the Youth in the Mid-70's project to determine how many jobs could be filled by 15- through 20-year-olds.

Schools, hospitals, waste recovery projects, day care centers, sanitariums, and other local agencies described hundreds of volunteer jobs waiting to be filled by young people. But indications were that high schools and community colleges need to know more about the ways in which educational objectives can be achieved through experience. They need to know more about developing, with the agencies and the students, work projects in which the experience would build upon more traditional learning and complement it.

The survey indicated that still more jobs would open up if the schools or some other agency could provide transportation to and from work, could cover costs of insurance and supervision and could prepare students, in advance, to meet entry-level skill specifications. *Under these circumstances, there would be enough jobs to provide every 15- through 20-year-old in the areas surveyed with almost three hours of service-learning opportunities a week, some in jobs that require only a few hours each week, others in full-time work for a half year or more.* Instead of working part-time over a six-year period, one-half of all young people in America could work full time for a school year as a part of growing up.

Public service employers interviewed expressed willingness to develop job descriptions and entry-level skill criteria, but they want to select and fire and to work closely with the sending institution in developing the programs. Some would provide on-the-job training, some would merely specify required skills such as typing speed; others would specify courses that must be taken in advance. The most common criterion mentioned was "genuine interest in the work." "We don't want people others are trying to save." Where a preference was stated, it was for action-learning volunteers who would serve part-time for an extended period—preferably a year—rather than full-time for a shorter period such as six weeks.

Some public service employers wanted volunteers only if money or personnel were provided for their supervision. If the sending institution—the high school, community college, or continuing education center—can't supply it, then some form of federal or local subsidy appears necessary, at least during the initial phase of action-learning programs. And most sending institutions appeared to need help in project development and in supervisor training.

Action-learning projects have been developed by secondary schools and colleges but also by state and local youth organizations such as the YMCA, YWCA, or Scouts. The schools would continue to do most of the accrediting, but other authorized agencies might award a high school certificate or could offer preparation, through service and related study, for the College Level Examination Program.

Generally, action-learning employment would be part-time and related to other study. Academic credit would be given for what was learned, not just for the experience itself. Participants would live at home, and would be unpaid except in cases that required an income for subsistence.

There are many who do need financial help when a paying job that offers learning opportunities is not available. As noted in the January 1969 *Manpower Report of the President,* over a third of the 11 million chronically poor in 1968 who could escape poverty through work were young people—"about four million are youth under 21, either out of school and facing peculiarly difficult problems of initial adjustment to the world of work, or still in school full-time and in need of a part-time job to meet their living expenses." And that was 1968 when the official unemployment level of those 16 to 20 was only 835,000. By early 1972, it was 1,350,000, and neither figure includes those who hadn't registered as unemployed.

Action-learning for many of the poor would have to be accompanied by a stipend, but, for most young people, it would require only out-of-pocket expenses for transportation or materials. The costs, including those of project development, of developing individual programs of learning for each student, and for supervision of work and study appear to be within range of the present costs for conventional high school and community college study.

Action-learning thus would provide another avenue for growing up, another way of transition from adolescence to adulthood. Action-learning offers an alternative not just for those who have little hope of making it in school and who would otherwise drop out, not just for those who pass on from grade to grade finally to graduate from high school or community college barely able to read with little sense of purpose or habit of self direction, and not just for those of the counter culture and the forerunners who reject what they view as an overly rigid process of socialization by a society they would oppose or amend. Action-learning offers an alternative for all, a needed alternative for the increasingly information-rich, action-poor world of the young. According to James Coleman:

Although the school is no longer necessary to provide information, it is more important than ever in developing skills for the management of information. The school of the future must focus on those activities that in the past have largely been accomplished outside school: first, productive action with responsibilities that affect the welfare of others, to develop the child's ability to function as a responsible and productive adult; and second, the development of strategies for making use of the information richness and information-processing capabilities of the environment . . . a much broader conception of learning is necessary: a conception in which the roles, constraints, demands, and responsibilities of adulthood in a complex society are central; a conception in which experience once again becomes important. (From "Education in Modern Society," an address by James S. Coleman, professor of social relations, Johns Hopkins University.)

Action-learning in volunteer public service would not replace on-the-job learning in private employment. Indeed, the separation between economic and educational institutions would become less pronounced. The educational benefits expected from work, or from a combination of work and related study, would be defined so that they could be assessed and attested to as learning as legitimate as that acquired through attendance at a school or college. As Coleman notes, "The conception of full-time education up to a given age, followed by full-time work, would be replaced by a continuing mix beginning at an early age and running through adulthood."

But, while the numbers of private sector jobs available to persons 20 and under could be increased substantially through educational vouchers or other forms of subsidy to private employers, the trend is now in the opposite direction. Fewer paying jobs are available to greater numbers of young people. The principal increases in opportunities for learning as a byproduct of work will, therefore, occur in volunteer service jobs. In the period from 1960 to 1970, the increase in service employment far outstripped overall employment (Table 5). The Census data of 1960 and 1970 indicates an overall increase in service employment of 49 per cent.

Table 5 Employment in Civilian Service Fields: 1970

| | | | Full-Time Equivalent | | |
| | | All | | | All |
	Total	Federal	STATE	LOCAL	Private
Total Services	22,373	1,653	2,302	6,226	12,192
Educational Services	5,489	19	803	3,455	1,212
Elementary and Secondary	3,766		16	3,335	415
College and University	1,537		722	119	696
Other Education	608		456	51	101
Health Services	4,284	193	482	469	3,140
Hospitals	2,746		433	398	1,915
Other Health	1,345		49	71	1,225
Environmental Services	730	221	131	328	50
Natural Resources	377	221	131	25	
Sewerage	61			61	
Sanitation, other	175			125	50
Local Parks and Recreation	117			117	

Table 5   (Continued)

	Total	All Federal	STATE	LOCAL	All Private
			Full-Time Equivalent		
Social Services	763		262	260	241
Public Welfare	250		97	153	
Housing & Urban Renewal	55			55	
Correction	142		90	52	
Employment Secur. Admin.	75		75		
Legal	241				241
Protection Services (Non-military)	670	30	56	584	
Police	480	30	56	394	
Fire, local	190			190	
Other Services	10,437	1,190	568	1,130	7,549
Highways	951	5	297	271	378
Postal	731	731			
Library, local	57			57	
Utilities & Transportation	4,787			267	4,520
Water	324			110	214
Electricity	341			56	285
Transit, local & inter-city	382			92	290
Tel and Tel	969				969
Gas	171			9	162
Railroad	621				621
Air Transportation	354			13	341
Radio and TV	141				141
Trucking & Warehousing	1,117				1,117
Other Utilities	240				240
General building contr.°	997				997
Special trade contr.°	1,654				1,654
Plumbing, Heating a–c	400				400
Painting, paper hanging	127				127
Electrical	286				286
Masonry, stonework, plaster	212				212
Roofing & sheet metal	120				120
Other	509				509
Other Services	1,260	454	271	535	

SOURCES:
Federal, State and Local columns from:
Public Employment in 1970, U.S. Department of Commerce, Bureau of the Census, Tables 1 and 3.
All private column from:
Employment and Earnings, Vol. 17, No. 6, December 1970, Table B-2.
Note: Certain private sector employment is included since it represents a source of supervisors.

The increase in action-learning opportunities is probably as great and, as indicated by the survey of three representative U.S. communities, perhaps greater. Educational institutions provide the most opportunities for service, as tutors, aides, and peer counselors. These opportunities can be expected to expand further as school principals and community agencies become aware of designs for volunteer service projects that are working well elsewhere. And in just the past few years, the opportunity for action-learning in other areas has increased extraordinarily: in work connected with environmental protection, in lead-based paint detection and removal, in water and air pollution control, in the reprocessing of waste products. In still other fields such as probationary work, drug rehabilitation, and recreational programs, well-prepared young people have shown that they can do as well as their elders. And they learn in the process, often as much and in some ways more than in school.

The survey of the three U.S. communities revealed that many, perhaps most, school administrators and local agency heads were unfamiliar with action-learning programs. Their estimates of the numbers of action-learning opportunities are, therefore, apt to prove conservative. There is then strong reason to have confidence in the survey data indications that some four million young people could be employed full-time for one year in action-learning programs (Table 6), or that almost every one of the 22 million young Americans 15 through 20 could be employed for over three hours per week. More likely, a mix would occur: some would be employed full-time for a spell; most would engage in part-time employment.

Table 6   Estimated Needs and Educational Requirements for
National Service Participants °
[Numbers in thousands]

		Minimum Academic Background			
	Need	H.S. DROPOUT	H.S. GRAD.	SOME COLLEGE	COLLEGE GRAD.
Total	4,030	1,340	1,470	935	285
Educational Services	1,000	205	420	270	105
Tutors	600	100	300	180	20
Teacher aides	300	100	100	80	20
Teachers	60	—	—	—	60
Public media aides	40	5	20	10	5
Health Services	900	215	405	230	50
Health aides	800	200	350	210	40
At hospitals	600	150	250	170	30
Outside hospitals	200	50	100	40	10
Mental health aides	100	15	55	20	10
At institutions	50	10	25	10	5
Outside institutions	50	5	30	10	5

Table 6   (Continued)

| | | Minimum Academic Background | | | |
	Need	H.S. DROPOUT	H.S. GRAD.	SOME COLLEGE	COLLEGE GRAD.
Environmental Services	800	600	110	50	40
Conservation aides	500	400	50	30	20
Pollution & sanitation aides	100	60	20	10	10
Beautification aides	100	70	20	5	5
Park development aides	100	70	20	5	5
Social Services	560	110	210	210	30
Day care aides	200	30	100	65	5
Welfare aides	200	30	50	110	10
Parole & Probation aides	20	5	10	5	—
Prison aides	20	5	10	5	—
Geriatric aides	50	20	20	10	—
Settlement house aides	50	20	20	10	—
Legal aides	20	—	—	5	15
Protection Services	300	60	155	65	20
Police aides	200	25	120	45	10
Fire aides	50	20	15	10	5
Highway safety aides	50	15	20	10	5
Other Services	470	150	170	110	40
Public works aides	200	100	70	25	5
Recreation aides	100	20	50	25	5
Library aides	50	—	15	30	5
Mayor's aides	20	5	5	5	5
Others	100	25	30	25	20

* Eberly, Donald J., *The Estimated Effect of a National Service Program on Public Service Manpower Needs, Youth Employment, College Attendance and Marriage Rates.* Russell Sage Foundation, January 1970, Table A.

Young people want this change. The 1970 National Institute of Student Opinion Poll showed that more than twice as many high school juniors and seniors would favor rather than oppose work in the community for academic credit as a requisite for graduation. And a recent poll of the participants in the University Year for ACTION program showed that 83 per cent of them felt that they had learned more in their year of service and job-related activities than in their conventional college study.

One effect of adding action-learning to the pattern of growing up in America would be a pronounced drop in the rate of unemployment. High school attendance or its equivalent would increase as potential dropouts come to view action-learning as a desirable alternative to classroom study, as an activity which complements it. Some would be persuaded to participate in action-learning because of the stipends paid on the basis of their need.

For them, as well as for others who received no stipend, action-learning would constitute a guaranteed employment opportunity program. Action-learning would, in effect, provide employment of first resort for the young, an opportunity to grow up in a world that is not only information-rich but action-rich as well.

Jacob Mincer

Youth, Education, and Work

Mincer, an economist, analyzes the current costs and social returns of education. His perspective on family, school, and workplace roles in the educational process coincides with those of other social scientists included in this text. Mincer believes that traditional schooling is a profitable investment. From the viewpoint of organizational efficiency, he calls for conjoining or "bringing the workplace to school and family, or any two of these institutions to the third," as well as conceptualizing and experimenting with new educational institutions.

Instructional Objectives
To review the economic components of school expenditures.
To describe such social returns of education as "informed and responsible citizenship, communication skills, lawful behavior, and standards of health."
To analyze secondary education as an economically profitable investment.

Until recently, full-time work rather than full-time education was the major activity of teenage youth. Very few Americans finished high school a century ago; today the proportion is nearly 75 per cent. Urbanization reduces the involvement of youth in a wide variety of work activities which are experienced in farm households. Even the acquisition of specific occupational work experience is progressively postponed as the period of schooling lengthens.

At the same time, the economic functions of the household are reduced by

FROM *Teachers College Record*, LXXIV (1973), pp. 309–316. Reprinted by permission of the author and the publisher.

economic growth, and its membership continues to decline, from the extended to the nuclear family and from large to small nuclear units. The family "work force" employed in household tasks diminishes even more rapidly than its membership as productivity growth induces shifts of labor from nonmarket to market activities.

Compared to the large farm households in which farm and household work and the learning of related skills were combined, the contemporary urban setting reveals a separation of family, school education, and work. Children are segregated in environments of peers in classrooms and in homes, where the few siblings are of similar age, and where fathers and, increasingly, mothers are absent most of the day. The factory, office, or store into which father and mother disappear for much of the day becomes increasingly remote as work experience of children is progressively delayed by lengthened schooling.

These trends are being noted with growing apprehension by many observers, especially by psychologists and sociologists. The apprehension is succinctly expressed by Coleman: "Due to changes in the institutions of family, school, and workplace, young people are shielded from responsibility, held in dependent status, and kept away from productive work—all of which makes their transition into adulthood a difficult and troublesome process." [1] Undoubtedly, apprehension has been intensified in recent years by highly visible and often destructive manifestations of youthful discontent, particularly in schools and campuses, and to some extent also by an apparently high level of youth unemployment.

If the lengthening of schooling and the associated delay in work experience are the sociological villains of the piece, in what light do they appear from an economic point of view? Has schooling become excessive and unduly long? What are the economic bases and interpretations of some of the trends in family, school, and working life? Though economics cannot provide a complete insight into, and even less a basic solution for, a complex societal problem, it can contribute to both by adding a perspective to those of the psychologists, sociologists, and educators.

In my attempt to do this, I want first to indicate the essentials of the economic analysis of education as an investment in human capital and its relevance to the questions posed about reasons and consequences of educational trends. Economists view education as an investment in human capital because it involves current costs and yields returns distributed over many periods. The capital embodied in man is accumulated knowledge and skill, both social and technical. This investment produces future satisfactions including augmented earning power.

The costs and returns of education might be evaluated from the vantage point of individuals (students), their families (parents), or society at large. Since the incidence of perceived costs and benefits is different for each of

[1] James S. Coleman, "How Do the Young Become Adults?" Report 130, Center for Social Organization, Johns Hopkins University, May 1972, p. 5.

these parties, some of the attitudes and some of the behavioral responses are also different. Since actual investments depend on effective access to financing, economists distinguish between private and public investment decisions in education and tend to ignore the distinction between the family and the dependent child (student), the family being viewed as a collective decision maker—whether or not the decisions represent a wholehearted consensus or an uneasy compromise. The latter distinction is not unimportant, either to the continuity or to the effectiveness of investment, but it has not as yet received sufficient analytical attention.

The costs and returns are monetary and nonmonetary, direct and indirect. The major elements of costs are schooling expenditures (tuition in the private account, total school costs in the public calculation) and foregone earnings of students. The returns are the incremental real incomes obtained in consequence of the investment by the individual and by society. The largely unobservable or difficult to evaluate components are effects of education on nonmarket ("consumption") productivities and so-called external effects. The latter occur when some benefits accrue to, or some costs are borne by, people other than the investors. Therefore, social returns (or costs) may be greater or smaller than the sum of private returns (or costs). The difference between the social and private sums is the value (positive or negative) of the externality. Given the concepts of costs and returns to educational investments, economists ask the following questions:

1. Are activities which produce education efficiently organized?
2. Are too few or too many resources allocated to these activities?

Economists have made no significant attempts to grapple with the first question. There is a tendency to equate education with school education, and the inquiry into the study of efficiency of schools as firms which produce education is relegated by economists to "educationists," just as the study of the organization and efficiency within business firms is left to engineers and "management scientists." The central concept which serves to provide answers to the second question is the (marginal) rate of return to the investment. This rate is the rate of discount (interest) which equates the discounted sum of costs to the discounted sum of returns at the time the (incremental) decision is made. The optimal amount of a particular investment is one at which the marginal rate of return is the same as in alternative activities. A dollar transferred from an investment activity with a lower rate of return earns more elsewhere, so total income is increased.

Externalities and Public Policy

If there are beneficial external effects of education and they outweigh the excess of social over private costs, the social rate of return exceeds the private rate. If so, and if the latter is not clearly lower in education than elsewhere, there is no educational overinvestment from a social point of view.

What are examples of such externalities? It is often suggested that they include, among others, informed and responsible citizenship, communication skills, lawful behavior, and standards of health. The existence of such externalities is invoked to justify public efforts to stimulate minimal educational investments by all families. Such efforts can take many forms. It is not clear, for example, that the best policy implied by the existence of externalities is a publicly owned school system rather than direct subsidies to students. The absence of competition among schools and the vast bureaucratic machinery in public school systems is likely to foster and perpetuate inefficiencies. Another question is the extent of minimal education implied by externalities, hence the extent of government support that is required. It is not clear that positive externalities can be attributed to mass, universal education beyond that of a general and elementary kind.

There are, of course, other reasons for public intervention, some of which also represent a response to a somewhat different kind of externality. This is the concern with the distribution rather than with the total volume of educational investments. Helping children of poor or of unloving parents to acquire a minimal degree of earning power is an objective for which schooling is viewed as an instrument. Private charity is not a dependable alternative, since it carries externalities as well: charity of givers is likely to reduce the giving of others, though it may induce the giving of some. Since poverty is viewed as a relative concept, the amount of minimal universal government-supported education has been progressively lengthening as average education (and income) have increased. It is not obvious, however, how long the span of such minimal education should be at any given time. Nor is it obvious that a legislated minimal age of compulsory and "free" schooling—it is not free, because of foregone earnings—is the best policy for a redistribution of wealth. An example of an alternative might be to provide a money equivalent of the desired increment in wealth for each child to be used for education or training at any time and possibly for some other purposes as well. This would reduce losses in foregone earnings and wasted opportunities for investment alternatives other than formal schooling.

If education positively affects not only earnings but also productivity in nonmarket (household, consumption) activities, the rate of return estimated from earnings data may be understated. The most important illustration is the education of girls. Since women on the average spend less than half as much time as men do in earning activities, it might seem that provision of equal amounts of schooling to them is wasteful, unless the nonmarket or consumption effects are strong. The fact that more educated women tend to spend more of their time in the labor market, at the same levels of husbands' income, is consistent with the hypothesis that education increases their earnings in the market more than their productivity in the home. This finding is reversed, however, when small children are present: more educated mothers curtail their work in the labor market to a greater extent than the less educated. Whether this phenomenon represents a productivity effect of mother's education in raising children is an open question which is important and researchable. If better educated mothers produce greater human capital in children and a better quality of family life, apart from contributing to family income, the provision of equal amounts of schooling to both sexes need not be questioned on economic grounds. Indeed, it is rarely questioned as a matter of public policy.

Though the real benefits to the family from educating men and women may be equal, their content is generally not the same. The relative importance of market earnings of men and of nonmarket production of women reflects a division of labor within families. Of course, the degree of specialization in family roles is not fixed across cultures or over time, though their sex linkage appears to be universal. The question for educational policy is whether it provides the appropriate preparation for the future family and occupational life of boys and girls, given the current division of labor in the family and the expected pace of change in it. The educational system tends to overlook this question, implicitly ascribing similar career expectations to both sexes, while parental models of behavior tend to impart expectations of differential roles which are likely to err in the opposite direction. A better understanding of the functions of the family, of the division of labor within it, and of forces producing change would contribute to more realistic aspirations and preparations for the expected or desired mix of market and nonmarket activities.

As long as the family will remain a viable institution, it will continue to imply a division of labor and a complementarity in the activities of its members. The nature of the family and its production function are subjects largely outside the economist's province at this stage of our knowledge. However, secular changes in the division of labor within the family as between market and nonmarket activities have been affected by known economic forces. Economic growth due to growing productivity in industry has meant that the same amount of time spent in the labor market purchases increasingly larger volumes of goods and services than can be produced at home. This induces shifts from work in households to work in the labor market.

Since childbearing and childrearing are time intensive activities, fewer children are born in successive cohorts, as mother's value of time rises in the labor market, and the demand for outside institutions, such as schools, to take over the childcare functions increases. At the same time, partly as a result of growing demands in the labor market and growing family income, and partly as a substitute of quality of children for reduced quantity of children, larger amounts (and longer periods) of education are demanded by families for each of their children.

Evidently, powerful economic forces are, at least in part, responsible for the increasingly prolonged separation of adults and of age graded children in the dissimilar environments of home, school, and workplace. These forces are the forces of economic growth, spurred by the growth of science and technology and producing growth in real incomes. If there is a need to ameliorate some of their consequences, it is not a call to stop economic growth.

Is There a Problem?

When we look at the massive trends in schooling in this century and in the past decades and years, we wonder whether we have not been overschooling our children. Certainly, there are signals of distress coming from the young and from many concerned parents and educators. Yet, if we view schooling as an investment process, there is no evidence that the profitability of that investment has declined as numbers of students have grown. The private rate of return to schooling has remained roughly constant around a respectable 10 per cent figure (with deviations depending on data and analysis) in the past three decades. This figure, as usually calculated, necessarily omits externalities and consumption effects, so it is probably understated. Evidently, during most of this period, demand for educated labor has been rising in step with its supply.

It appears that in the past few years this happy conjuncture has given way to a surplus of supply in the markets for highly educated labor, particularly in the sciences. Rates of return calculations do not immediately capture these changes, since relatively long streams of earning experience (at least a decade) are required for the calculation. Even if we imprudently ignore these latest and hopefully transitory developments, we must keep in mind that the calculated rate of return is an average over the student population, which conceals a wide dispersion. This means that for, say, 20 to 30 per cent of students at any level, the additional schooling has been a waste at least in terms of earnings. Assuming no change in the fraction of failures, and assuming that the distribution of results is reflected in attitudes even before graduation, the distress is more strongly felt and expressed today than in the past because the student population is older, therefore, more articulate, more educated, therefore, suffering a greater loss from overschooling, and much more numerous, therefore, more visible.

It should also be noted that when the overall schooling level was lower, the inability to obtain further education was the source of distress of many people. Only the privileged few continued schooling for prolonged periods. The locus of unhappiness was diffuse, outside of school. When few do not go on to higher levels of schooling, it is the reluctant or "captive" student that is unhappy, and the distress is strongly concentrated in schools.

The high and stable rate of return to schooling in the past decades is not safely extrapolated into the future. To begin with, the greatest expansion of high school completion and post-high school enrollment took place in the past twenty-five years, in a period of seeming insatiable and growing demand for educated labor, and in a period demographically favorable to the young in the labor market: young people, aged sixteen to twenty-four, constituted a declining proportion of the total labor force until quite recently. Most recently, job opportunities and starting relative wages of college graduates have begun to decline in some fields. It will not be clear for some time whether this phenomenon is of long-range significance beyond the recent sectoral and business cycle decline in demand.

One disturbing index of conditions in the general youth labor market throughout the sixties has been the rather high unemployment rate, which has actually risen in the past decade both absolutely and relative to the unemployment rate of the adult population. The fact that the unemployment rate of young people is higher than that of adults is not surprising. Entry into the labor force and job shopping during the early years of work experience are reflected in high unemployment counts. This is certainly true of the sixteen to nineteen age group and somewhat less so of the twenty to twenty-four age group.

There are several additional factors which contribute to the size and growth of the unemployment rate in the young population groups. First, the number of students working seasonally (in the summer) and otherwise part-time has increased greatly. The large turnover—between work and school—is associated with unemployment. As the proportion of students and of student job searchers grows, this component of unemployment increases in importance. Indeed, about 75 per cent of the unemployment observed in the sixteen to nineteen age group is associated with entry and re-entry into the labor force. Second, the young people in these age groups who left school have progressively shorter work experience, since the successive cohorts graduate later. High unemployment is typical of less experienced workers, so growing unemployment is the statistical reflection of diminishing experience in (fixed) young age groups.

None of these factors represent obvious distress. A worsening of employment conditions should be reflected in the duration of unemployment. But the duration of youth unemployment is short (most of it is less than six weeks), and has not increased together with the rate (except in recessions). However, some of the effects of unemployment may not show up in duration to the extent that lack of success results in dropping out of the labor force back to school or to other activities not in the labor market.

One factor which adversely affects the condition of young inexperienced workers in the labor market is the upward trend in minimum wages. Most sixteen to nineteen year olds are employed at or below minimum hourly rates. Each successive hike in the minimum wage, relative to the general wage level, and the progressive expansion of coverage, reduces employer demand for inexperienced, initially low productivity workers.

The particularly bad effect of minimum wage hikes is that they limit the opportunities for training or learning on the job. Apprentices and informal learners must accept initially low-paying jobs; their lower wages reflect not only lower productivity but also the costs of training which the firms provide, formally or informally. The minimum wage blocks this route to advancement and forces a detour via more school learning, at best.

Not all of those prevented from job experience at young ages stay longer at school. According to empirical analysis of minimum wage effects, the labor force participation rate of nonstudents has also been adversely affected. What happens to the double dropouts (out of school and work) may be guessed, but is not well documented.

The increasing tendency of bypassing relatively unskilled work experience via schooling is, of course, strengthened by the growth of public subsidies to universal schooling at progressively higher levels. The minimum wage hikes (and draft policies in the recent past) are additional factors producing a growing number of reluctant students. To some extent, the growth of a largely seasonal part-time student labor force represents an attempt to overcome the growing confinement of youth to schooling and the growing postponement of economic and personal independence.

If a social problem exists, its universality is probably overstated by the tendency of observers to focus on the more visible segments of the population. The analysis available to economists does not suggest any obvious persistent economic malfunctions in the growth of schooling. The rate of return to schooling appears to be reassuring thus far, though the average certainly conceals distributional problems, and the most recent developments are not clearly reflected. The review of youth labor market conditions does reveal some symptoms of distress, though the size and trend in the unemployment figures tend to convey an exaggerated picture of it.

One large area of ignorance makes the economic analysis far from complete: the question of efficiency of the educational production function, the effects of its "industrial," curricular, and pedagogical organization. The observed rate of return does not tell us whether activities which produce education could not be more efficiently organized. Economists are only now beginning to take an interest in studying the educational production function. Much of their interest, however, centers on the production function within schools, although education is a much broader concept than schooling. Once *educational* purposes or functions are defined, the place and nature of *schooling* as one of several (alternative and/or coexisting) institutions can be envisaged, in the light of changes in technology and in society.

Broadly speaking, education of the young involves transmission of knowledge, socialization, identification and encouragement of talent, preparation for work, and orientation toward future personal, household, and public responsibilities. It seems obvious that many, perhaps most, of these purposes cannot be achieved in the traditional classroom. Group or individual learning should depend on function and on available technology. Acquisition of social skills, and participatory activities such as sports, arts, and recreation require social, though not necessarily age segregated, environments. The same is true of the acquisition of information about and experience in a variety of work activities. The management of households, of health, of family finances are matters of social and individual learning. At the same time, the acquisition of intellectual knowledge through reading, listening to lectures, and writing can be pursued individually, without fixed schedules, and at the student's own pace. Certainly, present day technology should make the best teaching and teaching aids available to all students. Of course, provision must be made for feedbacks in form of discussions, testing, and guidance.

The institutional settings need to be envisaged and experimented with. It is not a matter of reversing trends and of somehow bringing the workplace to school and family, or any two of these institutions to the third. The progressively shrinking family, the increasingly abstract occupations, and the existing schooling which at best prepares for further schooling cannot simply be conjoined and revitalized for the education of the young. The new institutions will have to provide direction and guidance for all the functions, whose loci may well be diffused according to needs and technology while providing maximum autonomy and variety for individual patterns of growth.

David Rogers

Vocational and Career Education:
A Critique and Some New Directions

Nearly eight million young persons are enrolled today in public vocational schools and about five million of these youth are high-school students. In the following paper, Rogers starts from the premise that employer participation in vocational training is a key element in educational reform. Excerpts from his comprehensive analysis reprinted here include a discussion of (a) the effectiveness of several vocational training agencies— Neighborhood Youth Corps, Job Corps, public service career programs, vocational high school, and community college; (b) barriers to youth employment in America—competition for jobs, employers' negative attitudes, child labor laws, insurance requirements; and (c) various exemplary programs involving industry-school cooperation.

Instructional Objectives
To describe vocational training agencies in the United States.
To review the characteristics of the youth labor market and to consider barriers to youth employment.

FROM *Teachers College Record*, LXXIV (1973), pp. 471–511. Sections reproduced: pp. 477–483, 492–496, 499–504. Reprinted by permission of the author and the publisher.

To describe the merits of "cooperative education" programs and to discuss the significance of employer participation in them.

Occupational Training Programs for Youth

THOUGH vocational high schools have long been characterized as the "dumping ground" for minority students, and in fact are in some big cities, that pattern is not at all uniform. Aggregate national data comparing racial, ethnic, and economic characteristics of vocational education students with the general population suggest that they tend to reflect the population at large.[1] If these data are in fact valid, one reason may well be that in some states, Texas, Minnesota, and Ohio being examples, vocational education programs are developed as vehicles for economic development. The purpose is to attract industry by developing a skilled work force through vocational training. States that adopt this strategy do not recruit minority students and the handicapped in large numbers, since these students require more extensive remedial programs and supportive services and do not allow for a quick payoff.[2] The result, then, is that these vocational high schools are very selective and end up recruiting middle-class students—and there are many of them around the nation.

In view of these patterns, it is important not to perpetuate the dumping ground myth. The main dumping ground is, as indicated above, the general curriculum, which does not prepare its graduates either for work or college, and should be eliminated or radically upgraded as soon as possible. It is important to be able to disaggregate the national data on vocational education allocations by getting more information on a state and locality basis. Since the states and cities have so much power as major funding sources, they can set policy to a considerable extent. Unfortunately, extensive comparative data, pointing up such differences in program priorities and student enrollments among states and cities, and indicating why they exist and with what consequences, are not available.

Another important point about this sector is its tremendous growth in recent years, from four million students and roughly $332 million in federal, state, and local expenditures in 1964, to eight million students and $1.4 billion in 1969.[3] The Vocational Education Acts of 1963 and 1968 had a lot to do with it, and many new programs reflect increased efforts to reach the urban poor and to establish schools in rural areas, two priorities established by that legislation.

This increase has created very serious staffing and facilities needs that have not always been met. As the HEW study indicates, though the number

---

[1] *Report of the Analysis Group*, HEW Vocational Education Review Task Force (Silver Spring, Md.: Operations Research, Inc., September 25, 1970), Vol. 1, pp. 39–42.

[2] Personal communication with Leonard Lecht.

[3] *Vocational Education Study-Group*, Discussion Paper, July 1970, NAM, p. 1.

of vocational schools increased from 405 in 1965 to 1,296 in 1969, construction was still not keeping up with enrollment. The same can be said for teachers. Despite their increase from 109,136 in 1965 to 166,398 in 1969, there is an immediate need for many more.[4]

On the other hand, the increase seems to be leveling off, and the likelihood is that vocational high school enrollments may go down from their four million in 1969 to as low as 3.4 million in 1980. This is due largely to declining birth rates in the 1950s and 60s. The big growth sector, by contrast, will be in post-secondary technical education, much of it in community colleges which may increase from 710,000 in 1969 to as many as six million or more in 1980.[5] I will discuss the community college in greater detail below.

Within vocational high schools, there are several different types of programs, including cooperative education, distributive trades, home economics and agriculture, trades and industry, health, office, and technical education. As various studies have indicated, there is often a poor fit between these programs and local (metropolitan area) labor markets.[6] Despite improvements in this regard with the legislation of the 1960s, there is still a tendency to train a surplus of students for declining occupations and too few for expanding ones.[7] Obsolescent curricula as well as machinery remain quite common. Thus the health field is one of the most rapidly expanding in many cities, and yet it had only increased from 1.2 per cent of total enrollment in 1965 to 2.2 per cent in 1969. Conversely, home economics and agriculture accounted for 55 per cent of the enrollment as late as 1965, after the urban crisis, poverty, and youth unemployment in inner-city ghettos had become significant public issues. These courses still accounted for 41.4 per cent of enrollment in 1969, though there had been a gradual accommodation to shifting public needs.[8]

This lag between changes in the economy and those in vocational curricula indicates the tremendous importance of good manpower and labor force projections for vocational educators. The lag exists largely as a consequence of the isolation of vocational educators from labor market economists and employers.

The agencies on which the least adequate data exist are proprietary

[4] *Report of the Analysis Group*, op. cit., pp. 62–68.

[5] M. J. Feldman, "Opting for Career Education: Emergence of the Community College," in R. C. Pucinski and S. P. Hirsch, eds., *The Courage to Change* (Englewood Cliffs, N. J.: Prentice-Hall, 1971).

[6] B. L. Mangum, "Workpower for the Seventies," in Pucinski and Hirsch, op. cit., pp. 85–108; R. N. Evans, et al., *Education for Employment: The Background and Potential of the 1968 Vocational Education Amendments*. Institute of Labor and Industrial Relations, University of Michigan and Wayne State University and the National Manpower Policy Task Force, 1969.

[7] There was great concern to correct this serious defect in writing the legislation. Much emphasis was placed on training for "new and emerging" occupations. The 1963 legislation was too permissive, however, and OE did not exercise strong leadership in pressing for the new priorities it established. Even the 1968 legislation has not yet been acted upon the degree necessary.

[8] *Report of the Analysis Group*, op. cit., p. 22.

schools. Though they must get licensed through the state, these agencies have no reporting requirements, and none are monitored very closely by independent evaluators. What evidence exists suggests that these schools vary tremendously in quality and in the kinds of courses offered.[9] There are now over seven thousand of them and they operate on a budget of anywhere between two and thirteen million annually. The fact that the figures available include such a wide range is an indicator of the poor data in this field.

Proprietary schools have developed to fill a need that vocational high schools do not meet at all, or only very poorly. Thus the heavy emphasis in this field on training for employment in emerging occupations—in data processing, electronics, and medical services—illustrates this point. Several analysts of vocational education have even suggested that the proprietary schools are the most innovative and adaptive in their curriculum and are at the cutting edge of economic change. They seem to have greater flexibility, closer linkages with industry and prospective employers, and a much more effective placement, employment service, and follow-up procedure than do vocational high schools.[10]

On the other hand, the record is apparently quite uneven; and a recent FTC case against four large proprietary schools accuses them of misrepresentation to the public of their capacity to place graduates. There are no adequate data on how common this practice may be, if it is in fact demonstrated in these instances. And, of course, no similar type charges have ever been made and enforced in the public sector. This suggests a double standard that may be quite inappropriate, especially in view of the fact that the private schools serve students much better in terms of training and placement than do vocational high schools.

Employer OJT programs are still another occupational training agency for youth; and if the data are limited for proprietary programs, they are all but nonexistent in any aggregate sense for employer programs. Economist Fritz Machlup estimated that business training programs cost over $3 billion in 1958; but this was before the many manpower programs of the 1960s. On the other hand, Machlup's figure was for all programs and not just those for youth.[11]

Moving back to the public sector, there are three other major occupational training programs for youth. First, there are the Department of Labor and OEO-administered agencies including the Neighborhood Youth Corps (NYC); the Job Corps; the MDTA skills training (classroom and OJT); the Public Service Careers Program for paraprofessionals; the Concentrated Employment Program (CEP), and others. Over one million youth, between the ages of sixteen and twenty-two are served by these programs, most of

[9] Ibid., pp. 13–22; A. H. Belitsky, *Private Vocational Schools and Their Students* (Cambridge, Mass.: Schenkman Publishing, 1969). The discussion to follow comes from these sources.
[10] Ibid., pp. 16–17.
[11] *Report of the Analysis Group*, op. cit., p. 22.

them (650,000) in the Neighborhood Youth Corps and Job Corps alone. This amounts to roughly $2 billion a year, or between 30 per cent and 40 per cent of the total manpower training funds.[12]

These programs developed, in large part, because of the failure of the public schools to reach large numbers of ghetto and rural youth, or, if they did, to make them employable. They thus constitute a second chance, second-tier educational and manpower training system, taking many of the dropouts or even graduates from the general curriculum or vocational high schools and providing them with further basic education, supportive services, and skills training.

As for their performance, it is very mixed, much like that of other vocational and manpower agencies. Since they serve somewhat different populations of youth from vocational high schools, despite some overlap, it does not make much sense to make extensive comparisons. The Neighborhood Youth Corps was designed as a work experience, income maintenance, and training program for youth and has been heavily criticized for not concentrating more heavily on the first and especially on developing work habits and personal discipline in youth. It has remained largely an income maintenance program that functioned also to keep youth off the streets, especially in the summer ("anti-riot insurance"), and as an "aging vat." [13]

The Job Corps, a very costly program providing vocational and basic education to youths in a residential setting, came under heavy fire in the late sixties for its poor management and inefficiency, with the Nixon administration closing fifty-nine of 123 centers since 1968.[14] Unfortunately, those in the urban centers were cut the most drastically, even though their performance was generally better. MDTA skill centers offer training, counseling, and occupational information and are generally regarded as quite effective. Many train students for broad skill areas and have considerable flexibility, as they allow students to enter at frequent intervals and leave when they reach their training goal. There have been recent attempts to integrate these centers into community colleges to provide minority students with a broader selection of occupations than would otherwise be the case. These skills centers have provided many lessons for vocational high schools on program and administration, suggesting that a lot of skills training can be done in a much shorter time than the high schools usually take.[15]

All the criticisms of these programs have to take into account the fact that they attempt to reach the most disadvantaged of the hard-core poor and minority youth, who require tremendous help and a wide variety of supportive services. An intensive evaluation of manpower programs in several big

[12] *National Manpower Programs—An Overview*, from Harvard Graduate School of Business Administration case materials, adapted from Department of Labor statistics.

[13] S. A. Levitan and R. Taggart, *Social Experimentation and Manpower Policy: The Rhetoric and the Reality* (Baltimore, Md.: Johns Hopkins University Press, 1971).

[14] Ibid., p. 35.

[15] S. A. Levitan, "Manpower Programs for a Healthier Economy," unpublished paper, p. 11.

cities by Garth Mangum and his associates at Olympus Research Corporation indicates that these programs have successfully trained and placed many ghetto youths.[16]

Another vocational training agency is the community college, whose significance has mushroomed over the past decade and seems likely to continue to grow in the future. Referred to in the past as "bush league" universities, set up to "cool out" aspiring minority students, community colleges have become effective manpower training agencies in their own right. They play an increasingly effective role in preparing youth for employment and helping to place them, having become a new type of career development institution.[17] They often have close ties to employers, both public and private, and conduct many effective work-study and cooperative education programs. An indication of their growing importance is provided by the fact that there were one thousand community colleges in 1971, almost double the 1960 number. The present enrollment is roughly two million students, three times the 1960 enrollment, with estimates that the total may reach almost three and a half million by September 1973.[18]

The community college continues to have serious "image" problems, related to the elitism of American society discussed above. It also suffers from high drop-out rates, partly a result of its large minority student population, from poor administration at the state level, and from general confusion and disagreement as to its role and function. Jencks and Riesman suggest that the most serious indictment of the community college is the faculty and administration's "primary interest [is] still in traditional academic programs and in students who will eventually transfer to a four-year college." [19] It is important for community colleges to be geared to a four-year baccalaureate degree, keeping open this option for many upwardly mobile minority students who may develop academic skills much more readily in the empathic and flexible setting of the community college. At the same time, a strong effort must be made to give greater status and dignity to the two-year program.

On the more positive side, community colleges are rapidly becoming one of the most productive manpower training institutions in the nation. Cost-effectiveness studies, such as that by Somers and Fernbach, indicate that they are more efficient than other post-secondary vocational-technical agencies.[20]

---

[16] G. L. Mangum, et al., *Total Impact Evaluation of Manpower in Four Cities* (Washington, D. C.: Olympus Research Corporation, August 1971).

[17] Feldman, op. cit.; B. Clark, *The Open Door College: A Case Study* (New York: McGraw-Hill, 1960).

[18] Feldman, op. cit., p. 111.

[19] Ibid., pp. 114–115.

[20] G. G. Somers and S. B. Fernbach, *An Analysis of the Economic Benefits of Vocational Education at the Secondary, Post-Secondary, and Junior College Levels: A Preliminary Report on an Evaluation of the Effectiveness of Vocational and Technical Education in the U.S.* (Madison, Wis.: University of Wisconsin, Center for Studies in Vocational and Technical Education, 1970); G. G. Somers, *The Effectiveness of Vocational and Technical Programs* (Washington, D. C.: U.S. Department of Health, Education, and Welfare, Office of Education, Bureau of Research, 1971).

They do better than vocational high schools as well in terms of the occupations and earnings of their graduates.[21]

Finally, there is the military, which also has extensive occupational training programs. In 1969, the four services spent over $1 billion on occupational training for about 580,000 young men.[22] Many of the occupations for which the military trains are in considerable demand in the civilian sector. Thus in 1969, there were 34,000 paramedical personnel, 63,000 electronics technicians, and 31,000 craftsmen graduated from military training programs.[23] Several studies have indicated, however, that more highly educated men from higher status backgrounds tend to be assigned to the better military vocational schools. This suggests that the military is "creaming" more high achieving recruits and might well provide the same training to men from less favorable socioeconomic backgrounds.[24] Indeed, a careful study by Reaume and Oi comparing the educational attainment of males in the civilian sector with those in the Navy and Air Force in comparably detailed occupational categories suggests that the military does not require such highly educated trainees for moving into those occupations.[25]

These are the main agencies involved, then, in vocational education. They are generally isolated and fragmented from one another, when it would be important to begin to establish closer linkages among them. A particularly missing linkage is between employers and vocational high schools. In England, through its polytechnic system, employers work closely with technical schools, paying employees to go back to take further training. And in many other European nations, technical schools work closely with employers to ensure that the training is relevant to jobs. That has not been the case in the United States, though there are the beginnings of efforts in this direction. Generally, employers and schools have nothing to do with one another, and employers find the vocational training of youth of little relevance in their performance on the job. In addition, employers do not contribute financially to the cost of vocational and post-secondary training as they do in other nations. Ways have to be found to link them in, as will be discussed at some length below.

THE LABOR MARKET AND JOB EXPERIENCES OF YOUTH

Despite the fact that American youth come into the labor market much later than do their counterparts in European societies, that compulsory education extends to a later age, and that as many as 35 per cent of high school graduates now go on to college, there has been a sharp increase over the

[21] Again, care must be exercised in interpreting these findings, because different student populations are served by these agencies.

[22] *Report of the Analysis Group,* op. cit., p. 23.

[23] Ibid., p. 29.

[24] Ibid., p. 33.

[25] D. Reaume and W. Oi, "The Educational Attainment of Military Civilian Labor Forces," in Studies Prepared for the President's Commission on an All-Volunteer Military (Washington, D. C.: U.S. Government Printing Office, 1970).

past decade in the number of students in the labor force. Students with part-time jobs were 56 per cent of the teenage labor force in October 1971, compared with 41 per cent in 1960.[26] Serious question exists as to the capacity of the economy to absorb them, especially those still in school, as indicated by the fact that they constituted 54 per cent of the teenaged unemployed in 1971, compared with only 30 per cent in 1960.[27]

This dramatic increase is a result both of the post-war baby boom and of the growth in labor force participation of in-school youth. Most of the working students take part-time and summer jobs at low wages in service industries and retail trade. They are often entry level, low skilled, neighborhood jobs, what have been called "youth jobs," in contrast to the "career jobs" which dropouts or high school graduates tend to take.[28] Black and white students differ markedly in the kinds of jobs they take, with blacks going almost exclusively into service but not trade jobs, where discriminatory employment barriers exist.

There is no organized counseling and placement service in the schools that helps students get these jobs. They apparently get them on their own and find out about their availability through informal networks of communication, including peers, local households and employers, and in general "around the community." Taking these jobs reflects, among other things, a desire for independence, action, and service, as well as a need to escape from what many youth may well regard as the unreal, confining, and even coercive confines of the classroom. Apparently, these part-time jobs are of great importance to many students who derive considerable benefit from such early work experience. They develop disciplined work habits, greater sophistication in job hunting methods, and increased knowledge of the workings of the labor market.[29] And as the Ohio State data suggest, youngsters of all income levels participate, not just those in more acute financial need.[30]

A second group in this labor market are out-of-school youth, whose approach to work and actual work experience is quite different. Work has a much greater urgency for them in economic terms, and they tend to take a longer career view of it than in-school youth. They go into manufacturing, offices, and large stores to a much greater extent, where employment is more likely to be permanent and to lead to promotions.[31]

The unemployment among these youth has become a very serious social problem in the 1960s and 70s, especially for minority youth in urban ghettos, but including other population groups as well. The problem is especially acute for high school dropouts, who had an unemployment rate of 23.3 per cent in 1971, compared with 14.4 per cent for high school

[26] 1972 Manpower Report to the President, U.S. Department of Labor, Part 4, New Perspectives on Youth Unemployment, pp. 77–100.
[27] Ibid., p. 77.
[28] Ibid., p. 89 ff.
[29] Ibid., p. 81.
[30] Ibid.
[31] Ibid., p. 89.

graduates.[32] The development of such manpower training programs as the Neighborhood Youth Corps and the Job Corps in the 1960s was an attempt to deal with this problem. More fundamental programs geared toward job creation, income maintenance for families, and vastly improved education are obviously called for. But these bandaid programs, as indicated above, have at least provided some income, increased the employability of some, and probably helped curb some of the social unrest in inner cities.[33]

There are many serious barriers to youth employment in America that do not exist to anywhere near the same degree in Europe, and that have contributed to the high rates of unemployment.[34] One is the tremendous competition for jobs. The age group at this time is exceptionally large, and many of them want at least part-time jobs. There is competition as well from middle-aged working women and returning veterans, both of whom are moving into the labor force in increasing numbers. If the nation finally decides that it wants to put more of these youth to work, it may have to accept that older women will be put out of jobs, at least over the short run, given our anti-inflationary economic policies.

A second barrier is employers' negative attitudes toward many young workers. They tend to hire older, more experienced workers in preference to teenagers. They often require a high school diploma; and they cite the inexperience and immaturity of youth as major reasons for not hiring them.[35] They regard the constant changing of jobs by young people as evidence of such immaturity, though such changing is often a result of shifts in job opportunities and of jobs no longer being available. At least one major survey indicates, moreover, that young people are strongly work oriented, realistic in their wage expectations, and adapt quite readily to work discipline.[36]

Beyond this are child labor laws that bar workers under sixteen from many occupations that are defined as being involved in interstate commerce and bar those under eighteen from hazardous occupations. Labor market analysts indicate that the laws are often not nearly as restrictive as employers think, and many employers are apparently confused about their applicability. This suggests the importance of a program of employer education and not just new legislation.[37]

Other barriers include the requirement of social insurance for employers hiring youth, occupational licensing and fees as a form of credentialing over

[32] Ibid., p. 82.

[33] Manpower training programs have often been referred to as "anti-riot insurance," and the summer riots helped hasten the initiation of many, including the National Alliance of Business's JOBS program, established late in 1967.

[34] 1972 Manpower Report to the President, op. cit., pp. 85–88.

[35] D. E. Diamond and H. Bedrosian, *Industry Hiring Requirements and the Employment of Disadvantaged Groups.* New York University School of Commerce, 1970, research financed by the Department of Labor, Manpower Administration.

[36] V. C. Perrella, *Youth Workers and Their Earnings, October 1969* (Washington, D. C.: U.S. Department of Labor, Bureau of Labor Statistics, July 1971).

[37] *1972 Manpower Report to the President,* op. cit., p. 87.

and beyond just a high school diploma, and employer training requirements. And there is, of course, the failure of the economy to produce enough jobs, which requires fiscal and monetary measures that have not yet been forthcoming.

Many of these barriers, especially the negative attitudes of employers, operate as a self-fulfilling prophecy. Youth are rejected for jobs because of their inexperience; it is difficult for them to acquire it; and they continue to be denied access to later employment for that reason. There has to be a way of breaking through the cycle.

But even if there were improvements in that regard, fiscal and monetary measures to stimulate employment demand are essential. There is a danger in placing too much emphasis on the supply side, training and motivating youth for employment, without a corresponding emphasis on maintaining a full employment economy. Manpower training programs in the 1960s, as useful and effective as they were in many ways, were in reality just patchwork, precisely because of this overemphasis on the supply side.[38] Pathological labor markets as well as pathological poverty, bad work habits, and inadequate education were a key problem, and it was beyond the power of federal agencies involved in vocational and manpower training to deal with it. More national planning and a commitment to fit such training into a larger strategy of job creation are required. It is unrealistic to expect youth to hold onto the work ethic and to be motivated toward further education and training when jobs at decent wages are not available.

These issues have become increasingly important as more youths have been moving in and out of this labor market. The youth labor market in America is beginning to resemble that in European societies in this respect. European nations do not have anywhere near the problems of youth unemployment, however, that we do. This may be due largely to the fact that they do not have the same discontinuity from school to work, the same legal and attitudinal barriers to youth employment, and the poor linkages of schools and employers that we have in America. The English polytechnic system and the Russian vocational training system are particularly relevant as models of how to relate school and work much more productively than is done in America, with employers playing a much more active role and taking on many of the training costs. Indeed, some proposed solutions for the vastly inadequate vocational education system in America are suggested by an examination of these other systems.

In brief, there is no orderly or effective system of vocational training and supportive services for youth in America and none allowing for continuing interchange and movement between school and work. The many agencies involved do not function as if the schools are producing young workers, which in fact they are in increasing numbers, even though they are not doing a good job. No coherent delivery system exists, involving collaborative

---

[38] S. M. Miller and R. D. Corwin, "U.S. Employment Policy from the 1960s to the 70s," *New Generation*, (Spring 1972), pp. 2–13.

relations among the many agencies concerned. This, along with the failure of the economy to generate enough jobs, has contributed substantially to the very serious problems of youth unemployment, alienation, crime, withdrawal, and other similar forms of behavior. And the tremendous emphasis placed on more and more formal schooling, and within the schools on providing counseling and other supportive services for the college-bound, have compounded the problem. In this vacuum, where no institutionalized procedures exist to provide for an orderly transition from school to work, youth themselves are informally providing the service. And a lot can be learned not just by looking at how other nations have handled these problems, or at exemplary programs in America, but at how our youth have on their own as well.

Since the nation is now passing through an "end of growth" period, with the schools and the economy having to absorb fewer teenagers in the immediate future, it would be easy to regard many of these problems as transitional phenomena which might best be handled by a good dose of benign neglect. That such a view is quite common in some circles is evidenced by the limited federal attention to the urban crisis in recent years. Some of this results from the writings of scholars such as Forrester and Banfield who have suggested that the liberal solutions of the 1960s, far from solving the problems of poverty, urban decay, and unemployment, may well have made them worse.

Clearly, there were many shortcomings in the domestic programs of the 1960s, not the least of which was the failure to provide for efficient management, implementation, and the careful translation of program design into reality.[39] Furthermore, there existed the misplaced liberal notion that changed natural priorities and more money alone were the main solution to urban problems. Both would help, but much more attention will also have to be paid to problems of management, of implementation, and of politics than was done in the past. It may be better to waste money on domestic education programs than on missiles, but why waste it at all?

EMPLOYER PARTICIPATION

Cooperative education may well be one of the most effective of all the vocational programs to date, notwithstanding its high costs and the difficulties of getting employers to make jobs available. Every effort should be made to press state and local vocational educational administrators to increase the scope of these programs.

A key to success in such reforms is to have much more employer participation in secondary vocational schools—to help update their curriculum and machinery, by providing information on changing labor force conditions; to improve teacher training and instructional methods by providing work-

[39] D. Rogers, *The Management of Big Cities* (Beverly Hills, Calif.: Sage Publications, 1971).

study opportunities for educators; to provide work experience, work-study, and job placement opportunities for students; and to improve the management of schools as well. There is widespread agreement that employers are at best only passively involved in secondary vocational education,[40] but few productive strategies have yet been developed to promote more participation. Nobody has yet developed explicit norms as to what the nature and extent of that participation might be. And educators are often very wary of having employers come in, lest they be unreasonably critical of existing programs and management and attempt to take over.[41] Many negative stereotypes exist on both sides, with educators fearful of what one has called "creeping capitalism" and concerned that industrialists might try to limit the curriculum to meet only their narrow manpower needs. Some employers, on their side, have tended to be insensitive and tactless in the past as they freely voiced their criticisms of vocational schools.

The exemplary programs that now exist and involve industry-school cooperation should be examined in terms of the lessons implied for increasing it in the future. They include community resources workshops in which business and industry leaders work with teachers in in-service training programs to give them an opportunity to learn more about community agency resources, and to determine how they can be used effectively in schools; various industry-education partnerships, even though they have not had any significant impact as yet; particular coop education programs, as, for example, the one in Dayton, Ohio; the vocational and manpower consortium in Cleveland, called the Metropolitan Cleveland Jobs Council, which involves the Board of Education, employers, City Hall, the Employment Service, and community-based manpower training organizations, all cooperating to provide a variety of training programs and supportive services at an old GE plant donated to the Board of Education; and the many promising programs recently developed in New York City, most notably the satellite academies, involving training and job placement in health and clerical occupations and a direct linkage with employers; an executive internship program that gives high school students complete course credit for working a semester as an assistant to a top city agency administrator; the partnerships of the Economic Development Council of New York with four high schools that go considerably beyond most of the others around the nation in that they involve major efforts at institutional change through teacher development, career education, and management reform; and the New York Urban Coalition's minischool program in three other New York City high schools, involving the use

---

[40] M. U. Eninger, *Effectiveness Evaluation Data for Major City Secondary Education Systems in the United States*, Vol. IV, Survey of Class of 1970 Graduates, Vocational Programs, Report to Office of Program Planning and Evaluation (Washington, D. C.: U.S. Office of Education, Department of Health, Education, and Welfare, 1972), Ch. 10; *Report of the Analysis Group*, op. cit., p. 92.

[41] Ibid.; S. Burt, "Collaboration at the Crossroads," in Pucinski and Hirsch, op. cit., pp. 141, 144; M. Hamburger and H. E. Wolfson, *1,000 Employers Look at Occupational Education* (New York: Board of Education of the City of New York, 1969).

of street workers, various municipal agencies to provide social services to students, employers, and a teacher development center. Intensive clinical studies should be commissioned on these programs, so that we can begin to understand how best to link employers and the schools.

There is a much more receptive climate now for such cooperation than in the past, due largely to the high drop-out rates, the increasing student unrest, the dependence of inner-city employers on a poorly educated labor pool of minority youth, and employers' increasing concern about the poor management of public education.

In the past, the lack of leadership at the national and state education levels was probably a major reason why efforts by industry at initiating cooperative programs did not always meet with a warm reception in schools. A most promising suggestion of the National Association of Manufacturers (NAM's) educational department is to establish a full-time staff person in school systems to work just on that issue. As NAM officials note: "The Association advocates that a qualified person of appropriate rank be designated at the federal, state, and local government education levels, to coordinate and encourage business, industry-education cooperation. . . ." [42] Top Office of Education officials are interested in the idea, as are several state education departments that now have such coordinators. Their performance should be evaluated, improved, and the position spread, where relevant, to other states and cities. Incentives must be provided for this to work, and more funds for it are also needed. Even at the risk of having coordinators and liaison people tripping over each other, employers should establish such positions as well. School-industry cooperation will not take place just by talking about it. There have to be full-time people involved in making it work.

One of industry's biggest complaints is that the equipment and curricula in secondary vocational schools are obsolescent. The complaint is valid, and the absence of relations between schools and both public and private employers has a lot to do with it. Hamburger and Wolfson reported in 1969, in a survey of New York and nineteen other big city school systems, that formally organized school relationships with business, labor, and community groups were practically nonexistent in half the cities surveyed. [43] Only four school systems had citywide educational advisory committees to establish such ties. Industry has apparently been trying hard for years to collaborate with the schools, but only in the face of great resistance. As Burt indicated: "Thus, a major problem is that educators have cloistered themselves from counsel by outsiders; they have been unwilling to accept members of the business world or the community in general, either as participants in the process of analyzing educational issues and considering alternative policies, or as actors in the instructional process." [44]

Burt and Lessinger have documented numerous instances of educators'

[42] NAM, Public Policy Report, *Industry Education Coordinator*, p. 1.
[43] Burt, op. cit., p. 141.
[44] Ibid.

resistance to overtures from business to volunteer in assisting public school programs. The negative consequences of this insulation are also well documented. A study by General Learning, Inc. indicates that in 1967, only 12 per cent of vocational educational students were enrolled in "trades and industry," which was one third of the projected job market need for this type of training. At the other extreme, 37 per cent of vocational education students were enrolled in home economics courses, or six times as many as the projected need would be.[45] Furthermore, Hamburger and Wolfson note that Chicago, in the heart of the midwest industrial complex, had a lower proportion of students in trade and industrial courses than any of the nineteen big cities they studied. New York, the business center of the world, enrolled a smaller percentage of high school students in this area than four other cities. And though a well-established need exists for manpower in the health occupations, none of the cities had a significant program.[46]

The issue, then, is not whether schools can interest employers in education, but rather how educators can be induced to respond to the interest already there, to harness the resources business has to offer. Such assistance as providing internships for teachers; guaranteeing employment to graduates of particular vocational programs; coordinating OJT programs with high school training; developing prevocational occupational information curricula for elementary and junior high schools; improving the workings of industry-advisory committees; providing jobs for work-study and cooperative education programs; helping improve counseling and placement services; and follow-up studies of graduates may all be available. As business becomes more interested in providing such assistance to meet its own manpower needs, and as the educators become more besieged by student unrest and outside criticism, the time for such cooperation may well have arrived.

The same kinds of linkages necessary between secondary vocational schools and employers are required with manpower training agencies. Nowhere is the duplication and fragmentation in vocational training more evident. As Lowell Burkett has observed: ". . . one must conclude that links in communication, coordination, and understanding are missing in the chain of vocational education and manpower development."[47] There is much that vocational educators can learn from the MDTA skills training programs, which are more flexible and train youth much faster than do vocational high schools. Employment Service and Bureau of Labor Statistics economists are indispensible for providing data on labor market trends. Employment Service counselors are needed to assist vocational students in job choice and placement. And the need for expanding cooperative education programs often requires collaboration between manpower trainers and vocational educators.[48] A major study, commissioned by the Department of Labor in 1966,

---

[45] NAM, Secondary Vocational Education, p. 4.
[46] Hamburger and Wolfson, op. cit., p. 150.
[47] L. A. Burkett, "Marriage of Vital Skills: Vocational Education and Manpower Training," in Pucinski and Hirsch, op. cit., p. 150.
[48] Ibid., p. 154.

on relations between the Employment Service and vocational education, indicates that some efforts at cooperation have begun. School counselors now work summers in the Employment Service, and with some positive results. Unfortunately, there is much duplication between vocational schools and the Employment Service in labor market analysis. It seems unnecessary for vocational educators to take on added functions when other agencies already have the expertise and staff to work in the schools. The big question, of course, is how one develops incentives to ensure such cooperation. I will deal with that below.

A critical component of secondary vocational education is its supportive services, including guidance, occupational information, placement, and follow-up surveys and services. One of the reasons that vocational graduates do not do better and that programs are sometimes so obsolete is that these services are so inadequate in vocational schools. Some of them can and should be provided by other agencies, as has just been mentioned. Guidance poses special problems and requires more extended discussion.

Guidance, as a discipline, is roughly sixty years old, but it has only become widely practiced in the schools over the past couple of decades. The field has moved back and forth from a concern for career and job guidance in its early years, to one for psychotherapy and life adjustment. It is in the latter phase now, and counselors are poorly equipped to offer career advice to students. They are almost exclusively former teachers who have no training or expertise in that field.[49]

The recommendations of Eli Ginzberg and his associates for changes in the guidance function, based on a nationwide three year study, are particularly compelling in this regard. They suggest that many more people be recruited into the profession from outside teaching; that they get training in labor market analysis and supervised work in outside, non-classroom settings; that counselors abandon their exclusive concern with psychotherapy and place much greater emphasis on career and job guidance; that they coordinate a wide range of services, especially for minority youth, without having to provide all these services themselves; and that the government should provide occupational information services routinely to guidance counselors and the schools.[50]

An important question is how should the guidance counselor relate to students, to the school, and to outside agencies. Certainly, there is a great need for guidance counselors to work much more closely with the Employment Service, and with employers and labor market analysts from government agencies. Otherwise they will continue to be uninformed about the realities of the labor markets into which many of their students will be moving.

Beyond that, insofar as they will be concentrating much more than in the past on career and job guidance, counselors should not have to provide many other specialized services. This has been one of their problems for many

---

[49] E. Ginzberg, et al., *Guidance* (New York: McGraw-Hill, 1971), Chs. 16–18.
[50] Ibid.

years. The definition of the job was too global, with the guidance counselor having to provide every conceivable service related to the "life adjustment" and "human development" of students. As former teachers, they did not have the professional training required to provide those services. Instead, they should become the orchestrators of services, including psychotherapy and testing. If they manage the delivery of all these services and concentrate themselves on career guidance, the guidance function should be performed much better than in the past.

There is, however, serious question as to whether the services ought even to be delivered in the school itself; Martin and Harrison comment on the threat that the counselor poses for the teacher, since he deals with problems that could not be adequately handled in the classroom and is oriented toward serving the needs of students and parents.[51] They recommend subcontracting these services to a Community Guidance and Evaluation Center, thereby minimizing some of the conflict, or at least its immediacy and visibility. This recommendation is in line with the general view that the schools keep receiving more and more overlays of functions that they cannot adequately handle and that deflect their limited resources from their main mission, which is formal academic instruction. Another model, however, of the school as a multi-service center, and as the most logical site for concentrating these resources, should also be considered. In general, it may be most useful to experiment with many different models and through careful evaluations determine which is better, and under what conditions.

[51] J. H. Martin and C. H. Harrison, *Free To Learn* (Englewood Cliffs, N. J.: Prentice-Hall, 1972), pp. 43–68.

Lenore W. Harmon

The Childhood and Adolescent Career Plans of College Women

Harmon asked nearly twelve hundred college freshmen women to report, retrospectively, which of 135 occupational titles they had contemplated as careers during adolescence. Each girl was asked to indicate her age when a given occupation appealed to her, and, if she subsequently lost interest in it, her age when it happened. Each girl was also asked to indicate the

FROM *Journal of Vocational Behavior*, I (1971), pp. 45–56. Reprinted by permission of the author and the publisher.

reasons for her choices. The data, in brief, reveal that early choices persist into adolescence, and that, in general, adolescent girls accede to the cultural bias that women need not aspire to positions of leadership and responsibility.

Instructional Objectives
To review the popularity of various occupations among adolescent girls.
To note the median age at which various occupations are first considered by adolescent girls.
To analyze persistency of adolescent girls' occupational preferences.
To consider reasons why adolescent girls relinquish occupational aspirations.

M OST theories of vocational choice have been developed out of a desire to understand how men choose their lifework. Two recent developments make it necessary to expand theories of vocational choice to include women. The first is the increasing proportion of women, especially mature women, who do work and the increasing proportion of jobs held by them.[1] The second is the finding that contrary to time-honored opinion,[2] women in occupations from Sewing Machine Operator to Social Worker do have well defined sets of interests which can be measured using the revised SVIB for women.[3] Since women do work and choose their jobs purposefully, counselors can counsel them more effectively if they have some understanding of how their interests develop.

This paper, unfortunately, does not present a theory of vocational development or choice for women. Theory can be no more than speculation unless it develops after a long look at the way the world is. This study was an attempt to look at the childhood and adolescent career preferences of college women in a normative manner. The purpose was to provide information for counselors and clues for those who are seeking a theory of vocational development in women.

Research in the vocational development of women has traditionally not gone much beyond the career or noncareer motivations of women.[4] Ginzberg [5]

[1] U. S. Department of Labor, *1965 Handbook on Women Workers* (Washington, D. C.: United States Government Printing Office, 1966), Women's Bureau Bulletin No. 290.
[2] E. K. Strong, Jr., *Vocational Interests of Men and Women* (Stanford, Calif.: Stanford University Press, 1943).
[3] D. P. Campbell and L. W. Harmon, *Vocational Interests of Non-Professional Women.* Final report of Project No. 6-1820, Grant OEG 3-6-061820-07555. United States Department of HEW, Office of Education, Bureau of Research, 1968, pp. 1–255; D. P. Campbell, *SVIB Handbook* (Stanford, Calif.: Stanford University Press, 1971).
[4] E. E. Matthews and D. V. Tiedman, "Attitudes Toward Career and Marriage and the Development of Life Style in Young Women," *Journal of Counseling Psychology,* XI (1964), 375–384; L. E. Tyler, "The Antecedents of Two Varieties of Vocational Interests," *Genetic Psychology Monographs,* LXX (1964), 177–227.
[5] E. Ginzberg, S. W. Ginsburg, S. Axelrad, and J. L. Herma, *Occupational Choice* (New York: Columbia University Press, 1951).

is one of the few people who asked women specifically about their past vocational plans but he used an *N* of 10 and devoted most of his attention to the type of preferences reported rather than the preferences themselves. This study focuses upon the occupations previously considered by a large number of college freshman women.

METHOD

During the summer of 1968, all freshman women who participated in the preenrollment testing program at the University of Wisconsin—Milwaukee were asked to complete the Life Planning Questionnaire for Women. Eighty per cent of all freshman women (1188) did so. The questionnaire included questions designed to establish the educational level and vocations of the students' immediate family, including their mothers and sisters, and the attitudes of their families toward maternal employment. The students' educational, vocational, and marriage plans were also investigated. In addition, each woman was asked to read a list of 135 names of occupations, checking each one she had ever considered entering and recording her age when she first considered it, her age when she last considered it, and the reason she stopped considering each occupation. The occupations listed were simply the 128 titles in Part I of the SVIB for women (Form T398) with the title "Teacher—High School" expanded into various types of teaching and with Mathematician, Occupational Therapist, and Physical Therapist added.

One of the problems in using a retrospective approach is that women may not recall the past accurately. The results of a more correct longitudinal approach, however, may well be only history by the time they are available. In this case using the retrospective approach meant that the results could only be hazy approximations of reality. The number of subjects available seemed adequate to provide reliable indications of trends.

Some of the trends investigated included: (1) the overall popularity of various occupational preferences, (2) the median age at which each occupation was first considered, (3) the persistence of various occupational preferences, and (4) the reasons specific occupations were dropped from consideration.

In addition, the past preferences of women who are currently planning to become either social workers or medical technologists were studied more intensively.

SUBJECTS

The 1188 women were all entering the University of Wisconsin—Milwaukee as freshman. The age of the respondents ranged from 16–44, with a mean of 17.7 years. Only 2% of the group was over 20. Eighty-three per cent of the women were from the Milwaukee metropolitan area.

The median educational attainment of both the mothers and fathers of the subjects was high school graduation, although the fathers, more often than the mothers, had some education beyond high school. The fathers were more likely to be employed in the skilled trades (28%) or semi- and unskilled work (18%) than in the professions (12%) or management (13%). Only 31% of the mothers had never been employed during the daughter's lifetime. The mothers were more likely to have held clerical (23%) or service (15%) jobs than professional jobs (7%). Over half the freshman women whose mothers had been employed perceived their mothers' main motivation to be financial, and their fathers' attitude toward their mothers' work to be tolerant as opposed to enthusiastic or grudging.

The primary educational goal of the freshman women was to obtain a Bachelor's degree although 35% were planning to take advanced degrees. Most of them planned to get their degrees in Education (23%) or Liberal Arts (35%). Very few of them expected to get degrees in Business Administration (3%) or Engineering (less than 1%).

While the subjects as a group were probably more like the average woman in socioeconomic status than freshman on many university campuses, it is important to note that they were college bound and that they did come from a single geographical area.

RESULTS

The number of occupations considered ranged from 1 to 90, with a mean of 16. However, the modal number was 12 and the middle 50% of the women considered 11–30 occupations.

Table 1 shows the percentage of the women who ever considered each occupation. The most popular occupation is Housewife. It may be even more popular than it appears here (51%) because many women who do not consider it an "occupation" probably did not check it.

Only 45 (33%) of the occupational titles had been considered by more than 10% of these women. The job titles were arbitrarily grouped into occupational families which resemble the groups of occupational scales on the women's SVIB. Then the percentage of occupations in each family which had been considered by more than 10% of the freshman women was computed. Table 2 shows that Medical Service occupations were most often considered by more than 10% of the respondents, with Social Service and Verbal occupations also often considered. Business and Clerical occupations were seldom considered by more than 10% of the respondents. Both the occupational groupings and the 10% cutoff point are arbitrary, but Table 2 does present a meaningful way of looking at the information in Table 1.

The median age of the women who considered each occupation at the time when they first considered it was calculated as an indicator of the order in which occupations were considered. The results are in Table 3. Median age was used rather than mean age because ages 6–9 and 10–12 were tabulated as units. Table 3 does not include occupations considered by less than 5% of the women because the number involved (less than 60) didn't seem large enough to provide a reliable estimate of median age.

Table 1   Popularity of Various Occupations by Percentages of 1188 Freshman Women Who Have Ever Considered Them

Per Cent	Occupations
51	Housewife
44	Actress
36	Teacher—Elementary
33	Artist/Social Worker
31	Interior decorator
28	Nurse
27	Fashion model/Stewardess/Teacher—Kindergarten
26	Author—Novel/Beautician
25	Teacher—English
22	Psychologist
20	Private secretary/Psychiatrist
19	Author—Children's/Foreign correspondent
18	Dental assistant/Interpreter
17	Biologist/Missionary/Musician
16	Costume Designer/Teacher—Language
14	Architect/Athletic director/Medical technologist/Poet
13	Advertiser/Chemist/Librarian/Pro Dancer
12	College Professor/Lawyer—Criminal/Physical therapist/Physician/Secret Service/Teacher—Art/Teacher—Social studies
11	Artists model/Bacteriologist/Dressmaker/Occupational therapist/Veterinarian
10	Dramatist/Nurses' aid/Magazine writer
9	Dietitian/Florist/Mathematician/Receptionist/Teacher—Music/Typist
8	Buyer/Cartoonist/City-State employee/Editor/Composer/Scientific researcher/Teacher—Dance/Teacher—Math
7	Pilot/Comptometer operator/Manager—Children's nursery/Hostess/Illustrator/Playground director/Reporter—General/Sculptress/X-Ray technician
6	Educational director/Judge/Church worker/Pharmacist/Surgeon/Teacher—Science/Waitress
5	Bank teller/Bookkeeper/Bank cashier/Cook/Farmer/Supermarket check-out clerk/Manager—Women's style shop/Policewoman/Office clerk/Politician/Radio-TV singer/Reporter—Women's pages/Stenographer/Teacher—Domestic Science
4	Housekeeper/Lawyer—Corporation/Court stenographer/News photographer/portrait photographer/Radio announcer/Teacher—Commercial/Travel bureau manager/Vocational counselor
3	Income tax accountant/Governor/Inventor/Opera singer/School principal/Other
2	Dean of Women/Dentist/Employment manager/Engineer/Hospital records clerk/Landscape gardener/Museum director/Probation officer/Retailer/Weather forecaster
1	Caterer/Author—Technical/Draftsman/Electronics technician/Hotel manager/Life insurance saleswoman/Golf pro/Office manager/Railroad reservationist/Radio program director/Real estate sales/Sales manager/Scenario writer/Scientific illustrator/Speciality Sales/Statistician/Childrens' clothes designer
0	Supervisor—Telephone office

Table 2   Percentages of Occupations in Various Occupational Families Considered by More than 10% of 1188 Freshman Women

Occupational Family	N Occupations in Family	% Occupations in Family Chosen by > 10%
Performing	12	42
Artistic	13	38
Verbal	19	53
Social Service	16	56
Math-Science	17	35
Business	16	0
Domestic	6	17
Clerical-Secretarial	11	9
Medical Service	6	83
Nonprofessional	12	42

Table 3   Median Ages When Various Occupations Were First Considered

Age	Occupations [a]
6–9	Housewife/Actress/(1)
10–12	Artist/Nurse/Missionary/Musician/Professional dancer/Physician/Veterinarian/Composer/(6)
13	Teacher—Elementary/Beautician/Cartoonist/Teacher—Dance/(1)
14	Fashion model/Stewardess/Teacher—Kindergarten/Author—Novel/Private secretary/Author—Children's/Architect/Athletic director/Poet/Librarian/Lawyer—Criminal/Secret Service/Dressmaker/Dramatist/Mathematician/Pilot/Teacher—Music/Manager—Children's nursery/Illustrator/Playground director/Surgeon/(4)
15	Social worker/Interior decorator/Teacher—English/Psychiatrist/Foreign correspondent/Dental assistant/Interpreter/Biologist/Costume designer/Teacher—Language/Medical technologist/Chemist/Physical therapist/Teacher—Art/Artists' model/Magazine writer/Nurses' aid/Dietitian/Florist/Scientific researcher/Teacher—Math/Hostess/Reporter—General/Sculptress/Teacher—Science/(20)
16	Psychologist/Advertiser/College professor/Teacher—Social Studies/Bacteriologist/Occupational therapist/Receptionist/Typist/Buyer/City-State employee/Editor/Comptometer operator/X-Ray technician/Educational director/Judge/Pharmacist/Waitress/(20)
17	(4)

[a] Occupations considered by 5% or less of the total group are not listed. The numbers in parentheses indicate the number of such occupations at each age level. Occupations listed are in order of popularity within ages.

The most popular occupations from Table 1 tend to have been considered earliest. Occupations considered by only 5–8% of the women tend to have been considered later. Overall, a few occupations were considered by relatively large proportions of the group between ages 6–12 and more occupations were considered, each by a relatively small proportion of the group, between ages 13–17.

The occupations considered by older girls seem to be more specific and sophisticated. For instance, Nurse, Physician, and Veterinarian were first considered at a median age between 10–12. Biologist, Medical Technologist, Chemist, Physical Therapist, Nurses' Aid, and Scientific Researcher were first considered at a median age of 15.

An analysis of the median age at which girls stopped considering an occupation provided little insight because most of the median ages were 16 or 17. Only Actress, Farmer, and Policewoman were given up at a median age of 13 and Veterinarian and Inventor at age 14.

It is also important to note that the proportions of college women still considering each occupation varies. The respondents were presented with a list of possible reasons for ceasing to consider an occupation. They were: (A) I realized that I do not have the necessary talents or abilities; (B) When I found out what people in the occupation actually do I lost interest; (C) The training for this occupation is too long or difficult; (D) I did not wish to undertake the training for this occupation because it is not offered in a college or university; (E) My parents or other people who are important to me did not seem to approve the occupation wholeheartedly; (F) I discovered that most people do not place a very high value on this type of work; (G) The way of life associated with this occupation no longer appeals to me; (H) I found another occupation I liked better although I believe this occupation would be a good one for me, too; (I) This occupation is still one which I may decide to enter.

The modal response for 110 of the 135 occupations (81%) was, "This occupation is still one which I may decide to enter." For 58 of those 110 occupations the next most popular response was, "I found another occupation I liked better although I believe this occupation would be a good one for me, too."

Table 4 shows the approximate proportion of the women who ever considered an occupation who are still considering it. Again, occupations which had ever been considered by 5% or less of the women were omitted. Housewife, the most popular and earliest preference, is also the most persistent. However, other popular preferences such as Actress, Beautician, and Fashion Model were among the least persistent. Educational and Social Service preferences emerge as the most persistent. While the median age at which an occupation was first considered probably does have some effect on persistence measured at age 17, it does not account for all the variance in persistence. Note that the occupations chosen at a median age of 16 from

Table 4 Persistence of Preferences Approximate Percentages of Women Who Ever Considered an Occupation and Who Are Still Considering It

Approximate % of Women Still Considering	Occupations [a]
80–89	Housewife
70–79	Educational director/(3)
60–69	Teacher—Elementary/Teacher—Kindergarten/College professor/Teacher—Social Studies/Buyer/Scientific researcher/Church worker/(8)
50–59	Social worker/Teacher—English/Psychologist/Teacher—Language/Teacher—Art/City-State employee/Editor/Teacher—Math/(9)
40–49	Interior decorator/Author—Novel/Author—Childrens'/Foreign correspondent/Biologist/Medical technologist/Poet/Advertiser/Chemist/Bacteriologist/Occupational therapist/Dramatist/Receptionist/Comptometer operator/Manager—Nursery/Hostess/Illustrator/Playground director/Reporter—General/Sculptress/Judge/(8)
30–39	Artist/Nurse/Stewardess/Psychiatrist/Interpreter/Costume designer/Athletic director/Librarian/Physical therapist/Secret Servicewoman/Dressmaker/Florist/Mathematician/Teacher—Music/Typist/Cartoonist/Composer/Teacher—Dance/Pilot/X-Ray technician/Pharmacist/(15)
20–29	Fashion model/Missionary/Musician/Architect/Professional dancer/Lawyer—Criminal/Artists model/Nurses' aid/Dietitian/(16)
10–19	Actress/Beautician/Private secretary/Dental assistant/Physician/Veterinarian/Surgeon/(4)

[a] Occupations which were ever considered by 5% or less of the total group are not listed. The numbers in parentheses indicate the number of such occupations at each percentage level. Occupations listed are in order of popularity.

Table 3 are scattered from the 30–70% levels in Table 4. It appears that occupations which do not require college training, which require talent or great beauty, or which require long training are among the least persistent, although some occupations of these types occur in the 30–49% range as well as below 30%.

Table 5 shows the modal reasons for ceasing to consider an occupation. Since the modal response for most occupations was that it is still being considered, there are few entries in Table 5. Note that some of the reasons, i.e., the ones related to actual job duties, level of training required, parental approval, and status were not used enough to be the modal response for ceasing to consider any occupation. The reasons which were used often seem quite appropriate to the occupations for which they were used.

Table 5   Modal Reason for Giving Up an Occupation Previously Considered

Reason	Occupation [a]
Lack of talent or ability	Actress/Artist/Fashion model/Musician/Architect/ Professional dancer/Physician/Artists' model/ Music composer/Teacher—Math/Sculptress/ Surgeon/Radio-TV singer/(4)
Training too long or difficult	Veterinarian/Lawyer—Criminal/(1)
Way of life undesirable	Beautician/Pilot/Waitress/Policewoman/(2)
Like another occupation better	Dental assistant/Teacher—Language/Athletic director/Teacher—Science/Office clerk/(4)

[a] Occupations considered by 5% or less of the total group are not listed. The numbers in parentheses indicate the number of such occupations for each reason. Occupations listed are in order of popularity.

The only preferences expressed between ages 6 and 12 which persisted (that is, continued to be considered by a majority of women) were House-wife, Nurse, and Missionary. Preferences expressed at this age which did not persist included Actress, Artist, and Musician, which lends some credence to Ginzberg's contention that choices made before age 11 are phantasy choices, in the sense that the child believes he can do anything and does not know how to evaluate his own choices. Only those preferences which stand the tests of interests, capacities, and values persist.[6]

Each woman had recorded her current occupational choice. Two groups of women, those who had chosen social work ($N = 53$) and medical technology ($N = 30$), were selected for further study to determine whether they had similar or different histories of occupational preferences. A previous study showed that there were differences in adult career choices between groups of women who had measured interests in social work and medical technology as college freshman.[7] This finding suggested that there might be interesting differences in childhood preferences between women who express these two choices as college freshmen.

The mean number of preferences for the social work sample was 13.6 with a range from 3–39. For the medical technology sample the mean number of preferences was 11.8, with a range from 2–31.

[6] Ibid.
[7] L. W. Harmon, "The Predictive Power Over 10 Years of Measured Social Service and Scientific Interests Among College Women," *Journal of Applied Psychology*, LIII (1969), 193–198.

Table 6 Occupations Ever Considered by More Than 15% of Those Now Choosing Social Work or Medical Technology with Median Age Each Was First Considered

Occupations chosen SW group	% SW group (N=53)	Median age SW group	% Total group (N=1188)	Median age total group	Occupations chosen MT group	% MT group (N=30)	Median age MT group	% Total group (N=1188)	Median age total group
Social worker [a]	79 [b]	15	33	15	Medical tech	70 [b]	16	14	15
Housewife [a]	58	10	51	6–9	Housewife [a]	58	8	51	6–9
Actress [a]	45	8	44	6–9	Nurse [a]	53 [b]	11	28	10–12
Psychologist	40 [b]	16	22	16	X-Ray tech	47 [b]	16	07	16
Author—Novel [a]	38 [b]	13	26	14	Dental ass't	37 [b]	14	18	15
Teacher—Elem [a]	34	14	36	13	Biologist	37 [b]	15	17	15
Interior dec [a]	34	15	31	15	Actress [a]	33	8	44	6–9
Stewardess [a]	32	13	27	14	Chemist	33 [b]	15	13	15
Psychiatrist [a]	30	15	20	15	Artist [a]	30	12	33	10–12
Artist [a]	30	8	33	10–12	Physical ther [a]	27	15	12	15
Nurse [a]	28	10	28	10–12	Bacteriologist	27	16	11	16
Poet	28 [b]	14	14	14	Social worker [a]	27	15	33	15
Private sec	28 [b]	13	20	14	Occ ther	23	14	11	16
Beautician	26	14	26	13	Beautician [a]	23	14	26	13
Designer—Child	26	16	01	15	Judge	23	17	06	16
Fashion model [a]	26	13	27	14	Teacher—Elem [a]	23	10	36	13
Teacher—Eng	24	14	25	15	Athletic dir	20	15	14	14
Teacher—Kind	24	14	27	14	Interior dec [a]	20	12	31	15
Costume design	23	16	16	15	Psychiatrist [a]	20	15	20	15
Author—Child [a]	21	13	19	14	Stewardess [a]	20	15	27	14
Missionary	19	13	17	10–12	Sci Research	20	15	08	15
Dressmaker	17	14	11	14	Physician	17	12	12	10–12
Foreign corr [a]	17	14	19	15	Foreign corr [a]	17	15	19	15
Magazine writer	17	14	15	10–12	Mathematician	17	14	09	14
College prof	15	14	12	16	Fashion model [a]	17	14	27	14
Interpreter	15	15	18	15	Musician [a]	17	12	17	10–12
Musician [a]	15	11	17	10–12					
Physical ther [a]	15	14	12	15					
Teacher—Lang	15	16	16	15					
Teacher—Soc St	15	15	12	16					

[a] Designates 14 occupations which appear on both the SW and MT lists.
[b] Percentage choosing the occupation exceeds that of the other group by 20% or more.

Table 6 shows the occupations considered by the social work and medical technology groups in order of popularity with the median age at which group members first considered it. For contrast, comparable figures are presented for the total freshman group. Both the social work and medical technology groups chose their own occupational title more often than housewife.

The fact that the response to the occupational checklist was not perfect is highlighted by the fact that 21% of those who listed their current occupational choice as social work did not check it and 30% of those who listed medical technology as their current choice did not check it. One can only conclude that a check means the occupation was considered but the lack of a check doesn't mean the opposite. Hopefully, such errors are randomly distributed among the occupational titles on the list and not selective. If so, the data present the preferences in their proper order, but the percentages of women considering each occupation are probably too low.

Fourteen occupational names appear on both lists, but the social work list is more oriented toward verbal, aesthetic, teaching, and fashion occupations than the medical technology list, which is oriented towards science, math, and medical service. The social work list seems more like the list for all freshman women. The comparison percentages from the total freshman group descend from high to low for those occupations on the social work list. For those occupations on the medical technology list, the comparison percentages for the total group are much less orderly. An occupation considered by only 7% of the total group is near the top of the medical technology list, while an occupation considered by 27% of the total group is near the bottom of the medical technology list.

The median ages at which both groups first expressed various preferences were strikingly similar to the ages at which women in the whole freshman group expressed these preferences despite the fact that they are based on very small Ns. This suggests that relevant preferences are not expressed earlier for women who choose social work or medical technology than for the average college woman. Instead, the preferences of both groups seem to diverge in the early teenage years into paths which are typical of women who choose either social work or medical technology.

The comparison of the two groups suggests that they do indeed have different histories of vocational preferences.

DISCUSSION

The early vocational considerations of college freshmen tend to be few and general. Of course, the checklist left out some fantasy choices which might well have occurred during the 6–9-year age period. A place to fill in "other" occupations considered was used by only 3% of the women but their entries did include things like Cowgirl and Circus Performer.

Because early choices were somewhat restricted in range, occupations like

Actress, Artist, and Nurse which were considered early were quite popular. A broader range of occupations was considered later with each occupation being less popular. However, since there was no restriction on the number of occupations a girl could check, we might conclude that while older girls look at the world of work more broadly, they look at themselves more narrowly.

In terms of overall popularity the Medical, Social Service, and Verbal fields are considered by the largest proportion of the women, with Business and Clerical-Secretarial occupations considered by the smallest. The whole business world has been rejected by this group of college freshman women. Jobs at the higher levels of responsibility in business may well have been rejected on the basis of cultural bias against women in positions of authority. Jobs at lower levels of the business world have probably been rejected as being for noncollege girls only. While it is good for women to begin to define themselves in terms of their interests and desired life style, it is unfortunate if they rule out possibilities on the basis of social or family pressure.

The popularity and persistence of the choice Housewife suggests that marriage as an institution is not likely to go out of style with this age group despite medical, legal, and ecological developments which make it possible for the single girl to have the best of both worlds.

The most persistent preferences for women in this group (after Housewife) tend to be in educational and social service occupations. The least persistent preferences involve unusual talent, long periods of training, or short non-college training courses. Of course, the data collected here on persistence does not reflect the total picture because the median age of the respondents was only 17. Future studies might show that many of the preferences which appear persistent here do not persist past age 20 or 25.

Taken together these findings suggest that college women do not express many or varied early preferences, that their later preferences although more varied may be restricted largely to typical women's fields, and that women's current vocational choices give some clues to their earlier patterns of vocational thinking. This latter finding may mean that college women today do not choose careers as randomly as was previously thought and that expressed choices do follow a history of related interests. Unfortunately, this study does not even suggest how divergent patterns of vocational interests develop.

The implications for counseling seem to be twofold. First, if the counselor is indeed an agent of cultural change, he should do everything he can to encourage women to consider many types of occupational choices which cut across the boundaries of cultural and sexual stereotypes. Secondly, the counselor dealing with an adolescent girl will do well to listen to the unusual occupations she is considering. They may well provide clues to her future vocational behavior. Table 6 suggests that it would be wise to pay attention to a 15-year-old girl who says she is considering X-ray technology, scientific research, and mathematics, which are relatively unpopular choices, except for women entering medical technology (and perhaps other scientific occupations). It would be unwise to encourage her to enroll in Elementary Education because it's "a good field for women" without further exploration of scientific fields.

Again, it must be stressed that these data are based on the *recollections* of college *freshman* from one *locality*. They should be accepted only tentatively, as a suggestive of trends, until further validated.

Susanne M. Shafer

Adolescent Girls and Future Career Mobility

In the following selection, Shafer analyzes several long-standing factors that inhibit adolescent girls from planning systematically for future careers —sex-role identification, career models, regional limitations, school experiences, personality development, household responsibilities, employment practices, and legal barriers. The researcher, under the auspices of the Ford Foundation, conducted her research in England, West Germany, East Germany, and the United States. She says that "for all girls the fact should be emphasized that traditional barriers to various forms of professional or vocational-technical education have come down and that barriers to many forms of employment have been removed." Shafer believes that girls today should phase their lives in career stages, e.g., high school, work-experience, career choice, college, marriage, motherhood, re-education, and re-entry into productive work.

Instructional Objectives
To note the status of women in the workplace.
To describe several factors that shape adolescent girls' outlook toward careers and career mobility.
To suggest practices that might lead adolescent girls to think about future career mobility.

D o GIRLS give serious consideration to a career for themselves? Although a good many express the hope of becoming a nurse, a teacher, or a secretary, very few think in terms of career mobility. The notion of long term career plans in the United States as well as in England and West Germany

FROM Paper prepared especially for this volume.

is a concept cogitated upon by boys and by the more farsighted or ambitious parents of boys. If these same parents were questioned about career mobility for a daughter, whatever their socio-economic class, they might express the hope that she should enter upon a happy and an economically secure marriage, a step that would on the surface obviate further concern for career mobility.

But in the United States today nearly half the women over eighteen and under sixty-five are in the labor force. In 1968 "of those with no children under six, 51 per cent worked; of those with no children under three, 37 per cent worked; of those with children under three, 25 per cent worked." [1] Married or not, the likelihood that a girl will be in the labor force for a part of her adult life is indeed far greater than in the past. Not only are the chores of homemaking less arduous and families smaller than in the past, but the frequency of divorce and the cost of living have risen so steeply that many women find earnings from a job outside the home a vital necessity.

In the past women were greatly restricted in the occupations which were open to them. That number was in fact further reduced if one eliminates any in which women were not welcomed though legally they had a right to such employment. Although women have been used across the land as nurses, clerks, secretaries, and teachers, they encountered great resistance if they sought entry into medical schools or to positions in marketing, advertising, and other executive-type posts in business, to higher administrative positions in schools or in government, including the Foreign Service, or to university professorships—that is, any of the bastions of the white, male patriarchy in American society. Along with the "ignorant masses" of by-gone days or the Blacks in more recent times, they were turned away, often on the correct assumption that their education had not prepared them for advanced positions.

Although the civil rights movement and the women's liberation movement have brought down many barriers that once kept women from the broad range of occupations open to males, girls still are subjected to experiences which tend to keep them from systematically planning for a future career. Career implies progression toward a higher level of skillfulness, perhaps from a rather easily learned vocation to one that requires more know-how and decision-making skills. The proverbial rise from office boy to corporation executive may be a somewhat lurid example. The rise of a classroom teacher to a principalship and then a school superintendency is far more common, for males, that is. To a large extent girls and their parents and teachers are as yet uncertain about the opportunities that have opened to women today. In addition, many are uninformed about the earnings differential between the American male and female and about the likelihood of girls spending a large part of their adult years in the labor force. What then are the factors which shape the adolescent girl's view toward career and career mobility?

[1] R. W. Smuts, *Women and Work in America* (New York: Schocken Books, 1971), p. VIII.

Sex Role Identification

Since World War II social change in the United States has affected the American family. While the nuclear family is the basic economic unit, it is increasingly broken by divorce or separation. Remarriage may eventually occur. In contrast to the prewar depression period, employment opportunities have been comparatively plentiful except for the least skilled, a group that includes many Blacks and other minorities, as well as the rural poor displaced by the mechanization of agriculture. Since consumer goods became ever more varied and attractive, many married women went to work once the children entered school, primarily to supplement family income. In case of divorce or desertion, they became the head of the household and the main breadwinner.

Decisions of individual women to seek employment outside the home are usually based on economic reasons. Most women in the labor force work because they or their families need the money they can earn—some work to raise family living standards above the level of poverty or deprivation; others, to help meet rising costs of food, education for their children, medical care, and the like. The majority of women do not have the option for working solely for personal fulfillment.[2]

As a result of the fact that so many women are in the labor force, sex roles have become somewhat less distinct over the years.

The traditional obligations of married women in Western society have been to bear and raise children, to perform household chores, to subordinate self-interests to the needs of other family members, to accept the authority of the husband in decision-making, particularly that having to do with finances, and to stay close to home, at least while the children are young. They have had the right to support, security, alimony in the event of divorce, loyalty and fidelity of the husband, and gratitude from the husband and children for nurturing services performed.[3]

That concept of the role of wives and mothers is the one into which most middle class girls have been socialized. They, but not their brothers, are also taught certain social behaviors which reflect an unequal status of the sexes.

Assertiveness, constructive aggression and striving for achievement and excellence, all characteristics considered desirable in adults in this society, are discouraged for women; while tenderness, emotional warmth and expressiveness, equally valued in the abstract, are not encouraged for men.[4]

[2] U.S. Department of Labor, Employment Standards Administration, *Why Women Work* (Washington, D. C.: U. S. Department of Labor, 1971), mimeographed, p. 1.
[3] B. Yorburg, *The Changing Family* (New York: Columbia University Press, 1973), p. 28.
[4] B. R. McCandless, *Adolescents, Behavior, and Development* (Hinsdale, Illinois: The Dryden Press, 1970), p. 423.

Sex role stereotyping is confirmed for girls by the mother who is home all day while any of her children are still young. Her passive role outside the home contrasts sharply with her husband's activity which must center heavily on his income-producing function. Until the advent of the ecology movement and the women's movement a girl growing up in the middle class seldom was made aware of any incongruity in the sex role with which she was expected to identify. Not only should families now remain small that we may achieve "population-zero" growth, but the many women who work should have far greater opportunities in the labor market and be paid on a level with men.

A different picture has been placed before the girl in a poor home.

Married women have few rights and, often, both domestic and economic obligations. Security, support, or alimony in the event of divorce are not expected, primarily because they are not economically possible. Illegitimacy and common law marriages are a reflection of this fact. Companionship is almost nonexistent, as this is a luxury of time and economics. Contrary to stereotyped notions of impulsiveness and abandonment among the poor, the wife is less apt than her middle- and upper-class counterparts to enjoy sex and tends to regard it as a duty and a chore. Survival is the crucial value in these family relationships.[5]

The women's movement has also served these women. By calling for legal dissemination of birth control information, for legalized abortion, and an increase in day-care centers, the women's movement has initiated social changes which will permit the poor to avoid having unwanted children and to go to work more easily.

So far the society-at-large has not yet fully recognized that the sex-role stereotyping of the past is inappropriate both for the present and the future. Regardless of their socio-economic class, girls are socialized to expect and even to seek marriage, children, and a means of earning some money. Little mention is made of any future need to garner a living wage or to develop a career as a means of self-fulfillment.

MODELS

As a result of sex role stereotyping and an ignoring of the implications of the ecological pressures for population control and the current alterations in traditional marriage patterns, girls appear to suffer from a poverty of aspirations. Though boys are often forced into competitive situations early in life, i.e. sports, girls are not urged to explore or expand latent talents on any broad scale. Their most immediate models, their mothers, often have not done so. Where a mother works in an unskilled or semi-skilled capacity and acquiesces willingly to the low wages and monotony of her job, a daughter would seem less likely to object herself to doing such work. In the United States in 1971 the median annual income of full-time male employees was

---

[5] B. Yorburg, op. cit., p. 29.

$9,630 but only $5,700 for females.[6] In England 54 per cent of the women in the labor force in 1966 were classified in the lowest categories of manual and non-manual labor or as personal workers.[7] In 1971 the median income for males 21 years or over in Great Britain was £28.1 per week for manual workers and £34.4 for nonmanual workers. The medians for females 18 or over were £14.6 and £18.0 per week respectively.[8]

These women often left school at the conclusion of compulsory education at age fifteen. They ended their schooling without any kind of vocational education. Presumably, they expected to work until marriage and then become full time housewives when they bore their first child soon after marriage. By the time these women were ready to re-enter the labor market, they were still only eligible for unskilled work. They did not insist on any more complex form of employment. The incentive contained in receiving a good wage is also absent since equal pay is not yet a reality in England. For their daughters they represent models of social acquiescence to the male dominance of the labor market. The same must be said of the American mother who accepts a humdrum, ill-paying job when additional education available nearby would permit her to seek employment commensurate with her abilities and interests.

In East Germany a different situation exists. Population data show a disproportionate number of women, i.e., 117 to every 100 males.[9] Economic data indicate a continuous labor shortage. As a result, the government seeks to make full use of its women to expand the labor force.[10] Legally occupational choice is open for both males and females and the wage structure does not mediate against women. In keeping with Communist ideology, the government of East Germany prescribes polytechnic education for every pupil in the schools. Industry and agriculture cooperate with schools to provide polytechnic education, that is, an introduction to the fundamentals of technology, economics, and production in industry or agriculture. Boys and girls from grades seven to ten spend three to five hours once a week ". . . in a Socialist enterprise (industry or agriculture), in order to work while they learn and learn while they work." [11] In addition, "it is not only the established constitutional right but also the duty of every citizen to learn a vocation, that is, to complete a full vocational training or course of study after finishing school." [12] Though East German women still exceed men in

[6] J. R. Chapin and M. S. Branson, *Women: The Majority-Minority* (Boston: Houghton Mifflin Company, 1973), p. 19.

[7] Great Britain, Government Statistical Service, Central Statistical Office. *Social Trends.* No. 3, 1972 (London: Her Majesty's Stationery Office, 1972), p. 71.

[8] Ibid., p. 89.

[9] German Democratic Republic, State Central Administration for Statistics, *Statistical Pocket Book of the German Democratic Republic, 1972* (Berlin: Staatsverlag der Deutschen Demokratischen Republik, 1972), p. 132.

[10] A. Horneburg, Besucherszentrum, Haus des Lehrers, Alexanderplatz, East Berlin. Interview, December 5, 1972.

[11] H. Klein and E. Behling, *German Democratic Republic, Education* (Dresden: Verlag Zeit Im Bild, 1971), p. 22.

[12] Ibid., p. 18.

the clerical and sales occupations and as cleaners, nurses, and teachers,[13] a considerable number are found to have qualified as master craftsmen, technicians and engineers, and in the other professions.[14] "In the Soviet Union," to cite another example from the Communist world, "women account for 36 per cent of engineers and 45 per cent of scientific workers. . . ."[15] Schoolgirls in Communist countries in Europe are more likely to have mothers in skilled or managerial or professional positions than are their peers in England or the United States.

TEACHERS AND SCHOOL ADMINISTRATORS

Turning to the other model close at hand, that is, to teachers and school administrators, American girls may notice that "nine out of ten elementary school teachers are women, but eight out of ten principals of these schools are men."[16] Only 1.4 per cent of U.S. high schools have women principals.[17] In East Germany, too, more often than not girls will have a male principal at the head of their school. Though 70 per cent of their teachers are female, only 25 per cent of the schools are headed by women.[18] As teenage girls look up the administrative hierarchy of their school in England, the picture characteristically before them is a headmaster (principal) in charge of their school if it is a mixed, or coeducational school. He is assisted by a deputy headmistress (and, of course, a woman secretary). There are only 27 headmistresses of mixed secondary schools in England at present.[19] There are only two female chief education officers and two women deputy chief education officers in all of England.[20] These posts correspond to the American superintendent and associate superintendent of schools, positions rarely filled by women. In West Germany the higher a pupil advances in the school system, the fewer women teachers he will have. Women principals are very rare indeed. Full professors at universities are men 99 per cent of the time. That figure may be matched in America where in 1970 Harvard had ". . . two tenured women professors in its arts and science faculty . . ."[21] and Berkeley had only slightly more women full professors on its entire faculty. For girls the result of their observation of this unequal representation of

[13] Federal Republic of Germany, Bundesminister for Domestic Affairs, *Deutschland, 1971*. Bericht und Materialen zur Lage der Nation (Opladen: Westdeutscher Verlag, 1971), pp. 292–297.

[14] German Democratic Republic, Staatliche Zentralverwaltung für Statistik, Statistisches Jahrbuch 1972 der Deutschen Demokratischen Republik. 17th year (Berlin: Staatsverlag der DDR, 1972), p. 382.

[15] J. Chabaud, *The Education and Advancement of Women* (Paris: UNESCO, 1970), p. 100.

[16] *Time* (August 31, 1970), p. 17.

[17] *Scholastic Teacher* (January, 1974), p. 9.

[18] A. Horneburg, op. cit., December 5, 1972.

[19] M. Sowerby, Headmistress, Cheney School, Oxford. Interview, April 10, 1973.

[20] E. M. Byrne, "Education, Training and Equal Opportunity." Mimeographed (January, 1973), p. 4.

[21] *Time*, op. cit., p. 17.

women in decision-making posts must be a blunting of their potential aspirations for leadership roles in education.

Career aspirations of girls may be further stunted by the dearth of women at the professional level generally and in decision-making roles in particular. In the United States, in England, and in West Germany few women are found in elected offices at the national level. Here no woman has yet been appointed to the United States Supreme Court and for some time no woman has served in the Cabinet. "Women constitute only 9 per cent of all the professions, 7 per cent of the doctors, 3 per cent of the lawyers, 1 per cent of the engineers." [22] In England in 1966 less than one per cent of working women were classified as professional workers as compared with 4.5 per cent of males.[23] In the two Germanies one major difference is the relatively high percentage of female physicians, an occupation far less closed off to women than has been the practice in England and the United States.

SOCIAL FACTORS

Other factors affect the way in which an adolescent girl projects her life into the future. The impact of models as well as sex role identification are modified by locational elements, by school experiences, by the girl's personality, and by lingering traditions. In the United States a woman is legally becoming a free agent in her determination of career plans, but in fact her decisions involve others who may cut sharply into any wild dreams.

LOCATIONAL LIMITS

If a girl grows up in a community with one major industry, she may view her career opportunity strictly in terms of the role differentiation practiced in that industry. If men work on the production line and in higher management and women as office workers and cleaners, the adolescent girl expects to be limited in her career choice to those available to the women around her. She will have to move to another community to obtain other jobs. That alternative may also confront the girl who wishes to enter upon an occupation which is practiced in a restricted number of locations. Examples are acting, television production, publishing, or medical research. Hopes of entering such work will at the least be proportional to the self-confidence of a girl, the encouragement received from home and school, and her initiative.

A girl's vocational aspirations may be suppressed by her perception of the demands that her future role of homemaker may make on her time, energy, and resourcefulness. In West Germany, East Germany, England, and to some extent in the United States, especially in working class families, household chores are allocated to the wife. The husband is free of tending to household

---

[22] Ibid., p. 17.

[23] Labour Party, Opposition Green Paper. *Discrimination Against Women.* Report of a Labour Party Study Group (London: The Labour Party, 1972), p. 13.

chores after his day at work. Only as one moves into the middle class in England do husbands on Sundays mow the lawn and wash the car. The presence particularly of a car attest to the husband's, and therefore his family's, middle class status.

In these cultures there remain, too, accompanying mores that the wife should wait on the husband and make his life easier while he is not at work.

In the United States relatively greater affluence for a family means an easing of household chores for the wife and mother. Large refrigerators and freezers allow for long term shopping and storage of foods. The poor may lack the appliances and the cash to make any long term food purchases. They may also lack the car to drive to the supermarket for one or two weeks' supply of groceries. Cleaning and washing are also made easier and more efficient where modern appliances are available right in the home.

A housewife's duties may also be lightened if she can place her preschool children into a nursery school or day care center for at least part of the day. American institutions of this kind are private ventures with the exceptions of those established with government funds intended to serve working mothers in poor neighborhoods. Charges to parents and the quality of programs vary widely, as does availability. By way of contrast, "nursery places are provided [by the government] for over 50 per cent of three year-olds and over 80 per cent of four year-olds in France; for over 80 per cent of three year-olds and over 90 per cent of four year-olds in Belgium; for over 80 per cent of four year-olds in Holland, and for over 50 per cent of three and four year-olds in Italy.[24] Such facilities enable women seriously to develop or maintain their careers while their children are young.

PERSONALITY IDEALS

Is a career-oriented woman considered over-aggressive by those around her? In a number of cultures a female is supposed to be subservient to the male. She is looked upon as inferior to him in physical strength and in intellect, over-emotional and inefficient. The United States, England and West Germany today still contain these beliefs, and in East Germany, Communist ideology notwithstanding, these mores have not yet died out.

The idea of female inferiority becomes a reality in the matter of educational and vocational goals. If subservience is expected, a girl will seek occupations where she is clearly in an inferior position to the male. As a nurse she will follow the orders of doctors and male hospital administrators, as a secretary she will follow the orders of the male business executive, as a store clerk those of the male manager, and as a teacher those of the male principal. In Western countries the division of labor still largely follows those lines.

In view of the occupational situation ahead for a girl, she is likely to adjust

[24] Great Britain, Department of Education and Science, *Education: A Framework for Expansion* (London: Her Majesty's Stationery Office, 1972), p. 4.

her educational objectives to her opportunities in the labor market. She will seek that level of education which is required for the jobs available to her. If she believes access to decision-making roles to be unlikely, she will refrain from seeking the education and training that would qualify her for such roles. Until recently few American girls have attempted to push their way into the country's law schools, medical schools, or colleges of business administration because not only was admission difficult but subsequent entry into appropriate professional positions was problematical. Those who broke through the barriers ran the risk of being dubbed aggressive.

In their study *Women in Top Jobs*, Michael P. Fogarty and Robert and Rhona Rapoport identified reasons for difficulties in rising to senior posts. Women, they found, may be too quickly typecast into a single field of specialization; they are considered incapable of being successful managers; they are under much closer scrutiny than men; their appearance may be looked upon as disadvantageous; their past experience may be underrated; and an assumption may be made that they are not fully committed to work.[25]

The anticipation of being exposed to a great deal of criticism leads a girl either to guard against any possible attacks by developing excellence in her chosen field or by selecting from the beginning a more subservient kind of occupation. In Western societies the male is supposed to be aggressive to the extent that he seeks to improve himself on the job, that he expresses his point-of-view and does not blindly accept the attitudes of others, that he finds a wife, that he governs the home, and that he utilizes his physical prowess to the utmost to emerge the victor either on the athletic field or on the battlefield. Even when driving a car some males exhibit that aggression. But, women who join the professions or who reach managerial posts in government, business, or industry may be condemned for supposedly showing similar aggressive behavior.

RELUCTANT HUSBAND

The adolescent female's thoughts about a career may be influenced by the fear of male disapproval. A husband may feel threatened by a wife who either becomes his equal or surpasses him on the occupational ladder. He may be unwilling to release her from her responsibilities in the home and to have these taken over by himself or by another individual. In a West German study of working women in the Common Market countries, Helge Pross found that only 2 per cent of West German husbands of such women help with all household chores; 32 per cent assist with simple household duties.[26] In England as yet a large number of men do not undertake any household chores. A husband may also fear that whatever aggressiveness or

---

[25] M. P. Fogarty, Robert and Rhona Rapoport, *Women in Top Jobs, Four Studies of Achievement. Political and Economic Planning* (London: George Allen and Unwin, Ltds, 1971), ch. V, passim.

[26] H. Pross, *Brigitte* (Giessen. Helge Pross, October, 1972), mimeographed, p. 13.

frustration and tension is generated in his wife by her career may spill over into her relationship with him.

EMPLOYERS' PRACTICES

No individual is likely to rise in an organization, be it business or government, without the encouragement of those above him. He relies on their estimate of his competence for his promotions. Their judgment of his potential provides him with opportunities for further training since these are afforded generally to employees with promise. While formalized tests and qualification certificates may exist and may be utilized for job improvement, the employer by his actions substantiates the employee's efforts to move up the occupational ladder.

In the case of women employees, many employers often fail to consider any of them for long term job improvement. They expect a woman to have divided loyalties. A woman, they think, will always place her family first should a conflict between her responsibilities at home and those at work develop. Any young, unmarried woman is viewed as a temporary worker. Marriage and children will likely terminate her employment.

In England many of these considerations lie behind the fact that forty per cent of the boys who leave school enter apprenticeships but only seven per cent of the girls do. Of the women most of the apprenticeships are in hairdressing, hardly a step toward an eventual decision-making role in the world of work.[27]

In East and West Germany access to vocational education is far more open to girls on an equal basis. Such access is secured by law in East Germany,[28] and in West Germany from full time vocational schools to universities girls may enter on the same basis as boys. That measure of equality came with the general quest for democracy and equality instituted during the postwar period of military occupation.

LEGAL BARRIERS

Legal restrictions have also stood in the way of women who have sought professional or managerial positions. In World War II Americans tried to expand the country's manpower by declaring racial discrimination in employment to be illegal. To make equal employment opportunities a reality, the Congress passed the Equal Pay Act of 1963.

[It] . . . prohibits discrimination on the basis of sex in the payment of wages for equal work on jobs that require equal skill, effort, and responsibility, and

[27] C. Avent, Senior Careers Advisor, Inner London Education Authority, Interview. May 11, 1973.
[28] German Democratic Republic, *Vocational Training in the German Democratic Republic* (Dresden: Verlag Zeit Im Bild, 1972), p. 55.

that are performed under similar working conditions. Its provisions apply to "wages" in the sense of remuneration for employment (including overtime) and to employer contributions for most fringe benefits. In a landmark decision, a Federal court held that women performing work which is "substantially" equal to that of men should receive the same pay.[29]

The Civil Rights Act of 1964 also contained provisions which prohibit ". . . discrimination on the basis of sex, as well as race, color, religion, and national origin, by employers of 25 or more employees. . . ."[30] Such discrimination has become illegal when applied by an employer to ". . . hiring or firing; wages; fringe benefits; classifying, referring, assigning, or promoting employees; extending or assigning use of facilities; training, retraining, or apprenticeships; or any other terms, conditions, or privileges of employment."[31] More and more forms or places of employment are being included in these provisions.

Suggestions for the Improvement of Career Mobility

If girls are to be aided in their serious concern for a career and for career mobility, schools and parents might well recognize that social change in contemporary America points toward the wisdom of that step. Women can expect to spend many years in the labor market; they may need to do so and they may want to do so. Economic pressure on individual families appears to demand that participation. Already ". . . half the mothers of school-age children now work,"[32] and ". . . in 1970 half of all women 35 to 64 years of age were in the labor force, as compared with 1 out of 4 in 1940."[33] The need to acquire skills which may form the basis for later careers seems especially vital in the case of minority girls of whom in 1970 one-third of the 16–19 year olds were classified as unemployed.[34] For all girls the fact should be emphasized that traditional barriers to various forms of professional or vocational-technical education have come down and that barriers to many forms of employment have been removed. A girl's choice of future employment may be much more far-ranging than earlier.

To persuade girls to expand their thinking about careers, women need to be permitted to hold decision-making posts and other jobs once largely the domain of males. A recent study by Tidball confirms the value of role models for girls.

[29] S. Feldman, *The Rights of Women* (Rochelle Park, New Jersey: Hayden Book Company, Inc., 1974), p. 50.

[30] Ibid., p. 50.

[31] Ibid., p. 54.

[32] *The Chronicle of Higher Education* (March 12, 1973). Reprinted by Project on the Status and Education of Women, Association of American Colleges, Washington, D. C.

[33] U.S. Department of Labor, Employment Standards Administration. *Women Workers Today* (Washington, D. C.: U.S. Government Printing Office, 1971), p. 4.

[34] Ibid., p. 6.

She found that the number of "career successful women" was directly proportional to the number of women faculty present in the achiever's undergraduate institutions at the time they were students. In fact, the correlation was a practically perfect +0.953. A disproportionately high number of women achievers came from women's colleges. Dr. Tidball explains this in terms of the higher number of women faculty. Clearly, the visibility of women successfully performing highly professional jobs positively influences the career aspirations of female students.[35]

To organize her thinking about her future aspirations in the world of work, a girl may be able to sort out matters more easily if she delineates likely phases in her life. Each phase may highlight a particular role. After high school, she may first concentrate on additional work experience to be followed by a more precise career choice and formal preparation for that. There may follow a phase of marriage and motherhood. That phase will in time overlap with a re-entry into the world of work and re-education. Many Americans today find that if job improvement is to be continuous, they need to extend and revise their education periodically. At this point a woman joins others in the labor force in the various forms of adult education. In that way she, too, may attain career mobility.

[35] Project on the Status and Education of Women, *On Campus With Women* (May, 1973), p. 11.

Schools as Agents of Social Change, Instruction, and Learning

The American high school must simultaneously preserve traditions, serve as a custodian of the community status quo, and function as an agent of social change, instruction, and learning. The major problem facing high schools during the 1970s is that of developing equal instructional programs for all youth. Nearly all adolescents will, at least, enter high school, and America is committed to serving each of them. But even the most comprehensive high schools are challenged by the range of their abilities, interests, and backgrounds. The seven papers in Part 3 illustrate collectively how present-day high schools are functioning as agents of instruction and learning. The papers provide an overview of high-school programs, educators' attitudes toward dissent, teachers' perceptions of students' characteristics, high-school discipline, sex-stereotyping, and characteristics of dropouts.

In the first selection, a practicing high-school principal calls for truly comprehensive high schools to meet "the diverse needs of all the young people in our society." Walen notes that a trend that began at the turn of the century toward increasing the comprehensiveness of high schools has not been fast enough. Programs contingent on academic subject-matter, he says—drawing a position parallel to both Bakan's and Coleman's (Part 1)—must be shared more equitably with alternative learning opportunities. He envisages a setting in which youth are given opportunity to work closely with teachers in "total learning situations." The teacher-sponsor would advise adolescents on academic programs and consult with them regarding independent-study programs in community agencies and local businesses. Providing such options, Walen believes, would move the high school "a very realistic step" toward becoming a transitional structure in the process of socialization.

A discussion of the willingness of educators to include adolescents in the process of changing academic and extracurricular school policies leads in the next paper to consideration of the attitudes of school personnel toward change. Student dissent occurred in nearly 70 per cent of the high schools in the United States in the 1960s, but according to Morgan and Wicas, "comparative tranquility" prevails today. Many educators, they say, view student dissent as bordering on "civil strife and anarchy." Their findings suggest that, although many professional educators believe that one of their major missions is to facilitate change, "there have to be grave doubts whether high school faculties, especially principals, possess the appropriate attitudes to allow meaningful and legitimate change to take place."

McCandless and his colleagues, in the third paper, assess the validity of several widely held assumptions about how students' social-class, sex, and race relate to teacher biases, and in the process, demonstrate the precariousness of many longstanding beliefs. Teachers are generally more comfortable in teaching adolescents who share their attitudes, achievement ethics, and lifestyle. Since the majority of teachers are drawn from the middle-class, the researchers expected that (a) while intelligence measures would predict school achievement scores equally well for boys and girls, correlations would be higher for advantaged youth; (b) teachers' marks relative to achievement test scores would be more accurate for girls and advantaged youth than for boys and disadvantaged youth; and (c), although achievement test scores would be comparable for the two sexes, teachers would assign higher grades to girls than boys. A study of 450 seventh-grade youth's group intelligence scores, school achievement scores, and teachers' marks, however, failed to substantiate these stereotypes. Intelligence and achievement test scores were more highly correlated for the disadvantaged and the Black than for the advantaged and white youth. The prediction regarding teachers' marks also went awry; the expected correlations did not appear. Teachers seem to have marked the advantaged and the white on the basis of socialization and the disadvantaged and Black according to objective performance. The data did reveal that girls are marked higher than boys; contrary to expectation, however, girls also performed better on standardized achievement tests.

Walberg, House, and Steele, in the succeeding paper, focus on youth's perceptions of school classrooms. These researchers asked adolescents in grades six through twelve to rate twenty-three classroom activities in respect to cognitive (e.g. "discover many solutions") and effective (e.g. "great concern for grades") dimensions. Walberg and his colleagues advanced two informal hypotheses: (a) students in the higher grades would place greater emphasis on cognitive skills and independent learning; and (b) alienation toward school would increase as a function of encountering more difficult content in the higher grades. The researchers' data revealed, surprisingly, that youth in the higher grades stressed lower-level cognitive processes, like memorization and knowing-the-best-answer, whereas those in the lower grades emphasized higher-level processes, such as application, comprehension, finding consequences, and discovering solutions. The researchers identify grades nine and ten as particularly significant, because many of the emphases on cognitive and affective processes reach either a trough or peak during these two years. They suggest, too, that the changes may indicate the extent to which many youth have become alienated from school objectives. The researchers conclude that the school's "maladaptation" to students needs and *abilities may grow acute as students become especially concerned about grades, getting into college, or even getting out of high school.*

School discipline usually reaches the top of any list of problems about which prospective secondary-school teachers would like insight. Findley and O'Reilly, in the fifth paper, analyze school discipline in detail. These researchers call for a philosophy of school discipline derived from concepts of self-control and citizenship. They argue that the older, shopworn disciplinary procedures—corporal punishment, detention, fines, suspension and expulsion—should be avoided, and they insist that the best deterrent to student offenses are relevant curricula, excellent teaching, and personal examples of good conduct on the part of administrators and teachers.

The two selections on sex-stereotyping, one by Trecker and the other by Saario, Tittle, and Jacklin, should be read together. Each complements the other in showing the extent to which secondary-school curricula overwhelmingly favor boys over girls. Sex bias appears in textbooks; for example, in history, social studies, mathematics and science. Girls' athletic and physical education programs obtain a pittance of the financial resources when compared to those for boys. In vocational training, girls are tracked in large numbers toward homemaking, health occupations, and business. As Saario, Tittle, and Jacklin note, "the school curriculum has clearly functioned to reinforce rigid, educationally discriminatory, and sexually stereotypic attitudes in both students and school staff."

An adolescent will usually do well in high school if he feels that he can meet the expectations of his teachers, that his studies are relevant to his long-range objectives, and that required skills fit in with his lifestyle. Junior high schools and high schools in the United States, however, have failed to meet such expectations for fourteen per cent of the white, twenty-one per cent of the Black, and thirty-four percent of the Spanish-origin youth (see Young's paper, Part 2). How is it that so many youth are disabled in secondary schools? Fitzsimmons, Cheever, Leonard, and Macunovich, in the final selection of Part 3, trace the academic histories of both high-school dropouts and poorly performing graduates during the elementary through secondary school years. The study reveals that the poorly performing students could have been identified as early as the third grade, that dropouts began failing somewhat later than poorly performing graduates, and that certain early performance patterns are associated with later dropout status. The researchers believe that schools can make a difference in respect to reducing dropout rates, and they call for emphases on coordinated programs of academic assistance, counseling, and home visitations.

Harry L. Walen

America's High School Dilemma

A *principal of a suburban Boston high school suggests in the following paper how a high school can achieve sufficient comprehensiveness to assist all its students in developing academic skills, responsibility, and citizenship. He insists that contemporary high schools should adopt highly flexible classroom schedules and increase the availability of tutorial and independent-study programs. To function effectively as an agent in the process of socialization, a high school must enable its students to integrate academic subject-matter study with work-study, on-the-job programs, or community-service options.*

Instructional Objectives
To stress the need for comprehensive high schools.
To emphasize the importance of flexible classroom scheduling to the integration of academic and vocational subject-matter.
To describe student participation in program development as integral to comprehensiveness.

TODAY's high school attempts to prepare some students for higher education at the same time it prepares others for more immediate entry into work. Therein lies the dilemma. The predicament is not unlike that which faced the television manufacturers when color television became a commercial possibility in an industry committed to a black-and-white system. Phrasing the dilemma another way, the question is how to make the American high school truly comprehensive, offering programs geared to the diverse needs of *all* the young people in our society.

GO BEYOND THE SCHOOL'S WALLS

Whether the teacher, the student, the parent, or the school administrator stresses the need for school activities other than academic, what emerges is a need for schools to go beyond the school walls. Schools need to provide broad experiences for students who will not go to college, as well as for those who will.

FROM *The Bulletin of the National Association of Secondary School Principals,* LVI (1972), pp. 79–85. Abridged. Reprinted by permission of the author and the publisher.

I refer here not just to the art, music, woodworking, or home and family-living experience that can be structured into the school curriculum, but to working with people in the community developing independent study projects in fields of their own inquiries and emerging interests. The school and its curriculum, in other words, has an increasing need to stretch beyond the walls and to offer a different kind of learning experience to supplement the academic curriculum.

MEANING OF COMPREHENSIVE SCHOOLS

The course of the American high school since the turn of the century has been to become increasingly comprehensive, to become less the academic college preparatory school, less the purely vocational school, and more the school that can through size, through facilities, and through the flexibility of its teaching staff meet more and more different needs of young people.

One element that must be sacrificed through this true comprehensiveness is the earlier emphasis upon the status of academic subject matter achievement. School committees and boards of education, administrators, teachers, parents, communities, and colleges must learn to recognize an equal status, importance, and dignity between the designing, building, and flying of a model airplane in order to learn aerodynamics, and an advanced placement course in Latin.

A basic equality exists between the individual's need for a work-study program and a course in calculus. This is not to say that a calculus course has the same goal as the work study, that it requires the same kind of intellectual ability, or that it has as long a history of stability in schools. It is to say, however, that the school has a responsibility to provide for both students what is necessary for each one to prepare himself according to his emerging needs and goals. It is meeting these many needs satisfactorily that entitles a high school to be called truly comprehensive.

WORK-STUDY OPTION IS VIABLE

Many programs exist today in forward-looking high schools. One is the work-study or the vocational-study pattern. The school appoints a supervisor, the student elects his basic academic courses, the school schedules these as early in the day as practicable, and the student (with the help of his faculty advisor) finds a job in which he believes he can learn some skills that he does not already have.

In some schools the vocational study experience must be accepted as additional to the basic academic program in order to protect the student should he change his goals *before* becoming a senior. In such schools, the vocational study is frequently accepted as the final major course in the student's program on the assumption that he may be moving directly into employment upon graduation. This means that the student is basically on a very flexible kind of schedule, able to leave the school when his academic courses are over to continue his on-the-job program. This provides an intermediate step for the student emerging from school into society. It also gives an added relationship between school and community and relates school more directly to real life situations. This is an important step toward making the school more completely comprehensive and related to the needs of all students.

TUTORIAL OR INDEPENDENT STUDY

Another option is tutorial or independent study. In this program the student writes a prospectus for a special interest project he would like to complete with the help of a teacher or some authority in the community. He might, for instance, wish to do a special project on the Civil War with a history teacher; or he might wish to do a special project with a horticulturist in the community to learn how to graft one type of fruit tree to another. The project, complete with a description, a bibliography, and stipulation of a written or oral report and/or a finished product, would be evaluated by a sponsoring teacher and a director of a department. A program of this type provides a linkage between the school, the independent interest of the student, and the resources of the community.

Still another option in the truly comprehensive school is making experiences available in the skills or professions that a student would like over and above the straight employment possibilities in business. An example of this might be a teacher cadet program. Under the sponsorship of a faculty member, a student would apply to be either a part- or a full-time cadet working with a teacher in a junior high school or an elementary school not only to assist the teacher, but also to learn something about teaching.

The student again would write up his proposal as to what he hoped to learn through his teacher cadet experience, would be interviewed by his sponsor-teacher in the high school and by the principal of the school in which he would be a cadet, and finally meet the teacher with whom he would work. His schedule could be so arranged that he would be in the school at certain times during the day in preparation of materials for succeeding classes. The student in this kind of program is able to expand his horizons of activity as well as his horizons of learning.

EXPANSION INTO OTHER FIELDS POSSIBLE

This approach can be expanded into many different fields. One example is the field of either nursing in a hospital or practical nursing in a nursing home. Another might be as a police or as a fire cadet. There is also the possibility of community service developed through the student's participation in the various phases of community endeavor. The active mind will see many possible extensions of this principle.

A logical development of these projects would be an umbrella program to coordinate different extra-school experiences in a varied pattern for each student. The vocational study, the independent study, the cadet programs can be melded into one program which in effect combines the school building and its program with the potentials in the community. One can see here the development of a situation in which the student may take the utmost advantage of many different options in his local high school. The student moves naturally into a situation where he is personally responsible for meeting his commitments and his personal time schedule. In this way a solution emerges to the dilemma schools face today.

FOLLOWING THE CONCEPT TO ITS ULTIMATE EXTENSION

An ultimate extension of this concept is what could be called an alternate option in the high school, enabling a student to operate in a small academic community with individual attention from the faculty. For the student who needs the sense of intimate community and independence in determining his own progress on a day-to-day basis, such an option is important, yet nonexistent in most high schools today.

Some experiments, such as the Parkway Project in Philadelphia, the Murray Road Plan in Newton, Mass., and the School Within a School in Brookline, Mass., have appeared in many parts of the country. Some have been interpreted as a "letting go" on the part of the school; and, by nature of being experiments, may sometimes have emerged as too permissive. But the major thrust is that students have the option of working closely with teachers in total learning situations, with the sense of belongingness and identification in a small academic community, and with a continuing involvement in the determination of what and how to study in terms of growing understandings and definitions of goals.

In one such alternate option, students and teachers have rooms available for use as an intellectual community center. They meet regularly each week as a total community to discuss where they are going as a group. They also meet weekly in smaller groups to discuss their individual projects and concerns.

With the advice of their sponsoring teachers, students may elect regular courses in the school, they may occupy available seats in classrooms in a number of nearby colleges, they may develop and follow small group courses in various areas with their sponsor-teachers, or they may develop and write independent study projects with community volunteers or businesses and follow these through under the general supervision of the teacher-sponsors.

The teacher-sponsors regularly evaluate progress and submit statements of achievement as part of the school record. The school has a transcript which takes into account the level of achievement and the degree of accomplishment in the total program. This might be called an ultimate option in the comprehensiveness of the high school, and a very realistic step toward making the American high school a transitional structure into total adult citizenship.

ESPECIALLY GOOD FOR ALIENATED STUDENT

A special concern is the alienated student. Within the high school setting, it is possible to plan for so-called "rap sessions" in which teachers who have a particular empathy for young people may discuss with students matters that seem of particular interest. This experience enables the teacher to gain a deeper perception of the frustrations of young people and their true concerns, while giving the young person an opportunity to feel that he not only is heard but is heard in the context of his peers. Such sessions may not necessarily be activist, in that they are more sharings of feeling than plannings for solutions to problems.

A stage beyond this is to have a separate building, as in Bennington, Vt., in which a small group of understanding teachers can set up their own "school" in terms of students who have become so alienated that they cause disruption or are completely apathetic. This arrangement segregates students from the school building. Its purpose is to provide understanding and a program, frequently deeply work-centered, which probably would lead into continued employment after securing a high school diploma. A positive self-identification can be built to the point where a student might want to return for a final year in the regular high school, or where a student might feel qualified to go to some school of higher education.

CONCLUSION

All of these options need to be thought of seriously in terms of meeting all the needs of young people. Flexibility in school options and the placing of responsibility on the shoulders of the student by no means mean that therefore all control goes. The opposite is true. In a democratic society it is essential that each individual assume as much responsibility for himself as he practically can. It is of vital importance that he should have built-in values and built-in controls which enable him to be a free citizen in a free state. He must learn in a school setting to be responsible for his own use and assignment of time, for meeting his appointments, for being in condition to do his work, for accomplishing his goals and his agreed-upon contracts with other students, with teachers, and with employers, and for being responsible for his own appearance and conduct wherever he is. The inculcation of respect for the accepted rules of the society or group and the fulfillment of agreements one makes with others result in a self-discipline.

In the more flexible or open school, the student is held completely accountable for meeting his appointments and completing his obligations and agreements. He should know the penalties for not living up to them, and these penalties should be evenly and fairly administered. All of his teachers must hold the individual student responsible for reasonable rules of conduct, attendance, and achievement which are stipulated and agreed upon. The flexibility now required of the American high school requires accountability on the part of the individual student.

Lewis B. Morgan

Edward A. Wicas

The Short, Unhappy Life of Student Dissent

Student dissent emerged in the late 1960s in unprecedented fury and has dwindled today to become nearly unnoticeable. As Morgan and Wicas point out, the idea of dissent resembles in the minds of many educators "upheaval bordering on civil strife and anarchy." But high-school student dissent has centered largely on legitimate issues—students' rights, curricula irrelevance, civil rights, the war in Vietnam, and ecological concerns. The specific issues are underpinned by a gnawing demand: students want to be involved in "shaping their own education and future." Morgan and Wicas wondered how receptive school personnel actually are to students' concerns and administered a questionnaire to over 1,200 administrators, counselors, and teachers. Their data suggest that prospects for change are dim; educators in high schools most sympathetic to students, it appears, are those having the least power to effect change.

Instructional Objectives
To review issues associated with high-school dissent.
To compare attitudes of principals, counselors, and teachers toward students' demands for change.
To discuss responsiveness of school personnel to students' concerns.

THE very words *change* and *dissent* serve to conjure up in professional educators an awesome image of institutional upheaval bordering on civil strife and anarchy. Although 1971–72 saw a general tapering off of student activism and dissident behavior, educators remember well the storms and stresses that many of the nation's colleges and high schools underwent during

FROM *Personnel and Guidance Journal*, LI (1972), pp. 33–38, abridged. Copyright 1972 American Personnel and Guidance Association. Reprinted by permission of the authors and the publisher.

the late 1960s and early 1970s. Perhaps educators fear that this year is the lull before the next, more fatal, storm. In any event, in listening to and reading what educational administrators are currently saying, one gets the distinct impression that they are crossing all their fingers while rubbing a rabbit's foot with their palms in the hope that the students in their charge will stay cool, or calm, or apathetic, or whatever—as long as they don't start rocking the educational boat again.

The issues that stood at the core of the student rebellion of the past few years—the irrelevance of contemporary education, the institutions' unwillingness to allow students to be involved in shaping their own education and future, the rock-ribbed hypocrisy of elders in dealing with youth and social concerns—are, to a large extent, still issues. But perhaps now, because students feel even more helpless to effect any real, permanent, meaningful change, the issues have been forgotten or suppressed by all but the most radical members of the student population, with the result that most college campuses and high schools have returned to a period of comparative tranquility, and business and education go on as usual.

THE "STUDENT MOVEMENT"

Let us review briefly the recent past to study the evolution and dissolution of the so-called student movement, especially as it pertained to the nation's secondary schools. The Berkeley uprising, the commitment of many students to the civil rights cause, and the burgeoning anti-Vietnam war feeling of the mid-1960s all played a major part in triggering dissent and disorder on many of the college campuses in this country. And at first it was strictly that —a college-based phenomenon. Before too long, however, increasing evidence cropped up that these disturbances had filtered down into the high schools, especially in urban areas. Westin [1] reported that in the four-month period from November 1968 to February 1969, 348 *serious* disruptions took place in high schools in 38 states and the District of Columbia. Trump and Hunt [2] found that 67 per cent of urban and suburban high schools and 53 per cent of rural high schools surveyed were experiencing student protests of one kind or another.

To any but the most Pollyannish observer there seemed little doubt that high schools were destined to be, as one student put it, the "next battleground." [3] And many authorities feared that these would turn out to be even bloodier battlegrounds than the colleges and universities had been, simply because high school dissidents tended to behave more impulsively, less predictably, and more violently than their college-age counterparts.

[1] A. F. Westin, "Civic Education in a Crisis Age," *Proceedings of the Conference on the School and Democratic Environment* (New York: Columbia University Press, 1969).

[2] J. L. Trump and J. Hunt, "The Nature and Extent of Student Activism," *Bulletin of the National Association of Secondary School Principals,* LIII (1969), 151–154.

[3] C. Karpel, "High Schools: The Next Battleground?" *This Week,* (August 17, 1969), pp. 12–13.

The issues? They were in abundance, especially at the local level. Students were distressed over school dress codes, including such restrictions as limits on hair and skirt lengths. Blacks became militant about issues such as the lack of black culture courses, the institution of holidays for black nationalist events, and discriminatory practices of long standing. Students complained about an irrelevant curriculum, an unfair grading system, and insensitive teachers, counselors, and administrators. The school's code of discipline was attacked with vehemence, not only by many students and some of their parents, but by ACLU lawyers as well. Students asked for draft counselors, ombudsmen, representation on the board of education, an "open campus" system, and they began to form SDS chapters and publish underground newspapers. For a while, it seemed as though they wished to change almost every aspect of the school's structure.

In the year or two that has transpired since high schools have become the central "battleground," many educators have been forced to look carefully at some of the traditions, regulations, and procedures that had contributed to making so many of their schools so sadly outdated. Some things changed. Male students' hair was allowed to grow longer (as long as it was "clean"); illegal locker searches ceased; some disciplinary codes became more lenient and more reasonable; some black students' voices began to be heard. But in many locales the change was short-lived and even illusory. A case in point: Mark Shedd, the former superintendent of schools in Philadelphia, lost his job largely because of his liberal stance in promulgating a "Students' Bill of Rights," which later became the focal point in his critics' attack upon him and his policies. And so it begins to appear that the pendulum is now poised at a position where it can swing either forward or backward, depending in large part on what people—laymen, educators, and students—want their schools, and education, to be and become.

What precisely do these constituent groups want their schools to become? In an effort to determine what climate existed among the professional staff of the high schools, we decided to survey a number of educators—teachers, counselors, and principals—on their attitudes toward change and dissent as it applied on the local level. Obviously, the attitudes these educators had were bound to be crucial factors in either the facilitation or the deterrence of high school students' attempts at effecting some sort of change within their schools. That is to say, if enough educators were receptive to meaningful change, students would have a powerful ally in their efforts to make their schools relevant institutions for the 1970s. On the other hand, if a school's faculty was resistant to change, students would have a tough row to hoe, since they would be bucking the school's establishment.

THE STUDY

Inasmuch as there were no standardized measuring instruments available for this type of research, a 40-item questionnaire was developed through a series of pilot studies. The questionnaire sought to ascertain those areas of most immediate concern to high school students and faculties. The questionnaire was comprised of those items judged to be "most liberal, most innovative, most radical" by a panel of social psychologists. Four broad areas of change and dissent were readily identified: (a) changes in school policy, (b) changes in curriculum, (c) changes in disciplinary procedures, and (d) forms of student dissent.

The study sample consisted of 1,220 randomly selected educators from 97 public high schools in the states of Massachusetts, Connecticut, and Rhode Island. Three mailings of the questionnaire resulted in a return of 939 responses (693 teachers, 145 counselors, and 101 principals), an overall return of 77 per cent. There is some reason to believe that the attitudes of the nonrespondents were somewhat more traditional and less accepting than the attitudes of those who did respond, if we can generalize from the rather hostile, negative comments jotted by nonrespondents on returned but uncompleted questionnaires.

The educators in the study were asked to indicate, along a 5-point Likert-type rating scale, how desirable or undesirable each item was. The results are summarized in Table 1 which presents the desirability-undesirability of selected items in descending rank order, according to the item's average rating.

A majority (51 per cent or more) of teachers accepted 17 of the 40 questionnaire items; a majority of counselors accepted 14 of the 40 items; and a majority of principals accepted 12 of the 40 items. However, on only 9 items (those ranked 1, 2, 3, 4, 5, 6, 8, 13, and 18) did a majority of all three responding groups agree that a change would be highly or moderately desirable. Three of these items dealt with "due process of law" as it applies to the secondary school (a "convicted" student's right to a hearing, right to counsel, and right to an appeal). Two of these items dealt with increased student involvement in the governance of the school (establishing a student-faculty discipline committee and granting the student council shared power with the faculty-administrative council). The other four of these majority-accepted items (freedom to express personal views in class, the institution of mental hygiene courses, the institution of black culture courses, and political activism by students) are all rather innocuous in the context of the present study; in short, they represent areas that should have been accepted by the schools all along rather than becoming focal issues in 1970.

It appears that, of the 40 questionnaire items, the 9 mentioned above stand the best chance of being accepted now or sometime in the near future by educators participating in the study. The remainder of the items appear to have much less of a chance, or no chance at all, of being accepted now or in the foreseeable future.

Since in most schools the principal holds the real power, it is interesting to see on what items principals disagree significantly with counselors and/or teachers. (Significant disagreement is defined in this case as a difference of

Table 1   Educators' Preferences Toward Change and Dissent: Selected Items

			Per cent		
Rank Order	Item	Group	HIGHLY OR MODER- ATELY DESIR- ABLE	NEUTRAL OR UN- DECIDED	HIGHLY OR MODER- ATELY UNDESIR- ABLE
3	Establishment of student-faculty discipline committee	Counselors Teachers * Principals	83 84 65	8 7 13	9 9 22
4	Granting student accused of a serious rule infraction the right to a hearing	Counselors Teachers * Principals	81 78 71	10 8 7	9 14 22
7	Peaceful demonstrations, protests	Counselors Teachers * Principals	69 64 43	12 12 14	19 24 43
9	Draft counseling by guidance counselors	Counselors Teachers * Principals	48 59 46	20 18 16	32 23 38
12	Free or open dress code	Counselors Teachers * Principals	62 58 49	10 9 13	28 33 38
16	Institution of "pass-fail" grading system	Counselors Teachers Principals	48 54 54	20 14 12	32 32 34
17	Appointing ombudsman to handle student grievances	Counselors Teachers * Principals	46 48 40	26 27 20	28 25 40
20	Banning police interrogations of students within the school	Counselors * Teachers * Principals	48 39 41	25 24 16	27 37 43
23	Abolishing after-school detention hall system	Counselors Teachers Principals	37 38 40	21 12 12	42 50 48
27	Allowing students to choose their own teachers	Counselors Teachers * Principals	27 29 19	14 17 6	59 54 75
29	Abolishing compulsory class attendance	Counselors Teachers * Principals	25 26 12	10 9 7	65 65 81
32	Discontinuing school suspensions for students	Counselors * Teachers * Principals	22 13 7	12 9 11	66 78 82
34	Establishment of SDS chapter	Counselors Teachers * Principals	4 6 1	10 11 2	86 83 97

Note.—The complete table of 40 items is available from the senior author on request.
* Indicates a difference of 10 points or more in the Highly or Moderately Undesirable column.

139

10 or more percentage points under the column headed "Highly or moderately *un*desirable.") Sixteen items were found to be areas of potential disagreement among the principals and the counselors and/or teachers, with 13 of the 16 items falling under the broad areas of school policy and disciplinary procedures, areas over which the principals held most immediate jurisdiction. It appears from the figures that the principal is less accepting of change in the school structure than are counselors and teachers; and since he holds the trump cards, it will be exceedingly difficult for those who desire to institute and implement change to do so in areas where the principal does not deem it desirable.

It was also found that the educators' age and sex had a slight bearing on their attitudes toward change and dissent. Females and younger educators (those from 20 to 29) were generally more accepting in their attitudes than were males and middle- and older-aged educators. Ironically, neither of these two more accepting groups hold very much power in the current high school structure (women's liberation notwithstanding), thus again pointing to the unalterable fact that change in the high schools will probably be a very slow, painstaking process.

DISCUSSION

If, as so many professional educators state, one of the most important missions of the school is to facilitate change, then—at least on the basis of this study's findings—there have to be grave doubts whether high school faculties, especially principals, possess the appropriate attitudes to allow meaningful and legitimate change to take place.

During the past decade change has become almost the rule rather than the exception; yet most educational institutions have proven to be agonizingly slow in keeping up with the times, let alone forging ahead of them. High school educators could well afford listening to and seriously considering some of the requests of the students in their charge and, in so doing, allow those professionals among their ranks—especially those who seem to be most attuned to students and their very real concerns—to assist young people in seeking and implementing change that is reasonable and within limits. At the present time this does not appear to be happening in very many high schools, with the result that many students, over-anxious for change and frustrated by the lack of it, take matters into their own hands and bring about the revolution and dissent that have rent so many of our educational institutions these past few years.

All in all, it is not a very optimistic scene. Students are crying for meaningful change in the school, the institution that most directly affects their adolescent lives. But the majority of the professional faculty that staff that institution, at least in this study's sample, are resistant to change and almost totally intolerant of dissent. Those few staff members who are sympathetic to the students and their concerns happen to be those who do not possess any real power to effect change. And so, unfortunately, the prospects for change remain dim.

Boyd R. McCandless
Albert Roberts
Thomas Starnes

Teachers' Marks, Achievement Test Scores, and Aptitude Relations with Respect to Social Class, Race, and Sex

McCandless, Roberts, and Starnes, in this selection, reveal that conventional assumptions about relationships among teachers' attitudes and youth's achievement on aptitude and intelligence tests may be misleading. The researchers compared boys and girls, classified by both social class and race, in terms of correlations among measures of intelligence, school achievement, and teachers' marks. Teachers' accuracy in marking youth and teachers' partiality in assessing grades were also evaluated. The researchers presumed that teachers would favor girls and the advantaged in their marking. None of the stereotypes, however, was clearly supported by their findings.

Instructional Objectives

To study relationships among three school-related variables—intelligence, achievement, and teachers' marks—in a study of youth classified by social class, sex, and race.

To discuss differences among the youth classified by social class, sex, and race relative to the three school-related variables.

To consider implications of the findings for assumptions about teachers' biases.

FROM *Journal of Educational Psychology*, LXIII (1972), pp. 153–159. Copyright 1972 by the American Psychological Association. Reprinted by permission of the authors and the publisher.

W HEN the first author was writing *Adolescents: Behavior and Development*,[1] he looked in vain for coherent, comparable-sample applied research that dealt with all the following norms and relations in such a manner as to be useful to the many who need such information: (*a*) school aptitude (intelligence) and standardized achievement test results; (*b*) aptitude scores and teachers' grades; (*c*) teachers' grades and standardized achievement test results.

Useful information can be provided when all three variables are studied as they vary with respect to sex, social class, and ethnicity.

Logical predictions about results from such comparisons can be made from the literature (see McCandless[2] for a representative review). These predictions are: (*a*) Conventional school aptitude (intelligence) measures predict standardized achievement test scores equally well for boys and girls, but better for advantaged than disadvantaged children. (*b*) Teachers' marks are more accurate for girls than boys, when judged against the sexes' standardized achievement test scores; for middle-class than for disadvantaged children; and are (perhaps) least accurate for disadvantaged black males. (*c*) Teachers consistently give girls higher grades than boys, but there are no important differences between boys' and girls' achievement when measured by standard achievement tests. More tentatively, it can be predicted that disadvantaged black males receive the lowest teachers' marks of eight frequent major groupings of two social classes by two sexes by two races.

If these logical predictions are correct, their educational and social implications are clear: Teachers' practices differentially discourage lower social-class children, and particularly lower social-class males. These practices may exacerbate the frustrations that disadvantaged children experience in school and, among other things, may increase the rate of school dropout among the very group that most urgently needs to stay in school or, alternatively, may frustrate lower-class boys and girls in ways that result in scholastic inefficiency when they *do* persist in school.

METHOD

Subjects

Subjects were 443 Atlanta, Georgia, public school children for whom teachers' marks were available for the first two trimesters of their seventh-grade year. All subjects had taken the California Test of Mental Maturity in the spring of their seventh-grade year, and all had taken the Metropolitan Achievement Test in the fall of their seventh-grade year. Eight cells were filled by approximately 50 children each: advantaged black boys, white boys, black girls, and white girls; and disadvantaged black boys, white boys, black girls, and white girls.

[1] B. R. McCandless, *Adolescents: Behavior and Development* (Hinsdale, Ill.: Dryden Press, 1970).
[2] Ibid.

The advantaged or middle-class subjects attended five schools where fewer than 18% of the parent clientele had incomes below $3,000. Disadvantaged or lower social-class subjects attended five different schools. For each school, more than 47% of the parent clientele had incomes lower than $3,000. The five disadvantaged schools served poverty neighborhoods (Office of Economic Opportunity criteria), and three were included in the Atlanta Model Cities Project.

The final match from among the available schools was made by consulting two veteran Atlanta Public School officials who knew the city's communities from long, close personal experience.[3] They guided the authors in making the closest possible match within the formal statistical criteria, using such criteria as incidence of fatherless households, working mothers, and fathers and mothers holding two jobs.

Overall, the advantaged black and white schools are closely matched by objective and subjective criteria of "advantagement," but the disadvantaged schools may be slanted a bit to the effect that, as a group, the white pupils are more disadvantaged than the black pupils. With a very few chance (and unknown) exceptions, all children were taught by teachers from both races. Almost all teachers were female.

Procedure

All data were taken from pupils' records on file at the 10 different schools. The authors moved from school to school until the eight cells listed above were filled. The data consisted of the following: (*a*) The total score for each subject from the California Test of Mental Maturity from the spring of the seventh-grade school year was the aptitude (intelligence) datum. (*b*) Using 4.0 as an A, average teacher grades for the fall and winter trimesters of the seventh-grade year were averaged for reading, language, arithmetic, social studies, and science. (*c*) Metropolitan Achievement Test scores, converted to grade equivalents, comprise the achievement test data.

Following collection of data, relevant correlations and measures of central tendency were computed, and tests of homogeneity of correlation and means were performed.

RESULTS

The most interesting facts in Table 1 are: First, while school aptitude (intelligence) scores predict both standing for standardized achievement tests and teachers' marks fairly well (*r* for the total group of 443 subjects is equal to .45 and .56, respectively), standardized achievement test results account for

[3] The authors appreciate the help of John Blackshear and Otis White from the administrative staff of the Atlanta Public Schools for their help with this matching, as well as the cooperation of Jarvis Barnes, Superintendent for Research and Development, Atlanta Public Schools, and the principals and secretaries of the schools in which data were gathered.

less than 10% of the variance of teachers' marks (r for the total group is only .31).

Table 1   Correlation Coefficients for Intelligence, Standardized Achievement, and Teachers' Marks for the Total Group, and by Advantagement, Sex, and Race

Group	n	INTELLIGENCE VERSUS STANDARDIZED ACHIEVEMENT	INTELLIGENCE VERSUS AVERAGE TEACHERS' MARKS	STANDARDIZED ACHIEVEMENT VERSUS AVERAGE TEACHERS' MARKS
			r	
Total	443	.45	.56	.31
Advantaged	230	.20	.56	.11[b]
Disadvantaged	213	.74[a]	.60	.58
Boys	221	.36	.50	.20
Girls	222	.53	.66	.39
Blacks	225	.55	.64	.48
Whites	218	.19	.50	.13[b]

[a] All paired correlations (e.g., .20 and .74 for intelligence versus standardized achievement for advantaged compared with disadvantaged) differ significantly from each other at the .01 level or less (Snedecor [4] chi-square test for homogeneity of correlation).

[b] This correlation does not reach significance at the .05 level. All other correlations are significant at .05 or less.

Second, when the three major divisions of the sample are considered (advantaged versus disadvantaged, boys versus girls, and blacks versus whites), teachers with some consistency assign their grades according to intelligence test standing (Table 1, column 3). Each member of the pairs of correlations in column 3, rows 4, 5 and 6, 7 differs significantly from the other,[5] but the range of differences is only from .16 for boys and girls to the nonsignificant .04 for advantaged and disadvantaged. Maximum variance of teachers' marks accounted for by intelligence is about 45% (all girls), minimum is about 25% (all boys, all whites).

Third, correlations between intelligence and standardized achievement test results, and standardized achievement test standings and average teachers' marks (Table 1, columns 2 and 4) are remarkably low for the advantaged, for boys, and for whites (range in columns 2 and 4 is from .11 to .36, or from only about 1% to about 13% of the variance of one variable accounted for by the other).

[4] G. W. Snedecor, *Statistical Methods* (5th ed., Ames: Iowa State College Press, 1956).
[5] Ibid.

Correlations among the three school-related variables are shown in Table 2 for the Advantagement $\times$ Sex, Race $\times$ Sex, and Advantagement $\times$ Race subgroups.

Although the two sets of four Advantagement $\times$ Sex, and Race $\times$ Sex correlations in column 3, rows 1, 2, 3, 4 and 5, 6, 7, 8 are heterogeneous,[6] absolute differences are not great and thus the practical significance of the differences is slight. The range of variance predicted for teachers' marks by intelligence for all the correlations (Table 2, column 3) is from about 52% (for disadvantaged girls) to about 16% (for white boys).

Table 2 *Correlation Coefficients for Intelligence, Standardized Achievement, and Teachers' Marks for Sex by Advantagement and Race, and Advantagement by Race Subgroups*

| | | r | | |
Group	n	INTELLIGENCE VERSUS STANDARDIZED ACHIEVEMENT TESTS	INTELLIGENCE VERSUS AVERAGE TEACHERS' MARKS	STANDARDIZED ACHIEVEMENT TESTS VERSUS AVERAGE TEACHERS' MARKS
Advantaged boys	116	.17 [a, b, d]	.57 [c]	.03 [a, b]
Advantaged girls	114	.27	.61	.15 [a]
Disadvantaged boys	105	.56	.45	.46
Disadvantaged girls	108	.84	.72	.64
Black boys	115	.49 [b]	.64 [c]	.45 [b]
White boys	106	.08 [a]	.40	−.01 [a]
Black girls	110	.65	.67	.49
White girls	112	.30	.62	.21
Advantaged blacks	116	.45 [b]	.65	.37 [b]
Advantaged whites	114	−.25	.56	−.11 [a]
Disadvantaged blacks	109	.62	.60	.62
Disadvantaged whites	104	.71	.55	.50

[a] Does not reach significance at the .05 level. All other correlations are significant at .05 or less.

[b] This set of four correlations is not homogeneous, $p \leqq .01$.[7]

[c] This set of four correlations is not homogeneous, $p < .05$.[8]

[d] In sets of four correlations (e.g., column 2, rows 1, 2, 3, and 4), pairs of correlations differing from each other by .22 or less are from a homogeneous population; those differing by .25 or more come from heterogeneous populations at the .01 level or less; all others depart from homogeneity at less than .05.[9]

[6] Ibid.
[7] Ibid.
[8] Ibid.
[9] Ibid.

The correlations between intelligence and standardized achievement test standings are strikingly low for both advantaged boys and girls (column 2, rows 1 and 2) and for advantaged whites of both sexes (in column 2, row 10, the correlation between intelligence and standardized achievement is —.25!).

Teachers' marks bear little relation to standardized test performance for either advantaged boys or girls (Table 2, column 4, rows 1 and 2), for white boys or girls (rows 6 and 8), or for advantaged whites (Table 2, column 4, row 10).

Table 3   Correlation Coefficients for Intelligence, Standardized Achievement, and Teachers' Marks by Advantagement and Race and Sex Subgroups

		r		
Group	*n*	INTELLI-GENCE VERSUS STANDARDIZED ACHIEVEMENT TESTS	INTELLI-GENCE VERSUS AVERAGE TEACHERS' MARKS	STANDARDIZED ACHIEVEMENT TESTS VERSUS AVERAGE TEACHERS' MARKS
Advantaged black boys	59	.43[b, c]	.78[b]	.38[b]
Advantaged white boys	57	—.35	.56	—.17[a]
Advantaged black girls	57	.50	.55	.32
Advantaged white girls	57	—.14[a]	.67	—.07[a]
Disadvantaged black boys	56	.55	.47	.53
Disadvantaged white boys	49	.47	.40	.35
Disadvantaged black girls	53	.78	.83	.73
Disadvantaged white girls	55	.80	.60	.52

[a] Does not reach significance at the .05 level. All other correlations are significant at .05 or less.

[b] This set of eight correlations is not homogeneous, $p \leqq .01$.[10]

[c] In sets of eight correlations (e.g., column 2, rows 1 through 8), pairs of correlations that differ from each other .21 or less come from homogeneous populations; those that differ .28 or more check out as heterogeneous at the .01 level or less; all other pairs are heterogeneous at less than .05.[11]

A continuation of the picture drawn above can be seen in Table 3. The lowest correlation in Table 3, column 3, is between intelligence and teachers' marks for disadvantaged white boys ($r = .40$).The figure for disadvantaged black boys is only slightly higher ($r = .47$). Nor for either racial group of disadvantaged boys is actual achievement as judged from standard tests strongly reflected in teachers' marks ($r = .53$ for black boys, .35 for white

[10] Ibid.
[11] Ibid.

boys). However, the intelligence versus teachers' marks for disadvantaged black girls is a striking .83 (about 70% of the variance of one variable is accounted for by the other).

From Table 3, column 2, it can also be seen that intelligence and achievement test results are *negatively* correlated for both advantaged white boys and girls (significantly so for the former), but reach a high level in the expected direction for disadvantaged black and white girls of .78 and .80, respectively.

On the whole (Table 3, column 4), as has been noted earlier, teachers' marks bear little relation to children's standings on standardized achievement tests, although the correlations between the two run as high as .73 for disadvantaged black girls. However, the correlations are actually negative in direction but nonsignificant for advantaged white boys and girls ($rs = -.17$ and $-.07$, respectively).

Finally, for only one subgroup, disadvantaged black girls (row 7), are the three correlations among the school-related variables consistent and high in all three columns of correlations. Efficiency of prediction among the variables is next best for disadvantaged white girls (Table 3, row 8).

Central tendency data for the three school-related variables are included in Table 4 for the total group and for the advantagement, sex, and race groups. As was expected, the disadvantaged are lower than the advantaged for all three variables (although the disadvantaged perform closer to expectancy in standardized test achievement grade level, as established by intelligence, than do the advantaged).

Table 4 Means and Standard Deviations for School Aptitude (Intelligence), Standardized Achievement Test Results, and Average Teacher Marks in Academic Subjects for Total Groups, and by Advantagement, Sex, and Race

Group	n	Intelligence		Achievement Test Grade Level		Average Teachers' Marks (4.0 = A)	
		M	SD	M	SD	M	SD
Total	443	90.9	20.1	5.43	1.10	2.4	.87
Advantaged	230	99.1 *	18.5	5.54 *	1.19	2.5 **	.80
Disadvantaged	213	81.9	17.8	5.12	.95	2.3	.80
Boys	221	89.4	21.7	5.19 *	1.07	2.2	.80
Girls	222	92.3	18.3	5.48	1.11	2.6	.80
Blacks	225	84.3 *	19.8	5.00 *	1.05	2.3	.70
Whites	218	97.6	18.0	5.68	1.05	2.5	.90

* *t* is significant at .01 or less.
** *t* is significant at less than .05 but greater than .01.

There is no intelligence difference between boys and girls, but the latter are significantly higher than the former in both standard achievement test standing and teachers' marks (rows 4, 5).

Black children fall below white children in standing for all three variables but, compared to whites, achieve equally close to expectancy in standardized achievement test results (expectancy based on intelligence test scores).

From Table 5, it can be seen that disadvantaged boys, black boys, and disadvantaged blacks fare markedly less well than any of the other groups for all three school-related variables, and that (although not so strikingly in all instances) advantaged girls, white girls, and advantaged whites head the list in their standings on the three school-related indexes.

Table 5   Means and Standard Deviations for School Aptitude (Intelligence), Standardized Achievement Test Results, and Average Teacher Marks for Sex by Advantagement and Race, and Advantagement by Race Subgroups

Group	n	Intelligence		Achievement Test Grade Level		Average Teachers' Marks (4.0=A)	
		M	SD	M	SD	M	SD
Advantaged boys	116	99.4[a]	19.4	5.41[b]	1.23	2.2[c]	.80
Advantaged girls	114	98.7	17.6	5.67	1.14	2.7	.80
Disadvantaged boys	105	78.2	18.4	4.95	.81	2.1	.80
Disadvantaged girls	108	85.5	16.5	5.29	1.05	2.5	.80
Black boys	115	83.0[d]	22.4	4.88[e]	.99	2.1[c]	.70
White boys	106	96.2	18.6	5.53	1.07	2.2	.90
Black girls	110	85.6	16.7	5.12	1.10	2.4	.80
White girls	112	98.8	17.5	5.83	1.01	2.8	.80
Advantaged blacks	116	92.7[f]	18.2	5.26[b]	1.20	2.4[g]	.70
Advantaged whites	114	105.5	16.5	5.81	1.12	2.5	.90
Disadvantaged blacks	109	75.4	17.5	4.73	.77	2.1	.70
Disadvantaged whites	104	88.8	15.5	5.54	.95	2.5	.80

[a] For the set of four means in this column, employing the Scheffé test, means that differ by 12.1 or more are significantly different at the .01 level or less. Overall F significant at less than .01.

[b] For this cell, by Scheffé test, means differing by .72 or more differ significantly at the .01 level or less. Overall F significant at less than .01.

[c] For this cell, by Scheffé test, means differing by .5 or more differ significantly at the .01 level or less. Overall F significant at less than .01.

[d] For the set of four means in this column, employing the Scheffé test, means that differ by 12.7 or more are significantly different at the .1 level or less. Overall F significant at less than .01.

[e] For this cell, by Scheffé test, means differing by .67 or more differ significantly at the .01 level or less. Overall F significant at less than .01.

[f] For the set of four means in this column, employing the Scheffé test, means that differ by 11.4 or more are significantly different at the .01 level or less. Overall F significant at less than .01.

[g] For this cell, by Scheffé test, means differing by .4 differ significantly from each other at the .05 level.

In Table 6 are given the central tendency data for intelligence, standardized achievement, and average teachers' marks for the eight Advantagement × Race × Sex subgroups of the sample. While *F* for each of the three columns of means is significant at less than the .01 level, no difference between any pair of means in columns 4 and 6 is significant.[12] However, inspection of the rows and columns in Table 6 adds information to that obtainable from the grosser groupings of subjects, as reported in Tables 4 and 5.

Table 6   Means and Standard Deviations for School Aptitude (Intelligence), Standardized Achievement Test Results, and Average Teacher Marks for Advantagement by Race by Sex Subgroups [a, e]

Group	n	Intelligence		Achievement Test Grade Level		Average Teachers' Marks (4.0=A)	
		M	SD	M	SD	M	SD
Advantaged black boys	59	92.6[b]	20.1	5.05[c]	1.13	2.3[d]	.60
Advantaged white boys	57	106.5	16.1	5.78	1.23	2.2	1.00
Advantaged black girls	57	92.9	16.3	5.58	1.24	2.6	.80
Advantaged white girls	57	104.6	17.1	5.85	1.00	2.8	.80
Disadvantaged black boys	56	73.0	20.5	4.71	.78	2.0	.70
Disadvantaged white boys	49	84.3	13.6	5.23	.75	2.2	.80
Disadvantaged black girls	53	77.9	13.3	4.74	.78	2.3	.70
Disadvantaged white girls	55	92.9	16.0	5.81	1.02	2.7	.70

[a] *F* for each column of eight means is significant at less than .01.

[b] Pairs of means in this column that differ from each other by 27.5 points or more differ at the .01 level or less (Scheffé test); those differing 24.1 to 27.4 points or more, at less than .05 but greater than .01.

[c] In this column, means 1.65 or further apart differ at the .01 level or less from each other (Scheffé); those 1.45–1.64 at less than .05 but greater than .01. No individual pairs differ significantly.

[d] In this column, means 1.3 or further apart differ at the .01 level or less from each other (Scheffé); those 1.1–1.3 at less than .05 but greater than .01. No individual pairs differ significantly.

[e] It should be noted that these data come from achievement tests given early in the fall term of school, soon after the end of the summer recess.

It can be seen from Table 6, rows 1, 2, 3 and 4 (the advantaged groups), that teachers mark boys, regardless of race, more severely than girls of either

[12] W. L. Hays, *Statistics for Psychologists* (New York: Holt, Rinehart and Winston, 1963).

race, even though (as in the case of the advantaged white boys and girls) there is neither a statistically nor a practically significant difference in accomplishment as measured by standard achievement tests, and no difference in intelligence (mean IQ for advantaged white boys is 106.5; for advantaged white girls, 104.6).

Among the four advantaged groups, black boys are clearly worst off in achievement test standing, even though they stand at almost exactly the same intelligence level as advantaged black girls.

The picture for the four disadvantaged groups is not greatly different, except that disadvantaged black girls join disadvantaged black and white boys in the low intelligence, low achievement test mean, and low average teachers' marks category. The differences favoring disadvantaged white girls over the other three disadvantaged groups are consistent for all three school-related variables, and seem large enough to be of practical significance, particularly when the moderate strength and consistency of correlations for this group among intelligence, achievement test standing, and teachers' marks are considered (see Table 3, row 8). For the eight subgroups of the total sample, this level of consistency and strength of interrelations is exceeded only for the disadvantaged black girls, but for them the accuracy–consistency phenomena are linked to relatively low teachers' marks (Table 3, row 7).

DISCUSSION

First, it was hypothesized that a conventional group intelligence test will predict standardized achievement test results equally well for boys and girls, but better for advantaged than disadvantaged children. Results fail to bear out the hypotheses, strikingly so in the case of the advantagement–disadvantagement prediction: Girls' standardized test results are predicted better than those of boys, and disadvantaged children's results are predicted strikingly better than advantaged (for advantaged, 4% of the variance as opposed to about 55% for disadvantaged). Additionally, standard achievement test performance of black children was predicted much better by intelligence than it was for whites (about 30% of the variance for black children, about 3% for white children).

For the advantaged, for boys, and for whites in this sample, factors other than California Test of Mental Maturity IQ account for most of the variance of school accomplishment as measured by the Metropolitan Achievement Test. Speculatively, factors responsible may be attention, motivation, rapport with teachers, conformity, or any one of many other things that may possibly be correlated with intelligence for the disadvantaged, for girls, and for blacks, but not for the advantaged, for boys, or for whites. In any event and for whatever reason, tests of achievement and intelligence have very much more in common for a disadvantaged than for an advantaged Atlanta population, and substantially more in common for a black than a white population.

The second hypothesis was that teachers' marks, when judged against achievement test results, will be more accurate for girls than for boys, for middle-class than for disadvantaged children, and perhaps least accurate of all for disadvantaged black boys.

The prediction was supported modestly for girls versus boys (about 15% of the variance for girls, only 4% for boys). For neither sex is prediction satisfactory in the useful–accurate sense. The prediction was seriously awry in the case of social class (only about 1% of the variance for advantaged, about 34% for disadvantaged). Teachers' marks were related moderately to accomplishment as judged by standardized achievement test results for disadvantaged black boys ($r = .53$). The groups for which *no* relation was shown between teachers' marks and achievement test results were *advantaged* white boys ($r = -.17$) and *advantaged* white girls ($r = -.07$). Speculatively, it may be that teachers mark the advantaged and the white according to how well socialized they are according to teachers' standards, but mark the poor and particularly the black poor more according to their objective performance. It seems that neither group is altogether well served if this should prove to be the case.

The third set of hypotheses was that teachers consistently give girls higher marks than boys (this is clearly and consistently borne out by the data); that there are no important differences between boys and girls in their standard achievement test performance (*not* borne out by the data: Girls consistently performed better than boys); and that disadvantaged black boys will receive the lowest teachers' marks of any group (borne out by the data; but they were also lowest in intelligence and performance on standardized achievement tests. However, in standard tests of achievement, disadvantaged black girls were at almost the same low level).

Finally, the results provide a sobering caution about trying to predict *anything* for a special subgroup from the general population relationships: For example, intelligence and standardized achievement test standing are correlated .45 for the total population for this study, but $-.35$ for advantaged white boys and .80 for disadvantaged white girls. Similarly, correlations between teachers' marks and achievement test standings range from $-.17$ for advantaged white boys to .73 for disadvantaged black girls. To say the least, caution about special group prediction is indicated.

Herbert J. Walberg
Ernest R. House
Joe M. Steele

Grade Level, Cognition, and Affect: A Cross-Section of Classroom Perceptions[1]

Elementary and high-school students, grades six through twelve, were asked to rate emphases given to twenty-three cognitive and affective classroom activities in the paper presented here. Walberg, House, and Steele anticipated that, with increasing maturity, youth would place greater emphases on higher level cognitive processes—application, comprehension, finding consequences, and discovering solutions. They also expected that alienation toward high school would increase among the youth as they increasingly faced more difficult content. The researchers employ sophisticated statistical procedures to show that grade level is indeed a powerful predictor of emphases among the classroom activities; however, they fail to confirm that youth place greater stress on higher level cognitive processes in the upper grades of high school. Grades nine and ten are revealed to be especially critical in the formation of attitudes toward learning, and as a consequence of "educational maladjustment," many students may become alienated from school at about this time.

Instructional Objectives
To consider changes by grade level in emphases given cognitive activities in the classroom.
To consider changes by grade level in emphases given affective activities in the classroom.
To consider the significance of grades nine and ten to cognitive affective processes associated with educational maladjustment.

IN THE last few years, several groups of research workers have begun investigations of student perceptions of classroom processes. Rather than counting observable entities or behaviors such as the number of students or teacher

FROM *Journal of Educational Psychology*, LXIV (1973), pp. 142–146. Copyright 1973 by the American Psychological Association. Reprinted by permission of the authors and the publisher.
1 This research was supported by the Center for Instructional Research and Curriculum Evaluation (Urbana), the Office of Evaluation Research, and by the Center for Urban Educational Research (Chicago). Mark Bargen programmed the regression models and Robert Rippey, Barak Rosenshine, and Wayne Welch commented on a draft of the manuscript.

behaviors, the focus has been on measuring the student view of the class as obtained on rating scales. Perceptual measurements are relatively convenient and inexpensive to administer and process, and they have incremental validity in predicting learning outcomes.[2] To gain insight into the development of these perceptions, a cross-sectional study of sixth- through twelfth-grade student ratings of cognitive and affective processes in their classrooms was undertaken.

While there has been no research on the development of perceived cognitive processes in classrooms, there have been several cross-sectional and longitudinal studies of student affect—either general school morale or attitudes toward teachers and learning. One of the first reported was by Jordon[3] who administered a questionnaire to 23 London school boys, ages 11 through 15, and found that attitudes declined with age in three of the five subject-matter areas surveyed. In 1937 and again in 1949, Fitt[4] surveyed 1,244 Auckland, New Zealand, students, ages 7 through 18, and found declining school attitudes with age in both administrations. The generalization that student morale is less favorable in later grades is supported in recent studies by Wisenthal,[5] Gulo,[6] Kniveton,[7] Neale and Proshek[8] and Yamamoto, Thomas, and Karns.[9]

In a study of attitude development and its correlates, Guest[10] concluded that "certain standard personal and demographic characteristics are consistently related to attitude positions regardless of the content being measured [p. 738]." Kniveton[11] offered support for this contention; his results showed British grammar school children, usually high achievers from the professional and managerial classes, had more favorable attitudes than did children of the same age from lower socioeconomic strata. Similarly, beginning with Fitt,[12] a number of the studies cited above revealed that girls'

[2] H. J. Walberg and G. J. Anderson, "Properties of Achieving the Urban Class," *Journal of Educational Psychology*, LXIII (1972), 381–385.

[3] D. Jordan, "The Attitude of Central School Pupils to Certain School Subjects, and the Correlation Between Attitude and Attainment," *British Journal of Educational Psychology*, XI (1941), 28–44.

[4] A. B. Fitt, "An Experimental Study of Children's Attitudes to School," *British Journal of Educational Psychology*, XXVI (1956), 25–30.

[5] M. Wisenthal, "Sex Differences in Attitudes and Attainment in Junior Schools," *British Journal of Educational Psychology*, XXXV (1965), 79–85.

[6] E. R. Gulo, "Rural Students' Attitudes toward Their Teachers," *Journal of Educational Resources*, LXII (1968), 88–93.

[7] B. G. Kniveton, "An Investigation of the Attitudes of Adolescents to Aspects of Their Schooling," *British Journal of Educational Psychology*, XXXIX (1969), 78–81.

[8] D. C. Neale and J. M. Proshek, "School Related Attitude of Culturally Disadvantaged Elementary School Children," *Journal of Educational Psychology*, LVIII (1967), 238–244.

[9] K. Yamamoto, C. Thomas and E. A. Karns, "School-related Attitudes in Middle-school Age Subjects," *American Educational Research Journal*, VI (1969), 191–206.

[10] L. Guest, "Longitudinal Study of Attitude Development and Some Correlates," *Child Development*, XXXV (1965), 779–784.

[11] Kniveton, op. cit.

[12] Fitt, op. cit.

attitudes toward school are more favorable than those of boys. Marks [13] noted that perception is a function of personality and maintained that perceptions of classroom environments describe students, rather than the environment. However, Walberg and Anderson [14] showed that in eight subject-matter areas, perceptions of classroom environments obtained from a sample of class members predict achievements (adjusted for IQ) of students in the same classes who did not respond to the environment scales. Thus, while perception of the classroom environment is partially a function of personality, components of this perception independent of the individual can be validly measured.

The studies of the relation of grade level to attitudes and morale cited above offer no theoretical frameworks. Although the present study was viewed as an exploration of a new domain, it seemed useful to formulate two informal hypotheses for preliminary testing. On one hand, with increasing psychological and social maturity of students, [15] greater emphasis on high-level cognitive tasks and independent learning might be observed at higher grade levels. On the other hand, increasingly difficult content in higher grades [16] might lead to greater alienation and consequent demeaning of tasks and learning particularly at the time students most often drop out of school. A single cross-sectional study cannot provide confirmations or rejections of these hypotheses; however, tentative levels of credence might be alloted on the basis of the study subject to replication.

METHOD

Sample

Data were collected from 121 classes in 69 schools as part of a state-wide evaluation study in Illinois. Classes ranged from Grades 6 through 12 and represented the four subject areas of science, mathematics, social studies, and language arts as shown in Table 1. From the 121 classes, 52 were classified as "gifted" while the remaining 69 were classified as "ordinary." The differences between these groups are reported elsewhere.[17] Table 1 shows that the numbers of classes at different grade levels is fairly evenly distributed over class size, subject, and giftedness.

---

[13] E. Marks, "Personality and Motivational Factors in Responses to an Environmental Description Scale," *Journal of Educational Psychology*, LIX (1968), 267–274.

[14] Walberg and Anderson, op. cit.

[15] B. S. Bloom, *Stability and Change in Human Characteristics* (New York: Wiley, 1963); L. L. Thurstone, *The Differential Growth of Mental Abilities* (Chapel Hill, N.C.: University of North Carolina Psychometric Laboratory, 1955).

[16] B. J. Hodgkins and R. E. Herriot, "Age-grade Structure, Goals, and Compliance in the Schools: An Organizational Analysis," *Sociology of Education*, XLIII (1970), 90–105.

[17] J. Steele, E. R. House and T. Kerins, "An Instrument for Assessing Instructional Climate through Low-inference Student Judgments," *American Educational Research Journal*, VIII (1971), 447–466.

Table 1   Description of the Sample

| | | | | Grade Level | | | | | Number | |
Subject Area	6	7	8	9	10	11	12	Mean of Class Size	of Gifted Classes	Total
Science	2	2	3	0	13	0	1	22.8	7	21
Mathematics	2	0	1	8	6	4	3	23.0	7	24
Social studies	4	7	5	0	2	7	0	25.3	13	25
Language arts	8	5	9	5	4	14	6	22.8	25	51
Total	16	14	18	13	25	25	10	23.4	52	121

Instrument

Twenty-three items from the Class Activities Questionnaire were used to obtain the students' perception of prevailing patterns of cognitive and affective emphasis. Students were asked to agree or disagree on a 4-point scale to statements describing tasks and other activities which characterize their class. These activities imply either one of six levels of cognitive educational objectives derived from Bloom's *Taxonomy* [18] or one of nine affective conditions stressed in class. A description of the development of this instrument and reliability coefficients are presented by Steele et al.[19]

Statistical Analysis

To introduce as much statistical control as possible, all available covariates were employed in the analysis. "Dummy" (0 or 1 dichotomous) variables were employed to uniquely identify each class with each subject matter and with the giftedness designation. The three dummy variables for subject matter were grouped together in the analysis. The quadratic forms (squares) of grade level and class size were included to test for curvilinear relations. Finally, the products of all the linear predictors (main effects) were computed to test for heterogeneity of regression (interaction). (See Walberg [20] for a further explanation of the use of dummy variables, products, and quadratics in regression analysis.)

RESULTS AND DISCUSSION

The 23 criteria were regressed on the 12 predictor terms in Table 2 using 24 models; that is, each of the 12 predictors was entered first or last in one of the models. The test for increment in R^2 for each predictor entered first

[18] B. S. Bloom, *Taxonomy of Educational Objectives: Cognitive Domain* (New York: Longmans, Green, 1956).

[19] Steele et al, op. cit.

[20] H. J. Walberg, "Generalized Regression Analysis in Educational Research," *American Educational Research Journal*, VII (1970), 71–90.

indicates how much variance in a criterion it can account for irrespective of the other predictors. Table 2 reveals that by this standard all predictors but class size and its quadratic form are highly significant ($p > .001$) in a multivariate sense (across all 23 criteria). However, the test for increments in R^2 for a predictor entered last are far more stringent since it indicates how much variance it explains after the variance associated with all the other predictors are statistically removed from the criteria. By this standard, grade level is the most powerful predictor; its quadratic form is also significant. Class size was not significant on either of its entries in linear or quadratic form; of all the variables, it is the weakest. Giftedness and three interactions were significant; these are not reported in detail here because they were used mainly as statistical control variables.

Table 2   Multivariate F Ratios for the Regression of Twenty-Three Criteria on Twelve Predictors

Criteria	First Entry	Last Entry
Grade level (A)	5.2 ***	2.3 **
Class size (B)	1.4	1.4
Subject (C)	5.3 ***	1.1
Giftedness (D)	6.7 ***	1.8 *
A²	4.7 ***	1.9 *
B²	1.5	1.1
B × A	4.1 ***	2.1 **
B × C	4.6 ***	1.0
A × C	5.6 ***	1.2
B × D	5.3 ***	1.1
A × D	5.9 ***	1.9 *
C × D	3.0 ***	1.6 *

  * $p = .05$.
  ** $p = .01$.
  *** $p = .001$.

Table 3 shows the means of the 13 criteria significantly related to grade level. The last two columns in the table contain the variance (R^2) accounted for (*a*) by both linear and quadratic forms of grade level and (*b*) by the quadratic beyond that accounted for by the linear form. The last column shows that 8 of the 13 regression lines for the criteria have significant curvature.

Table 3 further shows that the lower level cognitive processes such as memorizing and knowing the best answer are seen as more emphasized in the higher grades, while the higher level processes such as application, comprehension, finding consequences, and discovering solutions are seen as more prominent in the lower grades. However, the plots are curvilinear; lower level processes tend to reach a peak and higher level processes reach a trough in Grades 9 and 10.

Table 3 *Means on Significant Criteria and Accountable Variance*

Criteria	Grade Level							R^2 L,Q	R^2 Q.L
	6	7	8	9	10	11	12		
Cognitive									
Put methods and ideas to use	2.26	2.15	2.11	1.84	1.73	1.79	1.84	24.3***	.7
Discover many solutions	2.19	2.19	2.12	1.82	1.85	1.93	2.01	20.5***	4.2**
Find trends and consequences	1.85	1.92	1.97	1.44	1.71	1.80	1.96	5.1*	3.3**
Restate ideas	2.01	1.91	1.81	1.63	1.61	1.80	1.84	17.4***	4.9**
Know the best answer	1.42	1.49	1.38	1.73	1.84	1.61	1.39	9.5**	3.1**
Practice methods to solve problems	1.84	1.73	1.63	1.63	1.44	1.50	1.39	18.5***	.0
Invent, design, compose, create	1.93	1.68	1.56	1.22	1.11	1.37	1.43	18.6***	.6
Memorize	.99	.83	1.03	1.47	1.63	1.19	.98	11.9***	5.6***
Affective									
Actively participates	2.33	2.36	2.26	1.63	1.58	1.69	1.86	30.1***	1.3
Independently explore and begin new activities	2.13	1.80	1.77	1.49	1.59	1.68	1.76	19.4***	2.1*
Excitement and involvement	2.02	1.69	1.68	1.33	1.15	1.23	1.45	25.2***	2.9*
Great concern for grades	1.53	1.54	1.51	1.85	2.06	1.86	1.70	12.1***	.3
Much opportunity to participate	2.69	2.62	2.64	2.18	2.07	2.29	2.47	22.9***	4.5**

$* p < .05.$ $** p < .01.$ $*** p < .001.$

On the affective criteria, class participation, independent activities, excitement, and involvement are perceived as more prominent in Grades 6 through 8 than in the higher grades, while great concern for grades is perceived as more pronounced in high school. Again, several of the criteria are curvilinear; independent exploration, involvement, and opportunity for participation are lower in the range of Grades 9 through 11 and concern for grades peaks at Grade 10.

The changes in perceptions across grade levels suggest educational maladaptation to student needs and abilities in high school, especially Grades 9 and 10. The changes may represent the institutional press of the high school on students to get high grades through memorization and getting the "right answers" to be admitted to college. Also, for many students, Grade 9 represents a transition from a small, intimate elementary school to a large, bureaucratic high school, and students begin dropping out in Grade 10, since the law requires them to stay till the age of 16.

Perceptions may turn favorable in the last 2 years of high school because by then alienated students have dropped out. While trends on the affective criteria confirm prior school attitude studies, the change in perceptions of cognitive emphasis may further suggest that students may psychologically or physically withdraw from high school because their classes appear to lack appropriate stimulation and intellectual challenge.

Dale Findley
Henry M. O'Reilly

Secondary School Discipline

Secondary school discipline is rarely discussed in the literature in adolescence, yet it is the topic about which prospective teachers usually claim that they want most to learn. The subject matter is exceedingly complex, involving questions of motivation, learning, and pedagogy, but Findley and O'Reilly offer a reasoned analysis of school discipline and its relationship to student behavior. The researchers identify the different interpretations that teachers assign to the meaning of discipline, suggest a workable philosophy, review forms of punishment—corporal, reprimand, conference,

FROM *American Secondary Education*, II (1971), pp. 26–31. Reprinted by permission of the authors and the publisher.

detention, fines, suspension and expulsion—and propose the development of an effective discipline program.

Instructional Objectives
To define three ways in which teachers interpret discipline.
To present a philosophy of discipline.
To suggest instructional practices that may facilitate classroom control.
To evaluate several forms of misconduct punishment.
To propose a procedure for developing an effective discipline program.

PROBABLY no one single issue recently has been of more concern to principals than the matter of student behavior. Of late the principal's authority has been seriously challenged. At least what principals have held to be their authority has been challenged.

In order to help children and youth develop the intellectual and moral discipline essential for being free people, we as adults and school administrators have to exercise discipline of mind. We must think through carefully and clearly what we mean by discipline, what kind of discipline we want, and by what methods we can best achieve it.[1]

In the face of uncertainty many persons tend to regress to simple and primitive ways of dealing with difficulties. In times of strain and anxiety there are demands for speeded-up action. Patient educational procedures in the making of complex judgements, are likely to be neglected. Instead, people begin to look for a less thought-requiring procedure. Some begin to look for a scale in which there is a prescribed form of punishment for every specific misdemeanor. Others advocate such coercive techniques as return to "woodshed" whippings, military marching in schools, more drills in the 3 R's, or fining the parents of children who get into trouble. These solutions are unappealing to most of us because they do not teach children the right ways of behaving when coercion is removed. It is because of such confusions that we as administrators must examine very carefully the concept of "discipline" and our own practices with the children and youth of today.[2]

There are mainly three different ways teachers talk about discipline. First of all teachers refer to the degree of order we have established in a group. Secondly, teachers define "discipline" as not the order we have, but the trick by which we have established order. And the third way teachers commonly use the word "discipline" is special ways of enforcing discipline by punishment.

Administrators must decide what goals we expect discipline to attain. Discipline is always connected with a goal or purpose. Individual discipline

---

[1] G. D. Sheviakor and F. Redl, *Discipline for Today's Children and Youth* (Washington, D.C.: Association for Supervision and Curriculum Development, National Education Association, 1956), p. 1.
[2] Ibid., p. 2.

is often thought of as an organization of one's impulses for the attainment of a goal, while group discipline demands control of impulses of the individuals composing a group for the attainment of a goal which all have accepted.

FORMULATING A PHILOSOPHY OF DISCIPLINE

In dealing with discipline and the adolescent in high school we must be prepared to change with the times and with changing conditions. Discipline, along with all other aspects of school life, is a changing phenomenon, reflecting the rapidly shifting community scene today. Policies relating to discipline often become outmoded. School regulations, like city statutes, become anachronisms with changing conditions. Thus policy evaluation and policy formulation become a continuous problem.

In formulating a philosophy of discipline the principal's role is one of advisory to the School Board. Formulating school discipline policies is a legal function of school boards. While it is true that the power to make policies are vested in the school board, recent history has seen changes wherein popular participation in policy formulation has broadened considerably. School boards have become sensitive to the desires of the people and have listened thoughtfully to interested groups of citizens, teachers, and to their administrators. There is a good deal of truth in the notion that America's schools are as good or as bad as the people want them to be.[3]

A principal and school board must remember that in our society and in our schools the individual citizen is granted certain inalienable rights, among them life, liberty, and the pursuit of happiness.[4] In light of recent court decisions it is very important that school boards act with reasonable exercise of their authority. The recent court decisions have tended to restrain the school from exercising many of the forms of control over student conduct which it and the community formerly accepted as normal and proper. But whatever the reasons for these legal actions may be and whatever their outcomes are, the impact of court decisions relating to control of student behavior is felt more immediately and heavily by the building principal than by anyone else in the administrative or teaching hierarchy.

It is worth mentioning at this point that some states have policies on school discipline which must be followed by local school boards. However, even when the state outlines school discipline policies, there is usually a degree of freedom, which permits the community to handle certain local problems.

The principal must take the lead in promoting a positive approach to discipline. To do this, the principal must be aware of the factors and practices

[3] K. G. Larson and M. R. Karpas, *Effective Secondary School Discipline* (Englewood Cliffs, N. J.: Prentice-Hall Inc., 1966), pp. 135–136.
[4] G. F. Ovard, *Administration of the Changing Secondary School* (New York: The Macmillan Co., 1969), p. 33.

that aid in developing good behavior patterns in schools. Lawrence E. Vredevoe, in his "Third Report on a Study of Students and School Discipline in the United States and Other Countries," indicated that practices that students and teachers believe to be most successful in developing good teacher-student relationships do not differ in size, location, or composition of the student body. In Vredevoe's report the schools selected as being representative of the best citizenship and teacher-student relationships, had the following common practices:

1. There was an understanding and apparent recognition of the purposes and values of the standards and rules in force by faculty and students.
2. Emphasis was placed on self-discipline by teachers and students.
3. Good citizenship and conduct were characteristic of the faculty as well as the student body. Courtesy, consideration, respect, professional dress and manner, and good speech were practiced by faculty members.
4. Standards and rules were subject to review and change, but were enforced until changed by due process.
5. The emphasis in treatment of all discipline cases was on the individual involved and not the act. This represents a significant change in the past 50 years. Today's society is more concerned with the transgression than the crime.
6. Students could expect fair but certain reprimand or punishment for violation of rules and standards.
7. The punishments meted out were fitted to the individual rather than the transgression.
8. Faculty and students cooperated in establishing, maintaining, and revising rules and standards.
9. The program was challenging to all groups.[5]

The kind of discipline which works in a democracy is self-discipline. Such discipline begins at the earliest years with external authority imposed by parents and teachers and is gradually relaxed as the student finishes the secondary school. From a sociological and psychological base, discipline is a learning process whereby the individual progressively learns to develop habits of self-control and recognizes his own responsibility to society.[6]

Generally speaking there are three to five per cent of the student body on whom corrective measures must be used, the general emphasis in schools should be on the prevention of misconduct and education toward self-control.[7]

Walter E. McPhie indicates that methods of preventing problems of control are divided into two categories: (1) things that should be done, and (2) things that should be avoided.

The following things should be done: use personal experience as a guide in

[5] L. E. Vredevoe, "School Discipline—Third Report on a Study of Students and School Discipline in the United States and Other Countries," *Bulletin of the N.A.S.S.P.*, (March 1965), 216–217.
[6] Ovard, op. cit., p. 334.
[7] Ibid.

identifying students as discipline problems, talk informally with the students at the beginning of the year about classroom procedures and expectations, permit students to see classes they choose, learn the students' names early, begin lessons promptly, be enthusiastic, provide each student an opportunity for success, admit error, make assignments reasonable and clear, occasionally do something nice for your students, and, above all else, be alert. The following things should be avoided: don't try to buy popularity, don't be a comedian, don't talk through noise, don't enter into arguments, and don't do things for students that they can do for themselves.[8]

The individual teacher is very important in school discipline. The better the teacher is in his preparation, teaching technique, personality, etc., the less likely are student conduct problems to arise. It is sometimes helpful to remember that many discipline problems can be solved through preventive correction by the teacher instead of a control penalty on the student.[9]

The specific causes of student offenses related to specific instances are many and varied, but most discipline problems can be attributed to a few fundamental reasons. Some of these are as follows: lack of general training and development, lack of interest in course work, poor teaching, poor school organization, unsatisfactory home conditions, lack of social adjustment, bad associates, physical defects, lack of responsibility, adjustment to adolescence.[10]

The school is a society in which the students and teachers interact with each other for a common purpose. Freedom exists but with it comes great responsibility, and as in all societies, there is a need for restrictions. Whenever restrictions are levied to govern the behavior of a group, rewards and penalties are necessary to support the restrictions. These restrictions should be spelled out in the student handbook so the students have full knowledge of the existing rules.[11]

Teachers and principals in the more difficult schools may long at times for autocratic methods of keeping order and forcing obedience that were available to the schoolmasters in earlier times. But even if today's students would submit to the harsher disciplines of the past, these methods would hardly suit the goals of modern education. The old disciplinary procedures served a society that held submission to authority to be a prime goal of childhood education. Today the ideal product of the mass schooling system is expected to possess an independent mind and a cooperative spirit, traits not likely to flourish in an atmosphere of institutional coercion.

Fear of the rod in traditional American schools was a major instrument of student discipline. Infliction of physical pain was justified on the same grounds as were the harsh penal codes of the day for adults. "Fear was

[8] W. E. McPhie, "Discipline Problems: An Educational Malignancy," *Bulletin of the N.A.S.S.P.,* (December 1961), 82–91.

[9] E. J. Brown and A. T. Phelps, *Managing the Classroom—The Teacher's Part in School Administration* (New York: The Ronald Press Co., 1961), p. 22.

[10] Ovard, op. cit., p. 337.

[11] Ovard, op. cit., p. 339.

conceived as the only force which would make men amenable to dominion
. . . It was natural (to believe) that children, too, should be controlled by
violence or the threat of violence." [12]

An historian of childhood, Philippe Aries, has traced the great change in
educational style that took place between the late Middle Ages and the 17th
Century, from a comradely association of teachers and learners to prisonlike
schools where "the birch became the mark of the schoolmaster . . . the
symbol of the subjection in which he . . . held his pupils." [13] Thus a humili-
ating disciplinary system—whippings at the master's discretion became widespread in schools in Europe. The American colonists, coming from a land
where flogging had become common in schools, took it for granted that
corporal punishment would be used to control the children in the schools
they established in the New World.[14]

The children in pre-Revolutionary America suffered not only pain of the
flesh, but the tormenting threat of eternal damnation. A catechism told him
he would be sent down to an everlasting fire if he were naughty. Evangelist
preachers told the child that he was born sinful and graphically described
what awaited them in the afterworld. This repressive attitude toward life,
this insistence on conformity to a moral and ethical code based purely on
religious sanction, was naturally reflected in the colonial schools and in the
discipline of children.[15]

The libertarian ideas and the humanitarian movements of the 18th and
19th centuries were slow to overcome the authoritarian spirit that still pre-
vailed in schooling of the young. Though whipping posts and other harsh
instruments of adult punishment gradually disappeared the tradition of the
rod remained fixed in the educational practice. The Rev. Francis Waylaid,
president of Brown University expressed the prevailing view in a public
address in 1830, "it is the duty of the instructor to enforce obedience and
the pupil to render it." [16]

Even Horace Mann, who crusaded during the 1930s against excessive
application of corporal punishment, did not approve of abolishing it altogether.

The pros and cons of corporal punishment have been debated for years.
And corporal punishment never quite dies as an educational issue. However,
corporal punishment hardly presents itself as an answer to the disciplinary
problems of the schools of today.

Such devices as detention periods have been initiated for the disobedient
child. However, upon taking a close look at detention periods it appears they
are not correcting the discipline problems of the times either. We must stress

[12] H. B. Shaffer, *Discipline in Public Schools*, Washington, D. C.: Editorial Research
Reports, 1969, p. 643.
[13] P. Aries, *Centuries of Childhood* (First Vintage Edition, 1965), p. 644.
[14] Shaffer, op. cit., p. 644.
[15] H. A. Falk, *Corporal Punishment: A Social Interpretation of its Theory and Practice
in the Schools of the United States*, 1941, p. 42.
[16] Shaffer, op. cit., p. 644

the prevention of student discipline problems. With the many social changes in the past decades we can see that the authoritarian atmosphere of the public school classroom is disappearing. The teacher is still the boss in the classroom, but the prevailing principle on discipline leans more toward a cultivation of self-discipline than toward rigid conformity to specific rules of conduct. Advances in the study of child psychology and the measurement of intelligence, growing recognition of emotional factors in learning, the rising influence of the scientific spirit, and the declining influence of Puritan morality over public education have all helped to free the student from the stern discipline of earlier times.[17]

Other types of punishment in common use in American school districts for student misconducts are the reprimand, conference, detention, fines, suspension and expulsion.

The reprimand is the most common device and the one most frequently resorted to as first choice of a teacher. If administered calmly and without the heat of anger it can be very effective.

Strickly speaking, the pupil-teacher conference should not be listed as a punishment device, but we must admit that it can have overtones of punishment when it is held after school as a result of the misbehavior. For one thing, the pupil is forced to remain after school for the appointment. This can be a very real punishment in itself if the student works after school or if he takes a bus. The conference can be a most effective means of getting to the bottom of misbehavior.

Another popular device, as old as education itself, and one which has met court approval is "staying after school—detention." As was mentioned earlier, many schools have abandoned detentions completely because it appeared that detentions have only annoyed the annoyer and didn't get to the root of the problem. Also, it is very difficult to assign certain punishments in the form of hours of detention to certain misconducts.

Fines are sometimes used in schools for certain adult type offenses like damaged books or failure to return books to library. However, principals should be aware that the courts have not looked with favor upon fining students without an alternative punishment such as the legendary "Ten dollars or ten days." The principal who excludes a pupil for failure to pay a fine and for which no alternative is offered, is on dubious ground if the matter goes to court.

It sometimes becomes necessary to exclude a student from class (suspension) for more than one day, this is entirely up to the principal. Suspension should be regarded as a fairly drastic punishment since it involves a definite academic penalty. However, in a school where students would rather be out of school than in, it hardly seems much punishment to suspend them from school.

[17] Ibid., p. 646.

Expulsion is the responsibility of the school board and should only be enforced if offense is grave enough.

To summarize, the principal shares with parents, guardians, teachers, district personnel, social workers, policemen, and juvenile judges the responsibility for teacher self-control and administering discipline to youth. The schools should supplement the role of parents and other agencies when these other agencies have a major responsibility in providing both teaching and corrective measures. The school has the major responsibility when the violation takes place within the framework of the schools program. It is important for the principal to understand the theory of effective discipline as well as the practical aspects of administering discipline.

A student, like other citizens in the community, has freedom, but the freedom is tempered by the responsibility that is involved in any given situation. In a free society restrictions are necessary to define the limits of both freedom and responsibilities. Because there are people who forget, or who place other values ahead of society's accepted values, or who are completely unwilling to accept responsibility, it is necessary to have penalties. Corrections should just be educative in nature to bring about self-discipline. But there are times when a penalty must be issued for control purposes. The principal should administer penalties that are in keeping with the nature of the violation; they should be administered as soon after the violation as possible. The penalty should be one that the principal feels just and at the same time can be successfully imposed.

Although corporal punishment has been in schools as long as schools have existed, the use of corporal punishment today is still a serious matter for the principal. Some states permit corporal punishment; other states do not. States that do permit corporal punishment do not make it mandatory. The teacher and the principal are still liable for their actions. As far as possible, both the teacher and principals should find other satisfactory penalties that will accomplish the same result as corporal punishment.

Presently we are facing many conflicts in the acceptance of new modes of maintaining student discipline. The consensus is that changes will come about nonetheless, and that when the schools have actually become better adjusted to the needs of the students, in both their instructional and their disciplinary functions, the anger and the alienation that lie behind adolescent violence will recede from the foreground of public education.[18]

A PROPOSAL FOR THE DEVELOPMENT OF AN EFFECTIVE DISCIPLINE PROGRAM

1. Provision should be made for involvement of the student governing body in the development of procedures to handle discipline matters.

[18] Ibid., p. 652.

(a) Decisions relating to the extent of student involvement in the development of school rules and regulations should be made.

(b) Decisions must be made relating to the extent of student involvement in the enforcement of school rules and regulations and the punishment resulting from the infraction of school rules and regulations.

2. The total faculty and staff must be involved in the development of the discipline program. The principal and his administrative staff must rely heavily on the teachers and supporting staff members to assist in carrying out the discipline program. It cannot be emphasized too strongly that the whole curricular program has a very important affect on the discipline program. A relevant curriculum can prevent many discipline problems.

3. The total program for handling discipline problems should be written. Caution should be exercised in the development of rules and regulations to insure enough flexibility to allow students to feel that they are being handled as individuals rather than inanimate objects. An appeal procedure should be established that allows students a fair and equitable hearing concerning their case. Time and money for supplies to develop and print the entire program should be allocated. All students, staff and faculty should receive a copy of the program.

4. The emphasis of the total program should be on prevention of misconduct, therefore, the principal must make an analysis of the cause of the misbehavior.

(a) Consideration must be given to the conditions which led to the misconduct.

1. What type of attitude do students have toward their total school experience?
   a. Do students feel teachers and administrators are "against" them?
2. What type of home background does the student have?
3. Was the misconduct an individual matter or was a group involved?
4. Is this a first offense or a repeat offense?
5. What facilities and services do you have available in the school system to provide assistance to the student involved so that he may adjust or so that the causal factors of misconduct may be removed?
6. What evidence exists to suggest that the student has achieved success in some way at school?

5. A periodic review of all rules and regulations should be undertaken to determine if the objectives of the discipline program are being met. Some record should probably be kept of the nature of offense and the disposition of the case to facilitate this analysis.

Janice Law Trecker

Sex Stereotyping in the Secondary-School Curriculum

The next two selections in Studies in Adolescence *describe the extent to which sex bias favors males in secondary-school textbooks, athletic programs, and vocational training. The paper by Trecker and the following paper by Saario, Tittle, and Jacklin call for redress of inequities. Trecker beseeches educators "to initiate and support efforts to evaluate school policies, curriculum, and educational materials with regard to sex bias and to work to eradicate stereotyping and bigotry in courses and programs." Saario, Tittle, and Jacklin see the first step as that of "changing the attitudes of administrators, counselors, and teachers."*

Instructional Objectives
To review the extent to which secondary-school textbooks are male-oriented.
To review the inequities that exist in girls' physical education and athletic programs.
To consider the constricted opportunities available to girls in vocational training programs.

O NE difficulty of dealing with sex bias in the public schools is that the integration of male and female students in most curriculum areas has led to a belief in educational equality. While such blatantly separate and unequal departments as physical education and vocational preparation are rationalized on the grounds of physical and attitudinal differences, other forms of bias are sufficiently subtle to be ignored altogether. At least until quite recently, stereotyped and biased curriculum offerings and materials were complacently accepted as either factually correct or not important enough to make changes worthwhile. The hidden assumption has been that girls, who were after all fortunate enough to have been admitted to secondary facilities over 100 years ago, could be adequately served by materials designed for boys.

Thus the standard in our secondary schools, after decades of coeducation,

FROM *Phi Delta Kappan*, LV (1973), pp. 110–112. Reprinted by permission of the author and the publisher.

is still male. Texts and programs are designed to enhance the male self-image, promote identification with male spokesmen and heroes, explore the developmental and intellectual growth of young males, and reveal masculine contributions to our culture. So far as the typical secondary school curriculum is concerned, humanity is masculine. This is evident whether one examines the literary style or graphic design of textbooks, the topics and individuals chosen for consideration and emphasis, the administration of the curriculum, the manner in which students are tracked, or the underlying assumptions of the course offerings. Current curricula and textbooks present perhaps the clearest demonstration of sex prejudice in our schools.

A look at current United States history textbooks, for example, raises the question of how our country has maintained itself with a 99% male population. These books consistently refer only to men, i.e., "our revolutionary forefathers," "the men who conquered the West," or "the men who built our nation." The pictures, photographs, and paintings chosen for inclusion are almost exclusively about male subjects. Women are rarely chosen as spokesmen, and even books with ample sections of documentary material allot women writers and thinkers no more than the most meager space—if any at all. A recent linguistic study of social studies texts, "Equal Treatment of the Sexes in Social Studies Textbooks," by Elizabeth Burr, Susan Dunn, and Norma Farquhar, details the more subtle manifestations of sex bias, including demeaning terms for women, exclusive use of male pronouns and generic terms, and a perpetuation of images of women as fragile and timid.

Nor are history and social studies texts the only offenders. Recently, the New York City Chapter of the National Organization for Women (NOW) prepared a *Report on Sex Bias in the Public Schools.* Josephine Milnar, a contributor to the report, examined a number of junior high school mathematics and science texts. She found that female mathematicians and scientists of note were ignored, and that illustrative and problem-solving materials were consistently characterized by sexual stereotypes. For example, while boys in mathematical problems show a variety of activities—gardening, building, sports, and painting—girls and women were virtually confined to sewing, cooking, and child care. In science books nonbiased texts were frequently accompanied by illustrations showing only males using scientific equipment or solving problems. Considering the large numbers of female students with scientific and mathematical potential who do not pursue careers in these areas, it seems unfortunate that texts and materials do not present young girls with positive female images and role models.

The exclusion of women from pictorial material, the stereotyped descriptions of those who do appear, and the linguistic conventions of the texts show how supposedly objective school texts subtly encourage female students to pursue their traditional roles—the home, silence, and subjection. Any doubt about this message is soon removed by a closer consideration of the topics emphasized in the various curriculum areas. Reviewing virtually any catalogue of supplementary texts and novels for secondary school students reveals how few novels and biographies feature female protagonists. While one can find a plentiful supply of novels built around the experiences of young men and boys from Alabama to Ankor Wat, one is fortunate to find even one-fourth as many dealing with young women. Supplemental texts typically include few biographies of outstanding women, and in volumes of collected lives, women receive only token representation. Both teachers and publishers seem to assume that males are involved in more interesting and important activities than females and that while girls are willing to read about boys, boys would be unconcerned about female protagonists.

Similar attitudes are evident in the social studies. Topics of particular interest to women are frequently omitted altogether, and the effects of sex bias and sex stereotypes on other problems and topics are ignored. How else can one account for the fact that, even today, young women are largely ignorant of their legal disabilities and of the prejudices they face in education, employment, and public policy, and that the general public remains uninformed about the role of sex bias in social problems? One reason is that very few social studies courses or text materials consider sex-role conditioning, women's current and historic legal status, social and philosophical attitudes toward women, or the connections between these attitudes and women's rights. It would be difficult to argue that citizenship courses are doing an adequate job when they fail to inform all students about the civic and legal disabilities affecting more than half of the student population.

Similarly, it seems difficult to justify the continuing neglect of the part that attitudes toward women play in other contemporary problems. Two-thirds of the adult poor are female, and the vast majority of the welfare population is comprised of women and children. For these reasons, it is impossible to discuss the problems of poverty without consideration of the status of women and of attitudes toward women and children. Similarly, now that 40% of the labor force is female, labor problems and unemployment cannot be explored realistically without consideration of the prospects of working women and of attitudes toward female employment. When women are trained virtually from birth to regard homemaking and child bearing as the primary and, in some cases, the exclusive "feminine" occupations, consideration of social attitudes and female roles would seem mandatory in any discussion of population control or ecology.

The same patterns of omission and neglect are evident in American history texts and courses, and it would be surprising if similar criticisms do not apply to European, Latin-American, and Afro-Asian history courses as well. Such topics as the evolution of the social and legal status of women, the importance of female and child labor in the industrial revolution, women's work in the wars and in social reforms, the women's movement, and the contributions of outstanding women are conspicuous by their absence. The typical U.S. history book generously devotes one out of its 500 to 800 pages to women, their problems, and their contributions. Looking at the typical history texts, the social studies programs, and the secondary school English and humanities reading lists, one must regretfully agree with the Pennsylvania report, "Sexism in Education." The authors, from the Pennsylvania Department of Education, the Human Relations Commission, and a state women's group, concluded that the Pennsylvania public school texts and library materials showed the following weaknesses:

> underrepresentation of women; representation in limited stereotyped roles— wives, mothers, teachers, nurses, secretaries, and other service-oriented jobs; reinforcement of culturally conditioned sexist characteristics showing as *female* such traits as dependency, passivity, noncompetitive spirit, and emotionality; and a very meager appreciation of women's contributions to history, literature, science, and other areas of American life. . . .

In light of current scholarly research on women's history and on the contributions of women to the arts, sciences, and ideas, it is simply no longer adequate to tolerate such weaknesses in American history texts.

Unfortunately, sex bias is not confined to the curriculum per se but extends to its administration and to the rationale of certain courses and procedures, especially with regard to athletics and vocational preparation courses. It would be difficult, for example, to defend most current athletic and physical education programs. In comparison with programs designed for male students, girls' athletic programs receive less money and equipment and show a narrower range in offerings. While some school systems offer no competitive programs for girls at all, many more show vast inequities in funding. *Let Them Aspire,* a report on the Ann Arbor (Michigan) schools, revealed that the budget for boys' interscholastic sports was 10 times as high as the corresponding female budget, a discrepancy by no means unique in this field. The view that boys' sports just happen to be more expensive is a frequent but inadequate justification. While school districts do not hesitate to introduce such costly boys' sports as football and ice hockey, the introduction of comparably expensive girls' activities as show jumping, horseback riding, or figure skating is almost beyond civic contemplation. It is not unusual for girls to be denied the opportunity for swimming, because pool time is limited, or for towns to reject funding for a girls' coaching staff, requiring talented young women either to abandon athletic excellence or to pay for private coaching.

In a number of cases, the neglect of female competitive athletics is paralleled by a neglect of physical education opportunities as well. Testimony from a 1971 New York City court suit against the administration of Junior High School 217 for sex bias included statements that girls were only rarely allowed to use outdoor recreation areas, that they were denied the opportunity to use the school's soccer fields, and that their indoor sports program was inferior in variety and quality to the corresponding boys' program.

Although there are glaring inequities in girls' physical education and athletic programs, they are of minor importance compared to the sexual inequities in vocational and technical education. It is still common practice to track students by sex for vocational training. Such tracking usually begins in the junior high school, where girls are steered into homemaking and boys into industrial arts. Even where sex prerequisites for these courses are absent, vocational training programs reflect rigid notions of appropriate masculine and feminine occupations. Thus females are an overwhelming majority in homemaking, health occupations, and business, while males predominate to an equally striking degree in agriculture, the skilled trades, and the industrial and technical fields. While as many girls as boys (indeed, more, if home-making is included) receive vocational training on the secondary level, their training prepares them for a very narrow range of occupations, mainly in low-paying women's fields. Nonvocational homemaking courses received the lion's share of federal funds for home economics until very recently, but young women are not prepared in these courses for paid employment but for unpaid labor as housewives.

Whether or not female students are deliberately excluded from vocational schools and courses, these sex divisions are justified on the ground that young girls are not interested in the traditionally masculine fields. Considering the economic disadvantages of their vocational choices—the low wages and worsening economic position of the American woman worker—materials and programs which might enlarge the career possibilities and raise the aspirations of young women should be a high priority item in any responsible school program. In addition to the legal and administrative changes needed to end tracking by sex, young women and men need information about the status of women in the labor force and about the new career opportunities available to women. Both ERIC and the Women's Bureau distribute informative material on women in the labor force, and the new interest in career education and vocational training will certainly make such material especially pertinent and useful. In perhaps no other area of the curriculum is there more need for nonstereotyped information and for positive role models for young women than in vocational training and career education. There is little doubt that traditional stereotypes about the proper work for women have combined with overt economic discrimination to greatly restrict the aspirations and opportunities of the female secondary school student.

Removal of bias in vocational training goes beyond a simple revision of textbooks and materials. It requires new ways of thinking about the needs of girls and women and revisions in thinking about their capacities. This is true of the curriculum as a whole, as well as of its constituent parts. School programs need to be evaluated from the point of view of female as well as male needs, and the supposition should not automatically be made that these are the same. For example, should the educational program include some form of women's studies, self-defense classes, the inclusion of material on contraception in sex education courses, and nonstereotyped courses about the family and marriage?

The removal of stereotypes and the development of a curriculum which is

appropriate for both female and male students is a complex procedure requiring the cooperation of teachers, administrators, counselors, and educational publishers. The role of teachers is especially important. While a few
subjects, such as history or science, lend themselves to a relatively small
number of standardized texts, other areas, such as the humanities, literature,
family life, and sex education, use such diverse materials as to require the
cooperation of several departments and teachers in researching material and
evaluating textbooks. In research and evaluation, in creating alternative
nonsexist books and materials, and in their dealings with the major textbook
houses, policy-making bodies and the public, teachers and teacher organizations can make major contributions to the elimination of sexual bias in the
secondary schools. Hopefully, educators will begin to initiate and support
efforts to evaluate school policies, curriculum, and educational materials
with regard to sex bias and to work to eradicate stereotyping and bigotry in
courses and programs.

Terry N. Saario
Carol Nagy Jacklin
Carol Kehr Tittle

Sex-Role Stereotyping in the Public Schools

Saario, Jacklin, and Tittle, here, and Trecker in the preceding selection,
describe the extent to which sex bias favors males in secondary-school
textbooks, athletic programs, and vocational training. The researchers
conducted a study of sex-role stereotyping in three major areas: "elemen-
tary school basal readers, educational achievement tests, and differential
curricular requirements for males and females." The curriculum section of
their comprehensive investigation, which is presented here, reveals clearly
how high-school curricula promote sex-role stereotyping and sex-discrimi-
nation.

Instructional Objectives
To review the inequities that exist in girls' physical education and athletic
*   programs.*

FROM *Harvard Educational Review*, XLIII (1973), pp. 386–416. Section reproduced:
"Curricular requirements," pp. 405–410. Reprinted by permission of the authors and
the publisher.

To consider the constricted opportunities available to girls in vocational training programs.

CURRICULAR REQUIREMENTS

The small amount of evidence available on school curriculum suggests it too may promote sex-role stereotyping and sex-discrimination. Acceptable avenues for the expression of a variety of interests are prescribed differently for males and females. Girls are told at an early age that boys are mechanically and scientifically inclined while girls excel at reading and language. To some extent this is reinforced by a division of males and females into seventh grade shop and home economics. Later vocational education tracks usually vary by sex; boys acquire a series of shop and mechanical skills while girls prepare for a life as a wife and mother, sometimes with secretarial skills on the side in case there is need to supplement a husband's income. Physical education classes for the most part are segregated by sex and as such often establish different physical expectations for individual performance by sex. All males are expected to be athletic superstars, while girls are not expected to aspire to anything beyond a good intramural fray. These expectations are often vigorously reinforced with substantially different financial allocations to boys' and girls' physical education programs.

Sex bias in vocational and physical education curricula is relatively easy to document and shall be the focus of this discussion. The deliberate segregation of the sexes according to preconceived notions of appropriate curricular activities is open to question in terms of the limitations it imposes on both sexes. Whose decision has led to sex-segregated classes? How pervasive is such segregation? Are such decisions made by students and their families or tacitly made *a priori?*

Education is not specifically mentioned in the United States Constitution, and hence its control constitutionally becomes the prerogative of each state. All fifty states have explicit constitutional provisions and numerous statutes and regulations which establish specific state responsibilities for the education of their citizenry. The National Education Association is one of the few existing sources of information about states' curricular and graduation requirements.[1] Most state requirements address only a limited number of academic subjects and a few non-academic ones like physical education, health, and practical arts. According to the NEA Educational Research Service,[2] no states patently discriminate by sex in the specification of their curricular requirements although variations by state do occur in those curricular items specified as mandatory and those considered to be the option

[1] M. Thompson, "Sex Discrimination in the Schools," Unpublished manuscript (Washington, D. C.: 3400 Dent Place, N. W., 1972).
[2] National Education Association Educational Research Service, *State Graduation Requirements* (Washington, D. C.: Author, May 1972).

of local school boards and administrators. Decisions about curricula and sexual composition of classes largely become the prerogative of local authorities.

Perhaps the most extreme form of discrimination in the exercise of local options occurs in metropolitan areas where a high concentration of students allows specialized high schools to appear. By design or default they usually become unisexual institutions and often male institutions. Given that public funds support these public schools, simple equity would require that male and female students have equal access to the programs offered. Females frequently are not admitted, and, when they are, often face more stringent entrance requirements, i.e., higher academic performance is demanded.[3] For example, of those courses listed in *Public High Schools, New York City*,[4] seventy-seven are designated as technical courses restricted to males and thirty-six are designated for females. Discrimination does not stop at the door to the classroom; as the New York City Board of Education (1972) notes, the system of vocational education in New York City discriminates against girls in three significant ways. First, more class slots are open to boys than to girls. Second, a "greater variety of more useful courses" are offered to boys than to girls, and, finally, even within a vocational program, such as fashion or dentistry, courses are labeled as being appropriate for one sex or the other. Such sex distinctions in vocational courses limit potential occupational roles for both males and females.

In the case of the vast majority of secondary schools in the United States local educational options are translated into some variation on the comprehensive high school theme James Conant advocated.[5] These options often result in a curriculum which is discriminatory in terms of specified vocational tracks and physical education courses. Frequently such discrimination occurs with the implicit consent of school boards. Data available from the USOE's Bureau of Adult, Vocational and Technical Education [6] substantially reflect this skewed sorting of students into "sex-appropriate" vocational tracks. Ninety-five per cent of all students registered in vocational agriculture courses are male. These figures represent the beginning of a new trend, for in 1970 no females were enrolled in agriculture. The field of health has also recently experienced a shift of minimal magnitude. In 1965, males constituted 4.9 per cent of those registered in health courses, as compared to 12.3 per cent of the health student population in 1971. Male and female distributions in

[3] G. Bryon, "Discrimination on the Basis of Sex in Occupational Education in the Boston Public Schools." Paper prepared for the Boston Commission to Improve the Status of Women, Eastern Massachusetts Chapter of N. O. W., 1972; New York Chapter, N. O. W., Education Committee, *Report on Sex Bias in the Public Schools* (New York: Author, 1972).

[4] New York City Board of Education, *Public High Schools, New York City 1970-71* (New York: Bureau of Educational and Vocational Guidance, 1970).

[5] J. B. Conant, *The American High School Today* (New York: Macmillan, 1959).

[6] U. S. Department of HEW, Office of Education, Bureau of Adult, Vocational and Technical Education, *Trends in Vocational Education* (Washington, D. C.: General Services Administration, 1972).

other categories for which the Bureau aggregates data conform to the same stereotypic pattern: ninety-three per cent of all students registered in consumer and homemaking courses are female; eighty-five per cent of those enrolled in home economics courses which lead to gainful employment are female; ninety-two per cent of those registered in technical courses—metallurgy, engineering, oceanography, police science—are male; seventy-five per cent in office occupations are female; and eighty-nine per cent of all registered in trade and industrial courses are male.

These issues take on particular urgency when it is realized that recently there has been renewed interest in questions of career education and choice. The year 1971 saw the largest investment ever in vocational education by federal, state, and local governments, a combined increase of twenty-two per cent over 1970 ($1,952,000,000 by state and local governments and $396,000,-000 by the federal government). In addition, career education has become a banner program of the current Secretary of Health, Education, and Welfare. Renewed interest in vocational and career education is thus reflected in financial and political support, and yet the distribution of the sexes into fields over the last decade has continued to follow traditional sex role patterns.

Perhaps such simple injustices could be accepted if labor market statistics revealed a different reality. In 1971, however, according to the Women's Bureau of the United States Department of Labor,[7] one-third of the thirty-two million women who were in the labor force were clerical workers. These figures included 3.6 million stenographers, typists, and secretaries. Seventeen per cent of the thirty-two million were service workers, fifteen per cent were professional or technical workers, of whom 1.9 million were teachers, and thirteen per cent were operatives, chiefly in factories. Women who were employed full-time in 1970 earned as a median income $5,323, or 59.4 per cent of the $8,966 median income earned by fully employed men. Surely no one would argue that women deliberately prefer such narrow, low paying, and low status sectors of the labor market. In fact, once given the opportunity, a noticeable insurgence of women is found in those fields which traditionally had been masculine domains. Soon these fields aggressively recruit female participation.[8]

As Crowley, Levitin, and Quinn [9] point out:

The "average woman" is a statistical creation, a fiction. She has been used to

[7] Women's Bureau, Employment Standards Administration, United States Department of Labor, *Highlights of Women's Employment and Education* (Washington, D. C.: Women's Bureau WB72191, U. S. Government Printing Office, March 1972).

[8] J. N. Hedges, "Women at Work: Women Workers and Manpower Demands in the 1970s," *Monthly Labor Review*, XCIII (June 1970), 19–29; H. Zellner, "Discrimination Against Women, Occupational Segregation, and the Relative Wage," *American Economic Review*, LXII (May 1972), 157–160; T. E. Levitin, R. P. Quinn and G. L. Staines, "A Woman Is Fifty-eight Per Cent of a Man," *Psychology Today*, VI (March 1973), 89–91.

[9] Ibid., p. 96.

defend the status quo of the labor market, on the assumption that knowing the sex of an employee reliably predicts his or her job attitudes. This assumption is false. Knowing that a worker is female allows us to predict that she will hold a job in a "woman's field," and that she will be substantially underpaid for a person of her qualifications. But knowing that a worker is female does not help us much to predict what she wants from her job.

While half of all women employed in 1969 were concentrated in 21 of the 250 distinct occupations listed by the Census Bureau,[10] an increasing proportion of these women assumed responsibility for some portion of their own or their household's income during their lifetime.[11] Thus to argue that women prefer low incomes and less secure positions in the labor market is fallacious. Unfortunately, the onus of such occupational distributions must lie at the feet of industries seeking unskilled cheap labor, and on the shoulders of schools which counsel and prepare women for limited future occupational roles.

Allocation of money to support sports and physical education programs represents another very clear instance in which resources are allocated differentially on the basis of sex. The tendency to support a major sports program for boys but not for girls starts early, often at the initiative of the local community. While there have been a few recent outstanding exceptions, communities typically organize Little League baseball and football teams, leaving young girls to their dolls. Eight-year-old girls quickly learn that only males "are proficient enough to form leagues, play regulation length games with paid umpires, uniforms, full schedules, and championship playoffs." [12] Such activities are usually neither sponsored nor organized by the elementary school, but do set the precedent for sex-segregated physical education after the fourth or fifth grade. Little rationale other than tradition exists for such segregation when students are being taught the same sport and are of approximately the same height, strength, weight, and skill level. Of course, young males are encouraged by their family, the media, and their peers to spend many hours a week on athletic activities outside of school, and by the time they are ten or eleven their athletic skills have been finely honed.

Real discrimination in the allocation of time, financial resources, and physical facilities is most evident in junior and senior high school. The largest swimming pool, the best playing fields, the finest tennis courts are usually reserved for male sporting events. Most schools offer male students a sports program composed of varsity competition in football, basketball, baseball, track, swimming, and other sports. These activities are considered to be an essential element in the comprehensive educational package offered

[10] J. N. Hedges, "Women at Work . . . ," op. cit.

[11] Levitin, Quinn and Staines, op. cit.

[12] R. Dunning, "Women in Sports," Unpublished Manuscript (Davis, California: F35 No. Campus Way, 1972), pp. 28–29.

by the school. Coaches are hired, uniforms purchased, and facilities built. Such expenditures are considered to be legitimate line-items in a school's budget. Seldom does a school's budget reflect comparable line-item expenditures for a girls' athletic program. Girls Athletic Associations (GAA) are usually voluntary, "out-of-school" programs. At a high school in California, for example, "the GAA must sell hot dogs at football games, bake cupcakes and other such things to support their limited program which . . . includes field hockey, basketball, volleyball, tennis and softball. In other words, there is no pre-existing program at the high school for female athletes or those girls who wish to become athletes. If the GAA cannot sell enough hot dogs and popcorn, there will be no field hockey team. If enough cupcakes aren't sold or bottles collected, basketball may have to go. The boys' programs do not face similar problems." [13]

Even the salary supplements that coaches receive highlight the school's discrimination in physical education. According to the N.E.A.,[14] in 1971-72 the extra-curricular salary supplements for head coaches ranged from a low of $1,226 to a high of $5,500. Intramural sports coaches received supplements which ranged from $554 to $1,920 and the cheerleader advisor received from a low of $347 to a high of $2,240. These salary supplements were not reported by sex but it is highly likely that the head coach is a male and the cheerleader advisor and possibly some of the intramural coaches are females. Schools do communicate in many ways that boys' athletic programs are of greater significance to the school's educational programs than are those for girls; the best physical facilities are reserved for male use, financial support of girls' programs is minimal, and an elaborate system of athletic options for girls and boys of varying abilities is nonexistent.

It is not our intent in this article to substitute one curricular prescription for another, nor do we suggest that any arbitrary concept of equal curricular opportunity is either desirable or feasible. We do assert that girls and boys should be treated by the school as individuals each with her or his own individual curricular interests and needs. Schools should make available to girls as well as boys a full range of options in physical education and inter-scholastic athletics. Shorthand and typing skills are at least as useful to boys as woodworking. The school curriculum has clearly functioned to reinforce rigid, educationally discriminatory, and sexually stereotypic attitudes in both students and school staff. Schools seeking to free the next generation of youth from the dysfunctional constraints of the past will have to change curricular requirements and redress inequities in the options open to boys and girls. But in order to accomplish these structural reforms schools must face the serious problem of changing the attitudes of administrators, counselors, and teachers.

[13] Ibid., p. 26.
[14] National Education Association, *Salary Schedule Supplements for Extra Duties, 1971-72* (Washington, D. C.: Research Memo, April, 1972).

Stephen J. Fitzsimmons
Julia Cheever
Emily Leonard
Diane Macunovich

School Failures: Now and Tomorrow[1]

Fitzsimmons, Cheever, Leonard, and Macunovich sought to determine whether future school failures could be identified in elementary and secondary school and whether the performance patterns of the eventual dropouts could be distinguished from those of youth who barely managed to graduate. The researchers report that poor performance can be identified as early as the third grade, that early problems in language may precipitate subsequent academic difficulties, and that early failure in one or two areas frequently spreads to later areas. The study concludes with a series of recommendations, based on programs of academic assistance, counseling, and home visitations, designed to decrease the dropout rates of high schools.

Instructional Objectives
To review dominant patterns of early poor performance—spread, parallel, hourglass, late failing, and random or incomplete.
To review patterns of failure by grade-level and subject matter.
To consider reasons given for dropping out of school and the grade at which dropouts leave school.
To consider relationships between elementary-school and high-school academic performances for, respectively, dropouts and poor performers.
To consider steps that might improve quality of student performances and reduce dropout rates.

FROM *Developmental Psychology,* I (1969), pp. 134–146. Copyright 1969 by the American Psychological Association. Reprinted by permission of the authors and the publisher.
[1] This study was conducted as part of a contract between Abt Associates, Inc. and the United States Office of Education (OEC–1–6–001681–1681). The United States Office of Education provides, under Title One of the Elementary and Secondary Education Act of 1965, "financial assistance to local educational agencies for the education of children of low-income families." But the United States Office of Education does not have unlimited funds for all programs which might improve the quality of this type of education and so needed a measure of the relative cost-effectiveness of alternate Title One programs placed in specific communities. The authors wish to express their sincere appreciation to Clark C. Abt for his many thoughtful suggestions.

THE PROBLEMS posed to contemporary American society by both high school dropouts and "low quality" high school graduates have been a subject of major national concern. Books,[2] magazines and journals, mass media coverage, and recent congressional action,[3] all indicate growing public awareness and determination to cope effectively with the dropout phenomenon. Cervantes[4] estimates the dropout rate among United States high school students to be between 30% and 40%. This estimate, if correct, means that more than 7½ million students will fail to complete high school in the 1960s, a figure which is both actually and proportionately greater than in the depression years of the 1930s. It does not even consider the problem of students whose performance records are poor but who still manage to graduate. It is also known that the greatest dropout rate exists among minority groups which can least afford to be educationally deprived.

These dropout statistics are important because of the social and personal problems associated with being a dropout in our society. It is known that crime, drug addiction, high unemployment, illegitimacy, welfare dependency, and alienation from the community exist in a disproportionate segment of this population. Lack of self-esteem and failure to participate in the social and political development of the community are further corollaries. When the direct cost of these problems to the public (police, health, welfare, etc.) is combined with cost-savings opportunities lost through failure to realize human potential (economic, social, and personal), the impact on society is enormous. While it cannot be argued that dropouts and poor performance *cause* these future problems, failure to complete high school successfully inevitably interacts with the critical factors which caused the dropout in the first place. Thus, it seems reasonable to assume that reversal of this trend could have many desirable consequences.

It has long been recognized that one characteristic of the high school dropout is a history of poor performance, probably beginning early in elementary school. While common sense suggests that there would be numerous published studies of individual student differences over the years, such has not been the case. In part, this may be due to the diversity of student populations in this country, and to different school policies, community characteristics, and different course curricula. It is also possible that a number of studies have been conducted which did not yield significant results and as a consequence were not published. To date, the best analysis of longitudinal research known to the authors has been developed by Bloom.[5]

This study[6] sought to determine the nature of the dropout's scholastic

[2] J. S. Cervantes, *The Dropout* (Ann Arbor: University of Michigan Press, 1965); D. Schreiber, *The School Dropout* (Washington, D. C.: National Education Association, 1963–64).

[3] The Elementary and Secondary Education Act of 1965.

[4] Cervantes, op. cit.

[5] B. Bloom, *Stability and Change in Human Characteristics* (New York: Wiley, 1965).

[6] Abt Associates, Inc. of Cambridge, Massachusetts, developed a computer planning model for estimating the relative cost-effectiveness of alternate Title One programs placed

behavior, as opposed to that of the poorly performing graduate, and to determine quantitatively the relationship of variables in *two* areas:

1. Did certain patterns exist with respect to poor performance in elementary and secondary school? A basic concern was the subject-grade interdependence. This question focused on the quality of education, regardless of whether a particular student graduated or failed to complete his education. The question also implied that certain patterns of early failure had "downstream" effects which could be analyzed and from which probability indexes could be derived. Such effects might have been subject specific, or have fallen into stages (e.g., seventh grade, ninth grade, etc.).

2. Were there certain patterns of performance which distinguished the dropout from his peers who, despite poor performance, managed to graduate? Here, it was recognized that while external conditions might be an important factor in dropping out of school, dropouts might also show different academic patterns corresponding to their ultimate failure to complete school. Cervantes [7] lists 20 characteristics which correspond to dropping out of school. These are broken down into areas of school, family, peer, and psychological test indexes. Cervantes notes that by the seventh grade, there is a depressed performance in math and reading (by 2 years); the majority of letter grades are poor; many have failed at least one grade in school; attendance is poor; students are frequently "underachievers"; there are frequent changes in school and many behavior problems. These were all acknowledged as being important, but the authors felt that it would be interesting to know more about both patterns of failure, and factors which distinguished the dropout from his peers who performed poorly but still managed to graduate.

Quantitative analysis of data on students regarding the above two question areas (covering their elementary and secondary school careers) provided the basis for initial predictions of the consequences of new educational programs.

Keeping in mind the above two considerations (patterns of poor performance and significant distinguishing factors which might identify dropouts)

---

in specific communities. It was assumed that different communities (possessing different socioeconomic characteristics), while frequently having similar problems or symptoms, were in need of different types of programs; since the causes of their problems were different, the solutions might be different. A computer model, serving as a planning aid, had to be able to integrate critical descriptors of a community, its school system, and the instructional process on the one hand, with various programs (e.g., remedial reading counseling, vocational training, new facilities) on the other. Such bringing together of data, if well programmed, would suggest probable outcomes, both qualitatively (better students, better community, etc.) and quantitatively (more graduates, more jobs, etc.). The present study made the necessary predictions about both the quality of graduates and the number of graduates (as opposed to dropouts). Actual records of student performance from which initial computer weightings could be determined were analyzed. Later experience with the consequences of specific Title One programs will provide refinement and validation of these weightings.

[7] Cervantes, op. cit.

the following questions were of primary importance, with respect to the onset of initial failures: (*a*) How early and in what subjects did initial failures occur among students who did poorly later in their academic careers? (*b*) What were the dominant patterns of failure in terms of grade of onset and by subject of origin? With respect to all failures: (*c*) What were the patterns of failure among graduates and dropouts by year? (*d*) What were the patterns of failure among graduates and dropouts by subject? (*e*) What were the patterns of failure among graduates and dropouts by subject and year? (*f*) In what grade did most dropouts occur? With respect to subject-grade failure interdependencies: (*g*) What were the interrelationships between early performance and midpoint performance? (*h*) What were the interrelationships between single- and multiple-course failures at the seventh-grade level and later graduation? What were the educational policy implications of the above findings?

METHOD

The data collected for this study were obtained in a suburban New England community of approximately 90,000 people. The median family income was $9,000. Students who were in attendance in the public school system came predominately from middle- to upper-middle-class homes, with a limited segment (perhaps 5 per cent) coming from relatively disadvantaged families (as defined by ethnicity, family education level, and income). Elementary schools served the first six grades; junior high schools served the seventh through the ninth grades; and the high school, the tenth through twelfth grades. The majority of students attending the public high schools went on to further education.

Data were collected on a total of 270 students, drawn from a parent population of approximately 2,500 students in attendance in the high school who graduated (or were scheduled to graduate) during the years 1966, 1965, 1964, and in a few cases, 1963. All students in this sample had attended high school at least long enough to have a record (entered upon the student's initiation of study at the school). The basic criterion of inclusion in the sample was serious performance difficulty during high school attendance or dropping out of school. *Poor performance* was defined as earning at least three Ds or Fs during high school career. Where students had only one or two failures, the grades were considered as "incidental" failures and were not included. Furthermore, data were gathered for only those students with histories which could be traced back through early elementary school. The 270 subjects in the sample included all students who classified as poor performers and for whom records were available back through early elementary school.

A common problem in analyzing data of this type is the "self-selective" nature of the sample; that is, the very students of greatest interest to the study are those most likely to have incomplete or sketchy records, due to moving around from one school to another, dropping back a grade, dropping out of school, etc. In contrast, students who may serve as comparison groups tend to be more stable in these respects. In essence the selection factor makes generalization somewhat more difficult. Certain shortcomings in the data were noted and served to place constraints on the generalizations drawn following analysis of data.

Limitations in generalization of results were imposed by the following considerations:

1. Students who performed poorly in early years of school, but who managed to improve their performance by high school, were not included in this study. Thus, there was no way to analyze the differences in performance patterns of students who remained as poor performers, in contrast to those who improved. Data collected in another survey by Abt Associates on achievement tests in Iowa suggest that students who initially perform poorly and then improve markedly in later years are in the minority.

2. Students who performed poorly in high school, but whose records had incomplete data for earlier years were not included. We have no reason to believe that they would have records "worse" than those included in the actual sample.

3. In some cases, students classified as "dropouts" may have completed their course work later and elsewhere without informing school officials. This is considered to be unlikely in most cases, however, since requests for records are necessary in cases of transfer and this is noted in the school records.

4. There is a tendency for high school students doing poorly to take less course work in the academic areas. Therefore, it was not assumed that the proportion of students failing English could be taken as comparable data to the proportion of students failing science (since the actual number of enrollees was different).

5. Finally, the data of elementary school records presented some problems. Many student records for elementary school had only limited data in the first through third grades (and in some cases, data were totally absent). In addition, grade-school teachers seemed to be less likely to differentiate performance abilities than were teachers in later grades. Grading was also done on a more objective basis in the later school years. Furthermore, while English and math had an "objective" scoring system for Grades 1 through 3, the same was not true of science and social studies. Because of these problems, considerable care has been taken in drawing conclusions about the exact nature of failure problems in the first and second grades.

Results

How early and in what subjects did initial failures occur among students who did poorly later in their academic careers? The uncorrected distribution of incidents of initial failure (a conservative measure) showed clearly that among high school students who did poorly the vast majority could have

Table 1 Point of Failure(s), by Subject and Year in School for 270 Poorly Performing High School Students

Subject	1 S	1 M^a	2 S	2 M	3 S	3 M	4 S	4 M	5 S	5 M	6 S	6 M	7 S	7 M	8 S	8 M	9 S	9 M	10 S	10 M	11 S	11 M
English																						
Reading	7	10	7	42	5	22	2	17	1	5		3	3	6			1	2	1	5		
Oral/written	3	7	5	22	2	26	2	19		4	1	1	3				1			3		
Spelling		5	4	34	3	20	4	15	1	4		3	1	2	2	4	2	4	2	4		
Mathematics	2	8	6	26	3	11	7	15	1	4	1	4	2	9		5		1		2		
Science		3	1	2		6		6		2	1	5	1	5	1	4	1	1				
Social studies	1			2		10		11	3	2	1	4	2	6	2	5	1	1		4		1
Miscellaneous													3		1	1		1				1
Total single: 98	13		23		13		15		6		4		12		6		5		1			
Cumulative percentage	13%		36%		50%		65%		71%		75%		88%		94%		99%		100%			
Total multiple: 457	33		28		95		83		21		20		28		19		10		18		2	
Cumulative percentage^b	6%		35%		56%		74%		78%		83%		89%		94%		95%		99%		100%	
Cumulative failures M & S	33%		53%		61%		75%															
Corrected for data 1–4^c	33%		53%		61%		75%															

Note: Column groups 1–11 represent *Year in School*.

a S = single initial failure; M = multiple initial failures

b It is assumed that the number of initial multiple failures, by student, is roughly comparable across the years. Thus, the cumulative percentages represent the incidents of failures rather than the percentage of subjects.

c See text discussion of "adjusted" failure incidence.

been identified early in their academic careers (see Table 1). Of these students, 3 out of 4 had already demonstrated poor performance in the fourth grade, and by the seventh grade, 9 out of 10 had performed poorly. The data indicate that by the time students passed through junior high school, 97 out of 100 students who received low marks had a previous record of failure. Clearly, then, among the high school students who did poorly, the vast majority could have been identified early in their academic careers (in elementary or junior high school).

The limitation of data from the first and second grades means that if anything, these estimates are conservative. In order to correct this distortion, the sample population was divided into subsamples by incidence of first year of data from Grades 1 through 5. For each subsample, the "adjusted" first failure data were assumed to begin the year after the data actually started. From the adjusted data cells, mean first failure occurrences and their standard deviation were determined. These figures were used to establish a probable range of first failure occurrences for the students for whom data were not available. In Grades 1 and 2 the number of occurrences was approximated using the Grade 1 to Grade 2 proportion from the more limited sample for which there were data. Not surprisingly, the adjustment did *not* change the cumulative percentage for the first four grades; that is, a total of 75% of the sample showed initial failures by the end of their fourth year. However, the adjustment did indicate that Grades 3 and 4 were too heavily biased in the unadjusted data to give the true year-by-year picture. The adjusted data (see Table 1) indicate that in fact slightly over 50% of the total initial failures had appeared by the end of the second grade (while the unadjusted data indicate that this point was not attained until midway through the third grade). This adjustment strengthens the case that performance difficulties appear quite early in the school career.

It is important to note the subject areas which provided the greatest difficulties. The critical performance difficulties fell in the English areas (reading, oral and written usage, and spelling, in that order) and in mathematics. These findings were somewhat biased, for teachers did not give letter grades to the sciences and social studies until the fourth grade. However, these latter two subjects failed to show up as important areas of initial failure at any point (even beyond the third grade, where objective grade scoring was available). Although these subjects were not the source of initial difficulty, this should not be confused with an absence of failures in these subjects. Many students did poorly in social studies and sciences, but they were not their areas of initial failure. This distinction will be discussed later in the paper in sections dealing with downstream effects of early failures.

The raw data were analyzed to determine if the percentage of onset failures differed for graduates and dropouts. The data revealed a clear but limited difference between these two groups. In 21 out of 24 cells representing the first four grades for six subject areas graduates exceeded dropouts in the proportion of initial failures recorded. Dropouts as a group tended to begin failing subjects somewhat later in their academic careers than did poorly performing graduates. (It should be remembered that "graduate" refers to students who completed school with very poor performance records, not to the entire student body.) This finding is important and will be dealt with further in the discussion of results.

What were the dominant patterns of failure in terms of grade of onset, and by subject of origin? It is reasonable to assume that not all children "fail" in the same manner. Some start to fail early in their careers, others do not fail until later on. Some begin having difficulty only in one subject, and still others in a number of areas simultaneously. Furthermore, some begin with many failures and improve themselves. Because of such individual differences, it was hypothesized that over a large sample of subjects, various "patterns" of failure would emerge. These included spread patterns—early poor performance in one or two areas, which later expanded to include other subjects (i.e., the long shadow of achievement gaps); parallel patterns—a pattern of failure which began in three or more areas and continued in those areas; hourglass patterns—early failure in three or more areas followed by improvement and then return to failures in many areas; late failing patterns —onset of failure which did not occur until the sixth grade; and random patterns—no apparent pattern.

No "converging" pattern of reduced failures is included here because such students, by virtue of the selection procedure, were excluded from the sample.

Data separated into these five categories (which contrasted dropouts to graduates) are shown in Table 2.

Table 2 *Analysis of Poor Performance According to Pattern of Failure*

Pattern	Total		Dropouts		Graduates	
	NO.	PERCENTAGE	NO.	PERCENTAGE	NO.	PERCENTAGE
Spread	108	40	29	40	79	40
Parallel	48	18	10	14	38	19
Hourglass	20	7	5	7	15	8
Late failing	57	21	18	25	39	20
Random or incomplete	37	13	10	14	27	14

Note.—$N = 270$.

Of the 270 records analyzed, 108 were found to have a spread pattern of poor performance. Collectively, this represented 40% of the total sample, the largest single grouping. This spread pattern was thought to be particularly significant, since even limited failures can be used as "early warning signs." [8]

With this in mind, the data were then examined to determine the areas which most typically were the origin points of the spread pattern. Analysis of the origins of both single and double area spread patterns revealed that

---

[8] There may be a number of children who do poorly in one or two areas, but then pull themselves up (these would be absent from this sample).

English, and particularly, reading, was the most frequent origin of failures. This was consistent with the data regarding the onset of failure for all students. Beyond English, only mathematics showed any sign of being an important indicator of future spread, and this was usually when in combination with English. The data demonstrated that by the third grade, two-thirds of the students who would have developed spread patterns in future years had their first failure, and these had their origins in English.[9]

Examination of the distribution of initial failures among dropouts as opposed to poorly performing graduates revealed no interesting differences.

What were the patterns of failure among graduates and dropouts by year? The total number of failures, when corrected for intermittent data in the first 2 years, and for the dropout occurrences in the last 3 years, did not suggest any significant "high points of failure," as for example, junior high school or high school. The occurrence of failure started early, rose rapidly, and then increased slowly over the years (the increase for dropouts being more pronounced than that of the graduates). However, there seemed to be a greater proportion of poor performance among dropouts in the ninth and tenth grades, suggesting that as students came closer to dropping out of school, they dropped further in their performance. (See Table 3.)

Table 3   Distribution of Failures by Year for Graduates and Dropouts

	Percentage of Poor Performance				
Grade	GRADUATES		DROPOUTS		TOTAL
1	.7	2.8[a]	.1	4.5	.8
2	3.6	5.7	3.3	5.5	3.5
3	6.2	7.5	5.7	6.4	6.0
4	9.2		9.7		9.3
5	10.2		10.7		9.8
6	7.4		9.7		10.1
7	9.3		10.2		8.2
8	9.3		11.1		9.8
9	12.4		13.7		12.8
10	10.5		13.4		11.3
11	11.8		8.2		10.8
12	9.3		3.2		7.6
Total	99.9		99.0		100%

Note.—$N = 270$.

[a] Approximations based on a full sample size population hypothesized for the first three grades.

[9] Specifically, English accounted for almost 70% of the single origin spreads (with math making up the remainder), and regarding double area initial failures, English was involved in every case. Reading in combination with other subjects was the most significant origin point of spread.

A comparison of dropouts to graduates suggested that year by year, the graduates did relatively better than the dropouts, and that dropouts, starting at about the fourth grade, did progressively worse each year.

What were the patterns of failure among graduates and dropouts by subject? Analysis of the data showed that English was by far the most significant area with almost 30% of the total failures. Mathematics and social studies each accounted for 18% of the failures. Languages (15%) and science (13%) made up the other important areas. Significantly, shop and business, even though started in the seventh grade (rather than in the first), still did not show many failures in this sample. Thus, despite the fact that many of these students were not "college bound," the academic areas still dominated their failure areas. The problem areas of dropouts and graduates were similar. The general finding was that pupils with poor performance records had the greatest difficulty with English, and that they seemed to fail other academic subjects somewhat uniformly.

While the distribution of failures for graduates and dropouts across subjects was similar, dropouts tended to perform more poorly than graduates in each subject. This was particularly true later in their academic career, starting clearly after the sixth grade.

What were the patterns of failure among graduates and dropouts by subject and year? Figure 1 presents a year-by-year analysis of the performance patterns for graduates and dropouts, for English, mathematics, science, and social studies. For Grades 1 through 3, the graduates received a higher percentage of low marks than the dropouts in both English and mathematics; in science and social studies the pattern was very similar. In Grades 4 through 6, the percentages diverged, with the dropouts having a greater number of failures in every subject. This difference was lost at the sixth grade, and it was at this point that the graduates tended to level off somewhat, while the dropouts began to increase progressively in their number of failures. In every subject (except math, 10–12) from Grades 7 through 12, the graduates had a substantially lower percentage of poor marks over the last 5 years. It is clear that the differences, while not large, consistently favored the graduates in terms of better performance.

Two more specific analyses of these data were possible. First, were there differences among the various subgroupings of courses for the first 3 years? Second, were there differences in the F to D mark ratios of the two groups for the last 7 years? With respect to the first three grades, no significant differences were found between graduates as compared and dropouts in English (spelling, reading, or oral and written usage) and in the various combinations of English, math, social studies, and science. Second, analysis of the ratio of Ds and Fs for dropouts versus graduates indicated that there was no noticeable difference in patterns. Both patterns showed a gradually increasing percentage of Fs, with the dropouts having a greater slope. However, in terms of the actual ratio of Ds and Fs, dropouts did have a larger percentage of Fs than graduates.

In what grade did dropouts leave school? Of the 270 students in the

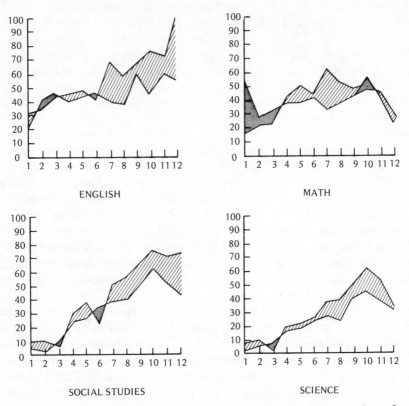

Figure 1. Percentage failing by subject by year for dropouts and graduates. (Percentage dropouts > percentage graduates ▨ ; > percentage dropouts ▧)

sample, 72 dropped out for various reasons. The majority of dropouts (56%) were boys. A general overview of the dropout rate in this sample indicated a fairly even attrition rate (see Table 4)—29% in the tenth grade, 36% in the eleventh grade, and 31% in the twelfth grade. (The 4% dropout figure in the ninth grade was disregarded here because few ninth grade students were old enough to drop out in accordance with State law.) However, such an overview hid some interesting distinctions between boys and girls in their dropout pattern. Boys tended to drop out at a fairly even rate from tenth grade through the twelfth grade. In contrast, the girls' dropout rate was much more varied during the four periods, with a high of 20% leaving during the twelfth-grade school year.

The reasons given for dropping out in some of the records may help explain this. Boys were most likely to drop out because of an alleged lack of interest in school and a desire to work. Girls, by contrast, frequently left for sudden personal reasons such as marriage, pregnancy, or illness, which occurred during the school year.

Table 4 Density of Dropouts Among Boys and
Girls for Grades 9–12

Grade	Boys [a]	Girls [b]
9 (Summer)	2	1
10 (School year)	4	4
10 (Summer)	8	5
11 (School year)	9	6
11 (Summer)	9	2
12 (School year)	8	14

[a] $N = 40$.
[b] $N = 32$.

What were the interrelationships between early performance and midpoint performance? It seemed reasonable to assume that if a child performed poorly early in his academic career, his failures there might have contributed to later difficulties in subjects requiring similar skills. For example, poor reading ability which was first recorded in elementary school English might have later contributed to failure in social studies where reading was also required. It seemed useful, however, to study first the relationships between early failure and midpoint failure (rather than failures as late as the twelfth grade), for there might be important relationships which were lost in the longer range comparisons. In addition, data from the junior high school level were more uniform since all students were required to take English, mathematics, science, and social studies. The chi-square (χ^2) test for two independent samples [10] provided an appropriate technique to examine this hypothesis. A variety of early and midpoint performance patterns were compared in this manner.

It already was evident that the areas of greatest interest for early year failures included English and math. Later failures in all areas were worth exploring. The following chi-square values were obtained.

Early performance in reading showed a significant relationship to later performance in English, social studies, and science; similarly, early performance in mathematics related significantly to later performance in ninth-grade English. Analysis of the actual distributions of these individual groups was necessary to interpret the reasons for this significance. Visual inspection of the data suggested that failure to pass reading in the fourth grade corresponded significantly to future failure in both social studies and English; however, passing reading in the fourth grade was no guarantee of later passing of courses. In short, poor reading might provide a real barrier to social studies proficiency, but the presence of early reading ability did not forecast later social studies success.

[10] S. Siegel, *Non-parametric Statistics* (New York: McGraw-Hill, 1956), p. 107.

Table 5 *Chi-Square Values for Early to Midpoint Performance*

Early Performance	Midpoint Performance	x^2	$r \phi$
Reading	English	17.34 **	.283
Reading	Social studies	8.14 **	.175
Reading	Science	5.34 *	.142
Reading	Mathematics	1.04	
Oral/Written	Social studies	2.37	
Oral/Written	Science	2.86	
Oral/Written	Mathematics	3.38	
Mathematics	Social studies	.95	
Mathematics	Science	2.67	
Mathematics	English	13.00 **	.226

* $p < .05$.
** $p < .01$.

Turning to the question of the relationship between fourth-grade reading and later performance in science, inspection of the distribution suggested that failure to pass English corresponded to later failure in science, but again passing English was not a guarantee of later passing science courses. Interestingly enough, failure to pass reading did not seem to assure failure in science, as much as passing English related to passing science. Thus, relative to science, there was a premium on passing reading, but less concern about failing it.

Finally, early mathematics performance showed a highly significant relationship with later English performance. Very few students (27 versus 85) failed early mathematics and later passed English. However, passing mathematics, again, was no assurance of passing English. This finding was examined in light of the correspondence of early reading to later English. A chi-square value of 17.34 (significant at the .01 level) suggested that the correspondence of early mathematics to later English might be more a function of grading procedures at the fourth-grade level than of subject-grade interdependency.

What were the interrelationships between midpoint single and multiple failures at the seventh-grade level and graduation? The second stage of analysis was concerned with how midpoint failures were related to graduation versus dropout among poorly performing students (see Table 6). The seventh grade was chosen for two reasons. First, it was at this point that nongraduates seemed to demonstrate increasing difficulty with their studies. Second, it might still be possible to do something to avert future dropout if the problem area could be identified and dealt with. Chi-square values were determined in the following areas as they corresponded to dropout versus graduation.

Table 6   Chi-Square Values for the Performance of Dropouts Versus Graduates on a Series of Single and Multiple Seventh Grade Performance Measures

Early Performance of Dropouts Versus Graduates	x^2	$r\ \phi$
English	4.31 *	.126
Mathematics	16.06 **	.244
Social studies	2.48	
Science	3.00	
English/Social studies	11.12 **	.208
English/Mathematics	6.83 **	.161
English/Science	6.90 **	.163
English/Social studies/ Mathematics	10.70	.202

* $p < .05$.
** $p < .01$.

Table 6 shows that performance in the seventh grade on a variety of measures bore a significant relationship to later graduation (or dropout). Inspection of the individual courses of English, mathematics, and social studies revealed that failure in seventh-grade mathematics corresponded most significantly to dropout at a later point in time. A significant number of dropouts failed this subject (62%), as contrasted with poorly performing students, 34% of whom failed the course but still managed to graduate. The same was true of English, but the tendency was not so pronounced. Social studies and science performance, however, failed to yield significant relationship with graduation.

Inspection of the relationship between multiple failures in the seventh grade with consequent graduation, not surprisingly, showed a highly significant pattern (all beyond the .01 level). However, inspection of the data indicated that this increased significance resulted in large part from the behavior of the graduates rather than that of dropouts; that is, a large number of graduates failed to do poorly in two or three courses simultaneously. About 50% of the dropouts did poorly in paired courses; that is, almost as many dropouts did well as did poorly and yet still dropped out. Thus, the multiple predictions must then be viewed with some skepticism. The source of significance was the disproportionate number of graduates who passed at least one of the subjects rather than a large number of dropouts who failed in two or three subjects.

Discussion

The majority of students who did poorly in their high school careers could have been identified early in elementary school. By the second grade, 50% had already experienced their first failure, 75% by the fourth grade, and 90% by the seventh grade. The critical areas of initial difficulty were English and mathematics.

Over 40% of the student records reflected a spread pattern (initially failing in only one or two areas) indicating that many children gave early warning signs of future academic problems in many areas. Not surprisingly, the majority of spreads began with English courses.

The distribution of failures over the years was fairly consistent. Beginning with an initial increase in failures in the first 3 years, the subject failures then showed a more gradual rise over the years, reaching a high point in the ninth and tenth grades. A comparison of dropouts with low achieving graduates tended to do somewhat better than dropouts; and that the dropouts tended to fall further and further behind after the seventh grade. Over the years, English was the most frequently failed subject, with mathematics and social studies being the next most difficult areas. However, the finding that the onset of initial failures among dropouts was later than for poorly performing graduates suggested that factors other than low ability contributed to actual dropping out of school. While the pattern of performance for graduates and dropouts across the subjects and across the years was similar, dropouts generally performed at a lower level.

Concerning the grade-subject interdependencies, it was found that the reading performance in the fourth grade corresponded to performance in ninth-grade English, social studies, and science; also, fourth-grade mathematics proved to correspond to ninth-grade English. With respect to the relationship between seventh-grade subject performance and ultimate graduation, English and mathematics separately, as well as when combined with social studies and science, showed significant correspondence to subsequent graduation or dropout.

These findings confirm some rather commonly held beliefs among educators. First, students having trouble in their high school academic performance usually have had a history of performance problems. This problem frequently goes back to early elementary school. Furthermore, this study indicated that while early failures may appear in only one or two areas (e.g., English or math subjects), many students (40% of this sample) show a downstream spread of effects (e.g., to social studies and sciences). Where many early failures existed, multiple failures tended to be continued. Most initial failures occurred in English or math, but this may be in part an artifact of the grading system since social studies and science were not objectively scored for the first 3 years. However, even when objectively scored, these subjects were only infrequently the source of initial failure.

English language development appears to be a focal point of academic failures throughout the scholastic career. For many years there has been a stress on the importance of verbal and reading-writing fluency. The findings of this study support the validity of the assumption that early general communication skills are vital to consequent success in other academic areas such as social studies and sciences.

While early performance is an excellent indicator of academic difficulty it is not as good an indicator of a student's dropout potential. The findings of this study indicate that poorly performing graduates produce a majority of early failing grades, which is consistent with the belief that dropouts do not come primarily from any "lower ability group." Many of the dropouts performed better than the poorly performing graduates in early years. Over 25% had no failures prior to the sixth grade. However, it should be remembered that dropouts are contrasted here to poorly performing graduates, not to the entire graduating class. Lack of ability alone cannot account for dropping out of school. Early assistance to poorly performing students may not, in this case, help students who will be dropping out of school, but it may increase the later performance of nondropouts who are already doing poorly. It should be remembered, however, that by the seventh grade most students who will have difficulty in high school (dropouts included) will already have difficulty, and at this point academic assistance (plus other types) can be applied.

Given these considerations, the following points seem applicable to educational planning:

1. Where students are found to be having difficulty with school during the first four grades, special remedial programs should be initiated to help improve the quality of their achievement.

2. Particular attention should be paid to the areas of English and math failures, not only to improve later performance in these areas, but to prevent a spread of performance difficulty to other areas.

3. Since in many cases dropouts fail to show performance difficulty in the first 2 or 3 years, such programs should be primarily directed toward improving quality of students' performance rather than toward increasing the quantity of graduates.

4. Where students show a reasonable performance pattern for the first few years, and then begin a sharp decline in performance, this should be taken as a warning sign of potential dropout. Assistance directed toward students at the seventh-grade level should be concerned not only with quality improvement, but also with increasing the number of graduates. Three types of assistance may be called for: academic assistance, in-school counseling assistance, and possible home visitation assistance (perhaps directed toward helping parents to provide better home atmosphere for study, and reinforcement of the child's improved performance where such occurs).

This study does not imply that preschool experiences [11] and experiences

[11] Bloom, op. cit.

during the school years which occur outside the school setting [12] are not vitally important in their influence on both the quality of graduates and the incidence of dropout. In many cases, changes in nonschool factors are decisive in changing the educational development of a given student.

There are three approaches to dealing with improvement of student performance and completion of schooling: education programs (e.g., Title I programs from the Elementary and Secondary Education Act), home and neighborhood improvement programs (e.g., various Office of Economic Opportunity programs), and selected combinations of the two. Application of educational programs alone implies that a problem is basically one of altering conditions in the school environment (through remedial instruction, better equipment, special counseling, etc.); that if one can alter certain characteristics of a student which affect his performance academically, he will improve and/or graduate.

Application of home and neighborhood programs alone to a problem (with associated school implications) implies that the problem is basically one of altering conditions in the home and peer environment external to the school (on both a preschool and during school basis), and that this will make it possible for the student to respond better to an already adequate education program.

Applying both educational and environmental programs in combination implies that effective change in student performance, and/or decreasing dropout rates, involves change in both the school and nonschool environment.

Determination of where either or both types of assistance is required is very difficult. It requires identification of the major contributing factors to poor student performance. In addition, the relative importance of both areas needs to be weighted and their interaction assessed. Will "curing" of one area be sufficient to override the negative impact of the other area? Conversely, is the interaction of both educational and environmental programs required to overcome performance problems and the likelihood of dropout for a given student?

Experience of Head Start Officials has shown that all of the effort to improve the preschool learning environment of the student may be futile unless there is follow-up in the schools (e.g., project "Follow Through").[13] Environmental improvement alone may be insufficient to improve student performance where the school fails to provide minimum necessary educational support. Conversely, administrators in the school who provide remedial instruction (and do a good job of this) may be totally frustrated when the nonschool environment negates their efforts (as in settings where there is severe malnutrition or where highly negative attitudes are held by parents and peer groups outside the school).

All this points to the conclusion that joint educational and environmental aid offer the greatest potential to improve student quality and decrease the

---

[12] Cervantes, op. cit.

[13] Indeed, even the Head Start Program may be unable to overcome certain prenatal and infancy deprivation experiences.

dropout rates. Unfortunately, both limited congressional funding and lack of clear understanding on the part of educators of the interaction between school and nonschool factors make it unlikely that many disadvantaged area schools will have the luxury of coordinated aid to cope with both school and nonschool problems.

Assume that in many instances the only aid which will be received by many local school districts will be educational assistance; that while it would be highly desirable to have environmental programs which would counteract negative home and neighborhood influences, such aid is unavailable. What should the educational program direction then be?

The findings of this study have suggested that aid early in the academic career has more impact than later aid. This is because it seems that many students who initially perform poorly only in one or two areas, may show a spread of failures in later years (thus compounding the problem). This is also consistent with the longitudinal research which suggests that the further along in a student's career, the greater is the amount of "end-career" variance already accounted for.

The findings of recent research by Coleman [14] and Urdal [15] both point to the importance of attitudes toward school. While home and peer groups (both preschool and during school) undoubtedly have great influence on attitudes, it seems reasonable that the experiences in the school setting contribute in their own right to attitudes regarding school. What happens when the student encounters dissonant attitudes and behaviors? Suppose that his experiences in school contradict what his family emulates and his friends say? Certainly this is better than when both school and nonschool experiences coincide in the negative!

It is hypothesized that assistance to students provided by educational programs should be both content and process oriented, and explicitly so. By process is meant the extent to which the teacher focuses on the student's feelings while the student is learning (Does a teacher reinforce improved performance? Is there peer group support for "doing better"? Are students helped to see how progress in school relates to improving their own lives? Is there genuine concern for the student's personal development and does the student sense this concern?). It is true that all of the "process" in the world will not help a student to perform better if he cannot read. However, although learning to read is essential, it is not a guarantee of improved performance. Therefore, a substantial part of the educational program emphasis should focus on *how* particular processes are to be used by teachers and counselors, that is, *programs should be oriented toward changing attitudes* (through positive experiences) as well as abilities. If attitudes toward school are vital, then programs must do more than change knowledge; they must change attitudes toward school.

[14] J. S. Coleman, *Equality of Educational Opportunity* (Washington: U. S. Office of Health, Education, and Welfare, 1966).

[15] L. B. Urdal, *Dropouts. An Analysis of Personal Variables Within the School Situation* (Olympia, Washington: State Superintendent of Public Instruction, 1963).

Socialization:
Theory and Practice

Socialization begins when the infant first attempts to imitate parental behavior. Role-taking later replaces imitation, and the child may act quite differently from his parents. Childhood is marked by emotional dependency, which usually yields in adolescence to an emotional commitment to meet the role expectations of parents, peers, teachers, and employers. The difficult challenge faced by every adolescent in acquiring responsible role behavior has led many observers to characterize adolescence as a time of identity crises. G. S. Stanley Hall gathered data from both evolution and folklore to declare that adolescence is "suggestive of some ancient period of storm and stress where old moorings are broken and higher level attained." Adolescence as a period in the life-cycle, however, probably is less synonymous with identity crises than identity formation. An adolescent develops identity by asserting one's self as a distinct human being, and one's sense of competence and selfhood depends upon the ways in which one learns obligations and assimilates earlier experiences. Socialization can be a trying process; an adolescent faces a series of important decisions in choosing a school program, a vocation, friends, and a mate. Choices are difficult to reverse, but the adolescent's sense of self-worth will be strengthened if he or she succeeds in meeting each challenge constructively; it may be diminished if choices limit future options and opportunities.

The five papers presented in Part 4 provide perspective on the identification process and indicate how parents in particular may influence the course of socialization. The first selection describes an empirical investigation of the venerable storm-and-stress hypothesis. Simmons, Rosenberg, and Rosenberg employed quantitative measure of four aspects of self-image—self-consciousness, stability, self-esteem, and accuracy of perceived self—to assess whether changes in self-image are accompanied by developmental stress. These researchers studied youth from third through twelfth grades and found that, relative to younger children, early adolescents, between twelve and fourteen-years-of-age showed a "higher level of self-consciousness, greater instability of self-image, slightly lower global self-esteem, lower specific self-esteem, and a more negative "'perceived self.'" Their data revealed, too, that twelve-year-olds already matriculated into junior high school suffered diminished self-images in comparison with twelve-year-olds still in elementary school, an indication that the transition from elementary school into junior high school may be a significant correlate of self-image stress. A comparable disturbance in the self-image, however, fails to materialize in the move from junior to senior high school.

In the second paper, Lynn derives from the concept of identification several implications for sex-role learning. He focuses on the significance of parental models, discussing both rewards and negative admonishments as influences on personality development and sex-role identity. Lynn contends that boys acquire relatively stronger sex-role identity than girls because the masculine role is accorded greater prestige, that boys are ridiculed more for adopting opposite sex roles, and that girls become increasingly disturbed with their lot, preferring instead the requisites of the masculine role. His analyses suggest coherent, plausible hypotheses to account for the complexities of identification during childhood and adolescence.

Every major developmental theory views the father as critically important in the process of sex-role learning. Paternal separation has been shown to exert a significant influence on sons' personality development, but Hetherington's study, included here as the third selection, is one of the few investigations conducted to assess the effect of paternal separation on daughters' personality development. Hetherington's study included girls from three kinds of household—father intact, divorced, and widowed. Separation from the father before age five was more severe on both groups of father-absent girls than at later ages. Although sex-role learning was relatively characteristic for the girls, father absence affected the two groups differently in adolescence when the girls began to interact with males. The daughters of divorcees tended to engage in more "proximity-seeking" and "attention-seeking" and "various forms of nonverbal communication associated with openness and responsiveness." The daughters of the widows manifested more inhibition, rigidity, avoidance, and restraint around males. The differences in the daughters suggest ways that divorced and widowed mothers view themselves, their marriages, and their lifestyles. Hetherington's study also raises several unanswered questions about the effects of father absence on the personality development of adolescent daughters; nonetheless, her data show that, henceforth, investigations of the effects of paternal absence must take into account reasons for the separation, the daughter's age at the time of the separation, and the current age of the daughter.

Families exercise a great deal of control over the destiny of children and adolescents, and recent studies have shown that the distribution of "conjugal power" between the mother and father can exert lasting effects on socialization. Adolescents appear in general to be more strongly oriented toward their same-sex parents. Girls tend to perceive their mothers and boys their fathers as the principal decision-maker in the family. Bowerman and Bahr, in the fourth paper, report the results of a survey of more than 18,000 adolescents, divided by sex into four age groups, dealing with relationship among conjugal power and adolescent identification with parents. These researchers asked whether youth who perceived their mother as dominant would, as a consequence, identify with her more than with their father, although in actuality identifying less *with either parent than youth who viewed the father as dominant or their parents as equal in power. They found, as had earlier investigations, that strongest identification occurs with the same-sex parent; however, "adolescents who perceived conjugal relations as equalitarian are highest in identification with parents while those who perceived the mother as dominant are lowest." Bowerman and Bahr's data are suggestive, too, of relationships between conjugal power and, respectively, marital happiness and parental personality characteristics. Their findings augment our understanding of the mechanisms of identification, and one may anticipate future investigators to elaborate on the provocative interpretations which they offer.*

To whom will youth defer when a choice must be made between either parents or peers as a source of reference? The news media proclaims that adolescents usually opt in favor of their peers. The image of a peer-dominant value structure, however, has yet to be substantiated. One of the earliest investigations in this area of adolescence suggested that adolescents tend to follow parental wishes in future-oriented situations and peer wishes in contemporary situations. In the final paper of Part 4, Larson indicates that most adolescents make parent-compliant choices whether the type of situation is future- or now-oriented. Moreover, those youth who are peer-oriented tend to make peer-compliant choices, whatever their orientation. A sizeable proportion of the youth described in Larson's investigation already had identified with future roles, i.e., to enter the university preparation program, and would permit neither parental nor peer pressure to deter them from their course of action. Role expectations derived from early socializing experiences obviously influence whether youth will select parents, peers, or others as sources of reference, and Larson calls for additional research to clarify these issues.

Roberta G. Simmons
Florence Rosenberg
Morris Rosenberg

Disturbance in the Self-Image at Adolescence

Adolescents, between twelve and fourteen, relative to younger children, are shown in the following paper to exhibit "heightened self-consciousness, greater instability of the self-image, slightly lower self-esteem, and a less favorable view of the opinions held of them by significant others." Simmons, Rosenberg, and Rosenberg reveal that disturbances in self-image are fairly common at adolescence, and that environmental factors may have a strong effect in producing them. Youth who enter junior high school appear to undergo more self-image stress than youth of the same age still in elementary school.

Instructional Objectives
To review explanations of developmental changes in self-image.
To illustrate four major dimensions of self-image.
To indicate changes that occur in self-image from childhood to adolescence.
To suggest the significance to self-image stress of matriculating from elementary to junior high school.

A MONG the most widely accepted ideas in the behavioral sciences is the theory that adolescence is a period of disturbance for the child's self-image. Hall [1] originally characterized the age as one of "storm and stress." Erikson [2] views it as a time of identity-crisis, in which the child struggles for a stable sense of self. Psychoanalytic theory postulates that the burgeoning sexual desires of puberty spark a resurgence of oedipal conflicts for the boy and pre-oedipal pressures for the girl.[3] To establish mature cross-sexual relationships in adulthood, the child must resolve these conflicts during

FROM *American Sociological Review*, XXXVIII (1973), pp. 553–568. Abridged. Reprinted by permission of the authors and the publisher.

[1] G. S. Hall, *Adolescence: Its Psychology and Its Relations to Physiology, Anthropology, Sociology, Sex, Crime, Religion, and Education* (New York: D. Appleton & Co., 1904).
[2] E. H. Erikson, "Identity and the Life Cycle," *Psychological Issues*, I (1959), 1–171.
[3] P. Blos, *On Adolescence: A Psychoanalytic Interpretation* (New York: Free Press, 1962); A. Freud, "Adolescence," *Psychoanalytic Study of the Child*, XIII (1958), 255–278.

adolescence. In the interim, the physiological changes of puberty and the increase in sexual desire challenge the child's view of himself in fundamental ways. Both his body-image and his self-image radically change.

Sociologists [4] traditionally characterize adolescence as a period of physical maturity and social immaturity.[5] Because of the complexity of the present social system, the child reaches physical adulthood before he is capable of functioning well in adult social roles. Adolescence becomes extremely difficult because the new physical capabilities and new social pressures to become independent coincide with many impediments to actual independence, power, and sexual freedom.

The resulting status-ambiguities, that is, the unclear social definitions and expectations, have been seen as engendering a corresponding ambiguity of self-definition. In addition, the need to make major decisions about future adult roles on the basis of what he is like at present further heightens the adolescent's self-awareness and self-uncertainty.[6]

From society's viewpoint, these external and internal pressures to plan for a future career, to become more independent, and to establish relationships with the opposite sex, all direct the individual away from his family of origin toward the creation of a new family. In the course of adolescence he changes from a dependent being whose prime emotional attachments are to his family of origin into a person capable of embarking on an independent existence, ready to establish his most important emotional allegiances outside of his present family. With all these physical, emotional and social changes, it is small wonder that social theorists assume that this period is difficult for the child's self-image.

Yet Offer,[7] on the basis of his longitudinal study of adolescent boys from ages fourteen to eighteen, suggests that for most boys these years are not characterized by stress or turmoil. Other investigators [8] also question the assumption of adolescent crisis. These studies, however, often do not deal with early adolescence; nor do they systematically measure differences in the self-image over age.

[4] K. Davis, "Adolescence and the Social Structure," *Annals of the American Academy of Political and Social Science*, CCXXXVI (1944), 8–16.

[5] For discussions of adolescence as a social phenomenon, see D. Bakan, "Adolescence in America: From Idea to Social Fact," *Daedalus*, C (Fall), 979–995; C. Gordon, "Social Characteristics of Early Adolescence," *Daedalus*, C (Fall), 931–960; L. Kohlberg and C. Gilligan, "The Adolescent as a Philosopher: The Discovery of the Self in a Postconventional World," *Daedalus*, C (Fall), 1051–1086.

[6] Erikson, op. cit.

[7] D. Offer, *The Psychological World of the Teen-ager* (New York: Basic Books Inc., 1969).

[8] R. R. Grinker, Sr., R. R. Grinker, Jr. and J. Timberlake, "A Study of 'Mentally Healthy' Young Males (Homoclites)," *American Medical Association Archives of General Psychiatry*, VI (1962), 405–453; F. Elkin and W. A. Westley, "The Myth of Adolescent Culture," *American Sociological Review*, XXIII (1955), 680–683; E. Douvan and J. Adelson, *The Adolescent Experience* (New York: John Wiley and Sons, 1966); I. B. Weiner, *Psychological Disturbance in Adolescence* (New York: John Wiley and Sons, 1970).

Aside from psychiatric case-histories, in fact, there is little evidence to refute or support the argument that the child's self-image changes from childhood to adolescence.[9] Since most work on adolescent disturbance has been clinical in nature, several fundamental questions on the self-image remain to be answered. First, do data support the belief that the adolescent's self-image differs from that of younger children? If so, could one term this difference a "disturbance," that is, a change which would cause the child some discomfort or unhappiness? In this paper we use the word "disturbance" as a milder term than "turmoil," "storm or stress," or "crisis," so that we can encompass less severe changes. It is not meant to imply psychopathology.

Second, if there is an adolescent self-image disturbance, when does it begin? This question is crucial to the evaluation of certain theoretical notions. Erikson[10] tells us that the adolescent must deal with the issues of a career decision and the establishment of his own family. While these concerns may be salient to the eighteen or nineteen year old, they do not concern the twelve year old. Conversely, it is the younger adolescent who is confronted with the body-image changes of puberty. This study tries to specify the onset of adolescent self-image disturbance.

Third, if there is an adolescent self-image disturbance, what is the course of its development? Do the problems appearing at the time it is precipitated continue to grow? Do they level off at a higher plane? Or do they decline as the adolescent learns to cope with them?

Finally, if it does exist, what triggers the adolescent disturbance? Typically, the onset of puberty is viewed as the trigger. But perhaps aspects of the social environment are at work.

Self-Image Dimensions

In this paper we adopt Gardner Murphy's[11] view of the self as "the individual as known to the individual." So conceived, the self-image can be viewed as an attitude toward an object; and like all attitudes, it has several dimensions.[12] We shall deal with four of these. In each case, there is reason to think that changes in these dimensions would be disturbing or uncomfortable for the individual.

The first dimension is self-consciousness; it refers to the salience of the self to the individual. As Mead[13] posited, in an interaction the ordinary individual must take account of others' reactions to himself and his behavior.

---

[9] M. Engel, "The Stability of the Self-Concept in Adolescence," *Journal of Abnormal and Social Psychology,* LVIII (1959), 211–215; E. V. Piers and D. B. Harris, "Age and Other Correlates of Self-Concept in Children," *Journal of Educational Psychology,* LV (No. 2) (1964), 91–95; E. C. Jorgenson and R. J. Howell, "Changes in Self, Ideal-Self Correlations from Ages 8 through 18," *Journal of Social Psychology,* LXXIX (June 1969), 63–67.

[10] Erikson, op. cit.

[11] G. Murphy, *Personality* (New York: Harper, 1947).

[12] M. Rosenberg, *Society and the Adolescent Self-Image* (New Jersey: Princeton University Press, 1965).

[13] G. H. Mead, *Mind, Self and Society* (Chicago: University of Chicago Press, 1934).

But people vary in the degree to which the self is an object of attention. Some people are more "task-oriented," i.e., more involved in the situation and less concerned with how they are doing or what others are thinking of them. For others, the self becomes so prominent that the interaction is uncomfortable. Do adolescents show more of this type of uncomfortable self-consciousness than younger children?

The second dimension of the self-image is stability. If an individual must take account of himself as an important part of a situation and if he is unsure of what he is like, then he is deprived of a basis for action and decision. Indeed, Lecky [14] described the self-concept as "the basic axiom of one's life theory," and Brownfain [15] showed instability to be associated with disturbance. The question is whether this stability is especially shaken during adolescence.

The third dimension is self-esteem, i.e., the individual's global positive or negative attitude toward himself. The importance of this feeling has been widely recognized.[16] Probably more research has been devoted to this aspect of the self-concept than to all others combined.[17] In part, this interest is probably attributable to the great relevance of self-esteem for emotional disturbance.[18] Is there evidence of self-esteem disturbance during adolescence?

The final dimension deals with the "perceived self." [19] While technically not an integral part of the phenomenal self, there is both theoretical and empirical reason to believe that the perceived self has an extremely important bearing on the self-image, particularly the self-esteem. Mead's [20] and Cooley's [21] classic theories emphasized the importance to the individual of

14 P. Lecky, *Self-Consistency: A Theory of Personality* (New York: Island Press, 1945).

15 J. D. Brownfain, "Stability of the Self-Concept as a Dimension of Personality," *Journal of Abnormal and Social Psychology*, XLVII (July 1952), 597–606.

16 W. James, *The Principles of Psychology* (New York: Dover, 1950 Copyright, 1890 by Henry Holt and Co.); W. McDougall, *Introduction to Social Psychology* (London: Methuen and Co., 1908).

17 R. Wylie, *The Self-Concept: A Critical Survey of Pertinent Research Literature* (Lincoln, Nebraska: University of Nebraska Press, 1961).

18 H. B. Kaplan and A. D. Pokorny, "Self-Derogation and Psychosocial Adjustment," *Journal of Nervous and Mental Disease*, CXLIX (November 1969), 421–434; C. R. Rogers, *Client-Centered Therapy: Its Current Practice, Implications, and Theory* (Boston: Houghton-Mifflin, 1951); Rosenberg, op. cit.; R. H. Turner and R. H. Vanderlippe, "Self-Ideal Congruence as an Index of Adjustment," *Journal of Abnormal and Social Psychology*, LVII (1958), 202–206; Wylie, op. cit., Chapter IV.

19 There is no standard terminology to communicate the idea of the individual's perception of how others see and evaluate him. Different terms have been used, for example, by: C. H. Cooley, *Human Nature and the Social Order* (New York: Scribner's, 1912); S. F. Miyamoto and S. Dornbusch, "A Test of the Symbolic Interactionist Hypothesis of Self-Conception," *American Journal of Sociology*, LXI (March 1956), 339–403; L. G. Reeder, G. A. Donohue and A. Biblarz, "Conceptions of Self and Others," *American Journal of Sociology*, LXVI (September 1960), 153–159; C. W. Backman, P. F. Secord and J. R. Peirce, "Resistance to Change in the Self-Concept as a Function of Concensus Among Significant Others," *Sociometry*, XXVI (March 1963), 102–111. For want of a better term we shall use "perceived self."

20 Mead, op. cit.

21 Cooley, op. cit.

his perceptions of how others see him.[22] Our question is whether adolescents are more likely than younger children to see others as viewing them unfavorably?

METHOD

Sample

The data for this analysis were collected from public school children in grades three through twelve in Baltimore City in 1968. A random sample of 2,625 pupils distributed among twenty-five schools was drawn from the population of third to twelfth grade pupils. Each school in Baltimore City was initially stratified by two variables: (1) proportion of nonwhite students, and (2) median income of its census tract. Twenty-five schools falling into the appropriate intervals were randomly selected. From each school, 105 children were selected by random procedures from the central records.

Some children had withdrawn from school after the central records were compiled and were no longer available. However, we were able to interview 1,917 children, that is, 79.2 per cent of the sample children still registered in the school, or 73.0 per cent of all children originally drawn from the central records.[23] Closely reflecting the population, the present sample is 63 per cent Negro and more heavily working class than the national average. None of the findings presented here were found to be spurious when controlled for race or class.

Comparisons across ages, however, must take account of the fact that school dropouts are absent from our population of older adolescents. The fact that this study is a cross-sectional rather than panel design generally limits the conclusiveness of the findings. We cannot be certain that age differences represent actual changes, particularly in the higher school grades.

Each subject was interviewed directly after school in his school. For the elementary school children, objective background information was collected from the parents. Parents were reached either by a five to ten minute telephone interview or, when there was no telephone, by home interview. Almost all parents were extremely cooperative and in only sixty cases were we unable to locate the parent or conduct the interview.

[22] For empirical support, see: Miyamoto and Dornbusch, op. cit.; Reeder, Donohue, and Biblarz, op. cit.; J. J. Sherwood, "Self-Identity and Referent Others," *Sociometry,* XXVIII (March 1965), 66–81; M. Manis, "Social Interaction and the Self-Concept," *Journal of Abnormal and Social Psychology,* LI (November 1955), 362–370; M. Helper, "Learning Theory and the Self Concept," *Journal of Abnormal and Social Psychology,* LI (September 1955), 184–194; M. Rosenberg and R. G. Simmons, *Black and White Self-Esteem: The Urban School Child* (Washington, D.C.: The American Sociological Association, 1972).

[23] One school—a combined elementary and junior high school—was entered twice in the total population of schools and, by chance, was selected in both categories. It was not practicable to double the sample size of this school; hence, the responses of these thirty-five elementary school children and those of the thirty-six junior high school children were doubled in weight to better represent the total population. In our analysis, we have thus treated our sample as 1,988 children.

Measures

Indexes were developed to measure the four aspects of the self-image discussed above. "Self-consciousness" is based on a seven-item Guttman Scale. (Example: "If a teacher asked you to get up in front of the class and talk a little bit about your summer, would you be very nervous, a little nervous, or not at all nervous?") "Stability of self" is indexed by a five-item Guttman Scale. (Example: "A kid told me: 'Some days I like the way I am. Some days I do not like the way I am.' Do your feelings *change* like this?")

Since the self-esteem dimension is central, this concept was measured in two ways. First, we ascertained the individual's general, overarching feeling toward himself through a series of general questions; we call this the global measure of self-esteem. For this purpose, a six-item Guttman Scale was used. (Example: "Everybody has some things about him which are good and some things about him which are bad. Are most of the things about you good, bad, or are both about the same?")

As Murphy [24] has observed, however, the individual's self-attitude is both general and specific. He not only has attitudes toward himself as a totality but also attitudes toward his specific qualities, such as his looks or his intelligence. A different approach to measurement, then, is to infer the individual's general self-assessment from his specific self-evaluations; we call this the specific approach. Both the global and specific indices are designed to measure general self-esteem; they are simply founded on competing rationales. In this study, the specific approach to self-esteem measurement is based on the individual's average self-assessment on the following eight characteristics: being smart, good-looking, truthful or honest, good at sports, well-behaved, hard-working in school, helpful, and good at making jokes.

While certain investigators [25] speak of "the perceived self," clearly, the individual has many perceived selves since he interacts with many types of people who evaluate him. Some of these perceived selves were investigated by our asking these children what they believed the following people thought of them: their parents, their teachers, children of the same sex, and children of the opposite sex.

RESULTS

The Disturbance

Does adolescence produce a disturbance in the child's self-picture? Table 1 clearly suggests that the emergence of self-image problems in adolescence is no myth, and that these problems occur early in adolescence. In general, self-image disturbance appears much greater in the twelve to fourteen age group than in the eight to eleven age group.

In contrast to younger children, the early adolescents (twelve to fourteen

[24] Murphy, op. cit.
[25] Miyamoto and Dornbusch, op. cit.

year olds) show a higher level of self-consciousness, greater instability of self-image, slightly lower global self-esteem, lower specific self-esteem, and a more negative "perceived self" (that is, they are less likely to think that parents, teachers, and peers of the same sex view them favorably). The assumption that such changes are likely to be disturbing is consistent with the fact that early adolescents also show a higher level of depressive affect than do the younger children (Table 1).[26] The only area showing improvement in early adolescence involves the opposite sex: children see themselves as better liked by the opposite sex as they grow older.

While the early adolescents are more self-conscious and have a more unstable self-image, this self-consciousness appears to decline somewhat in later adolescence and the self-image becomes somewhat more stable. However, even in late adolescence, the subjects manifest greater self-consciousness and instability than do the eight to eleven year old children.

Only for global self-esteem is there an improvement in later adolescence marked enough for the youngsters from age fifteen up to score more favorably than the eight to eleven year olds. The older adolescents show higher global self-esteem than both the young children and the early adolescents. Earlier studies [27] have also shown an increase in self-esteem among senior high school students; furthermore, one of these [28] also demonstrated a decline in self-esteem in early adolescence as compared to childhood.

Although global self-esteem feelings decline only slightly in early adolescence, and rise conspicuously in later adolescence, this pattern is not true of self-esteem based on those specific qualities we have considered, such as intelligence, honesty, diligence and good behavior. If one simply averages the self-ratings on these qualities, he will find a relatively sharp decline between childhood and early adolescence; and this lowered self-evaluation continues into later adolescence.

While one may reasonably assume that the lowered self-evaluations of these specific qualities indicate some degree of self-image disturbance, this conclusion is not certain. For, as William James [29] long ago noted, it is not simply a question of how favorably the individual judges himself, but also how much he has staked himself on a particular quality. For example, an adolescent may agree that he is poor at sports or is plain; but if he cares little about these qualities, he will not be disturbed by their lack. Thus only a low self-rating on a quality that is valued highly is likely to be experienced as disturbing.

To take account of self-values, we asked our respondents how much they cared about each of these qualities, i.e., how important they were to them. Table 2 deals solely with children who care "very much" about whether they are smart, good-looking, helpful, etc. It is among these children that one

---

[26] The scale of "depressive affect" appears in the original article.

[27] Engel, op. cit.; Piers and Harris, op. cit.

[28] Piers and Harris, op. cit.

[29] James, op. cit.

Table 1   Children's Self-Ratings by Age

| | Age | | | |
| | Median Scores | | | |
	8-11 (N = 819)[a]	12-14 (N = 649)	15 + (N = 516)	Total: Median x^2 Test [b]
Self-consciousness (Low score = high self-consciousness)	3.8 ***	3.0	3.2	p < .001
Stability of the self-image (Low score = high instability)	2.6 ***	2.1	2.3	p < .001
Self-esteem (global) (Low score = low self-esteem)	4.0	3.8 ***	4.4	p < .001
Self-esteem (specific) (High score = unfavorable rating)	3.6 ***	5.0	5.0	p < .001
Perceived self (High score = unfavorable rating)				
Perceived opinion of parents	4.8 **	5.1	5.1	p < .01
Perceived opinions of teachers	3.2 ***	3.4	3.4	p < .001
Perceived opinions of peers of the same sex	1.6 ***	1.8 **	2.0	p < .001
Perceived opinions of peers of opposite sex	2.4 ***	2.1 **	2.0	p < .001
Depressive affect (High score = high depression)	2.3 ***	2.9	3.0	p < .001

* = p < .05 for adjacent age groups according to median x^2 test; ** = p < .01; *** = p < .001.

Tests between adjacent age groups are not entirely appropriate, in part, because of the nonindependence of comparisons (i.e., the 12-14 age category is compared with each of the other age groups). Since the test affords some indication of how seriously to take the observed differences, however, it is included for convenience. (See Blalock [30] for a discussion of this problem in the case of analysis of variance.)

a For missing data, total cases are reduced accordingly.

b Siegel.[31]

30 H. M. Blalock, Jr., *Social Statistics* (New York: McGraw-Hill Book Co., 1972), pp. 328–334.

31 S. Siegel, *Nonparametric Statistics for the Behavioral Sciences* (New York: McGraw-Hill Book Co., 1956), 111–116, 179–184.

would expect an unfavorable self-rating on a quality to be psychologically upsetting.[32]

Table 2   Proportion Rating Selves Very Favorably on Each Characteristic Among Those Who Care "Very Much" About That Characteristic, by Age

Respondent Rates Self Very Favorably on Following Qualities	Age			Total: x^2 Test
	8-11	12-14	15 OR OLDER	
Smart	26% *** (547)	9% (366)	5% (244)	p < .001
Good-looking	20% * (258)	13% * (197)	6% (121)	p < .001
Truthful or honest	54% *** (527)	38% (424)	38% (320)	p < .001
Good at sports	50% (339)	46% (266)	42% (163)	p < .001
Well-behaved	46% *** (474)	31% (332)	39% (239)	p < .001
Work hard in school	71% *** (494)	50% ** (373)	39% (231)	p < .001
Helpful	60% *** (506)	46% (329)	46% (225)	p < .001
Good at making jokes	49% (151)	40% (53)	46% (28)	p < .05

* = p < .05 for adjacent age groups according to χ^2 test;
** = p < .01;
*** = p < .001.

Tests between adjacent age groups are not entirely appropriate, partly because of non-independence of comparisons. Since the test affords some indication of how seriously to take the observed difference, however, it is included for convenience.

With respect to this criterion, Table 2 indicates that the early adolescents (twelve to fourteen) have a consistently lower self-image than the younger children (eight to eleven); i.e., they are less likely to rate themselves very favorably on the qualities they consider important. In some cases, such as being "good at making jokes," the differences are minor; for others they are large. On the other hand, there is little consistent difference between early and later adolescents in this regard. The consistent and clear age difference appears between childhood and early adolescence, with the early adolescents less likely to say they are performing well with respect to their self-values.

It may be contended that the lower self-ratings on these qualities simply

[32] Rosenberg, *Society and the Adolescent Self-Image*, op. cit., Ch. 13.

reflect the fact that adolescents are more "realistic" while the younger children tend to "inflate" their self-qualities. Other analyses of these data have shown that compared to older children, elementary school children do tend to inflate the prestige of their racial and ethnic group status and their father's occupational status.[33] Perhaps the adolescent does become more realistic about what he is like, but this does not mean that the adjustment to reality is not distressing for him. As Blos [34] has noted: "The difficulty of relinquishing the inflated self-image of childhood is usually underestimated." From the viewpoint of one's emotional state, "reality" is not the issue.

To summarize, the results show a general pattern of self-image disturbance in early adolescence. The data suggest that, compared to younger children, the early adolescent has become distinctly more self-conscious; his picture of himself has become more shaky and unstable; his global self-esteem has declined slightly; his attitude toward several specific characteristics which he values highly has become less positive; and he has increasingly come to believe that parents, teachers, and peers of the same sex view him less favorably. In view of these changes, it is not surprising that our data show early adolescents to be significantly more likely to be psychologically depressed.

The course of self-image development after twelve to fourteen is also interesting. In general, the differences between early and late adolescence are not large. There is improvement in self-consciousness, stability, and especially global self-esteem, but no improvement in assessment of specific qualities or in the perceived self. The main change occurs almost always between the eight to eleven-year-old children and the twelve to fourteen-year-old children.

Onset of the Disturbance

Can we be more specific about this change in the self-image from childhood to early adolescence? Does it occur gradually or suddenly? As Figure 1 shows, a noticeable difference appears between eleven-year-olds and twelve-year-olds. (Note that the eleven-year-old group includes children from eleven years, no months, to eleven years, eleven months; while the twelve-year-old group covers those from twelve years, no months to twelve years, eleven months.) Self-consciousness, instability of the self-image, low global self-esteem, and low specific self-esteem all rise relatively sharply among the twelve-year-olds compared to the eleven-year-olds, although in most cases some rise has begun earlier, particularly the year before. This movement from the eleven year old group to the twelve-year-old group is the only one-year period in which the children show an increase of disturbance on all these measures. In fact, on all four measures it is the largest yearly increase in disturbance up to that age. For three out of four measures, it is the largest increase between any two ages.

[33] R. G. Simmons and M. Rosenberg, "Functions of Children's Perceptions of the Stratification System," *American Sociological Review*, XXXVI (April 1971), 235–249; Rosenberg and Simmons, op. cit.
[34] Blos, op. cit., p. 192.

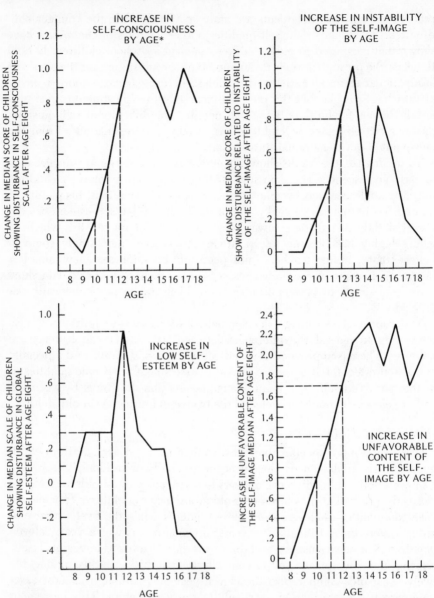

Figure 1. *For each scale, the median score of the eight-year-old group is subtracted from the median score of each subsequent age group. If the graph line rises, then disturbance along the dimension is said to increase. The points above "0" indicate a higher level of disturbance after age 8, while the points below "0" indicate a lower level.*

* The values at age 10, 11, and 12 are indicated by dotted lines. In the sample there are 98 eight-year-olds, 225 nine-year-olds, 233 eleven-year-olds, 237 twelve-year-olds, 213 thirteen-year-olds, 199 fourteen-year-olds, 150 fifteen-year-olds, 162 sixteen-year-olds, 130 seventeen-year-olds, and 56 eighteen-year-olds.

For almost all the dimensions considered here, disturbance continues to increase after twelve, but in most cases the high point of disturbance occurs either at age twelve, thirteen, or fourteen. In fact, stability of self-image and global self-esteem seem to improve after this point, particularly in late adolescence; while disturbances in self-consciousness and in specific self-esteem seem to level off and remain at early adolescent levels. The sole area of increasing disturbance in later adolescence involves the children's perceptions of the opinions of significant others.

The course of global self-esteem development deserves special mention. We noted earlier that the self-esteem level of the twelve to fourteen-year group was only slightly lower than that of the eight to eleven group. But this finding conceals an important change: the sudden dramatic decline in self-esteem among the twelve-year-olds (Figure 1: compare eleven- and twelve-year-olds). But during the following year, when the children reach thirteen, global self-esteem rapidly returns to its earlier level and continues to rise in later adolescence. Later we shall see some possible reasons for this dramatic but temporary shift.

In sum, the data suggest that when they are twelve-years-old (that is, between their twelfth and thirteenth birthdays), children tend to experience a more marked increase in self-image disturbance. For some dimensions, this relatively sharp increase continues among those who are age thirteen. It is relevant to note that early adolescence is also characterized by a corresponding increase in feelings of depression or unhappiness, though this rise has clearly begun earlier (Figure 2). After age thirteen, there is again a general leveling off.

Environmental Context

Placing the rise in self-image disturbance at some time after the twelfth birthday would seem to agree with the assumption that puberty is the chief determinant of this disturbance. But are there factors in the social environment which may also be responsible for these changes?

One important environmental change occurs for most children at this time. They generally begin their last year of elementary school (the sixth grade) when they are eleven and the first year of junior high school (the seventh grade) when they are twelve. Does the movement into junior high school itself contribute to the increase in self-image disturbance?

Obviously, one cannot examine the effects of change in environment by comparing sixth and seventh graders since one does not know whether such differences are due to the fact that the seventh graders are in junior high school or simply that they are older. It is, however, possible to disentangle the effects of age maturation and school contexts by comparing children of the same ages.

By the spring of the school year, when our data were collected, both the sixth and seventh grades held an appreciable number of twelve-year-olds. If the junior high school experience were particularly stressful for the child, then the twelve-year-olds in junior high should show greater disturbance of their self-images than the twelve year olds in elementary school.

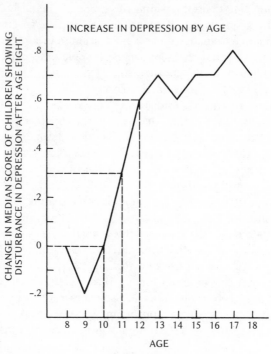

Figure 2.

Table 3   *Disturbance of the Self-Image by School Context, Among Twelve-year-old Children*

| Self-Image Disturbance | Twelve-year-old Children | | According to x^2 Analysis |
	IN ELEMENTARY SCHOOL	IN JUNIOR HIGH SCHOOL	
Per cent low self-esteem (global)	22% (167)	41% (59)	$p < .01$
Per cent low self-esteem (specific)	28% (151)	46% (57)	$.10 > p > .05$
Per cent high self-consciousness	27% (172)	43% (61)	$p < .05$
Per cent high instability of self-image	30% (158)	53% (60)	$p < .01$

Table 3 dramatically supports this hypothesis. The twelve year olds in junior high school have lower global self-esteem, lower specific self-esteem, higher self-consciousness, and greater instability of self-image than their age-peers in elementary school. For example, 41 per cent of the twelve-year-olds in junior high school indicate low global self-esteem in contrast to only 22 per cent of those in elementary school; 43 per cent of the former manifest high self-consciousness compared to only 27 per cent of the latter. All but one of the these differences are statistically significant beyond the .05 level.[35]

If these findings are valid, they certainly afford a vivid illustration of the way a social context can affect individual personality. Yet it is possible that these differences are spurious. Perhaps the sixth grade twelve-year-olds differ in other ways from the seventh grade twelve-year-olds. The sixth grade twelve-year-olds are more likely to have poorer grades, to be black, and to be from the lower social classes; but these factors do not appear likely to improve their self-images. In any case, controlling for these factors by means of test factor standardization,[36] we find that none of the original differences involving global self-esteem, specific self-esteem, self-consciousness, or stability of self-concept, can be explained by any of these variables. Even when standardized on race, class, or marks in school, all differences between elementary school and junior high school twelve-year-olds remain essentially unchanged. Furthermore, Table 4 shows that in general these findings hold for blacks as well as whites, for middle class as well as working class respondents, and for students with high as well as low grades.

Does this mean that the only remaining difference between these two types of twelve-year-olds is the school which they attend? One other possibility involves the relative ages of these two groups in their classes. The sixth grade twelve-year-olds are among the oldest and biggest children in their class, while the seventh grade twelve-year-olds are among the youngest and least physically mature. The self-pictures of the sixth grade twelve-year-olds could benefit from their relative advantage, while the self-images of their seventh-grade age peers could suffer from their age-rank in their group. If so, the sixth grade twelve-year-olds should have more positive self-images than the younger children in their classes; while the seventh grade twelve-year-olds should show more disturbed self-images than the older children in their grade.

Yet Table 5 shows there is virtually no difference between the self-image ratings of eleven and twelve-year-olds in the sixth grade, nor is there a difference between the self-pictures of the twelve and thirteen-year-olds in the seventh grade.

Thus, the transition into junior high school seems to represent a significant stress along several dimensions of the child's self-image; while aging from

[35] One's view of the opinions of Significant others, however, does not appear to be affected by movement into junior high school.

[36] M. Rosenberg, "Test Factor Standardization as a Method of Interpretation," *Social Forces*, XLI (October 1962), 53–61.

Table 4 Disturbance of the Self-Image Among Twelve-year-olds in the Sixth or Seventh Grade, by Race, Social Class, and Marks in School

Self-Image Disturbance	Race				Social Class				Marks in School			
	BLACKS		WHITES		MIDDLE CLASS		WORKING CLASS		A's AND B's		C's AND BELOW	
	6TH GR.	7TH GR.	6TH GR.	7TH GR.	6TH GR.	7TH GR.	6TH GR.	7TH GR.	6TH GR.	7TH GR.	6TH GR.	7TH GR.
Per cent low self-esteem (global)	18% (106)	33% (27)	30% (61)	47% (32)	14% (21)	44% (16)	21% (119)	36% (39)	20% (49)	37% (30)	23% (104)	42% (24)
Per cent low self-esteem (specific)	33% (92)	46% (26)	19% (58)	45% (31)	48% (21)	41% (17)	26% (108)	44% (36)	17% (47)	39% (28)	29% (91)	50% (24)
Per cent high self-consciousness	28% (109)	32% (28)	27% (62)	52% (33)	24% (21)	53% (17)	29% (122)	38% (40)	22% (50)	37% (30)	29% (106)	58% (26)
Per cent high instability of the self-image	31% (104)	50% (28)	26% (53)	56% (32)	35% (20)	71% (17)	27% (112)	44% (39)	30% (47)	52% (29)	28% (96)	54% (26)

eleven to twelve and twelve to thirteen does not in itself appear stressful. Within the same school class, age makes little difference; but within the same age group, school class makes a great difference.

Table 5   Disturbance of the Self-Image by Age, by Grade in School

	Grade in School			
	SIXTH GRADE		SEVENTH GRADE	
	AGE 11	AGE 12	AGE 12	AGE 13
Per cent low self-esteem (global)	29% (73)	24% (106)	40% (58)	36% (101)
Per cent low self-esteem (specific)	20% (69)	25% (93)	46% (56)	41% (90)
Per cent high self-consciousness	22% (76)	27% (106)	42% (60)	46% (101)
Per cent high instability of self-image	30% (76)	33% (102)	53% (59)	46% (92)

One further question is whether the self-image disturbance associated with the transition from sixth to seventh grade results from the general disturbance associated with transferring to any new school or whether it is specifically associated with entry into a junior high school. One way to examine this question is to look at those twelve-year-old sixth graders who have moved to their current schools this year. These children are identical with other twelve-year-old sixth graders in grade level but are different in being new students; conversely, they are similar to all twelve-year-old seventh graders in being new students, but are different in grade level.

Unfortunately, the number of twelve-year-olds in the sixth grade new to their schools is small; the results are thus no more than suggestive. Nevertheless, the data in Table 6 are particularly interesting. Though some differences exist between sixth graders new in the school and other sixth graders, the differences are inconsistent and would not suggest less disturbed self-images in either group. But the findings involving junior high students are clear and consistent. The twelve-year-olds in junior high are considerably more likely than either sixth grade group to show disturbances of the self-image, by scoring higher on self-consciousness, higher on instability of self-image and lower on global self-esteem. With regard to specific self-esteem, they are slightly higher than the sixth grade newcomer but much lower than the other sixth graders. The results as a whole suggest that a twelve-year-old child who moves from one elementary school to another may not find the experience as stressful as does the twelve-year-old who has entered a junior high school in the past year.

*Table 6   Self-Variables by Grade and Geographical Mobility,
Among Twelve-year-olds Only*

Self-Image Disturbance	Twelve-year-old Children		
	6TH GRADER; NOT NEW TO SCHOOL	6TH GRADER; MOVED INTO SCHOOL THIS ACADEMIC YEAR	7TH GRADER
Self-consciousness			
High	28%	25%	42%
Medium	50	40	48
Low	22	35	10
N = 100%	(67)	(20)	(60)
Instability of self-image			
High	36%	18%	53%
Medium	49	76	41
Low	15	6	7
N = 100%	(66)	(17)	(59)
Self-esteem (global)			
Low	23%	15%	40%
Medium	27	55	36
High	50	30	24
N = 100%	(68)	(20)	(58)
Self-esteem (specific)			
Low	23%	44%	46%
Medium	51	44	30
High	26	12	23
N = 100%	(61)	(16)	(56)

Note, incidentally, that the transition from junior to senior high school does not show a parallel effect on the self-image; fifteen-year-olds in senior high school do not show more disturbed self-images than fifteen-year-olds in junior high school. Why this should be so is not clear. Perhaps the difference between junior high school and elementary school is experienced as much greater than the difference between junior and senior high school.

In sum, the data indicate increased self-image disturbance associated with the transition from elementary to junior high school. The reason does not appear to be solely the age change (with its associated biological changes); for at ages roughly equivalent, the seventh graders still show greater disturbance. Nor does it simply appear to be the shock of transferring to a new school; although the number of cases is small, the newly arrived sixth graders generally show less disturbance than seventh graders and are not consistently worse off than other sixth graders (all at the same age). Furthermore, the transition from junior to senior high shows no such effect.

Perhaps puberty does not in itself disturb the self-image but heightens vulnerability to environmental circumstances which threaten the self-concept. Only further research can determine what it is about the junior high school experience that is stressful for the self-image.

SUMMARY AND DISCUSSION

This cross-sectional study has investigated several dimensions of self-image development in 1,917 urban school children in grades three through twelve. A definite disturbance of the self-image has been shown to occur in adolescence, particularly early adolescence. In some respects this disturbance appears to decline in later adolescence, while along other dimensions it persists. In many areas, a particular rise in disturbance appears to occur when the child is twelve, that is, between the twelfth and thirteenth birthdays. The rise often begins a year before, and may continue for the next year or so. Often, however, it seems to increase little, if at all, after age thirteen or fourteen.

During early adolescence, compared to the years eight to eleven, the children exhibited heightened self-consciousness, greater instability of self-image, slightly lower global self-esteem, lower opinions of themselves with regard to the qualities they valued, and a reduced conviction that their parents, teachers and peers of the same sex held favorable opinions of them. They were also more likely to show a high depressive affect.

These data agree with the findings of Offer,[37] who studied a somewhat older adolescent group (fourteen to eighteen), and who reports that both parents and adolescents agreed that the greatest amount of "turmoil" in their lives occurred between ages twelve to fourteen. The finding that instability of the self-picture increases during adolescence might appear to support Erikson's[38] views on adolescent problems of ego-identity. However, Erikson seems to place the ego-identity crisis in late adolescence; whereas our data indicate a rise in instability during early adolescence.

Our data do not completely explain the dynamic processes at work in adolescence. For example, they cannot measure the effects of hormonal and other pubertal changes on the self-image in early adolescence.[39] Yet they do show, dramatically, that the child's environment appears to have a stronger

[37] Offer, op. cit., Ch. 11.
[38] Erikson, op. cit.
[39] N. W. Shock, "Some Physiological Aspects of Adolescence," *Texas Reports on Biology and Medicine,* IV (1946), 289–310; J. M. Tanner, "Sequence, Tempo, and Individual Variation in the Growth and Development of Boys and Girls Aged Twelve to Sixteen," *Daedalus,* C (Fall 1971), 907–930.

effect than age-maturation on certain aspects of the self-image. One of the major reasons twelve-year-olds are more likely than eleven-year-olds to show an increase in self-image disturbance appears to be that the twelve-year-olds have moved into junior high school. Twelve-year-olds in the seventh grade are more likely to indicate disturbance on these self-image measures than are twelve-year-olds in the sixth grade. There are no comparable differences between eleven- and twelve-year-olds in the sixth grade, or between twelve- and thirteen-year-olds in the seventh grade.

Thus, movement into junior high school at puberty is a significant event for the child. He moves from a protected elementary school, where he usually has one teacher and one set of classmates, to a much larger, more impersonal junior high where his teachers, classmates, and even his rooms are constantly shifting. He moves from a setting where the teacher is a parent-surrogate, to a more impersonal environment. Here he is expected to behave more independently and more responsibly, and he must make his first career decision—whether to take an academic, commercial, or vocational course.

That a disturbance of the self-image does not occur in the move from junior to senior high school raises a question. Is this finding due to the fact that the difference between senior and junior high is quantitative and not qualitative; i.e., that the school is bigger but of similar type? Or is it that the move into a very different type of school roughly coincides with the onset of puberty, which makes the self-image of the early adolescent more vulnerable to the assaults of the junior high school environment? Our data do not answer these questions. Many of them might be answered by a study of a middle school covering the fourth to eighth grades. In such a school, one might expect a more gradual transition to departmentalization, a more gradual buildup in others' expectations for independence and responsibility. The shift would not necessarily coincide with the onset of puberty.

Knowledge about self-concept development is still pretty much an unknown land in social psychology. Our sample tells us something about what differences appear between the ages of eight and eighteen, but there is little information about development before and after these years. Whether the level or type of self-image disturbance which develops in early adolescence persists in adult life or changes in a positive or negative direction is still unknown. Nor does our study reveal the more dynamic processes of self-image change. That would require a long-term panel study. Given the importance of the self-concept to the individual, we hope that the required research will be forthcoming.

David B. Lynn

The Process of Learning Parental
and Sex-Role Identification

Sex-role behavior is made up of performances and attitudes that coincide with the cultural stereotypes of masculinity and femininity. Lynn presents four assumptions about sex-role learning and discusses how each accounts for aspects of the process of identification. Lynn's assumptions are: (1) both boys and girls initially identify with their mother; later boys must shift from this early identification to a masculine model; (2) young girls interact more with an appropriate sex-role model than young boys because the mother is more active in child-rearing; (3) by virtue of a highly developed reward system for typical masculine behavior and the many sanctions against feminine behavior, boys replace early maternal identification with masculine stereotypes; (4) American society is male-dominated and allocates more privileges and greater prestige to male than female sex roles.

Instructional Objectives
To indicate the different meanings inherent in the concept of identification.
To present a comprehensive theoretical framework of identification to account for sex-role learning.
To explain the bases for these theoretical formulations.

T HE purpose of this paper is to summarize the writer's theoretical formulation concerning identification, much of which has been published piecemeal in various journals. Research relevant to new hypotheses is cited, and references are given to previous publications of this writer in which the reader can find evidence concerning the earlier hypotheses. Some of the previously published hypotheses are considerably revised in this paper and, it is hoped, placed in a more comprehensive and coherent framework.

THEORETICAL FORMULATION

Before developing specific hypotheses, one must briefly define identification as it is used here. *Parental identification* refers to the internalization of per-

FROM *Journal of Marriage and the Family*, XVIII (1966), pp. 466–470. Reprinted by permission of the author and the publisher.

sonality characteristics of one's own parent and to unconscious reactions similar to that parent. This is to be contrasted with *sex-role identification,* which refers to the internalization of the role typical of a given sex in a particular culture and to the unconscious reactions characteristic of that role. Thus, theoretically, an individual might be thoroughly identified with the role typical of his own sex generally and yet poorly identified with his same-sex parent specifically. This differentiation also allows for the converse circumstances wherein a person is well identified with his same-sex parent specifically and yet poorly identified with the typical same-sex role generally. In such an instance the parent with whom the individual is well identified is himself poorly identified with the typical sex role. An example might be a girl who is closely identified with her mother, who herself is more strongly identified with the masculine than with the feminine role. Therefore, such a girl, through her identification with her mother, is poorly identified with the feminine role.[1]

Formulation of Hypotheses

It is postulated that the initial parental identification of both male and female infants is with the mother. Boys, but not girls, must shift from this initial mother identification and establish masculine-role identification. Typically in this culture the girl has the same-sex parental model for identification (the mother) with her more hours per day than the boy has his same-sex model (the father) with him. Moreover, even when home, the father does not usually participate in as many intimate activities with the child as does the mother, e.g., preparation for bed, toileting. The time spent with the child and the intimacy and intensity of the contact are thought to be pertinent to the process of learning parental identification.[2] The boy is seldom if ever with the father as he engages in his daily vocational activities, although both boy and girl are often with the mother as she goes through her household activities. Consequently, the father, as a model for the boy, is analogous to a map showing the major outline but lacking most details, whereas the mother, as a model for the girl, might be thought of as a detailed map.

However, despite the shortage of male models, a somewhat stereotyped and conventional masculine role is nonetheless spelled out for the boy, often by his mother and women teachers in the absence of his father and male models. Through the reinforcement of the culture's highly developed system of rewards for typical masculine-role behavior and punishment for signs of femininity, the boy's early learned identification with the mother weakens. Upon this weakened mother identification is welded the later learned identification with a culturally defined, stereotyped masculine role.

[1] D. B. Lynn, "Sex-Role and Parental Identification," *Child Development,* 33:3 (1962), 555–564.
[2] B. A. Goodfield, "A Preliminary Paper on the Development of the Time Intensity Compensation Hypothesis in Masculine Identification," paper read at the San Francisco State Psychological Convention, April, 1965.

(1) * *Consequently, males tend to identify with a culturally defined masculine role, whereas females tend to identify with their mothers.*[3]

Although one must recognize the contribution of the father in the identification of males and the general cultural influences in the identification of females, it nevertheless seems meaningful, for simplicity in developing this formulation, to refer frequently to *masculine-role identification* in males as distinguished from *mother identification* in females.

Some evidence is accumulating suggesting that (2) *both males and females identify more closely with the mother than with the father.* Evidence is found in support of this hypothesis in a study by Lazowick [4] in which the subjects were 30 college students. These subjects and their mothers and fathers were required to rate concepts, e.g., "myself," "father," "mother," etc. The degree of semantic similarity as rated by the subjects and their parents was determined. The degree of similarity between fathers and their own children was not significantly greater than that found between fathers and children randomly matched. However, children did share a greater semantic similarity with their own mothers than they did when matched at random with other maternal figures. Mothers and daughters did not share a significantly greater semantic similarity than did mothers and sons.

Evidence is also found in support of Hypothesis 2 in a study by Adams and Sarason [5] using anxiety scales with male and female high school students and their mothers and fathers. They found that anxiety scores of both boys and girls were much more related to mothers' than to fathers' anxiety scores.

Support for this hypothesis comes from a study in which Aldous and Kell [6] interviewed 50 middle-class college students and their mothers concerning childrearing values. They found, contrary to their expectation, that a slightly higher proportion of boys than girls shared their mothers' childrearing values.

Partial support for Hypothesis 2 is provided in a study by Gray and Klaus [7] using the Allport-Vernon-Lindzey Study of Values completed by 34 female and 28 male college students and by their parents. They found that the men were not significantly closer to their fathers than to their mothers and also that the men were not significantly closer to their fathers than were the women. However, the women were closer to their mothers than were the men and closer to their mothers than to their fathers.

Note that, in reporting research relevant to Hypothesis 2, only studies of *tested similarity*, not *perceived similarity*, were reviewed. To test this hypoth-

---

* Specific hypotheses are numbered and in italics.

[3] D. B. Lynn, "A Note on Sex Differences in the Development of Masculine and Feminine Identification," *Psychological Review*, 66:2 (1959), 126–135.

[4] L. M. Lazowick, "On the Nature of Identification," *Journal of Abnormal and Social Psychology*, 51 (1955), 175–183.

[5] E. B. Adams and I. G. Sarason, "Relation Between Anxiety in Children and Their Parents," *Child Development*, 34:1 (1963), 237–246.

[6] J. Aldous and L. Kell, "A Partial Test of Some Theories of Identification," *Marriage and Family Living*, 23:1 (1961), 15–19.

[7] S. W. Gray and R. Klaus, "The Assessment of Parental Identification," *Genetic Psychology Monographs*, 54 (1956), 87–114.

222   *Socialization: Theory and Practice*

esis, one must measure tested similarity, i.e., measure both the child and the parent on the same variable and compare the similarity between these two measures. This paper is not concerned with perceived similarity, i.e., testing the child on a given variable and then comparing that finding with a measure taken as to how the child thinks his parent would respond. It is this writer's opinion that much confusion has arisen by considering perceived similarity as a measure of parental identification. It seems obvious that, especially for the male, perceived similarity between father and son would usually be closer than tested similarity, in that it is socially desirable for a man to be similar to his father, especially as contrasted to his similarity to his mother. Indeed, Gray and Klaus [8] found the males' perceived similarity with the father to be closer than tested similarity.

It is hypothesized that the closer identification of males with the mother than with the father will be revealed more clearly on some measures than on others. (3) *The closer identification of males with their mothers than with their fathers will be revealed most frequently in personality variables which are not clearly sex-typed.* In other words, males are more likely to be more similar to their mothers than to their fathers in variables in which masculine and feminine role behavior is not especially relevant in the culture.

There has been too little research on tested similarity between males and their parents to presume an adequate test of Hypothesis 3. In order to test it, one would first have to judge personality variables as to how typically masculine or feminine they seem. One could then test to determine whether a higher proportion of males are more similar to their mothers than to their fathers on those variables which are not clearly sex-typed, rather than on those which are judged clearly to be either masculine or feminine. To this writer's knowledge, this has not been done.

It is postulated that the task of achieving these separate kinds of identification (masculine role for males and mother identification for females) requires separate methods of learning for each sex. These separate methods of learning to identify seem to be problem-solving for boys and lesson-learning for girls. Woodworth and Schlosberg differentiate between the task of solving problems and that of learning lessons in the following way:

> With a problem to master the learner must explore the situation and find the goal before his task is fully presented. In the case of a lesson, the problem-solving phase is omitted or at least minimized, as we see when the human subject is instructed to memorize this poem or that list of nonsense syllables, to examine these pictures with a view to recognizing them later. [9]

Since the girl is not required to shift from the mother in learning her identification, she is expected mainly to learn the mother-identification lesson as

[8] Ibid.
[9] R. S. Woodworth and H. Schlosberg, *Experimental Psychology*, New York: Henry Holt & Co., 1954, p. 529.

it is presented to her, partly through imitation and through the mother's selective reinforcement of mother-similar behavior. She need not abstract principles defining the feminine role to the extent that the boy must in defining the masculine role. Any bit of behavior on the mother's part may be modeled by the girl in learning the mother-identification lesson.

However, finding the appropriate identification goal does constitute a major problem for the boy in solving the masculine-role identification problem. When the boy discovers that he does not belong in the same sex category as the mother, he must then find the proper sex-role identification goal. Masculine-role behavior is defined for him through admonishments, often negatively given, e.g., the mother's and teachers' telling him that he should not be a sissy without precisely indicating what he *should* be. Moreover, these negative admonishments are made in the early grades in the absence of male teachers to serve as models and with the father himself often unavailable as a model. The boy must restructure these admonishments in order to abstract principles defining the masculine role. It is this process of defining the masculine-role goal which is involved in solving the masculine-role identification problem.

One of the basic steps in this formulation can now be taken. (4) *In learning the sex-typical identification, each sex is thereby acquiring separate methods of learning which are subsequently applied to learning tasks generally.*[10]

The little girl acquires a learning method which primarily involves (a) a personal relationship and (b) imitation rather than restructuring the field and abstracting principles. On the other hand, the little boy acquires a different learning method which primarily involves (a) defining the goal, (b) restructuring the field, and (c) abstracting principles. There are a number of findings which are consistent with Hypothesis 4, such as the frequently reported greater problem-solving skill of males and the greater field dependence of females.[11]

The shift of the little boy from mother identification to masculine-role identification is assumed to be frequently a crisis. It has been observed that demands for typical sex-role behavior come at an earlier age for boys than for girls. These demands are made at an age when boys are least able to understand them. As was pointed out above, demands for masculine sex-role behavior are often made by women in the absence of readily available male models to demonstrate typical sex-role behavior. Such demands are often presented in the form of punishing, *negative* admonishments, i.e., telling the boy what not to do rather than what to do and backing up the demands with punishment. These are thought to be very different conditions from those in which the girl learns her mother-identification lesson. Such methods of demanding typical sex-role behavior of boys are very poor methods for inducing learning.

[10] Lynn, "Sex-Role and Parental Identification," op. cit.
[11] Ibid.

(5) *Therefore, males tend to have greater difficulty in achieving same-sex identification than females.*[12]

(6) *Furthermore, more males than females fail more or less completely in achieving same-sex identification, but rather, they make an opposite-sex identification.*[13]

Negative admonishments given at an age when the child is least able to understand them and supported by punishment are thought to produce anxiety concerning sex-role behavior. In Hartley's words:

> This situation gives us practically a perfect combination for inducing anxiety —the demand that the child do something which is not clearly defined to him, based on reasons he cannot possibly appreciate, and enforced with threats, punishments and anger by those who are close to him.[14]

(7) *Consequently, males are more anxious regarding sex-role identification than females.*[15] It is postulated that punishment often leads to dislike of the activity that led to punishment.[16] Since it is "girl-like" activities that provoked the punishment administered in an effort to induce sex-typical behavior in boys, then, in developing dislike for the activity which led to such punishment, boys should develop hostility toward "girl-like" activities. Also, boys should be expected to generalize and consequently develop hostility toward all females as representatives of this disliked role. There is not thought to be as much pressure on girls as on boys to avoid opposite-sex activities. It is assumed that girls are punished neither so early nor so severely for adopting masculine sex-role behavior.

(8) *Therefore, males tend to hold stronger feelings of hostility toward females than females toward males.*[17] The young boy's same-sex identification is at first not very firm because of the shift from mother to masculine identification. On the other hand, the young girl, because she need make no shift in identification, remains relatively firm in her mother identification. However, the culture, which is male-dominant in orientation, reinforces the boy's developing masculine-role identification much more thoroughly than it does the girl's developing feminine identification. He is rewarded simply for having been born masculine through countless privileges accorded males but not females. As Brown pointed out:

> The superior position and privileged status of the male permeates nearly every aspect, minor and major, of our social life. The gadgets and prizes in

---

12 D. B. Lynn, "Divergent Feedback and Sex-Role Identification in Boys and Men," *Merrill-Palmer Quarterly*, 10:1 (1964), 17–23.

13 D. B. Lynn, "Sex Differences in Identification Development," *Sociometry*, 24:4 (1961), 372–383.

14 R. E. Hartley, "Sex-Role Pressures and the Socialization of the Male Child," *Psychological Reports*, 5 (1959), p. 458.

15 Lynn, "Divergent Feedback and Sex-Role Identification in Boys and Men," op. cit.

16 E. R. Hilgard, *Introduction to Psychology*, New York: Harcourt, Brace, and World, 1962.

17 Lynn, "Divergent Feedback and Sex-Role Identification in Boys and Men," op. cit.

boxes of breakfast cereal, for example, commonly have a strong masculine rather than feminine appeal. And the most basic social institutions perpetuate this pattern of masculine aggrandizement. Thus, the Judeo-Christian faiths involve worshipping God, a "Father," rather than a "Mother," and Christ, a "Son," rather than a "Daughter." [18]

(9) *Consequently, with increasing age, males become relatively more firmly identified with the masculine role.*[19]

Since psychological disturbances should, theoretically, be associated with inadequate same-sex identification and since males are postulated to be gaining in masculine identification, the following is predicted: (10) *With increasing age males develop psychological disturbances at a more slowly accelerating rate than females.*[20]

It is postulated that as girls grow older, they become increasingly disenchanted with the feminine role because of the prejudices against their sex and the privileges and prestige offered the male rather than the female. Even the women with whom they come in contact are likely to share the prejudices prevailing in this culture against their own sex.[21] Smith[22] found that with increasing age girls have a progressively better opinion of boys and a progressively poorer opinion of themselves. (11) *Consequently, a larger proportion of females than males show preference for the role of the opposite sex.*[23]

Note that in Hypothesis 11 the term "preference" rather than "identification" was used. It is *not* hypothesized that a larger proportion of females than males *identify* with the opposite sex (Hypothesis 6 predicted the reverse) but rather that they will show *preference* for the role of the opposite sex. *Sex-role preference* refers to the desire to adopt the behavior associated with one sex or the other or the perception of such behavior as preferable or more desirable. *Sex-role preference* should be contrasted with *sex-role identification*, which, as stated previously, refers to the actual incorporation of the role of a given sex and to the unconscious reactions characteristic of that role.

Punishment may suppress behavior without causing its unlearning.[24] Because of the postulated punishment administered to males for adopting opposite-sex role behavior, it is predicted that males will repress atypical sex-role behavior rather than unlearn it. One might predict, then, a dis-

[18] D. G. Brown, "Sex-Role Development in a Changing Culture," *Psychological Bulletin*, 55 (1958), 235.

[19] Lynn, "A Note on Sex Differences in the Development of Masculine and Feminine Identification," op. cit.

[20] Lynn, "Sex Differences in Identification Development," op. cit.

[21] P. M. Kitay, "A Comparison of the Sexes in Their Attitudes and Beliefs About Women: A Study of Prestige Groups," *Sociometry*, 3 (1940), 399–407.

[22] S. Smith, "Age and Sex Differences in Children's Opinion Concerning Sex Differences," *Journal of Genetic Psychology*, 54 (1939), 17–25.

[23] Lynn, "A Note on Sex Differences in the Development of Masculine and Feminine Identification," op. cit.

[24] Hilgard, op. cit.

crepancy between the underlying sex-role identification and the overt sex-role behavior of males. For females, on the other hand, no comparable punishment for adopting many aspects of the opposite-sex role is postulated. (12) *Consequently, where a discrepancy exists between sex-role preference and identification, it will tend to be as follows: Males will tend to show same-sex role preference with underlying opposite-sex identification. Females will tend to show opposite-sex role preference with underlying same-sex identification.*[25] Stated in another way, where a discrepancy occurs both males and females will tend to show masculine-role preference with underlying feminine identification.

Not only is the masculine role accorded more prestige than the feminine role, but males are more likely than females to be ridiculed or punished for adopting aspects of the opposite-sex role. For a girl to be a tomboy does not involve the censure that results when a boy is a sissy. Girls may wear masculine clothing (shirts and trousers), but boys may not wear feminine clothing (skirts and dresses). Girls may play with toys typically associated with boys (cars, trucks, erector sets, and guns), but boys are discouraged from playing with feminine toys (dolls and tea sets). (13) *Therefore, a higher proportion of females than males adopt aspects of the role of the opposite sex.*[26]

Note that Hypothesis 13 refers to *sex-role adoption* rather than *sex-role identification* or *preference. Sex-role adoption* refers to the overt behavior characteristic of a given sex. An example contrasting sex-role adoption with preference and identification is an individual who *adopts* behavior characteristic of his own sex because it is expedient, not because he *prefers* it nor because he is so *identified.*

SUMMARY

The purpose of this paper has been to summarize the writer's theoretical formulation and to place it in a more comprehensive and coherent framework. The following hypotheses were presented and discussed:

1. Males tend to identify with a culturally defined masculine role, whereas females tend to identify with their mothers.
2. Both males and females identify more closely with the mother than with the father.
3. The closer identification of males with their mothers than with their fathers will be revealed most frequently in personality variables which are not clearly sex-typed.
4. In learning the sex-typical identification, each sex is thereby acquiring separate methods of learning which are subsequently applied to learning tasks generally.

[25] Lynn, "Divergent Feedback and Sex-Role Identification in Boys and Men," op. cit.
[26] Lynn, "A Note on Sex Differences in the Development of Masculine and Feminine Identification," op. cit.

5. Males tend to have greater difficulty in achieving same-sex identification than females.
6. More males than females fail more or less completely in achieving same-sex identification but rather make an opposite-sex identification.
7. Males are more anxious regarding sex-role identification than females.
8. Males tend to hold stronger feelings of hostility toward females than females toward males.
9. With increasing age, males become relatively more firmly identified with the masculine role.
10. With increasing age, males develop psychological disturbances at a more slowly accelerating rate than females.
11. A larger proportion of females than males show preference for the role of the opposite sex.
12. Where a discrepancy exists between sex-role preference and identification, it will tend to be as follows: Males will tend to show same-sex role preference with underlying opposite-sex identification. Females will tend to show opposite-sex role preference with underlying same-sex identification.
13. A higher proportion of females than males adopt aspects of the role of the opposite sex.

E. Mavis Hetherington

Effects of Father Absence
on Personality Development
in Adolescent Daughters[1]

A seldom investigated aspect of socialization is that of the effect of father absence on the behavior of daughters. It is likely to vary as a function of why the father is absent and the timing of the separation. To explore the possibility of latent effects of paternal absence in daughters at adolescence, Hetherington compared adolescent girls from three kinds of households— father-intact, divorced, and widowed—on several measures of sex-role learning. The data revealed that timing and reasons for separation are indeed important. Early separation was relatively more severe, and the

FROM *Developmental Psychology*, VII, (1972), pp. 313–326. Copyright 1972 by the American Psychological Association. Reprinted by permission of the author and the publisher.

[1] The Author wishes to extend her appreciation to Jan L. Deur for his assistance in the data analysis of this study.

daughters of divorcees engaged in earlier heterosexual behavior, attention-seeking, and "forms of nonverbal communication associated with openness and responsiveness" whereas the daughters of widows manifested more inhibition, rigidity, avoidance, and restraint around males.

Instructional Objectives
To review effects as suggested by earlier investigations of paternal absence on boys and girls.
To indicate differences in nonverbal behavior—proximity in seating, posture, eye-contact, etc.—during interview sessions with father-absent girls.
To compare the sex-role attributes of father-absent girls.
To consider why father-absent girls fail to interact appropriately with males.

ALTHOUGH the absence of a father in the preschool years has been demonstrated to effect the sex-role typing of preadolescent sons,[2] few effects have been found with daughters. There has been some indication of greater dependency on the mother by girls who have limited access to their fathers;[3] however, this finding has not been reliable. For example, it is reported in a recent study by Santrock [4] that there were no differences in preschool black girls in dependency, aggression, and femininity as a function of father absence. This lack of disruption of feminine sex-role typing is surprising in view of the evidence of the salience of the father in the sex-role typing of daughters in intact families.[5]

All major developmental theories of sex-role typing attribute importance to the father's role in this process. Psychoanalytic theorists emphasize the daughter's competition with the mother for the father's love as a critical factor in identification. Role theorists have suggested that because of his differential treatment of sons and daughters, the father is the most important

[2] C. R. Bach, "Father-Fantasies and Father-Typing in Father-Separated Children," *Child Development*, XVII (1946), 63–80; H. B. Biller and R. M. Bahm, "Father-Absence, Perceived Maternal Behavior, and Masculinity of Self-Concept Among Junior High School Boys," *Developmental Psychology*, IV (1971), 178–181; E. M. Hetherington, "Effects of Paternal Absence on Sex-Typed Behaviors in Negro and White Preadolescent Males," *Journal of Personality and Social Psychology*, IV (1966), 87–91; D. B. Lynn and W. L. Sawrey, "The Effects of Father Absence on Norwegian Boys and Girls," *Journal of Abnormal and Social Psychology*, LIX (1959), 258–262; P. S. Sears, "Doll Play Aggression in Normal Young Children: Influence of Sex, Age Sibling Status, Father's Absence," *Psychological Monographs*, LXV (1951), 6, Whole No. 323.
[3] Lynn and Sawrey, op. cit.
[4] J. W. Santrock, "Paternal Absence, Sex Typing, and Identification," *Developmental Psychology*, II (1970), 264–272.
[5] E. M. Hetherington, "The Effects of Familial Variables on Sex Typing, on Parent-Child Similarity, and on Imitation in Children," *Minnesota Symposium on Child Psychology*, I (1967), 82–107; P. Mussen and E. Rutherford, "Parent-Child Relations and Parental Personality in Relation to Young Children's Sex-Role Preferences," *Child Development*, XXXIV (1963), 489–607.

figure in the reciprocal sex-role learning of offspring of either sex.[6] Social learning theorists have assumed that the daughter's acquisition of feminine behavior and of the specific skills involved in interacting with males is at least partly based on learning experiences and reinforcements received in interactions with the father.[7] This is reflected in the subsequent development of security and culturally appropriate responses in later heterosexual relations.[8] Since few effects of paternal absence on the development of daughters have been found in the preschool or elementary school years, it may be that such effects only appear at puberty when interactions with males become more frequent.

Studies of delinquent girls suggest that paternal absence may result in disruptions in heterosexual behavior. Although girls are less frequently arrested on delinquency charges than are boys,[9] girls who do become delinquent are more likely than delinquent boys to be the product of a broken home,[10] and their delinquency is more often due to sexual misconduct.[11]

It has been found that time of separation and reason for separation are important factors in determining the effects of father absence on boys. Separation before age 5 is more disruptive than later separation,[12] and a higher incidence of clinic problems,[13] delinquency,[14] and recidivism [15] is associated with separation due to divorce than with separation due to death of the father.

The present study was designed to explore the effects of time of and reason for paternal separation on the behavior of father-absent adolescent girls.

METHOD

Subjects

The subjects were three groups of 24 lower- and lower-middle-class, first-born, adolescent, white girls who regularly attended a community recreation center. They ranged in age from 13 to 17 years. None of the subjects had

---

[6] M. Johnson, "Sex Role Learning in the Nuclear Family," *Child Development*, XXXIV (1963), 319–333.

[7] Hetherington, "The Effects of Familial Variables . . . ," op. cit.; Mussen and Rutherford, op. cit.

[8] H. B. Biller and S. D. Weiss, "The Father-Daughter Relationship and the Personality Development of the Female," *Journal of Genetic Psychology*, CXVI (1970), 79–93.

[9] D. Glaser, "Social Disorganization and Delinquent Subcultures," in H. C. Quay, ed., *Juvenile Delinquency* (New York: Van Nostrand, 1965).

[10] T. P. Monahan, "Family Status and the Delinquent Child: A Reappraisal and Some New Findings," *Social Forces*, XXXV (1957), 250–258; J. Toby, "The Differential Impact of Family Disorganization," *American Sociological Review*, XXII (1957), 505–512.

[11] A. K. Cohen, *Delinquent Boys: The Culture of the Gang* (Glencoe, Ill.: The Free Press, 1955); Glaser, op. cit.

[12] Biller and Bahm, op. cit.; Hetherington, op. cit.

[13] J. Tuckman and R. A. Regan, "Intactness of the Home and Behavioral Problems in Children," *Journal of Child Psychology and Psychiatry*, VII (1966), 225–233.

[14] C. Burt, *The Young Delinquent* (New York: Appleton, 1929).

[15] F. I. Nye, "Child Adjustment in Broken and in Unhappy Unbroken Homes," *Marriage and Family Living*, XIX (1957), 356–361.

male siblings. The first group came from intact families with both parents living in the home, the second group from families in which the father was absent due to divorce and in which the child had had minimal contact with the father following the divorce, and the third group from families in which the father was absent due to death. None of the father-absent families had any males living in the home since separation from the father occurred. There were no differences between groups on mean age or education of the subjects, occupation, education, or age of the mothers or fathers, maternal employment, religious affiliation, or number of siblings. Six daughters of divorcees, five daughters of widows, and six daughters from the intact families were only children.

Procedure

The study was comprised of five sets of measures: (a) observational measures of each girl's behavior in the recreation center; (b) measures of each girl's nonverbal behavior in interacting with a male or female interviewer; (c) ratings based on an interview with the daughter; (d) ratings based on interviews with the mother; (e) scores on the California Personality Inventory Femininity Scale,[16] the Internal-External Control Scale,[17] the short form of the Manifest Anxiety Scale,[18] and the Draw-a-Person Tests for mothers and daughters.[19]

OBSERVATIONAL PROCEDURES IN THE RECREATION CENTERS. The frequency with which subjects exhibited 21 behaviors during 10 randomly sampled, 3-minute observations was recorded by two female observers. Observations were made in 1-minute units, yielding a total of 30 units. Two of the 3-minute observations were done at a recreation center dance. Interjudge agreement ranged from 84% to 100% across the various scales. The 21 behaviors recorded were prosocial aggression; verbal aggression toward males and females separately; separate measures for male peers, female peers, male adults, and female adults of instrumental dependence; seeking praise, encouragement, and attention; and subject-initiated physical contact and nearness. In addition, presence in male, female, or neutral areas in the center and participation in masculine, feminine, or neutral activities were obtained.

Measures of masculine, feminine, and neutral areas and activities were originally standardized on 20 girls and 20 boys. The frequency with which these adolescents participated in activities or were present in a given area of the center during 20 randomly sampled, 3-minute periods was recorded. Activities and locations were classified as masculine if boys obtained signifi-

---

[16] H. G. Gough, *Manual for California Personality Inventory* (Palo Alto, Calif.: Consulting Psychologists Press, 1957).

[17] J. B. Rotter, "Generalized Expectancies for Internal Versus External Control of Reinforcement," *Psychological Monographs,* LXXX (1966), 1, Whole No. 609.

[18] A. W. Bendig, "The Development of a Short Form of the Manifest Anxiety Scale," *Journal of Consulting Psychology,* XX (1956), 384.

[19] K. Machover, *Personality Projection in the Drawing of the Human Figure* (Springfield, Ill.: Charles C Thomas, 1957).

cantly higher scores than girls, feminine if girls' scores were higher than boys', and neutral if there was no sex difference in frequency.

PROCEDURE FOR THE ASSESSMENT OF NONVERBAL BEHAVIOR. When the subjects were first brought into the laboratory, they participated in a 15-minute interview involving neutral content about such things as movies, school, television, etc. Half of the subjects were interviewed by male and half by female interviewers. Three interviewers of each sex were used in the study. Two observers, seated behind a one-way vision screen, recorded the frequency of nonverbal behaviors occurring in 30-second units. Thus there were thirty, 30-second observation units in the 15-minute period. The interview was tape recorded and the number of seconds of subject and experimenter speaking time and silence was calculated. Since it was necessary to control the amount of interviewer looking behavior and since a fixed gaze was awkward, the interviewer was permitted to look down six times, for 5 seconds each, during the interview.

When the subject was initially ushered into the room by a female experimenter the interviewer was seated behind a desk with three empty chairs positioned with varying proximity to the interviewers. One chair was at the end of the desk adjacent to the interviewer, one was directly across the desk facing the interviewer, and one was across and about 3 feet down the desk from the interviewer. The subject was instructed to sit down and was permitted to select her own seat.

During the course of the interview the observers recorded eye contact when the subject was speaking, when the interviewer was speaking, and when there was silence by depressing telegraph keys which activated the pens of an Esterline-Angus multipen recorder. These procedures are described in greater detail by Exline, Gray, and Schuette.[20] The two observers agreed 96% of the time in their judgments of the subjects' visual fixations. Since eye contact is related to who is speaking, these measures were converted into proportions of eye contact relative to the amount of silence and speaking time by the interviewer and subject.

Five postural measures, adapted from those of Mehrabian,[21] were obtained: (*a*) shoulder orientation, in terms of 10-degree orientations away from the interviewer; (*b*) arm openness, as rated on a 7-point scale from 1 (arms crossed in front) to 7 (hands touching in the back); (*c*) leg openness on a 4-point scale from 1 (legs crossed) to 4 (legs and feet apart); (*d*) backward lean on a 5-point scale from 1 (more than 20 degrees forward) to 5 (leaning backward more than 20 degrees); and (*e*) sideways lean in 10-degree units. Interjudge reliabilities were .90 for shoulder orientation, .98

[20] R. Exline, D. Gray and D. Schuette, "Visual Behavior in a Dyad as Affected by Interview Content and Sex of Respondent," *Journal of Personality and Social Psychology,* I (1965), 201–209.

[21] A. Mehrabian, "Inference of Attitudes from the Posture Orientation and Distance of a Communicator," *Journal of Consulting and Clinical Psychology,* XXXII (1968), 296–308.

for arm openness, .94 for leg openness, .96 for backward lean, and .95 for sideways lean.

Finally, five expressive measures were recorded: [22] smiles, positive head nods, negative head nods, gesticulations, and self-manipulations. Interrater agreement varied from 89% to 100% across these measures. These postural and expressive measures were scored only once per 30-second interval.

DAUGHTER-INTERVIEW MEASURES. When the neutral 15-minute interview was concluded, a female interviewer entered the room, the previous interviewer left, and a structured interview proceeded. These interviews were tape recorded and later rated by two judges on a series on 7-point scales. The interjudge reliabilities for these scale scores ranged from .73 to .96 with an average reliability of .82. The scales were concerned with feminine interests; female friendships; positive attitude to the feminine role; security around female peers, female adults, male peers, and male adults; perceived warmth of mother; perceived restrictiveness-permissiveness of mother; conflict with mother; closeness to mother; similarity to mother; similarity to father; positive attitude to father; warmth of father; competence of father; masculinity of father; control in family decision making of father; conflict with father before separation; disturbance at separation; close relation with any available adult male substitutes; and self-esteem. The scale for disturbance at separation was omitted in the interviews of girls from intact families. Eight of the father-absent girls, mainly those early separated, could offer no information on conflict with father before separation and six could offer no information about disturbance at separation.

MOTHER-INTERVIEW MEASURES. Mothers were brought into the laboratory and given a structured interview by a female interviewer about child-rearing practices and attitudes toward her daughter, herself, and her spouse. Interviews were tape recorded and rated on a series of 7-point scales by two raters. Interjudge reliabilities ranged from .70 to .96 with a mean of .85. Some attempt to assess shifts in parent-child interaction over time was made by having separate ratings on 11 scales developed to assess maternal behavior before and after adolescence. This was done with the following scales: intrusiveness, overprotection, permissiveness for sexual curiosity and activity, permissiveness for aggression, punishment for sexual activity, punishment for aggression, warmth, ambivalence, psychological and physical punishment, consistency in discipline, and conflict with daughter. The interview was also rated for reinforcement of daughter for sex-appropriate behaviors, attitude toward spouse, attitude toward men, acceptance of feminine role, anxiety about female adequacy, anxiety about adequacy as a mother, happiness and fulfillment in life, happiness in marriage, frequency of contact with male adults, conflict with father preceding separation, intensity of disturbance following separation, length of disturbance following separation, support from friends and family following separation, resentment at being a single

[22] H. M. Rosenfeld, "Instrumental Affiliative Functions of Facial and Gestural Expressions," *Journal of Personality and Social Psychology,* IV (1966), 65–72.

woman with a child, negative shift in self-concept following separation, child's preseparation closeness to father, and child's disturbance at separation. The last 8 scales were given only to the divorced and widowed mothers. PERSONALITY MEASURES. Following their interviews both the mother and daughter were administered the Draw-a-Person Test, the California Personality Inventory Femininity Scale, the Internal-External Control Scale, and the Bendig Short Form of the Manifest Anxiety Scale. The Femininity Scale measures femininity of interests, activities, and preferences, whereas the sex of the first figure drawn on the Draw-a-Person Test is often used as a measure of unconscious sex-role identification or orientation. The Internal-External Control Scale measures the extent to which an individual feels she has control over the reinforcements that occur in association with her behavior. The Manifest Anxiety Scale is frequently assumed to measure generalized anxiety.

RESULTS

Observational Measures in Recreation Centers

Separate one-way analyses of variance for the three groups (father absence due to divorce, father absence due to death, and father present) were performed on the 21 observational measures. The means of variables for which significant F ratios ($p < .05$) were obtained are presented in Table 1. For significant factors in these and all subsequent analyses of variance, comparisons between means were made with two-tailed t tests, and, unless otherwise noted, the discussed results of these comparisons were significant at less than the .05 level.

Both father-absent groups showed more instrumental dependency on female adults than did the father-present group. Daughters of divorcees

Table 1 *Group Means for Observational Variables in the Recreational Center*

| | Group | | | | |
| | FATHER ABSENT | | FATHER | | |
Observational Variable	DIVORCE	DEATH	PRESENT	F	p
Instrumental dependency on female adults	3.17_a	3.17_a	1.62_b	4.00	.02
Seeking praise, encouragement, & attention from male adults	2.50_b	1.17_a	1.12_a	4.83	.01
S-initiated physical contact and nearness with male peers	3.08_b	1.71_a	1.79_a	3.03	.05
Male areas	7.75_a	2.25_b	4.71_c	7.91	.001
Female areas	11.67_a	17.42_b	14.42_a	5.37	.007

Note.—All row means which do not share a common subscript differ at least at $p < .05$ with two-tailed t tests.

sought more attention from male adults and initiated more proximity seeking and physical contact with male peers than did the other girls. This seeking of contact with male peers also was supported by their greater time spent in male areas of the recreation center. In contrast, an avoidance of male areas and preference for female areas by daughters of widows was found. The groups did not differ with respect to any of the other 16 measures.

The father-absent groups were divided into girls who had lost their fathers before age 5 and those who lost them later (divorced early, $N = 14$; divorced late, $N = 10$; widowed early, $N = 13$; widowed late, $N = 11$). Two-way analyses of variance for unequal Ns, with type of father absence and age of separation as the factors, were performed on each of the observational measures of the father-absent girls. All significant findings are reported below. In addition to the previous differences reported between daughters of widows and divorcees, the results of these analyses suggest that early separation from the father has a greater effect on daughters' behavior than later separation. Means for variables associated with significant F ratios are presented in Table 2. The only significant interaction occurred on prosocial aggression where girls from divorced early families exhibited more prosocial aggression than girls from divorced late or widowed early families. Early, in contrast to late, separation is associated with greater attention seeking from both male and female adults, greater subject-initiated physical contact with male adults and female peers, more time spent in male areas and less in feminine activities.

Table 2   Means for Observational Variables in the Recreation Center for Early and Late Separated Father-Absent Girls

Observational Variable	Father Absent			
	DIVORCED EARLY	DIVORCED LATE	DEATH EARLY	DEATH LATE
Prosocial aggression	5.14	2.60	2.15	3.54
Seeking praise, encouragement, & attention from male adults	3.14	1.60	1.46	.82
Seeking praise, encouragement, & attention from female adults	2.14	.80	2.31	1.27
S-initiated physical contact & nearness with male adults	2.28	1.50	2.69	.91
S-initiated physical contact & nearness with male peers	2.93	3.30	2.31	1.00
S-initiated physical contact & nearness with female peers	3.21	1.50	3.38	1.73
Male areas	9.14	5.80	3.23	1.09
Female areas	11.64	11.70	16.54	18.45
Female activities	12.78	18.00	15.38	16.91

Table 3 Position of Chair Selected with Male and Female Interviewers

	Male Interviewer			Female Interviewer		
	FATHER ABSENT		FATHER	FATHER ABSENT		FATHER
Position	DIVORCED	DEATH	PRESENT	DIVORCED	DEATH	PRESENT
1	8	0	1	1	2	1
2	3	2	8	8	7	9
3	1	10	3	3	3	2

Nonverbal Behavior in the Daughter's Interview

Presented in Table 3 is the frequency with which daughters from the three groups of subjects seated themselves with varying gradations of proximity from male and female interviewers. Position 1 is the seat immediately adjacent but at right angles to the interviewer, Position 2 directly across from the interviewer, and Position 3 across and further removed from the interviewer. There were no significant differences as measured through the index of predictive association [23] when the interviewer was a female; however, with a male interviewer the daughters of divorcees tended to choose the most proximate seat, the girls from intact families the seat directly across the table, and the daughters of widows the most distant seat.

The means of the summed scores in 30 observational units for the remaining nonverbal measures, plus amount of silence, and subject and interviewer speaking time for the three groups with male and female interviewers are presented in Table 4. A 3 (Father Status) × 2 (Sex of Interviewer) analysis of variance was performed on each of these measures. The analyses yielded either a significant main effect or interaction on all variables with the exception of gesticulations. There was a significant main effect for father status on all variables except for interviewer speaking time and positive head nods. Sex of interviewer had a significant main effect on subject speaking time, interviewer speaking time, eye contact when the subject was speaking, positive head nods, and manipulations. Interpretation of some of these main effects must be qualified by the significant interactions associated with subject speaking time, silence, shoulder orientation, arm openness, leg openness, backward lean, sideways lean, smiles, proportion of eye contact when the interviewer was speaking, and proportion of eye contact during silence. In general, few differences were found between father status groups with a female interviewer. Most differences were obtained with male interviewers and the means tended to be ordered with the divorced and widowed groups at the extremes and the intact family group in an intermediate position.

In spite of the fact that interviewers had been trained in a structured interview method, male interviewers talked more than female interviewers.

[23] W. L. Hays, *Statistics* (New York: Holt, Rinehart, and Winston, 1963), pp. 606–609.

Table 4   Mean Nonverbal Measures for Subjects with Male and Female Interviewers

	Male Interviewer			Female Interviewer		
	FATHER ABSENT		FATHER	FATHER ABSENT		FATHER
Nonverbal Variable	DIVORCED	DEATH	PRESENT	DIVORCED	DEATH	PRESENT
S speaks	619.17	463.92	601.58	614.50	632.67	624.25
Interviewer speaks	156.00	201.58	143.50	123.00	111.08	121.33
Silence	116.50	234.50	154.92	161.83	156.25	154.42
Shoulder orientation	496.67	1318.33	802.50	817.50	804.17	804.17
Arm openness	159.50	109.33	125.33	131.58	129.58	134.67
Leg openness	68.33	49.50	48.42	50.08	55.00	51.83
Backward lean	72.58	96.42	80.67	80.25	77.00	83.50
Sideways lean	434.17	300.83	399.17	406.67	400.00	402.50
Smiles	13.58	8.50	10.17	11.75	11.92	10.83
Positive head nod	7.25	4.75	6.00	7.83	8.00	6.83
Gesticulations	9.75	5.00	5.25	6.58	6.58	6.50
Manipulations	12.67	13.83	8.00	8.25	8.58	7.58
Negative head nods	2.17	2.50	2.42	2.08	2.08	2.33
Eye contact when interviewer speaking	.59	.31	.41	.44	.44	.43
Eye contact when S speaking	.68	.47	.66	.73	.67	.69
Eye contact during silence	.84	.29	.34	.34	.34	.37

This may have been because subjects talked less with male interviewers. Daughters of widows with a male interviewer spoke significantly less and were more silent than any other group of subjects. There was also a trend ($p < .06$) for daughters of divorcees to be less silent with a male than female interviewer.

Subjects in the divorced group with male interviewers tended to assume a rather sprawling open posture, often leaning slightly forward with one or both arms hooked over the back of the chair. In contrast, subjects in the widowed group sat stiffly upright or leaned backward with their back often slightly turned to the male interviewer, their hands folded or lying in their laps and their legs together. Compared to girls in any other group, daughters of widows with a male interviewer showed more shoulder orientation away from the interviewer, more backward lean, less arm openness, less sideways lean, and less eye contact during silence or when the interviewer was speaking. In contrast, daughters of divorcees with a male interviewer showed more forward lean, more arm and leg openness, more eye contact when the interviewer was speaking and during silence than did any other group of subjects. They also smiled more than did the other two groups with a male interviewer. Daughters of widows smiled less with a male than a female interviewer. It should be noted that there were no differences between means on these variables with a female interviewer.

Table 5 Means of the Nonverbal Measures for Early and Late Separated Father-Absent Girls with Male and Female Interviewers

Nonverbal Variable	Father Absent Early				Father Absent Late			
	MALE INTERVIEWER		FEMALE INTERVIEWER		MALE INTERVIEWER		FEMALE INTERVIEWER	
	DIVORCED (N = 7)	DEATH (N = 7)	DIVORCED (N = 7)	DEATH (N = 6)	DIVORCED (N = 5)	DEATH (N = 5)	DIVORCED (N = 5)	DEATH (N = 6)
S speaks	652.57	401.86	601.00	629.50	572.40	550.80	633.40	635.83
Interviewer speaks	158.00	259.57	137.71	118.33	153.20	120.40	102.40	103.83
Silence	89.43	238.57	106.14	152.17	154.40	228.80	164.20	160.33
Shoulder orientation	432.86	1340.00	864.28	801.67	586.00	1288.00	752.00	806.67
Arm openness	164.28	100.57	132.28	133.33	152.80	121.60	130.60	125.83
Leg openness	75.14	46.86	50.43	58.83	58.80	53.20	49.60	51.17
Backward lean	67.86	104.14	83.86	80.17	79.20	85.60	75.20	73.83
Sideway lean	508.57	270.00	392.87	406.66	330.00	344.00	426.00	393.33
Smiles	14.71	7.00	12.43	12.83	12.00	10.60	10.80	11.00
Positive head nod	8.43	4.14	8.00	8.33	5.60	5.60	7.60	7.67
Gesticulations	13.28	4.00	7.57	7.17	4.80	6.40	5.20	6.00
Manipulations	13.14	13.28	9.00	9.00	12.00	14.60	7.20	8.17
Negative head nods	2.28	1.71	1.71	2.17	2.00	3.60	2.60	2.00
Eye contact when interviewer speaking	.65	.26	.45	.44	.51	.39	.42	.44
Eye contact when S speaking	.77	.39	.67	.65	.55	.58	.83	.69
Eye contact during silence	.67	.28	.36	.36	.38	.31	.32	.33

There were more manipulations with a male interviewer than female interviewer, and manipulations were more frequent in both the father-separated groups than the intact group. There were more positive head nods and more eye contact when the subject was speaking and the interviewer was a female. Also, when the subject was speaking, there was less eye contact for daughters of widows than the other father-status groups. Although the interaction associated with this variable was not significant, an inspection of the means suggests that this finding was largely attributable to the small amount of eye contact when subjects in the widowed group were speaking to male interviewers.

Three-way analyses of variance with unequal Ns involving type and time of separation and sex of interviewer were performed on each of these same nonverbal variables for father-separated girls only. The means for this analysis are presented in Table 5. The results associated with type of separation and sex of interviewer paralleled those of the previous analyses and are not discussed again. In addition, significant main effects for time of separation were obtained on interviewer speaking time, gesticulations, and eye contact during silence. Significant interactions between type and time of separation were obtained on backward lean, gesticulations, eye contact when the interviewer was speaking, and eye contact during silence. Triple-order interactions were obtained on subject speaking time, backward lean, sideways lean, smiles, gesticulations, eye contact when the subject was speaking, and eye contact during silence.

Interviewers spoke more with early than late separated girls. Daughters whose fathers died early talked less to a male interviewer than did any other group of girls. When the interviewer was speaking, there was less eye contact in the widowed early group than in either the divorced early or divorced late groups. The late separated daughters of widows showed less eye contact when the interviewer was speaking than did the divorced early girls. When they were speaking to a male interviewer, the girls in the early widowed group showed a smaller proportion of eye contact than did girls in any other group. Girls whose parents were divorced late looked directly when speaking to a female interviewer more often than girls whose parents were divorced early, or than did either group of late separated girls with a male interviewer. However, in talking to a male interviewer, the divorced late girls showed less eye contact than the divorced early girls. During silence with a male interviewer, these divorced late girls showed more eye contact than did any other group of girls with either a male or female interviewer.

The openness and approach of the divorced early girls and inhibition of widowed early girls with a male interviewer was reflected in the differences between means in the significant triple interactions on some of the postural and gestural measures. The widowed early girls showed more backward lean with a male interviewer than did any other group of girls. In contrast, divorced early girls showed less backward lean with a male than a female interviewer.

Congruently, divorced early girls with a male interviewer showed more sideways lean than did the other three groups with a male interviewer or the divorced early group with a female interviewer. In addition, with a male interviewer, widowed early girls showed less sideways lean than did any group of subjects with a female interviewer.

The widowed early girls with a male interviewer smiled less than any other group of girls. The divorced early girls with a male interviewer not only smiled more than the widowed early girls, but also more than any late separated group except divorced with a male interviewer. In addition, they made more gesticulations than any other group.

Daughter-Interview Measures

Separate one-way analyses of variance with father status as the factor were performed on the 22 daughter-interview variables. Significant results were obtained for the 10 variables presented in Table 6 along with the group means. Deviations of the daughters with absent fathers appeared most often in relation to feelings and interactions with males. It is interesting to note that there were no differences on variables such as feminine interests, attitudes to the feminine role, or similarity to mother and father, each of which might have been related to sex typing or identification. There also were no differences with respect to relationships with other females including the mother. All groups reported themselves as equally secure around female adults and peers, equally close to their mothers, and their mothers as equally warm and permissive. The exception to this was that daughters with divorced parents reported more conflict with their mothers.

Table 6 Means for Daughter Interview Measures

| | Father Absent | | Father | | |
Interview Variable	DIVORCED	DEATH	Present	F	p
Security around male peers	2.71_a	2.62_a	3.79_b	4.79	.01
Security around male adults	2.12_a	2.12_a	3.66_b	11.25	.001
Heterosexual activity	4.83_a	2.62_b	3.83_c	12.96	.001
Conflict with mothers	5.08_a	3.62_b	4.08_b	5.64	.005
Positive attitude toward father	3.08_a	4.66_b	4.21_b	7.57	.001
Father's warmth	3.33_a	4.50_b	$3.87_{a\,b}$	2.82	.06
Father's competence	3.16_a	4.75_b	4.12_b	6.65	.002
Conflict with father	4.43_a	2.25_b	3.46_c	7.03	.002
Relations with other adult males	3.29_a	3.12_a	4.54_b	5.08	.009
Self-esteem	2.87_a	$3.58_{a\,b}$	4.04_b	3.34	.04

Note.—All row means which do not share a common subscript differ at least at $p < .05$ with two-tailed t tests.

Both daughters of widows and divorcees felt insecure around male peers and adults; however, this was manifested in different ways. The daughters of divorcees reported more, while the daughters of widows reported less, heterosexual activity than any other groups. There was some evidence of more negative feelings toward the father by daughters of divorcees than by daughters of widows. Girls of divorcees reported more negative attitudes toward the father, more conflict with the father, and regarded the father as less competent than either of the other two groups of girls. Girls of widows reported having less conflict with their fathers than did either of the other groups of girls and described their fathers as warmer and more competent than did daughters of divorcees. It is interesting that both groups of father-absent daughters reported less contact with other adult males than did children from intact families. Girls from intact families frequently reported being attached to their parents' male friends. Girls from father-present homes and from widowed families showed higher self-esteem than girls from divorced families.

Separate two-way analyses involving type and time of separation were performed on the father-absent daughters' interview data. These analyses yielded little additional information except that daughters of widows reported more disturbance at loss of the father than did daughters of divorcees. The effects for type of separation paralleled those in the previous discussion and no significant age effects or interactions were obtained.

Mother-Interview Measures

Separate one-way analyses of variance for the father-status groups were performed on each rating measure of the maternal interview. The means for groups on the variables for which significant F ratios were obtained are presented in Table 7.

Table 7   Group Means for Maternal Interview Rating Scales

Variable	Father Absent		Father Present	F	p
	DIVORCED	DEATH			
Overprotection before adolescence	3.62_a	3.71_a	2.67_b	3.39	.04
Punishment for sexual curiosity & activity after adolescence	3.87_a	2.79_b	3.00_b	4.32	.02
Consistency after adolescence	3.54_a	4.67_b	4.67_b	4.46	.02
Conflict before adolescence	4.25_a	2.92_b	3.71_a	4.06	.02
Conflict after adolescence	4.75_a	3.46_b	3.75_b	5.55	.006
Negative attitude toward spouse	4.67_a	3.30_b	3.33_b	5.46	.006
Anxiety about adequacy as mother	4.50_a	3.83_b	3.54_b	3.30	.04
Happiness & fulfillment in life	2.75_a	3.58_b	3.75_b	2.31	.05
Happiness in marriage	2.79_a	4.75_b	4.12_b	9.36	.001
Conflict with father	4.71_a	2.67_b	3.33_b	11.84	.001

Note.—All row means which do not share a common subscript differ at least at $p < .05$ with two-tailed t tests.

Divorced mothers appear to have had a negative attitude toward their ex-spouses, themselves, and life in general. Their lives and marriages had not been gratifying, and they were concerned about their adequacy as mothers. However, these mothers reported positive relationships with their daughters, and exhibited similar patterns of affection and discipline to that of the widowed and still married mothers in the preadolescent period. Most deviations followed and may have been a reaction to the daughters' adolescent behaviors. Both groups of mothers without husbands were overprotective and solicitous of their preadolescent daughters. High conflict with spouse before separation and with daughter after adolescence was found in divorced women. The lowest preadolescent conflict with the daughter was reported by the widowed group; however, there were no differences in preadolescent conflict between the divorced and intact groups. Divorcees reported themselves as being more punitive toward their daughters for sexual activity and as being inconsistent in discipline only after adolescence. This similarity in affection for their daughters, but difference in response to adolescent behavior, by widows and divorcees is reflected in the following portions of representative interviews by two mothers, the first from the widowed group, the second from the divorced group.

[Daughter's name] is almost too good. She has lots of girl friends but doesn't date much. When she's with the girls she's gay and bouncy—quite a clown but she clams up when a man comes in. Even around my brother she never says much. When boys do phone she often puts them off even though she has nothing else to do. She says she has lots of time for that later, but she's sixteen now and very pretty, and all her friends have boy friends.

That kid is going to drive me over the hill. I'm at my wits end. She was so good until the last few years then Pow! at eleven she really turned on. She went boy crazy. When she was only twelve I came home early from a movie and found her in bed with a young hood and she's been bouncing from bed to bed ever since. She doesn't seem to care who it is, she can't keep her hands off men. It isn't just boys her own age, when I have men friends here she kisses them when they come in the door and sits on their knees all in a very playful fashion but it happens to them all. Her uncle is a sixty-year-old priest and she even made a "ha ha" type pass at him. It almost scared him to death! I sometimes get so frantic I think I should turn her into the cops but I remember what a good kid she used to be and I do love her. We still have a good time together when we're alone and I'm not nagging about her being a tramp. We both like to cook and we get a lot of good laughs when we're puttering around in the kitchen. She's smart and good-looking—she should know she doesn't have to act like that.

Again, separate 2 (Type of Separation) $\times$ 2 (Age of Separation) analyses of variance were performed on ratings of separated mothers. In addition to the previously obtained differences for type of separation, early separation was found to result in greater overprotection preceding and following adolescence than does later separation. The only significant interaction was on intrusiveness following adolescence, which indicated that early divorced mothers were more intrusive than late divorced or early widowed mothers.

On the analyses of scales only rated for separated mothers, widowed mothers, in contrast to divorced mothers, reported greater intensity of disturbance following loss of husband, more emotional support from friends and family, and less resentment at being a woman bringing up a child alone. Many widowed mothers described having the child as "a blessing" or as "giving them something to live for."

Personality Measures for Mothers and Daughters

No differences were found among groups for mothers or daughters on the number of subjects drawing a female figure first on the Draw-a-Person Test (daughters: divorced, 18; death, 19; present, 16. Mothers: divorcees, 17; widows, 19; intact, 17). One-way analyses of variance for the three father-status groups were done separately for mothers', and daughters', scores on the California Personality Inventory Femininity Scale, Rotter's Internal-External Control Scale, and the Bendig Short Form of the Manifest Anxiety Scale.

Mother groups and daughter groups did not differ in their responses to the Femininity Scale. On the analyses for mothers, both divorced and widowed mothers were found to feel more externally controlled than mothers from intact families. No differences on the total Internal-External Control Scale scores were found for daughters. However, Mirels [24] has recently factor-analyzed this scale and has concluded that it is not unidimensional but includes two factors. The first factor is comprised of items involving a felt mastery over the course of one's life, the second concerns the extent to which an individual is capable of influencing political institutions. Five items which loaded heavily on each of the factors were selected, and separate analyses of variance were performed on scores on the five personal and political control items. There were no differences between groups for either mothers or daughters on the scores on political control, but both groups of separated mothers and daughters scored lower on internalization on the personal control items than did mothers and daughters from intact families. Both groups of daughters without fathers also reported themselves as more anxious on the Manifest Anxiety Scale than daughters with the father living in the home. Divorcees were more anxious than the other two groups of mothers. No time of separation effects were found on any of the scale scores when subsequent analyses of time and type of separation were performed.

DISCUSSION

The results of this study suggest that there are different patterns of effects of father absence on the development of girls and boys. Past research indicates that in boys, separation results in disruptions in sex-role typing during the

---

[24] H. L. Mirels, "Dimensions of Internal Versus External Control," *Journal of Consulting and Clinical Psychology*, XXXIV (1970), 226–228.

preschool years, but with increasing age and extrafamilial interaction these effects are attenuated or transformed into compensatory masculinity. In contrast, previous studies with young girls have demonstrated no effects of father separation except an occasional finding of greater dependency.

These studies in combination with the present one suggest that the effects of father absence on daughters appear during adolescence and are manifested mainly as an inability to interact appropriately with males, rather than in other deviations from appropriate sex typing or in interactions with females. There was little apparent disturbance in sex-typed behaviors or preference for the female role as assessed by observational or interview measures or the California Personality Inventory Masculinity-Femininity Scale. Father absence seems to increase dependency in girls, but this is viewed as an appropriately feminine attribute. It does not appear to be related to masculine behaviors such as aggression. Even when aggression appeared in the group of girls whose parents had been divorced early it took the form of prosocial aggression, which is a characteristically feminine form of aggressive behavior.[25] Although these girls also scored low in female activities, this seemed to be largely attributable to their spending time in seeking proximity with male peers by hanging around the male areas of the recreation center. These girls spent so much time in the carpentry shop, basketball court, and other male areas that they had little opportunity to sew, do beadwork, or participate in female activities usually located elsewhere. During recreation center dances they spent much of their time at the boys' end of the hall around the "stag line," in contrast to the daughters of widows who stayed at the girls' end, often at the back of the group of girls. Two of the girls in the widowed group hid out in the ladies room for the entire evening of one dance. This was not because of differences in popularity between the groups of girls. When they were present in the hall the two groups of father-absent girls were asked to dance equally often. It is interesting to note that in spite of their greater time spent in male areas, daughters of divorcees did not participate in masculine activities more than the other girls. There were also no differences between groups in sex-role orientation as measured by sex of the figure drawn first on the Draw-a-Person Test, although in father-absent boys disruptions in sex-role orientation tend to be more enduring than those in sex-role preference or sex-typed behaviors.

Except for greater dependency on female adults in the recreation center, girls with absent fathers showed few deviations in relations with females. The effects of father absence on relationships with males is particularly apparent in the nonverbal measures recorded during the girls' interviews with male and female interviewers. Few group differences were found with female interviewers; however, with male interviewers, clear group differences in nonverbal communication emerged. With male interviewers, daughters of widows demonstrated relatively infrequent speech and eye contact, avoid-

[25] R. R. Sears, "The Relation of Early Socialization Experiences to Aggression in Middle Childhood," *Journal of Abnormal and Social Psychology,* LXIII (1961), 466–492.

ance of proximity with the interviewer in seat selection and body orientation, and rigid postural characteristics. In contrast, daughters of divorcees again showed proximity seeking and a smiling, open, receptive manner with the male interviewer. This greater receptiveness to males by the girls whose fathers are absent because of divorce also is supported by their interview reports of earlier and more dating and sexual intercourse, in contrast to daughters of widows who report starting to date late and being sexually inhibited.

When effects of time of father separation were found, the effects of early separation were usually greater than later separation. This is in agreement with studies of the effects of father absence on sons and suggests that the first 5 years of life represent a critical period for the impact of father absence on children. This effect was most apparent in some of the nonverbal measures of communication in the daughter interview where early separation tended to increase the disparity between the behavior of the daughters of widows and divorcees. However, on the observational measures in the recreation center, time of separation tended to affect the behavior of the two groups of father-separated girls in a similar direction. It is interesting that few time of separation effects were found on interview or test measures; they emerged most frequently in observational measures.

It might be proposed that for both groups of father-absent girls the lack of opportunity for constructive interaction with a loving, attentive father has resulted in apprehension and inadequate skills in relating to males. Their tension in relating to males was supported by their reports in the interview of feelings of insecurity in interacting with male peers and male adults, and in their high rate of manipulations such as nailbiting, hair, lip, and finger pulling, and plucking at clothes and other objects while being interviewed by a male. Their general feeling of anxiety and powerlessness was also reflected in relatively high scores on the Manifest Anxiety Scale and relatively low scores on the factor dealing with a sense of personal control over the course of one's life on the Internal-External Control Scale. This may be intensified in daughters of divorced parents by their low sense of self-esteem.

If it is argued that both groups of girls were manifesting deviant behaviors in attempting to cope with their anxiety and lack of skills in relating to males, the difficult question that remains is how they developed such disparate patterns of coping mechanisms to deal with this problem.

It seems likely that differences in the behavior of the divorced and widowed mothers may have mediated differences in their daughters' behaviors. However, in relationships with their daughters, widows, divorcees, and mothers from intact families were remarkably similar in many ways. In affection, control, and discipline these mothers were similar. The differences between divorcees and the other two groups which appeared after adolescence in consistency, conflict, and punishment of the daughter for sexual activity could well have occurred as a reaction rather than a precursor to their daughter's disruptive adolescent behavior with males. However, there was less strife between widows and daughters than in any other family. All groups of mothers were equally feminine, reinforced daughters for sex-appropriate behaviors and, surprisingly, had equally positive attitudes toward men. Since these mothers were offering their daughters appropriately feminine models and rewarding them for their assumption of the feminine role, the finding that there were no disruptions in traditional measures of sex typing for the father-absent girls is compatible with expectations of social learning theorists.

The only measures on which both father-separated groups of mothers differed from those in intact families were on overprotection of the daughter before adolescence and in feeling more externally controlled. These too could be associated with loss of a husband.

It seems mainly in attitudes toward herself, her marriage, and her life that the divorcee differed from the widow. She is anxious and unhappy. Her attitude toward her spouse is hostile; her memories of her marriage and life are negative. These attitudes are reflected in the critical attitude of her daughter toward the divorced father. Although she loves her daughter she feels she has had little support from other people during her divorce and times of stress and with her difficulties in rearing a child alone. This is in marked contrast to the positive attitudes of the widows toward marriage, their lost husbands, the emotional support of friends and family at the loss of a husband, and the gratifications of having children. These attitudes are reflected in the happy memories their daughters have of their fathers.

Any explanation of the relationship between these maternal behaviors and the daughters' behavior in interacting with males is highly speculative. It may be that daughters of divorcees view their mother's separated lives as unsatisfying and feel that for happiness it is essential to secure a man. Their lack of experience in interacting with a loving father and their hostile memories of their father may cause them to be particularly apprehensive and inept in their pursuit of this goal. It might be argued that rather than being inept these girls are precociously skillful and provocative in their relationship with men. However, such things as their reported anxiety around males and the fact that they were no more popular than the other groups of girls at the recreation center dances suggests that their coping mechanisms are not effective. It may also be that life with a dissatisfied, anxious mother is difficult, and these daughters are more eager to leave home than daughters of widows living with relatively happy, secure mothers with support from the extended family. Daughters of widows with their aggrandized image of their father may also feel that no other males can compare favorably with him, or alternately may regard all males as superior and as objects of deference and apprehension.

It should be noted that the mothers in the father-separated groups are not representative of all divorcees and widows since they have not remarried. This might be more difficult for the divorcee than the widow, who reports more support by her family and even frequent closeness with her dead husband's family. The widow may have less to gain by remarriage, although both groups report an equal number of male friends and dates.

There are many questions about the effects of father absence on the development of daughters that remain unanswered. It is apparent that reasons for and age of separation, as well as current age of the daughter are important factors which must be considered in future investigations of this problem.

Charles E. Bowerman
Stephen J. Bahr

Conjugal Power and Adolescent
Identification with Parents[1]

Conjugal marital power—"the ability of one partner to influence the other's behavior" is usually described as patriarchal, matriarchal, or equalitarian. Bowerman and Bahr reveal how conjugal power affects the identification of adolescents with their parents. The study included over 18,000 youths from unbroken homes in grades seven through twelve. The data indicate primarily that "adolescents who perceive conjugal relations as equalitarian are highest in identification with parents while those who perceive the mother as dominant are lowest."

Instructional Objectives
To review relations suggested by earlier investigators between conjugal power and adolescents' identification with their parents.
To define conjugal power as a variable in socialization.

FROM *Sociometry*, XXXVI (1973), pp. 366–377. Reprinted by permission of the authors and the publisher.

[1] We express appreciation to Viktor Gecas for helpful suggestions in the preparation of this paper. The data on which the paper is based were obtained from the Adolescent Study, directed by Charles E. Bowerman while at the University of North Carolina, supported by Public Health Service Grant M-2045 from NIMH. Analysis of the data was supported by the Department of Rural Sociology, Washington State University, and is Scientific Paper No. 3968, Washington Agricultural Experiment Station.

To indicate by age/sex groupings the degree to which adolescents differentiate parental power.

To explain the relations revealed by the findings in this study between conjugal power and identification of adolescents with their parents.

M UCH socialization research and literature has focused on questions concerning the effects of various types of parental behavior on the child and his social development. Parental power and support are among the explanatory variables often used in the attempt to answer such questions. With the emphasis in socialization research on parental discipline and parent-child interaction, the effect that *conjugal* interaction may have on the child has been given only cursory examination. Yet research on the effects of conjugal interaction on the child might supply useful information for providing more adequate and complete theories of socialization. The present paper focuses on one aspect of this problem, namely the relation of conjugal power to adolescent identification with parents.

Identification has long been one of the major interests of social psychologists. With increased attention being given to "problems of youth," such as student riots, a seemingly large generation gap, and increased juvenile delinquency, even by children from "good homes," [2] parents and scholars are continually seeking to understand youth and why some identify with their parents and accept their values and others do not. Identification suggests a relationship which may be personally gratifying, and in which the possibility of influence and learning may be maximized. Hence, it may be viewed as an indicator of adequate socialization and internalization of parental norms and values. It is in this context that we wish to examine the possible effects of conjugal power differences on the adolescent's identification with his parents.

PREVIOUS RESEARCH

The dearth of research or theory concerning the relationship of conjugal power to adolescent identification with parents provides little basis for deriving specific research hypotheses. However, available research does direct us to some fruitful questions regarding this relationship. Bronfenbrenner [3] has studied those traits boys and girls tend to acquire under conjugal power structures that are patriarchal, matriarchal, and equalitarian. A summary of his results are as follows:

[2] H. L. Myerhoff and B. G. Myerhoff, "Field Observations of Middle Class 'Gangs'," *Social Forces*, XLII (March 1964), 328–336.

[3] U. Bronfenbrenner, "The Changing American Child—A Speculative Analysis," in John N. Edwards, ed., *The Family and Change* (New York: Alfred A. Knopf, 1969), pp. 236–250.

Both responsibility and leadership are fostered by the relatively greater salience of the parent of the same sex. . . . Boys tend to be more responsible when the father rather than the mother is the principal disciplinarian; girls are more dependable when the mother is the authority figure. . . . In short, boys thrive in a patriarchal context, girls in a matriarchal. . . . The most dependent and least dependable adolescents describe family arrangements that are neither patriarchal nor matriarchal, but equalitarian. To state the issue in more provocative form, our data suggest that the democratic family, which for so many years has been held up and aspired to as a model by professionals and enlightened laymen, tends to produce young people who 'do not take initiative,' 'look to others for direction and decision,' and 'cannot be counted on to fulfill obligations.'

Dager [4] suggests that in a democratic, equalitarian power structure the child is not able to clearly delineate and internalize important roles, and thus, such equalitarianism ". . . would seem to befuddle the child with subsequent implications for personality organization." In short, the Bronfenbrenner and Dager studies indicate that adolescent responsibility, initiative, and internalization of important roles may be greater when the same-sex parent is dominant than when the conjugal power structure is equalitarian. Is conjugal power related in a similar way to identification? This suggests the following research questions: (1) Do adolescents identify more with the same-sex parent when that parent is perceived as dominant? (2) Is the difference between male and female identification with each parent less when the conjugal relationship is perceived as equalitarian than when it is perceived as husband- or wife-dominant?

Several studies suggest that a mother-dominant power structure may possibly have negative consequences for children, especially for boys. Schulz [5] suggests, for example, that the indiscreet "free man" has little control over his children or wife, for he has nothing to legitimize his authority. Schulz points out the detrimental effects that such a situation has on children. In the traditional monogamous family or in the discreet "free man" type, the father has more authority and is given more respect. The implication is that in matriarchal families the children might have less identification with their father.

Mischler and Waxler [6] have studied family power and its relation to mental illness. They found that the biggest difference between healthy and schizophrenic children was not in the behavior of the children, but in the behavior of the parents. In normal families the parents formed a power coalition. In families with male schizophrenics the mother and son formed a

---

[4] E. Z. Dager, "Socialization and Personality Development in the Child," in H. T. Christensen, ed., *Handbook of Marriage and the Family* (Chicago: Rand McNally, 1964), pp. 740–782.

[5] D. A. Schulz, *Coming Up Black* (Englewood Cliffs, New Jersey: Prentice-Hall, 1969).

[6] E. G. Mischler and N. E. Waxler, *Interaction in Families* (New York: John Wiley, 1968).

coalition and the father was isolated and had little power. Girl schizophrenics were isolated and the mother was dominant over the father. Green [7] suggests that the absence of a male role model and wife dominance contributes to neurosis. Although the Mischler-Waxler and Green studies do not deal directly with identification and respect, they imply that identification might be less in wife-dominant families than in other families.

These studies suggest the following research questions: (1) Do adolescents who perceive the mother as dominant identify with their mother more than their father? (2) Do adolescents who perceive their mother as dominant identify less with either parent than do adolescents in other families?

Adolescents might identify with their parents more strongly when their parents have a satisfactory marital relationship. Blood and Wolfe [8] found marital satisfaction highest in equalitarian couples and lowest in wife-dominant couples. Does an adolescent identify with parents to a greater degree when conjugal power is perceived as equalitarian and to a lesser degree when it is seen as mother-dominant?

SAMPLE

The present study is a secondary analysis of data collected by Bowerman in 1960. Almost half the sample was obtained through public and parochial schools in central Ohio, while the remainder was obtained in public schools in central North Carolina. This sample included all adolescents in grades seven through twelve who were in school when a structured questionnaire was administered by teachers in the classroom in April and May of 1960. The final sample was 18,664 white students from unbroken homes. This sample contained 5393 junior high males, 5664 junior high females, 3755 senior high males, and 3852 senior high females.

CONCEPTS AND MEASURES

Although identification has been defined in various ways, Bandura states that ". . . it is generally agreed that identification refers to a process in which a person patterns his thoughts, feelings, or actions after another person who serves as a model." [9] Similarly, Gewirtz refers to identification as ". . . the child's acquisition of the values, ideals, roles, and conscience of an important other person (the model), particularly those of his parents and especially the same-sex parent." [10] When one identifies with another (the

[7] A. W. Green, "The Middle-Class Male Child and Neurosis," *American Sociological Review*, XI (February 1946), 31–41.

[8] R. O. Blood and D. M. Wolfe, *Husbands and Wives* (New York: The Free Press, 1960), p. 258.

[9] A. Bandura, "Social-Learning Theory of Identificatory Processes," in D. A. Goslin, ed., *Handbook of Socialization Theory and Research* (Chicago: Rand McNally, 1969), pp. 213–262.

[10] J. L. Gewirtz, "Mechanisms of Social Learning: Some Roles of Stimulation and Behavior in Early Human Development," in D. A. Goslin, ed., *Handbook of Socialization Theory and Research* (Chicago: Rand McNally, 1969), pp. 57–212.

model) he (1) sees the model as a significant other, (2) feels positive affection and admiration for the model, (3) takes on the model's norms and values, and (4) may perceive the direct control the model has over him as legitimate.[11]

Wide differences exist concerning the most appropriate way to measure identification.[12] In the present study we will define it in terms of the value orientation that adolescents have toward mother and toward father, as measured by the following eight items.

(1) Do you respect your mother's (father's) opinions about the important things in life?

(2) How much do you depend on your mother (father) for advice and guidance?

(3) Do you respect your mother's (father's) judgment about normal, everyday matters you face?

(4) Would you like to be the kind of person your mother (father) is?

(5) How much do your mother's (father's) opinions influence *your* ideas of right and wrong?

(6) Do you find your mother's (father's) advice helpful in deciding what you should do?

(7) Do you feel that you can trust your mother's (father's) judgments about important decisions you must make?

(8) Do you find the attitudes and opinions of your mother (father) helpful in deciding matters of right and wrong?

Each of these items had five response categories from very negative to very positive. A Guttman-type scale was constructed, combining non-differentiating responses to provide a quasi-scale with values ranging from 0 to 14 and a reproducibility index of about 75 per cent with simple scoring.

In this paper, power is conceptualized as the ability of one partner to influence the other's behavior. This definition is similar to the definition of power used by many researchers in the area of the family and is consistent with recent social power theorists who generally agree that ". . . social power is a person's potential for exerting a force toward change in another person."[13]

The following question was used as the measure of conjugal power: When important family problems come up, which parent usually has the most *influence* in making the decision? (Responses were "mother almost always," "mother much more often," "mother little more often," "about equal," "father little more often," "father much more often," and "father almost always.") Although there are unresolved problems concerning the concept of power

[11] R. J. Adamek and E. Z. Dager, "Social Structure, Identification and Change in a Treatment-Oriented Institution," in E. Z. Dager, ed., *Socialization* (Chicago: Markham, 1971), pp. 162–188.

[12] Bandura, op. cit.

[13] T. E. Smith, "Foundations of Parental Influence Upon Adolescents: An Application of Social Power Theory," *American Sociological Review*, XXXV (October 1970), 860–873.

and its measurement, this question would seem to be a reasonable indicator of the general concept of power as it is often used in the literature. It should be kept in mind that our measure of conjugal power is based on the adolescent's perceptions. Although some might say that a more objective or behavioral measure is preferable, this method seems justifiable from a symbolic interaction perspective. What is important for adolescent identity is the adolescent's perception of the conjugal power structure, for the adolescents act on that definition even if it is not entirely accurate. Furthermore, in light of the difficulty in getting reliable and valid measures of conjugal power, it seems that the intimate view that an adolescent has of his family may be one appropriate alternative way to "get at" conjugal power. Data from two recent studies suggest that there may be fairly high validity to adolescent perceptions of conjugal power.[14]

FINDINGS

Table 1 gives the mean scores on adolescent identification with parents by perceived husband-wife power, for each of the four adolescent subgroups. Identification with both parents is clearly higher, on the average, when the power structure is seen as equalitarian. The one exception is the attitude of older males toward father, where the average identification with dominant fathers is slightly higher than for the equalitarian situation. Beyond this, however, the relationship between power and identification is significantly different toward mothers than toward fathers. Scores of identification with mother average about the same whether mother or father is viewed as more dominant; identification scores when one parent is dominant average 1.00 below scores for the equalitarian situation, and the difference is fairly constant for all four age-sex groups. However, identification with father averages 1.91 lower when the mother is perceived as more influential compared with scores toward more influential fathers. Also compared with scores toward equalitarian fathers, fathers in mother-dominated families averaged 2.20 lower for the four age-sex groups, though dominant fathers averaged only .29 lower than those who were equalitarian.

The last column of Table 1 shows the differences in relation between power and mother versus father identification in another way. Females have higher average identification scores with mother than with father regardless of the perceived power structure. The difference in favor of mother, however, is greatest when the mother has more power, and least when the father is the dominant parent. Males, by comparison, identify more strongly with whichever parent is dominant, and have approximately equal scores toward mother and father when parents are perceived as equalitarian. This gradient

[14] S. J. Bahr, C. E. Bowerman and V. Gecas, "Adolescent Perceptions of Conjugal Power," *Social Forces*, LII (December 1973); G. H. Elder and C. E. Bowerman, "Family Structure and Child-Rearing Patterns: The Effect of Family Size and Sex Composition," *American Sociological Review*, XXVIII (December 1963), 891–905.

Table 1   *Mean Identification of Adolescent with Parents by Perceived Power of Parents* *

Age-Sex Group	Most Influential Parent	N	Mean Identification with		Difference a—b
			(a) MOTHER	(b) FATHER	
Males (7–9 grade)	Mother	874	7.65	6.26	1.39
	Both Equal	2490	8.46	8.59	—.13
	Father	1762	7.69	8.18	—.49
Females (7–9 grade)	Mother	990	8.56	5.38	3.18
	Both Equal	3001	9.58	7.76	1.82
	Father	1485	8.65	7.24	1.41
Males (10–12 grade)	Mother	717	6.27	5.09	1.18
	Both Equal	1350	7.24	7.08	.16
	Father	1580	6.30	7.23	—.93
Females (10–12 grade)	Mother	978	7.48	4.94	2.54
	Both Equal	1545	8.99	7.03	1.96
	Father	1256	7.93	6.67	1.26

* The standard deviations of scores for the four age-sex groups toward mother and father range from 3.80 to 4.45 with a mean of 4.10. With S = 4.10 and Ns of 700, the standard error of a difference would be .22. Since the differences discussed in the Findings section are much larger, and based on Ns over 700, they are obviously significant statistically.

in mother-father identification found for both males and females and in both age groups is due, of course, to the relatively low identification with fathers in mother-dominant homes noted previously.

Another comparison that can be made from Table 1 is between scores of male and female subjects, controlling for age of subject and parental power structure. In all comparisons, identification averages higher toward the same-sex parent. The closest sex balance is found among the junior high subjects where females average 1.00 higher than males in identification toward mother, and males are .88 higher than females in identification toward father. For senior high subjects, males and females have fairly similar identification with father—males averaging only .25 higher, but females average 1.53 higher with mother than do males. Within each of these comparison groups, however, sex differences in identification are approximately the same regardless of the type of parental power structure. In other words, when we control for age of subject, the relationship between parental power balance and identification to either parent is very similar for male and female adolescents.

In another set of comparisons, we note that the junior high subjects have higher average identification scores than the senior high students with both mother and father, for each sex and power type. For example, younger males are 1.38 higher than older males in identification with mothers in mother-dominant families. Although age differences do not vary greatly from one power type to another, differences in attitude toward mother are slightly smaller in equalitarian families and those toward father are a little *larger* in equalitarian families. In general the age differences in identification are smaller for females than for males.

In the tabulation that we have been discussing, a parent was classified as more powerful if the student checked any one of three responses to the question as to which parent usually has the most influence in making decisions about important family problems: "almost always," "much more often," or "little more often." Since these categories represent degrees of dominance, we were interested in whether there were differences in identification with the parent perceived as having slightly more power compared with a great deal more power. This question seems especially interesting because in a study cited earlier, Bronfenbrenner [15] states that:

> Extreme concentrations of power in one or another parent were comparatively rare. Had they been more frequent, we suspect the data would have shown that such extreme asymmetrical patterns of authority were detrimental rather than salutary for effective psychological development, perhaps even more disorganizing than equalitarian forms.

To make this comparison, we combined the responses "almost always" and "much more often" to form a high dominance category, and used the response "a little more often" for the low dominance category. Frequencies in these high and low dominance categories were roughly equal. With four age-sex groups of subjects, identification with mother and with father, and either mother or father dominant, there are 16 comparisons that can be made of identification with a parent with high versus low dominance. In 13 of these comparisons, adolescent identification was lower with the parent perceived as having high dominance rather than low dominance. The average of these 13 differences was .64. In the other three instances the differences were small and averaged only .11 in favor of high dominance, not a statistically significant difference. Recalling that identification is highest when parents are seen as having equal power, we have a gradient from equality downward toward lower identification as either parent becomes increasingly powerful over the other.

As a check on the reliability of results reported for the eight-item scale, and to provide a referent in terms of actual response, a tabulation was made of one of the component items: desire to be like mother (and like father). The conclusions (see Table 2) are essentially the same as those obtained from comparison of means for the entire scale: the per cent desiring to be like each parent is highest in families with equal parental power, it is highest toward the same-sex parent except for males reporting mother dominance, and the greatest comparative "loss" in identification is with fathers when

[15] Bronfenbrenner, op. cit., p. 245.

mother is seen as more dominant. The younger subjects of each sex had higher identification with both parents under all influence conditions than did older subjects (data not shown), but the differences were small, ranging from 1 to 7 per cent.

Table 2   Adolescent Desire to Be Like Mother and Father by Perceived Power of Parents (In Per Cent)

	Most Influential Parent	N	Desire to Be Like *	
			MOTHER	FATHER
Males	Mother	1591	71	65
	Equal	3840	79	85
	Father	3342	74	81
Females	Mother	1968	79	58
	Equal	4546	88	76
	Father	2741	82	71

* Those adolescents who checked "Yes, completely," "In most ways," and "In many ways" to the question "Would you like to be the kind of person your father (mother) is?" were placed in the "Desire to Be Like Father (Mother)" category; those who checked "In just a few ways," or "not at all" were *not* placed in this category.

Table 3   Comparison of Which Parent Adolescents Respect More, by Perceived Power of Parents (In Per Cent)

	Most Influential Parent	N	Which Parent Respected More *			
			MOTHER MORE	EQUAL	FATHER MORE	TOTAL
Males	Mother	1591	35	49	15	99
	Equal	3840	12	78	10	100
	Father	3342	15	59	26	100
Females	Mother	1968	50	41	9	100
	Equal	4546	25	71	4	100
	Father	2741	32	55	13	100

* Based on the question, "Whose ideas and opinions do you respect more, as a guide to your own behavior, your father's or your mother's?"

Comparisons between identification with mother and with father have been made up to this point by contrasting separate answers about mother and father. A different perspective on this comparison is given in Table 3 which shows the relationship between parental influence and a question asking for a direct comparison of which parent the adolescents respect more. In general, the data confirm generalizations previously made. Except for females with more-dominant mothers, subjects are most likely to say that they respect parents equally; however, this answer is most frequent when parents are seen as equally influential. Subjects of either sex are more likely to give greater respect to one parent if that parent is dominant, though the only instance where the father is respected more than the mother is by males who see him as the dominant parent. As in the data reported earlier, fathers fare worst, in comparison with mothers, when the mother is perceived as most influential. Under this condition, males respect mothers more than fathers by two and a third to one, whereas the father who is seen as dominant is given equal or greater respect by 85 per cent of the males.

SUMMARY AND CONCLUSIONS

It is clear that adolescents in this study who report being raised in families where parents have equal influence identify more strongly, on the average, with both parents than do adolescents in mother- or father-dominant families. This finding is of particular interest in view of evidence in two earlier studies of some possible negative consequences of an equalitarian power structure. The Bronfenbrenner data [16] indicate that adolescents from equalitarian families are low on dependability and initiative and Dager [17] concludes that equalitarian families may inhibit adequate role internalization. The findings are not necessarily inconsistent, and suggest the importance of investigating in this context the interrelations of identification and other personality variables.

When one parent is perceived as having less family influence than the other, we find that not only is identification of the adolescent lower with both parents but that the relationship is different for father than for mother. Identification with mother differs little, on the average, whether she is more influential or less influential; however, identification with father is considerably lower when he is perceived as the less influential of the two parents. This means not only a difference in identification with less powerful than with more powerful fathers (with consequences that this may have for father-child relations) but a significant difference in comparative identification with fathers and mothers within certain families. Variations in these relationships by age and sex of subject were reported. The unbalanced power relationship may also affect other structural aspects of the family. For instance, the finding by Blood and Wolfe [18] that marital happiness seemed to be lowest in a wife-dominant power structure, along with our finding that a lower proportion of adolescents in such families identify with both parents and have a large discrepancy in level of identification with mother and

16 Ibid.
17 Dager, op. cit.
18 Blood and Wolfe, op. cit.

father—suggests a relationship between marital happiness and equality of identification with parents. Such a relationship would be circular, with marital discord producing situations that resulted in differential attitudes toward parents, and conversely with wide differences in identification producing dyadic relationships resulting in discord, regardless of the reasons for level of identification. Support for this line of reasoning is provided by Farber [19] in his work showing that marital integration is a factor in transmission of family norms and values to children.

The explanation for our findings is not simple, and must be sought in a combination of factors, some of which may be more relevant for one subject than for another. For instance, the higher identification for adolescents with equalitarian parents may result from lower levels of marital conflict; the decision-making process may be more likely to entail exchange of views and clarification of principles that rationalize the values of parents; or such parents may reflect the emerging norms of equality between the sexes.

When one parent is perceived to have more influence than the other, the interpretation becomes more complex. The very low identification with less-dominant fathers is undoubtedly connected with the traditional norms of male dominance. In some instances the father may receive low respect merely because he does not follow the expected pattern. It is more likely, however, that this situation is related to higher marital and family conflict, to low self-esteem of the father, or to a partial withdrawal from family interaction. No such drastic loss of identification occurs when the mother is the least-dominant parent; this is expected or permitted in the norms. An important question can be raised at this point about the conceptualization of influence. We used an over-all indicator, whereas influence is exerted in a number of areas of the group relationship and the balance of influence may not be the same in one area as in another. Many of the subjects may view the mother as more influential in matters relating to child-rearing, although the father may be perceived as having more global influence. Reactions to influence, then, may be affected more by performance in certain roles than by the overall power that one or the other parent may have.

The relationship between conjugal power and identification of adolescents with parents would seem to have sufficient promise for theories of parent-child relations and socialization to suggest the need for elaboration of the research design by taking into account some of the kinds of explanatory variables suggested above. It should also be fruitful to examine the relationships among other conjugal interaction patterns and identification, as well as among conjugal power and other socialization variables.

---

[19] B. Farber, "Marital Integration as a Factor in Parent-Child Relations," *Child Development*, XXXIII (1962), 1–14.

Lyle E. Larson

The Influence of Parents and Peers

During Adolescence:

The Situation Hypothesis Revisited[1]

Larson's investigation tested assumptions derived from earlier investigations that youth comply with parental wishes in future-oriented situations and with peer wishes in now-oriented situations. Larson, however, reports that the significance of a situation, for example, a moral dilemma, affects choice of action more than pressures from either parents or peers. The data suggest that high-school youth conform less to either parents or peers than earlier interpretations of adolescent socialization have led us to believe. According to Larson, youth are in fact fairly realistic and are "well aware of future statuses and roles, the significance of decisions involving content issues, and have achieved a recent sense of independence."

Instructional Objectives
To review earlier research pertaining to the relative significance of either parents or peers as sources of reference.
To consider how adolescents might comply with the wishes of either parents or peers in seven hypothetical dilemmas.
To consider the stability of adolescent choice patterns when parents and peers are reversed as sources of reference.
To explain the significance of compliance patterns among youth.

THE RELATIVE influence of parents and peers during adolescence is the subject of a large body of literature but the beneficiary of little substantive research. The research that has been done illustrates an apparent problem: peers and parents are each found to be most salient to the adoles-

FROM *Journal of Marriage and the Family*, XXXIV (1972), pp. 67–74. Reprinted by permission of the author and the publisher.

[1] This paper is based on a study conducted in November, 1967, supported by the Cooperative Research Program of the United States Office of Education, DHEW Project 7-1-105, OEG-9-8-070105-00350(010). It is a revised version of a paper delivered at the 1969 Annual Meeting of the Canadian Anthropology and Sociology Association, Toronto, Ontario.

cent. One body of literature suggests that the family has little influence on youth.[2] Adolescents are said to reject their parents in preference for their peers.[3] Other studies, however, indicate that the family continues to have a major impact during adolescence.[4]

To this point, the major empirical attempt to bridge the gap between these somewhat polarized positions may be characterized as the situation hypothesis. Simply stated, adolescents are said to opt for the expectations of their peers in situations that have implications for current status and identity needs and for the expectations of their parents in situations that have implications for future statuses and roles.[5]

The situation hypothesis represents a large body of theoretical assumptions that are central to the sociological perspective.[6] More recently the situation itself is seen to alter predispositions to act, role-taking and role-modification processes, and other characteristics of action.[7] What a person thinks and does in a situation tends to reflect previous learning experiences, the influence of reference groups, the influence system and process of which they are a part, the person's personality, and the type of situation. The situation may be seen as the fleeting citadel of thought and action—"a still-life picture of the structure of an individual's social space." It is apparent that the situation is important in the determination of the choices adolescents exercise when there are cross-pressures emanating from both parents and peers.

The actual measurement of the influence of a situation, however, is quite difficult. Most research, in consequence, has relied on the so-called hypothetical situation: "what would you do if." Brittain's study is an example of this approach. A series of situational dilemmas involving current and future role

[2] E. A. T. Barth, W. B. Watson, and W. Blanchard, "Norms and Social Relations: Some Problems of Parent-Child Relations in Mass Society," in J. R. Folta and E. S. Beck, eds., *A Sociological Framework for Patient Care* (New York: John Wiley, 1966).

[3] James S. Coleman, *The Adolescent Society* (New York: The Free Press, 1961); B. C. Rosen, *Adolescence and Religion: The Jewish Teenager in American Society* (Cambridge: Schenkman Publishing, 1965); C. E. Bowerman and J. W. Kinch, "Changes in Family and Peer Orientation of Children Between the Fourth and Tenth Grades," *Social Forces*, XXXVII (February 1959), 206–211.

[4] B. G. Myerhoff and W. R. Larson, "Primary and Formal Aspects of Family Organization: Group Concensus, Problem Perception, and Adolescent School Success," *Journal of Marriage and Family*, XXVII (May 1965), 213–218; E. Douvan and J. Adelson, *The Adolescent Experience* (New York: John Wiley, 1966); W. L. Slocum, *Family Culture Patterns and Adolescent Behavior* (Pullman: Washington State University, 1963).

[5] C. V. Brittain, "Adolescent Choices and Parent-Peer Cross-Pressures," *American Sociological Review*, XXVIII (June 1963), 385–391; "An Exploration of the Bases of Peer-Compliance and Parent-Compliance in Adolescence," *Adolescence*, II (Winter 1967-68), 445–458; "A Comparison of Rural and Urban Adolescents with Respect to Peer vs. Parent Compliance," *Adolescence*, XIII (Spring 1969), 59–68.

[6] W. I. Thomas and F. Znaniecki, *The Polish Peasant in Europe and America* (Chicago: University of Chicago Press, 1918–20); K. Lewin, *Principles of Topological Psychology* (New York: McGraw-Hill, 1936); J. H. S. Bossard and E. Boll, *Sociology of Child Development* (New York: Harper and Row, 1966), pp. 31–104.

[7] E. Goffman, *The Presentation of Self in Everyday Life* (New York: Doubleday, 1959); G. J. McCall and J. L. Simmons, *Youth and the Social Order* (Bloomington: Indiana University Press, 1966).

implications were presented to a sample of adolescent girls. The dilemma created involved the pressure of parents to do one thing and the counter-vailing pressure of best friends to do the opposite. The situations were then reversed to ascertain the effect of the content of the situation (the substan-tive dilemma) and the effect of peer and parent pressure in two opposite situations with identical content (the influence dilemma). Brittain used a control group to insure confidence in the changes in the experimental group and a time interval (one to two weeks) to remove the possibility of a response set. The findings were clear. Parent-peer cross-pressures were found to be a function of the content of the alternatives and peer and parent conformity was shown to vary systematically across situations. Peers were seen as more competent guides in *current* situational dilemmas while parents were seen as more competent guides in *future* oriented situations.[8] It is assumed that the situations and procedures used permit the measurement of parent and peer orientations among youth.

Several questions may be raised about this approach. In the first place, the assumption that the choices of peer and parent compliant youth reflect reference group orientations may be unsound. Situational dilemmas may only measure the adolescent's choice of action, not the nature of his parent and peer relationships. Compliance may reflect fear, respect, appreciation, judgments of special competence, a reaction to recent events, and many other possibilities. Therefore, it would be helpful to establish the parent-peer orientations of youth independent of situations to adequately assess the relative meaning of the situational dilemma. As indicated earlier, the situa-tion is more likely a mediating rather than determining feature of the influ-ence process.

Second, the interrelationships among the situations were not considered. Do adolescents who opt for the wishes of their parents in a party dilemma also choose to be parent compliant in a moral dilemma? Similarly, do party-oriented adolescents tend to be college-orientated adolescents (the relation-ship among content choices)? Brittain identified content, parent, and peer compliant adolescents through the use of single situations and their reversals. He did not relate the response in one type of situation to another.

Third, Brittain utilized a "what do you think the person in the story is *likely* to do" technique rather than the "what would *you do* if" technique. The latter is deemed preferable in that it avoids the "everybody would do it except me" response and facilitates an "I would do it regardless of what others would likely do" response. The measurement of the relative influence of situations must (a) organize the adolescent's perceptions toward realistic self-experience, and (b) activate the adolescent's perceptions of *his* social experience rather than that of somebody else.

The preceding discussion of the situational approach lends credence to a reconsideration. This paper presents the results of a critical reassessment of

[8] Brittain, "Adolescent Choices and Parent-Peer Cross-Pressures," op. cit., p. 389.

the situation hypothesis with particular reference to two factors: (a) the relative effect of several hypothetical situations on parent and peer compliance, and (b) the impact of the parent and peer *orientations* of youth on their parent and peer choices in differing situations.

Accordingly, the following hypotheses will be tested.

> Hypothesis 1. In hypothetical situations where the decision has future implications, adolescents will tend to choose the parent compliant alternative.
>
> Hypothesis 2. Peer and parent compliant choices will vary positively with the adolescent's parent and peer orientations.

It should be emphasized, however, that this study is not designed to replicate Brittain's study, only to explore the implications of the weaknesses discussed above. The situational approach is seen as one aspect of a basic question in sociological analysis: Who has the most influence on youth and under what conditions is this influence mediated? The larger study, a part of which provides the data for this paper, deals with the structure and process of social influence during adolescence and specifically attempts to trace the interpenetrations and linkages among the central referents in the life space of the adolescent.

RESEARCH PROCEDURES

The data were collected in a community of 11,000 people in southern Oregon. The population includes all seventh, ninth, and twelfth grade students who were in the three Valleyview (the pseudonym selected) schools on the day the study took place. Pretested paper and pencil tests were administered to 1,558 students, 1,542 of which are useable.

The hypothetical situations presented to each adolescent are similar, though not identical, to those used by Brittain. Two situations are used to measure cross-pressures emanating from parents and peers that have current role implications: membership in a club and attendance at a party. The remaining two situations are designed to measure future-oriented situations: telling the principal who broke the glass in the school door (a moral dilemma) and the choice between college and general programs (a curriculum dilemma).

With the exception of the club membership situation, the remaining three situations were preceded by the following instructions:

> The following statements describe *hypothetical* situations in which you face an important decision. Read each statement carefully and indicate which of the two things you would *most likely* do if you actually faced the situation.

To illustrate the question, the party situation will be illustrated. The party situation involved a dilemma in which the adolescent is urged to go to a party by his best friends and urged by his parents to stay home. This situation is presented below.

You have been invited to a party which you want very much to go to. Your best friends have decided to go and are urging you to go, too. They will be very unhappy if you don't go. Your parents, however, do not approve of the party and are urging you not to go. Your parents will be very unhappy if you do go. What would you do?

1. (   ) Go to the party
2. (   ) Stay home

In order to ascertain the actual effect of the situation it was then reversed.

Suppose the situation above is reversed. Your parents are urging you to go to the party. However, your best friends have *not* been invited and are urging you not to go. You really don't want to go to the party. Your parents will be very unhappy if you don't go; your best friends will be very unhappy if you do go. What would you do?

1. (   ) Go to the party
2. (   ) Stay home

The first situation described above may be referred to as "party versus parents" in that to go to the party would be a violation of parental wishes. The second may be labeled "party versus friends" in that to go to the party would be a violation of the wishes of the adolescent's peer group. It may be emphasized that to consider only the first of these situations (or only one of them) could be measuring nothing more than "home orientation" or "party orientation" rather than parent and best friend compliance. However, in reversing the situation (considering both of them) the probability that the parent-peer orientations are being measured is increased. This technique follows Brittain's Cross Pressure Test (CPT) quite closely. No attempt was made in this study, however, to set up experimental and control groups due to the priority of more general research objectives. In addition, the respondent was presented the alternate situation (the reversed situation) in immediate sequence whereas Brittain used a one to two week delay. In this case, it was deemed useful to explore the frequency of response consistency. As will be seen later, only a minority remained either parent- or peer-compliant, indicating that the time interval may be unnecessary.

The moral character situation (whether to tell or not to tell the principal who broke the glass in the school door) and the curriculum situation dilemma (whether to enter the general or college preparatory programs) were presented to the respondent in the same way.

The parent and peer orientations of youth were measured by fifteen questionnaire items each of which provided three alternative response categories: parents, best friends, and both about the same. To the author's knowledge, this is the first time that any attempt has been made to allow the adolescent to opt for *both* his parents and his best friends. The questions were presented in the following form: Who *best* understands your problems. Utilizing the "hierarchical clustering technique," [9] five of the fifteen items were chosen to provide optimum classification of the adolescents into three statistical groups: Those who are parent oriented, those best friend oriented, and those who assign equal salience to both parents and best friends.

FINDINGS

Table 1 presents responses to each of the seven situations. The majority of adolescents chose to accept the wishes of their parents in three situations (parental pressure against joining a club, going to a party, and entering the general program in school) and the wishes of their best friends in one

Table 1   Adolescent Choice Patterns in Hypothetical Situations (in Percentages)

| | Adolescent Choice Patterns | | |
Hypothetical Situations	PARENT COMPLAINT	BEST FRIEND COMPLAINT	N [a]
Current Situations			
X_1 Club Membership [b]	65.9	34.1	(1508)
X_2 Party vs. Parents [c]	69.7	30.3	(1483)
X_3 Party vs. Best Friends [c]	47.9	52.1	(1491)
Future Situations			
X_4 Character vs. Best Friends [d]	52.6	47.4	(1499)
X_5 Character vs. Parents [d]	54.4	45.6	(1502)
X_6 College vs. Best Friends [e]	78.0	22.0	(1488)
X_7 College vs. Parents [e]	33.9	66.1	(1483)

[a] Non-responses are excluded.

[b] Joining club against Parents' wishes.

[c] In the party vs. parents situation the adolescent is urged by his parents to stay home and by his best friends to go to the party. The party vs. best friends represents a reversal of this situation to ascertain whether the situation or the parent/best friend cross-pressures are operating.

[d] In the character vs. best friends situation the adolescent is urged by his parents to tell the principal who broke the glass and by his best friends not to tell. This situation is reversed in the character vs. parents situation.

[e] In the college vs. best friends situation the adolescent is urged by his parents to enter the college preparatory program and by his best friends to enter the general program. The college vs. parents situation is a reversal of this situation.

[9] S. C. Johnson, "Hierarchical Clustering Schemes," *Psychometrika*, XXXII (September 1967), 241–254.

situation (best friend pressure against entering the general program in school). The remaining three situations show a fairly even split: about half of the adolescents chose the parent option, the other half the best friend option.

It is apparent that Hypothesis One must be rejected. The assumption that adolescents will opt for the wishes of their peers in situations that involve current status and identity needs is not supported in this study. Despite the pressure of the adolescent's best friends to join a club or go to a party (not to go separates the adolescent from his peers), the majority were parent compliant. Similarly, in only one of the four situations involving the future did adolescents opt for their parents wishes.

However, Table 1 does not permit an analysis of an individual's choices in different situations. In the curriculum situation, for example, it is unclear whether those who are parent compliant in situation six are also parent compliant or best friend compliant in situation seven. In addition, the character situation remains ambiguous. In this case, it is unclear whether moral principles, parent, or peer compliance has psychological priority. Table 2 permits an initial answer to these questions.

Table 2 Gamma Correlation Matrix

Situations	Symbol	X_1	X_2	X_3	X_4	X_5	X_6
Current Situations							
Club Membership	X_1						
Party vs. Parents	X_2	.82 °					
Party vs. Best Friends	X_3	.31 °	.16				
Future Situations							
Character vs. Best Friends	X_4	−.51 °	.48 °	.35 °			
Character vs. Parents	X_5	−.22	−.15	−.11	.88 °		
College vs. Best Friends	X_6	.33 °	.33 °	.10	.17	.02	
College vs. Parents	X_7	.16	.10	.15	.22	.02	−.58 °

° Gamma is significant at the .05 level or greater.

Gamma is used to assess the interrelationship among the situational dilemmas. In each case, the data are organized to insure covariability, *i.e.*, parent compliance appears as the first category in each cross tabulation.

The club membership situation is significantly correlated with four of the six situations indicating that: (a) adolescents who opted for parent compliance in the club situation tended to choose the parent-compliant alternative in the other situations; and (b) adolescents who opted for their best friends in the club situation tended also to opt for their best friends in the other situations. Adolescents who opt for parental wishes by staying home from the party (situation X_2) tend to opt for the wishes of their parents in telling the principal who broke the glass in the school door (situation X_4) and entering the college program (situation X_6). This finding either indicates that the pressure of parents and peers are predictive in situational dilemmas or that going to college and telling the principal are simply more important to the adolescent. It is likely that the situations create unrealistic pressures that fail to assess the impact of actual cross-pressurized situations. This explanation is given considerable credence in the relationship between the character versus parents and character versus best friends situations (situations X_4 and X_5). The correlation is inverse, —.88. It is clear that adolescents who opted for the wishes of parents in the first situation also opted to tell the principal who broke the glass in the school door in the second situation. Likewise, those who chose not to tell the principal in the first situation also refused to tell the principal in the other situation. It appears that the cross-pressures of parents or peers are less important than the adolescent's moral values.

Similarly, there is a pronounced negative relationship between the college versus best friends (X_6) and college versus parents (X_7) situations (—.58). Adolescents choosing the college prep program in the first situation also did so in the second; those choosing the general program in the first tended also to do so in the second situation.

Table 3   Stability of Adolescent Choice Patterns Where Parent/Best Friend Cross-Pressures Are Reversed (in Percentages)

	Adolescent Choice Patterns			
Combined Effect of Hypothetical Situations	REMAINED PARENT COMPLIANT [b]	REMAINED BEST FRIEND COMPLIANT [c]	REMAINED SITUATION COMPLIANT [d]	N [a]
X_8 Party Situation	34.8	17.7	47.5	(1452)
X_9 Character Situation	13.7	7.1	79.2	(1482)
X_{10} Curriculum Situation	21.3	9.2	69.6	(1471)

[a] Non-responses are excluded.

[b] Respondents who opted for the wishes of their *parents* in both the initial situation and its reversal.

[c] Respondents who opted for the wishes of their *best friends* in both the initial situation and its reversal.

[d] Respondents who opted for parents or best friends in the initial situation but who reversed their choice when the situation was reversed. These respondents are appropriately referred to as situation or content compliant.

Table 3 reveals the strength of the relationships suggested above. Adolescents who remain compliant to parents or peers when the situation is reversed are considerably outnumbered by those who remain situation or content compliant. The cross-pressures created by the party situations commands parent-compliant responses from 35 per cent of the adolescents. In contrast, 18 per cent chose the best friend-compliant alternative in both situations. The largest proportion (48 per cent) of the respondents may be described as situation-compliant. In this case, adolescents are either home-oriented (choosing to stay home from the party regardless of the direction or source

of "created" pressure) or party-oriented (choosing to go to the party irrespective of pressure). In both the character and curriculum situations it is clear
that the majority of adolescents have chosen what they consider to be the
appropriate option (telling or not telling the principal, entering the college
or general program) parent or best friend pressure notwithstanding. In all
three situations, among those who are influenced by the direction or source
of cross-pressure, about twice as many adolescents are parent compliant as
best friend compliant. The stability of these choice patterns across four or
more situations are presented in Table 4. As can be seen, the majority of
adolescents opted for the content of the situation. More than three times as
many remained parent compliant as remained best friend compliant in four
or more of six situations.)

**Table 4   Stability of Adolescent Choice Patterns Across Content Dilemmas:
The Effect of Situations**

Situational Effect	N [a]	Per Cent
Parent Compliant [b]	(220)	15.7
Best Friend Compliant [c]	(69)	4.8
Mixed Compliance [d]	(83)	5.9
Situation Compliant [e]	(1034)	73.6
	(1406)	

[a] Non-responses are excluded.
[b] Respondents who opted for the wishes of their parents in four or more of the six
situations.
[c] Respondents who opted for the wishes of their best friends in four or more of the
six situations.
[d] Respondents who opted for the wishes of parents *or* best friends in four of the six
situations and who remained situation compliant in the remaining two situations.
[e] Respondents who opted in terms of the situation (rather than the cross pressures of
parents and peers) in four of the six situations.

Brittain's central hypothesis has not fared well in this study. Adolescents
tend to choose parent compliant options in current-oriented situations. In
future-oriented situations, in contrast, content compliance appears to be
more predictive than either parent or peer pressures. The linkage of the
individual's response to differing situations seems to indicate that situational
dilemmas do not permit a measurement of the adolescent's relationship with
either his parents or peers. At best, situational dilemmas enable the adolescent to choose courses of action. Therefore, it will be helpful first to consider
the adolescent orientations to parents and peers independent of situational
measurement and, second, the impact of the adolescent's orientations on his
choices in situational dilemmas.

Table 5 shows that the majority of adolescents are pro-parent in their
orientations. Only a minority assign priority to their best friends. As antici-

Table 5   Parent and Peer Orientations of Youth

	N	Per Cent
Parent-Oriented	546	35.5
Parent/Best Friend-Oriented	605	39.3
Best Friend-Oriented	387	25.2
Total	(1538)	100.0

pated, a substantive proportion of youth see no reason to differentiate between parent and peer societies.

Tables 6 and 7 present the relationships between parent-peer orientations and choice patterns in the situational dilemmas. It is apparent that the hierarchical orientations of youth toward their parents and best friends do have consequences for their choice patterns. Adolescents who remained parent or friend compliant across the party situation are significantly influenced by their orientations toward their parents and peers. The character and curriculum situations reveal similar relationships even though the relative proportion of adolescents remaining parent or friend compliant is considerably

Table 6   Stability of Adolescent Choice Patterns Where Parent/Best Friend Cross-Pressures Are Reversed By Parent-Peer Orientations (in Percentages)

Parent-Peer Orientations	Adolescent Choice Patterns			
	PARENT COMPLIANT	BEST FRIEND COMPLIANT	SITUATION COMPLIANT	N [a]
Party Situation				
Parents	46.8	6.9	46.3	(521)
Parents/Best Friends	34.2	18.9	46.9	(565)
Best Friends	18.3	46.9	50.3	(366)
	Gamma = .64 *			
Character Situation				
Parents	21.5	3.8	74.7	(522)
Parents/Best Friends	11.0	8.7	80.3	(584)
Best Friends	7.2	9.0	83.8	(376)
	Gamma = .56 *			
Curriculum Situation				
Parents	28.3	5.8	65.8	(530)
Parents/Best Friends	19.9	10.1	69.9	(572)
Best Friends	13.0	12.5	74.5	(369)
	Gamma = .58 *			

[a] Non-responses are excluded.

* Gamma is significant at the .05 level or greater. Note: Gamma is computed for the first six cells only. The situation compliant category is not included because gamma is inappropriate. In addition, the significance of the impact of cross-pressures among those who remained parent and best friend compliant across situations is best illustrated by computing a measure of association for this part of the contingency table.

reduced. The significance of the impact of cross-pressures on those who remained parent or peer compliant in four or more situations with differing content is further illustrated in Table 7.

Table 7 Effect of Situations by The Salience Hierarchy

	Effect of Situations				
Parent-Peer Orientations	PARENT COMPLIANT	BEST FRIEND COMPLIANT	MIXED COMPLIANCE	SITUATION COMPLIANT	N [a]
Parent-Oriented	26.8	1.6	4.2	67.4	(496)
Parent/Best Friend-Oriented	12.6	5.8	6.9	74.7	(548)
Best Friend-Oriented	7.6	7.8	6.7	77.9	(357)
			Gamma = .72 [o]		

[a] Non-responses are excluded.
[o] Gamma is significant at the .05 level or greater. Note: Gamma is computed for the first six cells only. The situation-compliant categories are not included because gamma is inappropriate. In addition, the significance of the impact of cross-pressures among those who remained parent and best friend compliant across situations is best illustrated by computing a measure of association for this part of the contingency table.

Several relationships are particularly clear. First, parent-oriented youth seldom choose to comply with the wishes of their friends (varying from 6.9 per cent in the party situation to 1.6 per cent across several situations). Second, adolescents giving equal salience to their parents and friends are distinctly less parent compliant than their parent oriented age mates. Perhaps, this simply means that they have more freedom to choose what *they* consider to be appropriate. Third, and most important, neither the parent-peer orientations nor the pressures of parents and peers have a mitigating influence on the choices of the *majority* of adolescents. Nearly as many parent-oriented as friend-oriented youth opt for choices inappropriate to parental expectation.

DISCUSSION AND CONCLUSIONS

In contrast to Brittain's findings, the responses of youth in this study differ very little between future- and current-oriented situations. At best, only a weak relationship exists between the pressures of parents and peers and the type of situation. The club membership and party situations are more conducive to parent or peer compliance than the character and curriculum situations. Where youth did opt in favor of complying with the wishes of others, they more often opted to comply with parental than peer wishes. However, most youth chose in terms of the *content* of the situation, parental and peer pressure notwithstanding. These findings suggest that youth in this study are (a) well aware of future statuses and roles, the significance of decisions involving content issues, and have achieved a reasoned sense of independence; (b) able to sort content alternatives into levels of priority assigning lesser significance to issues of temporal importance; and (c) prepared to give credence and compliance to the pressures of parents and peers when they are realistic. In other words, whether one goes or doesn't go to a party is less important than whether one tells the principal who broke the door window or whether one enters the college preparatory program. In the first case, adolescents are able to comply with parent or peer wishes. In the latter two, their decision is more likely based on what they consider to be appropriate, parent and peer pressures notwithstanding.

It has also been seen that choices vary systematically with parent and peer orientations. Parent-oriented youth tend to make parent-compliant choices, best friend-oriented youth tend to make best friend-compliant choices. However, these relationships are sustained for the majority of adolescents in situations involving low priority content alternatives that have a temporal impact. Neither parent-peer orientations nor pressures preclude adolescent ability in decisions appropriate to the adolescent's sense of identity with future roles. It should be emphasized, of course, that content-oriented youth may well be influenced by family and friends alike in making content choices. For example, the content choice to enter the college preparatory program may be due to earlier parental encouragement and pressure.[10]

In conclusion, it appears that hypothetical situations provide limited insight into the structure of parent and peer orientations during adolescence. It may be reasonable in subsequent research on the parent-youth-peer relationship to use other methodological techniques. Elsewhere it has been shown that the inclusion of an equal salience category and a consideration of the quality of the adolescent's relationship with his parents virtually eliminates the parent-rejection theory of adolescence.[11] Further research is needed on the characteristics of youth that act independently of their parent-peer orientations and the pressures emanating from their reference group.

[10] R. A. Rehberg, *Selected Determinants of Adolescent Educational Expectations* (Eugene, Oregon: Center for Advanced Study of Educational Administration, 1967).

[11] L. E. Larson, *The Structure and Process of Social Influence During Adolescence: An Examination of the Salience Hierarchy* (Unpublished Doctoral Dissertation, University of Oregon, 1969).

Socialization:

Youth-Culture Commitments

The transition of adolescents through the peer world into adulthood encompasses major aspects of socialization. Peer interaction permits adolescents to see how friends respond to their parents and to assume a variety of roles—to be temporarily leaders or followers, deviants, or conformists. Values and behavioral norms held by peer-group members also enable adolescents to acquire perspective on their own values and attitudes. Untested social skills can be tried and impractical aspirations can be entertained. The values of a peer group pose certain strictures on its members, too. They represent reference points that define appropriate and inappropriate behavior, sanctioning peer-group members either through acceptance or rejection. Over the course of time, satisfying experiences with peers may contribute to strong identity formation, whereas unsatisfactory experiences may precipitate identity crises. The seven papers presented in Part 5 encompassing, respectively, slang vocabularies, peer-group structures, interpersonal attraction, peer statuses, sex information, sexual decision-making, and marriage values, describe the attitudes, sanctions, and norms that determine the nature of adolescents' youth-culture commitments.

The adolescent language system rarely becomes the subject of investigation, partly because social scientists have yet to devise satisfactory procedures for conducting research on it. Nelsen and Rosenbaum, in the first selection, describe an unusual study which indeed analyzes youth's knowledge of slang words—words commonly used by adolescents in conversing with peers. These researchers also offer a "slang and word association paradigm," which appears to be a useful technique for classifying adolescent vocabularies. Nelsen and Rosenbaum asked nearly 2000 adolescents, stratified on the basis of sex and grade level, to list all of the slang words that they could recollect which they associated, respectively, with money, cigarettes, alcohol, popularity, and so forth. The youth's slang production was found to correspond generally with recognized sex differences in adolescent interests. Boys produced more slang terms for "auto and motor bikes" and "money." Girls produced more slang for "clothes, styles, and appearance," "an unpopular person," and "boys." These researchers report, too, that slang production for many of the sex-differentiated topics increased with age, and they suggest that "a special language may play a role in determining both uniformities and differences among adolescent subgroups."

The role of peer groups in youth's transition from playgroup innocence to heterosexual prowess is one of several critical features in adolescent socialization. To explore how peer influence is exerted, Dunphy conducted a field investigation of the structure of adolescent groups. The methods by which he identified hierarchies of groups—crowds, cliques and networks of reciprocal role relationships—are especially impressive. Dunphy spent hours and hours at street corners, hangouts, homes, and beach parties until he gained the confidence of the adolescents. His careful and painstaking attention to the intricacies of peer-group interaction surely lends credence to his conclusion that "the social structure of urban adolescent peer groups has the effect of maintaining a high level of achievement which insures that most adolescents aggressively acquire an increasingly mature heterosexual role."

Interpersonal attractiveness tops virtually every listing of the attributes of adolescent popularity. Cavior and Dokecki start from the premise in the third selection that interpersonal attractiveness among adolescents is a function of physical attractiveness, attitude similarity, and academic achievement, and the researchers offer a provocative developmental analysis of these three variables. They divided fifth- and eleventh-grade boys and girls into groups on the basis of those who knew one another and those who were strangers to each other. The "knowers" judged classmates' photographs on physical attractiveness, perceived attribute similarity, and interpersonal attraction. The "nonknowers," who were youth in the same grades but different schools, judged identical photographs on physical attractiveness. The data revealed that evaluations of physical attractiveness tend to be based on cultural definitions of attractiveness that are acquired around age seven. Familiarity and awareness of popularity appeared to exert little effect on the youth's judgments. Since knowers and nonknowers exhibited high agreement in judging physical attractiveness, the data suggest, too, that physical attractiveness may be more significant in determining popularity than perceived attitude similarity.

Schwartz and Merten believe that the meanings adolescents assign to status terms and prestige categories constitute a cultural core that is sufficiently different to comprise an independent status system, distinct world view, and style of life. In a study of high-school youth from stable working-, lower-middle-, and upper-middle-class areas of a community, the researchers found that the students structured a status system and used the terms "hoody," "socie," and "conventional" to differentiate the life-styles, dress, speech, and interpersonal demeanor of youth. The terms may change from one region of the country to another or from one moment in time to another. In the Southwestern United States, for example, one hears "jocks," "cowboys," and "freaks" reverberate in the halls of high schools. Whatever the terms in vogue, they pertain to social virtues or defects and provide standards by which adolescents measure their own worth. They signify both moral *attributes, which make persons admirable or reprehensible, and moral dispositions, which indicate the kinds of things people say and do. Moreover, according to Schwartz and Merten, youth's status terminology "is embodied in a normative order predicated upon conceptions of those personal qualities which its members believe make a male admirable and a female desirable." An adolescent's estimation of his or her own competence and rank in the prestige hierarchy of the youth-culture depends on whether peers call him or her by a term that has laudatory or pejorative connotations. The term indicates whether or not the adolescent is able to present a "cool" self-image under highly competitive social conditions.*

Each of the preceding four papers emphasizes the significance of heterosexual prowess to peer status, and as one might expect, adolescents learn a great deal about sex during the high-school years. This knowledge, however, often is so confused that meaningful integration with wider systems of values is very difficult. Adolescents may learn about sex from printed literature and from high-school classes in health, physical education, and biology. But topics associated with premarital heterosexual behavior—making out, petting, how to handle a boy's advances, and birth control—seldom are discussed in high-school classrooms. These topics often are forbidden, perhaps because they prove emotionally threatening to school personnel and parental groups. In the fifth selection, Thornburg (a) identifies some prevailing sources of adolescents' initial sex information, and (b) reports on their perception of its accuracy. This researcher asked 451 students at four widely separated universities for their recollections on the following topics: abortion, contraception, ejaculation, homosexuality, intercourse, masturbation, menstruation, origin of babies, petting, prostitution, seminal emissions, and venereal disease. Thornburg's data confirm that peers are youth's major source of initial sexual information, but he shows, too, that youth rate sources differently with respect to accuracy; for example, they believe literature to have been their most reliable source of information on abortion; the school, venereal diseases; their mothers, menstruation; and their peers, homosexuality, intercourse, and masturbation.

The chain of decisions that adolescents face in assuming personal responsibility for sexual conduct is discussed in elaborate detail by McCreary Juhasz. This author presents, in the sixth selection, an original model for sexual decision-making, including choices associated with intercourse, whether to have children, birth control, abortion, child adoption, and marriage. McCreary Juhasz reviews the changes in patterns of sexual behavior that have occurred among adolescents in recent years and suggests that both attitudes and actual behavior are vastly more open today than ever before. She believes that youth can respond constructively to the temptations and demands of sex only when they accept responsibility for their actions and logically think through each of the decision-making stages.

Students of adolescent behavior usually regard adult marriage as one of the benchmarks signifying a youth's commitment to adult responsibilities and statuses. However, as Dreyer points out in the seventh selection, many adolescents today view marriage as an optional relationship, less a means to attain certain ends than an opportunity for innovative, psychological growth. Consequently, the conventional fusion of sexual behavior and marriage is pulling apart and sex-type roles associated with traditional expectations about how husbands and wives should respond to one another are changing.

Edward A. Nelsen
Edward Rosenbaum

Language Patterns Within the Youth Subculture: Development of Slang Vocabularies[1]

The investigation presented here describes the role of unconventional language in the youth culture. Nelsen and Rosenbaum hypothesize that slang enables adolescents to transmit values and norms, express approval and hostility, and reinforce selective perceptions and categorizations of the social environment, all of which contribute to cultural distinctness in the youth culture. The researchers created a "slang word association paradigm," a scheme for asking adolescents to list the slang words that they use in talking about "school," "exams," "success," "popularity," and so forth. They investigated the slang production of nearly 2,000 youth, grades seven through twelve, and found that both sexes produced more slang in reference to unpopular than popular words; and the discrepancy increased with age. Moreover, general knowledge of slang increased with age for both sexes. In late adolescence, for example, both sexes produced more slang for topics like alcohol and drinking, cigarettes and smoking, drugs, and the opposite sex. Sex differences appeared, too; older girls acquired more slang for clothes, styles, and appearance; boys, more slang for autos, motorbikes, and money. Nelsen and Rosenbaum thus conclude that the number of slang words produced by a given stimulus reflects the social saliency of the topic in the youth culture.

Instructional Objectives
To substantiate the hypothesis that slang contributes to the "subcultural differentiation" of adolescents.

FROM *Merrill-Palmer Quarterly of Behavior and Development*, XVIII (1972), pp. 273–284. Reprinted by permission of the authors and the publisher.

[1] This investigation was partially supported through a grant from the Wisconsin Alumni Research Foundation. Many students and colleagues influenced the research. A study by Joseph Mason provided much of the original impetus. Janice Freeman Adams served as research assistant for the project. Discussions with Alexander Astin, Robert Davidson, Frank Farley, John Giebink, and Roger Severson contributed to the development and interpretation of the study. Suggestions by Robert Grinder and Don Seaver clarified the manuscript at various stages.

To compare slang usage by adolescent boys and girls.

To describe slang usage by both high-school grade-level and sex for personal and nonpersonal topics.

To suggest that slang may indicate the social saliency of topics in the youth culture.

SINCE Sapir's [2] and Whorf's [3] classical analyses of relationships between language and culture, a growing body of theory and research has reaffirmed the central role of language in the socialization process. The analyses of Kluckhohn,[4] Bernstein,[5] Brown,[6] and Hymes [7] all support Bossard's assertion that "the acquisition of language is necessary to set into motion the two conditioning factors of social interaction and cultural background which mold the personality of the child." [8]

While research is beginning to clarify the role of conventional language in socialization, the special role of nonstandard language, that is, slang or argot, within distinct subcultures has been noted only recently by social scientists. Schwartz and Merten,[9] for example, have conceptualized youth culture as consisting of "those adolescent norms, standards, and values which are discussed in language particularly intelligible to members of this age grade." Lewis [10] also has suggested that the child is a member of "two linguistic communities," one employing a language of adults, another employing a language of peers. He suggests that the slang of the adolescent culture serves to identify youth as culturally distinct; to transmit values and norms; to express approval, hostility, and other attitudes; and to reinforce the selective perceptions and categorization of the social environment.

If a special language does thus play a role in the social development and subcultural differentiation of adolescents, then measures of familiarity with that language should reflect variations due to cultural age-grading and participation within differential subcultural roles. Lerman,[11] for example, found

[2] E. Sapir, *Language* (New York: Harcourt, Brace and World, 1921).

[3] B. Whorf, *Language, Thought, and Reality* (Cambridge: Technology Press; New York: Wiley, 1956).

[4] C. Kluckhohn, "Culture and Behavior," in G. Lindzey, ed., *Handbook of Social Psychology* (Reading, Mass.: Addison-Wesley, 1954), II, pp. 921–976.

[5] B. Bernstein, "Social Structure, Language, and Learning," in J. DeCecco, ed., *The Psychology of Language, Thought, and Instruction* (New York: Holt, Rinehart and Winston, 1967), pp. 89–103.

[6] R. Brown, *Social Psychology* (New York: The Free Press, 1965); *Words and Things* (New York: The Free Press, 1958).

[7] D. Hymes, "The Functions of Speech," in J. DeCecco, ed., op. cit., pp. 78–84.

[8] J. Bossard, *The Sociology of Child Development* (New York: Harper, 1948), pp. 177–178.

[9] G. Schwartz and D. Merten, "The Language of Adolescence: An Anthropological Approach to Youth Culture," *American Sociological Review*, LXXII (1967), 453–469.

[10] M. Lewis, *Language Thought and Personality in Infancy and Childhood* (New York: Basic Books, 1963).

[11] P. Lerman, "Argot, Symbolic Deviance, and Subcultural Delinquency," *American Sociological Review*, XXXII (1967), 209–224.

that males had greater knowledge of argot referring to gang fighting, theft and robbery, drugs, and organized rackets; for both sexes knowledge of argot was greater for older than for younger adolescents. He notes, however, "the key issue concerning sex differences in verbal comprehension may be *not* which sex is superior but, rather, under what conditions different *types* of linguistic references are more likely to be known by boys or by girls. Further exploration of this issue would aid greatly in understanding the differential socialization of boys and girls and its impact on cognitive functioning."

Other than Lerman's study, there have been almost no empirical investigations of such issues. Previous investigators of adolescent language [12] have interrogated informants informally in quasi-naturalistic settings, but the data could not be analyzed quantitatively.

Although empirical studies, such as Lerman's, did employ slang vocabulary tests to measure individual and group differences in knowledge of specific terms, there are several limitations to this method of assessing familiarity with slang expressions. First, the number of terms and the variety of topics considered in slang vocabulary tests are necessarily restricted. Separate tests or subtests are needed to assess familiarity with terms referring to specific topics or phenomena. Second, new slang terms are continually introduced within youth subcultures, and other terms become unfashionable. Moreover, expressions that are common in one school or community may be unfashionable or unheard of in another setting. Thus, construction of separate vocabulary tests would be necessary for different groups, and the tests would not be directly comparable. Indeed, these limitations of vocabulary testing techniques may be a major reason for the current lack of scientific data on slang.

This report concerns research to develop a broad and flexible method for assessing familiarity with slang for various topics. A modified word association technique was employed to elicit slang from groups of adolescents, so as to determine the number of expressions associated with given stimulus topics. It was assumed that the number of slang responses produced in this context would measure the extent of familiarity with terms referring to each topic.

The report also concerns relationships of basic socialization variables, age and sex, with the slang familiarity measures. The study compared adolescent males and females at successive grade levels according to the number of slang associations given in response to selected stimulus topics. The stimulus topics were: (a) money; (b) cigarettes and smoking; (c) autos and motorbikes; (d) alcohol and drinking; (e) clothes, styles, and appearance; (f) boys; (g) girls; (h) a popular person; and (i) an unpopular person.

Although the study was exploratory in nature, it was predicted in general that the number of slang responses would vary systematically according to cultural age-graded and sex role characteristics. With reference to age and grade level, it was predicted that a relatively great amount of slang would be

[12] I. Opie and P. Opie, *The Lore and Language of School Children* (Oxford: Clarendon Press, 1959); Schwartz and Merten, op. cit.

emitted by older adolescents, particularly for the topics pertaining to alcohol and autos, because legal prohibitions limit involvement of younger adolescents in these areas.

METHOD

SUBJECTS.   The sample was drawn from junior and senior high schools in four semi-rural communities located within 30 miles of Madison, Wisconsin. A total of 1,000 males and 916 females, grades 7 through 12, participated in the study. Subjects were drawn from several different communities in order to provide more general representation, since pilot testing revealed idiosyncratic patterns of performance within individual schools and classes. The sample consisted of participants in physical education classes on the day of testing. Physical education is required of all students in the four school systems, and no special criteria, such as ability level, determine class placement. Hence, the sample was presumably representative of high school students from communities similar to those included in the study.

PROCEDURE.   Subjects participated in the testing session during regularly scheduled physical education classes ranging in size from about 20 to 60. Subjects within each grade level were randomly assigned to groups of four same-sexed persons by a "counting off" procedure. (Occasionally a group of 3 or 5 was used when an odd number of Ss was encountered.) In two of the school systems males and females were tested separately by Es of the same sex. In the other two systems the sexes were tested concurrently, but in widely separated areas of the gymnasiums, and they had no opportunity to communicate during the testing. In these latter schools a male E read the instructions to all Ss; he also passed out the materials to male Ss, but a female assistant distributed the materials to female Ss.

After the Ss were assigned to four-person groups, each group was given an 8" × 11" test booklet consisting of 9 pages, with a stimulus topic and 46 black spaces (two columns) on each page. One familiar slang term and one relevant nonslang term were presented as examples along with each topic. The topics and examples were printed on the top of each page as follows: "List all the slang words that kids your age use when talking about _____. For example, _____ is a slang word, but _____ is not. Write one word or phrase on a line. Do not use phrases with more than three words." The order of presentation of the topics was varied randomly, except that "money" was always presented first to simplify the task instructions.

The assembled groups were told:

> We are making a collection of slang words used by teenagers and would like your assistance today in telling us the slang words you know. Each group should work together to make a list of the slang terms teenagers know and use when talking about different topics.
>
> By slang I mean words that just teenagers use in their own way, or words

that are commonly used by teenagers in their crowd. For example, in talking about money, the words "buck" and "scratch" are slang words, but the words "cash" and "dollar" are not slang.

We will give you a chance to list all of the slang words you know dealing with money. But first, each group should take a few seconds to pick out a person to write the words on the list. This person should be able to write clearly and quickly. [Pause]

When I say go, you will have five minutes to work. Do not turn to the next page until you are told to. Try to write as many words as you can think of, but be sure they are slang words used by your age group. You will not be asked to put your names on the questionnaires because we are only interested in finding out the words that your age group uses. [Five minute work period]

Additional topics are listed on the following pages. We will give you exactly five minutes to write on each topic. Do **not** turn the pages until you are told to, and don't add words to lists on different pages. Remember, list all of the slang words you can think of—if they are used by your group. Ready, begin.

Response periods were 5 minutes per topic, with no inter-item intervals, except for a brief question period after the first topic (money).

The protocols were scored by counting the number of responses for each topic. The recording procedure was highly objective and presented little problem in the analysis. A few responses with illegible writing were omitted. There were some problems with perseverative responses, that is, repeated listings with slight variations, such as 36-26-36, 37-25-36, 38-24-36 etc., for "girls" or 350cc's, 400cc's, etc. for "autos." However, these problems were handled simply by counting all responses of a given type as a single response. One protocol was rejected due to failure to follow the instructions.

Rationale for the Design and Procedures

Several methodological considerations influenced the decision to gather data collectively from small group units rather than from individuals. First, the study was concerned with subcultural variables; hence there was no need to assess individual differences. Second, pilot testing revealed that the group format allowed for some social interaction and stimulation, and Ss tended to have a motivating and/or disinhibiting effect upon one another. Generally, it appeared that a greater number and variety of responses were produced under the group conditions. Third, although the data were actually recorded in written rather than spoken form, the responses of the group were typically given orally before they were recorded by the group scribe. This approximates more closely the natural conditions of slang usage in that slang is primarily a phenomenon of spoken rather than written language. Fourth, some individuals, especially younger Ss, were uncertain about the meaning of some terms, and occasionally failed to differentiate slang from conventional terms. On the other hand, the groups in effect screened the responses for appropriateness to the topic (meaning) and for slang versus nonslang usage, thereby providing an operational criterion for classifying the terms as slang.

Another methodological issue concerns the selection of stimulus topics. Ideally, an a priori, systematic basis for selecting or sampling the topics would have provided an important control parameter in the study. However, there is no recognized a priori basis for sampling verbal stimuli such as these, and the topics were therefore selected arbitrarily by the investigators on the basis of the apparent relevance to adolescent culture. Casual observation as well as pilot testing revealed that adolescents were acquainted with a variety of terms referring to the topics included in the study.

Although the stimulus topics were not selected on a systematic basis, it would be desirable to compare the number of slang terms elicited by the various stimuli that were used. However, such stimulus effects are rather complex and may reflect several confounded variables. For example, more slang responses for the topic "unpopular person" than for "cigarettes" could mean that youths were less familiar with terms for cigarettes; but the difference might also reflect greater category breadth of the topic, a greater number of possible denotative meanings, and/or greater complexity of the topic. Therefore, direct statistical comparisons across topics would be equivocal and difficult to interpret, unless some form of control over the category breadth, complexity, and other such extraneous variables could be provided.

A degree of control over such extraneous aspects of the topics could be provided by determining the number of nonslang associates for each topic, representing baseline measures against which the number of slang associates could be compared. However, the slang versus nonslang terms pertaining to a given topic may refer to different phenomena, that is, to qualitatively different domains. For example, the domain of conventional (nonslang) terms referring to cigarettes includes numerous proper nouns, such as names of brands. Since brand names are not typically expressed in slang, the inclusion of brand names could arbitrarily inflate the baseline measure of conventional terms. It would be desirable, nevertheless, to have such baseline measures of standard word associations, not only to provide partial statistical control for the number of word associations associated with the topics, but also to control for age and sex differences in fluency and vocabulary. For example, older adolescents presumably have larger vocabularies pertaining to many topics and would generally emit a greater number of word associations than younger adolescents. Such measures could not be obtained, however, due to exigencies of the testing arrangements in the schools, and these issues must await further research.

In spite of the failure to obtain such baseline measures on the number of standard (nonslang) associations in relation to age or grade level, one can regard the slang association measure for each topic as a statistical control (i.e. a basis for comparison) for age-related differences on the other topical measures. In other words, the slang measures can be compared with one another on the basis of the amount of change associated with grade level.

General developmental changes in verbal ability, word fluency, and other extraneous variables, in effect, influence all of the slang measures to the same degree.

The design that was selected compared the number of slang responses to each topic according to school (4 levels), sex (2 levels), and grade level (6 levels). The nine dependent variables consisted of the slang response frequencies (the number of slang expressions listed) for each of the nine stimulus topics. The over-all effects of stimulus topics were not directly compared because of the problems mentioned above.

RESULTS

A multivariate analysis of variance (MANOVA) of the slang response frequencies was computed with a program [13] based on Bock's [14] model for non-orthogonal multivariate designs. The multivariate F tests indicated that the slang response frequencies for certain topics varied significantly ($p < .001$) in relation to schools, grade levels, and sexes. The multivariate Fs were also significant ($p < .05$ level) for the school x grade level and the school x sex interactions; the grade level x sex and school x grade level x sex interactions were not statistically significant.

The univariate tests on the sources which were significant indicated that school differences were related significantly beyond the .001 level to the number of responses to "clothes, styles, and appearance," "boys," and "girls." Grade level differences were related significantly beyond the .001 level to the number of responses to all nine topics. Sex differences were related significantly with the number of responses to six of the nine topics, specified in Table 1. The school x grade level interaction was significant for "money" ($p<.01$), "cigarettes and smoking" ($p<.01$), "alcohol and drinking" ($p<.05$), "boys" ($p<.05$), and "unpopular person" ($p<.05$). The school x sex interaction was significant for "money" ($p<.001$), "cigarettes and smoking" ($p<.05$), and "boys" ($p<.05$).

The main effects and interactions involving schools were of secondary interest in this analysis because effects involving schools per se could not be interpreted in relation to specified sociological or psychological variables. Nevertheless, these effects did indicate that the slang response patterns varied from school to school in complex ways. Hence the significant findings attributable to this factor point to the necessity of qualifying some of the generalizations as one considers populations based upon specific schools. Subsequent description and discussion of the results will focus upon the relationships of grade level and sex to the slang frequency measures.

[13] J. Finn, *Multivariance: Fortran Program for Univariate and Multivariate Analysis of Variance and Covariance* (Buffalo, New York: Department of Educational Psychology, State University of New York at Buffalo, May 1967).

[14] R. Bock, "Contributions of Multivariate Experimental Designs to Educational Research," in R. Cattell, ed., *Handbook of Multivariate Experimental Psychology* (Chicago: Rand McNally, 1966), pp. 820–840.

Table 1   Means and Standard Deviations of Slang Response Frequency for Males and Females

Stimulus Topic	Males		Females		
	M	SD	M	SD	F
Money	9.3	4.1	7.7	3.3	28.0 ***
Cigarettes	9.2	5.1	8.6	4.6	2.1
Alcohol	11.5	7.5	11.5	6.5	0.0
Autos, Bikes	14.4	8.9	11.4	6.7	22.0 ***
Clothes, Style	11.3	6.8	15.2	7.7	37.6 ***
Boys	13.3	9.2	16.5	10.7	14.9 ***
Girls	17.4	10.2	17.3	9.6	0.0
Popular	9.5	5.7	12.0	5.7	24.0 ***
Unpopular	18.4	9.3	21.9	9.7	18.6 ***

*** $p < .001$.

Table 1 compares the slang frequency means of males and females for each topic. These data show that males listed more terms than females for "money" and "autos and motorbikes." On the other hand, females listed more terms than males for "clothes; styles, and appearance," "boys," "a popular person," and for "an unpopular person." These sex differences were all significant beyond the .001 level.

The means at each grade level are presented graphically for males in Figures 1 and 2 and for females in Figures 3 and 4. Data for personal and nonpersonal topics were separated to facilitate interpretation of the graphs. Visual inspection of the figures reveals a tendency towards increasing mean values with successive grade levels, but the means increased much more for some topics than for others. Among males, for example, the means for "a popular person" ranged from 8.3 terms at grade seven to 11.4 at grade twelve, whereas means for the topic "girls" ranged from 10.4 terms at grade seven to 24.4 at grade twelve. In general among males, slang for "girls," "autos and motorbikes," and "alcohol and drinking" increased most from grade 7 through grade 12, while slang for "popular person," "clothes, styles, and appearance," "cigarettes and smoking," and "money" increased only slightly. Among females, on the other hand, "unpopular person," "alcohol and drinking," and "girls" increased the most, whereas "money," "cigarettes and smoking," and "popular person" increased little.

DISCUSSION

The results indicated that the numbers of slang terms and phrases associated with the different youth culture topics varied according to grade level, sex, and school. Thus, in general, familiarity with slang appears to be patterned according to age-grading and participation within certain subcultural roles and groups. Although the patterns of variation appear complex, several more

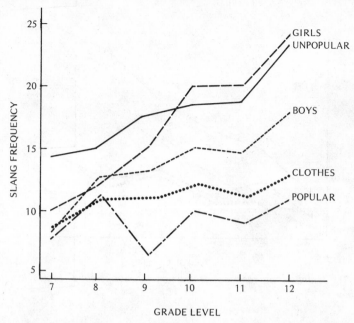

Figure 1. Males' slang response frequency for personal topics according to grade level.

specific conclusions regarding developmental and sex role differences can be offered on the basis of the results.

In accordance with the predictions, frequencies of slang associations increased with successive grade levels; moreover the frequencies increased more rapidly with successive grade levels for some topics than others. In general, there were relatively small increases in slang referring to "money," "cigarettes and smoking," "a popular person," and "clothes, styles, and appearance." Thus, the significance of these phenomena, as reflected by youth culture language, appeared to change only slightly during adolescence. On the other hand, there were relatively large increases for the topics, "alcohol and drinking," "unpopular person," and particularly among males, for "autos and motorbikes," and "girls." Thus, the data supported the hypothesis that there is a higher correlation of age with knowledge of slang for autos, motorbikes, alcohol, and drinking. This hypothesis was based upon the observation that age-related legal prohibitions and sanctions control involvements of adolescents in these areas.

Differences in performance on the slang measures also appeared to correspond with generally recognized sex differences in adolescent interests. First, males tended to produce more responses than females to the topics "autos and motorbikes" and "money." These topics refer to phenomena and behavioral domains which are integral to the adolescent male culture. Adolescent males are presumably more likely than females to own a car or motorbike, to be regularly employed, and to be primarily responsible finan-

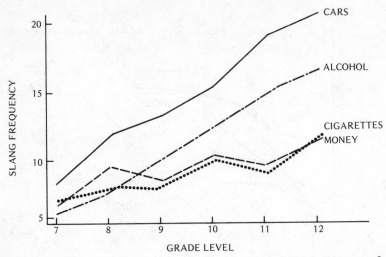

Figure 2. *Males' slang response frequency for nonpersonal topics according to grade level.*

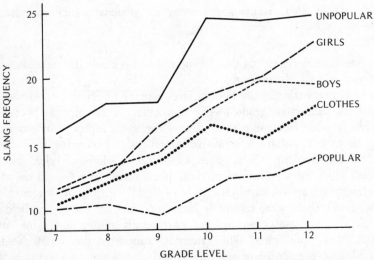

Figure 3. *Females' slang response frequency for personal topics according to grade level.*

cially for meeting expenses involved in dating, maintaining a car, and satisfying personal needs. Thus, males appeared more involved linguistically, as well as behaviorally, in these aspects of adolescent culture. In contrast to males, females tended to produce more responses to "clothes, styles, and appearance," "a popular person," "an unpopular person," and "boys." Thus, females appeared to be more linguistically oriented towards certain social aspects of their culture.

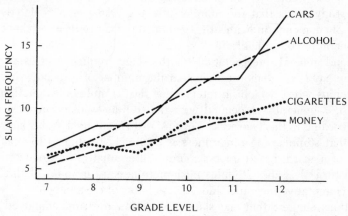

Figure 4. *Females' slang response frequency for nonpersonal topics according to grade level.*

These differential patterns of linguistic orientation for males and females correspond with sex differences in adolescent interests reported in a study by Harris,[15] which indicated that boys are more concerned with recreation and money, while girls are more concerned with social matters such as personal attractiveness, home and family relationships, and love and marriage.

The correlation of the slang familiarity measures with generally recognized age and sex role differences is consistent with the general notion that a special language may play a role in determining both uniformities and differences among adolescent subgroups. However, it would be hazardous to conclude that there is necessarily a direct correlation between the slang measures and specific socialization practices or social behaviors. The significance of the slang measure cannot be conceptualized so simply because language and socialization are related in complex ways.

The type of measure employed in the study describes but one aspect of adolescent language—the extent or size of special vocabularies which adolescents associate with given phenomenon. It is with the interpretation of this measure that we are concerned herein. Several suggestions for pertinent interpretations come from fields as disparate as cultural linguistics, experimental psychology, and psychology of personality.

First, from cultural linguistics comes the suggestion that the number of words and expressions relating to a given phenomenon may in some cases directly correspond with the importance or significance of the phenomenon for the culture that uses the set of terms. An example is provided by Whorf's [16] oft-cited observation that Eskimo language has various terms referring to snow, in contrast to standard English, which has only one general

[15] D. Harris, "Sex Differences in the Life Problems and Interests of Adolescents, 1935 and 1957," *Child Development*, XXX (1959), 453–459.

[16] B. Whorf, op. cit.

term for snow. Thus, one interpretation of the slang measure employed in the current study holds that the number of slang responses associated with a topic or phenomenon indicates the general significance or importance of the phenomenon for the subculture.

A second general interpretation for the slang frequency measure is suggested by Noble's [17] demonstration that the number of associative responses to a stimulus word, which he refers to as the "stimulus meaningfulness" of the word, is generally associated with the frequency of occurrence of that word according to the Thorndike-Lorge Word List. Zippel [18] also has demonstrated that stimulus meaningfulness is positively related to the evaluative polarity of a word, based upon semantic differential ratings of words. Carroll,[19] in turn, describes stimulus meaningfulness as an index of the "extent of . . . connotative meaning, and . . . richness of connotation. . . ." These observations suggest that the slang association measure employed in the current study, which is procedurally similar in many respects to Noble's measure, might be conceptualized similarly as an index of meaningfulness of the stimulus topics for a particular subculture or group.

A third possible interpretation of the slang measure is based upon Kelly's [20] theory, which views personality in terms of "personal constructs" that are integral to the social and psychological functioning of individuals. Kelly suggests that "comprehensive" personal constructs subsume a relatively great variety of events. The number of slang associations may be interpreted similarly as an index of the "comprehensiveness" of various youth culture constructs, as signified by the stimulus topics. Kelly also suggests that personal constructs may vary according to the "level of cognitive awareness," and that a high-level construct is one which is readily expressed in socially effective symbols. High scores on the slang measure might accordingly indicate a high level of social-cognitive awareness pertaining to a topic, because the measure is comprised of terms common to many members of the adolescent subculture. This interpretation implies that the slang measure might be useful for studying relationships between culture and personality.

Of course, such attempts to interpret the slang association measure are highly speculative. More precise interpretation of the significance of the measure can come only with additional research that identifies the parameters affecting the measure. For example, to what extent do the slang response frequencies for given topics correlate with comparable word association measures employing standard English? To what extent do word fluency, intelligence, and/or other skills influence performance on the measure, especially in relation to developmental differences? Does socioeconomic status have a general relationship to familiarity with slang for various topics?

[17] C. Noble, "An Analysis of Meaning," *Psychological Review*, LIX (1952), 421–430.

[18] B. Zippel, "Semantic Differential Measures of Meaningfulness and Agreement of Meaning," *Journal of Verbal Learning and Verbal Behavior*, VI (1967), 222–225.

[19] J. Carroll, *Language and Thought* (Englewood Cliffs, New Jersey: Prentice Hall, 1964).

[20] G. Kelly, *The Psychology of Personal Constructs* (New York: Norton, 1955).

Is the measure a sensitive index of any personality variables? Do situational parameters play an important role?

In conclusion, the research reported herein appears to have raised many questions. Nevertheless, the results do indicate that there are important differences in the sociolinguistic patterns of adolescent subgroups. These differences are clearly related to sex role and age-grading; membership in particular schools and classes also seems to be an important, but complex source of variation. More important than the specific findings, however, is the implication that the slang association paradigm employed in the study may represent a broad, flexible, and sensitive tool for surveying many facets of adolescent culture and personality.

Dexter C. Dunphy

The Social Structure of
Urban Adolescent Peer Groups

During adolescence, as at no other time in life, there is a tremendous increase in the volume of heterosexual social relationships. Whether or not an adolescent belongs to a peer group, his life is affected by one, either by the advantages inclusion provides or by the disadvantages that exclusion fosters. The personal qualities that make a male admirable and a female desirable are the prime objectives of participating in the youth culture. The development for this explicit purpose of two closely related peer groups, the clique and the crowd, has been carefully analyzed by Dunphy, and his masterful contribution to understanding adolescent peer groups is presented below.

Instructional Objectives
To define the characteristics and boundaries of adolescent cliques and crowds.
To discuss adolescent role differentiations in cliques and crowds.
To describe the significance of peer groups to the development of adolescent heterosexual prowess.

FROM *Sociometry*, XXVI (1963), pp. 230–246. Reprinted by permission of the author and the *American Sociological Association*.

M OST writers on adolescence emphasize the influence of peer groups on the course of adolescent social maturation. Indeed some regard the peer group as of comparable significance to the family and the school in the socialization of urban adolescents. Parsons, for example, states: "The family offers a wide enough range of role participations only for the young child. He must learn, by actual participation, progressively more roles than his family of orientation can offer him. It is at this point that the peer group and school assume paramount importance." [1] Existing research has established that a major difference in sex composition exists between typical preadolescent and adolescent groups. Preadolescent groups are almost universally unisexual in composition, with play centering around sex-categorized activities and role models.[2] The "gang age" thus appears to consolidate the oedipal crisis by reinforcing the child's learning of his basic sex role, such learning taking place mainly at this stage through identification with the parent of the child's own sex. Adolescence by contrast is marked by an increasing volume of heterosexual choices of preferred associates. During adolescence most persons achieve membership in a heterosexual group and acquire a heterosexual role.[3]

With some notable exceptions, field studies of adolescent peer groups have been few and inadequate and most studies of adolescent groups have aimed to assess the importance of isolated factors rather than to study groups as functioning entities. With the exception of studies of delinquent gangs, the literature is practically devoid of thorough analyses of particular groups and their dynamics. Consequently documented information on the forms and functions of adolescent peer groups is limited. Many writers distinguish two types of adolescent groups, usually referred to as "cliques" and "crowds." The most obvious difference between these two groups is their size. Hurlock, for instance, refers to the crowd as "the largest of the social units formed by adolescents." [4] The clique is usually regarded as smaller, more clearly defined and more cohesive than the crowd. Hollingshead states: "When there is a lack of homogeneity the peer group may be a clique, which is smaller and

---

[1] Talcott Parsons and Robert F. Bales, *Family, Socialization and Interaction Process* (London: Routledge and Kegan Paul, 1956), p. 38.

[2] David P. Ausubel, *Theory and Problems of Adolescent Development* (New York: Grune and Stratton), 1954; James H. Bossard, *The Sociology of Child Development* (New York: Rinehart, 1948); Paul H. Furfey, *The Gang Age: A Study of the Preadolescent Boy and His Recreational Needs* (New York: The Macmillan Co., 1926); Jacob L. Moreno, *Who Shall Survive?* (Washington, D.C.: Nervous and Mental Disease Publishing Company, 1934); Frederic M. Thrasher, *The Gang* (Chicago: Chicago University Press, 1936); William F. Whyte, *Street Corner Society* (Chicago: Chicago University Press, 1943).

[3] Luella Cole, *Psychology of Adolescence* (New York: Rinehart, 1948); William F. Connell, Elizabeth P. Francis, and Elizabeth E. Skilbeck, *Growing up in an Australian City* (Melbourne: Australian Council for Educational Research, 1957); Paul H. Furfey, "The Group Life of the Adolescent," *Journal of Educational Sociology*, 14 (Dec., 1940), 195–204; August B. Hollingshead, *Elmtown's Youth* (New York: McGraw-Hill Book Co., 1949); Elizabeth B. Hurlock, *Adolescent Development* (New York: McGraw-Hill Book Co., 1949); Jacob L. Moreno, op. cit.

[4] Op. cit., p. 173.

more purposefully organized than is the crowd. Exclusion of those who do not belong is the express purpose of the clique." [5] A wide survey of the use of these two terms in the literature on adolescence reveals no clear indication of the relative size limits of the two types of group nor agreement on what different functions, if any, these two groups perform for their members. While Hurlock suggests that cliques are the basic elements in a crowd,[6] Cole states that the clique "prevents many social contacts from taking place and reduces the effectiveness of those that do occur." [7] Similarly no clear picture exists of the internal structural properties of adolescent peer groups (e.g., leadership) nor of the dynamics by which groups function to induce the learning of a mature heterosexual role. The study reported here was therefore undertaken to provide some detailed information on the types, sizes, structure, and dynamics of adolescent peer groups in non-institutionalized urban settings.

THE RESEARCH DESIGN

This article summarizes some of the results of a field study undertaken in Sydney, Australia, between February, 1958, and December, 1960. Informal peer associations of adolescents were located in the community and studied in their natural settings. The research methods were developed in a pilot project with 60 adolescents. The subjects of the investigation itself were 303 adolescents among whom boys and girls were included in approximately equal numbers.[8] Ages ranged from 13 to 21 years. The groups were scattered throughout the Sydney Metropolitan area, were from differing socioeconomic backgrounds (although predominantly middle class) and were in most cases connected in some way with sponsored youth organizations. These clubs were used as points of departure for an exploration of the natural groups to which their members belonged, each group being studied for a period of from four to six months. Two natural associations of "unattached" youth were included to check a possible bias arising from the method of choosing subjects; no important differences were found between the structure and dynamics of these groups and the other groups in the study.[9]

The main problem in investigating the structural properties of adolescent groups is to find an appropriate method of research. Because of their informal nature, the most satisfactory method is participant observation. However, since these are adolescent peer groups, the adult observer is denied member-

[5] Op. cit., p. 448.
[6] Op. cit., p. 173.
[7] Op. cit., p. 264.
[8] In natural groups such as these, there are some membership changes over time. The numbers refer to the total membership of the groups at the time the sociometric questionnaire was administered.
[9] However, the extent to which this sample of Sydney youth is "typical" is not known. Of the "natural associations," one was a hierarchy consisting of two crowds, the other, a lower-class gang at Stage 1 (see Figure 1).

ship and full participation in them. A modified version of the participant observer approach was developed in a pilot study. This consisted in making initial contacts with youth through institutional settings, establishing rapport, and subsequently moving out into non-institutional settings. The author spent many hours on streetcorners, in milkbars and homes, at parties and on Sydney beaches with the groups being studied. All groups were informed of the nature of the study and agreed to cooperate. Other more formal methods were used in conjunction with informal observation and participation. Questionnaires were administered to all subjects, diaries were kept concurrently by the members of each group in which interaction with peers for a period of a week was recorded in detail; the majority of the subjects were interviewed at length, their answers to questions being recorded on tape. The result was a flexible method of observation designed to gather a large amount of detailed information with as little interference as possible to the normal functioning of the groups under study.

Results

Group Types

An initial attempt to locate group boundaries through sociometric means proved confusing because of a considerable lack of correspondence between individual subjects' responses when asked to list those who belonged to their "crowd." However, observation of interaction, and interviewing, revealed a high level of consensus on the boundaries of membership groups. Groups were clearly recognized as definite entities, and high status members of these groups could give accurate (i.e., verifiable by observation of interaction) descriptions of group boundaries and could also list members in status terms. In fact, while many members could not accurately describe their own positions in the group structure, they could usually describe the positions of others with some precision.

Two kinds of groups were located by participant observation, by interview, and by analysis of the diaries. These corresponded fairly closely with those referred to as cliques and crowds in the literature, and this terminology will be applied to them here. Both types of groups are true peer groups since group members are of similar age and regard each other as acceptable associates.

The first and most obvious basis of differentiation between the group types was size, the clique being smaller than the crowd. Forty-four cliques were located varying in size from three to nine members and having an average membership of 6.2. Crowds were considerably larger. Twelve crowds were located having a range of membership from 15 to 30 and an average size of 20.2. On the average then, the clique is only about one third the size of a crowd. No group was observed with a membership in the range ten to 14. Therefore, if these groups are typical, cliques and crowds are not two ends on a continuum of size but two distinct groups on a numerical basis alone.

An examination of the two types of groups shows why this is so. *The crowd is essentially an association of cliques.* There was little variation in the number of cliques within the twelve crowds. No crowd had more than four or less than two component cliques. The average number of cliques forming a crowd was 3.1.

The distinct upper limit of nine members for the clique suggests the intimacy of the relationships between members. The limited membership makes possible the strong cohesion which is a marked characteristic of these groups. Their similarity in size to the family possibly facilitates the transference of the individual's allegiance to them and allows them to provide an alternative center of security. The larger number in the crowd obviously precludes such close relationships between members. Interviews showed that from the point of view of a member within one clique within a crowd, members of other cliques are acceptable associates but not "real buddies" like the members of his own clique.

While the cliques are the basic units in crowd structure, not all cliques were associated in crowds. This held for five of the forty-four cliques in the study whose members either were not accorded or did not seek, status in a crowd. They were outside the crowd structure as some individuals (isolates) were outside the clique structure. Clique membership appears to be a prerequisite of crowd membership, since no case was found of an individual possessing crowd membership without at the same time being a member of a clique. On the other hand, one could be a clique member without being a crowd member. The members of cliques normally lived in close residential proximity and this appeared to be the main ascriptive requirement for clique membership. The cliques associated in a crowd were from adjacent residential localities and their members were of similar age and level of social development. Contrary to Cole's view, quoted above, cliques do not limit social contacts, but, on the contrary, the acquirement of clique membership is virtually the only way in which such contacts can be established and expanded.

Within localities, crowds were differentiated on an age basis, with two or three crowds associated in a status hierarchy. Five of these hierarchies, each in a different suburb, were objects of investigation in the study. Invariably the mean age of members of a crowd higher in the hierarchy was higher than the mean age of members of a crowd lower in the hierarchy. All but one of the crowds in the study formed part of a hierarchy of two or three crowds, and in some hierarchies, upper status members of one crowd occupied low status positions in the crowd above. The difference between age means of crowds adjacent in such hierarchies varied from seven months to three years and seven months, but averaged about two years.

Since age was a major factor underlying crowd differentiation, it is not surprising that where two crowds were adjacent in a crowd hierarchy, the social distance between them (as measured by relative frequency of interaction) varied with the difference between the mean ages of their members.

When there was a large gap between the mean ages of adjacent crowds, interaction between the members of the two crowds was extremely limited. Where the gap was small, interaction was far more frequent and the upper status members of the lower crowd tended to hold low status positions in the crowd above.

All crowds were heterosexual, and within crowds there was a consistent difference between the ages of boys and girls. In all crowds boys were older on the average than the girls with whom they associated. Differences between the mean ages of boys and girls in the same crowd ranged from three months to one year and ten months but averaged ten months. Many of the cliques of later adolescents were heterosexual and in all these the same age relationship between the sexes was apparent. The differentiation of the sexes along age lines parallels the typical age relationship between spouses in marriage.

Cliques and crowds perform different functions for their members. The clique centers mainly around talking. The members of one hierarchy, for example, recorded 69 clique settings and 25 crowd settings in their diaries. Of the 69 clique settings, the predominant activity in 56 of them was talking, while it was the main activity in only five of the 25 crowd settings. A similar trend was found in all groups. Analysis of the content of conversation in the clique shows that it performs an important instrumental function in that it is the center for the preparation of crowd activities, for dissemination of information about them, and for their evaluation after they are over. The crowd, on the other hand, is the center of larger and more organized social activities, such as parties and dances, which provide for interaction between the sexes. It acts as a reservoir of acceptable associates who can be drawn on to the extent required by any social activity. Thus cliques and crowds are not only different in size; they are also different in function.

There is a tendency for clique and crowd settings to be distributed differently throughout the week. In the hierarchy mentioned above, 16 of the 25 crowd settings took place at the weekend and only nine during the week. Of the clique settings, however, 47 occurred during the week and only 22 at the weekend. In all hierarchies the majority of crowd settings occurred at weekends, while the majority of clique settings occurred on weekdays.

Structural Change

In considering the hierarchical arrangement of crowds, certain general trends in the structural development of peer groups through the adolescent period become apparent. Some structural characteristics consistently appear before others in all hierarchies. An abstract ideal-typical outline of structural development is portrayed in Figure 1.

The initial stage of adolescent group development appears to be that of the isolated unisexual clique: i.e., isolated in terms of any relationship with corresponding groups of the opposite sex. This primary stage represents the persistence of the preadolescent "gang" into the adolescent period. Stage

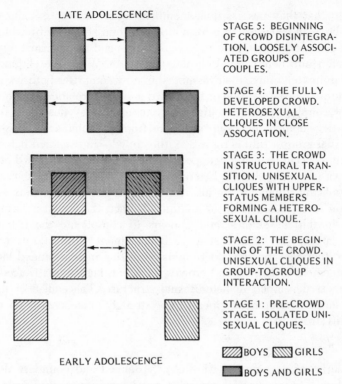

LATE ADOLESCENCE

STAGE 5: BEGINNING OF CROWD DISINTEGRA-TION. LOOSELY ASSOCI-ATED GROUPS OF COUPLES.

STAGE 4: THE FULLY DEVELOPED CROWD. HETEROSEXUAL CLIQUES IN CLOSE ASSOCIATION.

STAGE 3: THE CROWD IN STRUCTURAL TRAN-SITION. UNISEXUAL CLIQUES WITH UPPER-STATUS MEMBERS FORMING A HETERO-SEXUAL CLIQUE.

STAGE 2: THE BEGIN-NING OF THE CROWD. UNISEXUAL CLIQUES IN GROUP-TO-GROUP INTERACTION.

STAGE 1: PRE-CROWD STAGE. ISOLATED UNI-SEXUAL CLIQUES.

EARLY ADOLESCENCE

▨ BOYS ▨ GIRLS
■ BOYS AND GIRLS

Figure 1. *Stages of group development in adolescence.*

2 introduces the first movement towards heterosexuality in group structure.[10] Unisexual cliques previously unrelated to cliques of the opposite sex now participate in heterosexual interaction. At this stage however, interaction is considered daring and is only undertaken in the security of a group setting where the individual is supported by the presence of his own sex associates. Interaction at this stage is often superficially antagonistic. Stage 3 sees the formation of the heterosexual clique for the first time. Upper status members of unisexual cliques initiate individual-to-individual heterosexual interaction and the first dating occurs. Those adolescents who belong to these emergent heterosexual groups still maintain a membership role in their unisexual

[10] I have deliberately not specified modal ages for the onset of the stages outlined in Figure 1. The variation in the ages at which these phases of group development are encountered is so great that measures of central tendency, by themselves, would be mis-leading; and any useful estimate of standard deviations would require a much more comprehensive study than that described here. The average age of members in one isolated clique of girls (Stage 1), for example, was 16 years 0 months. On the other hand, Stage 3 had been reached by another clique of girls with an average age of only 13 years 10 months, and the average age of the interacting clique of boys was 14 years 6 months. The figure suggests the order of structural changes in the adolescent peer group but the differing rates, and conditions affecting these rates, need further, more extensive investigations.

clique, so that they possess dual membership in two intersecting cliques. This initiates an extensive transformation of group structure by which there takes place a reorganization of unisexual cliques and the reformation of their membership into heterosexual cliques (Stage 4). While the cliques persist as small intimate groups, their membership now comprises both sexes. Stage 5 sees the slow disintegration of the crowd and the formation of cliques consisting of couples who are going steady or engaged. Thus there is a progressive development of group structure from predominantly unisexual to heterosexual groups. In this transition, the crowd—an extended heterosexual peer group—occupies a strategic position. Membership in a crowd offers opportunities for establishing a heterosexual role. The crowd is therefore the most significant group for the individual, but crowd membership is dependent upon prior membership in a clique. In fact, the crowd is basically an interrelationship of cliques, and appears to consolidate the heterosexual learning appropriate to each stage of development. The majority of clique members, therefore, possess a determinate position in an extended hierarchical arrangement of cliques and crowds, in which high status is accorded to groups most developed in heterosexual structure. The course of the individual's social development appears to be strongly influenced by his position within this structure.

Internal Properties

Boundaries of peer groups were clearly defined and boundary definition operated as a form of social control. Crowd boundaries were most rigidly defined. When peer group members were asked to choose associates to join them in a number of situations, only 4 to 8 per cent of choices were directed outside the crowd. On the other hand 37 to 47 per cent of choices were directed outside the members' own cliques to members of cliques within the same crowd. The majority of choices were made within the respondent's own clique. Clique boundaries were less sharply defined than crowd boundaries since some individuals were willing to choose members of other cliques in the same crowd. Very few were prepared to choose outside their own crowd.

Boundary definition was a constant process which could be observed in recurring decisions such as who would be invited to parties or on swimming excursions. The meaning of boundary definition in practice can be illustrated by describing a party in which members of two crowds from the same hierarchy were involved. The hierarchy consisted of three crowds, the upper and middle crowds being fairly narrowly differentiated by age and therefore having two "marginal" members in common. At the instigation of the author, members of these two crowds were invited to a party held by one of the members of the upper crowd. Clique boundaries were most obvious at the beginning and the end of the evening. Members arrived and left in cliques. At the party itself, however, the cliques within each crowd showed a tendency to merge and members interacted across clique boundaries. The crowds were strongly differentiated. Although everyone was initially in the lounge room, the younger crowd gradually relegated itself to the kitchen, leaving the upper crowd in possession of the lounge room. This arrangement persisted throughout the rest of the evening. The two marginal members were clique leaders in the middle crowd, low status followers in the upper. Their behavior reflected their position in the hierarchy, for they oscillated from one room to the other throughout the evening. Two isolates, whom the author had arranged to be invited, showed contrasting ways of adjusting to the situation. The girl made no attempt to relate herself to either group, remained seated in one corner of the lounge room all evening, rarely spoke, and was left to make her own way home, unaccompanied. The boy attempted to relate himself to the upper crowd leader, was ignored, and remained on the fringe of those who gathered around this status figure. Thus both cliques and crowds are boundary-maintaining systems in certain situations. When together, cliques in the same crowd tend to merge. However, only boundaries between cliques are relaxed. Those who did not possess membership in a component clique were not accepted into the crowd, whether or not they attempted to relate themselves to it.

In order to acquire a membership role, an individual has to pass from outside through the boundary into the group. This is definitely a matter of achievement. Members of groups reported that they had to "push themselves forward" to enter a group. A typical statement was: "Someone who gets in and pushes, gets into a group easiest. You just have to get in and push. People who stand back just don't make the grade." Acceptance into a group was not just a matter of achievement but also of conformity. It was reported by those who had achieved membership that a new member had to "fit in," "be the same to us." Or, as one boy put it: "All groups have a certain temperament of their own. Anyone new has to fit in; he must have similar aspects and outlooks and like similar things." By demanding initial conformity to peer group standards, members ensured that the group would be a cohesive entity capable of controlling the behavior of those in it in the interests of the dominant majority. The basic consensus of values which results is a major factor in the strong *esprit de corps* of most adolescent peer groups.

It is possible to lose a membership role and to pass through the group boundary out of the group. This was due to one of two causes, as was shown by an examination of a number of concrete cases. Firstly, ostracism was sometimes the result of a member's rejection of the authority of the group. A member who regarded himself as superior to others in the group, or his judgment as superior to the judgment of the group, was quickly cut down to size. Persistence in such an attitude involved exclusion from the group and the redefinition of the boundary to exclude the offender. Loss of a membership role could also occur where an individual failed to maintain achievement, especially heterosexual achievement, at the level of his peers. This involved at first a loss of status. Continued failure to achieve meant that the member was simply dropped from the group with a consequent readjustment of the group boundary.

Entrance to a peer group depends on conformity, and failure to continue to conform at any stage means exclusion from the group. Thus the definition of the group boundary is an important means of social control which ensures the maintenance of a high level of achievement in social development.

Role differentiation: Leader and Sociocenter

Most adolescents claimed that their groups did not possess leaders. ("We don't like to think that there's a boss over us.") However, cliques were normally referred to by the name of one person in the group, e.g., "John Palmer's group." Other statements showed that while adolescents strongly denied that they had leaders, they did in fact implicitly recognize one person in the group as the incumbent of a leadership position. The following statement is typical of many made when adolescents discussed the groups they knew. "Rod has a group at Waverton, Joanne down there at North Sydney, and Julia up at Crow's Nest. The groups revolve around them." In each peer group in the study there was one individual who occupied the major leadership position and who played an important and distinctive role in relating the group to its environment.

The structure of the external system of the cliques was basically composed of the relationship of the clique leaders' positions to each other, and these positions were integrated primarily through a common relationship with a crowd leader. In fact, the clique leaders assumed group representative roles in the external system of the clique. They were better known outside their group than any of their followers—a finding consistent with Whyte's account [11] of gang structures. Thus there were two types of leadership position differentiated, corresponding with the two main types of adolescent groups. There were both clique and crowd leaders. Clique leaders were more socially mobile than their followers and were in more frequent contact with others outside the clique. The communication structure of the crowd consisted in the interrelationship of the clique and crowd leadership positions. Consequently clique leaders were better informed than their followers about what was going on in the crowd, and played a decisive part in decision making. The high status accorded the crowd leader's position is reflected in verbal and written comments about those who occupied these positions. The crowd leader appeared to be a coordinating and integrating figure in the social structure of the crowd whose presence set the seal of success on a crowd event. The incumbent of this position was always a male, and usually the leader of the largest and most heterosexually advanced clique in the crowd. Thus he had already shown his organizational capacity in a clique setting. Each clique leader was also the focus of intra-clique interaction. He was thus not only the best informed person in his clique about events and people in the crowd but also the best informed person about what was going on in his own clique. As such, he occupied a strategic position between the external and the internal systems of his own group. His followers realized

[11] Op. cit.

this and relied on the leader for information about others in the clique and in the crowd and about clique and crowd activities. While the clique leader's position is subordinate to that of the crowd leader, it is also invested with power and high status.

The clique leader's role in the coordination of his clique with others in the crowd exposes him to two sources of role expectations. In his position as leader of the clique he is expected by members of the clique to perform essential leadership functions. As a key figure in the crowd structure, he is subject to the expectations of the other clique leaders in the crowd. His subordinate position in relation to the crowd leader means that he is particularly susceptible to influence from that source. He is thus in a position where he relays the general wishes and attitudes of his followers to others in the crowd and the influence of others, particularly status superiors, to his followers. The leader role consists of organizational skills required for the coordination of clique activities with the activities of other cliques in the crowd. It also consists of personality traits allowing the leader to mix freely with others outside his clique and maintain friendly relations within the clique. *Most importantly he has to play an advanced heterosexual role since the crowd is essentially a heterosexual association.* Leaders dated more often, were more likely to be going steady, and had achieved this relationship earlier than other members of their cliques. Where a follower attained a superior level of heterosexual achievement than the leader, there was a change of leadership or a splitting of the group structure. The admired form of heterosexual role varies with the stage of structural development of the group. For instance, an aggressive role towards the opposite sex is admired at Stage 2 (see Figure 1), but results in loss of a leadership position if maintained by the leader at Stage 3.

Leaders were not only superior in heterosexual development but were responsible for maintaining the general level of heterosexual development in their cliques. They acted as confidants and advisors in matters of heterosexual behavior and even organized "partners" for "slow learners." They thus brought about a progressive development in heterosexual relationships on the part of those in their groups. The clique leaders, one of whom is also the crowd leader, form an elite within the extended peer group or crowd. An elite is a small proportion of the population who together exercise a degree of control over persons and resources disproportionate to their number. The leaders are an elite in this sense in that, together, they strongly influence the behavior of those in their cliques by consistently maintaining the pressure to achieve higher levels of social development. They do this through their centrality in the communication structure and their possession of the most valued "resources" of their groups: organizational skills, desired personality traits, and the ability to play an advanced sex role.

Within the crowd, role differentiation occurred also along the expressive dimension. Just as there was a central instrumental role in the crowd (the crowd leader), so there was a major expressive role referred to here as a "sociocenter." The sociocenter was a specialist in humor. While the status accorded this position varied from one crowd to another, the position was well established in all crowds. The incumbent was always popular, well-liked and the most extroverted member of the crowd. When the crowd gathered he usually dominated the center of the group's attention with a continual flow of witticisms and practical jokes. Because of the attention paid him in crowd settings, adults frequently regarded the sociocenter as the leader and inferred that the group was therefore essentially frivolous in character.

The degree to which the sociocenter role was differentiated varied considerably from one crowd to another, and the extent of the differentiation appeared to be influenced by the character of the crowd leader's role. In crowds where the crowd leader was seen by the members as playing an authoritarian, directive role, the sociocenter was highly differentiated. Where the crowd leader was seen as non-directive, as leading simply by virtue of superior social skills, the role was less differentiated. The more the crowd leader directly or indirectly forced the pace of social achievement in the crowd, the more highly differentiated the role of the sociocenter appeared.

This bears a similarity to R. F. Bales' finding [12] that differentiation in small problem-solving laboratory groups occurred along two axes, instrumental and expressive, and resulted in the emergence of a "task specialist" and a "best-liked man." These types appear to correspond to the "crowd leader" and the "sociocenter" reported above. Bales suggested that [13]

> a certain amount of ambivalence tends to center on the task specialist. He tends to be liked because he is satisfying needs in relation to the task area. But he also tends to arouse a certain amount of hostility because his prestige is rising relative to the other members, because he talks a large proportion of the time, and because his suggestions constitute proposed new elements to be added to the common culture, to which all members will be committed if they agree. Whatever readjustments the members have to make in order to feel themselves committed will tend to produce minor frustrations, anxieties and hostilities. These are centered to some degree on the object most active in provoking the disturbance—the task specialist.

In the adolescent peer group, the leader is the person who plays the most advanced heterosexual role. He moves the group to participate in heterosexual activities and encourages members to develop more mature heterosexual roles. While the members are generally motivated to achievement, this still implies new levels of conformity and commitment. The crowd leader's role is therefore particularly analogous to that of the task specialist who is similarly concerned with increased performance and similarly induces culture change. Like the task specialist, also, the peer group leader is the center of

[12] Parsons and Bales, op. cit.
[13] Ibid., p. 297.

the communication pattern and high in status relative to the other members. It seems likely that the sociocenter performs the system function of relieving the tension created in the group by the leader, tension which is at its highest in the heterosexual crowd situation. His specialization in humor, a form of tension release, supports this interpretation. The more the leader dominates, the more tension is created and the more differentiated the sociocenter role becomes. If this did not occur, the tension would tend to destroy the cohesion of the group and thus impede progress towards higher goals. Bales has noted the interdependence of these two roles in his groups and this was apparent in the peer groups. They are by nature high consensus groups since only members who conform to the culture of the group are admitted. The crowd leader and the sociocenter play mutually supportive roles in the crowd structure, the complementarity of the two roles preserving the equilibrium of the crowd.

Socialization Process in the Adolescent Peer Group

The primary stage of socialization, which occurs in the family, is largely achieved through the identification of the child with his parents and his consequent incorporation of their norms. This stage has a strong effect on the acquisition of a basic sex role. The peer group at adolescence assumes many of the functions previously performed for the individual by the family and is thus of considerable significance in promoting his increasing independence from the family. If there is an internal consistency in the whole process of socialization through childhood and adolescence, we would expect socialization to take place through an identification with the peer group leaders similar to that with the parents. At the beginning of this article it was mentioned that discrepancies were observed when subjects were asked to name those in their crowd. The list given by an individual usually did not match very well the group others named as his associates and which could actually be observed in concrete situations. However, in the social structure of these membership groups as identified by participant observation, through interviews, and through analysis of diary records, these discrepancies showed up as a highly consistent and meaningful trend. When clique members were asked to name those in their crowd, they tended to name those in their own clique and the leadership elite of their crowd. The leadership elite was in fact highly "overchosen" in the sense that they received many more choices than they themselves made. There was a consistent discrepancy in the direction of high status between the groups in which the individuals actually participated and the groups to which they referred themselves.

By using a chi square technique, the probability of this trend occurring by chance could be tested. However, the test could be applied only to hierarchies where there were proportionately few intercrowd choices so that the crowds could be treated as if they were independent entities. Four of the five hierarchies met this criterion. Two hypotheses were tested. (1) Leaders, when choosing outside their own clique and within the same crowd, choose other clique leaders significantly more than they choose followers, when allowance is made for the relative proportion of leaders to followers. (2) Followers, when choosing outside their own clique and within the same crowd, choose clique leaders significantly more than they choose followers, when allowance is made for the relative proportion of leaders to followers. Hypothesis 1 was supported in three of the four hierarchies at the 0.1 per cent, 1 per cent, and 2 per cent levels respectively, but the chi square was not significant in the fourth. Inspection of the fifth hierarchy shows that those choices made within the crowd boundaries show the same trend. Hypothesis 2 was supported in all four hierarchies at the .1 per cent, .1 per cent, .01 per cent, and 5 per cent levels respectively. Inspection of those choices made within crowd boundaries in the fifth hierarchy shows the same trend.

In some cases, choices were made of members of other crowds in the same hierarchy. These were usually choices between high status members of one crowd and low status members of another older crowd. Fifty-three choices of this kind were made in all hierarchies. Forty-nine of these were directed upwards to members of crowds higher in status than the ones to which the choosers belonged. The remaining four were directed downwards to members of crowds lower in status. Thus an examination of all extra-clique choices reveals a strong and highly significant tendency to list clique leaders in the same crowd and members of a crowd higher in the status hierarchy when naming associates. In particular, those lower in status than the chooser tend to be omitted. Members of the leadership elite within crowds were particularly overchosen. These results can be interpreted as showing a general upward trend in status terms in the pattern of identification in these groups. In naming those who belong to their "crowd," therefore, these adolescents apparently listed their *reference* rather than their *membership* groups, suggesting that the social structure is stabilized by the ego-involvement of clique members with the clique and crowd leaders.

These data lend support to Freud's notion, advanced particularly in his *Group Psychology and the Analysis of the Ego*,[14] that a primary group is a number of individuals who have taken the same person, the leader, as their ego-ideal. "We already begin to divine that the mutual tie between members of a group is in the nature of an identification of this kind, based upon an important emotional common quality; and we suspect that this common quality lies in the nature of the tie with the leader."[15] Thus Freud's view emphasizes that the bond with the leader is of more importance to group stability than are the ties between the members and that, in fact, it is the former which confers significance on the latter. "A primary group of this kind is a number of individuals who have put one and the same object in the place of their ego ideal and have consequently identified themselves with each other in their ego."[16] Freud regarded the family as the prototype of every human group and the leader as a parent substitute. Certainly the

14, 15, 16 Sigmund Freud, *Group Psychology and the Analysis of the Ego* (New York: Liveright, 1922), pp. 108, 120.

position of the leader in the peer group is analogous in some ways with that of the parent and a similar identification appears to occur. However, the evidence above does suggest that there is identification not only with the leader of one's clique, but beyond that an identification with a number of status figures in the wider peer group—the crowd. The interviews suggested that there is a progressive differentiation of this object system. Generally speaking, the lower a member's status in the social structure, the less differentiated the mental picture he possessed of the positions of others and their relationships with each other. It seems reasonable to deduce from this that the first stage of socialization into a group of peers, the clique, is dependent on the differentiation by the initiate of the leader, and his identification with him. From this stage the pattern of identification suggests that there is a progressive differentiation of the whole object system and a single reference idol (the clique leader) is replaced by a system of social objects which consists basically in the pattern of crowd leadership positions and roles in their interrelationships.

DISCUSSION

In the socialization of the individual his transition from the nuclear family to wider adult society can take place in many ways. In western urban society, the peer group is one important avenue through which this can occur. In Sydney, for instance, where this study was undertaken, it appears that about 70 per cent of boys and 80 per cent of girls at ages 14 and 15 belong to peer groups similar to those dealt with here.[17] If the groups reported are typical, socialization within the peer group system is an extension of socialization within the family system and shows important resemblances in pattern. There is, for instance, a similar differentiation of structure along instrumental and expressive lines with both high status instrumental and expressive roles functioning to preserve the equilibrium of the peer group system. As in the family, the individual proceeds through a series of successively more complex systems of relationships and in the process identifies with status figures, internalizing their roles. Thus his personality continues to expand through the progressive differentiation of his object system.

It appears of some significance that socialization within the adolescent peer group system begins as the stable state the individual enjoyed as latency child in the family is upset by new social expectations at puberty, leading him to establish an increased dependence on the peer group. Initially this group is the unisexual clique, which represents the continuation of the preadolescent "gang" and at this stage is a group comparable in size to the family. In order to achieve and maintain membership in this group, the individual must show his readiness to conform to the group's authority. This is made easier through his identification with the clique leader who embodies

---

[17] Connell et al., op. cit.

many of the social skills and personality traits admired in the group. The clique establishes and reinforces the individual's drive to achieve hetero-sexuality, since it is, or becomes, a subsystem of the crowd: the crowd in its turn is only a subsystem of a hierarchy of crowds. Thus through clique membership the individual is inducted into an extended peer group system markedly different from the family in size. About middle adolescence there is a major transformation of the clique system which has persisted in a rela-tively stable form. A new clique system evolves from this structurally unstable stage. Groups become heterosexual, members having established a significant relationship with a member of the opposite sex. The crowd persists long enough to ensure that the basic role characteristics underlying this relation-ship are thoroughly acquired. It then breaks up into cliques of loosely associated couples as members move towards marriage. The social structure of urban adolescent peer groups has the effect of maintaining a high level of achievement which ensures that most adolescents progressively acquire an increasingly mature heterosexual role.

Norman Cavior
Paul R. Dokecki

Physical Attractiveness, Perceived Attitude Similarity, and Academic Achievement as Contributors to Interpersonal Attraction Among Adolescents

The study presented below is among the first empirical investigations of the interrelationships between physical attractiveness and perceived attitude similarity—two major determinants of adolescent popularity. Cavior and Dokecki asked (a) one group of fifth- and eleventh-grade boys and girls who knew each other to judge classmates' photographs on physical attractiveness, perceived attitude similarity, and interpersonal attraction and (b) another group of comparable youth who did not know each other

FROM *Developmental Psychology*, IX (1973), pp. 44–54. Copyright 1973 by the American Psychological Association. Reprinted by permission of the authors and the publisher.

to judge the same photographs on physical attractiveness. The data yielded support for seven hypotheses: 1) ranking and rating methods of evaluating physical attractiveness are highly correlated; 2) boys and girls employ comparable criteria in judging physical attractiveness; 3) judgments of knowers and nonknowers are highly correlated; 4) familiarity exerts greater influence on judgments of popularity of persons of average attractiveness— less on those most and least attractive; 5) correlations of physical attractiveness and perceived attitude similarity, respectively, and interpersonal attraction are about the same at both grade levels; 6) physical attractiveness and perceived attitude similarity also are positively correlated at both grade levels; 7) physical attractiveness enhances perceived attitude similarity in judgments of popularity more than the latter enhances the former in such judgments.

Instructional Objectives

To describe correlates of popularity—physical attractiveness, perceived attitude similarity, and academic achievement.

To discuss the extent to which each of seven hypotheses about interpersonal attraction among adolescents is supported by empirical data.

To advance plausible explanations for the contribution of physical attractiveness, perceived attitude similarity, and academic achievement, respectively, to popularity among adolescents.

THREE factors which are plausibly related to interpersonal attraction (popularity) in school-aged children are (*a*) physical attractiveness, (*b*) attitude similarity, and (*c*) academic achievement. A potential fourth factor, global personality, as in "he has a nice personality," is far too nebulous to be useful in understanding popularity. Such popular conceptions of personality seem to suggest that the other person's attitudes and behaviors are considered desirable, perhaps indicating that the person making the statement has similar attitudes and sees himself behaving similarly to the person he is encountering. Although the three factors considered here have been dealt with in previous studies of interpersonal attraction, in none have these factors been examined simultaneously, from a developmental perspective, and in naturally occurring groups whose members have known each other over an extended period of time.

Previous research in which a variety of methods have been utilized has indicated a significant relationship between physical attractiveness and popularity.[1] It should be noted that the subjects in almost all of these studies

[1] D. Byrne, C. H. Ervin, and J. Lamberth, "Continuity between the Experimental Study of Attraction and Real-Life Computer Dating," *Journal of Personality and Social Psychology,* I (1970), 157–165; D. Byrne, O. London, and K. Reeves, "The Effects of Physical Attractiveness, Sex, and Attitude Similarity on Interpersonal Attraction," *Journal of Per-*

did not know each other prior to the research, and it is possible that physical attractiveness may be more important at the beginning of a relationship than after the person is known for a period of time. With extended contact, factors such as attitude similarity may become more important than physical attractiveness in determining popularity, and it might be expected that over time the relationship between physical attractiveness and popularity weakens, at least in situations such as school, where persons are to some extent required to interact with each other.

Cavior and Dokecki [2] studied the relationship between physical attractiveness and popularity in a naturally occurring group of fifth graders; boys and girls made judgments of the physical attractiveness of the boys. Significant correlations were found between physical attractiveness and popularity. This study was replicated [3] cross-culturally with fifth-grade Mexicans boys and girls in Monterrey, Mexico. Physical attractiveness and popularity were again found to be closely correlated. The present investigation was directed in part toward replicating and extending the previous findings of Cavior and Dokecki by including older children and considering other possible determinants of popularity.

Byrne and his associates, working within a reinforcement paradigm, have demonstrated the existence of a relationship between attitude similarity and interpersonal attraction.[4] One of the problems with Byrne's methodology is that even when there is face-to-face interaction, which has usually not been the case, confederates or stooges are used. Also, it is immediately clear to the subject in most of Byrne's research whether his attitudes are in actual agreement with those of the nonexistent, absentee "stranger." In real life, after much time and discussion, one person may believe his attitudes are congruent with another's while in fact this may or may not be the case. This

---

sonality, XXXVI (1968) 259–271; R. H. Coombs and W. F. Kenkel, "Sex Differences in Dating Aspirations and Satisfaction with Computer-Selected Partners," *Journal of Marriage and the Family*, XXVIII (1966), 62–66; F. A. C. Perrin, "Physical Attractiveness and Repulsiveness," *Journal of Experimental Psychology*, IV (1921), 203–217; B. Pope, "Socio-Economic Contrasts in Children's Peer Culture Prestige Values," *Genetic Psychology Monographs*, XLVIII (1953), 157–220; M. Roff and D. S. Brody, "Appearance and Choice Status During Adolescence," *Journal of Psychology*, XXXVI (1953), 347–356; W. Stroebe, C. A. Insko, V. D. Thompson, and B. D. Layton, "Effects of Physical Attractiveness, Attitude Similarity, and Sex, on Various Aspects of Interpersonal Attraction," *Journal of Personality and Social Psychology*, I (1971), 79–91; E. Walster, V. Aronson, D. Abrahams, and L. Rottman, "Importance of Physical Attractiveness in Dating Behavior," *Journal of Personality and Social Psychology*, IV (1966), 508–516.

[2] N. Cavior and P. R. Dokecki, "Physical Attractiveness and Popularity Among Fifth Grade Boys." Paper presented at the meeting of the Southwestern Psychological Association, Austin, Texas, April 18, 1969.

[3] N. Cavior and P. R. Dokecki, "Physical Attractiveness and Interpersonal Attraction Among Fifth Grade Boys: A Replication with Mexican Children." Paper presented at the meeting of the Southwestern Psychological Association, St. Louis, Missouri, April 25, 1970.

[4] For an extensive review, see G. Lindzey and D. Byrne, "Measurement of Social Choice and Interpersonal Attractiveness," in G. Lindzey and E. Aronson, eds., *The Handbook of Social Psychology*, 2nd ed. (Reading, Mass.: Addison-Wesley, 1968), Vol. 2.

phenomenon is the issue of actual versus perceived similarity.[5] As Byrne and his co-workers [6] have noted, there is evidence suggesting that perceived attitude similarity is generally more important than is actual similarity.

Results of studies relating academic achievement and intelligence to interpersonal attraction and popularity are conflicting, but the "box score" analysis performed in the Lindzey and Byrne [7] review indicated a low but positive correlation between the two variables.

From our previous research [8] and from a consideration of the literature, seven hypotheses were formulated and investigated. They are listed in the Results section, with the data relevant to each.

METHOD

Subjects

Two grade levels (age groups) were studied: fifth graders (18 boys, 12 girls) aged 10 to 12 with a modal age of 11 and eleventh graders (14 boys, 14 girls) aged 16 to 18 with a modal age of 17. These age groups were selected as representing relatively maximum physical development prior to and subsequent to puberty. All subjects were white, of western European ancestry, and members of the upper-lower to lower-middle socioeconomic class. The data were collected within a 3-week period, during the spring, from schools that were from 5 to 15 miles north of Houston, Texas. All subjects within each grade level were used and all had known each other for a period of time. Seventy per cent of the fifth graders had been in the same class since first grade, one child had been in the class for 9 months, and the others for at least 17 months. Most of the eleventh graders had known each other for many years, most since first grade, and none of them had been in the class for less than 9 months. Thus, the eleventh graders knew each other longer than the fifth graders knew each other. Because of these degrees of acquaintance, these four groups, composed of boys and girls at two grade levels, are referred to here as the "knowers" groups. Four additional "nonknowers" groups, composed of 15 boys and 15 girls at each of the two grade levels, from different schools than the knowers groups, were similar to the knowers groups with respect to age, race, ancestry, and socioeconomic background. These nonknowers did not know the knowers but they knew each other for as long as the knowers had known each other. There were thus 16 groups or sets of data: Grade Level (2) × Knowing Condition (2) × Sex of Judge (2) × Sex of Pictures (2).

[5] R. Tagiuri, J. S. Bruner, and R. R. Blake, "On the Relation Between Feelings and Perception of Feelings Among Members of Small Groups," in E. E. Maccoby, T. M. Newcomb, and E. L. Hartley, eds., *Readings in Social Psychology*, 3rd ed. (New York: Holt, Rinehart and Winston, 1958).

[6] D. Byrne, "Attitudes and Attraction," in L. Berkowitz, ed., *Advances in Experimental Social Psychology* (New York: Academic Press, 1969), Vol. 4; Lindzey and Byrne, op. cit.

[7] Lindzey and Byrne, op. cit.

[8] Cavior and Dokecki, 1969, op. cit.; 1970, op. cit.

Procedure [9]

Black and white, 5 × 7 inch, full-length pictures were taken of the boys and girls in the four knowers groups. The boys' and girls' pictures were judged separately and only at their own grade level. It should be noted that the subjects in the knowers groups were judging pictures of their own class-mates. Each subject was seen individually and was asked to arrange (rank), from a random display, the photos from most to least attractive, and to rate, from a randomly ordered deck of pictures, each one as either "handsome (or pretty), average, or ugly." Both the method used to judge physical attrac-tiveness and the sex judged first were counterbalanced with each of the Grade × Sex groups. The ranking and rating methods of judging physical attractiveness were performed by all subjects in both the knowers and non-knowers groups; all other procedures described hereafter involved only sub-jects in the knowers groups.

All of the subjects in the knowers groups ranked (from most to least liked) and rated (like, sometimes like–sometimes dislike, dislike) their classmates, whose names were printed on cards, each sex separately. The method of judgment and sex judged first within each method were counterbalanced.

The subjects also filled out a 5-point attitude questionnaire, reflecting how similar they believed their attitudes were to those of each other boy and girl in their class, from almost none of our ideas and interests are the same; we almost never agree about things, 1, to almost all of our ideas and interests are the same; we agree about things almost all the time, 5. The order of presentation of the attitude scales and physical attractiveness judg-ment tasks was counterbalanced.

Cumulative grade point indexes and national achievement test scores were obtained for each student from school records. For the fifth graders, scores on the Science Research Associates Achievement Series, Green Level, Form D, Grade 5 were used. For the eleventh graders, scores on the College Entrance Examination Board Preliminary Scholastic Aptitude Test were used.

RESULTS

The order of presentation of the measures had no significant effects.

Hypothesis 1: Physical attractiveness is scalable; that is, there is high interjudge agreement on physical attractiveness. In order to test this hypothe-sis the Kendall coefficient of concordance was calculated for the rankings of physical attractiveness for each of the 16 sets of data. The judgments of physical attractiveness were reliable for all sets: The coefficients ranged from .43 to .74. The values of the chi-squares associated with the coefficients of concordance ranged from 51.59 to 162.62 ($p < .001$ in all cases); the mean chi-square for the 16 groups was 108.33. In addition, there was consistently greater agreement among nonknowers than among knowers, and judgments

---

[9] A complete description of these procedures is available from the first author.

of the opposite sex, with only one exception, yielded higher coefficients of concordance than judgments of the same sex. The data supported Hypothesis 1.

Hypothesis 2: There is a positive relationship between ranking and rating methods of judging physical attractiveness. The two methods were compared by using the Spearman rank-order correlation coefficient. The values of these coefficients ranged from .88 to .98 ($p < .001$ in all cases; mean $R = .94$), indicating that the two methods yield very similar results. These results supported Hypothesis 2. (Although all of the correlations similarly computed for the popularity measures were also significant, $p < .025$ or less, they were generally smaller in magnitude, ranging from .68 to .90.)

There were significant differences in the use of the three attractiveness categories by knowers and nonknowers. In all comparisons, the knowers used the handsome or pretty category significantly more and the ugly category significantly less than the nonknowers. Earlier research [10] indicated that the use of the three attractiveness categories (from high to low) was negatively related to one's self-concept in these areas; the lower the physical attractivness self-concept the more frequently was the attractive category used. Thus, although the two methods, ranking and rating, yield rank-order distributions that are substantially correlated, the ranking method appears to be less influenced by other factors. Consequently, the remaining analyses to be reported are based on the ranking method of judgment. In all cases, the rating method yielded similar results.

Hypothesis 3: Boys and girls use similar criteria in making their judgments of physical attractiveness. Within knower groups, the correlations between boys' and girls' rankings of physical attractiveness were all statistically significant, ranging from .82 to .98, with a mean of .91 ($p < .001$ in all cases). These results were interpreted as supporting Hypothesis 3.

Hypothesis 4a: Knowing the persons being judged has a small but significant effect on the judgments of their physical attractiveness. Investigation of the effect of knowing a person on the judgment of his physical attractiveness was somewhat involved. The results of the analysis of the effects of knowing are presented in Tables 1 and 2. In Table 1, it can be seen that among fifth graders the correlations between knowers and nonknowers (i.e., within-sex, between-school correlations) were significant for the judgments of the physical attractiveness of boys but not for the judgments of the physical attractiveness of girls. Among the eleventh graders, the correlations between knowers and nonknowers were all significant. If knowing had no effect on the rankings, these within-sex, between-school correlations would be expected to approach the values of within-sex, within-school correlations. Therefore, within each group subjects were randomly divided into two subgroups and within-group (within-sex, within-school) correlations were computed. These within-group correlations, each greater than .88, were com-

[10] N. Cavior, "The Relationship of Physical Attractiveness to Physical Attractiveness Self Concept and Popularity," unpublished manuscript, University of Houston, 1968.

Table 1 Spearman Rho Correlations Between Schools within Sex and Between Two Random Subgroups within Each of the 16 Groups of Subjects

Grade Level and Knowing	Sex of Judges	Sex of Subjects	Between-School Correlations: Knowers Versus Nonknowers	Within-Group Correlation	Z Test of Difference Between Within-Groups and Between-School rs
5: Knowers	Boys	Boys	.62 ****	.96 *****	3.34 ****
		Girls	.33	.90 *****	2.40 ***
	Girls	Boys	.68 ****	.93 *****	2.27 **
		Girls	.05	.89 ****	2.91 ****
5: Nonknowers	Boys	Boys	.62 ****	.98 *****	4.31 ****
		Girls	.33	.94 *****	2.96 ****
	Girls	Boys	.68 ***	.95 *****	2.75 ****
		Girls	.05	.91 *****	3.14 ****
11: Knowers	Boys	Boys	.86 *****	.93 ****	.86
		Girls	.61 ***	.94 *****	2.42 **
	Girls	Boys	.71 ****	.95 ****	2.22 **
		Girls	.63 ***	.94 *****	2.34 *
11: Nonknowers	Boys	Boys	.86 ****	.92 ****	.70
		Girls	.61 ***	.98 *****	3.73 ****
	Girls	Boys	.71 ****	.93 *****	1.81 *
		Girls	.63 ***	.93 ****	2.15 **

* = $p < .05$, one-tailed tests.
** = $p < .025$.
*** = $p < .01$.
**** = $p < .005$.

pared to the values of the between-school (knowers versus nonknowers) correlations, and the differences for all but two groups were found to be statistically significant. These differences suggest that, within limits, knowing does affect the judgments of physical attractiveness. The limits are the significant positive correlations between the knowers' and nonknowers' rankings of physical attractiveness.

Hypothesis 4b: The knowing variable has the greatest influence on judgments of average attractive persons as compared to persons at either extreme. In order to test this part of Hypothesis 4, three manipulations of the data were performed. First, the middle two-thirds of the nonknowers' physical attractiveness rankings were defined as average in attractiveness and the upper and lower one-sixths as most and least attractive, respectively. Mean discrepancy scores between the physical attractiveness rankings assigned by knowers and nonknowers of the persons depicted in the pictures were computed for the three attractiveness categories. Table 2 shows that in six of the eight comparisons the largest mean discrepancy scores were for the average

Table 2 *Mean Physical Attractiveness Discrepancy Scores Assigned by Knowers and Nonknowers of the Subjects for Three Categories of Physical Attractiveness*

Grade Level	Sex of Judges	Sex of Subjects	Level of Attractiveness		
			MOST	AVERAGE	LEAST
5	Boys	Boys	2.50 $n = 3$	4.33 $n = 12$	1.50 $n = 3$
		Girls	2.00 $n = 2$	3.00 $n = 8$	.50 $n = 2$
	Girls	Boys	5.33 $n = 3$	3.58 $n = 12$	2.00 $n = 3$
		Girls	6.25 $n = 2$	4.06 $n = 8$	1.00 $n = 2$
11	Boys	Boys	.67 $n = 3$	2.12 $n = 8$	1.67 $n = 3$
		Girls	1.17 $n = 3$	3.69 $n = 8$	2.33 $n = 3$
	Girls	Boys	1.67 $n = 3$	3.12 $n = 8$	2.67 $n = 3$
		Girls	.00 $n = 3$	3.75 $n = 8$	1.33 $n = 3$

attractive pictures. Only among the fifth-grade girl judges did the most attractive persons have larger physical attractiveness discrepancy scores than the average attractive persons. In all eight comparisons, the least attractive persons received lower discrepancy scores than the average attractive persons. Similar results were obtained using the physical attractiveness rankings of the knowers for determining the pictures assigned to the three attractiveness categories.

The second data manipulation involved combining the discrepancy scores for the most and least attractive persons. Following this operation, the fifth-grade girls' judgments of the boys was the only comparison in which the average attractive persons did not obtain higher discrepancy scores than the combination of most plus least attractive persons. These results can be seen by averaging the data in Table 2 for the most plus least attractive persons.

The third manipulation of the data was necessitated by small sample sizes in the most plus least attractive category. In order to compensate for this, the discrepancy scores were summed within each grade level. The mean discrepancy scores between knowers and nonknowers in the fifth grade were 3.79 for the average attractive and 2.68 for the most plus least attractive persons combined. The difference between these means was significant ($t = 1.722$, $p < .05$, one-tailed test). For the eleventh graders, the means were 3.17 and 1.44, respectively. The difference between these means was also statistically significant ($t = 3.576$, $p < .001$, one-tailed test).

The result of these three operations indicated that knowing had a significantly greater effect on the average attractive persons than on the combination of most plus least attractive persons.

Hypothesis 5: There is a positive correlation between popularity and physical attractiveness, between popularity and perceived attitude similarity, and between physical attractiveness and perceived attitude similarity. Hypothesis 6a: There is a positive correlation between physical attractiveness and popularity at each of two age levels. Hypothesis 6b: The correlation between attractiveness and popularity is significantly lower among the older than younger groups. A perceived attitude similarity score was calculated for each subject by first summing the ratings assigned him by each of his classmates. Separate scores were obtained for each sex within the class. The sums were then converted into rank data from the most similar attitudes (highest sum of ratings) to the most dissimilar attitudes (lowest sum of ratings). Thus, the person with the highest sum (Rank 1) was seen by his classmates as having attitudes most similar to everyone in the class, while the person with the lowest sum (Rank n) was seen as having attitudes which were most dissimilar from his classmates.

Eight multiple regression analyses were computed (one for each Grade × Sex of Judge × Sex of Picture combination within the knower condition), using popularity as the criterion variable and rankings on physical attractiveness, perceived attitude similarity, cumulative grade average, and achievement test scores as predictor variables. In Table 3 are the correlations between the popularity rankings and each of the four predictor variables. The results were interpreted as supporting Hypothesis 5. Inspection of the table reveals that both physical attractiveness and attitude similarity were consistently correlated with the popularity rankings. Academic performance was not so related. Physical attractiveness and perceived attitude similarity were positively correlated.

Table 3   Correlations between Popularity Rankings and Physical Attractiveness (PA) Perceived Attitude Similarity (ATT), Cumulative Grade Averages (CGA), and National Achievement Test Scores (NATS), and Between PA and ATT

Grade Level	Sex of Judges	Sex of Subjects	PA	ATT	CGA	NATS	Correlation Between PA and ATT
5	Boys	Boys	.96 ****	.92 ****	.15	.35	.88 ****
		Girls	.94 ****	.84 ****	.36	.32	.71 ****
	Girls	Boys	.89 ****	.76 ****	.10	.37	.75 ****
		Girls	.67 ***	.74 ****	.23	.23	.83 ****
11	Boys	Boys	.64 ***	.90 ****	.12	.06	.45 *
		Girls	.87 ****	.83 ****	.31	.15	.75 ****
	Girls	Boys	.74 ****	.96 ****	.03	.20	.66 ****
		Girls	.47 *	.92 ****	.09	−.08	.63 ***

* $p < .05$, one-tailed tests.
** $p < .025$.
*** $p < .01$.
**** $p < .005$.

The amount of variance in the criterion variable, popularity, accounted for by each of the predictor variables, is presented in Table 4. In general, there were major differences between the two grade levels which also involved differences between the sexes. Specifically, physical attractiveness accounted for most of the variance in the popularity rankings for the fifth-grade boys' rankings of both boys and girls, the fifth-grade girls' rankings of the boys, and the eleventh-grade boys' rankings of themselves. Perceived attitude similarity accounted for most of the variance in girls' rankings of themselves at both age levels, and for both sexes' judgments of the eleventh-grade boys. In general, these two variables accounted for a substantial portion of the variance in popularity rankings. In six of the eight regression analyses, the cumulative grade average made a small but statistically significant contribution to the variance of the popularity rankings. Achievement test scores made small but significant variance contributions in five of the eight analyses. A comparison of Tables 3 and 4 indicates that the amount of variance contributed to popularity by physical attractiveness and attitude similarity corresponds directly with which of these two predictors was more highly correlated with popularity as indicated in Table 3. This finding reflects the strong correlation obtained between physical attractiveness and perceived attitude similarity also indicated in Table 3.

Table 4   Percentage of Variance Accounted for by the Predictors of the Criterion Variable Popularity

Grade Level	Sex of Judges	Sex of Subjects	Total Variance Accounted for	Predictors [a]			
				PA	ATT	CGA	NATS
5	Boys	Boys	96	.93 ****	.02 ****	.01 ****	.01 ****
		Girls	99	.87 ****	.02 ****	.01 ****	.10 ****
	Girls	Boys	83	.79 ****	.02 ****	.01 ****	.01 ****
		Girls	59	.01 *	.54 ***	.01	.03
11	Boys	Boys	89	.07 ****	.81 ****	.01 ****	.01 ****
		Girls	88	.76 ****	.08 ****	.04 ****	.00
	Girls	Boys	95	.01 ****	.91 ****	.03 ****	.00
		Girls	86	.02 ****	.84 ****	.01 ****	.01 ****

[a] PA = physical attractiveness, ATT = perceived attitude similarity, CGA = cumulative grade averages, and NATS = national achievement test scores.
  * $p < .05$, one-tailed tests.
  ** $p < .025$.
  *** $p < .01$.
  **** $p < .005$.

With respect to the amount of variance contributed by academic achievement to interpersonal attractiveness, it can be seen in Table 4 that the cumulative grade point average (student's grades in class) consistently made very small but significant variance contributions; but the National Achievement test scores made no contribution when heterosexual judgments were involved, that is, boys' judgments of girls and girls' judgments of boys. However, for these same judgments, cumulative grade point averages made larger variance contributions to popularity than for same-sex judgments.

From the developmental perspective, inspection of Table 3 clearly indicates that even after the children had known each other for long periods of time, there was a significant positive correlation between physical attractiveness and popularity, particularly for heterosexual friendship selections. Although the correlations between physical attractiveness and popularity tended to be lower among the eleventh graders than among the fifth graders, only for the boys' judgments of boys was the decrease statistically significant (.96 versus .64, $t = 3.00$, $p < .05$). There were no significant changes in the correlation values between perceived attitude similarity and popularity from fifth to eleventh grade. Therefore, the results lend support for Hypotheses 5 and 6a but in general fail to support Hypothesis 6b.

Hypothesis 7: Physical attractiveness determines popularity for the most and least attractive subjects, while for average attractive subjects there is a Physical Attractiveness × Popularity interaction. The average attractive subjects had significantly higher discrepancy scores between physical attractiveness and popularity rankings than the most and least attractive subjects. Mean discrepancy scores between physical attractiveness and popularity rankings assigned to each group of subjects were determined in order to assess the relationships between these two variables. These mean discrepancy scores by grade, sex of judge, sex of subjects, and level of attractiveness are presented in Table 5. Inspection of the table indicates that in five of the eight comparisons the discrepancy scores were largest for the average attractive subjects. As in Hypothesis 4b, the discrepancy scores of the most and least attractive subjects were combined and then summed across sex of judge and sex of subject within each grade level. For the fifth graders, the mean discrepancy score between rankings of physical attractiveness and popularity was 1.89 for the average attractive subjects and .68 for the extreme attractive subjects. The difference between these means was statistically significant ($t = 3.313$, $p < .01$). For the eleventh graders, the mean discrepancy score for the average attractive subjects was 2.89 and for the combined most and least attractive subjects, 1.48. The difference between these means was also significant ($t = 2.248$, $p < .05$). In addition, post hoc analyses indicated that in the average attractive groups, people who were liked by the knowers were judged as significantly more attractive than by the nonknowers and those who were disliked were seen as less attractive by the knowers than by the nonknowers. However, the changes in rankings of physical attractiveness associated with liking or disliking were not very large, although they were statistically significant. These results support Hypothesis 7.

Discussion

Judgments of Physical Attractiveness

The high interjudge agreement on physical attractiveness indicates that beauty is not in the eye of the beholder; rather, there are cultural definitions

Table 5   Mean Discrepancy Scores between Physical Attractiveness and
Popularity for Three Levels of Attractiveness

Grade Level	Sex of Judges	Sex of Subjects	Level of Attractiveness		
			MOST	AVERAGE	LEAST
5		Boys	.67 $n = 3$	1.17 $n = 12$	1.33 $n = 3$
	Boys				
		Girls	1.00 $n = 2$	1.00 $n = 8$	1.00 $n = 2$
		Boys	.67 $n = 3$	2.33 $n = 12$	.00 $n = 3$
	Girls				
		Girls	.75 $n = 3$	3.19 $n = 8$	.00 $n = 2$
11		Boys	2.00 $n = 3$	3.00 $n = 8$	.67 $n = 3$
	Boys				
		Girls	.17 $n = 3$	2.69 $n = 8$	.33 $n = 3$
		Boys	3.33 $n = 3$	2.25 $n = 8$	1.33 $n = 3$
	Girls				
		Girls	3.00 $n = 3$	3.62 $n = 8$	1.00 $n = 3$

of physical attractiveness which males and females learn and use. The cultural definitions appear to be acquired at about age 7.[11]

Knowing the person being judged exerts a relatively small but significant effect on judgments of physical attractiveness, with a greater effect on judgments of average attractive persons compared to persons at the extremes. Nevertheless, there was a large positive correlation between the judgments of knowers and nonknowers, except in judgments of fifth-grade girls. The absence of a significant relationship between knowers and nonknowers judging the attractiveness of fifth-grade girls needs to be replicated before any definite conclusions can be drawn. However, it can be speculated that if actual persons rather than their photographs were judged, the correlation between knowers and nonknowers would be higher than those obtained in the present study because knowers are presumably judging actual persons when they are arranging the photographs.

11 N. Cavior and D. A. Lombardi, "Developmental Aspects of Judgment of Physical Attractiveness in Children," Developmental Psychology, VIII (1973), 67–71; J. F. Cross and J. Cross, "Age, Sex, Race, and the Perception of Facial Beauty," Developmental Psychology, V (1971), 433–439.

Correlates of Popularity

Physical attractiveness and popularity are strongly correlated. The findings thus far have revealed a high correlation between these two variables from age 6 [12] through college age.[13]

Perceived attitude similarity and popularity are also strongly correlated. Which of these two variables, physical attractiveness or perceived attitude similarity, is the more important determinant of popularity cannot be determined definitely at this time because, although perceived attitude similarity had the stronger effect in four of the eight analyses, physical attractiveness had the stronger effect in the other four. In the four groups in which perceived attitude similarity was stronger, the physical attractiveness of the subjects was more homogeneous than in the other four groups. This was shown by a comparison of the coefficients of concordance in judging physical attractiveness relative to the regression analyses predicting popularity, which indicated that as the homogeneity of physical attractiveness increased its predictive power relative to popularity decreased. Tentatively, then, it is concluded that physical attractiveness has the stronger effect on popularity.

It is possible that perceived attitude similarity is part of a halo effect that develops from physical attractiveness. If so, then physical attractiveness should have the more important effect on popularity. It appears, however, that in North American society at least, it is culturally acceptable for men to select women on the basis of physical attractiveness or sex appeal but not for women to select men on the same bases. Instead, women are taught to value things such as security rather than physical attributes. In a computer dating study, Coombs and Kenkel [14] found that college males placed more importance on physical attractiveness than females in date selection before the dates were arranged. However, these authors also found that females, after the date was terminated, reported greater dissatisfaction with the physical attractiveness of their dates than did the males; thus, it appears that women in this study understated the importance of physical attractiveness and may have been reflecting socially approved cultural stereotypes which they did not follow in their personal behavior.

Physical attractiveness and perceived attitude similarity are highly correlated and, although a correlation implies no particular direction of causality, the high agreement between knowers and nonknowers in judging physical attractiveness suggests that the direction is from physical attractiveness to perceived attitude similarity. This position is in accord with the findings of Walster et al.,[15] who found that among college females and males who had known each other for several hours via a computer date, only physical attractiveness was related to being liked, whereas selected person-

[12] J. R. Staffieri, "A Study of Social Stereotype of Body Image in Children," *Journal of Personality and Social Psychology,* I (1967), 101–104.
[13] Perrin, op. cit.; Walster et al., op. cit.
[14] Coombs and Kenkel, op. cit.
[15] Walster et al., op. cit.

ality measures of the Minnesota Multiphasic Personality Inventory, the Minnesota Counseling Inventory, and Berger's Scale of Self-Acceptance were not so related.

It was not possible in this study to compare actual versus perceived attitude similarity. If Byrne [16] were correct, then one would expect to find that the most popular people actually have a higher proportion of attitudes in common with most of their peers and, consequently, there would be a significant correlation between actual and perceived attitude similarity. However, a recent study by Cavior and Miller [17] found little support for the hypothesis that actual attitude similarity and perceived attitude similarity are correlated among tenth- and twelfth-grade males and females. Their study also found that physical attractiveness and perceived attitude similarity contributed more to the variance in interpersonal attraction than did actual attitude similarity and length of acquaintance and that physical attractiveness and perceived attitude similarity were positively correlated. In addition, Davitz [18] found that sociometric choices among children were positively correlated with perceived attitude similarity but not with actual attitude similarity; and Levinger [19] found no relationship between actual attitude similarity and interpersonal attraction in a longitudinal study of changing attraction between roommates.

Aronson and Worchel [20] found that a positive or negative evaluation (like–dislike) of a subject by a confederate was more important than actual attitude similarity in determining the subjects' attraction toward the confederate. This finding was confirmed by Byrne and Griffitt,[21] but it appears to have limited applicability in light of the results of the present study. It is difficult to imagine many people liking, especially for dating and marriage, an unattractive man or woman no matter how positively he or she evaluates them. One would expect that positive evaluations are important in contributing to interpersonal attraction only when the physical attractiveness of each person is acceptable to the other. Acceptability may be due to constructs such as adaptation level, drive states, objective attractiveness of the persons involved, and past experience with respect to rejection by highly attractive persons.

The above arguments seem to provide ample justification for concluding that physical attractiveness determines popularity. However, there is some

---

16 Byrne, "Attitudes and Attractions," op. cit.

17 N. Cavior and K. Miller, "Physical Attractiveness, Attitude Similarity, and Length of Acquaintance as Contributors to Interpersonal Attraction Among Adolescents," unpublished manuscript, West Virginia University, 1972.

18 J. R. Davitz, "Social Perception and Sociometric Choice of Children," *British Journal of Psychology*, L (1955), 173–176.

19 G. Levinger, "Little Sand Box and Big Quarry: Comment on Byrne's Paradigmatic Spade for Research on Interpersonal Attraction," *Representative Research in Social Psychology*, III (1972), 3–19.

20 E. Aronson and P. Worchel, "Similarity Versus Liking as Determinants of Interpersonal Attractiveness," *Psychonomic Science*, V (1966), 157–158.

21 D. Byrne and W. Griffitt, "Similarity Versus Liking: A Clarification," *Psychonomic Science*, VI (1966), 295–296.

evidence for a reciprocal effect of these two variables; in the average attractive range, the physical attractiveness of popular persons was judged higher and that of unpopular persons judged lower by people who knew them as compared to persons who did not know them (see the Results section, Hypotheses 4b and 7). Thus, average attractive persons may become popular because of their physical attractiveness, as the general conclusion suggests, but once they become popular their judged physical attractiveness is increased by their being liked. However, from the data (Table 1, correlations between knowers and nonknowers), it appears that the extent to which popularity can change judgments of physical attractiveness is limited.

Gary Schwartz

Don Merten

The Language of Adolescence: An Anthropological Approach to the Youth Culture[1]

Schwartz and Merten view youth culture as a unique cultural system. To them it is less a rivalrous contraculture than a genuinely independent subculture. Youth, the researchers point out, possess a status terminology

FROM *The American Journal of Sociology,* LXXII (1967), pp. 453–468. Slightly abridged. Reprinted by permission of the authors and the University of Chicago Press.

[1] This paper reports on the first part of an on-going anthropological study of the youth culture in an urban community which is supported by the National Institute of Mental Health grant MH 12172-01. Our data are derived from field observation of peer groups operating in their natural habitats and from intensive, free-flowing interviews with selected informants. Initial contacts were made with this youth population through an established youth-serving agency, and subsequent relationships were established by following out friendship networks, i.e., meeting and talking with friends of our initial contacts. We found that these networks seldom bridged the several strata of the status system; thus, it was necessary to establish new contacts and follow out friendship networks in each of the strata. Thus far, most of our informants have come from the higher reaches of the adolescent status system (24), rather than its lower levels (10). There are more girls (23) than boys (11) at present in our formal interview sample. Much of our data on the boys came from less structured contexts such as conversations in cars. Although the number of interviews with each informant varies, we find that some of our more articulate informants have remained with the study for a year on the basis of two or three hour-and-a-half tape-recorded interviews per month. The interviews were usually with individual informants, although occasionally small groups of 2–4 students were interviewed. A considerable portion of our data was gathered in talks with students at dances, parties, hangouts, card games, etc.

or argot that contributes meaning to their world view, life-style, and personal standards. Their analyses, predicated on David Reisman's observation that adolescent social life is partially hidden from adults by linguistic devices, show the youth culture as consisting of norms, standards, and values communicated by a language system essentially unintelligible to adults. Nonetheless, they argue that youth reference groups are also dependent on adult orientations. For example, youth status systems, described by such terms as "hoody," "socie," "snob," "stuck-up," "greaser," and "scragg" reflect the different social-class segments of the adult society. The researchers illustrate how youth-culture norms for dating may be interpreted to explain inconsistencies inherent in such cultural categories as "cool," "cute," and "elite." In brief, "cuteness," and "coolness" are shown on the one hand to be complementary social categories from the boys' perspective, but relatively contradictory from the viewpoint of girls' standards, where "coolness" is more highly idealized.

Instructional Objectives

To understand why youth tend to measure self-worth against youth-culture standards.

To describe adolescent status terms and prestige categories as forming the cultural core of the adolescent social system.

To define the meaning of key status terms or categories in the youth culture.

To discuss the motives and norms of adolescent dating from youth-culture perspectives.

The Problem

The question of whether there is a relatively self-contained adolescent subculture in this society stimulates recurrent, inconclusive sociological controversy. Contrary to the model of the youth culture as a contraculture, we hold that its reality as a subculture does not rest upon its power to repudiate or undermine basic adult values. We shall argue that peer-group interaction is guided by expectations which do not govern the behavior of other members of the community. And we claim that the understandings which transform what might otherwise be transitory encounters into stable peer-group relationships are not fully comprehensible to the rest of the community. More simply, adolescent social relationships are predicated upon premises not completely accessible or intelligible to adults.[2]

---

[2] In a comparatively recent view of the "adolescent society," Bennett Berger, "Adolescence and Beyond," *Social Problems,* Vol. X (1963), asserts that "there is absolutely no good body of data on adolescents, Coleman's included, which indicates the existence of a really deviant system of norms which govern adolescent life" (p. 395).

From our point of view, the specifically subcultural aspects of adolescent social life reside in those symbolic elements (values, beliefs, and standards) which integrate various concrete norms [3] into a coherent system of action. Later in this paper we will examine some of the symbolic resolutions of adolescent role dilemmas and ambiguities, for example, adolescent beliefs about their own social world which reduce logical and moral inconsistencies between incongruous orientations to various social situations.

As Reisman suggests, the significance of much of adolescent social life is partially hidden from adults by linguistic devices. Consequently, the data which can best reveal the character of the youth culture are linguistic, and the relevant aspect of adolescent language is obviously semantic.

Language and Action

In this paper, we will show that adolescent perceptions and assessments of their own social universe are embodied in a distinctive argot, their status terminology. These status terms refer to moral attributes (those qualities which make some persons admirable, others reprehensible, etc.) and moral dispositions (the kinds of things these people are likely to do and say). The members of a status category are thought to possess common social virtues and defects. Status terms, then, are not affectively neutral labels for structural positions in the youthful social system. They bestow either negative or positive esteem on those who manifest or exemplify these personal characteristics. Consequently, an individual's rank in the local prestige hierarchy is partly a function of the meanings inherent in those terms his peers use to describe his character and his group affiliations. . . .

The linguistically conditioned ways in which the members of a group perceive and evaluate their social environment have determinant consequences for their behavior. Here we follow Clyde Kluckhohn, who says that "the *vocabularies* of different languages both reflect and perpetuate habitual and distinctive ways of categorizing experience or modes of thought." [4] He goes on to say that "how people behave toward one another is, in part, a function of what they call each other and of *how* they conceive objects, themselves, other people and types of events which enter into their relations." [5] Elucidation of the meanings implicit in the adolescent status terminology will illuminate the complex relationships between the norms of this subculture and the behavior of its members in various social settings.

Stated in functional terms, cultural categories contained in language do not usually determine the particulars (i.e., the who, how much, and when) of any behavioral sequence but, rather, provide the cognitive and evaluative

---

[3] By concrete norms we mean specific prescriptions and proscriptions which refer to particular types of social contexts (e.g., dating) and which govern or which actors feel ought to govern behavior (e.g., sexual) in these kinds of social settings.

[4] "Culture and Behavior," *Handbook of Social Psychology*, Vol. XX, ed. Gardner Lindsey (Reading, Mass.: Addison-Wesley Publishing, 1954), p. 938, italics in original.

[5] Ibid.

parameters of social interaction in any social setting.[6] These categories identify the appropriate motives, values, roles, and rules which transform the actor's external physical world into what Hallowell calls the behavioral environment of the self. "A *second* function of all cultures is the orientation of the self to a diversified world of objects in its behavioral environment, discriminated, classified, and conceptualized with respect to attributes which are culturally constituted and symbolically mediated through language. The role of language in object-orientation is as vital as in self-orientation." [7] As we shall see in the case of the meaning of the term "cool," these categories tie both the actor's moral orientations and cognitive definitions of social situations to the critical motivational dimensions of the self, that is, his judgments about his own worth—"Any kind of self-depreciation, loss of self-esteem, or threat to the self impairs the complex motivational systems that focus upon the self and its needs. At the same time, self-evaluation through culturally recognized norms is inescapable." [8]

THE STRUCTURAL ORIGINS OF THE YOUTH CULTURE

Considered as a phenomenon indigenous to modern societies, the youth culture can be traced to the problem of socialization in industrial societies.[9] Certainly adolescent norms refer to these structural problems at various levels of meaning. But this does not exhaust the cultural connotations and the behavioral implications of distinctively adolescent modes of communication. For there is great latitude in the selection of the cultural forms which provide adequate solutions to these structural exigencies and concomitant developmental crises—witness the differences in the content of the peer-group norms in various communities and classes.[10] Therefore, it is not possible to account for the substance and imagery of the youth culture solely

[6] For a persuasive statement of a somewhat different point of view, see Frake, "A Structural Description of Subanum 'Religious Behavior,'" *Explorations in Cultural Anthropology,* ed. Ward Goodenough (New York: McGraw-Hill Book Co., 1964).

[7] A. I. Hallowell, "The Self and Its Behavioral Environment," *Culture and Experience* (Philadelphia: University of Pennsylvania Press, 1955), p. 91, italics in original.

[8] Ibid., p. 106.

[9] S. N. Eisenstadt's classic study, *From Generation to Generation* (Glencoe, Ill.: The Free Press, 1956), points out that there is a radical social-psychological transition between childhood and adulthood in industrial societies. Thus, every child in our society must eventually leave his family circle where he is appreciated for *who* rather than *what* he is. According to this theory, the youth culture serves as a "halfway house" between a young person's particularistic and universalistic associations. While youth groups are based upon ascriptive ties, the youth culture enables adolescents to try out roles and form relationships which involve more universalistic considerations: An adolescent must *earn* his status in the peer group. The youth culture, then, allows the adolescent to experiment with objective, universalistic standards without sacrificing the psychological security of highly solidary primary groups.

[10] For a very detailed account of the attitudes and activities of various types of adolescent peer groups, see Muzafer and Carolyn Sherif, *Reference Groups: Exploration into Conformity and Deviation of Adolescents* (New York: Harper & Row, 1964).

in terms of the difficult passage from childhood to adulthood in a highly differentiated society.

THE YOUTH CULTURE DEFINED

Part of our society's ideology about the nature of human growth asserts that youth must not prematurely assume adult roles. Thus, it is often said that adolescents need an exemption from the pressures of adult responsibilities in order to discover their individual talents. These ideological sanctions encourage adolescents to transform developmental necessities into aesthetically satisfying as well as socially adaptive modes of behavior. In other words, the efflorescence of adolescent styles results from this license to experiment with the possibilities inherent in adult roles. In turn, the youth culture symbolically affirms and celebrates its freedom from conventional restraints on social behavior which have little or no immediate practical significance. For example, many of our informants lavishly praise what they call "idiot" [11] behavior: actions and attitudes which are childish or foolish from an adult point of view and which sometimes treat situations from seemingly incompatible perspectives, for example, dealing with a love relationship in a manner that is at once flippant and romantic. According to some of our most articulate informants, the ability to engage in any sort of silly collective action requires a certain amount of inner freedom and *joie de vivre*. In general, these informants tend to associate these sorts of peer-group activities with independence from adult supervision and with actions which demonstrate this autonomy. [12]

Stated more formally, the youth culture consists of those adolescent norms, standards, and values which are discussed in a language particularly intelligible to members of this age-grade. At this point, we should note that members of the youth culture do not deal with or even "talk" about all the concerns which vitally interest or agitate adolescents, and they may even ignore or overlook those concerns which are of enduring significance to the members of this society. [13] Yet the youth culture continues a distinctive

[11] Words enclosed by quotation marks (e.g., "cool") are terms used with considerable frequency by our informants. This is not to say, however, that the notions contained in these words are not also expressed by circumlocution. These terms are ordinarily used in reference and rarely in address.

[12] According to some of our informants, "idiot" should not be equated with childish behavior. We have been told that those persons who are able to act this way are often the same people who appear most sophisticated (i.e., adult-like) in other social contexts. Perhaps, this connection between silly and sophisticated personal styles is a symbolic means of demonstrating what Erving Goffman (*Encounters* [Indianapolis: Bobbs-Merrill Co., 1961]), calls role distance. They seem to say that we now have mastered the developmental tasks of childhood, and hence these sorts of performances (playing games which have no extrinsic social significance) can now be slightly ridiculed because it no longer constitutes a vital part of our social identities.

[13] This idea was stimulated by James F. Short's remarks on delinquent gangs in "Social Structure and Group Processes in Gang Delinquency," *Problems of Youth: Transition to Adulthood in a Changing World*, ed. Sherif and Sherif (Chicago: Aldine Publishing, 1965), esp. p. 173.

vision of social reality. It is embodied in a normative order predicated upon conceptions of those personal qualities which its members believe make a male admirable and a female desirable.

THE YOUTH CULTURE AS A CONTRACULTURE

The sociological conception of the youth culture as a contraculture assumes that the cultural and structural aspects of the youth culture are inextricably linked. Thus, evidence which reveals serious structural discontinuities between the generations is also supposed to show a set of youth norms which are opposed to adult values.[14] According to the contraculture model, if adolescents substantially accept core adult roles and values, then the youth culture is essentially epiphenomenal.[15] But if they doubt the legitimacy of societal values, then the youth culture is the appropriate label for this truly rebellious posture. In contrast, our approach to the youth culture holds that the symbolic components of adolescent social life form a relatively coherent subculture *irrespective* of whether its norms eventually subvert, reinforce, or have no lasting effect upon adult values. Our position rests upon a basic theoretical assumption: that the cultural categories which shape adolescent orientations to their own social milieu are largely autonomous inasmuch as they are embodied in systems of meanings whose implications are not immediately apparent to adults.[16]

The structure of advanced societies generates a certain amount of adolescent rebelliousness against adult authority.[17] But this does not mean that opposition to the goals of the older generation is the only, or even the most important, disjunction between adolescent and adult views of social reality. Nor is it true that the norms of the youth culture derive their subcultural attributes from intergenerational conflict.

In fact, the traditional cycle of intense intergenerational conflict followed

---

[14] Cf. James Coleman, *The Adolescent Society* (New York: The Free Press, 1961), and F. Elkin and W. Westley, "The Myth of Adolescent Culture," *American Sociological Review*, Vol. XX (1955), who have tried to determine whether the norms of the youth culture impede or inhibit the socialization of adolescents into adult occupational roles.

[15] As subordinate and quite powerless members of our society, youth are said to experience social and psychological deprivation because of the conflicting demands which are placed upon them. Viewed as a contraculture, the youth culture evolves out of a normative "reaction-formation" to these pressures. According to Milton Yinger, "Contra-Culture and Subculture," *American Sociological Review*, Vol. XXV (1960), it involves "the creation of a series of inverse or counter values (opposed to those of the surrounding society) in the face of serious frustration or conflict" (p. 627).

[16] For example, most adults in this community are aware of, and many approve of, the fraternity and sorority system which operates despite an official school ban on such activity. However, if our adolescent informants are correct, very few adults know why one person is "rushed" and another is not. Though many parents seem to want their children to succeed in this social world, most adults are ignorant of the specific social criteria fraternity and sorority youth use to select certain kinds of persons for their exclusive social circles.

[17] See K. Davis, "The Sociology of Parent-Youth Conflict," *Social Perspectives on Behavior*, ed. H. D. Stein and R. A. Cloward (Glencoe, Ill.: The Free Press, 1958).

by reconciliation when the younger generation takes its place in society seems less common today than in the past. Instead of direct confrontations over the moral validity, the relevance, and the appropriateness of the other generations' goals and aspirations,[18] both the older and younger members of this society subscribe to a laissez-faire ideology. This encourages generational segregation, rather than opposition. Keniston notes that "another salient fact about young people today is a relative lack of *rebelliousness* against their parents or their parents' generation. . . . The result is frequently an unstated 'gentleman's agreement' between the generations that neither will interfere with the other." [19] According to one of our informants, a senior girl:

(Q) Do you know what adults in this community think about various issues?
(A) I'd say there is a very small amount of contact between the teen-agers and the adults because we're self-centered, I think, and the adults are too. We think "I'll leave them alone," and they do too.

Our informants almost instinctively measured their own worth against the standards of the youth culture. And the cardinal concerns of the youth culture are in those domains over which they exercise direct control: friendships, relations with the opposite sex, and various types of expressive activities. This sort of partial cultural isolation is reinforced by the paucity of enduring intergenerational contacts outside of formal socializing agencies, such as the school and family.[20] Thus most of the adolescents we have observed accept a socially imposed hiatus in their life cycle, regardless of whether they are eager, reluctant, or uninterested in becoming an adult; and most of them assume that only their peers can truly understand those kinds of interpersonal accomplishments and failures which make their lives in the adolescent world either gratifying or mortifying.

Open intergenerational conflict in this community revolves around the question of how much control adults rightfully can exercise over adolescents.[21] Both sides in these disputes agree that intrusion into private genera-

18 See Walter Laquer, *Young Germany* (New York: Basic Books, 1962), for a description of youth movements which opposed the prevailing ethos of their society in their early stages of development.
19 K. Keniston, "Social Change and Youth in America," *Daedalus*, XCI (1962), 151–156, italics in original.
20 See F. Musgrove, *Youth and the Social Order* (Bloomington: University of Indiana Press, 1965), for an interesting historical perspective on the present separation of the generations.
21 According to the data collected by Henry McKay for the Institute for Juvenile Research, this area, in the 35-year period from 1927 to 1962, had the lowest mean delinquency rate in the city (these rates are based upon official Juvenile Court cases). However, this low rate of delinquency should not be interpreted as evidence of a complete lack of intergenerational conflict. We have observed that behavior which slightly violates adult norms, such as surreptitiously playing poker for high stakes or putting a fraternity picture in the school annual (fraternities and sororities are forbidden), is often sufficient to demonstrate one's autonomy vis-à-vis adult controls. Since the tolerance of deviant youth behavior in the community is small, one can establish one's autonomy through relatively minor acts of defiance of adult authority.

tional matters is generally unwarranted, for example, adults usually allow adolescents to arrange their own social affairs. The issue, then, concerns the definition of those aspects of adolescent behavior which are legitimately public and hence subject to adult control.

THE RELATIONSHIP BETWEEN ADULT VALUES AND YOUTH NORMS

In our study of this upper-middle-class urban community,[22] we found that these adolescents successfully internalized adult occupational goals. None of our informants questioned the notion that a high school diploma was a minimal requirement for even a half-decent job, and comparatively few students in the local high school dropped out before graduation. Most of these adolescents intended to go to college, and many of them worked reasonably hard to get good grades. They wanted a college degree because they felt it would help them get the professional job or husband which insures a middle-class way of life. However, very few of these adolescents, even the best students, had marked intellectual or scholarly interests. In short, we discovered that adolescent conceptions of the validity of adult roles and values are, at least, largely independent of the standards they use to estimate the relative excellence of their peers.[23]

The youth culture in this area is not completely oblivious to an individual's potential capacity to assume his adult roles. But, as far as his peers are concerned, his success or failure in the academic system of the high school (i.e., his grades) is a relatively minor component of his social identity, although very negative connotations are associated with the status of a "brain"—a person who devotes all his energies to getting high marks. Our informants usually call such a person "twinky," which implies that his demeanor manifests an underlying effeminacy. The choice of a term which

[22] The community we studied is located in a large midwestern city and has a population of approximately 25,000. It has most of the socio-economic characteristics commonly associated with upper-middle-class residential areas. Since it may be useful to compare this community to the city as a whole, the figures for the latter will be given in parentheses; and the figures for both will be given in approximate percentages. According to data from the 1960 Census, the median family income in this community was $11,000 ($6,700). Only 5 per cent (14 per cent) of the families earned less than $3,000 a year, and 58 per cent (21 per cent) had an income of $10,000 a year or more. Eighty-six per cent (24 per cent) of the families lived in single-dwelling units, and of these 82 per cent (33 per cent) were owned by the occupants. For this population the median number of years of education was almost 13 (10), and 21 per cent (6 per cent) had four years of college or more. Seventy-two per cent (37 per cent) of this population held white-collar jobs.

[23] In "Values and Gang Delinquency: A Study of Street-Corner Groups," *American Journal of Sociology*, Vol. LXIX (1963), R. A. Gordon, J. F. Short, D. S. Cartwright, and F. L. Strodtbeck report that even the most socially disadvantaged, delinquent youth not only evaluate a middle-class way of life very highly but that they also see the conventional path to this end—saving, working at a steady job, and education—as a legitimate, although not always realistic, way to attain a respectable adult status. Yet, as Short, *op. cit.*, points out, these adolescents do not use these values to regulate peer-group life. Similarly, it is wrong to infer that, just because middle-class adolescents are even less ambivalent about adult values, these standards determine the norms of their peer groups.

connotes less-than-manly behavior follows a peculiarly subcultu
The standards of the youth culture are focused on those sorts of
which its members think reflect one's sex-role identity. Their judgments of
personal worth are closely linked to general conceptions of those attributes
and performances which are thought to reveal a person's masculinity or
femininity. For boys, the crucial external signs of inner manhood are physical
strength, athletic talent, courage in the face of aggression, a willingness to
defend one's honor at all costs, and sexual and drinking prowess. According
to girls, the most admirable feminine traits are physical attractiveness,
personal vivacity, and the ability to delicately manipulate various sorts of
interpersonal relationships.

As a cultural system, the youth culture in this area consists of those norms,
life styles, and ideals which are intimately associated with a *variant*, age-
graded system of cultural meanings. Of course, the youth culture does not
emerge out of a cultural vacuum. Adolescent social patterns obviously are
based upon adult conceptions of the desirable types of social relationships
and upon adult images of personal virtue. Adolescents, however, do not
slavishly copy these general cultural norms. The youth culture experiments
with and elaborates on some of the partially unrealized or alternative possibilities in the adult moral order. This is particularly true in the interpersonal
realm: Adolescents distinguish various kinds and degrees of trust among
friends. Our informants habitually discriminate among "good," "best," and
"casual" friends. One informant distinguished among these types of friends
in the following terms:

(Q) What are some of the things you expect of a friend?
(A) When you leave [a group], when you walk out, they don't all of a sudden
start stabbing knives in your back. It all depends upon the degree of
friendship you want [in response to the question].
(Q) What are the various degrees of friendship?
(A) With some girls you just have a casual friendship, and she's got her friends
and I've got mine, but we'll sit down and talk. Then like the girls in my
club, we are pretty good friends. We know who we are going out with.
With the casual friend you don't sit and talk about your boyfriend to them.
I have one best friend.
(Q) Are there certain things you share with a best friend that you don't share
with a fellow club member [i.e., a "pretty good friend"]?
(A) You talk about your boyfriends if you had an argument, but you wouldn't
tell them personal things [i.e., to a "pretty good friend"]. I could tell my
best friend anything, and she wouldn't think badly of you. You don't have
to worry that, will she tell anybody else? While the members of my club,
I expect them not to stab knives in my back when I leave, *but my best
friend, if someone else does, I expect her to stand up for me. My club
members, I wouldn't expect them to stand up for me.*

From a comparative point of view, then, the differences among the cultural categories which shape adult and adolescent orientations to some

social situations are admittedly slight. Nevertheless, and this is the important point, the differences between àdult standards of personal worth and the meaning of adolescent status terms are great enough to sustain an independent adolescent status system. The multitude of discrete norms which regulate a person's relations with his peers are integrated into a meaningful system of action by distinctively adolescent conceptions of personal worth. The cultural core of the adolescent social system is formed by the meanings of adolescent status terms and prestige categories. An adolescent's estimation of his own interpersonal competence depends, to a great extent, upon whether the particular terms his peers use to describe his status have laudatory or pejorative connotations. These terms indicate whether he is able convincingly to present a "cool" self-image in highly competitive social contexts.

THE MEANING OF KEY STATUS TERMS

The adolescents in this community do not see their status system as a perfectly linear, clearly defined series of hierarchically arranged status positions. Rather, they perceive it as a set of ranked, slightly ambiguous prestige categories which are internally differentiated. This status system is structured along two dimensions. First, there are horizontal social strata defined by differentially evaluated life styles, that is, modes of dress, speech, and interpersonal demeanor. In general, our informants perceive two salient life styles which they refer to as "hoody" and "socie." However, we see another way of life which lacks an explicit folk designation, though most of our informants distinguish it from "socie" and "hoody" styles. For the lack of a better term, we call this the conventional way of life. It is an essentially residual category which includes all those patterns which are neither clearly "socie" nor "hoody."

The dominant values institutionalized in the status system of the local high school are those held by the majority of the upper-middle-class segment of this youthful population (the high school draws students from a stable working- and lower-middle-class community as well as from our upper-middle-class area).[24] Consequently, most adolescents in this area perceive the "socies" as the top stratum of this prestige system. Since "hoody" and "socie" youth do not agree about who has the most valuable way of life (e.g., our "hoody" informants tell us that "socies" are hypocrites, etc.), an individual's estimation of his own status depends, in part, upon his particular adolescent reference group. From an observer's point of view, the "hoody"

[24] In numerical terms, this upper-middle-class group does not constitute a majority of this school population. Yet, through the fraternity and sorority system which it dominates and through less overtly stratified, adult-sponsored youth groups which it co-opts as a recruiting ground, these adolescents control both the formal (e.g., the cheerleaders at this high school are not only restricted to sorority girls but to the members of one sorority) and informal activity systems which emerge out of school associations but which are definitely not confined to this location.

adolescents have evolved a truly independent style of life. Nevertheless, our "hoody" informants see their own life style as at least a partly antagonistic response to "socie" values and material advantages. "Hoody" adolescents, by and large, refuse to and often cannot financially afford to compete with "socies" on the latter's terms, and they feel that their mode of life is not accorded general esteem in this system. Those who adopt what we have called a conventional way of life gain some social recognition only to the extent to which they can imitate "socie" patterns.

The vertical component of this status system locates an individual's rank within one of these horizontal strata. As far as we can ascertain, a person's rank is a function of how well he is known by the other members of his stratum, and this, in turn, seems closely related to his ability to conspicuously live up to its standards of excellence. This vertical dimension, then, is quantitative rather than qualitative and refers to what our informants mean when they say someone is more or less "popular." Since public renown is a basic value in the "socie" world, those who achieve fame are called "elites." This, however, says nothing about their commitment to one of the various substyles available to the members of this stratum. Although all our informants subscribe to a highly egalitarian social ideology (no one is inherently better than anyone else), "hoody" adolescents take it very seriously. Though many of our "hoody" informants admitted that certain persons in their social circle are more "popular" than others, they have no term which designates high position.

An adolescent's socioeconomic status certainly affects his ability to assimilate "socie" styles. Nevertheless, the decisive factor is his ability to act in terms of these standards whatever his family background. In other words, an adolescent's status identity is created by his overt commitment to an adolescent life style.[25] Some of our lower-middle- and stable working-class informants are among the most influential "socies," while a few of our informants from upper-middle-class homes are labeled "hoods" by their peers. "Socies" tend to associate "hoody" life styles with very stereotyped conceptions of the attitudes and aspirations which distinguish the lower and middle classes. For instance, even those "socie" informants from stable working- and lower-middle-class families, repeatedly tell us that "hoods" are the sort of people who do not care about their grades, about school activities, about their personal appearance, about morals, etc. In essence, they believe that the "hoods" incorporate what they think is the critical lower-class social-psychological attribute—a complete lack of interest in "bettering oneself."

[25] Most of the adolescents who fall into the conventional category seem more oriented to "socie" than "hoody" dress styles, and some have attempted and failed to join "socie" groups. In contrast to "socies" and "hoods," conventionals have a life style which does not appear to involve a code of honor vis-à-vis other groups. Conventionals, however, tend to define the local social system in terms of what all its members perceive as polar, antagonistic social categories, i.e., "socie" and "hoody." Hence conventionals are difficult to place unambiguously in the status system and lack the definite social identities ascribed to "socies" and "hoods."

At this point, we should note that there are alternate terms for these status categories; for example, the words "socie" and "socialite" are used interchangeably. Also, certain status terms change over time. For instance, many of our informants feel that it is more "in" to use the term "mellow" in those contexts where they formerly used the term "cool," but they also agree that these terms have the same meanings. Status terms also take on special meanings according to the structural position of the speaker. Thus, a "socie" speaker will use the term "hoods" interchangeably with "greasers," "scraggs," etc.; all of these terms have very derogatory implications. Similarly, "hoods" use the terms "snob" and "stuck-up" as synonyms for "socie."

"Hoods" and "socies" very rarely use these terms to describe themselves but almost obsessively use them to describe each other. It is difficult for adults to appreciate the discrepancy between the adolescent meaning of a term like "hoody" and its conventional referents, that is, to delinquents. For example, one of our most articulate informants belongs to the "hoody" stratum, and she accepts this designation insofar as she defines her own personal style as one which consistently opposes "socie" styles. Yet adults would not ordinarily call her "hoody" because she takes a college mathematics course in her spare time and participates in a tutoring project for culturally deprived children.

These status terms do not refer directly to bounded social units which have a clearly demarcated membership. Yet membership in certain cliques, clubs, fraternities, and sororities makes it very likely that a person will be considered a "socie" by his peers. The precise meaning of these terms, however, cannot be understood apart from the nature of the youth culture in an upper-middle-class community. Here adolescents have a dual orientation to the standards of the youth culture and to the values of the adult world.[26]

The adult world is represented by the achievement orientation of the high school. Our "socie" informants claim that this stratum is divided into the "clean-cut" or "all-around" and the "hoody-socie" segments. The "clean-cut socies" stress role performances which are explicitly linked to the school's activity system. They usually do well in team sports, get fairly good but not necessarily high grades, and most importantly, know how to get along with their teachers and classmates—they are very "sociable."[27] In fact, it seems

[26] N. Riley, J. Riley, and M. More, "Adolescent Values and the Riesman Typology: An Empirical Analysis," *Culture and Social Character,* ed. Seymour M. Lipset and Leo Lowenthal (Glencoe, Ill.: The Free Press, 1962), found this same dual orientation to parental and peer-group standards. Also see C. V. Brittain, "Adolescent Choices and Parent-Peer Cross Pressures," *American Sociological Review,* Vol. XXIII (June, 1963), and in Part Three of this book.

[27] Being "sociable" often means that a person is able to articulate previously unconnected persons or cliques into larger and sometimes bounded social networks. This trait, in turn, is closely related to a person's standing in the "socie" world. For example, one of our informants who actively aspired to this stratum told us that part of her lack of success was due to her inability to bring her various, disparate friendship groups together. She sat in the middle of the lunch table between these two groups but could not promote social intercourse between them and felt marginal to both. However, another informant, who lacked the usual physical attributes of a "socie" girl, was an "elite" largely because

that part of a non-"socie" social identity involves the belief that one does not have enough social skill and organizational ability to give a "swinging" or "cool" affair, and non-"socie" social gatherings generally reinforce this self-fulfilling prophecy.

"Clean-cut socies" must also realize the "cool" patterns of adolescent social life. They must succeed in the intense competition for dates with high-status persons; the social circle from which a person selects his dating partners partially establishes his or her standing in the larger social system. After the second year of high school, "socie" boys must be "conditioned" drinkers, which means not getting prematurely or obnoxiously inebriated in social situations. Sexually, "socie" boys must "make out" and thereby provide some concrete evidence for their frequent and exaggerated boasts about their sexual prowess.

For these boys, drinking and dating are the definitive areas in which one's manhood is tested and proven. They talk a great deal about and admire toughness but studiously avoid situations where they might have to fight. Buying liquor or beer in a store is viewed as a potential threat to their image as autonomous "men," and, conversely, it is seen as a challenge which, if handled properly, can add greatly to one's stature in the group. As our informants perceive it, buying beer in a bar or package store is a battle-ground reserved only for the courageous: the risks to one's self-esteem are great. If a boy reveals that he is afraid to show a false identification card or otherwise bluff his way through demands that he prove his age, then he loses considerable face within his peer group. But if he stands his ground when accused of being under age and does not give in to his desire to flee the situation, then he proves that he has "guts" regardless of whether the store ultimately sells him the beer. Our informants tell us that it is crucial not to "lose your cool" in these situations, and anyone who fails to rise to the occasion has his claims to "coolness" ruthlessly deflated by his peers.

Girls prove their worth in a more contracted arena. They must attract many high-status boys as dates, and to do so they must occasionally engage in rather intense petting without endangering their "reputations." While their prestige depends partly on the status their presence bestows upon their dating partners, it can be compromised if they give sexual favors to all who request them.

The "socies" (our informants usually employ the term "socie" and qualify it when they want to refer to those who adhere to the "clean-cut" or "hoody" variant) fully realize the adolescent dimensions of this social system. Though a member of the "clean-cut socies" adopts many "cool" patterns, he never

---

she could not only integrate separate dyads into larger friendship networks, but could then combine these networks into a named group whose membership was drawn from both the sorority world and from those girls who were by and large sorority "material" but who were excluded by the "blackball" system—one vote against a prospective member was enough to reject her. This girl provided the rationale, the occasions (e.g., "hen parties"), and most importantly, the contacts which enabled some girls to validate their status in the larger social system through membership in this group.

relinquishes his commitment to adult standards of accomplishment. On the other hand, the "hoody-socies" devote themselves wholeheartedly to adolescent conceptions of excellence. They are the most enthusiastic fraternity and sorority members and are not usually very interested in academic pursuits. Instead they spend a good deal of time and energy systematically refining their dating and drinking techniques. And they are the avant-garde leaders in musical tastes, dress styles, etc.

The "hoods" and the "hoody-socies" should not be confused. The latter represent the furthest an adolescent in the "socie" stratum can move away from adult values without openly rejecting them, that is, they rarely openly defy adult authority in acts of serious delinquency, and, unlike some of the "hoods," they rarely drop out of high school before graduation.

"Socies" have developed a special set of status terms which distinguish various social segments among those who occupy the lower orders of the status system. These terms have depreciatory connotations because they imply that these social types are represented by persons with morally defective or socially underdeveloped personalities. From the "socie" perspective, the "hoods" belong to the more encompassing social category of "out-of-its." One informant described the "out-of-its" as follows: "They're misfits; they're insecure, they don't think they're cute enough, or they're awkward, or they have a lisp or something." This is a heterogeneous category; here one finds the rebels, the retarded or slow learners, the intellectuals, and anyone else who is deviant from the point of view of the prestige criteria which define this status system.

"Socies" also perceive another category of persons who are not attached to or even loosely associated with "socie" cliques and yet who do not fit into the "out-of-its." Some of our "socie" informants call them the "others," and they are just ordinary students who are not distinguished by some success or blatant failure in the adolescent social system. One student described the "others" in this way: "Some of them may not come out of their shell until they get to college, and they may find a group whether it's intellectual or social. These kids will usually gravitate toward getting the higher grades— some don't concentrate on anything at all. They just go along and get by in school and don't join activities, but just sit home and watch television all the time." The derogatory implications associated with the term "others" do not simply derive from exclusion from "socie" social circles: It means that a person has no definite social identity in this social system. As far as "socies" are concerned, these people are faceless because they are not demonstrably attached to a discernible adolescent style. As one of our informants put it, "others" are people you do not notice or know anything about unless you happened to go to elementary school with them.

As we have seen, the process of status attribution is quite complex and does not result simply from objective talents and characteristics, for example, a boy's athletic ability, a girl's physical attractiveness, etc. Thus, an individual must take the esteem he has gained in a variety of contexts and transform this diffuse prestige into a subculturally validated image of the successful adolescent. He must present himself as "cool," and our informants tell us that if a person truly believes he is "cool" he generally acts "cool." In other words, concrete achievement buttresses the crucial mode of presentation of self in the adolescent subculture, and *it is this self-image and not the concrete role performance which ultimately interests adolescents. Confidence about one's essential masculinity or femininity and the ability to manifest this in smooth performances in many spheres is the essence of high status in this social system.*

One might expect a normative shift toward adult success standards over time in a youthful population largely oriented to college. But as an adolescent progresses through high school he discovers that the tension between adult and adolescent patterns increases rather than decreases. By the final year of high school the social category of the "clean-cut socies" has very few members. Those who cling to "clean-cut" patterns and hence are not trying to be "cool" no longer dominate the status system. In fact, those "clean-cut socies" who do not perceive this shift toward "cool" patterns are called "milk and cookies boys" and rapidly descend in the status system. One informant described what happened to a fraternity which did not make the shift to the "socie" patterns: "The Lambdas aren't well liked now because the Lambdas don't drink, and the other kids are all getting to drink, and they [the Lambdas] are not that well liked anymore because they look down upon it [drinking]. So now if you want social prestige with the kids, you wouldn't dare mention the Lambdas." The former members of the "clean-cut socies" who retain their social supremacy do so by appearing to adhere to responsible adult standards while, at the same time, actively participating in covert adolescent patterns.

CULTURE SOURCES OF INTEGRATION IN THE YOUTH CULTURE

Every cultural system has internal normative inconsistencies. In this section, we will show how certain cultural categories partially resolve some of the paradoxical or contradictory behavioral implications of the norms which govern dating. "Cute" and "cool" are prestigeful terms in this system, and an "elite" girl should be both. Girls see these as consistent personal attributes when they refer to the norms which regulate the ways in which a person achieves pre-eminence in the prestige system. But when girls talk about the ideal norms which should control relationships between members of the opposite sex, these two terms assume partly antagonistic meanings.

Both our male and female informants define a "cute" girl as a person who exudes a certain kind of sexual attractiveness but who does not demonstrate her sexual superiority in intercourse. In fact, if it is widely known that a high-status girl has had sexual intercourse, she very likely will be dropped from the "elite" circles even if she did not get pregnant. Yet, if she is "cool," a girl must be quite adept in the dating system. This means that she must

" with a comparatively large number of boys without, on the \, being "made." She must allow herself to reach a relatively high ˼ʋ or sexual excitement and intimacy without giving in to what are described as persistent demands for greater sexual favors. Consequently, if a girl is considered both "cool" and "cute" by her age mates, she must not only be physically attractive but also confidently manage the sexual self-aggrandizement which marks these temporary unions.

So far, "cuteness" and "coolness" are somewhat different but essentially complementary social categories. But girls have their own moral standards which form part of the meaning of these terms. When the social context is restricted to feminine interests and when the norms of proper behavior vis-à-vis males are at issue, "cool" and "cute" become partly contradictory categories.

Adolescent girls in this community discuss the motives and the norms which should govern dating in terms of "good clean fun." A good dating partner should be companionable, have similar interests, and should be a sympathetic and lively person. In this context, the "cute" girl is viewed as the friendly, "all-American girl" whom everyone likes and admires. She is vivacious, attractive, and, above all, not overly interested in the leverage one can obtain over boys through the judicious allocation of her affections. In short, she is a very wholesome girl. However, this category of the "all-American girl" quickly drops out of the picture when the girls talk about the realities of the power struggle which almost invariably accompanies dating. Incidentally, "going steady" is an institutionalized way of emphasizing the solidarity rather than the individualism of dating oriented to the status system. But among "elites" the dominant concern of who is going to control the relationship—all of our informants were convinced that long-term dating was an intrinsically asymmetrical relationship and were afraid that their peers would see them as the subordinate partner [28]—almost inevitably leads to its dissolution in a relatively short time. One girl viewed dating as follows:

(Q) You see this [dating] as pretty much of a game of strategy?
(A) Definitely! It's one of the most fun games around too. Because you never know what's going to happen. . . . It's up to you. There are no rules really. There might be a couple of rules that you take for granted, but basically. . . .
(Q) Like what [rules]?
(A) Well, not to do anything really nasty. Like go out with his best friend— break a date with him and go out with his best friend or something like that. Nothing really drastic, but aside from that there aren't too many rules, and you've just always got to make sure that you're on top, that you're winning because otherwise if you're not winning you're losing and there's no tie. So you always make sure you're winning.

---

[28] Many of our male informants expressed what seemed to us an almost pathological fear of being "pussy whipped," but we shall let psychoanalysts reveal the psychological implications of this term.

According to ideal feminine norms, real sex, as distinguished from the "good-night kiss," is out of place, undesirable, and, in some sense, morally wrong on a good date. The feminine vision of a romantic relationship holds that a date should come from mutual concern with the other partner's true or inner qualities. As even a cursory glance at love comics and true romance magazines will attest female ideology maintains that it is possible to appreciate the true worth of another person only if one is willing to rise above the ordinary trivial absorption in the competitive aspects of cross-sex relations, that is, with the other person's physical appearance, with his or her superficial manners (usually with their sophistication or lack of it), with the other person's prestige value (whether one's peers think he or she is "cool"), etc.

In light of these norms, "coolness," which is manifest in an attachment to "making out," is apparently incompatible with purely feminine conceptions of "cuteness." Thus when girls talk solely in terms of their own moral standards, the "cute" girl is defined less by reference to her physical attractiveness than by her attractive "personality." Nevertheless, if a "cute" girl is to retain or achieve a position among the "elite" of the adolescent social system, she must attract high-status boys. How, then, does she retain her image of "cuteness" and the esteem that goes with it in the eyes of her girlfriends if she must also engage in a wide range of petting activities with many boys? Or, to phrase this in motivational terms, how does she keep her "cool" orientation toward sex within the moral boundaries of the feminine universe? That is, how can she participate in a rather promiscuous pattern of sexual intimacy with many boys and, at the same time, exercise considerable control over her sexual encounters?

This somewhat contradictory pattern of normatively encouraged sexual promiscuity and restraint is resolved by a higher-order cultural category. This category defines the sexual nature of boys in both cognitive and evaluative terms. Our girl informants tell us that boys "naturally" try to "get all they can" sexually because boys are born with uncontrollable sexual urges.[29] One girl discussed the issue in the following terms:

(Q) Whose responsibility is it [regarding how far things go sexually on a date]?
(A) The girl's. I mean because guys can't help it. I mean they are born that way, but then girls get carried away because guys can't help themselves and girls can. To a point, but once past that point there's no hope.
(Q) Are all guys like this or just particular guys?
(A) Some guys would get as far as they could get, just for kicks, but there are other boys who are just as nice as they can be, but any boy who likes a girl enough . . . I don't think he would do it intentionally to hurt her, but just can't help to get as far as he can get. I don't think even the nicest guy can help being that way.

[29] The Ngulu, by way of contrast, are convinced that women are born sexually unsatisfiable (see T. Beidelman, "Pig [Gulwe]: An Essay on Ngulu Sexual Symbolism and Ceremony," *Southwestern Journal of Anthropology*, Vol. XX [1964]).

In terms of dating norms, girls say that it is their responsibility both to satisfy part of this inborn male desire for continual sexual satisfaction and to keep the situation from getting out of hand. Though girls admit that they also have strong sexual feelings, they agree that they and not the boys are capable of rational control, of setting limits.[30] Thus, girls claim that nature has burdened them with the responsibility of keeping petting relationships within the prescribed moral limits. In a basic sense, girls see boys as morally defective—or, if not as morally defective, at least as morally immature. Boys are said to be simply incapable of realistically assessing the negative consequences of giving free rein to sexual impulses in a dating situation. And, from what we have been able to observe, boys often fulfil these cultural expectations which have been phrased in such biological terms.

Although success in dating seems superficially completely tied to ascriptive criteria, there are important performance aspects to dating. Female competence is culturally defined as the ability to manipulate the sexual component of dating relationships to one's own advantage. Some girls have told us about a technique of "dumping" which they use to entice boys and yet keep them in a dependent position, never certain of whether they will be abandoned for a more attractive partner. One girl described her dating relationship in the following way:

> Like when Jim and I first started dating, we got along just fine. Then I started to dump on him, being a little snotty once in a while and stuff like this. Then I decided to be nice because it would be nice to be nice for a while, just as a change. Then I figured if he was so nice to me when I was dumping on him, just think if I was nice to him, he would really be nice to me. Well then he decided that wasn't such a hot idea [and] that he would start dumping on me which I didn't think was such a good idea either. So when he started dumping on me, I just decided to give him the shaft.

One of the latent and unintended consequences of this dating system is the widespread fear among "popular" girls that they are being exploited by the boys. A "popular" girl often feels that if she becomes too attached to a boy he may, in reality, be dating her only for the prestige which comes from being in the company of a "cool" and "cute" girl or, what is worse, he may play upon her romantic proclivities to seduce her.

Incidentally, we have found that many of the girls who "fall in love with" a popular entertainer, such as one of the Beatles, are often marginal in a very special way. They may have all the prerequisites for success in the dating system; they are often physically attractive and personable. But these

[30] For a long time we were puzzled about the reasons why one of our informants was systematically excluded from the girls' group mentioned above. Our other informants in this group told us, at first, that her clinical attitudes toward sex repulsed them, but upon reflection they admitted that they too collectively discussed sex in a similar manner. Upon further investigation, we found that this girl revealed her desire for sex, she "needed it," and hence she violated these norms.

girls reject the hostility and exploitation inherent in the dating system and prefer an imaginary but romantically perfect relationship with these remote figures.

CONCLUSION

In conclusion, we do not hold that the youth subculture is a closed normative system. The normative integrity, coherence, and identity of a subculture is not always based upon estrangement from the larger culture nor does it always reside in social organizations which resist integration into the larger society. On the other hand, in a discussion of the reality of the youth culture, Berger declares that subcultures must not only have "relatively distinctive styles of life, but styles of life which are to a great extent self-generated, autonomous, having institutional and territorial resources capable of sustaining it in crisis and insulating it from pressures from without." [31] In our opinion, this limits the concept of a subculture to very special, and possibly almost non-existent, cases of cultural differentiation in this society. The high degree of interdependence of functionally differentiated subsystems in this society makes it unlikely that many subcultures will fulfil all of Berger's stringent prerequisites.

In contrast to Berger's strictures, we propose a more catholic and perhaps more fruitful view of a subculture. Rather, we suggest that the core of the youth culture resides in its distinctive evaluative standards. They endow the adolescent status terminology (and thus the social categories through which the members of this age-grade orient themselves to their peers) with qualities and attributes which do not dominate adult status judgments. Here we follow Anselm Strauss' view of the connection between social categories linked to a person's position in age and other societal structures and the ways in which people perceive social reality:

> These changes in conceptual level involve, of course, changes in behavior, since behavior is not separate from classifying. Shifts in concept connote shifts in perceiving, remembering and valuing—in short, radical changes in action and person. . . . Terminological shifts necessitate, but also signalize new evaluations: of self and others, of events, acts and objects; and the transformation of perception is irreversible; once having changed, there is no going back. One can look back, but he can evaluate only from his new status.[32]

From our point of view, then, the members of a subculture can be integrated into basic societal institutions even though their definitions of ordinary social situations are predicated upon a special set of cultural meanings. Consequently, the crucial criterion for the identification of a youth sub-

---

[31] Berger, op. cit., p. 396.
[32] Strauss, *Mirrors and Masks: The Search for Identity* (Glencoe, Ill.: The Free Press, 1959), p. 92.

culture is whether its norms provide its members with a distinctive world view, a style of life, and the standards against which they can measure their own worth. Here again it is worthwhile to quote Strauss on age-graded perceptions of the world: "But the world is different for persons of different age and generation even if they share in common sex, class, and nationality, and occupation." [33]

Finally, our approach emphasizes the element of free cultural play in the genesis of the youth culture. Of course, we do not deny that the typical psychological and role problems of this age-grade provide the raw materials out of which youth culture is built. But we do point to the ways in which the meanings inherent in this adolescent normative order transcend the requirements of simple adjustment to these exigencies. In other words, these adolescent cultural inventions and innovations impose a discernible order upon the crises and dilemmas of adolescence.

[33] Ibid., p. 138.

Hershel D. Thornburg

Adolescent Sources of Initial Sex Information[1]

Although much disagreement prevails as to whether sexual promiscuity and premarital sexual indulgence are increasing among adolescents, the fact remains that sex is an exceedingly salient issue with youth. The extent and accuracy of their knowledge about human sexuality have been the subject of considerable speculation, but only limited data have provided bases for school policies on sex education. In this selection, Thornburg adds substantially to our understanding of adolescents' sexual behavior by providing information regarding youth's initial sexual knowledge. The findings, derived from a study of students at four universities, indicate that peers are youth's major source of sexual information; however, on matters of accuracy regarding abortion, venereal disease, and menstruation, youth look also to, respectively, printed literature, school programs, and their mothers. Thornburg's informative investigation reveals, too, that initial sources of sexual knowledge differ for the two sexes.

FROM Paper prepared especially for this volume.

1 The author wishes to thank William Looft, Pennsylvania State University; Dwight Jeffrey, Louisiana State University in New Orleans; Mary Jane McFate, Bakersfield College; and Robert Karabinus, Northern Illinois University for their assistance in data collection.

Instructional Objectives
To describe sources of adolescents' initial sexual information.
To analyze sex differences in adolescents' sources of initial sexual information.
To discuss adolescents' perception of the accuracy of their initial sexual information.

THE CONTROVERSY that raged in the late 1960s over the teaching of sex education in the schools had a direct bearing on preadolescent and adolescent youths because it reduced the opportunities for them to receive sex information from legitimate, knowledgable sources.[2] Although there were parental groups who opposed sex education so strongly that many programs in the United States were abandoned, the attention given to it indicated that parents, educators, physicians, and psychologists were concerned that adolescents today are being subjected to pressure for heterosexual involvement at an earlier age.

A social puberty precedes the physiological puberty known to most twelve to fourteen-year-olds.[3] Social puberty refers to heterosexual involvement being thrust on the preadolescent prior to his developmental physiological basis that would make such behavior more natural. It generally occurs as a result of highly suggestive social stimuli that our youth confront in their daily environment. Their exposure to different sexual behaviors is common through the media of television, motion pictures, literature, music, and advertising. Because of its materialistic emphasis, sex is generally presented in an enticing, luring, get-involved way. Combined with peer pressure to become sexually active, even prior to puberty, the naturalness of sex and its consequences, whether positive or negative, are rarely understood or realistically presented to the preadolescent.

What type of early sex information do youth have and from whom do they generally gain such information? Four hundred and fifty-one students enrolled in major universities in California, Illinois, Louisiana, and Pennsylvania were asked to state to the best of their knowledge the age, accuracy, and first source from which they received information on the following sex topics: abortion, contraception, ejaculation, homosexuality, intercourse, masturbation, menstruation, origin of babies, petting, prostitution, seminal emissions, and venereal disease. While those given the questionnaire were asked to recall back into their preadolescence or adolescence, such information probably reflects trends among contemporary adolescents. Further, this sample was selected because of its contrasting geographical distribution from

[2] H. D. Thornburg, "Educating the Preadolescent About Sex," *Family Coordinator,* (January, 1974).
[3] H. D. Thornburg, *Adolescent Development,* (Dubuque, Iowa: W. C. Brown, 1973).

a larger study being done by this author,[4] consisting of 970 students from eleven different geographically located universities.

The tabulated data of first source information for the 451 students is found in Table 1. Analysis of the data indicates that with the exception of "origin of babies" and "menstruation," the parents' role in sex information is quite limited (15.3 per cent). The schools, generally thought of as a reliable information source, contributed 19.5 per cent of the knowledge. Literature provided an additional 20 per cent. Peers, however, tended to be the primary information source for youth (39.4 per cent). The combined categories of father, physician, and minister, contributed 2.6 per cent of the information, just half as much as was gained by experience (5.0 per cent). The data in this study has a striking resemblance to studies done two and three decades ago [5] as well as to current studies.[6]

Table 1   A Comparative Study of Initial Sex Information Sources

Source	Pennsylvania N=99	Louisiana N=111	California N=135	Illinois N=106	Total % N=451
Mother	13.9	14.6	12.5	13.3	13.5
Father	1.4	1.3	2.1	2.6	1.8
Peers	40.8	38.9	38.2	40.3	39.4
School	18.7	18.4	22.5	17.5	19.5
Literature	20.4	21.1	16.7	22.3	20.0
Physician	.4	.8	.5	.0	.4
Minister	.0	.3	.7	.7	.4
Experience	4.5	4.6	6.7	3.3	5.0

Evidence from the author's earlier investigations indicates that literature is making a more significant contribution than it did two and three decades ago. The data do not support an increase in parental and school contributions to sex information. As can be seen by looking at Table 2, adolescents gain significant, somewhat comparable, amounts of information from literature, with abortion being the most frequently sought item.

A somewhat distorted statistic is the 13.5 per cent of information provided

[4] H. D. Thornburg, "Regional Differences in Sources of Sex Information." in H. D. Thornburg, *Contemporary Adolescence*, 2nd edit. (Monterey: Brooks/Cole, 1973).

[5] H. Angelino and E. V. Mech, "Some 'First' Sources of Sex Information as Reported by Sixty-seven College Women," *Journal of Psychology*, 39 (1955), 321–324; H. M. Bell, *Youth Tell Their Story*, (Washington, D.C.: American Council on Education, 1938); M. R. Lee, "Background Factors Related to Sex Information and Attitudes," *Journal of Educational Psychology*, 43 (1952), 467–485; C. V. Ramsey, "The Sex Information of Younger Boys," *American Journal of Orthopsychiatry*, 13 (1943), 347–352.

[6] H. D. Thornburg, "Age and First Sources of Sex Information as Reported by 88 College Women," *Journal of School Health*, 40 (1970), 156–158; H. D. Thornburg, "A Comparative Study of Sex Information Sources," *Journal of School Health*, 42 (1972), 88–92.

Table 2 Sources of Sex Information (in per cent)

Source	Abortion	Contraception	Ejaculation	Homosexuality	Intercourse	Masturbation	Menstruation	Origin of Babies	Petting	Prostitution	Seminal Emissions	Venereal Disease	Total
Mother	7.4	9.5	5.9	7.0	16.8	4.2	43.2	44.6	4.6	7.4	4.7	5.3	13.5
Father	.7	2.0	1.6	1.6	2.7	.5	.9	4.4	.5	3.3	1.7	1.8	1.8
Peers	19.6	42.4	46.1	52.9	55.9	48.8	22.7	26.1	60.0	50.5	30.0	18.5	39.4
School	30.0	22.9	17.1	12.9	9.8	14.4	18.2	15.5	6.4	6.0	28.9	52.1	19.5
Literature	40.0	20.4	20.9	23.0	8.4	22.8	11.5	9.2	8.7	31.2	26.7	20.1	20.0
Physician	.5	1.6	.2	.0	.2	.2	.7	.2	.2	.2	.3	1.1	.4
Minister	.2	.2	.2	.5	.0	1.4	.2	.0	1.2	.2	.0	.2	.4
Experience	1.6	.9	8.0	2.1	6.1	7.7	2.7	.0	18.7	1.2	8.0	.4	5.0

by mothers. In actuality, mothers' contribution is quite low if one excludes the topics of menstruation (43.2 per cent) and origin of babies (44.6 per cent). These two topics account for 58 per cent of the total information, a figure highly comparable to the 52 per cent in Thornburg's 1972 study.[7] Studies by Ramsey [8] and Angelino and Mech [9] reported that information on origin of babies and menstruation accounted for 47.5 per cent and 48 per cent respectively of the mother's information output.

There were little regional differences in sources of sex information from the literature, schools, or one's mother. The one exception which merits some discussion is within the California sample where it appears that the youth were somewhat more dependent on the schools (22.5 per cent) and less on literature (16.7 per cent) than the other three groups.

If the two most prevalent adolescent sexual expressions, petting and intercourse are examined, peer influence is obviously dominant. Peers provided 60 per cent of the information on petting, 56 per cent on intercourse. More reliable sources accounted for little information here. While schools and parents exert interest in some sexual concepts, they are hesitant to discuss sexual behavior. Earlier studies also support this finding.[10]

The data were also analyzed to determine if boys and girls are likely to seek out different sources of information to learn about sex. Table 3 provides a breakdown of such information. There are two major differences between the sexes as girls were more dependent upon their mothers (19.3 per cent compared to 5.4 per cent for males) and boys were more dependent on peers for information (45.2 per cent compared to 35.3 per cent for girls). There were also some percentage gaps in using the schools and experience as information sources.

One final consideration in this study was the degree of accuracy perceived

Table 3   Sex Differences in Initial Sex Information Sources

Source	Male % N=180	Female % N=271	Total % N=451
Mother	5.4	19.3	13.5
Father	3.0	1.0	1.8
Peers	45.2	35.3	39.4
School	17.2	21.1	19.5
Literature	20.3	19.7	20.0
Physician	.3	.5	.4
Minister	.6	.4	.4
Experience	7.9	2.7	5.0

[7] Thornburg, *Journal of School Health*, 1972.
[8] Ramsey, *American Journal of Orthopsychiatry*, 1943.
[9] Angelino and Mech, *Journal of Psychology*, 1955.
[10] Thornburg, *Journal of School Health*, 1970, 1972.

in the adolescent's initial contact with each term. These findings are summarized in Table 4. The students were asked to score the accuracy of their information as highly accurate, accurate, distorted, or highly distorted. Combining the categories of accurate and highly accurate, the overall accuracy percentage for the 12 sexual concepts was 73.75 per cent. If one compares these data with those of previously reported studies,[11] the percentage of accuracy is quite high, a finding that indicates today's youths are seeking more reliable information. The greatest accuracy was found for abortion, menstruation, and venereal disease, which is especially interesting. First, students gained most information about abortion from literature; second, venereal disease was learned mainly in school; third, mothers provided most information about menstruation. This indicates that peers are by no means the only source of information. It also indicates a high degree of reliability in the various sources.

Table 4   Accuracy of Obtained Information *

Topic	Highly Accurate %	Accurate %	Distorted %	Highly Distorted %
Abortion	32.7	55.0	11.9	.4
Contraception	26.4	50.8	21.4	1.4
Ejaculation	27.2	46.7	23.7	2.4
Homosexuality	17.5	43.2	32.6	6.7
Intercourse	24.4	42.0	26.9	6.7
Masturbation	21.8	41.6	30.0	6.6
Menstruation	45.5	38.0	13.1	3.4
Origin of Babies	33.5	41.7	18.8	6.0
Petting	26.0	44.7	25.0	4.3
Prostitution	21.2	50.8	21.8	1.9
Seminal Emissions	25.3	50.0	21.8	2.9
Venereal Disease	37.3	43.7	16.1	2.9

* The percentages represent the combined totals for all four universities (n=451) in each category.

Three sexual concepts fell within the 60 per cent accuracy range: homosexuality, intercourse, and masturbation, and in each instance peers were the significant contributors to accuracy. These accuracy percentages are quite high, giving some indication that the level of peer information is apparently more accurate than may have been true in the past. The studies by Elias and Gebhard and Schwartz reported higher incidences of distorted information. This may be due, in part, to the differences in the populations

[11] J. Elias and P. Gebhard, "Sexuality and Sexual Learning in Children," *Phi Delta Kappan*, 50 (1969), 401–406; M. S. Schwartz, "A Report on Sex Information Knowledge of 87 Lower Class Ninth Grade Boys," *Family Coordinator*, 18 (1969), 371–381.

studied. Elias and Gebhard sampled the general population; Schwartz investigated lower-class junior-high-school boys; and the study described here considered college youth.

With sexual-social stimuli so prevalent, ways should continue to be sought in which reliable information can be transmitted to adolescents. It is presumed herein that shifts from peer sources to parental, school, and literature sources increase the potential for more accurate information being obtained. Naivete is an expensive, sometimes unfortunate, price that our youths pay for being thrust into sexual behavioral roles with limited or inaccurate information. Further, one cannot disregard the social impact of the peer group and mass media, both of which tend to make sexual activity attractive and exciting to adolescents. Increased credibility of authority sources among peers involving sexual issues should enhance the adolescents' understanding and responsibility toward his own sexual behavior.

Anne McCreary Juhasz

Sexual Decision-Making:
The Crux of the Adolescent Problem

Whether to have intercourse, have children, practice birth control, have an abortion, give up a child for adoption, and marry are among the issues adolescents face as they begin to assume responsibility for expression of sexual impulses. McCreary Juhasz believes that youth must become aware of the critical questions to be asked, consider the implications of available alternatives, and anticipate a precipitating chain of reactions. In the following paper, the researcher poses a series of likely questions adolescents will ask, organizes them in terms of a comprehensive model, and reviews systematically the considerations raised by each. Adults, McCreary Juhasz holds, are obligated to assist adolescents in dealing effectively with life and attain proficiency in problem-solving and decision-making.

Instructional Objectives
To review contemporary changes in the sexual behavior patterns of youth.
To describe a model of sexual decision-making involving six critical issues.

FROM Paper prepared especially for this volume.

D URING past decades, choices of sexual behavior and decisions about sexual activity have become increasingly important, both to the individual and to the society. At the same time, the responsibility for choice and decision has shifted from society to the individual. Concurrently, awareness of the basic nature of "man's" sexuality has resulted in increased opportunities and expectations for a wide variety of sexual experience. This has occurred at a time when young people have few guidelines or restrictions. In this context the area of sexual decision-making is crucial.

Recently, evidence has been accumulating to suggest that important sex-related decisions are being made at increasingly younger ages. Decisions which were previously made primarily at the young adult stage in life now are being preempted by the adolescent. For example, Erikson [1] assigns the task of establishing an intimate relationship to the young adult. However, increasing numbers of adolescents are attempting this task. Examination of some of the research from only the past decade provides a striking illustration of this. Until recently, adults, college students and unwed mothers were the subjects of surveys or studies dealing with sex. This is understandable. Existing taboos made adult participation in such research more probable and more acceptable. Also, availability of specific groups as captive participants explains the emphasis on college students and unwed mothers. Underlying all this could be the idea that sex was not really a suitable topic for research, and that even if it were, adolescents would not be suitable subjects. They were not supposed to know anything about sex, and they were not supposed to have had sexual experiences. However, reports on adolescent sexual behavior are now beginning to appear. The aspects of sex which have been studied have also changed. Early surveys dealt with factual knowledge, source of information, attitude toward premarital sexual activity, and attitude toward various degrees of sexual intimacy. Now the questions deal with types and frequencies of specific sexual behavior, aspects of interpersonal relationships, and types of group-family structure. In summary, sex-related research now includes younger and younger people. Also the focus is on what they think and do rather than on what they know.

CHANGES IN SEXUAL BEHAVIOR: SELECTED RESEARCH

As early as 1965, Glassberg [2] noted that premarital intercourse had become a perfunctory aspect of the adolescent dating system. Hurlock,[3] in 1966, wrote that teenagers no longer have any regard for virginity. Rainwater,[4]

[1] E. H. Erikson, *Childhood and Society* (New York: W. W. Norton and Company Inc., 1963).

[2] B. Y. Glassberg, "Sexual Behavior Patterns in Contemporary Youth Culture: Implications for Later Marriage," *Journal of Marriage and the Family*, XXVII (1965), 190–192.

[3] E. B. Hurlock, "American Adolescents Today—A New Species," *Adolescence*, I (1966), 17–21.

[4] L. Rainwater, "Some Aspects of Lower Class Sexual Behavior," *Social Issues*, XXII (1966), 96–108.

at the same time, reported that lower class youngsters are more likely to have premarital sexual relations than are middle class boys and girls. However, even in the lower class, the double standard exists with fewer girls than boys having intercourse. Reiss [5] investigated sexual permissiveness in terms of type of relationship and degree of religiosity. He concluded that there had been no appreciable increase in the proportion of nonvirginity among unmarried young people from the 1920s up to 1967 when his report was published. Also, he found that affection was the prerequisite for permissiveness for most young people.

Approval and acceptance of nonvirginity in others and approval of coitus for the unmarried have been major issues. College students and unwed mothers have been the subjects most frequently used for investigation. Reports on men have remained stable in terms of number. However, since World War I, there has been a 20–30 per cent increase in the number of studies of college girls. Approximately forty per cent of those questioned now report having had sexual intercourse.[6] Vance Packard [7] points out that in Kinsey's report 20 years previously, 20 per cent of college women admitted premarital sexual intercourse as compared with 43 per cent in 1968, an increase of 60 per cent.

The few available studies of adolescent sexual activity do not support the assumption that adolescents are promiscuous and sexually active to an alarming extent. A 1970 survey conducted by The Merit Publishing Company [8] involved 22,000 high-achieving high school juniors and seniors. This study revealed that, while 42 per cent expressed approval of premarital sexual intercourse, only 18 per cent of the boys and 15 per cent of the girls reported having participated in intercourse. Offer's [9] longitudinal study of adolescent boys reported similar results.

Kantner and Zelnik,[10] reporting in 1972 on the sexual experience of young unmarried women in the United States, found evidence that premarital intercourse is beginning at younger ages and that its extent among teenagers is increasing. At age 15, approximately 32 per cent of blacks and 11 per cent of whites had had sexual intercourse. By 19 years of age the percentages were 80 per cent for blacks and 40 per cent for whites. Interestingly, these

[5] I. Reiss, *The Social Context of Premarital Sexual Permissiveness* (New York: Holt, Rinehart and Winston, 1967).

[6] E. B. Luckey and G. D. Nass, "A Comparison of Sexual Attitudes and Behavior in an International Sample," *Journal of Marriage and the Family*, XXXI (1969), 364–379; G. R. Kaats and K. E. Davis, "The Dynamics of Sexual Behavior of College Students," *Journal of Marriage and the Family*, XXXII (1970), 390–399; R. R. Bell and J. B. Chaskes, "Premarital Sexual Experience Among Coeds, 1958 and 1968," *Journal of Marriage and the Family*, XXXII (1970), 81–84; H. T. Christensen and C. Gregg, "Changing Sex Norms in America and Scandinavia," *Journal of Marriage and the Family*, XXIX (1970), 616–627.

[7] V. Packard, *The Sexual Wilderness* (New York: David McKay Company Inc., 1968).

[8] Merit Publishing Company, "National Survey of High School High Achievers," (1970).

[9] D. Offer, D. Marcus and J. Offer, "A Longitudinal Study of Normal Adolescent Boys," *American Journal of Psychiatry*, CXXVI (1970), 917–924.

[10] J. F. Kantner and M. Zelnik, "Sexual Experience of Young Unmarried Women in the United States," *Family Planning Perspectives*, IV (1972), 9–18.

sexually-experienced teenagers appear to have relatively stable relationships. In about 60 per cent of the cases a single partner was involved and intent to marry was a factor. Also, these subjects were not very sexually active. Seventy per cent of them had had sexual intercourse only once or twice during the month interviewed. This study revealed that higher socio-economic status, higher level of education, and faithful church attendance were associated with a lower rate of premarital intercourse. Poverty and residence in the central cities of metropolitan areas, on the other hand, was highly correlated with sexual intercourse. A high correlation also held for girls who were raised in a rural area and then migrated to the city.

Sorensen's [11] report provides figures which are fairly similar to those reported above. He notes that 45 per cent of all girls ages 13 to 19 have had sexual intercourse. Before age 17, one-third of all girls have had first intercourse. The findings from his survey lend strong support to the concept of sex as permissable with love. In his study, 80 per cent of all boys and 72 per cent of all girls agreed that premarital intercourse with someone you loved prior to marriage was acceptable. Seventy-six per cent of males and 67 per cent of females felt that two people should not feel obligated to marry just because they lived together.

Today's adolescents, freed from parental, societal, and clerical controls, moving away from parents in search of some form of internal guide for their decisions, presented with pressures and opportunities for sexual experience at increasingly early ages, will be faced with sexual decisions. They will have to assume the responsibility for these decisions. In this last half of the twentieth century, adults can not make decisions for youth. Nor can they be expected to assume responsibility for the actions of young people. Each individual must make his or her own choice and must then accept responsibility for the results. However, adults *can* and *must* serve a twofold function; first, to prepare the next generation to deal effectively with life, and second, to provide knowledge and training in problem-solving and decision-making. These are the premises on which the model of sexual decision-making is presented below.

THE MODEL FOR A CHAIN OF SEXUAL DECISION-MAKING

The model for a chain of sexual decision-making is based on the following six questions.

Question	*Choice or Result*
1. Intercourse or no intercourse? [12]	1. Intercourse
2. Children or no children?	2. Either [13]
3. Birth control or no birth control?	3. Pregnancy
4. Delivery or abortion?	4. Delivery
5. Keep the child or give it up?	5. Either [14]
6. Remain single or marry? [15]	

[11] R. Sorensen, *Adolescent Sexuality in Contemporary America* (New York: World Publishing, 1973).

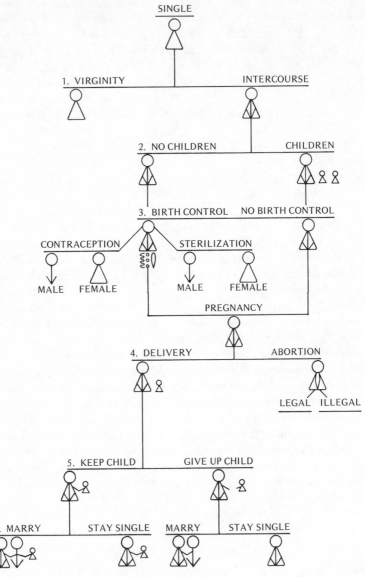

Figure 1.   *A model for sexual decision-making.*

The model (see Figure 1) demonstrates the way in which the individual must be able to follow logically, the cumulative ramifications of a single

---

12 Each decision, except "no intercourse," leads to consideration of the next question.

13 A decision about the use of birth control is relevant for those who plan a family as well as for those who do not want children.

14 Whether or not a child is involved, couples may consider the possibility of marriage.

15 The question, "to remain single or marry?" could have been the first link in the chain. However, it seems more realistic to begin with the question, "to have sexual intercourse or not?"

sex-related decision. For each of the six questions in this chain, the adolescent should understand factors which could influence decisions. In addition, for each possible choice, he or she should be aware of the questions which will arise, the additional problems which must be faced and the implications of subsequent actions. In other words, a logical, systematic consideration of the knowns and unknowns is required.

For each individual there will be unique aspects in his or her own situation. Also, the complexity of the questions which must be considered will vary from person to person, depending upon background, personality, and value system. Similarly, decisions will vary from individual to individual. However, there are some general factors, and some well-established facts which can be used as a basis for this problem-solving approach to the sexual decisions which are precipitated by the initial question which every adolescent will have to face, "To have sexual intercourse or not?"

1. To Have Sexual Intercourse or Not?

Three major influences on this decision are (1) individual needs, (2) respect and concern, and (3) fear. *Individual needs* usually provide the motivation for sexual encounter and often the young person finds it difficult to pinpoint the specific reason for the decision to have intercourse. Often it is not a preplanned, premeditated action. It is more likely to be either an impulsive, spur-of-the-moment act or the result of gradual drifting into a situation where it almost seems to be inevitable. Studies of unwed mothers have revealed an unconscious, neurotic need to become pregnant, but for the emotionally-healthy young person this would not apply. Similarly, reasons given by adults for sexual activity would not necessarily be true for youth.

Currently, the most frequently cited justifications for sexual intercourse appear to be the following: (a) the individual's rights to freedom and self-fulfillment, (b) the need to learn through experiencing in order to have a better adult relationship, and (c) the means of obtaining peer approval and acceptance. Certainly, freedom, self-fulfillment and individual rights are ultimate goals of the self-actualized individual in our society. At the present time, traditional values are being challenged by youth, attempting to achieve these aims. However, often the maturity and responsibility implicit in these goals are lacking. These two questions are rarely considered: "Responsible for whom? and Freedom for what?"

Learning through doing and experiencing is a pedagogically-sound principle. However, the stakes are high in the game of sexual intercourse. There is scant evidence that sexual intercourse leads to improved relationships. Similarly, there is little evidence on the negative side.[16] However, doubts

[16] Glassberg, op. cit.; D. Shope and C. Broderick, "Level of Sexual Experience and Predicted Adjustment in Marriage," *Journal of Marriage and the Family*, XXIX (1967), 424–427; H. Miller and W. Wilson, "Relation of Sexual Behavior Values and Conflict in Avowed Happiness and Personal Adjustment," *Psychological Reports*, XXIII (1968), 1075–1086; J. F. Kantner and M. Zelnik, "Contraception and Pregnancy: Experiences of Young Unmarried Women in the United States," *Family Planning Perspectives*, V (1973), 21–35.

have been expressed concerning the ability of the person with a history of many and varied sexual contacts to form a stable and satisfying relationship. Thus the individual, learning through doing, must run the risk of unknown consequences and unforeseen reactions.

Peer approval and acceptance are powerful motivational forces at the time of adolescence. Thus, one finds a higher rate of premarital sexual experience among those who have little support from family, church, and social groups.[17] It is easier to resist peer pressure if one can present some justification in terms of parental rules and regulations or group sanctions. In a way, this is "passing the buck," placing the responsibility on someone else. In another way it is an indication of respect for parental opinions and values. However, Kantner and Zelnik[18] found that the incidence of premarital sexual intercourse for those living in college dormitories was no higher than for those living at home. In an earlier study, college girls living on campus told interviewer Gael Greene[19] that, in order to escape peer pressure and avoid rejection by the group, it was easier to say that they had had intercourse when they actually hadn't. Probably this same pressure is applied wherever one resides, and at the high-school level as well as at the college level. For some girls, the pressure to lose their virginity becomes such a burden that they find any male stranger, have intercourse and get it over with. Then they can say that they have done it.

Fear, respect, and concern are also strong motivational forces. Unlike individual needs, which serve to attract one toward sexual intercourse, they tend to motivate one to avoid it. Feelings of fear, respect and concern may be closely interwoven in relation to the specific family, social, and religious background of the individual. Attitudes and values are firmly established by adolescence and they will have a bearing upon feelings of achievement, satisfaction, guilt or anxiety experienced by the individual in relation to his sexual behavior. Most adolescents like and respect their parents. Even when they are not in complete accord with parental beliefs and convictions, most would hesitate to knowingly hurt or deeply displease their parents.

Fear and concern for oneself and for the outcome of the relationship can also be deterrents to sexual intercourse. Important questions will be these: "Who will be hurt? Who will treat me differently? How will I feel toward my partner? How will my partner feel toward me?" These are some of the unknowns. In addition, there is the fear of physical hazards, either immediate or long term. Physical fears are associated with pregnancy and venereal disease. Both are possible outcomes of sexual intercourse; both can be prevented and controlled. Certainly, easy accessibility of contraceptives lessens the fear of pregnancy. This has not lead to a corresponding rise in contraceptive use, however.

At present, there is a rise in the rate of VD. Some of this increase may be

17 Kantner and Zelnik, op. cit., 1973.
18 Ibid.
19 G. Greene, *Sex and the College Student* (New York: Dell Publishing Company, 1964).

attributed to oral-genital sexual activity. However, actual sexual intercourse is the primary method of contact. Early detection and treatment can be effective, but new strains are much more resistant to previously effective drugs.[20] In addition, apprehension is warranted by increasing evidence of the hazards to both the adult and to the new-born infant.[21]

RELATED QUESTIONS

Hopefully, the individual who thinks through the first question and decides to have sexual intercourse has also formed a philosophy, some set of standards, that will enable him to live happily and effectively with himself and with his decision. Three questions which appear to be very practical but which are nevertheless, highly relevant in terms of maintaining a positive self-concept, will accompany the decision to have intercourse: "With whom? Under what circumstances? and In what manner?"

For young people today, type of relationship and degree of affection appear to be important aspects of the choice of partner. Degree of commitment is less important. In some cases, because affection is seen as "good" in itself, multiple partnerships may not be viewed as promiscuous. For some people, degree of responsibility and type of family or group structure may be important considerations.[22]

The question, "Under what circumstances?" is tied closely to some aspects of the first one, "With whom?" For some individuals, commitment such as engagement will be a requirement. Goals, values, self-concept, and individual needs—all will influence the decision.

CHOICE OF SEXUAL OUTLETS FOR VIRGINS

Sexual expression usually is normal, natural, and healthy. Thus, the individual who selects virginity rather than intercourse must find some satisfactory sexual outlet. However, certain behavior might be considered to be deviant or abnormal, *e.g.*, exhibitionism, fetishism, sadism, necrophilia, beastiality, or excessive preoccupation with pornographic material. Other outlets include masturbation, homosexuality, and petting up to the point of intercourse without going all the way.

2. CHILDREN OR NO CHILDREN?

Should the first decision be to have intercourse, then the second major question must be considered: "To have or not to have children?" Parents,

---

[20] H. M. Wallace, "Venereal Disease in Teenagers," *Clinical Obstetrics and Gynecology,* XIV (1971), 432–441; Todays *VD Control Problem* (Washington: American Social Health Association, 1972).

[21] L. Nazarin, "Gonorrhea in Children," *Medical Aspects of Human Sexuality,* V (1972), 64; G. Martin, "The Innocent Aspect of Congenital Syphillis," *Hospital Physician,* IV (1973), 75–76.

[22] E. Macklin, "Heterosexual Cohabitation Among Unmarried College Students," *The Family Coordinator,* XXI (1972), 463–472.

infant, extended family and society as a whole will be affected by this decision.

Over-population, adequate child care, quality of family life, and utilization of human potential: these are concerns of the total society. All prospective parents, married or unmarried, should take these into consideration when deciding whether or not to have a child. Unfortunately, in many instances, couples responsible without forethought for pregnancies tend not to care how frequently illegitimacy occurs.[23] On the other hand, in intact families, the implications of a baby being born to an unmarried teenage relative may be traumatic. Certain families will react with grief and shame; others will provide support, both economic and emotional. Some will raise the child as their own.[24] Each couple will have to try to predict the impact on their own family members and the possible repercussions in terms of their established relationships with these significant others.

Considerations for the infant involve physical, emotional, and social aspects. The young unmarried mother is a poor risk as far as her infant is concerned. Babies born to such girls have more physical problems at birth and in early infancy. The unwed mother is likely to have poor prenatal care and diet and this affects the infant.[25] Emotionally, the young parents may be less able to deal with the task of raising the child, because many of them are still developing themselves and attempting to solve their own problems. While there are no firm statistics indicating that the battered baby is more likely to have unwed or young parents, there is some supporting evidence to this claim.[26]

The next point has both emotional and social implications. Society still labels the child of unwed parents a bastard, and this label can be emotionally and socially damaging. Malinowski [27] has set forth his *Principle of Legitimacy,* and it still holds today in much of our culture.

> The most important moral and legal rule concerning the physiological side of kinship is that no child should be brought into the world without a man—and one man at that—assuming the role of sociological father, that is, guardian and protector of the male link between the child and the rest of the community.

Adolescent parents should consider both present and future implications for

[23] P. M. Barglow, D. Bornstein, M. Exum and H. Visotsky, "Some Psychiatric Aspects of Illegitimate Pregnancy in Early Adolescence," *Am. Journal of Orthopsychiatry,* XXXVIII (1968), 672–687; M. Wessel, "A Physician Looks at Services for Unmarried Parents," *Social Casework,* XLIX (1968), 11–15.

[24] M. LaBarre, "Emotional Crisis of School Age Girls During Pregnancy and Early Motherhood," *Journal of Child Psychiatry,* XI (1972), 537–557.

[25] H. J. Osofsky and J. Osofsky, "Adolescents as Mothers," *American Journal of Orthopsychiatry,* XL (1970), 825–834.

[26] D. Gill, *Violence Against Children: Physical Child Abuse in the United States* (Cambridge: Harvard University Press, 1970).

[27] B. Malinowski, "Parenthood—the Basis of Social Structure," In R. W. Roberts (Ed.), *The Unwed Mother* (New York: Harper and Row, 1966), 36–37.

themselves, irrespective of the child. These encompass educational opportunities, economic stability, emotional reactions, and physical aspects. It has been shown that if a teenaged couple marry when the wife becomes pregnant, they fail to catch up with their peers in terms of education and income because of the investment at the time of pregnancy and birth.[28] This often involves dropping out of school for the parents.

Emotionally and physically the young adolescent is least well prepared to handle the multiple responsibilities of home and family. Physically, the young mother has more complications. Emotionally, she rarely has the support needed to carry her through the pregnancy, delivery, and child-raising stages.[29] Also, there is the long-range effect on future relationships, either with the partner or with others. Each additional individual in any relationship, even an infant, complicates the picture, compounds the interactions, and increases the possibility of problems and crises.[30]

The decision, to have or not to have children is an individual one in terms of responsibility. However, the effect is not limited to the decision-maker. The repercussions are felt by many to whom the individual also has some degree of responsibility.

3. BIRTH CONTROL OR NO BIRTH CONTROL?

The third decision, the use of birth control methods applies both to those who want children and to those who do not want children. For the latter, this should be an imperative decision. For the former, planning is involved so that the child will be really wanted from the moment of conception, and not just after it arrives. This applies to the many couples who want to have children, but for some reason decide to wait for a period of time which will best fit into their overall long-range plans. The unmarried who fail to consider this an imperative decision are immediately precipitated into the next decision-making situation: "If I don't use birth control, don't want children, and become pregnant, what will I do?"

This discussion will focus on two methods of birth control: contraception and sterilization. Both can be effective in limiting children. Responsibility for both can rest with either the male or the female. There are positive and negative aspects to both. Comprehensive literature is readily available to adolescents through Planned Parenthood and similar organizations.

CONTRACEPTION

Individuals faced with a decision about the use of contraceptives should know both the positive and negative factors. On the positive side, through

---

[28] L. Coombs, R. Freedman, J. Friedman and W. Pratt, "Premarital Pregnancy and Status Before and After Marriage," *Am. J. of Sociology*, LXXV (1970), 800–820.

[29] Barglow, Bornstein, Exum, Wright, Visotsky, op. cit.

[30] J. Menken, "The Health and Social Consequences of Teenage Childbearing," *Family Planning Perspectives*, IV (1972), 45–53.

the use of contraceptives, one can lessen the fear of pregnancy and presumably encourage more relaxed enjoyable sexual intercourse. Also, there should be a lower incidence of unwanted pregnancy and fewer cases of illegitimacy. If the condom is used there should be less risk of contacting venereal disease.

On the other hand, there are negative aspects of contraception. Some of these are tied to emotions, attitudes, and values. Religious and parental regulations or customs may act as deterrents. Some individuals feel that the use of contraceptives indicates the intent to have intercourse and this causes guilt feelings. Others feel that the use of contraceptives detracts from the sexual experience. Adults fear that widespread use of contraceptives will encourage promiscuity.

For some individuals, the more practical aspects of the problem still remain: "Whose responsibility is birth control? Who should use the contraceptive? How does one get it? What is the best type to use?" The female, especially, should be aware of the possible side effects of the various methods, and also should know of the long-range effects of consistent use. Medical literature reports regularly on the necessity for individualized attention to the type of birth control used.[31]

STERILIZATION

The second alternative for ensuring "no children," sterilization, has many of the same pros and cons as does the use of contraceptive measures. However, there is one difference. With present methods this procedure is irreversible. However, research is proceeding now which may allow reactivation in the male.[32] Again, questions arise: "Should the male or female be sterilized? What will be the psychological effects? What of future mating or remarriage? Should use of the sperm bank be considered? How important is zero population growth?" One would assume that questions relating to sterilization would rarely be considered seriously by the adolescent. The implications are vastly different for the 40-year-old father of ten children than for the 16-year-old unmarried male with no offspring.

4. DELIVERY OR ABORTION?

Should pregnancy occur, either planned or accidental, a decision must be made whether or not to deliver the child. Background factors which influ-

---

31 F. Kane Jr., R. Daly, J. Ewing, and M. Keller, "Mood and Behavioral Changes with Progestational Agents," *British Journal of Psychiatry*, CXIII (1967), 265–268; S. Sturgis, "Oral Contraceptives and Their Effects on Sex Behavior," *Medical Aspects of Human Sexuality*, II (1968), 4–9; B. Herzberg, A. Johnson, and S. Brown, "Depression Symptoms and Oral Contraceptives," *Br. Medical Jnl.*, IV (1970), 142–145; "Risk of Pill," M.D., 10 (1973), 2.

32 "Urologists Differ on Reversibility of Vasectomy," *Hospital Practice*, October (1973), 36–41.

enced decisions at the previous links of the chain will apply here. The major points concern illegitimate children, population problems, young parents as bad risks, negative effects upon the young parents' present and future, and loss of potential to society. However, the question of abortion raises additional considerations.

General Considerations

It is a fact that with more liberal laws, abortion is now accepted and practiced with increasing frequency. However, religious and social mores remain important influences in this decision. For many individuals this will be a moral decision, and firmly established attitudes, beliefs, and teachings will serve to direct behavior. The second general consideration is an unknown. The psychological and physical effects of abortion can not be predicted. Research indicates that abortion, under ideal circumstances and barring complications, is physically as safe as pregnancy to term and delivery. Psychological effects will be highly individualized and can not be predicted accurately.[33]

The following points are related to responsibility and thoughtful decision-making. Abortion is a remedial rather than a preventive action. Careful planning and reliable action could eliminate this issue for most people. Exceptions may arise, for instance in the case of rape or mental deficiency. Failure to accept responsibility for prevention of pregnancy and ready acceptance of abortion as a remedy can lead to an established pattern of repeated pregnancy and abortion. The ramifications of this for the individual and for society are considerable.

Specific Considerations

The specific considerations related to abortion are mainly practical in nature: legality, availability, safety, cost, secrecy, and security. Each could be elaborated upon. If the trend of the past few years is indicative, it appears that all of these practical aspects will become easier to manage. At present, however, all must be considered. Any one may be problematical.

5. KEEP THE CHILD OR GIVE UP THE CHILD?

Should the single pregnant girl decide to deliver the child, she must decide whether to keep it or to give it up. Rarely does the father have to make this decision. Again, the same general considerations related to the welfare of the child and the impact upon all concerned individuals are relevant. Added to these are specific points pro and con for giving up the child for adoption.

On the plus side for the infant, presumably "it" would be wanted by the adoptive parents and would most likely have an advantage in terms of

---

[33] Kantner and Zelnik (1972), op. cit.; C. Schaffer, "Pregnancy, Abortion, and the Developmental Tasks of Adolescence," *Journal of Child Psychiatry*, XI (1972), 511–536.

support, education and care. On the negative side are possible psychological effects upon the mother, and at a later date, upon the child.

6. REMAIN SINGLE OR MARRY?

If the young mother chooses to keep the child, she may consider marriage as an alternative to remaining single. In selecting marriage she will meet the requirements set forth in Malinowski's *Principle of Legitimacy*—providing the infant with a male link to society. She may receive physical and emotional support. On the other hand, marriage entered into because of a child can be problematic. Love, affection, and responsibility may be absent, thus the solution to the problem may be a bad one.

For the girl who keeps the child and remains single, the following points must be considered: (1) continuation of the relationship; (2) provision of care and support for the child; (3) planning for the future of the mother; (4) determining the father's responsibility; and (5) deciding upon the type of family or group structure. Each of these considerations is multi-faceted and complicated even for the traditional, two-parent, married family group. For the single adolescent, the problems are multiplied many times over.

Philip H. Dreyer

Changes in the Meaning of Marriage Among Youth: The Impact of the "Revolution" in Sex and Sex Role Behavior

The advent of effective birth control measures, adoption of less constraining abortion laws, and growth of equalitarian attitudes between men and women have led during the past decade to increased sexual behavior outside the traditional marriage-family unit. In the next selection, Dreyer discusses how changes in norms and attitudes towards sexual behavior have altered the meaning of marriage for youth. Premarital intercourse

FROM Paper prepared especially for this volume.

appears to be acceptable today within the framework of an emotionally-involved relationship. He argues that a "sexual revolution" is in the making, especially among women, whose frequency of premarital sexual involvements in recent years has risen relative to that of men. His review also reveals that youth's knowledge of sex and reproduction generally is inadequate and that their use of contraceptives often is haphazard. Dreyer observes in his noteworthy essay that perhaps one-third of youth are "actively seeking new forms and meanings in marriage." Marriage for many youth, he says, has become a goal in itself—an "affirmation of personal identity, psychological intimacy, mutual pleasure giving, the promise of continued personal growth, and a transcendent relationship between two human beings."

Instructional Objectives
To review marriage and divorce rates among adolescents.
To discuss whether a "sexual revolution" is occurring.
To discuss youth's interpretation of premarital sexual behavior.
To discuss youth's view of marriage.

INTRODUCTION

THE INSTITUTION of marriage appears in the 1970s to be undergoing changes which are complex and profound. According to the U.S. Bureau of the Census a larger percentage of people in the U. S. were married in 1970 than at any other time in the nation's history. In 1971 22.2 per cent of the women aged 18 to 19, 60.5 per cent of those aged 20–24, and 83.0 per cent of those aged 25–29 were married. Among men in 1971 7.5 per cent of those aged 18–19, 42.9 per cent of the 20–24 year olds, and 75.3 per cent of the 25–29 year olds were married. Despite this apparent popularity, marriage rates have declined and leveled off in the last twenty years, from a high of 166.4 marriages per 1000 unmarried women aged 15 to 44 in 1950 to 148.0 in 1960 and 149.1 in 1969. At the same time divorce rates have increased sharply from 10.3 divorces per 1000 married women 15 years or older in 1950 to 13.4 divorces in 1969. Among young women in 1971 0.2 per cent of 18–19 year olds, 2.4 per cent of 20–24 year olds, and 4.3 per cent of 25–29 year olds were divorced, while for men the divorced percentages were 0.1, 1.0, and 2.5 for the same respective age groups. Finally, the median ages for brides and grooms in the United States, i.e., the age at which 50 per cent of the people in an age group are married, which had been declining steadily for most of the twentieth century, has begun to increase in the last decade, from a low of 20.3 years for women and 22.8 years for men in 1960 to 20.8 years for women and 23.2 years for men in 1970.[1]

[1] United States Bureau of the Census, *Current Population Reports*, series P-20, 1970.

From these statistics it seems clear that marriage as an institution is still very popular among young people and is not about to become extinct. But what is also clear is that for today's youth marriage does not carry with it all of the same assumptions, prerequisites, obligations, and meanings that it did for their parents or grandparents. For example, the census data given above indicate that young people today are waiting longer and are marrying at older ages than their parents did twenty years ago. They also indicate that young people are more likely to be divorced than their parents were at the same age.

The explanation of these assorted facts appears to be that for a sizeable proportion of young people the entire meaning of marriage seems to be changing, with greater emphasis being given to the opportunities marriage provides for personal growth and satisfaction, rather than the functions marriage has traditionally served in promoting social stability and continuity. At this point it appears that the majority of young people still cling to traditional notions of marriage; however, there appears to be a growing minority who are seeking to define new meanings for marriage. It is this sizeable minority who seem to be bringing about change and from whom we can begin to understand what new meanings marriage has today and what it is likely to mean in the future.

The changes which are occurring within the institution of marriage have been caused by changes in norms and behaviors with regard to sex behavior and sex-role playing. In the past sexual intercourse and the definition of sex roles took place almost exclusively within the context of the legal marriage contract. To engage in sexual intercourse before or outside of marriage was considered wrong and to think about adult sex roles outside of the context of one's marriage partner and children was uncommon and openly discouraged.

In recent years the invention of effective birth control techniques, along with the legalization of abortion, have become part of a new set of norms regulating sex behavior, making adult sexual behavior possible for unmarried persons and effectively separating sex behavior from the exclusive domain of marriage. New attitudes about sex typed social roles, the cultural influences on the social roles played by men and women, and the impact of the civil rights movement among blacks and women have led to a reevaluation of sex roles and to a tendency for such roles to be defined outside of the marriage-family socialization unit. These changes have fundamentally altered the meaning of marriage for youth, and it is necessary for us to review in detail these changes before returning to consider what marriage means today.

1. Sex Behavior Among Youth

Perhaps nothing has caught the imagination of Americans in the last decade so much as the vision of young men and women bathing together nude at the Woodstock Rock Festival of 1968. For many the scene gave meaning to the vague phrase "the new morality" and for others it confirmed the old moralists' fear that "counter-culture" values had indeed infected all of youth. In the years since Woodstock, clothing styles among youth have become more informal with an emphasis upon clothing which allows more freedom of movement. In many cases these styles of dress also give more exposure to the body, although the "unisex" look, where both men and women wear pants and shirts and have long hair, does not expose the body so much as provide for freer movement. Looser clothing and greater body movement has been accompanied by a change in attitude about the body and the image that one person conveys to another. Youth thus seem to be less concerned with "putting on a good front" than with appearing "real" and "natural." The body is seen less as an object to be decorated, corseted, and changed to conform to some norm of beauty, than it is to be accepted and presented in its natural state. Sex behavior among youth is seen in the same light, as a natural and acceptable part of life, where many of the older restrictions and rituals no longer seem appropriate or meaningful.

Research in the area of sex behavior among youth has stressed three general topics. First, there have been a number of studies in the last twenty-five years which have attempted to describe the number of persons in various groups who engage in such activities as petting, masturbation, and sexual intercourse. These studies have generally been used to answer the question of whether or not there has been a change in sex behavior among young people, or to what extent has there been a "sexual revolution?" Second, several studies have measured the attitudes of young people about sex behavior, attempting to answer the question, to what extent are young people in the 1970s more accepting of premarital and extra-marital sex behavior than were their parents and grandparents? Third, studies have investigated the meaning of sex behavior among young people who do engage in sexual intercourse. These studies generally have been aimed at describing the quality of interpersonal relationships which lead to sexual intercourse and the feelings and attitudes of those people who have engaged in such activities. These studies have tried to answer the question of what effect does sex behavior have upon those who engage in it? In all three of these areas of research there has been a great deal of controversy, so that it is necessary to review some of the literature to understand where the controversy stands at this point in time.

The "Sexual Revolution" Among Youth

The question of whether or not there has been a "sexual revolution" among youth usually is debated in terms of changes in percentages of various groups of young men and women who report having engaged in premarital sexual intercourse. Those who feel that there has been no real change argue that the "sexual revolution" began with the beginning of industrialism one hundred years ago and that youth in the 1960s and 1970s are not really more active sexually but are merely more willing to admit their activity than their parents and grandparents. Those who feel that there has been a "sexual revolution" in the last twenty-five years compare the results of recent studies to Alfred Kinsey's monumental studies of the sex behavior of men and women, published in 1948 and 1953.[2]

At this point in time there have been enough studies to begin to answer the question about whether there has been a "sexual revolution." As reviewed by Cannon and Long,[3] Kantner and Zelnik,[4] and Sorensen,[5] the results of twenty-eight studies of premarital sex behavior conducted since Kinsey's report in 1953 clearly indicate that there has been an increase in the percentages of young people who engage in premarital sexual intercourse, but that this change has been most "revolutionary" for women rather than for men. In general, the percentage of white men aged 15 to 25 who have had sexual intercourse before marriage has not increased very much in the last twenty-five years, but the number of white women aged 15 to 25 having premarital sexual intercourse has risen dramatically until today there is virtually no difference between the proportions of young men and women who engage in such behavior.

One of the first studies to show the nature of the change in sex behavior was that of Christensen and Gregg[6] which compared similar samples of college age men and women from Utah and the Midwest in 1958 and again in 1968. Their study revealed that in 1958 39.4 per cent of the men and 9.5 per cent of the women in Utah and 50.7 per cent of the men and 20.7 per cent of the women in the Midwest had had premarital sexual intercourse. By 1968 36.5 per cent of the men and 32.4 per cent of the women in Utah and 50.2 per cent of the men and 34.3 per cent of the women in the Midwest had had premarital sexual intercourse. These data indicated two important points about changes in sex behavior among youth. First, it is difficult to generalize about sex behavior for the entire American population. The percentages in this study clearly showed regional differences between the Intermountain (Utah) and Midwestern samples. Second, in both regions men's behavior changed very little, while women's sexual behavior showed a dramatic increase.

Although there have been few other studies that have made direct com-

---

[2] A. C. Kinsey, W. B. Pomeroy, and C. E. Martin, *Sexual Behavior In The Human Male* (Philadelphia: W. B. Saunders, 1948); A. C. Kinsey, W. B. Pomeroy, C. E. Martin, and P. H. Gebhard, *Sexual Behavior In The Human Female* (Philadelphia: W. B. Saunders, 1953).

[3] K. L. Cannon and R. Long, "Premarital Sexual Behavior In The Sixties," *The Journal of Marriage and the Family,* 33 (1971), pp. 36–49.

[4] J. F. Kantner and M. Zelnik, "Sexual Experience of Young Unmarried Women in the United States," *Family Planning Perspectives,* 4 (1972), pp. 9–18; J. F. Kantner and M. Zelnik, "Contraception and Pregnacy: Experience of Young Unmarried Women in the United States," *Family Planning Perspectives,* 5 (1973), pp. 21–35.

[5] R. C. Sorensen, *Adolescent Sexuality in Contemporary America: The Sorensen Report* (Cleveland: World Publishing Co., 1973).

[6] H. T. Christensen and C. F. Gregg, "Changing Sex Norms in America and Scandanavia," *The Journal of Marriage and the Family,* 32 (1970), pp. 616–627.

parisons of similar samples at different points in time, there have been a number of studies which report relatively large proportions of college women who have had premarital sexual intercourse, despite differences in samples, methodology, and geographical regions. Robinson [7] found that 28.7 per cent of 115 college women in Georgia had had premarital sexual experience. Luckey and Nass [8] reported that 43.2 per cent of women studied at 21 colleges across the United States had had premarital sexual intercourse. Davis [9] found that 26.9 per cent of college women in Kansas and 37 per cent of those over age 19 were nonvirginal. He also reported that out of a sample of 178 college women in Colorado 56 per cent had had premarital sexual intercourse. Kaats and Davis [10] found that 41 per cent of 222 college women in one sample and 44 per cent of 97 college women in another sample in Colorado had had premarital coitus. In one of the best studies of sex behavior among young women, Kantner and Zelnik [11] found that 14 per cent of unmarried women aged fifteen and 46 per cent of the unmarried nineteen-year-old women had had sexual intercourse.

Most of these studies have surveyed the sex behaviors of young men and women without attempting to compare findings with those of Kinsey. In a recent study reported by Hunt [12] such comparisons were made, and changes in sex behavior were discussed in detail. In this report, which studied the sex behaviors of 2,026 people of all ages in the United States, about 80 per cent of the single white men under age 25 and 75 per cent of the single white women under age 25 had had sexual intercourse. Compared to data from white subjects reported by Kinsey in 1953 this represented a slight increase in premarital sexual intercourse for men but a large increase for women, one-third of whom reported premarital sexual intercourse in 1953. Among married women under age 25 approximately 50 per cent in both 1953 and 1972 reported premarital sexual intercourse. Among younger people in this study premarital sexual intercourse was more frequent, with 80 per cent of the youngest women who married before age 25 reporting premarital sexual intercourse. The incidence of premarital sexual intercourse among noncollege men under the age of 17 was reported at 66 per cent in 1953 and 75 per cent in 1972; however, the percentage of young men aged 18 to 24 who reported having sexual relations with prostitutes dropped from about 33 per cent in 1953 to 3 per cent in 1972.

The rate of sexual intercourse also has increased in the last 20 years with

[7] I. E. Robinson, K. King, C. J. Dudley, and F. J. Clune, "Change In Sexual Behavior and Attitudes of College Students," *The Family Coordinator*, 17 (1968), pp. 119–123.

[8] E. B. Luckey and G. D. Nass, "A Comparison of Sexual Attitudes and Behavior in an International Sample," *The Journal of Marriage and the Family*, 31 (1969), pp. 364–379.

[9] K. E. Davis, "Sex on Campus: Is There a Revolution?" unpublished paper (Boulder, Colorado: Institute of Behavioral Sciences, University of Colorado, 1969).

[10] G. R. Kaats and K. E. Davis, "The Dynamics of Sexual Behavior of College Students," *The Journal of Marriage and the Family*, 32 (1970), pp. 390–399.

[11] Kantner and Zelnik, 1972.

[12] M. Hunt, "Sexual Behavior in the 1970s," *Playboy Magazine*, (October, 1973), pp. 85–207.

Kinsey reporting sexual intercourse 23 times a year by young single men and between 10 and 16 times a year by single women aged 16 to 25, while the Hunt study found that single men who had sexual intercourse did so at a median rate of 33 times a year and single women who had sexual intercourse did so at a median rate of more than 50 times a year. Young married persons between the ages of 16 and 24 also increase in rate of sexual intercourse, from a median of 130 times a year in Kinsey's study to 154 in the Hunt study.

The incidence of extra-marital sex behavior among young married men under age 25 has increased slightly in the last 20 years, with 32 per cent of young husbands reporting such behavior; however, there has been a marked increase in extra-marital sexual intercourse among young wives under age 25, with 9 per cent of Kinsey's sample reporting such behavior, but 24 per cent of Hunt's sample engaging in this activity.

While heterosexual sex behavior has increased generally and particularly among young women, homosexual sex behavior among young people appeared to have shown little change in the last 20 years. Approximately 20 per cent of the men and 10 per cent of the women aged 18 to 24 in the Hunt study reported ever having had a homosexual relationship. These figures were very similar to those presented by Kinsey in 1953 and were difficult to interpret, since for many of the subjects there had been only one brief homosexual contact in early adolescence which was more indicative of experimental trial behavior than of a long range preference for homosexuality.

The results of all of the studies of sex behavior among youth not only support the notion that there has been a "sexual revolution" but also point to the fact that there seems to have been a general leveling out of differences among various groupings of young people in terms of sex behavior. For example, the old concept of a "double standard" of sex behavior that made it somewhat more acceptable for men to engage in sexual intercourse before marriage than for women has apparently disappeared. The current data reveal that the percentages of men and women who have premarital sexual experience are about the same. Second, social class differences in sex behavior do not appear to be so great as reported in studies made in the 1940s and 50s. In the past it was often noted that lower class youth began sexual activity earlier than middle and upper class youth and that larger proportions of lower class youth were sexually active before marriage than either middle or upper class youth. The recent data seem to show that in terms of the age at which sexual activity begins, the percentages of men and women engaging in sexual intercourse, and the variety of sex acts practiced, the middle and upper classes are not much different than the lower classes. In fact, Kantner and Zelnik [13] found that among white women between the ages of 15 and 19, girls from affluent homes were somewhat more likely to have had premarital sexual intercourse than girls from poorer homes.

[13] Kantner and Zelnik, 1972.

A third trend, which is supported by data from Kantner and Zelnik, is that racial differences in sex behavior patterns appear to be disappearing also. Black women aged 15 to 19 tend to begin having sexual intercourse at an earlier age than whites, with 80 per cent of the blacks and 40 per cent of the white women reporting having had sexual intercourse by the age of 19; however, this racial difference tends to decrease and level out after age 20. In the State of Georgia the Governor's Special Council on Family Planning estimates that of the 33 per cent of the women aged 15 to 19 who are sexually active half are black and half are white.[14]

It must be remembered in light of these findings about the lessening of sex, social class, and racial differences in sex behavior among youth that there still remain significant regional differences in patterns of sex behavior. For example, Packard [15] found that among white college students 69 per cent of the men at Southern schools and 46 per cent of the men at Midwestern schools reported having had premarital sexual intercourse, while 57 per cent of the women at Eastern schools and 25 per cent of the women at Midwestern schools reported such activity. Thus, Eastern women were more active sexually than Midwestern men but less active than Southern men. In another case, Reiss [16] studied sex behavior of black and white men at high schools and colleges in New York and Virginia, finding that in both states black men were more active sexually than white men; however, white men in New York were more active sexually than black men in Virginia.

One finding of particular importance in the recent studies of changes in sexual behavior among youth is that knowledge about sexual reproduction and the use of adequate birth control techniques has not kept up with the increase in sexual activity, especially among youth aged 15 to 19.

The use of contraceptives by youth does not appear to be as universal as is often believed and varies greatly by age group. In the study by Kantner and Zelnik,[17] using a national probability sample of teenagers 15 to 19, it was found that over 75 per cent of the 1,300 sexually active teenagers in the sample had used contraception at some time; however, 53 per cent failed to use any method the last time they had had intercourse and less than 20 per cent said that they always used some method. More than 50 per cent of the contraceptive users in this study relied primarily upon the male controlled methods of withdrawal and the condom. Slightly more than 20 per cent of the sexually active teenage women, both whites and blacks, used the pill; however, the regularity of pill usage varied greatly by age, with regular usage being associated with greater age and frequency of sexual intercourse. As with sexual behavior itself, there were no significant differ-

[14] R. Bahr, "Questions and Answers Concerning Teenage Pregnancy in Georgia," unpublished paper (Atlanta, Georgia: Georgia Department of Human Resources, The Governor's Special Council on Family Planning, October, 1973).

[15] V. Packard, *The Sexual Wilderness* (New York: David McKay Co., 1968).

[16] I. L. Reiss, *The Social Context of Premarital Permissiveness* (New York: Holt, Rinehart, and Winston, 1967).

[17] Kantner and Zelnik, 1972.

ences in the use of contraceptives between social class or racial groups. Among sexually active subjects 40 per cent of the poor and 49 per cent of the nonpoor used contraception at last intercourse, while 43 per cent of black teenagers and 48 per cent of white teenagers reported using some method at last intercourse. For younger teenage girls, aged 15 to 17, blacks were more likely than whites to be using an effective method of birth control, such as the pill or an interuterine device (IUD), a finding which was attributed to the fact that young black women are more likely to be enrolled in public family planning clinics.

The consequences of this haphazard usage of contraception by teenagers are that six out of ten first births to teenagers aged 15 to 19 are conceived premaritally. In Georgia, it is estimated by the Governor's Special Council on Family Planning that one out of every three teenage mothers bears her child out of wedlock and that half of all illegitimate births in 1972 were to teenage mothers.[18]

Teenagers' knowledge of sex and reproduction is generally inadequate. Only 40 per cent of Kantner and Zelnik's sample of sexually active teenage women had a generally correct notion of the period of greatest risk of pregnancy in their monthly cycle; the majority thought that it was during their menstrual period. Among these same women 28 per cent of the whites and 55 per cent of the blacks thought they could not become pregnant easily, even when they had unprotected intercourse. It seems clear that, given these data and the fact that the most popular contraceptive techniques are those which are male controlled, there is a pressing need for greater sex education among youth with an emphasis upon the facts of reproduction and the use of contraceptives by both men and women.

Among youth aged 20 to 25 contraceptives and adequate knowledge about sexual reproduction appear to be more prevalent, because the majority of this age group are married, are more experienced, and are more likely to be enrolled in birth control programs sponsored by family planning centers. Fertility rates dropped 8.8 per cent for all women in the late 1960s, from 91.1 births per 1000 women in 1967 to 83.1 births per 1000 women in 1972; however, the teenage fertility rate declined only 3.7 per cent during this period, while the rate for women aged 20 to 44 declined by 9.9 per cent.[19]

Changing Attitudes About Sex Among Youth

Regardless of whether one wishes to accept the evidence of a radical change in sexual behavior itself as supporting the concept of a "sexual revolution," it is hard to dispute the evidence that there has been a radical change in the ways in which young people think about sex and their widespread acceptance of sexual intimacy as a valid form of behavior. Stated bluntly, sex is "in," and virginity is "out." Or, as Jarl E. Dyrud has written,

[18] Bahr, 1973, p. 3.
[19] Ibid., 2.

We are all aware that in the past decade there has been something special about the way the popular culture has taken up sex as a preoccupation, or rather as an obsession. I don't mean pornography either. I mean the new sexual mythology that views orgasm as a panacea for all of life's dreariness.

. . . Even if sexual behavior has not changed dramatically, the meanings have. Words are powerful determinants of how we think of ourselves—how we feel about ourselves. They define success and failure. As Ogden Nash, the poet laureate of Baltimore, put it:

> Sticks and stones may break my bones
> But words can break my heart.[20]

Although there is some evidence that the attitudes of high school students toward sexuality have not changed in the last decade, studies of college students seem to reveal that there has been a general liberalization of attitudes about what is acceptable sexual behavior. Christensen and Gregg,[21] cited earlier, found that among college students in Utah 23.3 per cent of the men and 2.9 per cent of the women approved of premarital sexual intercourse in 1958, while in 1968, 38.4 per cent of the men and 23.5 per cent of the women approved. For the Midwest, 46.7 per cent of the men and 17.4 per cent of the women approved of premarital sexual intercourse in 1958, while 55.4 per cent of the men and 37.7 per cent of the women approved of such behavior in 1968. In a poll of over 2,000 college students representing a cross-section of American universities, the Yankelovich[22] survey conducted in 1969 and again in 1971 found that only 34 per cent in 1969 and 25 per cent in 1971 felt that "casual premarital sexual relations" were morally wrong. Forty-two per cent in 1969 and 26 per cent in 1971 felt that "relations between consenting homosexuals" were morally wrong. While 77 per cent in 1969 and 57 per cent in 1971 felt that "extra-marital sexual relations" were morally wrong. With regard to changing the values of society this poll found that 43 per cent in 1969 and 56 per cent in 1971 said that they would welcome "more acceptance of sexual freedom," while 24 per cent in 1969 and 13 per cent in 1971 said that they would reject such a change.

While there do not appear to be comparable data for the noncollege population of youth, it seems clear that attitudes about the morality of sexual behavior and the social acceptability of sexual freedom have been changing very rapidly in the direction of greater acceptance of sexual freedom, especially among unmarried persons.

The Context and Meaning of Sex Behavior Among Youth

The context in which this increased sexual behavior among youth occurs is most often that of a serious and potentially long term relationship between

---

[20] J. E. Dyrud, "The Sexual Revolution: Fact or Fantasy?" *The University of Chicago Magazine*, LXVI (January–February, 1974), p. 21.

[21] Christensen and Gregg, 1970.

[22] D. Yankelovich, *The Changing Values On Campus* (New York: Pocket Books, 1972), pp. 37–42.

a young man and woman. In most cases both men and women seem to feel that premarital sexual intercourse is acceptable within the framework of an emotionally involved relationship, and the extent to which they agree that such behavior is acceptable is directly related to the intensity of the emotional involvement.

Perhaps the best data supporting the relationship between approval for sexual relations and level of interpersonal involvement have been provided by Reiss.[23]

Approval of Petting and Full Sexual Relations by Stage of Relationship

	Adults %		Students %	
	FOR MEN	FOR WOMEN	FOR MEN	FOR WOMEN
Petting:				
When engaged	60.8	56.1	85.0	81.8
In love	59.4	52.6	80.4	75.2
Strong affection	54.3	45.6	67.0	56.7
No affection	28.6	20.3	34.3	18.0
Full Sex Relations:				
When engaged	19.5	16.9	52.2	44.0
In love	17.6	14.2	47.6	38.7
Strong affection	16.3	12.5	36.9	27.2
No affection	11.9	7.4	20.8	10.8
N	1390	1411	811	806

In the study reported by Hunt [24] it was found that among young women, ". . . the contemporary norm is 'permissiveness with affection.' In Kinsey's study, almost half of those married women who had had premarital intercourse had had it only with their fiancés; in our own sample, while twice as many have had premarital intercourse, an even larger proportion—slightly over half—limited it to their fiancés; and among the youngest women in our study, the figure is still higher. It is very likely that there are more single women today who are willing to have intercourse on a purely physical level, without emotional ties, but most sexually liberated single girls still feel liberated only with the context of affectionate or loving relationships." The increases which this study found in extra-marital sexual relations among the young were not indicative of a sensation oriented, carefree disregard for emotional ties, but were signs of a breakdown in some marriages. Such extra-marital affairs were considered a major violation of trust and commitment, resulting almost always in divorce. Practices given much publicity, such as

23 Reiss, 1967, p. 29.
24 Hunt, 1973, pp. 200–201.

mate swapping or "swinging," were engaged in by less than 2 per cent of the married men and women under 25.

The meanings which are attached to sexual behavior by those youth who engage in it before marriage are not entirely positive, and there is a growing body of literature pointing to the uncertainties and anxiety which accompany sexual behavior for some youth. In a study by Maslow and Sakoda [25] positive self-esteem was shown to be associated with participation in premarital sexual intercourse; however, a later study by Stratton and Spitzer found that "permissive sexual attitudes are associated with an unfavorable self-concept." [26] Offer concluded from his eight-year longitudinal study of middle class high school students that,

> The data demonstrate a tremendous variability among adolescents in their attitudes toward sex. About 50 per cent are comfortable about it and 50 per cent are not.
>
> Another study shows that when college students were asked about their current love affairs, 25 per cent of the females and 35 per cent of the males responded that they were more active sexually than they want to be.
>
> This bit of information can be interpreted in many ways. Possibly they feel guilty about their behavior, or they do more things, because they think the adult world expects it from them. Possible, too, is that each young adult believes that his or her partner demands more sex than either really wants to give. But no matter how the data are interpreted, we end up with the young adult in conflict over his or her sexual behavior. [27]

In another study of unmarried women who sought birth control advice at a large Midwestern university, Zweben and Bardwick [28] found that most young women sought the pill because their boy friends wanted them to. As summarized by Douvan, "Many of them said that they were not so eager for a sexual relationship, but felt that if they refused they would lose the boy friend. Others showed fear of abandonment on projective measures. These young women were in a double bind and no-win game: if they refused the boy friend sex, they will lose him, and if they agree to sex protected by the pill, they fear he will take the sex and *then* they will lose him. It was quite clear in the interviews that the girls wanted love and commitment and were giving sex as a gift of love or in hope of obtaining commitment. They were

[25] A. Maslow and J. M. Sakoda, "Volunteer Error In the Kinsey Study," in J. Himeloch and S. F. Fava (eds.), *Sexual Behavior In American Society* (New York: W. W. Norton, 1955), pp. 119–125.

[26] J. R. Stratton and S. P. Spitzer, "Sexual Permissiveness and Self-Evaluation: A Question of Substance and A Question of Method," *The Journal of Marriage and the Family*, 29 (1967), pp. 434–441.

[27] D. Offer, "Attitudes Toward Sexuality in a Group of 1500 Middle Class Teen-agers," *The Journal of Youth and Adolescence*, 1 (1972), pp. 81–90.

[28] J. M. Bardwick, "A Predictive Study of Psychological and Psychosomatic Responses to Oral Contraceptives," in J. T. Fawcett (ed.), *Psychological Perspectives on Population* (New York: Basic Books, 1972).

anxious about the threat of abandonment to an extent that does not mesh with concepts of recreational sex and the new morality." [29]

In summary, sexual behavior among youth is not representative of a disregard for emotional ties and is not promiscuous thrill seeking. Instead it appears to be part of the attempt by youth to achieve a sense of identity through affectionate, emotionally involved forms of physical intimacy. At the same time that the general culture seems to be caught up in what Dyrud calls the "current doctrine of sexual fulfillment as salvation," youth are finding that the increasing acceptability of premarital sexual behavior is not a total blessing but carries with it anxieties and tensions which their parents and grandparents seldom experienced. This increase in the amount and acceptability of sexual behavior is a new phenomenon for the current generation of youth, and, while the roots of this behavior remain firmly in the deepest emotions and loyalties of one person's attachment to another, it poses a unique challenge to the structure and meaning of the institution of legal marriage.

2. Sex Roles for Youth

The term "sex role" refers to those social behaviors and attitudes about expected behaviors which have been assigned by the dominant culture to one sex or the other. In our culture, for example, the role of "homemaker" involves both a set of behavioral skills and a set of attitudes about who one is and what one does that predisposes an individual to act out those skills. It is possible for the "homemaker" role to be played by both men and women; however, in our culture this role has been sex typed as more appropriate for women to play than for men. Women are encouraged and taught how to act out this role and are rewarded for doing so, while men who act out this role are discouraged and even punished for doing so. Not all social roles are sex typed in this way; however, it is one of the major tasks of youth to distinguish which sex-typed roles are appropriate for them and which sex roles they will act out in the process of becoming adults in our society.

The literature on this subject has been confusing because often the term "sex role identity" has been used synonomously with the term "sex role preference." "Sex role identity" usually refers to a person's awareness and acceptance of one's biological gender. This involves both a recognition that one is physiologically male or female and an awareness that there are culturally defined attitudes and behaviors which go with one's gender. As Kagan[30] and Kohlberg[31] have shown, most Americans develop such a "sex

29 E. Douvan, "Sex Differences in the Opportunities, Demands, and Developments of Youth," in R. J. Havighurst and P. H. Dreyer (eds.), *Seventy-fourth Yearbook of the National Society for the Study of Education: American Youth in the Seventies* (Chicago: The National Society for the Study of Education, 1975).

30 J. Kagan, "The Acquisition and Significance of Sex-typing and Sex-role Identity," in M. Hoffman and L. Hoffman (eds.), *Review of Child Development Research*, Vol. 1. (New York: Russell Sage, 1964), pp. 137–168.

31 L. Kohlberg, "A Cognitive-Developmental Analysis of Children's Sex Role Concepts and Attitudes," in E. Maccoby (ed.), *The Development of Sex Differences* (Stanford, California: Stanford University Press, 1966), pp. 82–172.

role identity" by the age of six or seven and hold it for the rest of their lives. The term "sex role preference" has been used to refer to an individual's conscious choice of a certain set of sex-typed attitudes and behaviors. Developmentally, this process follows the formation of a "sex role identity" and may change from time to time, whereas "sex role identity" is stable and unchanging. A sixteen-year-old woman, for example, with a "sex role identity" of a woman may prefer to act out what have traditionally been defined as male sex role attitudes and behaviors, giving her what some would call a "masculine sex role preference." For all but a few youths there is little ambiguity or choice in their "sex role identity"; however, in the area of "sex role preference," which implies a choice of socially sex-typed role behaviors and attitudes, there is increasing flexibility as our society changes its notions of how roles should be sex typed.

In an affluent society the family, as described by Parsons and Bales,[32] has two primary functions: to socialize the young and to stabilize adult personality development. Increased leisure time gives men more time to spend with their families and encourages men to play more of the expressive, interpersonal roles. At the same time, the use of mechanical devices to perform housework chores and the greater availability of education gives women the time and preparation for the acting out of task roles outside the home. These opportunities for greater role flexibility by both men and women did not lead to the actual playing of different sex roles in the years shortly after World War II however. Instead, the family unit became a source of recreation both in the sense of providing the social environment for the use of leisure time and in the sense of becoming a focus for the care and raising of children. The flight to the suburbs revived some of the characteristics of the agrarian era, but even though suburban living gave each family its own land again, there was no real economic function to be fulfilled by using this land. In this environment men channelled their efforts into do-it-yourself projects, while women concentrated their efforts on raising children, a process which Slater called the "ultradomestication of the American female."[33]

The children of these ultradomesticated families have become the youth of the 1970s, and like so many generations before them they are looking for new and better ways to fulfill themselves as people. These youth, unlike their parents, take economic affluence, technological skill, and leisure time for granted because they have never known any other way of life. For them the ultradomesticated family seems rigidly materialistic and narrow in its role possibilities. Thus, they seek to take advantage of the possibilities for flexible sex role playing and alternative life styles which their parents chose to overlook.

The actual changes in sex role preference patterns have primarily involved the roles available to and preferred by women. Shortly after World War II

---

[32] T. Parsons and R. F. Bales, *Family, Socialization, and Interaction and Process* (New York: The Free Press, 1955).

[33] P. Slater, *The Pursuit of Loneliness: American Culture at the Breaking Point* (Boston: Beacon Press, 1970), pp. 53–80.

Mirra Komarovsky [34] pointed out that college women of that era seemed to fall into two basic sex role preference types, the first of which was the "feminine role" which had a "common core of attributes defining the proper attitude to men, family, work, love, etc., and a set of personality traits often described with reference to the male sex role as "not as dominant, or aggressive as men" or "more emotional, sympathetic." The second sex role type was the "modern" role. According to Komarovsky this "other and more recent role is, in a sense, no *sex* role at all, because it partly obliterates the differentiation in sex. It demands of the woman much the same virtues, patterns of behavior, and attitude that it does of the men of corresponding age." In studying these sex role types among college women of the 1940s, Komarovsky noted that,

> The generalization emerging from these [studies] is the existence of serious contradictions between two roles present in the social environment of the college women. The goals set by each role are mutually exclusive, and the fundamental personality traits each evokes are at points diametrically opposed, so that what are assets for one become liabilities for the other, and the full realization of one role threatens defeat in the other. [35]

For Komarovsky the "serious contradictions" in the sex roles available to educated women were an "intrinsic" part of the adolescent woman's development and often resulted in feelings of anxiety, emotional problems, and confusion about personal goals, aspirations, and achievement behavior.

Parsons and Bales noted that family roles tended to fall into two general categories. The first of these were the "instrumental" or "task oriented" roles which required a concern for dealing with the world outside the family, providing the resources necessary for family survival and welfare, and an ability to tolerate the hostility which such activities were likely to elicit from others outside the family. The second of these were the "expressive" or "group maintenance" roles which focused upon interpersonal harmony and satisfactions within the family, requiring emotional sensitivity and an ability to give others pleasure. Within the family "instrumental" roles were usually played by men, while "expressive" roles were usually played by women, and to some extent the "instrumental-expressive" distinction corresponded to sex-typed roles. Yet, as Parsons and Bales noted, both husbands and wives played each role at some time, depending upon the nature of a specific situation. [36] Thus the two role orientations often were sex typed but were not mutually exclusive and did not lead to the same type of "serious contradictions" that Komarovsky had found.

By the 1960s the discussion of sex roles tended to revolve around the

[34] M. Komarovsky, "Cultural Contradictions and Sex Roles," *American Journal of Sociology*, 52 (1946), pp. 184–189; M. Komarovsky, *Women in the Modern World, Their Education and Their Dilemmas* (Boston: Little Brown, 1953).

[35] M. Komarovsky, 1946, p. 186.

[36] Parsons and Bales, 1955.

stated preferences and aspirations of young women and men with regard to the relative importance they attached to their family as opposed to their occupational career. For young men the options had not changed very much. As Douvan and Adelson [37] found, the basic orientation of young men was around the question of "What will my occupation be?" Involved in the answer to this question were educational aspirations, upward social mobility, job security, and income level, while issues of marriage, children, and home were of lesser importance, usually thought to be matters which would be resolved after the occupational and status issues were resolved. For young women the central concern seemed to be, "Who will my husband be?" This question carried with it the primary assumption that a woman would see her husband and family as most important to her, with her own status, security, and satisfaction being derived from her ability to establish and maintain a family. According to Adelson and Douvan, the sex role behavior of the adolescents they studied were quite traditional, and they found relatively few subjects of either sex who seemed to be in great conflict over these issues.

Other studies in the 1960s began to focus on the sex role preferences of young women and the relationships between those preferences and various types of attitudes and behaviors. These studies found that among women sex role preferences were changing as more women expressed interest in a "modern," "instrumental," "liberal," or "career" role orientation than ever before, and that a young woman's sex role preference was related to other attitudes and behaviors, such as motivation, educational achievement, occupational plans, desire for children, and rewards deemed desirable. In addition, it was found that the contradictions in sex roles which Komarovsky described for the college women were becoming more widely felt by all sectors of the population of women.

One of the most interesting findings with regard to young women's sex role perception has been the observation that how a young woman perceives of herself acting out various sex roles is related to attitudes about achievement goals and to actual behavior in settings requiring competitive behavior in order to achieve a goal. In some cases it has been shown that women who have had experience with "success" and who score high on projective measures of "need for achievement" also seem to inhibit their own achievement behavior when competing against men. Horner [38] described this behavior as "fear of success," noting that for women, "success," as traditionally defined in terms of being academically superior and receiving awards for excellence, was often accompanied by "negative consequences," such as social ostracism, feelings of guilt, and conflict with peers. Presumably this fear was based

[37] E. Douvan and J. Adelson, *The Adolescent Experience* (New York: John Wiley and Sons, 1966).

[38] M. Horner, "Sex Differences in Achievement, Motivation, and Performance in Competitive and Noncompetitive Situations," unpublished doctoral dissertation, The University of Michigan, 1968; M. Horner, "The Motive to Avoid Success and Changing Aspirations of College Women," in J. Bardwick (ed.), *Readings on the Psychology of Women* (New York: Harper and Row, 1972), pp. 62–67.

upon the conflict in sex roles which women raised in a society which stresses noncompetition for women felt when they tried to achieve goals which required aggressive and competitive behavior against men. This research pointed up the fact that traditional sex roles for men and women tended to minimize competition between the sexes by assigning different task roles to men and women. As sex roles become more diffuse and flexible, issues of competition become more relevant and anxiety producing for both sexes. While Horner's study found that over 60 per cent of the women in her sample showed "fear of success," as opposed to 10 per cent of the men, a more recent follow up by Hoffman,[39] which studied the same variables at the same university, found that the same percentage of women showed "fear of success" (over 60 per cent) but that a larger number of men (over 70 per cent) showed "fear of success."

Komarovsky's recent study of sex role contradictions among men [40] included data on changes in the extent to which women deliberately minimized their intellectual competence when with men. Comparing answers to the same questions given to college women in 1950 by Wallin [41] and in 1970 and 1971, she found that women in the 1970s were much less likely to hide their ability than the women in 1950. In response to the question, "When on dates how often have you pretended to be intellectually inferior to the man?" 32 per cent said "very often, often, or several times," 26 per cent said "once or twice," and 42 per cent said "never" in 1950, as compared with 15 per cent, 30 per cent, and 55 per cent respectively in 1971.[42]

These studies have begun to clarify the nature of the conflicts and problems involved with the changes in women's sex role preferences; however, we are only beginning to understand the complexities of this change. The important point of all this seems to be that many young women are not playing the "traditional" role nor even expecting to play that role, but are working out various types of role combinations, permutations, and innovations. It is no longer the norm for young women to aspire to the classical "traditional" role. Instead there seems to be a great deal of interest in young women to do more than get married and have a family and to transcend the ultradomesticated role.

Young women today seem to be involved in a process of defining sex roles in a new way. The "serious contradictions" inherent in the choice of "feminine" or "modern" roles described by Komarovsky have not disappeared. If anything these contradictions are felt by most young women, not just the college educated elite. What has changed, however, is that young women

[39] L. Hoffman, "Fear of Success in Males and Females: 1965 and 1972," *Journal of Consulting and Clinical Psychology*, 1974, in press.

[40] M. Komarovsky, "Cultural Contradictions and Sex Roles: The Masculine Case," *American Journal of Sociology*, 78 (1973), pp. 873–884.

[41] P. Wallin, "Cultural Contradictions and Sex Roles: A Repeat Study," *American Sociological Review*, 15 (1950), pp. 288–293.

[42] M. Komarovsky, 1973, p. 878.

are attempting to go beyond a choice of playing either the "feminine" role OR the "modern" role and are developing a combined role where they go to school, take up a career AND get married, have children, and make a home. Thus the dilemma which their mothers faced of having to choose between a family or a career has been replaced for young women today by the dilemma of trying to have both a family and a career. To resolve this latest dilemma requires a young woman to be goal directed, self-assertive, and highly adaptable. In order to enjoy the best of both the instrumental and expressive roles, she must be able and willing to tolerate the tension and hostility which role experimentation sometimes produces and must be resourceful enough to resolve role conflicts in creative and personally meaningful ways. There are few models for young women today, for no other American generation has sought to synthesize sex roles, but in a technologically advanced society with an affluent economy and ideals which encourage independence and mobility, young women are finding a suitable environment for role experimentation which promises to have sweeping consequences for the entire society.

One of the most important consequences of young women's sex role innovations has been that the sex role choices of men have begun to change. As women begin to take up occupations which in the past were sex typed as appropriate only for men and as the nature of the economy shifts towards an emphasis upon service occupations which require expressive and interpersonal skills, the pattern of sex-typed occupational roles has become less clear and less functional. Some biological attributes of sex roles, such as distinctions made on the basis of physical strength requirements for the successful completion of jobs, have become irrelevant in an economy where machines do most of the heavy work. Other biological attributes of sex roles, such as personality traits or physical stamina thought to be important for certain jobs, have been proved false, as women have displayed the same traits and stamina on the job as men. The effect of these facts has been to destroy many old notions about sex differences and sex related job requirements, so that in a service based economy most occupations can be successfully performed by both men and women. The effect of this upon men has been to vastly increase their own occupational choices, and young men today are seeking careers in fields previously dominated by women, such as nursery and elementary school teaching, nursing, physical therapy, social work, and telephone operating.

At this point in time, however, the changes in men's sex role preferences has not been so global as have been those of young women. Men tend to play more different types of roles but they do not appear to have changed their basic attitudes about their role making the way women have. Most young men still think about their own roles in terms of traditional educational and occupational stereotypes, requiring aggressive, analytical, instrumental behavior. They also still tend to see as ideal the family roles which their parents and grandparents experienced.

Komarovsky [43] found that among men at an Ivy League college 55 per cent said that they wanted their future wives to combine a career and family in some way, while 40 per cent said that they did not want their wives to have careers outside of the home. In general she reported that these men's attitudes about wives' roles were full of inconsistencies. While 70 per cent seemed to desire women who were their intellectual equal and said that they felt no stress when in the company of intellectually equal or superior women, almost all seemed to feel that after marriage the wife should bear full responsibility for the children and should stay at home while the children were young. Only 7 per cent said that they would modify their own role behavior in order to share homemaking and child care roles so that the wife could have a career. Thus, the men in this study appeared to be ambivalent about their future family roles, saying that they held "liberal" attitudes about women's roles in general but also saying that their own wives should in fact act out a more "traditional" set of role behaviors. As Komarovsky summarized, "The ideological support for the belief in sharp sex role differentiation in marriage has weakened, but the belief itself has not been relinquished." [44]

It seems clear that the major changes in sex role behaviors among youth in the immediate future are going to be brought about by women, and that women will struggle with the conflicts present in sex role choice for some time. It also seems clear that young men's sex role choices will continue to expand but that their attitudes and behaviors in this area will not change much until their basic attitudes about marriage and the sharing of the responsibilities of caring for children also change. In the case of both young men and women the crucible in which these changes in sex role preferences and behaviors is acted out will be the institution of marriage, and it is to the structure and meaning of that institution that we must now turn.

3. MARRIAGE AMONG YOUTH

At the outset of this paper it was noted that the legal institution of marriage seems to be as popular among Americans in the 1970s as ever before. Yet among youth it was noted that marriage no longer seems to carry with it the same prerequisites and prerogatives that it formerly did and that youth were approaching marriage more tentatively, marrying at later ages than their parents and apparently revising the meaning of marriage. It was noted that premarital sexual intercourse was becoming almost normative for today's youth and that these youth were using such sexual relationship not promiscuously but as serious attempts at coping with problems of identity, intimacy, and human sexuality. Furthermore, previously described changes in patterns of sex role preferences among young men and especially among young women pointed to fundamental shifts in family activities and the fact that

[43] M. Komarovsky, 1973.
[44] Ibid., p. 879.

role functions were being defined outside of the context of marriage. All of this information raises questions of whether marriage is an obsolete institution and what marriage means for youth today and in the future.

The new attitudes about marriage are perhaps best expressed in studies of college students. Among these young people in institutions of higher education across the country there seems to be a universal set of values which stress the importance of love, autonomy, knowledge, and family. The Yankelovich [45] profile of college youth in 1971 found that out of a list of 18 value choices students listed as the most important, "love," "friendship," "education," "expressing your opinion," and "family," while rating as least important "living a clean, moral life," "religion," "patriotism," "beauty," and, last of all, "money." Thus, while there appears to be consensus about value, particularly high value given to "love" and "family," there is not such agreement about the place of marriage or the effectiveness of the traditional family structure. In response to the question, "Is marriage obsolete?", 24 per cent of the Yankelovich sample in 1969 agreed, while 76 per cent disagreed. By 1971 the same question was agreed on by 34 per cent of college youth questioned, while 66 per cent disagreed, an important change in attitude over such a short period and one which indicated how rapidly views about marriage were being revised. Also in the 1971 study, Yankelovich's college sample asked, "Does the traditional family structure work?" To this question 71 per cent said "yes," but 12 per cent said "no," and another 17 per cent were not sure. Questioned about attitudes towards being married, 61 per cent said they looked forward to being married, but 14 per cent said they did not look forward to being married, and 18 per cent said that they "didn't know." To a question about interest in having children, 79 per cent said they were interested, 9 per cent said they were not interested, and 12 per cent were unsure. Finally, when asked about interest in living in communes and collectives, 51 per cent said they were not at all interested, while 36 per cent expressed interest (31 per cent for short term and 5 per cent as a permanent choice), and 13 per cent were unsure. [46]

What is striking in these figures is not the fact that the majority holds traditional views about marriage, but the fact that there is a sizeable and growing minority of young people who do not hold traditional views and who are actively interested in exploring alternative life styles to those implied by traditional marriage. Where past generations generally held marriage and family as important life goals and seemed to agree about what they meant, among today's youth there is not the same unanimity of opinion about either the desirability or the meaning of marriage. As an estimation, it seems reasonable to say that about two-thirds of all youth today continue to hold fairly traditional views about marriage, while one-third are actively seeking new forms and meanings in marriage.

[45] Yankelovich, 1972, pp. 37–39.
[46] Ibid., pp. 43–45.

Marriage As a Means

In the traditional sense marriage has served as a *means* to achieving certain personal and social ends. Entered into as a legal contract by means of a ritualized social ceremony, marriage was seen as the only way to achieve legitimate sexual gratification, to have children, and to be admitted to full status as an adult. Within the family instrumental or task accomplishment roles were usually played by husbands, while expressive or group maintenance roles were usually played by wives. Normative behavior within this traditional view of marriage requires women to abstain from sexual behavior before or outside of marriage and requires that children can only be borne "legitimately" by married women. Men are required to act in a responsible fashion, looking after the financial security and general welfare of his family. These expectations were rigid, allowing for little variation, and were based upon a conception of marriage which saw it as a permanent contract between two people.

This traditional marriage served as a means for individuals to achieve certain personal goals, such as parenthood, adult status, security, and independence from parents. It also served as a means for society to achieve certain group goals, such as the control of sexual impulses, the socialization of children, the stabilization of adult personality, and the preservation of social customs and norms which were considered essential to the group's survival. As a means to these personal and group goals marriage required individuals to obey social custom and ritual at the expense of individual psychological needs. So great were the social rewards for being married that women sacrificed personal ambitions and talents to act out traditional roles as wife, homemaker, and mother, and men gave up mobility and independence to act out the roles of husband, provider, and father. In many schools and colleges women who were married were not allowed to continue in school with their peers, apparently because they had advanced in status to adulthood by the fact of being married and thus were expected to share a different set of goals that somehow made further schooling unnecessary.

It is interesting that in the United States marriage has most often been seen as a voluntary contract entered into by the bride and groom, with the consent, but not necessarily the initiative of the parents; whereas, in many Asian and some European cultures marriages are entirely arranged by the parents, without even the knowledge of the bride and groom. This perhaps explains why in America there has always been a romanticism about "falling in love" and "marrying for love." Given little or no parental guidance and refusing to accept the sociological reality that marriage was a means to an end and not an end itself, young people traditionally have fantasized about "love" and "being in love" as a convenient defense against the possibility that marriage meant giving up part of oneself in order to attain social respectability, security, and the opportunity to produce a legitimate heir.

What perhaps most distinguishes the traditional majority of young people today from the minority who seek new forms and meaning in marriage is their attitude towards the necessity of marriage. The traditional majority see marriage as a necessary part of their lives, without which they will not be able to accomplish their life goals and feel truly "successful." The growing minority, however, do not see marriage as necessary and consider it to be only one alternative among several other life styles. For this group life goals and satisfactions can be attained with or without marriage; therefore, marriage is not a necessary means to certain goals but becomes itself an end, deliberately chosen because it offers rewards not found in unmarried life no matter how sexually liberated and open such a life might be.

To a large extent the attempt to find new meaning and purpose in marriage is a result of the fact that marriage is no longer a social necessity to the same extent that it formerly was. A person today can live with another person, can participate in sexual intercourse, can have children—either naturally or by adoption—and can be accepted by many groups as a fully functioning adult without being married in the legal or official social sense. The legal benefits of marriage, such as joint ownership of property, protection from liability, increased credit, inheritance guarantees, and dependency protection for wives and children, are not available without marriage, but these benefits of marriage do not seem important to most youth and are likely to become less significant with the passage of the Equal Rights Amendment to the U.S. Constitution. Without the necessity of marriage, the reasons for marrying become personal and psychological, rather than institutional and sociological.

Marriage As an End

For the growing proportion of youth seeking to find new meaning in marriage, marriage has become a goal representing affirmation of personal identity, psychological intimacy, mutual pleasure giving, the promise of continued personal growth, and a transcendent relationship between two human beings. As an end, rather than as a means, marriage becomes a commitment to another person and to one's own sense of personal identity.[47] Through such a commitment, which all youth hope will be permanent, the individual is free from the uncertainty of choosing from among alternative partners and life styles, so that the effect of marriage is not to restrict or stabilize personal growth but to open it up to complete self-expression and development. Because both members are committed to themselves as well as to each other, each is free to play whatever roles seem most comfortable and practical in the marriage. Stereotypic family roles become obsolete in such a marriage, because both members may be in school or working and must share roles of provider, homemaker, and child socializer. In such a marriage children are not required but may well be desired as the couple grow to form a relationship which can take proper care of children.

[47] "The conscious feeling of having a personal identity is based on two simultaneous observations: the immediate perception of one's selfsameness and continuity in time; and the simultaneous perception of the fact that others recognize one's sameness and continuity." E. Erikson, "Identity and the Life Cycle," *Psychological Issues*, 1 (1959), p. 23.

The essence of marriage as a goal is in the identity formation process described by Erik Erikson [48] and elaborated by Kenneth Keniston.[49] The adolescent, faced with the psychosocial conflict between "identity formation and role diffusion," enters the stage of life called "youth" with an acute sensitivity to his own state. Among other characteristics this archetypical youth lacks the ability to make "commitments" and to experience psychological "intimacy," so he spends a great deal of his time play acting roles, being enthused by various ideologies, and being physically intimate with others as he attempts to realize his or her own identity. The act of making a "commitment" to another person, as in marriage, thus represents a crucial step in identity formation. It is for this reason, not because the legal contract is inviolate or because divorce is impossible, that young people who see marriage as an end take it so seriously. Marriage represents the most significant and public statement of personal identity in the young person's life to that point. Given the commitment to one's own identity and to the sharing of that identity with another person, the young person is able to experience psychological intimacy and feelings of joy, self-confidence, and competence. Since both partners have the same ability to make such a commitment, marriage as an end becomes the mutuality of identity formation and intimacy between two persons.

Critics of this new approach to marriage have claimed that it tends to glorify hedonism and selfishness with a highly romanticized and unrealistic set of attitudes about the nature of society today. These critics claim that seeing marriage as an end is merely another form of traditional romanticism which substitutes psychological terms like "identity" for older words like "romance." It is the contention of this paper that this current emphasis upon marriage as personality growth is not so much a representation of unrealistic romanticism as it is a sensitivity to the rapidly expanding opportunities for human development which are present in contemporary society. The youth who see marriage in this way are notable for the cool and rational fashion in which they contemplate marriage. These youth see marriage as a viable alternative among several other ways to achieve personal development and fulfillment. They are not "star-struck" or "love-sick," but are cautious and deliberate, choosing marriage only when it appears to be the only form of commitment which will be satisfactory to the mutual identity, intimacy, and continued growth of two individuals.

---

[48] E. Erikson, *Childhood and Society* (New York: W. W. Norton, 1950); E. Erikson, "Identity and the Life Cycle," *Psychological Issues*, 1 (1959); E. Erikson, *Identity: Youth and Crisis* (New York: W. W. Norton, 1968).

[49] K. Keniston, *The Uncommitted: Alienated Youth in American Society* (New York: Dell Publishing Co., 1965); K. Keniston, *Youth and Dissent* (New York: Harcourt Brace Jovanovich, 1971).

Socialization:
Value Commitments

Adolescents acquire an understanding of social values by observing, imitating, and adopting the attitudes of persons who are significant to them. Role-taking the attitudes of others helps to transform concepts of rules from external observations to internal principles. Value commitment finds expression in socialization as the myriad experiences the adolescent encounters eventually coalesce into meaningful patterns, providing a consistent and rational outlook. The first of the four papers in Part 6 offers a developmental analysis of "moral character" or "conscience." The ensuing three papers, dealing with political socialization, religiosity, and protest music, respectively, describe adolescents' socialization from the viewpoint of attitude formation and outlook.

Conscience refers to functioning in accordance with societal precepts, and Kohlberg, in the first selection, believes that the developmental level of children and adolescents' capacity to make moral judgments influences moral conduct. He presents a typology of moral structures comprised of three distinct levels of moral thinking; each level has two related stages. He considers each level and stage as a separate moral philosophy. The preconventional level and Stages 1 and 2 characterize children from ages four to pre-adolescence. According to Kohlberg, children may be well-behaved and responsive to cultural concepts of good and bad, but may be oriented toward these concepts because of the threat of punishment, hope for reward, or simply because of the physical power of those who articulate behavior expectations. At Stage 1, a child's conduct is determined more by physical consequences of action than by the elementary concepts of morality. At Stage 2, right action tends to be defined in relative, hedonistic terms. At the second level, an adolescent's moral expectations of his family, peer group, community, etc. have significant value in their own right. At this level young people are inclined to conform, justify, and support values of social sharing and love. At Stage 3, a youth is more likely to judge behavior by intention—"he means well"—rather than by consequences; and at Stage 4, an adolescent has acquired a sense of duty and respect for authority and an ability to catagorize moral values. At Stages 5 and 6, mature morality is a function of having learned to make right decisions on the basis of self-chosen ethical principles.

In the second paper, Merelman employs the term adolescence to refer to the development of political socialization as a field of inquiry and to the actual political socialization of youth. He traces the efforts of political and psychoanalytic theorists to fashion a sophisticated outlook of the political socialization of youth, and in the course of his analysis, he reveals how each viewpoint affected the nature of research questions. Merelman also discusses the developmental pattern of children and youth's political orientations. His review starts with "system-specific" (interpersonal) attitudes toward authority structures, institutions, personalities, and issues in the American political system. He suggests that young children's political outlook is diffusive; children, for example, appear to apply their identification with their parents to the President, viewing him as a father and regarding the country as a large family nurtured by a benevolent leader. Political socialization in adolescence appears to become more differentiated, and adolescents appear better able to disengage "images and evaluations of political authorities" from their assessments of parental qualities. Political orientations in adolescence, however, tend to be unstable, and Merelman asks rhetorically whether the more critical political attitudes are formed in childhood, leaving little of significance to be learned in adolescence? Merelman addresses himself, too, to adolescent attitudes toward the fundamental or universal principles of political systems: legitimacy, law, obedience, rights, and community obligations. He observes, first, that adolescents possess more relativistic attitudes toward the law than children. He then alludes to several psychological models that should prove useful in explaining changes, and finally, discusses the effects that the family, school, peer-group, and mass media may have on the political socialization of youth.

The third paper in Part 6 offers an explanation for the rapidly growing Jesus Movement. The radical political movements of the 1960s yielded early in the 1970s to what has been variously labeled a New Mysticism, New Reformation, or New Spiritualism. Graham points out that proponents of recent counterculture movements differ among themselves in the role they assign to technology in their quest for peace of mind. He includes "disciples of the Maharishi and researchers in brain-waves-cum-meditation" among the youth-culture religious groups that stress technology in their search of "new consciousness." On the other hand, he says the striking characteristic of the Jesus Movement is its strong antitechnological bias. Graham identifies a parallel between youth in the Jesus Movement and non-Christian youth in the counterculture; both groups equally eschew materialistic society. Youth in the Jesus Movement equate conventional churches with idolatry, traditional American ethics with rivalry and competitiveness, sexual impulses with hedonism, and western intellectual thought and rationalism with irrelevance. Graham sees in the Jesus Movement "a narrowing and de-institutionalizing of traditional Christian theology." It appears that the Jesus Movement is the

*latest idealistic effort among adolescents to disaffiliate themselves from ma-
terialistic society and create a culture of fulfillment.*

One major expression of youth's alienation from industrialism occurred in
an outpouring of protest music during the 1960s. When Eve of Destruction
reached the best-seller charts in 1965, a radical change took place in rock'n'
roll. Suddenly the big beat music acquired significant message lyrics. In the
early 1960s, adolescents were busy frugging to unintelligible wails, but
during the social turmoil of the late 1960s, protest music became an expression of youth's longing for ways to confront the dilemmas posed for them by
an unheeding society. As Rodnitzsky observes in the final paper of Part 4,
folk writer-performers became important models for youth "obsessed with
individuality." Youth today continue to strive for individuality, albeit with
less urgency than only a few years ago, but protest music has tapered in
appeal to become, at least temporarily, a youth-culture relic. Rodnitzsky
asserts that protest music "has been fragmented by its commercial success,
cultural acceptance, and failure to establish relationships with specific social
reform movements." Whether protest music returns in force during the 1970s
may depend on how effectively youth in general meet the challenges of
socialization.

Lawrence Kohlberg

Moral Education in the Schools:
A Developmental View

A generation or two ago, descriptions of character education programs appeared often in pedogogical literature. Optimism among educators ran high, for the anticipation of effecting meaningful change in children's moral character seemingly conveyed deep social significance. Kohlberg observes, however, that traditional, formal moral educational programs have been largely ineffective, and he suggests that a new approach is in order. He rejects the two common interpretations "that moral behavior is purely a matter of immediate situational forces and rewards" and "that moral character is a matter of deep emotions fixed in earliest childhood in the home." As an alternative, he offers the outlook that, although a specific act of cheating may be determined by situational factors, predisposition to acts of misconduct is related to children's capacity for judgment, ability to predict consequences, delay gratification, and focus attention. He describes six, age-related sequencial stages through which children and adolescents presumably proceed step by step, and he argues persuasively that the concept of "moral character" is meaningful if moral character is conceived of as developmental rather than as a set of fixed traits of honesty. This stimulating analysis of problems of moral education is complemented with pointers on how teachers might facilitate children's and adolescents' moral development.

Instructional Objectives
To explain why ethical instruction in schools has traditionally had little influence on moral character.
To suggest that levels of ego strength and capacity to make moral judgments are fundamental components of moral conduct.
To describe six stages in the development of capacity to make moral judgments.
To review two major aims of moral education: to stimulate development of moral judgment ability and to provide guidance and criticism of action in the application of higher levels of judgment.

FROM *The School Review*, LXXIV (1966), 1–29. Modified and updated for the second edition of this volume by the author. Reprinted by permission of the author and the University of Chicago Press.

For many contemporary educators and social scientists, the term "moral education" has an archaic ring, the ring of the last vestiges of the Puritan tradition in the modern school. This archaic ring, however, does not arise from any intrinsic opposition between the statement of educational aims and methods in moral terms and their statement in psychological terms. In fact, it was just this opposition which the great pioneers of the social psychology of education denied in such works as John Dewey's *Moral Principles in Education* [1] and Emile Durkheim's *Moral Education*.[2] Both of these works attempted to define moral education in terms of a broader consideration of social development and social functions than was implied by conventional opinion on the topic, but both recognized that an ultimate statement of the social aims and processes of education must be a statement couched in moral terms.

Unfortunately, the educational psychologists and philosophers who followed Dewey's trail retained his concern about a broad phrasing of the goals of education in terms of the child's social traits and values (e.g., cooperation, social adjustment, "democraticness," mental health) without retaining Dewey's awareness that intelligent thought about these traits and values required the concepts dealt with by moral philosophers and psychologists. More recently, however, thoughtful educators and psychologists have become acutely aware of the inadequacies of dealing with moral issues under cover of mental-health or group-adjustment labels. We have become aware, on the one hand, that these mental-health labels are not really scientific and value-neutral terms; they are ways of making value judgments about children in terms of social norms and acting accordingly. On the other hand, we have come to recognize that mental-health and social-adjustment terms do not really allow us to define the norms and values that are most basic as ideals for our children. The barbarities of the socially conforming members of the Nazi system and the other-directed hollow men growing up in our own affluent society have made us acutely aware of the fact that adjustment to the group is no substitute for moral maturity.

It is apparent, then, that the problems of moral education cannot be successfully considered in the "value-neutral" terms of personality development and adjustment. In this paper, I shall attempt to deal with some of the value issues involved in moral education but will approach these issues from the standpoint of research findings. I believe that a number of recent research facts offer some guide through the problems of moral education when these facts are considered from Dewey's general perspective as to the relationship between fact and value in education.

[1] J. Dewey, *Moral Principles in Education* (Boston: Houghton Mifflin Co., 1911).
[2] E. Durkheim, *Moral Education* (Glencoe, Ill.: The Free Press, 1961; originally published in 1925).

RESEARCH FINDINGS ON THE DEVELOPMENT OF MORAL CHARACTER
RELEVANT TO MORAL EDUCATION IN THE SCHOOLS

One of the major reasons why the social functions of the school have not been phrased in moral-education terms has been the fact that conventional didactic ethical instruction in the school has little influence upon moral character as usually conceived. This conclusion seemed clearly indicated by Hartshorne and May's findings that character-education classes and religious-instruction programs had no influence on moral conduct, as the latter was objectively measured by experimental tests of "honesty" (cheating, lying, stealing) and "service" (giving up objects for others' welfare).[3] The small amount of recent research on conventional didactic moral education provides us with no reason to question these earlier findings. Almost every year a professional religious educator or community-service educator takes a course with me and attempts to evaluate the effect of his program upon moral character. While each starts by thinking his program is different from those evaluated by Hartshorne and May, none comes away with any more positive evidence than did these earlier workers.

While recent research does not lead us to question Hartshorne and May's findings as to the ineffectiveness of conventional, formal moral education, it does lead us to a more positive view as to the possibility of effective school moral education of some new sort. In particular, recent research leads us to question the two most common interpretations of the Hartshorne and May findings: the interpretation that moral behavior is purely a matter of immediate situational forces and rewards and the interpretation that moral character is a matter of deep emotions fixed in earliest childhood in the home. Instead, recent research suggests that the major consistencies of moral character represent the slowly developing formation of more or less cognitive principles of moral judgment and decision and of related ego abilities.

The first interpretation of the Hartshorne and May findings mentioned was essentially that of these authors themselves. Their conclusions were much more nihilistic than the mere conclusion that conventional moral-education classes were ineffective and essentially implied that there was no such thing as "moral character" or "conscience" to be educated anyway. Hartshorne and May found that the most influential factors determining resistance to temptation to cheat or disobey were situational factors rather than a fixed, individual moral-character trait of honesty. The first finding leading to this conclusion was that of the low predictability of cheating in one situation for cheating in another. A second finding was that children were not divisible into two groups, "cheaters" and "honest children." Children's cheating scores were distributed in bell-curve fashion around an average score of moderate cheating. A third finding was the importance of

---

[3] H. Hartshorne and M. A. May, *Studies in the Nature of Character* (3 vols.; New York: Macmillan Co., 1928–30).

the expediency aspect of the decision to cheat, that is, the tendency to cheat depends upon the degree of risk of detection and the effort required to cheat. Children who cheated in more risky situations also cheated in less risky situations. Thus, non-cheaters appeared to be primarily more cautious rather than more honest than cheaters. A fourth finding was that even when honest behavior was not dictated by concern about punishment or detection, it was largely determined by immediate situational factors of group approval and example (as opposed to being determined by internal moral values). Some classrooms showed a high tendency to cheat, while other seemingly identically composed classrooms in the same school showed little tendency to cheat. A fifth finding was that moral knowledge had little apparent influence on moral conduct, since the correlations between verbal tests of moral knowledge and experimental tests of moral conduct were low ($r = 34$). A sixth apparent finding was that where moral values did seem to be related to conduct, these values were somewhat specific to the child's social class or group. Rather than being a universal ideal, honesty was more characteristic of the middle class and seemed less relevant to the lower-class child.

Taken at their face value, these findings suggested that moral education inside or outside the school could have no lasting effect. The moral educator, whether in the home or in the school, could create a situation in which the child would not cheat, but this would not lead to the formation of a general tendency not to cheat when the child entered a new situation. Carried to its logical conclusion, this interpretation of the findings suggested that "honesty" was just an external value judgment of the child's act which leads to no understanding or prediction of his character. It suggested that concepts of good or bad conduct were psychologically irrelevant and that moral conduct must be understood, like other conduct, in terms of the child's needs, his group's values, and the demands of the situation. "While from the standpoint of society, behavior is either 'good' or 'bad,' from the standpoint of the individual it always has some positive value. It represents the best solution for his conflicting drives that he has been able to formulate." [4] This line of thought was extended to the view that moral terms are sociologically as well as psychologically irrelevant. From the standpoint of society, behavior is not clearly good or bad either, since there are a multiplicity of standards that can be used in judging the morality of an action. As sociologists have pointed out, delinquent actions may be motivated by the need to "do right" or conform to standards, to both the standards of the delinquent gang and the great American standard of success. [5]

---

[4] I. M. Josselyn, *Psychosocial Development of Children* (New York: Family Service Association, 1948).

[5] It is evident that the cheating behavior so extensively studied by Hartshorne and May does not represent a conflict between unsocialized base instinctual impulses and moral norms. The motive to cheat is the motive to succeed and do well. The motive to resist cheating is also the motive to achieve and be approved of, but defined in more long-range or "internal" terms. Moral character, then, is not a matter of "good" and "bad" motives or a "good" or "bad" personality as such. These facts, found by Hartshorne and May,

382 Socialization: Value Commitments

A second interpretation of the Hartshorne and May findings was somewhat less nihilistic. This interpretation was that suggested by psychoanalytic and neopsychoanalytic theories of personality.[6] In this interpretation, moral instruction in the school was ineffective because moral character is formed in the home by early parental influences. Moral character, so conceived, is not a matter of fixed moral virtues, like honesty, but of deep emotional tendencies and defenses—of love as opposed to hate for others, of guilt as opposed to fear, of self-esteem and trust as opposed to feelings of inadequacy and distrust. Because these tendencies are basically affective, they are not consistently displayed in verbal or behavioral test situations, but they do define personality types. These types, and their characteristic affective responses, can be defined at the deeper levels tapped by personality projective tests, but they are also related to other people's judgments of the child's moral character. This point of view toward moral character was mostly clearly developed and empirically supported in the writing and research of Robert Havighurst and his colleagues.[7]

While both the "situational" and the "psychoanalytic" interpretations of moral-character research have some validity, recent research findings support a different and more developmental conception of moral character with more positive implications for moral education.[8] While a specific act of "misconduct," such as cheating, is largely determined by situational factors, acts of misconduct are also clearly related to two general aspects of the child's personality development. The first general aspect of the child's development is often termed "ego strength" and represents a set of interrelated ego abilities, including the intelligent prediction of consequences, the tendency to choose the greater remote reward over the lesser immediate reward, the ability to maintain stable focused attention, and a number of other traits. All these abilities are found to predict (or correlate with) the child's behavior on experimental tests of honesty, teacher's ratings of moral character, and children's resistance to delinquent behavior.[9]

---

have not yet been fully absorbed by some clinical approaches to children's moral character. If a child deviates a little he is normal; if he deviates conspicuously, he is believed to be "emotionally disturbed," i.e., to have mixed good and bad motives; if he deviates regularly or wildly, he is all bad (a "psychopathic" or "sadistic" personality).

[6] E.g., S. Freud, Civilization and Its Discontents (London: Hogarth Press, 1955; originally published in 1930); E. Fromm, Man for Himself (New York: Rinehart, 1949); and K. Horney, The Neurotic Personality of Our Time (New York: W. W. Norton & Co., 1937).

[7] R. J. Havighurst and H. Taba, Adolescent Character and Personality (New York: John Wiley & Sons, 1949); and R. F. Peck and R. J. Havighurst, The Psychology of Character Development (New York: John Wiley & Sons, 1960).

[8] L. Kohlberg, "Moral Development and Identification," in H. Stevenson, ed., Child Psychology (Chicago: University of Chicago Press, 1963): "The Development of Children's Orientations Toward a Moral Order: I. Sequence in the Development of Moral Thought," Vita Humana, VI (1963), 11–33; and "The Development of Moral Character and Ideology," in M. Hoffman and L. Hoffman, eds., Review of Child Development Research (New York: Russell Sage Foundation, 1964).

[9] Kohlberg, "The Development of Moral Character and Ideology," op. cit. These factors are also stressed in the works of Peck and Havighurst, op. cit., who found extremely high correlations between ratings of moral character and ratings of ego strength.

The second general aspect of personality that determines moral conduct is the level of development of the child's moral judgments or moral concepts. Level of moral judgment is quite a different matter from the knowledge of, and assent to, conventional moral clichés studied by Hartshorne and May. If one asks a child, "Is it very bad to cheat?" or "Would you ever cheat?" a child who cheats a lot in reality is somewhat more likely to give the conforming answer than is the child who does not cheat in reality.[10] This is because the same desire to "look good" on a spelling test by cheating impels him to "look good" on the moral-attitude test by lying. If, instead, one probes the reasons for the moral choices of the child, as Piaget and I have done,[11] one finds something quite different. As an example, we present the child with a series of moral dilemmas, such as whether a boy should tell his father a confidence about a brother's misdeed. In reply, Danny, age ten, said: "In one way, it would be right to tell on his brother or his father might get mad at him and spank him. In another way, it would be right to keep quiet or his brother might beat him up." Obviously, whether Danny decides it is right to maintain authority or right to maintain peer "loyalty" is of little interest compared to the fact that his decision will be based on his anticipation of who can hit harder. It seems likely that Danny will not cheat if he anticipates punishment but that he has no particular moral reasons for not cheating if he can get away with it. When asked, the only reason he gave for not cheating was that "you might get caught," and his teacher rated him high on a dishonesty rating form.

Danny's response, however, is not a unique aspect of a unique personality. It represents a major aspect of a consistent stage of development of moral judgment, a stage in which moral judgments are based on considerations of punishment and obedience. It is the first of the following six stages found in the development of moral judgment: [12]

Level I—Premoral

Stage 1. Obedience and punishment orientation. Egocentric deference to superior power or prestige, or a trouble-avoiding set. Objective responsibility.

Stage 2. Naïvely egoistic orientation. Right action is that instrumentally satisfying the self's needs and occasionally others. Awareness of relativism of value to each actor's needs and perspective. Naïve egalitarianism and orientation to exchange and reciprocity.

Level II—Conventional Role Conformity

Stage 3. Good-boy orientation. Orientation to approval and to pleasing and helping others. Conformity to stereotypical images of majority or natural role behavior, and judgment of intentions.

Stage 4. Authority and social-order-maintaining orientation. Orientation to

[10] L. Kohlberg, *Stages in the Development of Moral Thought and Action* (New York: Holt, Rinehart and Winston, 1969 [in preparation]).

[11] J. Piaget, *The Moral Judgment of the Child* (Glencoe, Ill.: The Free Press, 1948; originally published in 1932); Kohlberg, "The Development of Children's Orientations Toward a Moral Order: I," op. cit.

[12] Kohlberg, "The Development of Children's Orientations Toward a Moral Order: I," op. cit.

"doing duty" and to showing respect for authority and maintaining the given social order for its own sake. Regard for earned expectations of others.

Level III—Self-accepted Moral Principles

Stage 5. Contractual legalistic orientation. Recognition of an arbitrary element or starting point in rules or expectations for the sake of agreement. Duty defined in terms of contract, general avoidance of violation of the will or rights of others, and majority will and welfare.

Stage 6. Conscience or principle orientation. Orientation not only to actually ordained social rules but to principles of choice involving appeal to logical universality and consistency. Orientation to conscience as a directing agent and to mutual respect and trust.

Each of these stages is defined by twenty-five basic aspects of moral values. Danny's responses primarily illustrated the motivation aspect of Stage 1, the fact that moral motives are defined in terms of punishment. The motivation for moral action at each stage, and examples illustrating them, are as follows:

Stage 1. Obey rules to avoid punishment. Danny, age ten: (Should Joe tell on his older brother to his father?) "In one way it would be right to tell on his brother or his father might get mad at him and spank him. In another way it would be right to keep quiet or his brother might beat him up."

Stage 2. Conform to obtain rewards, have favors returned, and so on. Jimmy, age thirteen: (Should Joe tell on his older brother to his father?) "I think he should keep quiet. He might want to go someplace like that, and if he squeals on Alex, Alex might squeal on him."

Stage 3. Conform to avoid disapproval, dislike by others. Andy, age sixteen: (Should Joe keep quiet about what his brother did?) "If my father finds out later, he won't trust me. My brother wouldn't either, but I wouldn't have a *conscience* that he (my brother) didn't." "I try to do things for my parents; they've always done things for me. I try to do everything my mother says; I try to please her. Like she wants me to be a doctor, and I want to, too, and she's helping me to get up there."

Stage 4. Conform to avoid censure by legitimate authorities and resultant guilt. Previous example also indicative of this.

Stage 5. Conform to maintain the respect of the impartial spectator judging in terms of community welfare or to maintain a relation of mutual respect. Bob, age sixteen: "His brother thought he could trust him. His brother wouldn't think much of him if he told like that."

Stage 6. Conform to avoid self-condemnation. Bill, age sixteen: (Should the husband steal the expensive black-market drug needed to save his wife's life?) "Lawfully no, but morally speaking I think I would have done it. It would be awfully hard to live with myself afterward, knowing that I could have done something which would have saved her life and yet didn't for fear of punishment to myself."

While motivation is one of the twenty-five aspects of morality defining the stages, many of the aspects are more cognitive. An example is the aspect

of "The Basis of Moral Worth of Human Life," which is defined for each
stage as follows:

Stage 1. The value of a human life is confused with the value of physical
objects and is based on the social status or physical attributes of its possessor.
Tommy, age ten: (Why should the druggist give the drug to the dying woman
when her husband couldn't pay for it?) "If someone important is in a plane and
is allergic to heights and the stewardess won't give him medicine because she's
only got enough for one and she's got a sick one, a friend in back, they'd
probably put the stewardess in a lady's jail because she didn't help the important one."
  (Is it better to save the life of one important person or a lot of unimportant
people?) "All the people that aren't important because one man just has one
house, maybe a lot of furniture, but a whole bunch of people have an awful lot
of furniture and some of these poor people might have a lot of money and it
doesn't look it."
  Stage 2. The value of a human life is seen as instrumental to the satisfaction
of the needs of its possessor or of other persons. Tommy, age thirteen: (Should
the doctor "mercy kill" a fatally ill woman requesting death because of her
pain?) "Maybe it would be good to put her out of her pain, she'd be better off that
way. But the husband wouldn't want it, it's not like an animal. If a pet dies
you can get along without it—it isn't something you really need. Well, you can
get a new wife, but it's not really the same."
  Stage 3. The value of a human life is based on the empathy and affection of
family members and others toward its possessor. Andy, age sixteen: (Should the
doctor "mercy kill" a fatally ill woman requesting death because of her pain?)
"No, he shouldn't. The husband loves her and wants to see her. He wouldn't
want her to die sooner, he loves her too much."
  Stage 4. Life is conceived as sacred in terms of its place in a categorical
moral or religious order of rights and duties. John, age sixteen: (Should the
doctor "mercy kill" the woman?) "The doctor wouldn't have the right to take
a life, no human has the right. He can't create life, he shouldn't destroy it."
  Stage 5. Life is valued both in terms of its relation to community welfare
and in terms of life being a universal human right.
  Stage 6. Belief in the sacredness of human life as representing a universal
human value of respect for the individual. Steve, age sixteen: (Should the
husband steal the expensive drug to save his wife?) "By the law of society he
was wrong but by the law of nature or of God the druggist was wrong and the
husband was justified. Human life is above financial gain. Regardless of who
was dying, if it was a total stranger, man has a duty to save him from dying."

We have spoken of our six types of moral judgment as stages. By this we
mean more than the fact that they are age-related. First, a stage concept
implies sequence, it implies that each child must step by step through
each of the kinds of moral judgment outlined. It is, of course, possible for
a child to stop (become "fixated") at any level of development, but if he
continues to move upward he must move in this stepwise fashion. While the

findings are not completely analyzed on this issue, a longitudinal study of
the same boys studied at ages ten, thirteen, sixteen, and nineteen suggests
that this is the case. Second, a stage concept implies universality of sequence
under varying cultural conditions. It implies that moral development is not
merely a matter of learning the verbal values or rules of the child's culture
but reflects something more universal in development which would occur
in any culture. In order to examine this assumption, the same moral-judgment
method was used with boys aged ten, thirteen, and sixteen in a Taiwanese
city, in a Malaysian (Atayal) aboriginal tribal village, and in a Turkish
village, as well as in America. The results for Taiwan and for America are
presented in Figure 1.

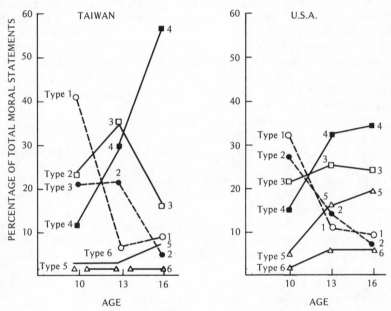

Figure 1. *Mean per cent of use of each of six stages of moral judgment at three
ages in Taiwan and the United States.*

Figure 1 indicates much the same age trends in both the Taiwanese and
the American boys. It is evident that in both groups the first two types
decrease with age, the next two increase until age thirteen and then stabilize,
and the last two continue to increase from age thirteen to age sixteen. In
general, the cross-cultural studies suggest a similar sequence of development
in all cultures, although they suggest that the last two stages of moral thought
do not develop clearly in preliterate village or tribal communities.

In the third place, the stage concept implies personality consistency. We
said that there was little consistency to honest behavior as such. There is,

however, a high degree of consistency, a "g-factor" of moral stage, from one verbal moral situation to the next.[13]

In order to consider the relevance of these moral-judgment stages for our conceptions of moral character, we must consider a little further their relationship to moral conduct. We have already noted that verbal agreement to moral conventions does not generally predict to moral behavior. We noted that when Hartshorne and May measured the child's "knowledge" of the society's moral conventions (as opposed to his response to moral-attitude tests, assessing strength of verbal assent to these convictions), slightly better predictions were obtained; tests of moral knowledge correlated with experimental tests of cheating in the low 30's, about as well as a single cheating test correlates with another. These tests of moral knowledge require somewhat more cognitive understanding of cultural moral prescriptions than do verbal moral-attitude tests, and they are somewhat more age developmental. Our tests of moral judgment, which are more genuinely developmental and reflective of basic cognitive structuring of values than moral-knowledge tests, are still better predictors of moral conduct, however, if moral conduct is conceived in developmental terms.

In referring to a definition of moral conduct, in developmental terms, we refer to the implications of the fact found by Hartshorne and May and corroborated by more recent investigations [14]—the fact that such behaviors as honesty (resistance to cheating) do not increase with age during the elementary school years.[15] In contrast, we saw that moral judgment and values were developing in sequential fashion during these years. For the majority of these elementary school years, however, the child has not developed any clear or internal moral values or principles that condemn cheating, so it is not surprising that cheating behavior does not decline in these years. While most elementary school children are aware of, and concerned about, the harm done others by acts of aggression or theft,[16] their only reason for not cheating is their fear of being caught and punished. Even at older ages, teachers give children few moral or mature reasons to think cheating is bad. Sixth-grade children tell us their teachers tell them not to cheat because they will get punished (Stage 1) "or because the person you copied from might have it wrong and so it won't do you any good" (Stage 2, expediency). In these years, then, resistance to cheating is not so much a matter of internal moral principles as of the situational and expediency factors stressed by Hartshorne and May. With regard to the type of cheating test situation used

[13] L. Kohlberg, "Stage and Sequence: The Developmental Approach to Moralization," in M. Hoffman, ed., *Moral Processes* (Chicago: Aldine Press, 1966).

[14] Kohlberg, "The Development of Moral Character and Ideology," op. cit.

[15] This has sometimes been viewed as consistent with the psychoanalytic view that character is fixed at an early age in the home. In fact, this does not seem to be true, as there is little predictability from early moral conduct to later adolescent moral conduct (ibid.).

[16] R. Krebs, "The Development of Moral Judgment in Young Children" (Master's thesis, Committee on Human Development, University of Chicago, 1965).

by Hartshorne and May, the critical issue for the subject's moral judgment is that of trust, what the experimenter or the teacher expects and what he has the right to expect. The experimenter explicitly leaves the subject unsupervised in a situation where he ordinarily expects supervision. This abandonment of control or authority is interpreted in varying ways. A very high degree of cheating in such a situation seems to primarily reflect a naïve abandon to the surface impression that the experimenter doesn't care. A lesser degree of cheating seems to reflect the child's belief that the experimenter doesn't care very much about his not cheating or he wouldn't leave him unsupervised and that a little cheating isn't too bad anyhow, so long as it is not too obvious and excessive or more than the others do.

In one study of sixth graders [17] almost all (80 per cent) of the children cheated somewhat. The majority of children at the premoral level of moral judgment (Stages 1 and 2) cheated a great deal, and the majority of the children at the conventional level of moral judgment (Stages 3 and 4) cheated a slight or moderate amount.[18] In contrast, adolescents at the level of moral principle (Stages 5 and 6) do interpret the opportunity to cheat as involving issues of maintaining trust, contract, social agreement, and equality of reward for equal effort and ability. The one sixth grader in the Kohlberg study at this level did not cheat at all.[19] Among a group of college students also studied, only one of nine principled-level subjects cheated on an experimental test while about one half of the twenty-six conventional-level subjects did so. (There were no premoral-level subjects in this group.)

Cheating, then, is not a good indicator of moral character until the child has developed in adolescence a set of inner moral principles that prohibit it. By that time, cheating behavior may reflect a lack of full development of moral values (i.e., a failure to reach the level of moral principles) or a discrepancy between action and moral values (a discrepancy due to a variety of possible deficits in ego strength or ego abilities).

More generally, then, there is some meaning to "moral character" as an aim of moral education if moral character is conceived of in developmental terms rather than as a set of fixed conventional traits of honesty, responsibility, etc.

Hartshorne and May's critique is justified insofar as it is a critique of a tendency of teachers to respond to isolated acts of deviance as indicating the child's bad or dishonest character. Specific acts of conformity or deviance in themselves reflect primarily situational wishes and fears rather than the

[17] R. Krebs, "Relations between Attention, Moral Judgment and Conduct" (Unpublished Ph.D. dissertation, University of Chicago, 1966).

[18] The attitude of this latter group is probably well expressed by the following anonymous student article in a British school paper written after a siege of experimental studies of honesty: "The next test reminded me of the eleven plus exam. I had great fun doing these but they are sure to think I am barmy. But then they made a fatal mistake; they actually gave us our own papers to mark. We saw our mistakes in time and saved the day by changing the answers."

[19] Kohlberg, *Stages in the Development of Moral Thought and Action,* op. cit.

presence or absence of conscience or moral character. Nevertheless, there is evidence that repeated misconduct tends to indicate general deficits or re- tardation of general moral-judgment capacities, or related guilt capacities, and the lack of internal ego control rather than simply situational values or emotional conflicts. While everyday judgments of moral character and worth are often psychologically erroneous, they do correlate with important con- sistencies in personality and development, which are positive from almost any viewpoint.

In addition to giving new meaning to notions of moral character, recent research also suggests that it may be possible to stimulate the development of moral character in the school. We said that there has been no recent research evidence to suggest revision of Hartshorne and May's finding that conventional moral- and religious-education classes had no direct influence on moral conduct as usually conceived. (More recently, ongoing research by Jacob Kounin also suggests that the teacher's use of various techniques of punishment and reward for misconduct has no relationship to the amount and type of misconduct that occurs in the classroom.) These negative results have usually been interpreted as indicating that only the home can have any real effect in moral teaching, because only the home teaching involves the intense and continuing emotional relationships necessary for moral teaching or for induction of potential guilt feelings for wrongdoing. In fact, the failure of conventional moral education in the school is probably not the result of the powerlessness of the school to influence the child's character but the result of the inadequacy of prevalent American conceptions of character education. These conceptions usually center on the training of good "habits" of honesty, responsibility, etc., through preaching, example, punishment, and reward. This conception of character education appears to be just as ineffective in the home as it is in the school. Extensive research on parental practices has found no positive or consistent relationships between earliness and amount of parental demands or training in good habits (obedience, caring for property, performing chores, neatness, or avoidance of cheating) and their children's actual obedience, responsibility and honesty. Amount of use of praise, of deprivation of physical rewards, or of physical punishment is also not found to relate consistently or positively to measures of moral character.[20]

There are, of course, a number of unique influences of the home on the development of character which the school cannot reproduce. These are not matters of specific moral training, however, but of the emotional climate in which the child develops. The only parent-attitude variables consistently found to relate to children's moral character are not "moral training" vari- ables but variables of parental warmth.[21] These emotional-climate variables, however, only account for a very small percentage of the differences between

[20] Findings reviewed in Kohlberg, "Moral Development and Identification," op. cit., and "The Development of Moral Character and Ideology," op. cit.
[21] See footnote 20.

children in moral development or moral character. Many of the environmental influences important in moral development are more cognitive in nature than either the "good habits" or the "early emotions" views have suggested. In part, this cognitive influence is meant in a relatively conventional mental-age or I.Q. sense. Intelligence quotient correlates well with maturity of moral judgment (31 to 53 at varying ages) and almost equally well with behavioral measures of honesty. At the kindergarten level, the capacity to make judgments of good or bad in terms of standards rather than in terms of punishment and egoistic interests is a capacity almost completely determined by cognitive development on Piaget tests of cognition.[22]

We have discussed the influence of general intellectual advance upon the development of moral judgment. In addition, advances in a number of aspects of social concepts customarily thought of as part of the social-studies curriculum are correlated with advance in moral judgment. Children in the original Kohlberg study were asked to say how much and why various occupations (such as judge, policeman, soldier, artist, senator) were respected by most people, an apparent question of comprehension of social fact and function. Responses to this task could be scored in a fashion similar to the moral-judgment questions, and individual children's levels were similar on the two tasks.

This task pointed up the fact that some of the difficulties in moral development of lower-class children are largely cognitive in nature. Sociologists and social critics like Paul Goodman and Edgar Friedenberg have stressed the notion that the school not only transmits middle-class moral values at the expense of lower-class moral values but that there is a certain fundamental "immorality" or "inauthenticity" about these middle-class values to the lower-class child in comparison with lower-class values. While sociologists are correct in stressing class-linked value systems, they are not correct in postulating class-based differences in *basic moral* values. The lower-class parent and the middle-class parent show little difference in the rank order of moral values desired for their children; for example, both put honesty at the top of the list.[23] In the Kohlberg studies of moral ideology middle-class and working-class children (matched for I.Q.) differed considerably. These differences, however, were developmental in nature. At one age, middle-class and working-class children differed in one way, at another in a different way. At all ages, however, the middle-class children tended to be somewhat in advance of the working-class children. The differences, then, were not due to the fact that the middle-class children heavily favored some one type of thought, which could be seen as corresponding to the prevailing middle-class pattern. Instead, middle-class and working-class children seemed to move faster and farther.

This finding becomes intelligible when it is recalled that the institutions

[22] Krebs, op. cit.

[23] M. Kohn, "Social Class and Parental Values," *American Journal of Sociology,* LXIV (1959), 337–51.

with moral authority (law, government, family, the work order) and the basic moral rules are the same regardless of the individual's particular position in society. The child's position in society does to a large extent, however, determine his interpretation of these institutions and rules. Law and the government are perceived quite differently by the child if he feels a sense of understanding and potential participation in the social order than if he does not.[24]

The slower development of moral judgment of the working-class boys seemed largely accountable for by two factors, lesser understanding of the broader social order and lesser sense of participation in it. Both factors showed up especially in the social-concept task conceiving occupations but were apparent in their moral judgments as well. It seems likely that social-studies programs in the school could have considerably more positive effect upon these class-differentiating aspects of moral development than is true at present.

Our discussion of social class stressed opportunities for social participation and role-taking as factors stimulating moral development. Perhaps a clearer example of the importance of social participation in moral development is the finding that children with extensive peer-group participation advance considerably more quickly through the Kohlberg stages of moral judgment than children who are isolated from such participation (with both groups equated for social class and I.Q.). This clearly suggests the relevance and potential of the classroom peer group for moral education. In pointing to the effects of extra-familial determinants upon moral development, we have focused primarily on their influence upon development of moral judgment. However, these same determinants lead to more mature moral behavior as well, as indicated by teachers' ratings and experimental measures of honesty and of moral autonomy.[25]

---

[24] The effect of such a sense of participation upon development of moral judgments related to the law is suggested by the following responses of sixteen-year-olds to the question, "Should someone obey a law if he doesn't think it is a good law?" A lower-class boy replies, "Yes, a law is a law and you can't do nothing about it. You have to obey it, you should. That's what it's there for." For him the law is simply a constraining thing that is there. The very fact that he has no hand in it, that "you can't do nothing about it," means that it should be obeyed (Stage 1).

A lower-middle-class boy replies, "Laws are made for people to obey and if everyone would start breaking them. . . . Well, if you owned a store and there were no laws, everybody would just come in and not have to pay." Here laws are seen not as arbitrary commands but as a unitary system, as the basis of the social order. The role or perspective taken is that of a storekeeper, of someone with a stake in the order (Stage 4).

An upper-middle-class boy replies, "The law's the law but I think people themselves can tell what's right or wrong. I suppose the laws are made by many different groups of people with different ideas. But if you don't believe in a law, you should try to get it changed, you shouldn't disobey it." Here the laws are seen as the product of various legitimate ideological and interest groups varying in their beliefs as to the best decision in policy matters. The role of law-obeyer is seen from the perspective of the democratic policy-maker (Stage 5).

[25] Kohlberg, "The Development of Children's Orientation toward a Moral Order: II," op. cit.

A Developmental Conception of the Aims and Nature of Moral Education

The facts, then, suggest the possibilities of useful planning of the moral-education component of schooling. Such planning raises more fundamental value issues, however, the issues as to the legitimate aims and methods of moral education in the American public schools. The writer would start by arguing that there are no basic value problems raised by the assertion that the school *should* be consciously concerned about moral education, since all schools necessarily are constantly involved in moral education. The teacher is constantly and unavoidably moralizing to children, about rules and values and about his students' behavior toward each other. Since such moralizing is unavoidable, it seems logical that it be done in terms of conscious formulated goals of moral development. As it stands, liberal teachers do not want to indoctrinate children with their own private moral values. Since the classroom social situation requires moralizing by the teacher, he ordinarily tends to limit and focus his moralizing toward the necessities of classroom management, that is, upon the immediate and relatively trivial behaviors that are disrupting to him or to the other children. Exposure to the diversity of moral views of teachers is undoubtedly one of the enlightening experiences of growing up, but the present system of thoughtlessness as to which of the teacher's moral attitudes or views he communicates to children and which he does not leaves much to be desired. Many teachers would be most mortified and surprised to know what their students perceive to be their moral values and concerns. My seven-year-old son told me one day that he was one of the good boys in school, but he didn't know whether he really wanted to be. I asked him what the differences between the good and bad boys were, and he said the bad boys talked in class and didn't put books away neatly, so they got yelled at. Not only is it highly dubious that his teacher's moralizing was stimulating his or any of the children's moral development, but it is almost inevitable that this be the case in an educational system in which teachers have no explicit or thought-out conception of the aims and methods of moral education and simply focus upon immediate classroom-management concerns in their moralizing.

The value problems of moral education, then, do not arise concerning the necessity of engaging in moral education in the school, since this is already being done every day. The value problems arise, however, concerning the formulation of the aims and content of such education. At its extreme, such a formulation of aims suggests a conception of moral education as the imposition of a state-determined set of values, first by the bureaucrats upon the teachers, and then by the teachers upon the children. This is the system of "character education" employed in Russia, as described by U. Bronfenbrenner.[26] In Russia, the entire classroom process is explicitly defined as

[26] "Soviet Methods of Character Education: Some Implications for Research," *American Psychologist*, XVII (1962), 550–565.

"character education," that is, as making good socialist citizens, and the teacher appears to have an extremely strong influence upon children's moral standards. This influence rests in part upon the fact that the teacher is perceived as "the priest of society," as the agent of the all-powerful state, and can readily enlist the parents as agents of discipline to enforce school values and demands. In part, however, it rests upon the fact that the teacher systematically uses the peer group as an agent of moral indoctrination and moral sanction. The classroom is divided into co-operating groups in competition with one another. If a member of one of the groups is guilty of misconduct, the teacher downgrades or sanctions the whole group, and the group in turn punishes the individual miscreant. This is, of course, an extremely effective form of social control if not of moral development.

In our view, there is a third alternative to a state moral-indoctrination system and to the current American system of moralizing by individual teachers and principals when children deviate from minor administrative regulations or engage in behavior personally annoying to the teacher. This alternative is to take the stimulation of the development of the individual child's moral judgment and character as a goal of moral education, rather than taking as its goal either administrative convenience or state-defined values. The attractiveness of defining the goal of moral education as the stimulation of development rather than as teaching fixed virtues is that it means aiding the child to take the next step in a direction toward which he is already tending, rather than imposing an alien pattern upon him. An example of the difference may be given in terms of the use of the peer group. In Russia the peer-group structure is created by the teacher (i.e., he divides the classroom into groups), and the peer group is then manipulated by punishments and rewards so as to impose the teacher's or the school's values upon its deviant members. If one took the stimulation of the moral development of the individual child as a goal, one would consider the role of the peer group in quite a different way. In the previous section we discussed the fact that classroom isolates were slower in development of moral judgment than were integrates. This suggests that inclusion of the social isolates in the classroom peer group might have considerable influence on their moral development, though not necessarily an influence of immediate conformity to teacher or school demands.

The implementation of this goal would involve various methods to encourage inclusion of isolates such as are under investigation in a research project at the University of Michigan conducted by Ronald Lippett. Some of these methods involve creating a classroom atmosphere encouraging participation rather than attempting to directly influence sociometric integrates to include isolates. Some of these methods involve more direct appeal to integrated members of sociometric groups, but an appeal to the implementation of already existing social and moral values held by these children rather than an effort to impose the teacher's values upon them by reward or punishment. The process raises many valuable issues potentially stimulating the moral development of the integrates as well, since they must cope with the fact that, "Well, we were finally nice to him and look what he did." These issues involve the opportunity for the teacher to play a different and perhaps more stimulating and open role as a "moral guide" than that involved in supporting conformity to school rules and teacher demands.

A definition of the aims of moral education as the stimulation of natural development is most clear-cut in the area of moral judgment, where there appears to be considerable regularity of sequence and direction in development in various cultures. Because of this regularity, it is possible to define the maturity of a child's moral judgment without considering its content (the particular action judged) and without considering whether it agrees with our own particular moral judgments or values or those of the American middle-class culture as a whole. In fact, the sign of the child's moral maturity is his ability to make moral judgments and formulate moral principles of his own, rather than his ability to conform to moral judgments of the adults around him.[27]

How in general, then, may moral maturity as an aim of education be defined? One general answer starts from the conception of maturity in moral judgment and then considers conduct in terms of its correspondence to such judgment. Maturity levels are most clearly apparent in moral judgment. Furthermore, the general direction of maturity of moral judgment is a direction of greater morality. Each of the Kohlberg stages of moral judgment represents a step toward a more genuinely or distinctly moral judgment. We do not mean by this that a more mature judgment is more moral in the sense of showing closer conformity to the conventional standards of a given community. We mean that a more mature judgment more closely corresponds to genuine moral judgments as these have been defined by philosophers. While philosophers have been unable to agree upon any ultimate principle of the good that would define "correct" moral judgments, most philosophers agree upon the characteristics that make a judgment a genuine moral judgment.[28] Moral judgments are judgments about the good and the right of action. Not all judgments of "good" or "right" are moral judgments, however; many are judgments of esthetic, technological, or prudential goodness or rightness. Unlike judgments of prudence or esthetics, moral judgments tend

[27] A research indication of this comes from the Kohlberg study. After individual moral-judgment interviews, the children in the study were subjected to pressure from an adult and from disagreeing peers to change their views on the questions. While maturity of moral judgment predicted to moral behaviors involving conformity to authority (e.g., cheating), it predicted better to behaviors involving maintaining one's own moral views in the face of pressure from authorities (r = .44). Among college students, not only were principled subjects much less likely to cheat, but they were much more likely to engage in an act of moral courage or resistance when an authoritative experimenter ordered them to inflict pain upon another subject (Kohlberg, *Stages in the Development of Moral Thought and Action,* op. cit.).

[28] R. M. Hare, *The Language of Morals* (New York: Oxford University Press, 1952); I. Kant, *Fundamental Principles of the Metaphysics of Morals,* trans. T. K. Abbott (New York: Liberal Arts Press, 1949); and H. Sidgwick, *Methods of Ethics* (London: The Macmillan Co., 1901).

to be universal, inclusive, consistent, and to be grounded on objective, impersonal, or ideal grounds.[29] "She's really great, she's beautiful and a good dancer"; "the right way to make a Martini is five to one"—these are statements about the good and right that are not moral judgments since they lack these characteristics: If we say, "Martinis should be made five to one," we are making an esthetic judgment, and we are not prepared to say that we want everyone to make them that way, that they are good in terms of some impersonal ideal standard shared by others, and that we and others should make five-to-one Martinis whether they wish to or not. In a similar fashion, when Danny answered our "moral should" question, "Should Joe tell on his older brother?" in Stage 1 terms of the probabilities of getting beaten up by his father and by his brother, he did not answer with a moral judgment that is universal (applies to all brothers in that situation and ought to be agreed upon by all people thinking about the situation) or that has any impersonal or ideal grounds. In contrast, the Stage 6 statements quoted earlier not only specifically use moral words, such as "morally right" and "duty," but use them in a moral way; for example, "regardless of who it was" and "by the law of nature or of God" imply universality; "morally, I would do it in spite of fear of punishment" implies impersonality and ideality of obligation, etc. Thus the value of judgments of lower-level subjects about moral matters are not moral responses in the same sense in which the value judgments of high-level subjects about esthetic or morally neutral matters are not moral. The genuinely moral judgment just discussed is what we mean by "judgments of principle" and "to become morally adult is to learn to make decisions of principle; it is to learn to use 'ought' sentences verified by reference to a standard or set of principles which we have by our own decision accepted and made our own." [30]

How can the teacher go about stimulating the development of moral judgment? We have already rejected the notion of a set curriculum of instruction and exhortation in the conventional moral virtues, a conception killed by Hartshorne and May's demonstration of ineffectiveness. Dewey [31] pointed to the inadequacy of such a conception long ago and traced it to the fact that it assumed a divorce between moral education and intellectual education on the one side, and a divorce between education and real life on the other. To put Dewey's critique more bluntly, both conventional character-education classes or preaching and conventional moralizing by teachers about petty school routines are essentially "Mickey Mouse" stuff in relationship to the real need for moral stimulation of the child. To be more than "Mickey Mouse," a teacher's moralizings must be cognitively novel and challenging to the child, and they must be related to matters of obvious, real importance and seriousness.

[29] L. Kohlberg, "The Development of Modes of Moral Thinking and Choice in the Years Ten to Sixteen" (Ph.D. dissertation, University of Chicago, 1958).
[30] Hare, op. cit.
[31] Op. cit.

It is not always necessary that these matters be ones of the immediate and real-life issues of the classroom. I have found that my hypothetical and remote but obviously morally real and challenging conflict situations are of intense interest to almost all adolescents and lead to lengthy debate among them. They are involving because the adult right answer is not obviously at hand to discourage the child's own moral thought, as so often is the case. The child will listen to what the teacher says about moral matters only if the child first feels a genuine sense of uncertainty as to the right answer to the situation in question. The pat little stories in school readers in which virtue always triumphs or in which everyone is really nice are unlikely to have any value in the stimulation of moral development. Only the presentation of genuine and difficult moral conflicts can have this effect.

We have mentioned that the stimulation of moral communication by the teacher should involve issues of genuine moral conflict to the child and represent new cognitive elements. There is also an important problem of match between the teacher's level and the child's involved in effective moral communication. Conventional moral education never has had much influence on children's moral judgment because it has disregarded this problem of developmental match. It has usually involved a set of adult moral clichés that are meaningless to the child because they are too abstract, mixed up with a patronizing "talking down" to the child in concrete terms beneath his level. In fact, the developmental level of moral-education verbalizations must be matched to the developmental level of the child if they are to have an effect. Ideally, such education should aim at communicating primarily at a level one stage above the child's own and secondarily at the child's own level. Experimental demonstration of this principle is provided in a study by E. Turiel.[32] Turiel ascertained the moral level of sixth graders on the Kohlberg stages, matched them for I.Q., and divided them into three experimental groups (and a fourth control group). All the groups (except the controls) were then exposed to short role-playing and discussion sessions with the experimenter centered on hypothetical conflict situations similar to those used in the Kohlberg tests. For one experimental group, the experimenter presented a discussion using moral judgments and reasons *one level above* the child's own. For a second group, the experimenter used moral judgments *two levels above* the child's own. For the third group, the experimenter used moral judgments *one level below* the child's own. All the children were then retested on the original test situations as well as on the situations discussed with the experimenter. Only the children who were exposed to moral judgments one level above their own showed any appreciable absorption of the experimenter's moral judgments. The children exposed to judgments one level below their own showed some absorption (more than those exposed to judgments two levels above) but not nearly as much as those exposed to one level above. Thus, while children are able to understand moralizing that

[32] "An Experimental Analysis of Developmental Stages in the Child's Moral Judgment," *Journal of Personality and Social Psychology*, 3 (1966), 611–618.

is talking down beneath their level, they do not seem to accept it nearly as much as if it is comprehensible but somewhat above their level. It is obvious that the teacher's implementation of this principle must start by his careful listening to the moral judgments and ideas actually expressed by individual children.

The two principles just mentioned were used by Blatt [33] to develop a four month program of once-weekly moral discussions for a class of twelve children aged 11 to 12. Children discussed and argued hypothetical dilemmas. The teacher supported and clarified the arguments of the children which were at an average (Stage 3) level as against those one step below that level (Stage 2). When these arguments seemed understood, using new situations, the teacher would challenge the level (Stage 3) previously supported, and support and clarify the arguments of those one stage above (Stage 4) the previous concensus. The children were given a pre- and post-test, using different stories than those involved in the classroom discussions (with some new stories given only for the post-test). Fifty per cent of the children moved up one stage, 10 per cent moved up two stages, the remainder staying the same. In contrast, 10 per cent of a control group moved up one stage during this period, the remainder staying the same. Blatt and others are continuing this experimental work in varying settings (e.g., ghetto schools) and at varying ages.[34] The potential value of such educational efforts appears in terms of some recent longitudinal findings (on a small sample of middle class males), which indicate that moral maturity at age 13 is an extremely good ($r = 78$ to 92) predictor of adult moral maturity (at age 24 to 27).[35] This is not because moral judgment development stops at age 13, it continues past college in most of this group. (As an example, while none of the 13-year-olds were primarily at the principled level, 36 per cent of the 24-year-olds in this sample were at the principled level (Stage 5 and 6).) Those who did not develop some (over 15 per cent) thinking by later high school, however, did not develop into the principled stage in young adulthood. In general, then, while moral development continues into adulthood, mature 13-year-olds retain their edge in development, presumably because development is stepwise and the advanced boys have less further steps to go through. Blatt is now conducting longitudinal follow-ups to see if those whose moral judgment was raised in his group retain this developmental advantage in subsequent years.

So far, we have talked about the development of moral judgment as an aim of moral education. The sheer ability to make genuinely moral judgments is only one portion of moral character, however. The remainder is the ability to apply these judgmental capacities to the actual guidance and criticism of action. We have pointed out that advance in moral judgment

[33] M. Blatt, and L. Kohlberg, "The Effects of Classroom Moral Discussion upon Children's Level of Moral Judgment," submitted to *Merrill Palmer Quarterly*, 1968.
[34] M. Blatt, "Experimental Studies in Moral Education Using a Developmental Approach" (Unpublished Ph.D. dissertation, University of Chicago, 1959).
[35] L. Kohlberg, *Stages in the Development of Moral Thought and Action*, op. cit.

seems to produce more mature moral action. Principled subjects both cheat much less and resist pressures by authorities to inflict pain on others much more than do less mature subjects. We do not yet know whether educational stimulation of moral judgment advance would actually produce more mature conduct in conflict situations. In any case, in addition to stimulating the development of general moral judgment capacities, a developmental moral education would stimulate the child's application of his own moral judgments (not the teacher's) to his actions. The effort to force a child to agree that an act of cheating was very bad when he does not really believe it (as in the case of the author of the school-newspaper article) will only be effective in encouraging morally immature tendencies toward expedient outward compliance. In contrast, a more difficult but more valid approach involves getting the child to examine the pros and cons of his conduct in his own terms (as well as introducing more developmentally advanced considerations).[36]

In general, however, the problem of insuring correspondence between developing moral judgments and the child's action is not primarily a problem of eliciting moral self-criticism from the child. One aspect of the problem is the development of the ego abilities involved in the non-moral or cognitive tasks upon which the classroom centers. As an example, an experimental measure of high stability of attention (low reaction-time variability) in a simple monotonous task has been found to clearly predict to resistance to cheating in Hartshorne and May's tests ($r = .68$).[37] The encouragement of these attentional ego capacities is not a task of moral education as such but of general programming of classroom learning activities.

Another aspect of the encouragement of correspondence between the child's moral values and his behavior is more difficult and fundamental. In order to encourage the application of his values to his behavior, we need to make sure that the kinds of behavior demands we make have some match to his already existing moral values. Two major types of mismatch occur. One type, which we have already mentioned, occurs when teachers concentrate on trivial classroom routines, thus moralizing issues that have no moral meaning outside the classroom. If the teacher insists on behavioral conformity to these demands and shows no moral concerns for matters of greater relevance to the child's (and the society's) basic moral values, the child will simply assume that his moral values have no relevance to his conduct in the classroom. It is obvious that the teacher must exert some influence toward conformity to trivial classroom rules, but there are two things he can do to minimize this sort of mismatch. The first is to insure that he does communi-

---

[36] This is actually more valuable for acts of good conduct than for acts of bad conduct. We expect children to justify defensively acts of misconduct. If we take the trouble to find out, however, we will often be surprised that the acts of good conduct we praise are valued by the child himself for immature reasons and that we are really rewarding "selfish" rather than moral values. In such cases it is relatively easy to foster the application of developmentally more advanced values in the child's repertoire to his own behavior.

[37] P. Grim, L. Kohlberg, and S. White, "Some Relationships between Conscience and Attentional Processes," *J. Pers. Soc. Psychol.*, 8 (1968), 239–253.

cate some of his values with regard to broader and more genuinely moral issues. The second is to treat administrative demands as such and to distinguish them from basic moral demands involving moral judgment of the child's worth and moral sanctions. This does not imply that no demands should be treated as moral demands but that the teacher should clearly distinguish his own attitudes and reactions toward moral demands from his more general conformity demands.

The most serious and vital value issues represented by school life are not moral values per se but are intellectual in nature. As Dewey points out in discussing moral education, the serious business of the school is, and should be, intellectual. The principal values and virtues the teacher attends to are intellectual. However, the teacher may attend to these values and virtues either with awareness of their broader place in moral development or without such awareness. If such awareness is not present, the teacher will simply transmit the competitive-achievement values that dominate our society. He will train the child to think that getting a good mark is an absolute good and then suddenly shift gears and denounce cheating without wondering why the child should think cheating is bad when getting a good mark is the most important value. If the teacher has a greater awareness of the moral dimensions of education, his teaching of the intellectual aspects of the curriculum will illustrate the values of truth integrity, and trust in intellectual affairs and intellectual learning in such a way as to carry over to behaviors like cheating.

The second form of mismatch between the teacher's moral demands and the child's moral values arises from the fact that the teacher feels that certain behavioral demands are genuine moral demands, but the child has not yet developed any moral values that require these behaviors. We gave as an example the fact that resistance to cheating on tests does not derive from anything like moral values in young children aged five to seven, whereas resistance to theft and aggression do correspond to more spontaneous and internal moral values at this age. Given this fact, it does not seem wise to treat cheating as a genuine moral issue among young children, while it may be with older children. In general, the teacher should encourage the child to develop moral values relevant to such behavior as cheating but should not treat the behavior as a moral demand in the absence of such values.

It is clear, then, that a developmental conception of moral education does not imply the imposition of a curriculum upon the teacher. It does demand that the individual teacher achieve some clarity in his general conceptions of the aims and nature of moral development. In addition, it implies that he achieve clarity as to the aspects of moral development he should encourage in children of a given developmental level and as to appropriate methods of moral communication with these children. Most important, it implies that the teacher starts to listen carefully to the child in moral communications. It implies that he becomes concerned about the child's moral judgments (and the relation of the child's behavior to these judgments) rather than about the conformity of the child's behavior or judgments to the teacher's own.

Richard M. Merelman

The Adolescence of Political Socialization

*This paper employs the term "adolescence" to refer both to the develop-
ment of political socialization as a field of inquiry and to the actual political
socialization of youth. Merelman evaluates research on political socialization relative to theoretical adequacy and descriptive merit. He also describes the developmental pattern of childhood and adolescent political
orientations, and he shows how socializing agencies such as the family,
school, peer-group, and media affect the socialization of youth's political
attitudes.*

Instructional Objectives
To review the development of political socialization as a field of inquiry.
To describe the developmental pattern of political attitudes in childhood.
To describe the developmental pattern of political attitudes in adolescence.
To consider the socializing influence on political attitudes of the family,
*   school, peer-group, and media.*

C HILDHOOD, according to psychologists, is a time when the world is
experienced afresh each day and when nascent talents press upon each
other. Childhood is also a time of faith and enthusiasm: faith in the natural
order of family and society, enthusiasm for the living and learning of life.
Of course, much of little consequence is mixed with the critically important.
Healthy optimism occasionally deteriorates into illusions of omnipotent
certainty.

The adolescent, however, takes stock of his youthful enthusiasms, search-
ing for an identity amidst the eddies of change. Some adolescents become
savagely critical of their childhood; others spy in the interstices of youth
some defining thread of personality to be grasped eagerly as a confirmation
of maturity. To most, however, adolescence is a time for skeptical and not
entirely humorless contemplation of youthful vanities. Such a period of
adolescent disarray and skepticism typifies the field of political socialization
today. Like the adolescent, it too awaits confirmatory signs of its authenticity,
identity and scholarly worth.

The adolescence of an academic field has four general characteristics:

FROM *Sociology of Education*, XLV (1972), 134–166. Abridged. Reprinted by permission
of the author and the publisher.

1) the compiling of histories and bibliographies of the field, 2) the emergence of standard course offerings, 3) the appearance of "young turks," and 4) the publication of anthologies. As Greenstein [1] notes in his brief historical account of political socialization, course offerings in political socialization have soared over the last 10 years, so much so that political socialization has now superseded such old warhorses as public opinion in attracting graduate students.[2] This upsurge of interest has not been confined to political scientists; such leading psychologists as Lawrence Kohlberg and Robert Hess also have been enthused. And, a second generation of socialization investigators, including Edward Greenberg, Elliott White, and Pauline Vaillencourt, has begun to make some impact on the field. Finally, in 1970 alone three anthologies of political socialization appeared.[3]

As is often true of rapidly growing disciplines, synchronization of development is significantly and ironically absent. Just as the mass of graduate students attracted by the early successes of political socialization bursts upon the field, their questionnaires and computers in hand, political socialization itself confronts the self-doubt of adolescence. Small wonder that many investigators feel a slight vertigo. I shall try to evoke the mood of political socialization today by tracing the field's origins, some of its major findings, the questions currently dividing it, and the implications these questions raise for political scientists and educators.

Origins

The appearance of political socialization as a distinct field of inquiry usually is dated from the publication, in 1959, of Herbert Hyman's *Political Socialization*.[4] Hyman does not report original research but, rather, an interpretation of many quite disparate earlier studies. Originally these studies had been conducted under the rubrics of social psychology, public opinion, electoral behavior, and political recruitment; Hyman developed a new framework for them to which he gave the name "political socialization." More importantly, Hyman helped stamp a particular cast of assumptions and research strategies upon the field he named. It is necessary, therefore, to investigate Hyman's approach.

As a sociologist, it was natural for Hyman to think of political socialization primarily as one facet of social structure. Political socialization was crucial to society because it was the means by which political values perpetuated

[1] F. I. Greenstein, "Political Socialization," in *International Encyclopedia of the Social Sciences* (New York: Macmillan and the Free Press, 1968), pp. 551–555.

[2] F. I. Greenstein, "A Note on the Ambiguity of 'Political Socialization': Definitions, Criticisms, and Strategies of Inquiry," *Journal of Politics*, XXXII (November 1970), 969–979.

[3] N. Adler and C. Harrington, *The Learning of Political Behavior* (Glenview, Ill.: Scott, Foresman, 1970); E. S. Greenberg, ed., *Political Socialization* (New York: Atherton, 1970); R. S. Sigel, ed., *Learning About Politics* (New York: Random House, 1970).

[4] H. Hyman, *Political Socialization* (Glencoe, Ill.: The Free Press, 1959).

themselves across the generations. Not surprisingly, therefore, Hyman organized his book around findings related to the agencies of socialization, for he shared the assumptions of most sociologists that human development is almost exclusively a process by which the environment, conceptualized in terms of social agencies, impresses itself upon the helpless, formless child. This approach provided the foundation for two vital assumptions about socialization: 1) socialization should be conceived mainly as a process by which social institutions inculcate political values, rather than as a learning process by which innately different individuals develop their own brand of political orientations; 2) because social institutions and agencies change more slowly than the individual, political socialization inevitably acts as a brake upon political change. In short, the vulnerability of the child and the relative stability of social institutions destined political socialization to be an important conservatizing force in the polity. As Hyman [5] noted, socialization is the "learning of social patterns corresponding to . . . social positions as mediated through various agencies of society."

Hyman's sociological perspective had the unfortunate side-effect of encouraging later investigators to think of socialization research mainly as the measurement of youthful political preferences, rather than as the illumination of psychological processes by which socialization agencies operated. Soon political socialization research became the study of political preferences at particular points in childhood and adolescence. rather than the longitudinal study of political maturation.

Other investigators tried to fill the psychological void that Hyman bequeathed to political socialization, but they had little with which to operate. Political scientists in the late fifties and early sixties utilized few forms of psychological theorizing; two major approaches dominated the field. There was the work of Harold Lasswell and his students,[6] who applied Freudian analysis to the study of political motivation. In addition, the Survey Research Center at the University of Michigan had made good use of a rudimentary associative conditioning model.[7] Political scientists had done little with the cognitive theories of Leon Festinger and Kurt Lewin; Piaget was unrecognized; and, important thinkers such as Albert Bandura, Robert Sears, and Erik Erikson had yet to make their mark.

Fred Greenstein did most to adapt the Freudian framework to the study of political socialization. Greenstein [8] not only built heavily upon Lasswell's analysis of authoritarian and democratic personality structures, but also followed Freudian assumptions by choosing to focus upon attitudes towards

[5] Ibid., p. 25.

[6] H. D. Lasswell, *Psychopathology and Politics* (New York: Viking Press, 1930) and *Power and Personality* (New York: Norton, 1948); A. George and J. George, *Woodrow Wilson and Colonel House* (New York: Dover, 1956); R. E. Lane, *Political Ideology* (New York: The Free Press, 1962).

[7] A. Campbell, et al., *The American Voter* (New York: Wiley, 1960), ch. 2.

[8] F. I. Greenstein, "Personality and Political Socialization: the Theories of Authorization and Democratic Character," *Annals*, CCCLXI (1965), 81–95.

political authorities.[9] The Freudian framework also had the virtue of complementing the structural approach followed by Hyman, because psychoanalytic theory assumes that environmental pressures usually win out over instinctual energies, albeit at considerable psychic cost. For our purposes, however, the important thing was that the choice of a Freudian framework for political socialization temporarily decided two important research questions.

First, political orientations would be conceived mainly as diffuse, deep-set responses to environmental stimuli; this implication followed from the Freudian emphasis upon unconscious motivation. Second, political socialization research would focus primarily on childhood, the major formative period according to psychoanalytic theory.

The Freudian and neo-Freudian emphasis upon authority structures in the family and polity also dovetailed nicely with the political situation at the time the first generation of political socialization researchers undertook their work. American politics in the late fifties was dominated by the benign paternal authority figure of President Dwight Eisenhower, whose unprecedented political appeal drew little of its sustenance from the partisan groupings that normally energize our politics.[10] It also was an era of bi-partisanship in foreign policy and of but marginal party competition in domestic affairs, as Lyndon Johnson, the leader of Senate Democrats, strove to forge a policy consensus with President Eisenhower. It most emphatically was not a time of overt racial tension; the only visible student disorders were quasi-institutionalized panty raids and football celebrations. "Pot" was a word applied to the ample girths of certain corporate executives and labor leaders.

The election of President Kennedy did not immediately disturb this picture. Kennedy symbolized few of the fiercely partisan Democratic associations that shaped the images of well-known party regulars such as Hubert Humphrey; moreover, the "Kennedy image" in power was one of high culture, grace, wit, and youthful energy, aristocratic fare normally too rich for American palates.

The fact that neither of these Presidencies was typical of American politics sometimes escaped the notice of socialization researchers. Few stopped to consider whether political conditions might not be coloring their findings about the child's attitudes towards political authority; many generalized further from the data they gathered during this period than in time would appear to have been prudent.

Although these conditions aided the adoption of a Freudian framework to explain individual political learning, there remained the problem of making political socialization a worthwhile endeavor for the political scientist in-

[9] F. I. Greenstein, *Children and Politics* (New Haven: Yale University Press, 1965), ch. 3.

[10] A. Campbell, et al., *Elections and the Political Order* (New York: Wiley, 1965), ch. 15; J. Davies, "Charisma in the 1952 Campaign," *American Political Science Review*, XLVIII (1954), 1083–1102.

terested in the macro-structure, the political system itself. How could an investigation of political attitudes among children be justified from the macro-political perspective, rather than from the sociological perspective? Three answers to this question can be found in the literature.

First, some political socialization investigators simply relied on classical political theorists, such as Plato, who pointed out the importance of a political education.[11] Unfortunately, however, this argument reduces to the statement, "Socialization is worth study because . . . . thinks it is." The poverty of this justification soon became apparent to all; a search for other arguments ensued.

Greenstein constructed a second rationale from some of the early socialization findings by employing the Freudian framework. He argued that the child's political orientations were so deeply embedded that they could not help but influence his adult stance towards politics; moreover, adult political attitudes, Greenstein assumed, influenced the political system.[12] But as Greenstein himself points out in a recent book, this justification ignores the problem of "aggregation," or the *way* in which individual attitudes accumulate to constrain the political process.[13] Some aggregative mechanism had to be discovered.

A mechanism finally emerged from the systems theory of David Easton. Easton was concerned about how political systems managed to persist and transform themselves in a world of violent change. The major cause of political instability, according to Easton,[14] is the problem of scarcity. Government's material and symbolic allocations always constitute a choice between competing interests; consequently, some groups are disadvantaged by almost every government decision. Indeed, even groups that profit from direct, specific allocations rarely gain enough to induce them to forge binding ties to the regime. Therefore, any political theory that focuses mainly upon the system's allocation of scarce resources will not explain systems persistence adequately.

The solution to the problem, according to Easton, is diffuse support.[15] Diffuse support consists of deeply held positive citizen affect towards the political system. Disadvantaged groups that lack diffuse support for the system become disaffected enough to revolt. By contrast, the presence of diffuse support provides an emotional cushion for the political system. Easton [16] conceives diffuse support to be latent and inaccessible to rational examination or discussion. The origins of diffuse support obviously are to be found, following the Freudian model, in childhood. Not surprisingly, therefore, Easton soon began, with others, a search for diffuse support in

---

11 See, for a critique, Greenstein, "Political Socialization," op. cit.
12 Greenstein, *Children and Politics*, op. cit., p. 157.
13 F. I. Greenstein, *Personality and Politics* (Chicago: Markham, 1969), pp. 20–40.
14 D. Easton, *A Systems Analysis of Political Life* (New York: Wiley, 1965), ch. 3.
15 Ibid., ch. 17.
16 Ibid., p. 274.

children.[17] This body of work differs markedly from that of Greenstein, for the former mainly is concerned about the macroconsequences of political socialization, while Greenstein talks primarily about the formation of political attitudes, leaving their articulation with the political system a somewhat more open question. An approach similar to that of Greenstein's, though drawing upon the Easton-Dennis data basis, is that of Hess and Torney. . . .[18]

SYSTEM-SPECIFIC ATTITUDES IN CHILDHOOD

By the fourth grade, most American children have developed two important political orientations, one towards the President[19] and the other towards political parties.[20] Let us discuss each orientation.

Easton and Dennis[21] believe that youthful orientations towards the President are an offshoot of the positive identifications the child established with his parent. Not surprisingly, the President appears powerful, benevolent, sensitive, aware of the child's needs, and capable of handling the demands of the Presidential role.[22] Of course, children do not have a clear conception of what being President entails, but most, by identifying the President with the father, apparently see the country on the model of a very large family cared for by a compassionate leader. According to Easton and Dennis,[23] (1969:190), Hess and Torney,[24] and Greenstein,[25] youthful supportive attitudes toward Presidential authority grow out of the child's vulnerability to and dependence upon parental largesse. Transfer of parental image is conceived to underly the fact that positive attitudes towards Presidential authority apparently develop irrespective of the occupant of the Presidential office. Of course, the Eisenhower phenomenon might account for this set of findings, but only one study, by Sigel,[26] validates this contention. Sigel found that the young child's partisan identification conditioned his view of President John Kennedy.

[17] D. Easton and J. Dennis, "The Child's Acquisition of Regime Norms: Political Efficacy," *American Political Science Review,* LXI (1967), 25–38; D. Easton and J. Dennis, *Children in the Political System* (Chicago: McGraw-Hill, 1969); D. Easton and R. D. Hess, "Youth and the Political System," in S. M. Lipset and L. Lowenthal, eds., *Culture and Social Character* (Glencoe, Ill.: The Free Press, 1961); D. Easton and R. D. Hess, "The Child's Political World," *Midwest Journal of Political Science,* VI (1962), 229–246; R. D. Hess and D. Easton, "The Child's Changing Image of the President," *Public Opinion Quarterly,* XXIV (1960), 632–644.

[18] R. D. Hess and J. V. Torney, *The Development of Political Attitudes in Children* (Chicago: Aldine, 1967).

[19] Greenstein, *Children and Politics,* op. cit., ch. 3; Hess and Torney, op. cit., ch. 3; Easton and Dennis, *Children in the Political System,* op. cit., ch. 8.

[20] Greenstein, op. cit., ch. 4.

[21] Easton and Dennis, op. cit., p. 201.

[22] Ibid., ch. 8.

[23] Ibid., p. 190.

[24] Hess and Torney, op. cit., pp. 20–21.

[25] Greenstein, *Children and Politics,* op. cit., pp. 46–48.

[26] R. S. Sigel, ed., "Image of a President: Some Insights into the Political Views of School Children," *American Political Science Review,* LXII (1968), 216–227.

Easton and Dennis [27] believe that the child's early positive evaluation of the Presidency is pivotal to the development of later supportive political orientations. However, they also stress the importance of the child's positive image of the policeman, an image based upon the policeman's role as protector of children.[28] Easton and Dennis' emphasis upon the socializing capacity of the policeman finds few echoes in the literature, although Greenberg [29] reports that young black children manifest more positive attitudes towards the police than they do towards the President.

Positive attitudes towards the President comprise the bulk of the child's diffuse support for the political system. Such support is augmented, however, by the early growth of partisan identification. After all, the child's attachment to a political party cements him to the political system by involving him intimately with a major system component. It is significant, therefore, that both Greenstein [30] and Hess and Torney's studies [31] show that large numbers of fourth graders claim a partisan identification. But there is some doubt about these findings. Greenstein's data base is a single city, New Haven, Connecticut. New Haven normally has a strong party politics that, at the time of Greenstein's field work, was dominated by a popular and highly partisan mayor, Richard C. Lee. Therefore, it is worth considering whether or not Greenstein's findings are situation and time-specific. Hess and Torney's findings also are inconclusive, for, though their data come from an eight-city sample, they do not assess subjective partisan identification itself, preferring instead to infer such identification from the child's self-reported voting expectations. This procedure insures error, in view of the widespread tendency of adults to deviate from partisan identification in voting.[32]

The extent to which early partisanship can be overstressed is suggested by Merelman's recent study. Merelman [33] discovered little partisan identification among 6th graders in two Los Angeles suburbs. Of course, the political culture of Southern California is not as party-dominated as is that of Connecticut; moreover, the nature of the political times altered radically between Greenstein's study and Merelman's 1967–68 field work. Specifically, Southern California is famous for voter instability, and in recent years strong attacks have been aimed at the party system nationally. But these caveats only emphasize the point. Research has not yet been comprehensive enough either in time or in space to yield firm conclusions about the role of youthful partisanship in the socialization of diffuse support.

There also is uncertainty about the development of other political orienta-

---

27 Easton and Dennis, *Children in the Political System*, op. cit., 198–207.
28 Ibid., chs. 10 and 11.
29 Greenberg, op. cit., p. 183.
30 Greenstein, *Children and Politics*, op. cit., ch. 4.
31 Hess and Torney, "The Development of Political . . . ," op. cit., p. 90.
32 R. M. Merelman, "Electoral Instability and the American Party System," *Journal of Politics*, XXXII (1970), 115–139.
33 R. M. Merelman, *Political Socialization and Educational Climates: A Study of Two School Districts* (New York: Holt, Rinehart and Winston, 1971); ch. 3.

tions in childhood. For example, Easton and Dennis [34] report a substantial increase in the child's political efficacy from the 4th through the 8th grade. But, this finding runs counter to Hess and Torney's argument [35] that the grade school emphasizes obedience to authority rather than political participation. An obedience orientation hardly encourages the growth of political efficacy. In his Los Angeles study Merelman [36] found political efficacy not at all well-formed by 6th grade; moreover, efficacy grew little from 6th through 9th grades. Unfortunately, Merelman's measure of political efficacy is less convincing than is that of Easton and Dennis. Still his data are consistent with recent findings reported by the Harveys.[37] Of course, these ambiguities may signify a changed political climate that leads today's child to political cynicism as early as grade school. The point, of course, is that we do not know what to conclude from the literature.

Certainly there are other findings which suggest that young children still manifest a diffusely positive attitude towards the political system. For example, over 30 per cent of Merelman's 6th graders admitted a desire to run for political office.[38] This proportion undoubtedly exceeds by far the fraction of adults who harbor political ambitions and bespeaks a youthful faith in the political system as a career channel. On a very different front, Wolfenstein and others [39] discovered that the assassination of President Kennedy had a profound and occasionally traumatic effect on young children. The depth of the reaction to the assassination would be incomprehensible without admitting that the President plays a central role not only in the child's conceptions of politics, but also in his view of a natural world resistant to sudden disturbance. Orren and Peterson [40] report that careful parental dissemination of assassination information reduced the severity of the child's reaction, but evidence of trauma remains.

Other tendencies toward diffuse support are existent in the child's identification with historical personages and national symbols, such as George Washington and the flag. Indeed, by the 6th grade, children in many countries find their nation's flag more attractive than those of other nations; [41] most American youngsters also avow their belief that the United States is the "best country" in the world.[42] Perhaps the safest conclusion to draw from these contradictory findings is that young children usually incline towards

[34] Easton and Dennis, "The Child's Acquisition of Regime Norms . . . ," op. cit.

[35] Hess and Torney, op. cit., p. 110.

[36] Merelman, *Political Socialization* . . . , op. cit., chs. 3 and 4.

[37] S. K. Harvey and T. G. Harvey, "Adolescent Political Outlooks: The Effects of Intelligence as an Independent Variable," *Midwest Journal of Political Science*, XIV (1970), 583.

[38] Merelman, Political Socialization . . . , op. cit., p. 87.

[39] M. Wolfenstein and G. Kliman, *Children and the Death of a President* (New York: Doubleday, 1965).

[40] K. Orren and P. Peterson, "Presidential Assassination: A Case Study in the Dynamics of Political Socialization," *Journal of Politics*, XXIX (1967), 388–405.

[41] E. A. Weinstein, "Development of the Concept of Flag and the Sense of National Identity," *Child Development*, XXVIII (1957), 166–174.

[42] Hess and Torney, op. cit., p. 29.

diffuse support, but that political events and situational contingencies can affect profoundly the depth and persistence of supportive tendencies.

SYSTEM-SPECIFIC ATTITUDES IN ADOLESCENCE

There are relatively few studies of political attitudes during adolescence, but there also is surprising agreement among these few. Adolescence emerges as a period of political uncertainty during which strong developmental patterns usually are absent. Jennings and Niemi [43] argue that the instability and malformation of adolescent political attitudes signifies a need for more study of adolescents. It could be argued as well, however, that the ambiguity of adolescent political orientations should serve as a warning to investigators that most of the important political orientations are formed in childhood, and that little of consequence is to be learned from further attention to adolescence.

Three aspects of adolescent socialization bear particular discussion: its slowed rate, its crystallization as a distinct form of socialization, and its change of affectual tone. Let us consider each of these facets.

Merelman [44] presents evidence that support for most democratic norms develops less between 9th and 12th grades than between 6th and 9th grades; Easton and Dennis [45] show that the young adolescent brings with him from childhood a relatively crystallized and highly developed sense of political efficacy. Merelman [46] also demonstrates that 12th graders are only slightly more sophisticated in their conceptions of public policy than are 8th graders, though his pilot study sample can support only tentative generalizations. Finally, evidence on the character and prevalence of adolescent political rebellion also suggests a slowing of development. There is little hard evidence for the popular belief that adolescent political rebellion in America is common or affect-laden.[47] Apparently, few adolescents use politics to act out aggressions against their parents. Indeed, those students most involved in radical, anti-establishment political activities rely heavily upon inherited political orientations [48] even as they substantially reshape those orientations. In short, there is little evidence that widespread political rebellion accelerates political socialization in adolescence. It is well to point out, however, that most hard data on this subject are restricted to a very narrow range of political orientations. The evidence of current student unrest calls for a broader approach to the question than the literature provides.

[43] M. K. Jennings and R. Niemi, "Patterns of Political Learning," *Harvard Educational Review*, XXVIII (1968), 443–468.

[44] Merelman, *Political Socialization* . . . , op. cit., ch. 4.

[45] Easton and Dennis, "The Child's Acquisition of Regime Norms: . . . ," op. cit.

[46] Merelman, op. cit.

[47] R. Middleton and S. Putney, "Political Expression of Adolescent Rebellion," *American Journal of Sociology*, LXVIII (1963), 527–535; D. W. Ball, "Covert Political Rebellion as Resentment," *Social Forces*, XLIII (October 1964), 93–101.

[48] K. Keniston, *Young Radicals* (New York: Harcourt, Brace and World, 1968); R. Flacks, "The Liberated Generation: An Exploration of the Roots of Student Protest," *Journal of Social Issues*, XXIII (1967), 52–75.

There also is evidence that during adolescence political socialization becomes differentiated from other forms of socialization. Easton and Dennis [49] show that as the child matures, his images and evaluations of political authorities disengaged themselves from his assessments of his parents. This divergence, according to Easton and Dennis, is the result of reduced parental control over the adolescent and the increasing salience of such system-regulated socialization agencies as the school. Additional significant evidence in support of the differentiation assertion is the fact that most 8th grade students have completed the institutionalization of politics, that is, the transfer of perceptual focus from key political personages and symbols to political institutions and roles. For example, adolescents have been found to be more likely than younger children to associate American politics with the Presidency rather than with a particular President; [50] in addition, adolescents pay attention to such important political institutions as the Congress and the Supreme Court, while at the same time the policeman fades from their consciousness as a symbol of authority.[51] Institutionalization obviously is a different perceptual and cognitive dimension from that usually employed in the adolescent's evaluation of his parents.

Still, it must not be assumed that all forms of political thinking become autonomous in adolescence. Valid evidence has yet to accumulate, but Kohlberg and Lockwood [52] report that such key forms of adolescent political thinking as the evaluation of policy dilemmas are related closely to nonpolitical moral judgment.

Lastly, adolescence is a time of political skepticism, as favorable orientations towards authority recede from the high points attained in childhood. Substantial numbers of adolescents believe that political authority is unresponsive, malevolent, and incompetent.[53] This withdrawal of support by no means wholly reverses the tide of childhood approval, but it does indicate system reassessment during adolescence.

Evidence from Merelman's Los Angeles study is particularly revealing on this subject. Merelman [54] found relatively little pro-democratic movement during adolescence along such attitude dimensions as freedom of speech, civic obligation, majority rule, and minority rights. Indeed, many adolescents simply refuse to endorse democratic norms, a surprising finding in view of the widespread reference to such values by radical student spokesmen. Merelman's findings are acutely reminiscent of Remmers' pessimistic conclusions [55] about adolescent support for democracy during the 1950's.

[49] Easton and Dennis, *Children in the Political System,* op. cit., pp. 249–254.

[50] Ibid., ch. 9.

[51] Ibid., pp. 254–270.

[52] L. Kohlberg and A. Lockwood, "Cognitive-Developmental Psychology and Political Education—Progress in the Sixties." Unpublished paper, 1970.

[53] R. M. Merelman, "The Development of Policy Thinking in Adolescence," *American Political Science Review,* (December 1971); Hess and Torney, op. cit., p. 76.

[54] Merelman, *Political Socialization and Educational Climates: . . . ,* op. cit., ch. 3.

[55] H. H. Remmers, *Anti-Democratic Attitudes in American Schools* (Evanston: Northwestern University Press, 1963), ch. 2.

Another indication of adolescent skepticism comes from the study of partisan identification. Jennings, and Niemi [56] report a sizeable rate of independence among their 12th grade sample; somewhat more adolescents than adults refuse to take sides in the party system. Hess and Torney [57] also report a sharply increasing independent rate during adolescence, though their particular index of partisanship prevents firm conclusions. Finally, over half of Merelman's 12th grade Los Angeles sample called themselves either Independents or "don't know," a figure exactly equal to the 9th grade percentage.[58] Adolescence apparently produces anything but commitment to parties.

Recent political events have, of course, focused attention upon the policy perspectives of adolescents, but any conclusions about this subject would be premature. There are two main hypotheses about the problem. First is the view that adolescent issue orientations are far closer to the views of parents than many casual observers believe; [59] second is the better known hypothesis that young people generally fall to the left of their parents but turn right with age.[60]

Unfortunately, neither view is supported adequately by the data. One reason is the difficulty of sorting out genuine life-cycle effects from idiosyncratic generational effects. The available cohort and longitudinal findings do indicate a slight trend to the left among adolescents in most generations and in many countries, but usable studies are too few and fragmentary to permit firm conclusions.[61] Only the Jennings-Niemi investigation comes near meeting methodological canons, for its data are drawn from interviews conducted with both parents and children. Conclusions, therefore, do not run into problems of recall accuracy. Jennings and Niemi [62] do find 12th graders somewhat to the left of their parents on most political issues. Unfortunately, the findings pertain to but one generation and shed no light upon the process by which left political attitudes are formed.

Merelman [63] was surprised to discover that policy views among ninth and twelfth graders fall along a cohesive liberal-conservative dimension, possibly

[56] M. K. Jennings and R. Niemi, "The Transmission of Political Values from Parent to Child," *American Political Science Review*, LXII (1968), 173.

[57] R. D. Hess and J. V. Torney, "The Development of Basic Attitudes and Values toward Government and Citizenship During the Elementary Years, Part 1." Report to the United States Office of Education, Cooperative Project No. 1078, p. 172.

[58] Merelman, *Political Socialization* . . . , op. cit., p. 82.

[59] E. Douvan and M. Gold, "Model Patterns in American Adolescence," in L. and M. Hoffman, eds., *Review of Child Development Research* (New York: Russell Sage Foundation, 1966), p. 485.

[60] For an extreme statement, see Jennings and Niemi, "The Transmission of Political Values . . . ," op. cit., p. 172.

[61] J. Crittenden, "Aging and Party Affiliation," *Public Opinion Quarterly*, XXVI (1962), 648–657 and "Reply to Cutler," *Public Opinion Quarterly*, XXXIII (1969), 589–592; N. Cutler, "Generation, Maturation, and Party Affiliation," *Public Opinion Quarterly*, XXXIII (1969), 583–589.

[62] Jennings and Niemi, "The Transmission of Political Values . . . ," op. cit., p. 174.

[63] Merelman, *Political Socialization* . . . , op. cit., ch. 3.

indicating an unusually tight ideological structuring among contemporary adolescents. But he also notes that among these students the proportion of Democrats, third party supporters, and Republicans are similar to those in the general population. The usage of left *ideology*, therefore, does not automatically lead leftward in party support.

FUNDAMENTAL ORIENTATIONS

So far we have been reviewing the literature on youthful attitudes toward the authority structures, institutions, personalities, and issues of our own political system. These attitudes are system-specific. But other political orientations are more fundamental, in the sense that they are directed towards fundamental aspects of *all* political systems, such as legitimacy, law, obedience, rights, and community obligations. What do we know about the growth of these orientations? According to Adelson and his colleagues,[64] whose articles are the foundation of this sub-field, pre-adolescents cannot bring themselves to question laws even though they envisage no general community interest superior to the interest of the self. The reason for this disjunction is that young children see law as a compelling emanation of mystical tradition, rather than as an instrument for the accomplishment of limited, specific ends. Individual rights, on the other hand, fall under no general moral principles, but are simply the products of idiosyncratic hedonistic calculation.

The picture changes abruptly in adolescence. By the end of their teenage years most adolescents have a considerably more relativistic sense of law. They comprehend its man-made origins and no longer believe it to be an emanation from the supernatural. Most also master a conception of community welfare that permits cooperation with the state in the absence of direct personal benefits. Thus, the purely hedonistic conception of individual rights fades. Adolescents do retain their commitment to individual welfare, but they prefer to see problems in the relationship between individual and community as necessitating the case-by-case balancing of equities rather than the blind application of inflexible laws.

Adelson and his colleagues discovered considerably more movement in these orientations during adolescence than did Merelman [65] in his study of some related forms of political thought. Merelman investigated four modes of policy thinking about poverty: moral, causal, sociocentric, and imaginative. Of these four, only moral thinking advanced significantly during adolescence. However, Merelman's youngest respondents were 8th graders, and

---

[64] J. Adelson and R. P. O'Neil, "Growth of Political Ideas in Adolescence: The Sense of Community," *Journal of Personality and Social Psychology,* VI (1966), 295–306; J. Adelson, B. Green, and R. P. O'Neil, "Growth of the Idea of Law in Adolescence," *Developmental Psychology,* I (1969), 327–332; J. Gallatin and J. Adelson, "Individual Rights and the Public Good: A Cross-National Study of Adolescents," *Comparative Political Studies,* III (1970), 226–243.

[65] Merelman, "The Development of Policy Thinking . . . ," op. cit.

Adelson's work suggests that much substantial movement in fundamental orientations occurs before this time. Merelman also shows that forms of policy thinking are less well-developed by the end of adolescence than are orientations towards law, the community, and individual rights.

More investigation of fundamental orientations clearly is needed. The field undoubtedly has been hampered by the general reliance of political socialization research upon the survey method, to the detriment of the depth interview approach required by studies of fundamental orientations.

Our review of the political orientations exhibited in childhood and adolescence permits us to speculate sensibly about sequence in political socialization. Little attention has been paid to this question, despite its importance as a means of allying political socialization to the psychological study of learning and maturation. However, the literature does take three rather different approaches.

First we encounter an implicit assumption that political socialization follows no particular sequence. This premise appears to guide the Survey Research Center group, for how else can we explain their almost exclusive concentration on socialization agencies? The structural characteristics and comparative importance of socialization agencies change spasmodically. Therefore, if socialization agencies are as important as the SRC implies, no single sequence of socialization could repeat itself for long.

Universal sequences of socialization can be postulated only if the investigator believes that individual maturation follows a more or less repetitive course dictated by characteristic interactions between environmental constraints or facilitations and developmental uniformities. Two such approaches have been advanced. One is the Freudian perspective enunciated by Greenstein,[66] Easton and Dennis,[67] Jaros,[68] and Hess and Torney; [69] the other is the cognitive-developmental model advanced by Merelman,[70] Hess and Torney,[71] and Dawson and Prewitt.[72]

Strictly speaking, of course, the orthodox Freudian framework cannot be applied rigorously to the findings we have reviewed. Most psychoanalytic theory assumes that fundamental attitudes towards parental authority form by the sixth year of life, although few children this young have a clear image of Presidential authority. Therefore, the Freudian framework requires a codicil of developmental lag. Still, a psychoanalytic approach expanded by

[66] Greenstein, *Children and Politics,* op. cit., p. 46.

[67] Easton and Dennis, *Children in the Political System,* op. cit.

[68] D. Jaros, "Children's Orientations Toward the President: Some Additional Theoretical Considerations and Data," *Journal of Politics,* XXIX (1967), 368–388.

[69] Hess and Torney, *The Development of Political Attitudes . . . ,* op. cit., p. 20.

[70] R. M. Merelman, "The Development of Political Ideology: A Framework for the Analysis of Political Socialization," *American Political Science Review,* LXIII (1969), 750–767.

[71] Hess and Torney, *The Development of Political Attitudes . . . ,* op. cit., p. 21.

[72] R. E. Dawson and K. Prewitt, *Political Socialization* (Boston: Little, Brown, 1969), pp. 51–52.

Erikson's discussion of identity [73] explains well both the child's idealization of and the adolescent's skepticism about political authority.

But a Freudian framework has difficulty predicting the differentiation of attitudes towards parental authority from attitudes towards political authority. The lack of parallelism between these two sets of orientations suggests that political socialization does not depend upon the developmental mechanisms described in psychoanalytic theory. Moreover, psychoanalytic theory treats subordination to parental authority as a source of neurotic defenses, but there is little evidence that such defenses play a major role in political socialization.[74] For these reasons, among others, recent theory has turned towards a cognitive-developmental approach.

Dawson and Prewitt [75] were among the first investigators to apply Piaget's cognitive-developmental model to political socialization; Merelman [76] attempts to elaborate that model into a comprehensive framework for analyzing socialization. No one can doubt the resemblance between the child's movement from concrete to formal-operational thought in Piaget's scheme and the child's passage from a diffusely, supportive, personalistic, traditional view of politics to a more institutional, skeptical perspective. Moreover, the development of fundamental orientations towards law, the community, and individual rights also seems to follow the Piagetian-Kohlbergian sequence.

But at this point the argument encounters difficulties. For one thing, as Gallatin and Adelson [77] point out, the development of political orientations lags as much as two or three years behind the main body of cognitive development. This lag can only indicate how peripheral politics is to the child. In turn, the peripheral character of politics may loosen political socialization from cognitive development, thereby opening socialization to as yet unknown influences. Moreover, large numbers of adolescents apparently never structure their political orientations as fully as Kohlberg [78] might expect. Finally, cognitive-developmental theory fails to account for the purely affectual, motivational side of political socialization. This failure can have serious consequences. For example, we would be wrong to view the early idealization of authority as a cognitive universal, for as Jaros and his associates [79] show, idealization also depends upon a positive relationship with parents.

Conspicuously lacking from the socialization literature is any concerted attempt to apply to political maturation recent theories or findings about

[73] E. H. Erikson, *Childhood and Society* (New York: Norton, 1950), pp. 261–263.

[74] An exception is F. A. Pinner, "Parental Overprotection and Political Distrust," *Annals,* CCCLXI (1965), 59–70.

[75] Dawson and Prewitt, *Political Socialization,* op. cit., pp. 51–52.

[76] Merelman, "The Development of Political Ideology: . . . ," op. cit.

[77] Gallatin and Adelson, op. cit., p. 239.

[78] L. Kohlberg, "The Cognitive-Developmental Approach to Socialization," in D. Goslin, ed., *Handbook of Socialization Theory and Research* (Chicago: Rand McNally, 1969).

[79] D. Jaros, et al., "The Malevolent Leader: Political Socialization in an American Sub-Culture," *American Political Science Review,* LXII (1968), 564–575.

imitation, modeling, and role playing.[80] The absence is unfortunate, primarily because these forms of learning may have much to do with the impact of such socialization agencies as the school, the peer group, and the mass media, whose representatives rarely establish enduring relationships with the child.

[80] A. Bandura and R. H. Walters, *Social Learning and Personality Development* (New York: Holt, Rinehart and Winston, 1963); L. Thomas, "Role Theory, Personality, and the Individual," in E. Borgatta and W. W. Lambert, eds., *Handbook of Personality Theory and Research* (Chicago: Rand McNally, 1968).

W. *Fred Graham*

Technology, Technique, and the Jesus Movement

Counterculture religious movements are distinguished in this paper on the basis of their endorsement of the technological age. Graham places youth in the Jesus Movement among those groups which denounce both industrialism and traditional Christianity. He says that they believe themselves to be living in a "cold, meaningless universe." Sorrow rather than joy characterizes them, and they appear to understand "the world to be at least provisionally in the hands of the prince of the power of darkness." They turn off the world, "grooving (as they would say) on essentials: salvation, sanctification, prayer, witness, fellowship and the work of the Holy Spirit in their lives."

Instructional Objectives
To distinguish between counterculture religious movements on the basis of whether technology is endorsed or repudiated.
To offer a plausible explanation for the appeal of the Jesus Movement.
To describe the characteristics of the Jesus Movement.

PROPONENTS of "counterculture" styles of thought and life differ critically regarding the place of technology in the new or "green" world that is nearing parturition. On the one side are those who—like Charles Reich [1] or

FROM *Christian Century*, XC (1973), pp. 507–510. Copyright 1973 Christian Century Foundation. Reprinted by permission from the May 2, 1973 issue and the author.

[1] C. Reich, *The Greening of America* (New York: Random House, 1970).

Jean-François Revel [2]—laud the products of technology and insist that the new society will use them without being dominated by them. Indeed, they hold that some of these products—the pill and the tape deck, for instance— were a major influence in creating the new consciousness and that they are necessary if Western man is to topple the Corporate State and come into new openness and freedom. On the other side are those who—like Theodore Roszak,[3] the compilers of the *Whole Earth Catalog* and admirers of Carlos Castaneda's three books on the Yaqui Indian *brujo* Don Juan—believe that technology is the enslaver of modern man and that, unless we shrug off its products as well as the rationalistic mind-set which gave rise to technological society, there is little hope for the future. Century readers will see the shadow of Jacques Ellul (*The Technological Society* and a spate of related books) behind this position.

In the more specifically religious field, these two attitudes toward technology and its manipulative corollary are much in evidence. Broadly speaking, it can be said that disciples of the Maharishi and researchers in brain-waves-*cum*-meditation represent the "pro" side of machinery and know-how, and the Jesus movement represents the polar opposite. Let us look first at the former.

I

In classic Eastern mysticism the aim is *moksha*, the existential realization that the essence of the individual (*atman* or soul) and the Essence of the universe (*brahman*) are one. The Buddhist term for this realization is Buddha-consciousness, though Buddhism holds to a greater philosophical skepticism concerning what it is that is united to the Holy Nothingness of Nirvana. The route in either case is long and difficult and somewhat painful. In Hinduism, such realization can be attained only by one who has studied long under a guru and has followed one or other of the arduous yogas or disciplines (the "yogas-yoke"). In Buddhism, the choice of yogas has been narrowed down to *raja* or "royal" yoga; i.e., the discipline of meditation.

But when the West really got into the Eastern thing, it was not through the long discipline of a yoga. Not at all surprisingly, the West achieved instant enlightenment by way of drugs. More recently, it has invented Transcendental Meditation as a way of getting quick results. This way looks genuinely Oriental, but whereas no Eastern religion has ever promised practitioners of its disciplines that kind of rapid success, Transcendental Meditation guarantees peace of mind to those who practice it for two 20-minute periods per day. Thus efficiency, the chief mark of technique, links up with Eastern religion the very moment it begins to have widespread effect in the West. In other words, it would appear that Eastern religion will not have even a ghost of a chance in the quick-production, quick-consumption West unless

[2] J. Revel, *Without Marx or Jesus* (New York: Doubleday, 1971).
[3] T. Roszak, *The Making of a Counter Culture* (New York: Doubleday, 1969).

it streamlines itself to the point of caricaturing its historical and philosophical integrity.

How easily technique, with its good efficiency, can move into religion is illustrated by the current scientific study of altered and expanded consciousness. Here one runs into the tangled wires of devices that measure skin temperatures and brain waves.[4] However interesting they may be, a caveat is in order regarding all such "scientific" studies. Remember, for instance, Masters and Johnson's research on sexual intercourse. It is probably true that because of their pioneering work people can be taught to have more satisfying sexual experiences; but it seems equally true that this may have little or nothing to do with loving another person. I am saying that we of today tend to substitute what technique *can* do for what it cannot do; we substitute sexual technique for love—and then wonder why love falls short and sexual techniques finally fail.

II

One of the interesting things that electroencephalographology has demonstrated is that the human brain puts out at least four kinds of electrical current, which researchers dub alpha, beta, delta and theta waves respectively. It is the theta waves that technicians are particularly excited about. They believe that these are the same waves that account for the visions of the great mystics, and they say that people who have been practicing meditation for a long time also produce theta waves. To be sure, these scientists find that alpha waves too indicate a turning-off of outside stimuli and concentration on one's own thoughts; but they think the former are more common and represent a level of consciousness lower than that indicated by theta waves. Anyway, serious research is now going on to discover what the connection between science and religion is in the human brain. One quotation may be sufficient to suggest the importance of this research for religious practice. In the article by Bill Schul, Dr. Elmer Green of the Menninger Foundation says: [5]

> The electroencephalograph, along with other devices, for the first time has provided science the opportunity to examine human consciousness. We are learning a great deal about the human mind, how it functions, how it learns, and this, in time, should have quite an impact on the whole educational process. But perhaps of even greater importance, science is beginning to confirm many of our religious and mystical traditions. In the past science has been criticized as the antithesis of religion, but today a body of evidence is growing which indicates that the higher levels of conscious awareness are not only a reality but also a legitimate business of science.

[4] For a summary of what is happening in this field see B. D. Schul, "Altered Consciousness: What the Research Points Toward," *The Christian Century*, January 19, 1972.
[5] Ibid.

A friendly statement indeed from the scientific community! But suppose you examine religious experience by way of the techniques described (plus "brainwave feedback training") with a view to enabling a person to attain in a few weeks a point of development in reaching higher modes of consciousness that (as Schul quotes researcher Erik Hoffman as saying) would have taken "three years under any other discipline." I wonder whether this is not to bend religious experience to the technique you are using. No doubt the techniques will work; no doubt people can be taught to put out theta waves at a rate not matched since Isaiah saw the Lord "high and lifted up." I can hear technicians exclaiming: "Man, look at those theta waves! It's a new record, and set not by some Zen master but by a white middle-class Jewish sophomore from MIT who trained hard two hours a day for six weeks." But just as I know from 20 years of marriage that love includes but is infinitely and almost undefinably more than sexual technique, so I suspect that anyone who is serious about man or God, about *moksha* or Buddha-consciousness, will not see in that wavy line any evidence for what he is passionately concerned about. Most people, however, *will* see that line as evidence. Because what technology and know-how cannot get you, and get you quickly, is not to be got; anyone who disagrees is simply afraid that the secrets he has worked for so long and hard can be appropriated by the masses in six easy lessons. Technology and propaganda of a well-meaning sort have programmed us to respond this way, for you can't sell the products of our industrial process by telling people they are hard to get! But so far in human history the result of technique has been not a heightening but rather a narrowing and flattening of human experience.

III

So we come to the antitechnology group of the counterculture—to the Jesus movement as representing the amorphous, many-faceted, anti-institutional and fundamentalist ferment among college-age youth today. The first thing to note is the soil in which this particular "greening" has grown. Many of our young people find it difficult to be as optimistic about life in our changing society as Reich and Revel profess to be. Indeed the optimism of *The Greening of America* seems remote from the mood of introspection and pessimism that many of my students express in talks with me. As they see it, their own perceptions are systematically ignored by the world, and their only alternatives are to drop out—and thus give up any ideas of influencing the system; or to stay in—and thus run the risk of having their minds so warped that they won't want to influence the system.

But I think I detect an even deeper pessimism in my students: their feeling that they are living in a cold, meaningless universe in which man emerged from the haphazard evolutionary process by accident, and a sorry accident at that. Either the universe "means something" or it does not; and the suspicion of many is that it does not.

This, of course, is the starting point of nontheistic existentialism. The message of Jean-Paul Sartre is, in effect: "The only meaning you will find in an accidental universe is the one you impress upon it." But that is quite an effort when the end is not rebirth or life with God, but disappearance into the earth—"enriching the humus," as theologian Sam Keen says. Our destiny is the same as that of the billions of people who have come and gone on this planet since personality came into existence—most of whom never had leisure to look up from their toil, to become "self-actualized" and thereby find some fleeting meaning for themselves. With God dead, the sacred cosmos of the past rendered utterly profane, and once-great theologies, East or West, turned into caricatures, man is thrust back upon his own tiny resources for creating and holding onto meaning. Is it any wonder that sorrow rather than joy and happiness seems to characterize American youth? There is pathos in what is dead: "Bye, bye, Miss American pie."

The Jesus movement seems to be an answer to this emptiness—an answer by way of a narrowing and deinstitutionalizing of traditional Christian theology. And perhaps inevitably such. For on American soil the church never held a place comparable to that which it held in Europe. Moreover, traditional theology has always been simplified here. People who had a continent to conquer could spend little time shaping and elaborating a theology. Their question was: How much do you need to know to be saved?

Modern youth's questions are less direct. One can imagine the following dialogue: Q.: What good are my efforts to change the world when nothing changes? A.: God will change it in his time, not ours. Q.: What good are theta waves if they only amount to psychic masturbation to the rhythm of a machine? A.: Jesus shows us that God is the Encountered One in every religious experience; but he needs no machines, only trust and prayer. Q.: What good are sensitivity groups if the world remains insensitive? A.: Be part of a movement whose aim is love, whose foundation is love, whose Exemplar is love. Q.: What about the hole in my life when all I can find to fill it with is ultimately empty too? A.: God promises you eternal wholeness. Q.: How can I live in a world, whether under capitalism or communism, whose methods deface the beautiful and crucify the good? A.: Come, you'll see that with God's power every crucifixion can become a resurrection.

IV

Writers about the Jesus movement are quick to point to its origins in biblical Christianity and to emphasize that the young are trying to live out what their parents professed to believe but did not practice. But the strong anti-technological bias of these college-age Christians is often missed. In their search for a simple Christian existence, they are like their non-Christian fellows in the counterculture who eschew as much of modern society as they possibly can. It is as if they had a sure instinct that today's unfaith is rooted largely in an industrial process; that—as Ellul has argued so persuasively and as most of us experience existentially—the technological society is radically incapable of faith.

How so? Well, we hear a great deal about agricultural and fishing communes which attempt to reroot people in nature and make them marginal to industrial—or, if you prefer, postindustrial—society. But it is more instructive just to observe and listen to these young men and women (they are neither shy nor dumb). They are not interested in jobs which take time from witnessing; for them, as for St. Paul, work is a means of holding body and soul together so that they can carry on the real purposes of life. Their quarters lack the expensive stereo equipment that you will find in every college dormitory or student apartment. They speak of a world which is passing away. As Roger Palms points out in *The Jesus Kids*,[6] their most quoted biblical texts have to do with the end time, the imminent disappearance of the world as we know it, the possibility of the "rapture" of the saints—all those apocalyptic passages that we rational, mundane Christians tend to dismiss as cryptic. They do not believe in the myth of progress. Their sexual mores are not "puritanical," but they do not consider sex highly important. They seem simply to have turned off the world of advertising and its glorification of sex, and they are grooving (as they would say) on essentials: salvation, sanctification, prayer, witness, fellowship, and the work of the Holy Spirit in their lives. Indeed, they remind one of the real Puritans, who lived so deeply that sex and all physical pleasures, while important, were not the focus of existence. Here again the "Jesus kids" flout the technological society. Where many of us do everything in our power to enhance our own attractiveness and keep our youth, where we pursue life as though it were about to slip from between our fingers, these "kids" are just "simple." Obviously, pleasure is *not* what life is all about; so they give it little thought and less time. They do not "buy into" modern society.

Intellectual historians cite many reasons for the demise of the invisible world of God, which men made visible by building cathedrals, organizing society, developing commerce and fighting the crusades. The Protestant work ethic, religious pluralism, the rise of modern science and its attendant philosophies (Cartesian rationalism and skepticism), the building of cities—all these have been blamed for the disappearance of the "sacred canopy" of the Middle Ages. Probably these did play a part, but observers as different as Thorstein Veblen, Peter Berger and Bishop E. R. Wickham place the major blame on the industrial process. For, they say, this process made the workingman perceive the world as a cause-and-effect machine, chained him to a god more efficient and powerful than any possible extraworldly power, and uprooted him from the rural society in which he had a role he understood. The process itself—the means of production—did more to fragment that invisible world than all the Humes or La Places with their philosophy or science.

---

[6] R. Palms, *The Jesus Kids* (Judson, 1971).

In any case, the Jesus movement people are rejecting that process. It is too time-consuming and demanding; it requires allegiances they will not make because they consider them idolatrous. Indeed, their often shrill denunciation of the churches issues from their conviction that we church people have sold our simple faith in Jesus for a mess of pottage; that is, for a production and sales system with a reciprocating consumer mentality which cannot allow us to seek first the kingdom of God and his righteousness. The jobs they do take in order to live are jobs that demand of them a minimum of loyalty and time. In contrast to standard-brand Pentecostals, at whose services there are frequent references to people "moving up" to better, more responsible jobs with bigger rewards, these youngsters keep only a tenuous relationship to education and job so that nothing can rob them of the time and energy they need to be active in the Lord.

That's where the Jesus kids are now. Not for them a meditative process that, presumably, would enable them to live sanely in our mad world. Nor are they interested in hitching machines to people to measure the quantity of their religious experience. Their approach to modern life is semieremitic or communal or Anabaptist in that it understands the world to be at least provisionally in the hands of the prince of the power of darkness. They can feel right in living with that world only by being marginal to it. The radicals of the late '50s and '60s talked about being "marginal men." The Jesus youth *are* marginal men. Whether they can keep on that way will be the real test.

Jerome L. Rodnitzky

The Decline of Contemporary Protest Music

Protest music arose in the mid-1960s as a major counterculture expression of youth's longing for personal fulfillment. Rodnitsky observes that folk writer-performers who function as social rebels, refusing to cater to the press, fans or music fads, develop credibility with "young radicals" and other youth who seek models upholding individuality. Rodnitsky, however, acknowledges that protest music has virtually disappeared today and advances such reasons for its cessation as "commercial success, cultural acceptance, and failure to establish relationships with specific social reform movements."

FROM *Popular Music and Society*, I (1971), pp. 44–50. Reprinted by permission of the author and the publisher.

Instructional Objectives
To describe the characteristics of contemporary protest music.
To suggest reasons why protest music has declined markedly as an expressive mode in the counterculture.

D URING the last five years, protest music has increasingly lost its meaning. It no longer suffices to suggest that a song protests. One must also inquire whether its protest lies primarily in its lyrics, music, style, or even in the performer's manner and dress. In short, does the song have an obvious message, or does it drive home its point in some subtle, symbolic, cultural code? Blatant message music has long since been driven to the cultural fringes by sophisticated ridicule and dwindling commercial success. It is no longer stylish or profitable to sing directly about social evils. Muckraking lyrics now often insult an audience's intelligence. The young ears that strain to pick up the vibrations of protest music are usually already convinced that the nation is hung up, corrupt, and decaying. They want to know how to confront the situation or at least how to live with it.

At the same time, the new generation shrinks from the syrupy phrase, the tired cliché, and the maudlin play on emotions. Those critics who caustically attacked the romantic emotionalism of Erich Segal's *Love Story* usually overlooked the generally unemotional, understated, low-keyed conversation of the novel's collegiate couple—especially Jenny's aversion to the Madison-Avenue superlative. *Love Story's* dialogue is typical of this generation's desire to mutely complete conversational blanks and make communication a veritable crossword puzzle. Thus, *Love Story* aptly illustrates an important new generational myth—the notion that people who really understand one another do so intuitively rather than verbally.

This tendency is easily observed in contemporary, popular message music —in the hazy lyrics of Bob Dylan, Paul Simon, and Joni Mitchell, for example, or the frenetic beat of the Rolling Stones or Jefferson Airplane. The words, style, and music are all open to various poetic interpretations. They are really do-it-yourself protest songs, since you can read your own problems into them and reap existential answers or solace in return. Another symptom of the breakdown of meaning lies in the relationships between the performer, the song, and the audience. Whereas one primary characteristic of the traditional folk-protest singer was an inclination to spend as much time introducing and explaining the song as singing it, if the contemporary singer speaks to the audience at all, he tends to talk about everything except the song.

Another striking development of contemporary protest music is the terminal illness overtaking various folk-protest orthodoxies. The arty attitude of *The Little Sandy Review,* which in 1962 could condemn a "Protesty song" as one that was "neither true protest nor true song," is necessarily suspect to a generation that identifies "true" anything with rigid ideology or social brainwashing.[1] Meanwhile, *Broadside,* the major butt of *Sandy Review's* barbed wit, because of the former periodical's tendency to protest with every line of every topical song it published, has now largely become a literary forum. The mostly mediocre topical ballads it presently prints are secondary to its often stimulating commentary on the musical scene and its usually sophomoric social criticism. *Sing Out* has made a valiant attempt to bridge the gap between the ideological and artistic traditionalists on the one hand and the loose, diverse counter-culture enthusiasts on the other, but the compromise does not satisfy many. Probably *Rolling Stone,* the psychedelic newspaper, more accurately reflects the vague amorphous nature of today's protest music. Amidst this cultural chaos, it is not surprising that Irwin Silber, former editor of *Sing Out* and a leader of protest-song movements since 1945, recently concluded that "the once vital folk song movement in America" was now "either hopelessly co-opted by the market-place or reduced to the level of a white, middle-class suburban hobby." [2]

That folk-rock increasingly means all things to all people is ironically illustrated by equally vigorous attacks on the new music from both the Right and the Left. Thus, such fiercely fundamentalist and anti-Communist groups as the Tulsa-based Christian Crusade attack folk-rock as a Marxist plot to subvert the nation's youth. This view is particularly explicit in such Crusade publications as Reverend David Noebel's book, *Rhythm, Riots, and Revolution* and his pamphlet, *Columbia Records: Home of Marxist Minstrels.* However, Irwin Silber, a Marxist-oriented cultural critic and one of Noebel's major villains, recently concluded that popular music threatened radical reform. Silber argued that American workers intuitively sense that electronic folk-rock "is basically a middle class trip." He further noted that the music's invitation to do your own thing was a capitalist, "bourgeoisie trait" and that "groovy life styles" induced the masses to ignore the system that oppressed them rather than struggling to change it.[3] No doubt, the anti-Communist Christian fundamentalists now fear electronic music less as a vanguard of atheistic Marxism and more as an emotional substitute for religious fundamentalism. Both fundamentalism and psychedelic music have a sensory stress that appeals to emotion over reason and the heart as opposed to the intellect.

There now seems little or nothing to revere. Some still popular topical singers like Tom Paxton, Joan Baez, and Phil Ochs may consider themselves to be "Woody's Children," but the young audiences who listen to their slickly-arranged, orchestrated ballads usually find Woody Guthrie's songs corny, simplistic, and irrelevant. Pete Seeger can still occasionally spring his sing-

[1] Jon Panake and Paul Nelson, "P for Protesty," *Little Sandy Review,* XXV (April, 1962), p. 18.

[2] Irwin Silber's column in *The Guardian,* May 9, 1970, p. 7.

[3] For the Christian Crusade's views see David Noebel, *Rhythm, Riots, and Revolution* (Tulsa, 1966) and *Columbia Records: Home of Marxist Minstrels* (Tulsa, 1967). Silber's comments appear in *The Guardian,* December 6, 1969, p. 17.

along charisma at an anti-War or anti-pollution rally, but on television and records the youth generally find him quaint and dull. Thus, it is perhaps logical that songs sung in the simple unvarnished Guthrie-Seeger style are now most often country-and-western topical ballads that appeal to the prejudices of an older, middle-America—songs like "Please Mr. Professor," "Welfare Cadillac," and "Okie from Muskogee." [4] These new protest songs on the right are destroying another folk-protest myth—specifically, the legend that topical songs appealing to the discontented common "folk" were almost by definition ballads sympathetic to social reform.

Increasingly, the classic protest-song tradition lives not in the folk, but in the memory and articles of academicians and folklorists who continue to inquire about the roots, ideology, and continuity of the folk-revival. Of course, one can do away with distasteful arguments about cultural continuity by adopting Bob Dylan's conclusion that "it's all just music." Yet, this hardly satisfies those intellectual scholars who Richard Hofstadter described as compulsive generalizers, nor does it calm those remnants of the Guthrie-Seeger tradition who see topical music as a lever for social reform.

That overt protest music has declined is universally acknowledged. However, there is less agreement and more significance in regard to the reasons for its demise. The causes of collapse are literally legion. They range from the commercial to the creative to the psychological. Protest music declined because guru Bob Dylan continually refused to lead some new magical protest renaissance. It degenerated as it became clear that the poetic songs of Paul Simon and other writers were messageless patchwork creations that reflected only the author's desire to create artful songs.[5] Protest music declined when a gifted singer like Judy Collins cut "preachy" songs from her repertory because she was tired of "finger pointing" at people she recognized "from the last rally." For, as Arlo Guthrie had noted: "You don't accomplish very much singing protest songs to people who agree with you. Everybody just has a good time thinking they're right." [6] Thus, Gordon Friesen, editor of *Broadside,* recently complained that although a number of good protest songs were being written, many folksingers sold out by singing "meaningless fluff about . . . clouds, flowers, butterflies . . . Suzannes . . . and the like." Indeed, some former topical singers even avoid the term folksinger by describing themselves as singers of "contemporary art songs." As Donovan Leitch put it in November, 1969, the "best writers" had "evolved to the point" where they "left protest behind and beauty" crept in.[7] Perhaps a 1970

---

[4] On the rise, style, and impact of these songs, see R. Serge Denisoff, "Kent State, Muskogee, and the White House," *Broadside,* no. 108 (July, 1970), pp. 2-4.

[5] On Simon's songs see Robert Christgau's "Rock Lyrics Are Poetry (Maybe)," in Jonathan Eisen (ed.), *The Age of Rock* (New York, 1969), pp. 236–239. In 1970 on both the Dick Cavett and Johnny Carson television talk shows, Simon frankly commented on his random method of songwriting.

[6] "An Interview with Judy Collins," *Life,* May 2, 1969, pp. 45–46. Arlo Guthrie quoted in "Woody's Boy," *Newsweek,* May 23, 1966, p. 110.

[7] Editorial, *Broadside,* no. 107 (June, 1970), pp. 9–10. Donovan quoted in UPI dispatch in *Fort Worth Press,* November 2, 1969.

New Yorker cartoon summed up the new attitude best. It pictured a young female folksinger (guitar in hand) about to begin her performance at a coffeehouse, however, before commencing she advised her audience that since her songs had no "social or political significance" she would like to assure them that she was opposed to the Vietnamese War and in favor of legalizing marijuana, boycotting California grapes, and Federal control of the economy.[8]

Whereas in 1967, topical singer Phil Ochs could fire up sophisticated radical activists, by 1969 Ochs was incapable of firing himself up. For example, in 1967 James Kunen, radical Columbia student, attended an Ochs concert in Central Park and wrote in his diary: "After listening to Phil Ochs, I'm ready not only to burn City Hall, but to charge out and stuff envelopes or distribute leaflets or even sit at a meeting." [9] However, the same general frustrations that had radicalized activist youth had also driven protest writers like Ochs to despair and destroyed their creativity. Ochs' songs have steadily become more revolutionary in spirit and more pessimistic about the future of American society. In a 1969 album, *Rehearsals for Retirement,* he sang an apocalyptic song titled, "A New Age" which aptly reflected his new mood. The ballad noted that considering the soldier's sorrow and the rage of the wretched, Americans should "pray for the aged," since we were approaching "the dawn of another age." The song later commented that while America was "born in a revolution," it "died in a wasted war." On the record jacket, Ochs bemoaned the fate of an America "imprisoned by" its "paranoia" and he concluded:

> My responsibilities are done, let them come, let them come. And I realize these last days these trials and tragedies were after all, only our rehearsal for retirement.[10]

Perhaps Theo Bikel was right back in 1967, when he asserted that "the protest song movement . . . had been shattered on the realities of American politics." [11] Moreover, as the despair of radicals mounts, it is becoming harder to decide whether formerly activist songwriters are using pessimism and sarcasm as a vehicle of protest or are simply dropping out politically.

There is increasingly less interest in arguing about what song lyrics mean. For example, the so-called "Dylanologists" are losing their audience. The youth do not seek meaning but mystique. Simultaneously they search for an all-encompassing oneness and individuality. They drop out of a conformist establishment society only to fall into a rigidly, non-conformist youth culture. Faced with such contradictory aims, it is better not to talk about meaning. Since the now generation has the illusion of unanimity, trying to define what they agree on is more likely to produce division than accord. For each individual, it is enough that the music fills a personal need.

[8] Cartoon by Charles Saxon in *New Yorker,* January 24, 1970, p. 30.
[9] James Simon Kunen, *The Strawberry Statement* (New York, 1969), p. 94.
[10] Phil Ochs album, *Rehearsals for Retirement,* A & M Records, 1969.
[11] Theo Bikel's comment made at 1967 Newport Folk Festival, quoted in *Broadside,* no. 87 (December, 1967), p. 12.

Nevertheless, if the songs have become less important, the folk writer-performers themselves have become more important as models for youth obsessed with individuality. Traditionally, the folksinger was a brawny laborer, an ex-convict, a hobo, or perhaps, a college-educated, amateur folklorist. Today's folksinger, however, is more likely an alienated college drop-out or graduate, seeking self-identity, money, or both through his own music. More importantly many singers symbolize personal integrity. Youth feel that Joan Baez, Phil Ochs, or Bob Dylan cannot be bought in the traditional show business sense. Thus, even though Dylan renounced protest music, he remains popular with practically all young radicals, because he consistently functions as a social rebel and refuses to bow to the press, or fans, or musical fads. Many preach doing your own thing, but Dylan lives it. Thus, he remains a credible existential hero.

Naturally, all this hero worship, mystique, and charisma are big business and with the expanding youth market very profitable. Indeed, commercialism is the one charge that all the new folk heroes must avoid. Some social reformers, however, do not fear the dangers of the marketplace, rather they welcome the struggle for the youth market. For example, Simon Kunen, a young radical writer, feels that capitalism has "a self-destruct mechanism." He argues that media conglomerates that dominate our popular culture seek only profit, and if radical revolutionary materials are profitable, corporations gladly disseminate radicalism and revolution.[12] Most reformers are far more pessimistic and feel that the mass media co-opt radical reform by diluting content and dulling fervor. For example, when protest songs are accompanied by a full orchestra, art may be improved but the message and the ardor may suffer.

However, the question is not whether protest music is alive and well commercially. The influence of protest music cannot be measured statistically. The few it does affect may be particularly vigorous activists who influence many others. The real present problem is that protest music has been fragmented by its commercial success, cultural acceptance, and failure to establish relationships with specific social reform movements. Thus, the most gifted topical writers and singers are striking out in several directions for personal reasons.

The folk revival and its offspring, the protest-song renaissance, have not died, but both are badly disintegrated. Perhaps this is appropriate in an age of polarization, fragmentation, and general discord. In any event, early in this new decade, students of protest music will necessarily have to focus their investigations on narrower areas of concern, if they are to follow the new music and artists and continue to draw useful conclusions. Some will argue proverbially that we will thus not see the wood for the trees. However, one may answer with the wisdom of philosopher Robin Collingwood: ". . . who wants to? A tree is a thing to look at; but a wood is not a thing to look at; it is a thing to live in."

[12] James Simon Kunen quoted on CBS' "Camera Three" television show, July 12, 1970.

Part

7

Imperfections in Socialization:
Drugs, Deviant Behavior, and Delinquency

Students of adolescence generally agree that youth who indulge in drugs, deviancy, and delinquency flout conventional morality and reveal, in many instances, imperfections in the processes of their socialization. Drug usage is prohibited by federal and state authorities; deviant behavior and delinquency are usually inhibited by the dictates of citizenship and conscience. The social unrest during the past decade, however, has stimulated revisions in legislation and more humaneness and tolerance in judging transgressions of morality. Six papers are presented in Part 7 that indicate collectively how swiftly social interpretations of the significance of drugs and delinquency are changing.

When drugs first appeared on a massive scale in the youth culture in the mid 1960s, most law enforcement officials espoused punitive, rigid, and moralistic attitudes. Medical officials commonly believed that drug use outside of a medical context was undesirable, and thus, any nonmedical use was "abuse." Parents and school authorities generally accepted these viewpoints at face value. The inclusive, almost wholesale condemnation of adolescent drug usage, however, is fading today in the adult society. Widespread publicity has been given objective, empirical investigations of both the physical consequences and the social significance of drug usage among adolescents, and the first three papers in Part 7, each of which deal with drugs, are characteristic of reports appearing in the 1970s. Each paper recognized a critical need for clinical rehabilitative services, and each acknowledges the necessity of developing efficient diagnostic procedures for distinguishing drug-use propensities among adolescents. Further, each investigation emphasizes that study of relationships between personality development and drug-usage may prove invaluable in understanding how to predict adolescents' susceptibility to drugs. First, drawing from their experiences in an inner city clinic, Proskauer and Rolland identify three categories of adolescent drug user: Experimental—*who appear "normal" in personality development;* depressive—*who manifest neurotic symptoms associated with feelings of emptiness, loneliness and worthlessness; and* characterological—*who exhibit major disabilities, perhaps related to serious deprivation or rejection early in their socialization. The researchers suggest a different clinical approach for each*

427

of the three categories. The experimental drug user, for example, may be responsive to either counseling or informal educational programs. The depressive drug users may benefit from psychotherapy, and the characterologically crippled drug users may require residential treatment.

Victor, Grossman, and Eisenman, in the second paper, describe relations between marijuana use and personality traits of predominantly middle-class, white, high-school youth. The researchers found that four per cent of eighth graders and fifty-five per cent of twelfth graders had tried marijuana at least once. They depict the marijuana user as being inclined toward an "openness to experience"; nonetheless, these researchers point out that frequent marijuana use is associated with increased propensity to experiment with other drugs, and that multiple-drug users relative to other youth tend to be more anxious and to earn lower grades. The succeeding paper evaluates alcohol and drug use and extends the range of demographic, social, and personal factor covered by Victor et al. Milman and Su administered a questionnaire to 551 middle-class, white, urban adolescents attending private secondary schools. Slow social and psychosexual development, good school performance, and interest in higher education, appear to deter interest in drugs and alcohol. On the whole, high-school youth who indulge in illicit drug use tend also to deviate from conventional norms of behavior and adjustment. These researchers found the use of alcohol, tobacco, and drugs intercorrelated. Alcohol usage was found to be about three times that of drugs; however, patterns of alcohol and drug use were similar.

One is reminded of the venerable adage, "The more one learns, the less one knows," after comparing sophisticated present-day analyses of delinquency with the simpler efforts of several generations ago. Research on delinquency has advanced swiftly, and the three papers included in Part 7 on deviancy and delinquency are indicative both of the progress that has been attained and the questions still to be answered. Deviancy—behavior that departs from accepted norms, and delinquency—the commission of unlawful acts—are subject to social observation, detection, and definition. Of the deviant and delinquent acts that come to the attention of the police, some are officially recorded and others are ignored. Dismissal may be a consequence either of trivial or insufficient evidence or of parental pressure on law-enforcement agencies. Many factors affect administrative decisions to note, report, and classify deviant or delinquent acts. Thus, trying to answer the question, "How many adolescents commit deviant or delinquent acts in a given year?" is like delving into the mysteries of life itself. Klein, in the first of the series, analyzes adolescent deviancy in automobile driving. He defines several forms of deviance—predation, deviant consumption, deviant appearance, deviant belief, deviant performance—and asserts that because of youth's relative isolation from both adult social norms and the productive sector of the economy, a driver's license often becomes the major rite of passage into adulthood. After a thorough analysis of the characteristics of adolescent driving, Klein suggests that we should look at "the adolescent driver not as a deviant, but perhaps as a forerunner of the society of the future."

Empey offers a comprehensive examination of evidence relating to contemporary delinquency theory. He questions three of its basic assumptions: (1) the universality of a relationship between social-class status and delinquency involvement; (2) the characterization of delinquent groups as having high "internal cohesion—esprit de corps, solidarity, cooperative action, shared tradition, and a strong group awareness"; and (3) the idea of a "singularly-focused," oppositional and autonomous delinquent subculture. He argues convincingly that researchers need (a) perspective on the differences that exist in rates of apprehension and kinds of violations across social classes; (b) baselines for evaluating the cohesiveness of delinquent groups; and (c) understanding of the extent to which the delinquent subculture is part of "a more amorphous and widespread tradition of deviance." Empey hopes that through a study of these issues better insight will be gained into "the total mosaic composed of delinquent values, actual behavior, and official reaction."

Ganzer and Sarason attempt to isolate sociological, family background, and personality variables among 100 boys and 100 girls, who previously had been institutionalized, to determine which would discriminate between recidivists (parole violators or recommited youth) and nonrecidivists. The study revealed that recidivists had gotten into trouble and were first institutionalized at earlier ages, possessed lower estimated verbal intelligence, and were more frequently diagnosed as having sociopathic personalities than were nonrecidivists. Moreover, the data also indicated that female delinquents in general came from "more disorganized and socially less adequate families than did males." The researchers hope that they have identified "a number of variables, which, when cross-validated, may be of practical value in predicting recidivism."

Stephen Proskauer
Ruick S. Rolland

Youth Who Use Drugs

Three classes of drug user—experimental, depressive, and character-ological, and the psychosocial bases of each classification, are described in the following paper. Proskauer and Rolland argue that drug usage usually is "an adaptive and defensive choice. . . ." They reject the conventional practice of stereotyping drug users, showing that drug usage for some youth results in " 'moving in' on society in a way that is often ethical and courageous." For other youth it may lead to "a life time of dereliction." As a consequence of their belief in a broad range of outcomes from drug usage, these researchers insist that careful diagnoses precede rehabilitative efforts.

Instructional Objectives
To define drug usage as an adaptive and defensive choice.
To describe three classes of drug user—experimental, depressive, and characterological.
To describe patterns of socialization characteristic of persons in each of the drug-user groups.
To discuss treatment planning for persons in each drug-user group.

D RUG USE has become an integral part of current youth culture. Experimentation with marijuana, amphetamines, barbiturates, LSD, other hallucinogens, and even narcotics which began in colleges and universities has sprung up in high, junior high, and elementary school populations.

When drugs appear in their schools and communities, parents, teachers, and others often react first by denying the phenomenon until it can no longer be ignored, then by applying indiscriminate repressive measures in response to a panic state. When it is possible to explore the underlying attitudes and feelings of the parental generation toward drug use, we often discover in adults, in addition to a legitimate concern about the effects of dangerous drugs on youth, envy of and resentment toward the younger generation for indulging in new kinds of forbidden pleasure which are felt to be closed to responsible adults. There is also a fear of the unknown experience and of the

FROM *Journal of the American Academy of Child Psychiatry*, XII (1973), pp. 32–47. Reprinted by permission of the authors and the *American Journal of Child Psychiatry*.

children's escaping into an uncharted realm where parental protection and authority have no sway. Under the influence of such strong feelings, even reasonable adults have resorted to massive denial or outbursts of ill-conceived action serving more to express anxiety than to meet the needs of our youth.

The medical profession for its part has focused primarily on the psychopharmacology of the drugs in question. Sometimes forgotten is the fact that individual young people are using drugs for a variety of reasons and under a variety of circumstances.

The Roxbury Court Clinic is a state-supported outpatient psychiatric facility located in the Roxbury District Court. It provides consultation, diagnostic, and treatment services to the Court and to a district in metropolitan Boston which has a crime rate unexceeded anywhere in Massachusetts as well as a high prevalence of alcoholism and heroin addiction. The Clinic staff have had the opportunity to interview a number of adolescents and young adults entangled with the law because of illegal drug use, primarily use of narcotics. The staff have also gleaned information from former drug users, probation officers, street workers, and mental health professionals in a variety of agencies collaborating with the Roxbury Court Clinic in the effort to arrange for each drug user the treatment program most likely to help him.

In the course of discovering the various motives behind many young people's use of drugs, we have encountered very few cases fitting psychiatric stereotypes, such as "the hard-core drug addict who cares only for immediate narcissistic gratifications." Drug taking is more usefully described, in our experience, as *an adaptive and defensive choice made by a young person for a combination of intrapsychic, familial, and social reasons.* While we have been vitally concerned with social and familial factors, the main purpose of this paper is to set forth a rough *psychodynamic* classification of youth who use drugs, to aid in selecting the most appropriate intervention for those who need our help, and to prevent our complicating the lives of those whose healthy development is not threatened by their use of drugs.

PROPOSED CLASSIFICATION

1. EXPERIMENTAL DRUG USERS. This category comprises a large segment of the youthful population who have taken drugs at one time or another under the influence of peer pressures, defiant feelings toward adult authority, curiosity, or desire for new sources of aesthetic and sensual experience. These influences are universal during adolescence and not even the manifestation of them in the use of drugs is a new phenomenon. Alcohol and tobacco have for generations been the subjects of adolescent experimentation, peer-group prestige, and rebellion against parental and societal rules. Today, however, young people are utilizing a wider range of drugs for the same purposes—drugs foreign to their parents' experience and, therefore, all the more upsetting to the older generation.

The young people in this category, however, have no compelling need for the drug experience and cannot be said to have a "drug problem" as such. As Wieder and Kaplan [1] put it: "Exposed to the appropriate drug, the one which fulfills his particular needs, the adolescent may experience temporary relief from distress and conflict. However, this is not a stable adaptation. The healthy adolescent eventually finds the sense of passive enslavement to the drug insufferable, and his progressive wish for development, active mastery, identity, and object relationship more urgent and satisfying than the drug's effect. Drug use will then be reduced to casual, intermittent employment of alcohol or marijuana, as in the manner of the adult."

2. DEPRESSIVE DRUG USERS. This group comprises a vast number of young people who are seeking adaptive and defensive solutions primarily to feelings of emptiness, hopelessness, loneliness, and worthlessness through drug experiences. The depressive mood is often not obvious to a casual observer and may be intrapsychically based, externally determined (e.g., through lack of opportunity in the urban ghetto), or both.

Dora Hartmann [2] regards this type of drug user as one for whom easy availability of drugs can become very dangerous. He is vulnerable to drugs as an easy way out; drug taking appears an attractive way of avoiding pain and of bypassing the active work needed to establish more mature object relations, a task which every adolescent must face for healthy emotional development.

3. CHARACTEROLOGICAL DRUG USERS. This much smaller group of young people were exposed in early life to deprivation, inconsistency, and rejection. These experiences have resulted in major ego deficits, and they seek to quell the intense pain imposed by developmental and environmental stresses through whatever dependable satisfactions are possible. Drug users in this group are at least psychologically addicted, and, as Wieder and Kaplan [3] point out, the drug stabilizes many of them the same way that reliance on an adult for external ego control maintains the adult borderline or psychotic.

We wish to emphasize that these categories are not proposed as tight compartments into which youthful drug users can be sorted, but rather as guidelines to help in planning effective therapeutic intervention for those cases in which intervention is required.

We anticipate that other workers and clinics will develop their own diagnostic scheme or improve upon ours, so that a more sophisticated and useful aid to treatment planning may result. Ultimately, careful research involving prospective studies of youthful populations and follow-up of those receiving various therapies will be needed to establish the validity of any pragmatically derived diagnostic approach.

We are also aware that our classification does not provide a discussion of

[1] H. Wieder and E. H. Kaplan, "Drug Use in Adolescents: Psychodynamic Meaning and Pharmacogenic Effect," *The Psychoanalytic Study of the Child,* XXIV (1969), 399–431.
[2] D. Hartmann, "A Study of Drug-Taking Adolescents," *The Psychoanalytic Study of the Child,* XXIV (1969), 384–398.
[3] Wieder and Kaplan, op. cit.

the enormous personal and social cost specifically of heroin addiction, nor does it describe syndromes associated with pharmacologic effects of particular drugs. It has been amply demonstrated in the case of amphetamines, for instance, that chronic drug use can lead to self-destructive and even violent behavior and possible organic brain damage. Recent data also suggest that the chronic use of hallucinogens or amphetamines can result in "burned out" states resembling chronic schizophrenia. Important psychopharmacologic findings such as these are widely discussed in the medical and psychiatric literature; our focus here, however, is upon the drug user and what he is looking for.

THE PSYCHOSOCIAL BASIS OF THE CLASSIFICATION

Experimental Drug Users

Peer-group standards are a potent influence during latency and an overriding force during adolescence in shaping human behavior. If drugs are the "in" thing, there will be a pressure on all members of the peer group to try them. If there is no compelling inner need for the drug experience, and the young person perceives the act of taking drugs as ego-alien ("People like me don't do this") or strongly disapproved of by those he loves and respects (and who love and respect him), then it is unlikely that a fixed pattern of drug use will develop.

It is crucially important to distinguish the young person who is simply experimenting with drugs from other drug users, for at least two reasons. First, the experimenter may not have a problem at all. In many areas, experimentation with marijuana in high school and junior high school has become commonplace, and there is no conclusive evidence of physical, psychological, or social damage from this casual experimentation. The idea that marijuana must lead to "harder" drugs or to delinquency is not supported by conclusive scientific data.

Secondly, the very process of labeling an experimenter as a confirmed "drug abuser" and subjecting him to overly strong legal or disciplinary action and rejection by loved ones may confirm a fear about himself: "Maybe I really am that bad." The experimenter may then continue along the path of drug use, fulfilling the prophecy of his family and community; whereas, treated with understanding or just left to himself, he would have dropped out of the drug scene in due time none the worse, and possibly the better, for the experience.

Apparently certain hallucinogenic drugs in the hands of young people who seemed emotionally healthy prior to intoxication can create a derangement which complicates the process of normal development, disastrously in cases of suicide or persisting psychosis after LSD ingestion.[4] So great has

[4] R. G. Smart and K. Bateman, "Unfavorable Reactions to LSD: A Review and Analysis of the Available Case Reports," *Canadian Medical Association Journal*, XCVII (1967), 1214–1221.

been the concern over these cases that few adults have seriously considered the possibility that drug experience could be a growth-promoting alternative for some young people. Although we have no evidence that any drug can produce permanent enhancement of measured performance in any sphere of activity, regardless of the subjective feelings of the drug taker, we know that objective performance alone is no reliable measure of internal growth processes, especially during adolescence.

The writings of Erik Erikson, Anna Freud, Edith Jacobson, Peter Blos, Irene Josselyn, and many others have drawn our attention to the intricacies of psychological development during the adolescent period. Much of this complexity has to do with shifts in the intrapsychic balance of forces and with restructuring of the ego, all occurring at an uneven and unpredictable pace. Intensified self-consciousness, labile self-esteem, and high sensitivity to the stress of narcissistic injury are characteristic of the adolescent phase of development.

There are limited periods of indulgence which act gradually to modify the obsessive-compulsive defenses erected during latency in the direction of more flexible and adaptive ways for dealing both with inner needs and with the realities of the external world. In the process, there may be a seeking after fulfillment of wishes for nurturance, aggressive power, and unrestricted gratification. Experimentation with certain drugs may occur in this context as one alternative among many forms of aesthetic and sensual pleasure.

Moderate doses of marijuana and some hallucinogens can intensify the conscious experiencing of fantasy, while tending to inhibit motor expression of impulses.[5] In this sense, it is possible that certain drug experiences permit gratification of aesthetic needs when direct satisfaction of sexual and aggressive drives would in reality be a more difficult or hazardous activity for the adolescent. If this be the case, then "mind-expanding drugs" may be for some a useful adaptive tool for managing the psychologically strenuous and biologically difficult psychosocial moratorium imposed on youth in our civilization.

Bergman,[6] for example, has presented evidence that peyote use by American Indians in the Native American Church is accompanied by an extremely low rate of adverse reactions and may have positive adaptive functions for its users.

The fact that many of the politically aware and effective youth of today have also been users of marijuana and hallucinogens should not be forgotten. For them the drug experience did not lead to "dropping out" but to a profound reorientation of values followed by "moving in" on society in a way that is often ethical and courageous.

[5] R. C. Pillard, "Marijuana," *New England Journal of Medicine,* CCLXXXIII (1970), 294–303.
[6] R. L. Bergman, "Navajo Peyote Use: Its Apparent Safety," *American Journal of Psychiatry,* CXXVIII (1971), 695–699.

At the very least, it must be an oversimplification to regard moderate drug use as merely a passing phase for such young people with no consequences for their psychological development or for the growth of their society. Encounters with drugs which intensify the awareness of internal stimuli may have especially contributed to the greater weight given to introspective experience in youth culture than in the wider American society, where attention to the inner life has been implicitly discouraged by stress upon material productivity and competitiveness.

Depressive Drug Users

Depressive moods occur universally during normal adolescence and are often overlooked by adults, who see withdrawal, surliness, and self-neglect as reflecting only intentional efforts by teen-agers to "be difficult." Many experienced clinicians believe that the mood swings of adolescence render even the healthy person more vulnerable to experiencing pervasive (but usually brief) feelings of emptiness, hopelessness, and intense loneliness than at any other time of life. When a young person suffers from a neurosis, unresolved grief over a loss, strained intrafamilial relations, or problems imposed by social conditions, the normal bouts of depression or emptiness may be much intensified.

We recognize the quest for relief from depressive moods as a major force behind many kinds of adolescent activity. The more profound the empty feeling, the more stimulating these compensatory activities must be in order to fill the void. Therefore, teen-agers prone to severe and prolonged depressive states often find drug use most appealing. There seems to be a great burden of depression among children and adolescents now, a phenomenon for which we have at least some partial explanations.

First, middle-class culture relentlessly demands the outward show of "mature" interests and behavior (both occupational and sexual), often before a child has entered puberty, while simultaneously expecting a prolonged adolescence devoted to higher education, a period during which the young person has been given no sanctioned sexual or occupational role in his society. Being asked to rush on into his future with no opportunity to be valued, gratified, and productive for what he is *now*, the young person naturally feels worthless and perpetually out of place. Recent social and political reinvolvement of youth may be reversing this trend.

Secondly, there is an aspect of American family life which bears a close relationship to increased depression in children and youth: emotional isolation of parents from each other and from their children. There is a failure to maintain a community of interest and an active mutual concern in many families and communities that seems to have developed along with the mass media (passive entertainment) and with large businesses and bureaucratic institutions (passive occupations). Children feel unrelated to and unsupported by their parents and increasingly depressed, while parents see the child's withdrawal as rejection or "badness." Both children and parents back off from one another, thus increasing the children's sense of emotional abandonment as well as the parents' feelings of frustration and helplessness.

It is in this setting of mutual alienation between parents and youth that the young person will frequently turn to drugs or run away. Parents who react either with panic or overindulgence fail to provide the understanding and support that is needed. Thus, a young person's involvement with drugs may be a signal that he feels vulnerable and alone in his family and community.

The social causes for childhood depressive states in poverty and ghetto areas need little elaboration here, since so much has been written about the damaging effects of economic and social impoverishment on child development. Pervasive family disorganization associated with chronic depression; ready availability of drugs and the drug-taking peer group; the bitterness, helplessness, and rage engendered by racism—all these add greatly to the pressure toward drug use in the ghetto. Recently, the increased expectations of improved living conditions and opportunities for urban populations, followed by repeated disappointments as programs fail or close for lack of funds or expertise, have created even greater frustration than existed before hopes were raised, making drugs all the more inviting as an escape.

Then there is the widespread and increasingly understandable disaffection about plastic culture, social problems, and discordant national priorities: the Vietnam war, racial inequalities, starvation amid abundance, etc. Many young people today feel chronically dismayed because they cannot realistically foresee a livable future.

Thus, depressive moods among youth today can have multiple causes: intrapsychic, familial, and social. What is more, depression may not manifest itself in easily recognizable forms, but rather may be expressed in "depressive equivalents" such as somatic complaints, irritability, poor school performance, and frantic pleasure-seeking or self-punishment, including excessive drug use. It is often difficult to assess how important a role depressive phenomena are playing in an adolescent's use of drugs. Especially when a long-standing pattern of drug use exists, the depressive feelings may have become well masked. Diagnosis is difficult, but experience suggests that the young person who displays a more than casual use of drugs but does not show severe long-standing character pathology is probably reacting to underlying depression.

There are also several forms of neurotic conflict against which the drug experience may provide a defense. Those who have intense conflicts about gender role and sexual identity, especially, may retreat into a passive drug experience, warding off an anxiety-provoking confrontation with the inevitable instinctual pressures and responsibilities of sexual maturation.

"Copping out" with drugs for some neurotic young people reflects the inhibition of successful performance arising from unresolved oedipal conflicts. It is not primarily the intoxicated state but the need to avoid normal productive life which draws them to drugs.

There are other youths for whom the resurgence of aggressive drives in adolescence is especially threatening because of fears of losing control or because of guilt-laden unconscious ideas which are linked to the aggressive impulses. Drugs which can produce a passive, self-absorbed state, accompanied by motor quiescence, serve to relieve young people for a time of anxieties about the emptiness, conflict, or violence within.

Characterological Drug Users

This category applies to the relatively few young people for whom profound disturbances in personality development are primarily responsible for an addictive pattern of drug use. These young people were in serious difficulty in childhood, well before they started on drugs, and usually experienced deprivation in early infancy, multiple losses of significant persons during childhood (especially fathers), and hostile-dependent relationships with their mothers. As adolescents and adults, they must contend with low tolerance for frustration, poor impulse control, a relatively poor capacity to bear anxiety and depression, trouble relating to others in a mutual way, and unreliable reality testing, especially under internal or external stress. They often have major disturbances of sexual identity. It is no wonder, then, that the usual events of life cause overwhelming difficulty for them and a reliable source of satisfaction, such as a drug, becomes mandatory in order to achieve transient contentment in an otherwise unstable and ungratifying existence.

Wieder and Kaplan [7] postulate that drug users with ego deficits may be using a particular drug experience as a kind of "prosthesis" to make up for these deficits. From another vantage point, they view "states of intoxication as chemically induced regressive ego states . . . different drugs induce different regressive states that resemble specific phases of early childhood development." It appears that drug use for those with severe ego deficits may occur *both* to satisfy a profound wish for regression *and* to prop up and support, however temporarily, certain inadequate ego functions.

It is important to stress that in our experience with an urban ghetto population, the characterological drug user group so defined accounts for only *a small minority* of the total youth involved with drugs. A much larger number are actually depressive users who only *appear* to have major character problems because they imitate patterns of behavior from drug-taking subcultures or have adopted regressive modes of behavior in reaction to loss of self-esteem and surrender of ego ideals. These pseudo ego defects disappear relatively early in the course of definitive treatment for the sources of depression. Because of the failure to make this differentiation, many depressed young people found to be using drugs may be stereotyped by society as "drug

[7] Wieder and Kaplan, op. cit.

fiends," jailed, and cast into a tragic mold—a lifetime of dereliction which need not have been their lot.

IMPLICATIONS FOR TREATMENT PLANNING

Experimentation with different modes of doing and being is part of normal adolescence. The healthy young person will find a solution to the question of drugs, just as he will to other issues such as standards of sexual behavior. His solution will not interfere with his growth into productive adulthood, provided support and understanding are available when he needs it. Formal treatment is unnecessary.

Many teen-agers who try drugs need only the presence of a trusted older person with whom they can discuss their experiences, both discoveries and misgivings, in a relatively nonjudgmental atmosphere. This may be an understanding parent, a teacher, or an older sibling or friend; it need not be a professional drug expert, though it would be helpful for as many people as possible to know the facts about drugs so that they can be of greater help when young people turn to them.

Just as important as knowledge, however, is the attitude of the person to whom a youth turns. If this individual condemns all drug use or attempts to frighten the young person into giving up drugs, he can be of little help. A sympathetic ear, expression of concern when it is warranted, and implicit recognition throughout that the young person will have to make his own decisions can provide crucial support to one who is experimenting with drugs. We have found that such a tolerant and truly respectful attitude can be very difficult to maintain consistently, especially for *professionally trained* counselors and therapists. Nonetheless, it remains the only way to warrant the kind of trust which will enable young people to discuss their experiences openly.

"Drug education" is often presented as *the* preventive solution to the problem of drug abuse. Clinical experience, quite predictably, suggests that only the experimental group of drug users is likely to be affected significantly by a purely educational approach. For depressed and characterologically crippled young people, the "facts about drugs" are not the main issues. Their needs are deeper and will not be countered by fear of harmful effects discussed at school or at home. Furthermore, it is primarily teachers and parents who need to be educated. Young people, especially in ghetto communities, are quite well informed by their own observations about the effects of drugs.

Nonetheless, a psychoeducational approach combined with special opportunities to develop useful skills could be decisive in helping a particular group which is at high risk for drug use: the potential school dropout. These young people may turn to drugs early, in the context of alienation from sources of gratification through mastery at school, and subsequently may lean more heavily on drugs after they have dropped out. While some may later prove to have depressive or characterological problems and therefore require special help, a large number of potential school dropouts might be prevented from giving up on mastery and turning to drugs in a destructive way if their educational programs really engaged their interest and if they were actively involved toward self-development in socially viable directions.

A critical factor in the prevention and treatment of depressive drug use is the availability of satisfying interpersonal relationships and activities to fill the painful void. For those young people with neurotic conflicts contributing in a major way to their use of drugs, some form of psychotherapy may be necessary before they can take advantage of those relationships and activities which are readily available to them.

The usual therapeutic skills of mental health personnel are applicable, since the drug taking serves as a defense against intrapsychic conflict as well as a potentially reversible reaction to familial or social problems. Family, group, or individual psychotherapy with this population may be effective, depending on circumstances in each case. In planning treatment, we find it important to clarify the specific precipitants to neurotic use of drugs and the pre-existing state of more effective functioning, as well as the particular adaptive modes which the young person has developed most successfully in dealing with the world and which offer alternatives to the defensive use of drugs.

For many young people in the depressive category, a rehabilitation program aimed at promoting individual skills and creating peer-group mutual support can be a crucial aid to therapy or an effective therapeutic modality in itself. A boost in self-esteem through a successful group experience may carry a highly vulnerable adolescent through a difficult period when he might otherwise have resorted to maladaptive solutions. Therefore, *community-based, goal-directed group activity programs* designed for and by the depressive type of drug-vulnerable youth may be the most practical and effective measures to meet the problem on a large scale. The mental health professional can contribute by encouraging the formation of these groups, by providing consultative services, and by gathering data about skills and interests in his diagnostic evaluations of youthful drug users, data which will help him make an informed referral to a youth group when appropriate.

A youth group can develop into a self-perpetuating therapeutic milieu helpful both to old members and new arrivals. The tribal cohesiveness of the hot-line volunteer group illustrates the potency of task-oriented peer-group experiences for teen-agers.

Cultural and social forces which engender emotional isolation and despair promote maladaptive use of drugs and are major public health hazards. Many of our youth who are struggling to deal with these malignant forces in their personal lives are now doing what they can to influence our political and cultural growth in more healthy directions. Promoting a young person's commitment to work toward positive changes in the world as he finds it is the treatment of choice for the young person and for his society as well.

Mental health professionals can help youth in this effort not only by providing therapy when it is needed and by training lay therapists to help the great numbers of disturbed youth, but also by joining in calling society's attention to real problems which require solution, such as the Vietnam war and unequal opportunity for minority groups, and by emphasizing the positive and healthy implications of constructive youth activism. Professionals must also strive to promote within their local communities a spirit of involvement in enterprises that will engage the interest of youth groups and enable young people to participate in and enrich the life around them.

The characterological group of drug users are usually said not to profit from traditional methods of insight psychotherapy on an out-patient basis. The Roxbury Court Clinic has had some success in treating such patients with severe character disorders, so long as a flexible therapeutic stance is maintained and cultural differences between therapist and patient are taken into account. It is crucial to employ ego-supportive interventions and available community resources in fostering new coping capacities and in compensating for the potentially regressive pull of the therapeutic relationship.

We are reluctant to consign an adolescent to the characterological category without long-standing evidence of prominent ego deficits in frustration tolerance, impulse control, object relations, capacity to bear anxiety and depression, and reality testing, together with evidence of major difficulties in sexual identifications, arrest of adolescent growth processes, and rigid negative identity formation.

Many of these young people become heavily addicted to narcotics or amphetamines. Often they use several drugs simultaneously and excessively. Only if life becomes miserable enough with drugs will they show motivation for change. Their rehabilitation requires long, difficult work, and relapse is common. It is inviting lifelong trouble both for these individuals and for society to treat their drug problem merely as a neurotic symptom or a criminal act.

There was little treatment for narcotic addicts of this type until the advent of self-help groups, such as Synanon, Day-Top, and others, and until the emergence of methadone blockade for maintenance.

The self-regulating communities owe much of their success to the involvement of former addicts in rehabilitation of others, an activity which directly enhances self-esteem and strengthens reaction formations against relapse, while providing an example of success to the newcomer. For adolescents especially, group programs need to include opportunities for successful participants to guide newcomers and take on vital roles in a supportive community over a sustaining period until, hopefully, new patterns of coping may become internally stabilized. As Wieder and Kaplan [8] state, however, "Some severely habituated users can safely become abstinent for long periods of time only in the confines of a regulated, protected milieu. This milieu replaces the drug as the homeostatic factor. Relapse, suicide, or psychotic episodes

[8] Ibid.

are the more usual sequelae to prolonged abstinence outside of the protective, anaclitic environment." Synanon and other self-help groups incorporate many of their members permanently into staff jobs, thus avoiding the potential disaster of separation.

An important subgroup of the characterological category includes those who would be psychotic were it not for the drug habit. Such drug users may function adequately with methadone maintenance for very long periods, much as chronic schizophrenics can be maintained on major tranquilizers. The two classes of drugs appear to have similar normalizing effects for these two groups of patients. Since methadone itself is addicting, the clinician must be reasonably sure of his diagnosis before he undertakes a long-term methadone maintenance program to prevent the young person's ego disintegration. This scruple is all the more important in treating adolescents for whom chronic use of a drug may contribute to the formation of an "addict identity" and a lifelong pattern of drug dependence.

Mental health professionals should involve themselves directly in the treatment of characterological drug users for several reasons. First, an ego-supportive type of therapy can be very helpful, demands considerable skill, and requires the professional to work through his own attitudes and feelings toward drug use in order to deal positively with his patients. Second, it is from the most severely afflicted that we have most to learn about the compelling forces which create a fixed pattern of drug use. Third, intimate knowledge of characterologically disturbed drug users is a necessity for effective consultation with other agencies which try to help them. If the mental health professional confines himself to treating the less difficult cases of depressive drug use, he will miss the opportunity to develop more effective approaches for helping characterological drug users.

SUMMARY

When faced with a youthful drug user, we must ask not only which drugs, but who is taking them and why. Effective treatment or judicious withholding of treatment requires a diagnostic understanding of the individual and of his life situation. On the basis of our clinical experience in an inner city court clinic, we have proposed three rough psychodynamic categories into which the population of youthful drug users can be separated for purposes of treatment planning.

We offer this classification as a basis for rational provision of clinical services, a foundation to which more detailed and sophisticated diagnostic criteria can be added as experience accumulates.

The three categories correspond approximately to other psychiatric diagnoses as follows:

1. *Experimental drug users:* normal developmental crisis or no significant psychopathology.

2. *Depressive drug users:* psychoneurotic or situational reaction, usually with depressive phenomena.
3. *Characterological drug users:* personality disorder (including severe neurotic character), borderline psychosis, schizophrenia, psychotic character.

A distinct set of interventions is appropriate to each category. For experimental drug users, deliberate noninterference, informal counseling, or educational and activity programs are usually sufficient. Depressive drug users can benefit from various types of psychotherapy and goal-directed peer activity group programs, including particularly those directed at political or social goals, such as youth hot-lines. Characterologically crippled drug users often require residential participation in a self-help program or methadone maintenance and may gain from a flexible psychotherapy which balances the quest for insight with equal attention to ego support and to constructive utilization of environmental resources.

We feel that community mental health clinics and child guidance clinics have a crucial role to play in providing diagnostic evaluation and therapy and in coordinating community resources for individual young people who use drugs. Though much remains unknown and uncertain in the field of drug use, psychological understanding of the individual drug user must be one foundation for treatment planning in order to give rehabilitative efforts the best chance of success and to prevent harmful interference by society with spontaneous processes of healthy maturation.

Hope R. Victor
Jan Carl Grossman
Russell Eisenman

Openness to Experience and Marijuana Use in High-School Students

The study presented here suggests that adolescents who possess certain personality traits are more open to experiencing marijuana. Victor, Grossman, and Eisenman dispute the view that marijuana use strongly affects

FROM *Journal of Consulting and Clinical Psychology,* XLI (1973), pp. 78–85. Copyright 1973 by the American Psychological Association. Reprinted by permission of the authors and the publisher.

*personality development. These researchers administered a variety of per-
sonality scales to marijuana users and nonusers enrolled in grades eight
through twelve in a predominantly middle-class, white high school. Their
findings reveal that personality characteristics associated with adventuresomeness, nonconformity, and creativity are related to marijuana use
among youth. Although these findings fail to substantiate a widespread
belief that long-term marijuana use impairs personality functioning, they
do indicate that frequent marijuana use leads to increased experimentation
with other drugs, and multiple drug users appear to be more anxious and
to earn lower grades.*

Instructional Objectives
*To review relationships between personality variables and marijuana use
   reported by earlier investigators.*
To describe the extent of marijuana use among high-school students.
To describe personality and behavioral correlates of marijuana use.
*To describe the predictive value of personality-profile research in identi-
   fying potential drug users.*

I N RECENT years, public concern over the increasing incidence of marijuana
use has prompted researchers to try and determine if marijuana use is
associated with psychopathology. Most results indicate that individuals who
are only casually or moderately involved with marijuana do not differ from
those who do not use the drug in incidence of psychopathology. It is only
when use becomes more frequent or other drugs are involved that differences
emerge. In some studies, excessive marijuana use has been found to be
significantly related to increased likelihood of involvement with other drugs,
poor social and work adjustment, increased hostility, greater difficulty in
mastering new problems, and the desire for a "psychotomimetic" experience
in marijuana use, rather than simple tension reduction or pleasurable stimulation.[1] Frequent marijuana users and multiple-drug users have been found to
score significantly more pathological than controls on the Minnesota Multiphasic Personality Inventory.[2] Chronic marijuana users have been described
as having more "personality aberrations," being more anxious, paranoid,
dependent, nonconforming, hysterical, and negativistic toward society than

---

[1] M. H. Keeler, "Motivation for Marijuana Use: A Correlate of Adverse Reaction,"
American Journal of Psychiatry, CXXV (1968), 386–390; S. Mirin, L. Shapiro, R. Meyer,
R. Pillard, and S. Fisher, "Casual Versus Heavy Use of Marijuana: A Redefinition of the
Marijuana Problem," *American Journal of Psychiatry,* CXXVII (1971), 54–60.
[2] N. Brill, E. Crumpton, and H. Grayson, "Personality Factors in Marijuana Use,"
Archives of General Psychiatry, XXIV (1971), 163–165; C. McAree, R. Steffenhagen,
and L. Zheutlin, "Personality Factors in College Drug Users," *International Journal of
Social Psychiatry,* XV (1969), 102–106.

moderate users.[3] In these studies, no significant differences were found between casual marijuana users and nonusers.

Even though there is little reason to suspect any clinical differences between moderate marijuana users and nonusers, some evidence does suggest that within the normal range there are definite personality and attitudinal distinctions between these groups. McGlothlin, Arnold, and Rowan [4] found that adult marijuana users were more likely than nonusers to be involved in various means of altering consciousness (e.g., stronger tendency to try other drugs, higher hypnotic susceptibility, interest in meditation, yoga, Zen). Users demonstrated a more unstructured and relatively unstable style of life than nonusers, preferring "a high level of stimulation, uncertainty, and risk, rather than security and structure" (more residential mobility, higher scores in sensation seeking). Users were also more tolerant of protest actions, more opposed to legal control of behaviors and actions to limit freedom, and more critical of "Establishment" policies and actions. Hogan, Mankin, Conway, and Fox [5] reported that college student marijuana users, as compared to nonusers, were self-confident, socially poised, adventuresome, skilled in interpersonal relations, and had high achievement motivation and wide interests. Along with these qualities went greater impulsivity, narcissism, irresponsibility, nonconformity, hostility to rules and conventions, and high pleasure seeking. In this study, nonusers were more rule abiding, responsible, inflexible, conventional, lacking in spontaneity, and narrower in interests. The idea that the marijuana user may be more flexible, creative, or open to experience is also subscribed to by Norton, who described the user as intelligent but narcissistic, expressing "a preference for aesthetic experiential values."

Some studies using high-school student samples have yielded similar results. Robinson [6] found marijuana users to be warmhearted, enthusiastic, extroverted, and dependent on their peer group, as compared to nonusers who were more reserved, slow, conscientious, introverted, and self-reliant. She suggested that users find satisfaction in peer relations, demonstrated by "struggle against authority, repudiation of 'Establishment' values, and the use of marijuana." Shetterly [7] found marijuana users to have been raised in permissive atmospheres with loose or inconsistent discipline, to have a more passive life style, and to reject formalized religion. Hager [8] reported that drug

[3] N. Zinberg and A. A. Weil, "A Comparison of Marijuana Users and Nonusers," *Nature*, CCXXVI (1970), 119–123.

[4] W. McGlothlin, D. Arnold, and P. Rowan, "Marijuana Use Among Adults," *Psychiatry*, XXXIII (1970), 433–443.

[5] R. Hogan, D. Mankin, J. Conway, and S. Fox, "Personality Correlates of Undergraduate Marijuana Use," *Journal of Consulting and Clinical Psychology*, XXXV (1970), 58–63.

[6] L. Robinson, "Marijuana Use in High-School Girls: A Psycho-Social Case Study," *Dissertation Abstracts International*, XXXI (1970), 2196.

[7] H. Shetterly, "Self and Social Perceptions and Personal Characteristics of a Group of Suburban High-School Marijuana Users," *Dissertation Abstracts International*, XXXI (7-A)(1971), 3279.

[8] D. Hager, "Adolescent Drug Use in Middle America: Social-Psychological Correlates," *Dissertation Abstracts International*, XXXI (11-A) (1971), 6158.

use is correlated with negative orientations toward traditional values (authoritarianism, college plans, ability to defer gratification, family orientation, school grades, peer orientation, political views, religious orthodoxy, and status aspirations).

Suchman [9] found college drug use (particularly the use of marijuana) to be closely associated with a pattern of behavioral, attitudinal, and personality variables which he termed a "hang loose" ethic. Behavioral correlates consisted of various "nonconformist" activities, such as participating in "happenings," mass protests, reading underground newspapers, and getting lower grades (rejection of the "hard work–success" ethic of conventional society). Typical attitudes of users were rejection of traditional educational, social, and political attitudes, that is, a "rejection of the established order." Again, in personality, marijuana users were rebellious, cynical, and anti-establishment, as compared to the more conforming, well-behaved, moral nonuser.

Grossman, Goldstein, and Eisenman [10] wrote that many reported characteristics of marijuana users seem to be indicative of the creative personality (unconventional, socially poised, aesthetic, adventuresome, nonconforming, flexible), while the descriptions of nonusers are similar to the authoritarian individual (conventional, inflexible, responsible, narrow in interests, rule abiding, traditional in values). Using the Personal Opinion Survey [11] as a measure of creativity and adventuresomeness and the California F Scale [12] as a measure of authoritarianism, the authors found that in a college student population as marijuana use increased, creativity and adventuresomeness increased significantly and authoritarianism decreased significantly. No significant differences were found in manifest anxiety or social desirability at any level of marijuana use. The authors described the personality profile of the marijuana user (creative, adventuresome, nonauthoritarian) by an "openness to experience" concept.

A subsequent study [13] additionally included Pearson's [14] five scales of novelty seeking (internal cognitive, external cognitive, internal sensation seeking, external sensation seeking, and desire for novelty). Again, marijuana use was found to be positively correlated with creativity and adventuresomeness and negatively correlated with authoritarianism, although the latter

[9] E. Suchman, "The 'Hang-Loose' Ethic and the Spirit of Drug Use," *Journal of Health and Social Behavior*, IX (1968), 146–155.

[10] J. C. Grossman, R. Goldstein, and R. Eisenman, "Openness to Experience and Marijuana Use: An Initial Investigation," *Proceedings of the 79th Annual Convention of Psychological Association*, VI (1971), 335–336. (Summary)

[11] R. Eisenman, "Values and Attitudes in Adolescents," in J. F. Adams, ed., *Understanding Adolescence* (Boston: Allyn and Bacon, 1968).

[12] T. W. Adorno, E. Frenkel-Brunswick, D. J. Levinson, and R. N. Sanford, *The Authoritarian Personality* (New York: Harper, 1950).

[13] J. C. Grossman, R. Goldstein, and R. Eisenman, "International Sensation Seeking and Openness to Experience as Related to Undergraduate Marijuana Use." Presented at the Annual Meeting of the Eastern Psychological Association, Boston, April 1972.

[14] P. Pearson, "Relationships Between Global and Specified Measures of Novelty Seeking," *Journal of Consulting and Clinical Psychology*, XXXIV (1970), 199–204.

relationship did not reach significance. The only dimension of novelty seeking significantly related to frequency of marijuana use was internal sensation seeking, a variable which other studies have also found to be associated with marijuana use.[15] In both Grossman et al. studies, males used marijuana more frequently than females, and Jews used marijuana more frequently than Protestants or Catholics—results that the authors interpreted by citing the greater adventuresomeness of males in our society and the low authoritarianism of Jews as compared to Protestants or Catholics. In both studies, grade point averages did not differ among level of use groups, and frequent marijuana users tended toward multiple-drug use.

In both Grossman et al. studies, the only significant intercorrelations between tested variables were $-.18$ ($p < .05$) between authoritarianism and creativity, .53 ($p < .001$) between creativity and internal sensation seeking, .50 ($p < .001$) between internal sensation seeking and adventuresomeness, and .63 ($p < .001$) between creativity and adventuresomeness. Depending on the specific intercorrelation, there is generally little, or at most moderate, common variance between subtests.

The present study represents an attempt to see if personality characteristics, similar to the profile in the Grossman et al. college samples, are associated with marijuana use in high-school sudents. The Personal Opinion Survey, its subtest for adventuresomeness, Pearson's Internal Sensation Novelty Seeking Scale, and the California F Scale were used in this study, with the expectations that creativity, adventuresomeness, and internal sensation seeking would be positively correlated with marijuana use, and authoritarianism, negatively correlated with increasing use. A test of acquiescent response set was included, both to act as a control for response set and to measure impulsivity, since Couch and Keniston [16] found a strong relationship between yeasaying and impulsivity. Although Grossman et al. found no relationship between acquiescent response set and marijuana use, a positive relationship was predicted here because of the greater impulsivity of marijuana users reported by Hogan et al.[17] The Manifest Anxiety scale was given as a general indicator of adjustment, with the prediction that high-school marijuana users, especially heavy users or multiple-drug users, might show more evidence of maladjustment than nonusers, reflected in greater manifest anxiety and possibly lower grades in school. We expected frequency of marijuana use to increase with grade level, with heavy marijuana users exhibiting an increased tendency to experiment with other drugs.

Concern has sometimes been expressed that long-term usage of marijuana

---

[15] Brill et al., op. cit.; McGlothlin et al., op. cit.; M. Zuckerman, R. S. Neary, and B. A. Brustman, "Sensation-Seeking Scale Correlates in Experience (Smoking, Drugs, Alcohol, 'hallucinations,' and Sex) and Preference for Complexity (Designs)." *Proceedings of the 78th Annual Convention of the American Psychological Association*, V (1970), 317–318. (Summary)

[16] A. Couch and K. Keniston, "Yeasayers and Naysayers: Agreeing Response Set as a Personality Variable," *Journal of Abnormal and Social Psychology*, LX (1960), 151–174.

[17] Hogan et al., op. cit.

might lead to reduced personal functioning and a higher level of maladjustment and apathy. Therefore, this study also analyzed all personality variables as a function of length of marijuana use to see if any changes occur over time. If maladjustment does increase with length of use, this might be reflected in decreases in some of the "positive" measures (e.g., creativity, adventuresomeness) or increases in the "negative" ones (e.g., manifest anxiety, lower grades) in the longest using groups.

Because both Grossman et al. results were based on college student samples, it is conceivable that their findings are only characteristic of the college-oriented individual. In terms of the present study, these students would be those who are in college-oriented courses of study such as academic or commercial–academic. It has been suggested that the use of marijuana in this type of individual represents a special type of motivation, reflecting "anticipatory socialization" to expectations of what college life will be like.[18] Thus, the possibility that marijuana users in non-college-oriented courses of study might not completely fit into the personality profile mentioned above was suspected.

The authors believe that the personality characteristics associated with marijuana use may explain the desire for the experience of using marijuana, and hence be an antecedent rather than a consequence of its use. In order to test this hypothesis, a differentiation of the nonusers was made into those who felt they might try marijuana in the future and those who stated they would not. It was predicted that the former group of nonusers would resemble present marijuana users in personality, rather than the nonusers whose sentiments toward personal marijuana use were negative.

METHOD

Subjects

The Ss were 984 male and female students between the eighth and twelfth grades. This sample represents approximately one fifth of the total population of a large high school located in a predominantly white, middle-income neighborhood in Philadelphia. Due to sampling procedures, students in college-oriented courses of study (academic, commercial–academic) were overrepresented, numbering 871. The remaining 113 Ss were working in non-college-oriented courses (general, commercial, trade preparatory). Unless otherwise mentioned, all results and data refer to the former college-oriented group.

Procedure

The Ss were tested anonymously in their classrooms with assurances that admission of drug usage would in no way penalize them, and that their teachers would not have access to the questionnaires. The Ss were told of the nature of the research and asked to fill out a form requesting demographic data and in-

---

[18] A. Mauss, "Anticipatory Socialization Toward College as a Factor in Adolescent Marijuana Use," *Social Problems,* XVI (1969), 357–364.

formation about their personal drug usage. Information was obtained on Ss' sex, age, birth order, religion, grade level, course of study, and approximate scholastic average. The Ss also reported whether they had ever experimented with marijuana, their present frequency of use (number of times per month), and the duration of their use of marijuana (number of years and months since the first experience with the drug). They additionally reported whether they had ever experimented with hashish, amphetamines, LSD, heroin, opium, or barbiturates. Nonusers were asked to estimate whether they thought they would ever try marijuana in the future. Questions were read aloud to insure understanding, especially in the lower grade levels. A battery of tests was then administered, including the Personal Opinion Survey, the California F Scale, Pearson's Internal Sensation Novelty Seeking Scale, a 12-item test for acquiescent response set, and the Manifest Anxiety scale.

Approximately 1,100 students were tested, but any forms that were incomplete or showed evidence of lying or exaggeration concerning drug usage were discarded. The Ss were subsequently divided into four categories of frequency of marijuana use: "nonusers," who had never tried the drug; "experimental users," who had tried marijuana but discontinued its use: "moderate users," who presently use the drug five times per month or less; and "frequent users," who use marijuana in excess of five times per month. Nonusers were additionally divided into two subgroups: those who stated they never expected to try marijuana (Nonuser A) and those who said that they might try it at some future time (Nonuser B). This final division yielded a total of five levels of marijuana use.

RESULTS AND DISCUSSION

Extent of Marijuana Use

When considering the percentage of students who have had some experience with marijuana, consonant with our predictions, we found that among eighth graders, 4% reported having tried the drug at least once; among ninth graders, the figure rose to 21%; among tenth graders, 33%; among eleventh graders, 49%; and among twelfth graders, 55% reported some experience. It is interesting to note that Grossman et al.[19] reported that approximately 56% of their college sample had experimented with marijuana, thus continuing the progression. This pattern also appeared in our measures of frequency of use and length of use. The number of times marijuana was smoked per month increased with higher grade levels ($F = 13.57$, $df = 4/861$, $p < .0001$), as did the length of time since the first marijuana experimentation ($F = 28.65$, $df = 4/861$, $p < .0001$).

Figure 1 indicates the differences between the sexes in marijuana use through all grade levels. Most researchers, including Suchman[20] and Grossman et al.[21] have consistently found that males do much more drug experi-

[19] Grossman et al., "Openness to Experience and Marijuana Use," op. cit.
[20] Suchman, op. cit.
[21] Grossman et al., "Openness to Experience and Marijuana Use . . . ," and "Internal Sensation Seeking and Openness to Experience . . . ," op. cit.

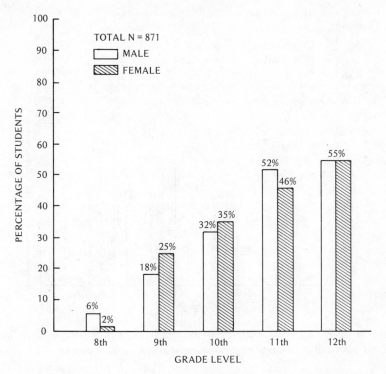

Figure 1. *Percentage of students from eighth through twelfth grades having tried marijuana at least once as a function of sex.*

mentation than females, sometimes attributing this finding to our society's tendency to selectively reinforce the male for adventuresome behaviors. In the present study, this relationship did appear in the youngest group, but by the ninth and tenth grades the trend reversed, and females were more active than males in marijuana usage. Since this reversal phenomenon disappeared by the eleventh and twelfth grades, it seems likely that the dating behaviors of ninth- and tenth-grade girls might account for the differences. That is, high-school girls tend to date older boys and are consequently exposed to opportunities for drug experience prior to their male classmates. By the time the upper grade levels are reached, more boys have experimented on their own, and the temporary trend disappears.

Steffenhagen, McAree, and Zheutlin [22] and Grossman et al.[23] found religion to be an important factor in the extent of drug usage. In both cases, Jews were found to use drugs more than Protestants or Catholics in college populations. Figure 2 illustrates the relation of religion to extent of marijuana use

[22] R. Steffenhagen, C. McAree, and L. Zheutlin, "Social and Academic Factors Associated With Drug Use on the University of Vermont Campus," *International Journal of Social Psychiatry*, XV (1969), 92–96.

[23] Grossman et al., "Openness to Experience . . . ," and "Internal Sensation Seeking . . . ," op. cit.

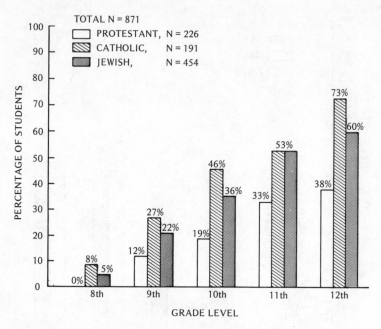

Figure 2. Percentage of students from eighth through twelfth grades having tried marijuana at least once as a function of religious background.

in the present study. We found that across all grade levels, Protestants were quite low in marijuana usage, Jews, slightly higher than the mean, with Catholics reporting the most experience with marijuana. This relationship was also significant when we considered differences among religions in the frequency of marijuana use ($F = 3.91$, $df = 2/859$, $p < .01$). In length of use, however, Jews reported longer histories of marijuana use than either Catholics or Protestants, the latter still being the lowest ($F = 4.95$, $df = 2/959$, $p < .007$). It has been hypothesized that the nonauthoritarian, open, and liberal child-rearing practices of Jewish families might account for more openness to the marijuana experience in Jewish Ss.[24] The high incidence of usage found among Catholics may be explained by the fact that these students are probably from more liberal Catholic families who chose to send their children to public school rather than the stricter, more traditional parochial school. Studies cited above that reported Jews to be more frequent users than Catholics may have had Catholic samples consisting of more graduates of parochial high schools. However, if the upbringing of the Catholic portion of our sample conformed to the traditionally stricter, more rigid Catholic model, a high percentage of marijuana users might be reflective of a reaction against an overly strict background in the form of rebellion against traditional values. This explanation seems tenable in light of the many previously cited studies describing the marijuana user as "rebellious," "non-

[24] Grossman et al., "Openness to Experience and Marijuana Use," op. cit.

Table 1   Mean Levels and Analysis of Variance Results of Personality Variables at Five Levels of Marijuana Usage

Personality Variable	Level of Marijuana Use					F
	NON-USER A [a] (n = 514)	NON-USER B [b] (n = 81)	EXPERI-MENTAL (n = 87)	MODER-ATE (n = 107)	FRE-QUENT (n = 82)	
Creativity	13.11	15.43	15.08	15.29	16.98	21.13***
Adventuresomeness	5.06	5.85	5.59	5.76	6.13	5.28**
Authoritarianism	14.75	12.06	12.87	12.40	10.94	9.28***
Internal sensation novelty seeking	7.67	12.91	11.33	12.51	13.98	33.77***
Manifest anxiety	8.74	10.21	9.47	9.71	9.15	—
Acquiescent response set	5.45	5.63	5.91	6.35	6.12	4.79*

[a] Those nonusers who said that they would never try marijuana.
[b] Those nonusers who said that they might try marijuana at some future time.
    * $p < .001$.
   ** $p < .0006$.
  *** $p < .0001$.

conforming," and having negative orientations toward traditional values, including the rejection of formalized religion.

Personality and Behavioral Correlates of Marijuana Use

A factorial analysis was done with five levels of frequency of marijuana use, two levels of sex, and two levels of birth order (firstborns and later borns). The results of this analysis are presented in Table 1. As in the previous studies, and consonant with our predictions, as the frequency of marijuana use increased, the levels of creativity, adventuresomeness, and internal sensation novelty seeking also increased significantly. Conversely, as marijuana use increased, authoritarianism decreased significantly. There is one consistent exception to these trends, namely, in the group of nonusers who said that they might someday try marijuana (Nonuser B). Instead of producing scores similar to the other nonusers in the sample, as predicted, these nonusers appeared more on the level of the moderate users in the four personality scales mentioned. This "before the fact" phenomenon lends support to the belief that the possession of certain personality characteristics, namely, creativity, adventuresomeness, nonauthoritarianism, and a desire for internal stimulation, tend to make an individual more open to the marijuana experience.

Unlike Grossman et al.,[25] who found no differences in acquiescent response set among the user groups, results of the present study indicate that as marijuana use increased, yeasaying increased significantly, with a slight drop in

[25] Ibid.

the heaviest user group. If, as previously mentioned, this scale is indicative of impulsivity, we see that marijuana users are more impulsive than nonusers, with the moderate users scoring the highest in this variable. Contrary to expectation, and repeating the findings of Grossman et al., no differences in manifest anxiety were found among any of the user groups, showing that there is no difference in level of adjustment using this measure between marijuana users and nonusers in this population.

All personality variables were also related to four levels of length of marijuana use (under 1 year, 1–2 years, 2–3 years, and over 3 years). Analysis showed only one significant relationship in any of the six personality scales. Scores on the internal sensation novelty seeking scale increased significantly in moderate users in the longest using group ($F = 3.53$, $df = 3/181$, $p < .01$). That is, in those Ss who had been using marijuana once a week or less, after a three-year period there was an increased desire for internal stimulation. Thus, there was no evidence that continued or long-term use of marijuana results in reduced personal functioning, at least as indicated by the personality measures employed here.

Our results contradict some research relating academic performance to marijuana use. Steffenhagen et al.[26] reported that the college drug user was "slightly above average" in academic standing. Grossman et al.[27] found no differences in grade point average between marijuana users and nonusers. Suchman,[28] however, reported that "drug use is more likely to occur among the poorer than the better students." In the present study, as the frequency of marijuana use increased, there was a significant decrease in reported scholastic average across all grade levels ($F = 9.78$, $df = 4/851$, $p < .0001$). It is interesting to note that Shetterly's [29] study of high-school students showed that marijuana users tended to possess more scholastic aptitude than most other students, but the majority were "functioning below expectancy levels in terms of earned grades." Shetterly explained this curious finding by stating that the marijuana users tended to be dissatisfied with school, especially their coursework, and this disenchantment interfered with performance at optimum level. It is possible that this explanation applies here as well. There was no relationship between academic performance and length of marijuana use.

The increased tendency of heavy marijuana users to experiment with other drugs is a finding that has been apparent in most studies of drug use. The numbers and percentages of students in each of the five marijuana user groups who have experimented with various other drugs are presented in Table 2. As expected, we found that as the frequency of marijuana use increased, the extent of reported experience with hashish, amphetamines, LSD, opium, and barbiturates also increased. However, only the heaviest marijuana

26 Steffenhagen et al., op. cit.
27 Grossman et al., "Openness to Experience . . . ," op. cit.
28 Suchman, op. cit., p. 150.
29 Shetterly, op. cit., p. 3279.

Table 2 **Numbers and Percentages in Each Frequency of Use Group**
Experimenting with Other Drugs

	Type of Drug											
	HASHISH		AMPHET-AMINES		LSD		HEROIN		OPIUM		BARBITU-RATES	
User Group	n	%	n	%	n	%	n	%	n	%	n	%
Nonuser A ($n = 515$)	0	0	3	.6	0	0	3	.6	0	0	4	.8
Nonuser B ($n = 80$)	0	0	1	1.3	0	0	0	0	1	1.3	2	2.5
Experimental ($n = 87$)	35	40.2	16	18.4	3	3.4	1	1.1	4	4.6	18	20.7
Moderate ($n = 107$)	92	85.9	32	29.9	12	11.2	0	0	11	10.3	32	29.9
Frequent ($n = 82$)	78	96.3	57	70.7	41	50.0	12	14.6	36	43.9	64	78.0

users showed any increased tendency to experiment with heroin. In most cases, females in each frequency of use category were much more likely to have experimented with other drugs than males in the same group.

Results of McAree et al.[30] and Mirin et al.[31] suggest that multiple-drug users or heavy marijuana users show more evidence of maladjustment and pathology than those who use marijuana alone or are only casually involved with the drug. Since analogous results were not present in the frequent marijuana user group in this study, a post hoc analysis was done with all Ss who reported current marijuana use (moderate and frequent users). Two levels of drug use, a marijuana-only group and a group who had experimented with marijuana and other drugs as well, were compared along each personality variable and on academic average. There were no significant differences between the two groups in level of creativity, adventuresomeness, authoritarianism, or yeasaying. The multiple-drug users, however, scored much higher than the marijuana-only group on internal sensation novelty seeking ($F = 6.84$, $df = 1/268$, $p < .009$). The multiple-drug users had lower scholastic averages than those who used marijuana alone ($F = 6.04$, $df = 1/268$, $p < .01$), and although the relationship did not reach significance, multiple-drug users also tended to score higher on the Manifest Anxiety scale ($F = 1.73$, $df = 1/268$, $p < .18$). Multiple-drug users generally were older than marijuana-only users, and they had used marijuana for longer lengths of time and with greater frequency—these relationships all being significant.

College-Oriented versus Non-College-Oriented Marijuana Users

Results of an analysis of the 113 Ss in non-college-oriented courses indicated that some variables seem to be specific to the college-oriented individual, while others are applicable to the high-school marijuana user in general. In this small sample, as frequency of marijuana use increased, internal sensation

[30] McAree et al., op. cit.
[31] Mirin et al., op. cit.

novelty seeking increased significantly ($F = 2.54$, $df = 4/103$, $p < .04$), and authoritarianism decreased significantly ($F = 3.34$, $df = 4/103$, $p < .01$). Adventuresomeness also increased with increased marijuana use, but this trend was not significant ($F = 1.47$, $df = 4/103$, $p < .21$). As in the college-oriented sample, Ss in the Nonuser B group consistently scored at the level of the moderate users in the three scales mentioned. No differences in manifest anxiety were found among any frequency of use category.

Unlike the college-oriented sample, this smaller group showed no differences in acquiescent response set across user groups, but this variable has not been consistent in its relation to marijuana use in the past. There was also no difference in scholastic average among the user groups, a finding that might be explained by the relatively small amount of variance in the reported averages of this group. The one personality variable that most clearly demonstrated a different relationship to marijuana use in the two samples was creativity as measured by the Personal Opinion Survey. In the non-college-oriented sample, no differences in creativity were found at any level of marijuana use, contradicting the very consistent positive relationship between this variable and frequency of marijuana use present in the Grossman et al. undergraduate samples and the college-oriented portion of this study. It seems that creativity, as a correlate of marijuana use, is only a relevant variable when considering college students or those individuals who anticipate going to college.

CONCLUSION

The "openness to experience" concept, consisting of high creativity, adventuresomeness, internal sensation novelty seeking, and low authoritarianism, seems to describe the marijuana user in the college-oriented high-school population as well as previous college samples. Most aspects of this profile also apply to the non-college-oriented marijuana user, with the exception of increased creativity scores. It is possible that the creativity aspect of the openness to experience concept does not apply to non-college-oriented individuals, but the sample used here was quite small and perhaps not representative. Future research is indicated in this area. It must be remembered that at the present time the results of this study can only be generalized to populations similar to the sample employed here (white, middle-income, college-oriented high school students in a large city). Obviously the motivational patterns of a rural marijuana smoker or a user in the black ghetto might be quite different.

The ultimate goal of this and similar research is to determine if there is a consistent personality profile associated with marijuana use that can possibly be used as a predictive tool to identify potential drug users. In this way, drug education programs could be specifically directed toward these individuals by employing teaching approaches found most successful with these personality types in the past. Adding validity to the idea that possession of this personality pattern might be predictive of future drug experimentation are the results of the nonuser group who stated that they might try marijuana in the future. These nonusers demonstrated personality traits at levels comparable to the present moderate marijuana users. It must be emphasized that all of the results reported here are correlational and not causal, as this last result implies. Moreover, the present findings suggest that the use of marijuana is not causal of any personality change, and does not create the type of personality associated with marijuana use in this study, but simply states that the possession of such traits tends to make an individual more open to the experience of marijuana use.

Doris H. Milman

Wen-Huey Su

Patterns of Illicit Drug and Alcohol Use Among Secondary-School Students

An attempt to identify the personality and demographic characteristics of adolescent alcohol and drug users is described in this selection. Over 500 middle-class, white, urban youth, grades nine through twelve, attending private secondary schools, responded to a self-administered, anonymous questionnaire. More than half of the youths reported having used alcohol, but less than 20 per cent had smoked tobacco and only 15 per cent had tried one or more drugs. Three-fourths of the drug users started with marijuana, and more than half of the users had tried one or more drugs. According to Milman and Su, patterns of drug and alcohol use are highly correlated and are most pronounced in youth who deviate from "currently accepted norms of behavior and adjustment."

Instructional Objectives
To discuss drug, tobacco, and alcohol use among adolescents.
To describe drug and alcohol use among adolescents in relation to such demographic factors as sex, age, and religion.

FROM *Journal of Pediatrics*, XXCIII (1973), pp. 314–320; copyrighted by The C. V. Mosby Company, St. Louis, Missouri. Reprinted by permission of the authors and the publisher.

To describe drug and alcohol use among adolescents in relation to academic achievement and interest in college.

To describe drug and alcohol use among adolescents in relation, respectively, to peer use and to extent of dating, petting, and sexual intercourse.

To describe drug and alcohol use among adolescents in relation to psychological adjustment.

THE EPIDEMIOLOGY of illicit drug usage has been a subject of increasing interest over the past seven years, an interest generated by changing practices and attitudes and the resultant problems. Current studies have focused mainly on usage by college and university students, among whom the phenomenon of drug use gained wide acceptance during the decade of the 1960s. It was logical to anticipate that, with wide acceptance by middle class youths in colleges, eventually drug usage would filter down into the high schools, a situation which became evident at least by 1967.[1] Since then many surveys have been undertaken for the purpose of defining the extent of the problem in secondary schools.[2]

The present study is concerned not only with illicit drugs but also with alcohol, and with demographic, social, and personal factors associated with users. Thus, as with our studies of university students,[3] we can apply our data to draw a profile of the characteristic user and nonuser. Such profiles, it is anticipated, can have both educational and clinical applicability. With respect to educational programs aimed at prevention of drug abuse, a knowledge of the population at risk might aid in designing a program which would address itself specifically to that particular population. Additionally, if one can identify the least susceptible population, one can design a program aimed at confirming that group's resistance to drugs. A clinician might make use of such a profile to identify the susceptible student and thus be in a position to offer guidance. It was also anticipated that identification of the alcohol user might have a similar clinical application and might shed additional light on the use of psychotropic agents.

---

[1] C. F. Sinnott, " 'Teens'—A Survey Summary," *American Journal of Catholic Youth Work*, IX (1968), 11.

[2] E. J. Salber, B. MacMahon, and B. Welsh, "Smoking Habits of High School Students Related to Intelligence and Achievement," *Pediatrics*, XXIX (1962), 780; J. T. Gossett, and J. M. Lewis, "Extent and Prevalence of Illicit Drug Use as Reported by 56,745 Students," *Journal of the American Medical Association*, CCXVI (1971), 1464; E. Josephson, P. Haberman, A. Zanes, and J. Elinson, "Adolescent Marijuana Use." Report on a National Survey, Proceedings of the First International Conference on Student Drug Surveys, College of Medicine and Dentistry of New Jersey at Newark and the Institute for the Study of Drug Addiction, September 14, 1971; M. Brown, "Stability and Change in Drug Use Patterns Among High School Students," *Congressional Record* CXVII (September 27, 1971), 10064.

[3] J. R. Lombillo and J. L. Anker, "Patterns of Drug Use in a High School Population," *American Journal of Psychiatry*, CXXVIII (1972), 836.

METHOD

The present study was undertaken in January, 1969, to determine patterns of drug use by middle class students in secondary school. Students in high-school grades 9 through 12 of two urban private schools were surveyed. The total enrollment, 551 students, was included in a universal sampling.

A self-administered, anonymous questionnaire consisting of 76 items was employed. Inquiry was made about tobacco, alcohol, marijuana, hashish, amphetamines, barbiturates, glue and cleaning fluid, dimethyltryptamine, mescaline, psilocybin, *d*-lysergic acid diethylamine, codeine, heroin, tetra-hydrocannabinol, cocaine, and gasoline. The questionnaire was presented simultaneously to all of the classes in order to minimize the possibility that discussion or prior knowledge among the students would influence the results. The administration of the survey was conducted by medical students in order to promote cooperation and to reassure the respondents of anonymity and immunity. By this means 100 per cent compliance was obtained.

The data were quantitated by tabulations and cross tabulations. Associations between variables were analyzed statistically by the chi square test and were considered significant when the p value was 0.01 or less. Those variables which failed to reach statistical significance were noted in the text. Intra-questionnaire reliability was estimated to be 0.95 for drug-related questions.

RESULTS

DEMOGRAPHY (TABLE 1). The sample was predominantly male (56 per cent), white (97 per cent), and Jewish (86 per cent). Ninety-two per cent of the families were intact. Eighty-one per cent of fathers were in business or professions. Fifty-seven per cent of the mothers were not employed outside the home. Forty-two per cent of fathers and 31 per cent of mothers were

Table 1   Demography

	No.	*%*
Total sample	551	100
Male	307	56
Female	244	44
Religion		
Jewish	473	86
Catholic	38	7
Protestant	24	4
Other	15	3
Race		
White	535	97
Other	15	3

college educated. Although in no respect representative of the total youth population of the locality, the study group was representative of the private school population.

Ninety-six per cent of the students were planning to go to college. Seventy-two per cent maintained an A or B average. Seventeen per cent held part-time jobs. Three per cent reported having been in trouble with the police. Again, these characteristics applied to private school students rather than to a public high-school population.

PREVALENCE OF DRUG USE (TABLE 2). Alcohol was the most commonly used drug; it was used by 52 per cent of students, occasionally (less than once a month) by 14 per cent and regularly (weekly) by 11 per cent of students. Tobacco was smoked by 18 per cent. Illicit drugs had been used at least once by 14 per cent. Among illicit drugs marijuana was the most commonly used; it was used by 12 per cent. Six per cent of students smoked it occasionally (less than once a month) and 5 per cent regularly (twice a month or more). Seventy-five per cent of drug users had tried marijuana as the first illicit drug. Four students (1 per cent) used cocaine and two students (less than 1 per cent) used heroin.

Table 2 Prevalence of Usage of Individual Drugs

Drug	No. using	% using	% also using alcohol
Alcohol	282	52	—
Tobacco	100	18	80
All illicit drugs	79	14	83
Marijuana	64	12	88
Hashish	38	7	84
Amphetamines	26	5	81
Barbiturates	17	3	82
Glue/cleaning fluid	15	3	87
LSD	10	2	70

Multiple drug use (Table 3) was the rule; 59 per cent of users (19 per cent of the total population) used two or more drugs and 7 per cent used as many as seven drugs.

The frequency of alcohol use among illicit drug users was much greater than in the sample as a whole (83 per cent compared with 52 per cent).

DEMOGRAPHIC FACTORS (FIG. 1). Boys outnumbered girls in the use of alcohol and illicit drugs; this was significant at the $p < 0.01$ level. A steady increase in the frequency of drug use was found with advancing age. Usage rates for alcohol and for illicit drugs were below average in 14-year-old

Table 3   Experience with Multiple Illicit
Drugs

No. of drugs used	% of drug users
1	41
2	19
3	12
4	8
5	5
6	8
7	7

students and well above average in 18-year-old students. Significant differences were found between Jewish students and those of other denominations, the Jewish students having the lowest usage rates for drugs and alcohol. Catholic and Protestant students had similar rates for experiences with alcohol, but among Protestants usage rates for illicit drugs were greatly in excess.

ACADEMIC ACHIEVEMENT AND INTEREST (FIG. 2).   There was a correlation between poor grades and use of alcohol ($p < 0.05$) and illicit drugs ($p < 0.01$). The greater use of alcohol ($p < 0.05$) and illicit drugs ($p < 0.01$) among non–college-bound students was consistent with this observation in relation to academic grades.

SOCIAL AND SEXUAL BEHAVIOR (FIG. 3).   For both alcohol and illicit drugs the influence of peers was very strong, whether measured by percentage of friends who used drugs or percentage of classmates estimated to be using drugs. Heterosexually oriented behavior was found to have a striking correlation with drug practices; the more advanced the behavior the greater was the prevalence both of alcohol and other drug usage.

PSYCHOLOGICAL ADJUSTMENT (FIG. 4).   Students reporting an excellent relationship with parents indicated lower use rates of alcohol and illicit drugs, reaching statistical significance for drugs but not for alcohol. Differences between self-designation as "happy" and "nervous" with respect to drug usage rate ($p < 0.05$) and between "happy" and "depressed" for alcohol, although short of statistical significance, suggested an association between drug use and negative mood states. A history of psychiatric difficulty was found to correlate positively with illicit drug use. The difference was not significant for alcohol but the trend was in the same direction. Antisocial behavior as indicated by arrests was strongly correlated with use of drugs but, again, was not significant for alcohol. Thus all of the examined indices of psychological maladjustment were significant for illicit drugs but were not significant for alcohol.

DRUG-RELATED BEHAVIOR (FIG. 5).   Smoking tobacco was strongly correlated with the use of alcohol and illicit drugs. Likewise, alcohol use was strongly

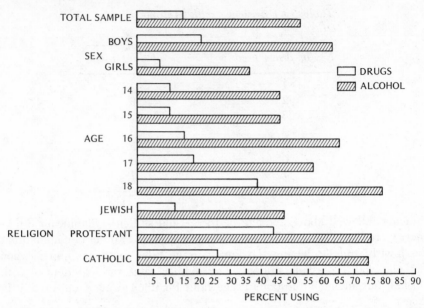

Figure 1. *Prevalence of illicit drug and alcohol usage in relation to demographic factors.*

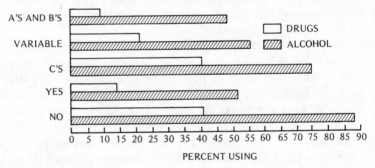

Figure 2. *Prevalence of illicit drug and alcohol usage in relation to academic achievement and interest.*

correlated with the use of illicit drugs. A reciprocal correlation was found between the use of illicit drugs and the use of alcohol, with the nonusers of alcohol having a much lower than average frequency of use of illicit drugs, the occasional users of alcohol having an average frequency, and the regular drinkers having a much higher incidence of use of illicit drugs.

DISCUSSION

The usage rates of tobacco, alcohol, and illicit drugs are somewhat lower on the whole in this study than those found by others.[4] The differences can

[4] Salber et al., op. cit.; Gossett et al., op. cit.; Josephson et al., op. cit.; Brown, op. cit.; Lombillo et al., op. cit.

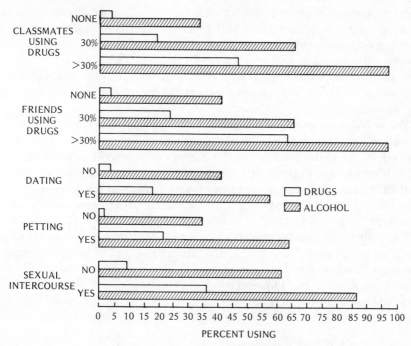

Figure 3. Prevalence of illicit drug and alcohol usage in relation to social and sexual behavior.

probably be accounted for by differences in the types of schools sampled, in geographic location, and in timing of the study. Our findings with respect to illicit drugs most closely approximate those of Sinnott [5] whose usage rate for marijuana of 13.5 per cent was very close to ours (12 per cent). Her study was performed on Catholic teen-agers from the same locale as our students and at about the same point in time. The similarity in results extends also to the breakdown by sex (boys 25 per cent in her study and 20 per cent in ours, girls 4 per cent versus 6.6 per cent), suggesting that, although our sample was preponderantly Jewish and Sinnott's was Catholic, religious differences were less important than class differences, her sample being drawn from Catholic parochial schools.

No correlation was found to exist for intactness of home, parents' occupation, or parents' education. The inference would appear to be that these kinds of situational factors have little influence on drug behavior. Moreover, although an "excellent" relationship with parents was found to be associated with a low incidence of drug usage, a "good" relationship was no different from a "poor" one, suggesting that parental influence, negative or positive, is of less significance in determining adolescent behavior than are factors outside of home and family.

Prominent among the factors inconsistent with drug usage are good school

[5] Sinnott, op. cit.

performance and interest in higher education. Even more significant in inhibiting drug use is slow social and psychosexual development; the young
person who follows a traditional, conservative path in other spheres during
the high-school years will very likely do the same with respect to drugs.
Conversely, social and sexual precocity, negative attitudes toward school,
and antisocial behavior appear to render the adolescent more receptive to
experimentation with drugs.

The correlation between drug use and psychiatric difficulty, per se, as
measured by a history of psychiatric consultation and/or treatment, suggests
a trend in the same direction as the aforementioned indicators of an anti-
establishment or independent attitude. As reported in studies of college
students,[6] drug usage can be an expression of adolescent rebellion and hence
is associated with other types of behavior which are at variance with adult
standards.

The high correlation between the percentage of friends or classmates using
drugs and high prevalence of drug or alcohol usage is of great importance
for understanding the dynamics of spread of drug usage. First of all, this
finding emphasizes the importance of peer influence and the tendency of
users to limit their contacts to other users, leading to what Brown [7] calls the

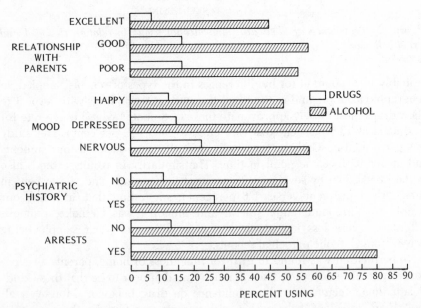

*Figure 4. Prevalence of illicit drug and alcohol usage in relation to psychological
adjustment.*

[6] D. H. Milman and J. L. Anker, "Patterns of Drug Usage Among University Students.
IV. Use of Marijuana, Amphetamines, Opium, and LSD by Undergraduates," *Journal of
the American College Health Association,* XX (1971), 96.
[7] Brown, op. cit.

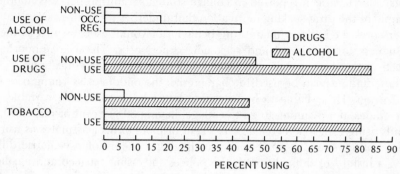

Figure 5. Prevalence of illicit drug and alcohol usage in relation to drug-related behavior.

"pattern of circular reinforcement." Second, the inflated perception of the prevalence of drug use by users tends to justify to the users their own drug use. Moreover, this inflated perception of use facilitates the induction of new users.

A most important finding is the parallel increase in the use of tobacco, alcohol, and illicit drugs in relation to factors which have a correlation with high rates of drug usage. Since these drugs are taken by different routes and have different subjective effects, one can conclude that the impetus for use is to be found not only in specific psychopharmacologic effects but also in the psychological and personal characteristics of the users. That is, drug-seeking behavior is a characteristic of a personality type or types rather than a response to the particular mind-affecting properties of specific drugs. This conclusion is in accord with the finding by Rosenberg [8] who reported that 52 per cent of young alcoholics also used illicit drugs.

The similarity in patterns of use between alcohol and illicit drugs leads to the inference that motivating factors are similar for the two groups of users. This could have important public health implications if marijuana were to receive legal sanction, since it is conceivable that a segment of abusers of marijuana would emerge as has been the case with alcohol. Then the question arises whether the marijuana abusers would be drawn from the same group as the heavy drinkers or whether they would constitute an additional problem group. The divergencies in this study between the psychological characteristics of drug users (unstable) and drinkers (more stable) suggest that, although there may be some overlap, there might also be an additional group of marijuana abusers emerging impelled by different psychological mechanisms.

Another important finding is the tendency toward use of multiple illicit

[8] C. M. Rosenberg, "Young Alcoholics," *British Journal of Psychiatry,* CXV (1969), 181.

drugs. This has been reported in college students [9] and probably is another example of the drug-seeking motivation that underlies much drug use. It also underscores the indiscriminate drug behavior of young users as well as their willingness to experiment and seek new experiences. These are important aspects of the drug problem for those concerned with drug education.

These findings can be used to characterize the middle class young user of illicit drugs. He is liable to be in mid-to-late adolescence, with variable or poor grades, not planning to go to college, having 30 per cent or more of his friends using drugs, perceiving 30 per cent or more of his classmates as using drugs, dating, sexually active, nervous, having a history of psychiatric difficulty, a history of difficulty with the police, and using tobacco and alcohol regularly. Contrariwise, the nonuser of drugs is in early adolescence, with high grades, planning to go to college, having no friends who use drugs, perceiving none of his classmates as using drugs, not dating or sexually active, not using tobacco, and showing no evidence of psychological disturbance.

[9] D. H. Milman and J. L. Anker, "Patterns of Drug Usage and Related Patterns of Behavior Among University Students. II. Multiple Drug Use," in W. Keup, ed., *Drug Abuse: Current Concepts and Research* (Springfield, Ill.: Charles C Thomas, Publisher, 1972), p. 190.

David Klein

Adolescent Driving as Deviant Behavior

Klein describes the characteristics of adolescent driving in the context of several categories of deviant behavior—predation, consumption, appearance, belief, and performance. He questions whether driver education programs for adolescents can be made to conform to adult standards of driving, and his provocative analyses suggest that deviant driving is to be expected of adolescents. Indeed, he argues that the relative isolation of adolescents from adult norms and the workplace ensures their deviancy.

Instructional Objectives
To define the meaning of deviance.
To describe types of deviance and to indicate how each is expressed in adolescent driving.

FROM *Journal of Safety Research*, IV (1972), pp. 98–105, a National Safety Council publication. Reprinted by permission of the author and the publisher.

To describe the adolescent as deviant and to illustrate how isolation from adult and workplace norms contribute to deviance.

To describe the role of the automobile in adolescents' achievement of individualism.

M ANY professionals in highway safety believe that current research on the young driver poses relevant and appropriate questions, but, because of methodological problems and inadequacies of data, answers them incorrectly or incompletely. The present paper, by contrast, offers the view that many current studies and action programs are based on inappropriate assumptions, address themselves to irrelevant questions, and hence achieve results that have little scientific validity or practical value—even though they have been obtained through impeccable methodology.

Four principal shortcomings of much of this research and practice illustrate its basic weakness.

First, many programs compare the numbers of citations and reported crashes accumulated by young drivers with similar data for the adult population and conclude that adolescents are substantially "worse." This may occur even though sophisticated investigators are aware that adolescents often receive citations or have their crashes reported because of personal appearance or social status rather than driving behavior.

Second, measurements of exposure, either quantitative or qualitative, are intended primarily to facilitate comparison of the young driver with the adult. Exposure is thus regarded as a means of making the findings more precise rather than as an *inherent part of the problem*. Although teen-age exposure is quite different in motivation and quality from adult exposure—and although it may be far more readily reducible, because much teen-age driving is not actually essential—few, if any, research or action programs are based on the self-evident assumption that crashes and violations can be reduced by reducing exposure.

Third, many investigators, because they attempt to use a representative sample, imply that their conclusions are applicable to "all teen-agers." In other areas of contemporary behavioral research, no professionally adequate investigator would generalize his findings to "all Negroes" or "all college freshmen." Yet much research on adolescent driving still tends to be generalized indiscriminately.[1] The few rough sortings that have been made—between males and females, between good and poor students, between those who have and have not taken courses in driver education—stem essentially from crude statistical associations and involve no causal relationships.

Finally, as an examination of virtually any textbook or state syllabus on driver education will indicate, both driver education curriculums and re-

---

[1] National Commission on Safety Education, *Summary of Results of Studies Evaluating Driver Education* (Washington, D. C.: Author, 1961).

habilitative measures aimed at the young driver are limited largely to improving driving-related skills and attitudes in the hope of modifying his behavior in the direction of the adult model. This approach embodies the dubious assumption that there is only one adult model and that it is a "good" one. A more serious limitation, however, is that it makes no effort to identify or change the wide range of social and psychological variables peculiar to the young driver that may influence his exposure as well as his driving behavior.

Clearly, each of these limitations warrants further examination; but the ultimate aim of most of the programs and related research is to devise methods that will make the adolescent drive as the adult does. Essentially, the question implicit in such research is "Why don't adolescents drive like adults?"—a question distressingly similar to (and no more useful than) the question "Why can't women be more like men?"

An alternative view is that adolescents are *not* adults and that efforts to make their driving resemble that of adults overlook a number of complexities. This view is by no means original. Sociologists and anthropologists have long recognized that adolescents constitute a deviant population in almost every industrial society. Thus, not only can they be expected to drive in a deviant fashion, but their deviant driving may, in fact, conform closely to the norms and values of their own (deviant) group. Any efforts to modify their driving in the direction of the adult model necessarily involve persuading them to deviate from group norms.

Having thus—simplistically for the moment and without documentation—labeled an entire age group as deviant, let us analyze deviance in order to understand why it may be a more useful concept than crashes and violations for the study of adolescent driving. We can then consider why adolescents constitute a deviant group and why some adolescents are more deviant than others.

DEVIANCE DEFINED.   In general, deviance may be defined as any behavior that departs substantially from what is regarded as normal or acceptable and that seems to threaten the welfare of society. Note that this definition specifies "what is regarded as acceptable" and not "what most people do," because deviance is defined not by actual behavior but by those members of our society who make its laws and define its values. Hence, certain behavior is regarded as deviant even though many people engage in it—a point that is extremely important with respect to adolescents. Note, too, the phrase "seems to threaten" rather than "actually threatens." Some kinds of behavior regarded as threatening (and hence deviant) only a few years ago—performing abortions or driving at 70 miles per hour—are now regarded as nonthreatening and perfectly legal by substantial segments of the population throughout the country.

Punishment for deviant behavior varies not only with time and place but also with the age and status of the person engaging in it. A 22-year-old girl who engages in premarital intercourse, for example, is subject to less censure or punishment than the 13-year-old who does the same thing. Similarly, blacks and other minority group members are more likely to be arrested and convicted for a wide variety of legal offenses than whites who commit the same acts.[2] Since adolescents are, by definition, young, and since they comprise a minority group, this differential definition of deviance becomes important.

The relationship between deviance and crime is also a complex one. Some deviant behavior, such as auto theft, is criminal since it violates a statutory law. But certain kinds of criminal behavior, such as the violation of a traffic law, are not actually regarded as deviant. For example, the annual *Uniform Crime Reports*,[3] which purports to tabulate all reported crimes in the United States, makes no mention of traffic offenses other than auto theft; and the exhaustive report of the President's Commission on Law Enforcement and Administration of Justice [4] ignores traffic offenses completely. Further, in most social circles the traffic violator is regarded as normal—"everybody gets a ticket once in awhile." As H. L. Ross [5] has pointed out, traffic crime is not taken seriously because it is "folk crime"; but, as we shall see shortly, adolescents are not regarded as "folk."

In viewing adolescent driving, then, we must distinguish among three distinct types of behavior: (1) a broad range of deviant behavior that is not in fact criminal; (2) a variety of behaviors defined as criminal; and (3) behaviors that actually threaten the safety or welfare of our society. These relationships will become clearer once we examine the various types of deviant behavior.

TYPES OF DEVIANCE. Deviance that is consistently criminal has been labeled *predation*, that is, behavior which destroys life or property or appropriates property that belongs to others. With respect to adolescent driving behavior, the two most common types of predation are auto theft and vandalism.

The consequences of auto theft are often aggravated by police response. When the police, on identifying a stolen vehicle, initiate a high-speed pursuit, the likelihood that the chase will end in a crash, often with fatalities or injuries, is multiplied manyfold.[6] The crash rate in such circumstances could be reduced if the police were to modify their response to juvenile thefts, acknowledging that a delay in recovering the vehicle (usually abandoned unharmed) is preferable to the injury and damage that may result from a dramatic pursuit. Such a modification seems unlikely, however, as long as the

---

[2] I. Piliavin and S. Briar, "Police Encounters with Juveniles," *American Journal of Sociology*, LXX (1964), 206–214.

[3] *Uniform Crime Reports: Crime in the United States* (Washington, D. C.: United States Government Printing Office, 1970).

[4] President's Commission on Law Enforcement and Administration of Justice, *The Challenge of Crime in a Free Society* (Washington, D. C.: United States Government Printing Office, 1970).

[5] H. L. Ross, "Traffic Law Violations: A Folk Crime," *Social Problems*, VIII (3) (1960–61), 321–341.

[6] E. F. Fennessy, T. Hamilton, K. B. Joscelyn, and J. S. Merritt, *A Study of the Problem of Hot Pursuit by the Police* (Hartford, Conn.: Center for the Environment and Man, Inc., 1970).

police (largely in response to society's mandates) place so high a value on property and so low a value on human life that they are willing to endanger life in an attempt to protect property. Nevertheless, ultimately, a reduction in the crash rate in this category may be achieved more easily by changing the behavior of the police rather than that of the adolescent.

A second form of deviance, some of it criminal, some legal, is *deviant consumption*—the consumption of goods and services (drugs, alcohol, non-standard versions of such standardized items as clothing, vehicles, or housing) that are not approved by society.

Whether or not certain types of consumption, for example, alcohol or sex, are labeled deviant depends on the age and status of the consumer. Both the age and status of the adolescent make him especially prone to types of deviant consumption that relate to his driving. Because his sexual activity, drinking, and drug use are per se deviant, he must engage in such activities in privacy; and few places lend themselves to privacy as conveniently as an automobile. Such use of an automobile inevitably means greater exposure and, therefore, a higher crash and citation frequency even if he drives as well as an adult.

The vehicle itself represents another area of deviant consumption. Although economic and technological changes have caused our society to become increasingly consumption-oriented, its more conservative elements—and these include many judges and traffic policemen—continue to look with disapproval on such examples of conspicuous consumption as the high-performance car and the so-called sports car, both driven preponderantly by young drivers. And, there is some evidence that the police issue citations to drivers of such vehicles more frequently than to other drivers for essentially the same behavior.

Adolescents are especially attracted to these cars for several reasons. First, the symbolic autonomy and power promised by advertisements for high-performance cars appeal to them. Second, they especially value the automobile as a status symbol because they are barred from other channels for the achievement of status. Finally, in an affluent society, many adolescents can spend a higher proportion of their disposable income on vehicles and accessories than adults can.

Yet another form of deviance involving adolescents is *deviant appearance*. Unconventional grooming or clothing often appears threatening; and, since unconventionality of appearance is largely restricted to adolescence, it is not surprising that both the bearded upper-middle-class college student and the leather-jacketed lower-class adolescent frequently complain of unjustified harassment by the police.[7]

Deviant belief often elicits a punitive response from society. And, to the extent that young people today are better educated than previous generations (a fact supported by a wide variety of evidence), many of their ideas and values inevitably seem deviant to their elders. They may appear especially

7 *New York Times,* May 11, 1971, p. 39.

deviant to those who are directly responsible for the enforcement of traffic regulation and who often tend to be less educated and more conservative. Heussenstamm [8] has demonstrated dramatically that this antipathy to the ideological positions of the young can result in punitive actions in a traffic situation. In her study, 15 adolescents with previously exemplary driving records received a total of 33 citations in 17 days after the investigator affixed Black Panther bumper stickers to their personal automobiles.

The final category of deviance—*deviant performance*—is both complex and difficult to define with respect to driving. Since all crashes have multiple, interrelated causes, our ability to identify specific behaviors that precipitate a crash is negligible. Theoretically, deviant performance is the kind of behavior that is supposedly discouraged by traffic laws. Correlations between crashes and citations in individual driving records are, however, too low to support the assumption that driving designated as illegal is in fact dangerous. And the wide variations among states in operator licensing criteria and driver education curriculums suggest that our notions of "good" and "bad" driving behavior are based on speculation rather than on data.[9]

Substandard (or deviant) performance is, of course, characteristic of the early stages of any learning process. In our society, adolescence happens to coincide with the time at which most persons learn to drive; thus, a certain number of so-called "teen-age" crashes are learning errors which have nothing to do with the age of the driver. Countermeasures restricting inexperienced drivers to a protective environment or conspicuously labeling such drivers (as with the British "L" for the driver's first year) for the protection of others as well as themselves have rarely been considered and have even more rarely been evaluated systematically.

Unfortunately, adolescence is also the time when most persons are learning to cope with alcohol; and a small error on the learning curve for driving, if it coincides with a small error on the learning curve for drinking, can produce rather serious consequences. The logical solution to this problem would be to permit adolescents to learn to drive and to learn to drink at different times in their lives, but the social feasibility of such a solution is low.

Other kinds of deviant performance by adolescents are not directly related to the precipitation of crashes but are nevertheless punished by the issuing of citations. Street dragging, for example, obviously contributes to noise, to atmospheric pollution, and occasionally to highway congestion—a charge that can be made with equal justice against the conventional cargo truck. But whether street dragging contributes disproportionately to the crash rate is not known. Nevertheless, in response to community pressures "to do something about it," police often issue citations for speeding or for vehicle defects that go unnoticed in other circumstances.

THE ADOLESCENT AS DEVIANT. Some types of deviance are clearly age-bound,

[8] F. K. Heussenstamm, "Bumper Stickers and the Cops," *Trans-action*, (February 1971), 32–33.
[9] D. Klein and J. A. Waller, *Causation, Culpability, and Deterrence in Highway Crashes* (Washington, D. C.: United States Department of Transportation, 1970).

and their concentration in the adolescent age group is self-evident. But other types are not necessarily age-bound; and we might well ask why unconventional clothing, excessive interest in high-performance cars, concern for speed and power, and motivation to defy authority are concentrated so heavily in the youth group that when these traits appear in older people we tend to label such people "adolescent."

There are two basic reasons for adolescents' high deviance rate. First, any social group that is isolated from the dominant group has little or no opportunity to learn the norms of the dominant group, to practice them, or to be rewarded for conformity to them. Hence the isolated group, whether it be an ethnic enclave, a sorority, or a ghetto-enclosed racial group, retains or develops its own language, clothing styles, music, and standards of behavior. And as adolescents have been increasingly isolated from interaction with adult society, "youth subculture" has become increasingly complex, conspicuous, and differentiated from the adult culture. Fifty years ago "youth culture" hardly existed, because the youth were highly involved in the adult culture.

This isolation has several causes. The shift from the extended family, replete with uncles, aunts, grandparents, and cousins, to the nuclear two-generation family consisting of two parents and one or two siblings has deprived the adolescent of meaningful day-to-day contacts with older people of various ages. The adults he does meet—teachers, dentists, storekeepers, auto mechanics—have a segmented, impersonal, and usually superordinate relationship with him. Even in the nuclear family, he tends to spend less time with his parents than he used to. This is especially true of the male because there is little that he can learn at home about his future occupational role. It is also especially true for the suburban male, since one or both of his parents may spend most of the working day away from home, and even meaningful interaction with his peers often necessitates considerable exposure in an automobile.

A similar shift in the productive sector of the economy from the family-owned store, farm, or shop to the large corporate enterprise prevents the adolescent from developing relationships in a work situation that facilitate his incorporation of the dominant social norms. As Urie Bronfenbrenner [10] has pointed out, today's adolescent has grown up with two basic sources of values and norms—his peers and a series of television heroes whose competitiveness, toughness, aggressiveness, and violence are always rewarded in the end.

Social isolation per se tends to produce norms that are different from those of the dominant group, but not necessarily *antagonistic* to them. What makes the youth culture a "contraculture" with norms clearly antagonistic to adult norms is the fact that our young people suffer not merely isolation but also deprivation of certain rights and privileges that adults enjoy. This deprivation becomes more severe as adolescence becomes increasingly prolonged—on

---

[10] U. Bronfenbrenner, *Two Worlds of Childhood* (New York: Russell Sage, 1970).

the one hand, puberty is occurring earlier and on the other, the increasing complexity of our technology has extended the length of schooling (and hence dependency) by several years.

The typical 17-year-old has been biologically mature for several years, is close to his peak physically, and yet is in many ways a second-class citizen. He is not permitted to work, vote, drink, engage in sexual activity, or make the kind of productive contribution to society that will earn him psychic gratification or social rewards. He is taught to work hard and to achieve; yet channels toward achievement, except in a narrow range of academic or athletic efforts, are rather restricted for him. (He cannot, as his grandfather could at his age, earn status by rearing a prize calf or by working at a job that contributes to his own development and to his family's standard of living.) He is urged to be individual and innovative, yet most opportunities for productive individualism and initiative are closed to him. (Today, building a better mousetrap requires a degree in mechanical engineering.) He learns, from books, television, and a variety of other sources, that a "real man" is tough, ingenious, and willing to take risks. Yet what aspects of his life can be coped with realistically through toughness, ingenuity, or risk-taking? He is taught that freedom is our most precious value, yet he feels that his own freedom is severely restricted—by parents, by schools, by laws— in ways that strike him as arbitrary. He is taught that all men are equal, yet he feels that he is not the equal of adults who, often enough, know less than he and are less willing to learn.

Given such a situation, it is easy to see the automobile's significance for the adolescent. His driver's license is, very often, his first rite of passage into the adult world. He can develop an expertise about automobiles or a virtuosity in handling them that matches or exceeds that of most adults. Customizing his car offers him a unique opportunity to innovate and to express his individualism. And on the highway, he is the equal of any adult—until he is stopped by a traffic policeman!

A physically handicapped woman once wrote of her joy in owning a car: "I could never in my life pass anyone on the street. But in a car, I can!" Small wonder that the adolescent feels likewise, or that he sees the automobile as offering him the only autonomy he can enjoy. And, since the media have taught him how precious a possession an automobile is, small wonder that he steals one if he can't obtain it legitimately or that he sees vandalism of an automobile as an effective way of striking out against adult society. One might venture to say that if the automobile had not existed, the contemporary teen-ager would have had to invent it.

THE MORE DEVIANT AND THE LESS. Although certain constraints apply to adolescents as a group, it seems clear that they apply more strongly to some adolescents than to others or that some adolescents have easier access to (or are more willing to accept) the rewards offered by adult society. Hence, if our hypothesis is correct, adolescents with greater access to socially approved activities should have a lower crash and citation rate.

There is some evidence (though it is far from adequate) to support this.

Carlson and Klein [11] have found that students whose academic performance, as measured by grades, is below the level of their predicted abilities
have a higher citation rate than those who perform at or above their predicted
level. Further, these underachievers demonstrate greater deviance in other
situations, that is, they are arrested more frequently for nontraffic offenses.
These findings do more than confirm the inverse relationship between grades
and traffic citations; they imply that the student who is able to do well
academically, but who rejects academic work as a route to success and reward, is the one most likely to be involved in a wide range of deviant
behavior. Schuman et al.[12] similarly note a degree of alienation in those
young drivers in their sample who had the highest crash frequencies.

Thus, it appears that the adolescent is less likely to involve himself in exposure, citations, and crashes if he can find satisfaction in a meaningful,
legitimate, socially useful task that might be offered by school or work but
often, apparently, is not. On the other hand, if society's expectations of the
adolescent are discrepant with his perception of his own capacities, he may
quite deliberately engage in deviant behavior that expresses his resentment
or defiance.

SOME IMPLICATIONS FOR RESEARCH AND ACTION PROGRAMS.   When adolescent
driving is recognized as almost inevitably deviant because of the adolescent's
social situation, one can understand why current punitive and educational
measures are unlikely to be effective in reducing citation and crash frequency. Our society might be able to reallocate substantial resources to more
effective countermeasures if it could only recognize that adolescent driving
is an integral part of the adolescent subculture and that it should not be
evaluated by adult standards.

Two obstacles make such a change in attitude unlikely. First, it would
eliminate the teen-age driver as a convenient scapegoat for our inability to
make inroads on the complex problem of highway losses—a position he
currently shares with the problem drinker. And, perhaps more important, a
more permissive approach to the teen-age driver problem is unlikely as long
as adult society maintains its basically hostile attitude toward adolescents.

One can find reasons for this hostility in both psychoanalytic theory and
ethology. But there are simpler explanations. First, as we have evolved from
an agricultural to an industrial society, children have become economic
liabilities instead of economic assets. Our own we may regard as emotional
assets; other people's children are simply an expense to us as taxpayers and
an environmental nuisance as neighbors. Second, when the current generation of adults grew up, money was more scarce, education was harder to
acquire, and full-time work occurred earlier in the life span. The presence of
well-fed, well-accoutred young people who seem neither to toil nor to spin

[11] W. L. Carlson and D. Klein, "Familial vs. Institutional Socialization of the Young
Traffic Offender," *Journal of Safety Research*, II (1) (1970), 13–25.
[12] S. H. Schuman, D. C. Pelz, N. J. Ehrlich, and M. L. Selzer, "Young Male Drivers,"
Journal of the American Medical Association (1967), 1026–1030.

offends all of us to some extent. Finally, when these "spoiled kids" generate ideas that threaten much of our own *raison d'être*, all of us tend to share the feelings of the traffic policeman who stops a bearded youth in a sports car that costs eight months of the policeman's salary and that carries a bumper sticker advocating fornication as a substitute for war.

But, although we may to some extent share the traffic policeman's feelings in such a situation, we must not allow ourselves as investigators, consultants, practitioners, or citizens to share his view that adolescent traffic violations are direct evidence of criminal intent. Nor should we assume that punishing the offender will make him a better driver or that we can teach him to drive "better" without changing other aspects of his life.

There is, in fact, some evidence that reducing hostility toward adolescents reduces their deviance. Numerous reports of volunteer programs indicate that, when adolescents are offered adult responsibilities, they respond in adult fashion. In Kaestner's [13] well-known study, in which a "soft-sell," personal letter replaced a stern, impersonal letter warning drivers about their accumulated violation points, the softer letter turned out to be more effective in reducing the drivers' crash frequency. This effectiveness was especially pronounced with younger male drivers. When, as happened in New York several years ago, a group of hot-rodders approached the police volunteering their service as a highway patrol to make free minor repairs for motorists disabled on expressways, acceptance of the proposal might have made a difference in the social attitudes as well as the citation rate of the group. Instead, it was summarily rejected by the New York Police Department.

A quite different approach would involve modifying the social and technological environment in order to offer the adolescent a more meaningful and rewarding role in society or, at least, to remove or modify those restrictions that infantilize or isolate him. (The recent reduction of the age of majority from 21 to 18 is an example that should be watched with close attention.)

To accomplish this, the educational system would have to learn how to motivate the large proportion of students that it currently succeeds only in alienating. And industry would have to be modified so that youths entering the work situation would see it as something more than a boring routine to be endured in order to earn enough money to buy a car or other physical or psychological necessities.

Adolescent behavior that is biologically "normal" should not continue to be labeled as legally deviant. A sociologist asked recently, "What would happen to the teen-age crash rate if every teen-ager had his own apartment where he could experiment with sex and alcohol or just talk with his friends in complete privacy?" One might also ask: What would happen to the crash rate if every adolescent were given the skills and the opportunities to involve

---

[13] N. Kaestner, E. J. Warmoth, and E. M. Syring, "Oregon Study of Advisory Letters: The Effectiveness of Warning Letters in Driver Improvement," *Traffic Safety Research Review*, XI (1967), 67–72.

himself in something that he would find substantially more meaningful and more rewarding than driving around in an automobile that he has modified with labor and ingenuity that might have been devoted to more productive purposes?

Obviously, such changes would involve all aspects of society—the school system, industry, laws, family structure, and residential patterns. Not only would they be difficult to effect, but the trends in many of these institutions appear to be in a direction opposite to what such changes would require.

This line of reasoning should not leave us with the depressing conclusion that we can do little about the young driver's crash rate and its consequences until vast and improbable changes occur in the total social system. If we shift our focus from changing the driver's behavior and the social environment that governs it to changing the driver's physical environment—making both the vehicle and the highway more forgiving of driver error and more protective of the driver when a crash occurs—we have grounds for optimism that are firmly based in good empirical data.

Promising as technological improvements are, however, it would be a serious mistake to concentrate exclusively on them and to dismiss our concern for adolescent driving behavior with the facile assumption that "they will grow out of it." Actually, there are reasons to believe that adolescents will *not* become "normal" adults in the present sense of the word, but that adult culture is likely to adopt increasingly some of the characteristics we now label "adolescent." Today's adolescents have already influenced our culture profoundly in terms of music, clothing styles, sexual attitudes and behavior, and communications media. Further, if current social and technological trends continue—the depersonalization and bureaucratization of work, the lack of meaningful relationships with non-peers, the decrease in feelings of personal autonomy in the community—then those characteristics that we now perceive as peculiarly adolescent, such as a detachment from meaningful work, an emphasis on hedonistic styles of consumption, a lack of interaction with members of other age groups, and a concern for "kicks" and "thrills" in recreational activities, may become characteristic of our society as a whole. For this reason, we should perhaps look at the adolescent driver not as a deviant, but perhaps as a forerunner of the society of the future.

LaMar T. Empey

Delinquency Theory and Recent Research

Empey raises a variety of questions below about middle-class delinquency. Are delinquent values widely shared and is delinquent behavior common? Does legal or semi-legal processing contribute to the solidification of delinquent groups? Is differential treatment of juveniles based less on actual behavior than other identifying characteristics? Empey suggests that answers to these questions would aid in determining whether delinquency stems from deviant or conventional traditions. On the one hand, he observes, theorists tend to view the delinquent subculture either as a contraculture—*where status is found through opposition to prevailing middle-class values*—*or as an* infraculture—*where status is derived from more deviant, less publicized versions of officially endorsed values in the overall culture.*

Instructional Objectives
To question the accuracy of official statistics regarding relationships between social class and delinquency.
To question the extent to which delinquent groups possess cohesiveness and influence.
To discuss the degree to which deviant traditions "occupy a symbiotic tie" with "conformist traditions."

ATTEMPTS to explain delinquency traditionally have been concerned with two fundamental sets of data: (1) evidence from official sources that delinquency is concentrated most heavily among lower-class juveniles [1] and (2) evidence that the delinquent act is typically a group phenomenon, not

FROM *Journal of Research in Crime and Delinquency,* IV (1967), pp. 28–42. Reprinted by permission of the author and the publisher.

[1] For examples see Ernest W. Burgess, "The Economic Factor in Juvenile Delinquency," *Journal of Criminal Law, Criminology and Police Science* (May–June, 1952), pp. 29–42; Joseph W. Eaton and Kenneth Polk, *Measuring Delinquency: A Study of Probation Department Referrals* (Pittsburgh: University of Pittsburgh Press, 1961), p. 4; Clifford R. Shaw and Henry D. McKay, *Juvenile Delinquency in Urban Areas* (Chicago: University of Chicago Press, 1942); Albert K. Cohen's analysis of several studies in *Delinquent Boys: The Culture of the Gang* (Glencoe, Ill.: The Free Press, 1955), pp. 37–44.

a solitary enterprise.[2] The result has been a number of influential theories which, despite many differences, have a common theme,[3] viz., that delinquency is primarily the product of provincial, lower-class gangs whose members share a common subculture. The factors which set delinquents apart from nondelinquents are thought to be their face-to-face interactions within gangs, the deviant norms and beliefs which the gangs engender, and the group rewards and publicity which the gangs provide.

Comparatively little attention has been paid to middle-class delinquency, principally because middle-class delinquency has not been considered serious, either in frequency or in form.[4] However, a growing number of empirical studies question both the basic facts which the theories must encompass and the theoretical constructs themselves. This paper reviews some of the questions that have been raised.

SOCIAL CLASS AND DELINQUENCY

The accuracy of official statistics regarding the relationship of social class to delinquency has long been a bone of contention. Many people have argued that official records are biased.[5] The reason, they say, that lower-class juveniles are overrepresented in delinquency statistics is simply that official agencies are more inclined to record the offenses of lower-class offenders.

[2] For examples see William Healy and Augusta F. Bronner, *New Light on Delinquency and Its Treatment* (New Haven: Yale University Press, 1936), p. 52; Sheldon and Eleanor Glueck, *Delinquents in the Making* (New York: Harper, 1952), p. 89; Clifford R. Shaw and Henry D. McKay, "Social Factors in Juvenile Delinquency," *Report on the Causes of Crime* (Washington, D.C.: National Commission on Law Observance and Enforcement, 1931), pp. 195–196; Joseph D. Lohman, *Juvenile Delinquency* (Cook County: Office of the Sheriff, 1957), p. 8; Norman Fenton, *The Delinquent Boy and the Correctional School* (Claremont: Claremont Colleges Guidance Center, 1935), as quoted by Karl G. Garrison, *Psychology of Adolescence* (Englewood Cliffs, N.J.: Prentice-Hall, 1956), p. 350; Peter Scott, "Gangs and Delinquent Groups in London," *British Journal of Delinquency* (July, 1956), pp. 4–26.

[3] Cohen, op. cit. *supra* note 1; Richard A. Cloward and Lloyd E. Ohlin, *Delinquency and Opportunity: A Theory of Delinquent Gangs* (Glencoe, Ill.: The Free Press, 1960); Walter B. Miller, "Lower-Class Culture as a Generating Milieu of Gang Delinquency," *Journal of Social Issues* (Summer, 1958), pp. 5–19. See also Frederic M. Thrasher, *The Gang: A Study of 1,313 Gangs in Chicago*, abridged and with a new introduction by James F. Short, Jr. (Chicago: University of Chicago Press, 1963); Lewis Yablonsky, *The Violent Gang* (New York: The Macmillan Co., 1962).

[4] For some discussions of the subject see Ralph W. England, Jr., "A Theory of Middle-Class Delinquency," *Journal of Criminal Law, Criminology and Police Science* (April, 1960), pp. 535–540; Herbert A. Bloch and Arthur Niederhoffer, *The Gang: A Study of Adolescent Behavior* (New York: Philosophical Library, 1958); Cohen, op. cit., pp. 81–91; William C. Kvaraceus and Walter B. Miller, *Delinquent Behavior, Culture and the Individual* (Washington, D.C.: National Education Association, 1959), pp. 77–84.

[5] Austin L. Porterfield, *Youth in Trouble* (Fort Worth: Leo Potishman Foundation, 1946), passim; Milton A. Barron, *The Juvenile in Delinquent Society* (New York: Alfred A. Knopf, 1956), p. 32; Lloyd Warner and Paul S. Lunt, *The Social Life of a Modern Community* (New Haven: Yale University Press, 1941), p. 427; William C. Kvaraceus, *What Research Says to the Teacher: Juvenile Delinquency* (Washington, D.C.: National Education Association, 1958), pp. 331–332.

But can this conclusion be substantiated by fact or is it, as Cohen asks, the product of "egalitarian proclivities and sentimental humanitarianism"? [6]

Universality of Inverse Relation between Class and Delinquency

The first issue that reflects on Cohen's question has to do with the universality of the supposed inverse relation between social class and delinquency. On one hand, the Short and Strodtbeck studies of delinquent gangs in Chicago tended to support official findings. Lower-class gang boys *were* the most delinquent. They were followed, in turn, by lower-class non-gang boys and then by middle-class boys. These differences held up for both Negro and white respondents, although Negro gang members were not so different from their Negro middle-class peers as were white gang boys from white middle-class peers.[7]

On the other hand, most studies of undetected delinquency in smaller cities and towns have not found significant differences among adolescents from different classes,[8] and those which have, have reported differences which are not nearly so strong as those indicated by official data.[9] For example, Gold, in a Michigan study, found a statistically significant, inverse relation between class and delinquency, but the strength of the relationship was extremely slight, a coefficient of $-.12$.[10] The degree of variance which could be explained by this relationship would be small indeed.

Empey and Erickson report similar findings from Utah.[11] The degrees of association between social class and three different delinquency scales were: for *general* theft, $-.20$; for *serious* theft, $-.17$; and for *common* delinquency, $-.17$. They discovered further that the inverse relationship was due more to a small amount of delinquency among upper-class respondents than it was to an excessive amount of delinquency among lower-class respondents. The lower- and middle-class groups did not differ significantly from each other while the degree of difference between each of them and the upper-class group was considerable.

---

[6] Cohen, op. cit., p. 42.

[7] James F. Short, Jr., and Fred L. Strodtbeck, *Group Process and Delinquency* (Chicago: University of Chicago Press, 1965), pp. 164–171.

[8] F. Ivan Nye, James F. Short, Jr., and V. J. Olsen, "Socio-Economic Status and Delinquent Behavior," *American Journal of Sociology* (January, 1958), pp. 318–329; John P. Clark and Eugene P. Wenninger, "Socio-Economic Class and Area as Correlates of Illegal Behavior Among Juveniles," *American Sociological Review* (December, 1962), pp. 826–834; Robert Dentler and Lawrence J. Monroe, "Early Adolescent Theft," *American Sociological Review* (October, 1961), pp. 733–743; Porterfield, op. cit. An exception is Albert J. Reiss, Jr. and Albert L. Rhodes, "The Distribution of Juvenile Delinquency in the Social Class Structure," *American Sociological Review* (October, 1961), pp. 730–732.

[9] LaMar T. Empey and Maynard L. Erickson, "Hidden Delinquency and Social Status," *Social Forces* (June, 1966), pp. 546–554; Martin Gold, "Undetected Delinquent Behavior," *Journal of Research in Crime and Delinquency* (January, 1966), pp. 27–46.

[10] Gold, op. cit., pp. 40–43.

[11] Empey and Erickson, op. cit., pp. 549–550. See also Maynard L. Erickson and LaMar T. Empey, "Class Position, Peers and Delinquency," *Sociology and Social Research* (April, 1965), pp. 271–272.

Actual Violation v. Apprehension

Empirical studies have indicated that the amount of undetected delinquency is great.[12] The degree of apprehension is extremely low, somewhere between 3 and 5 per cent of all self-reported offenses. Yet, when apprehension does occur, officials are more likely to record and process lower-class youngsters.[13]

The picture is further confused by the fact that the police and other officials are charged by juvenile court law to respond to poor home and family conditions, neglect, truancy, and other factors which may come to light when some "predatory" act is detected. Their interest is often solicitous rather than punitive, but since these factors are more often associated with lower-class than middle-class juveniles, the former are more inclined to be processed legally. These two conditions distort the idea of the epidemiological character of delinquency and probably lend credence to the notion of an inverse relation between class and delinquency.

Seriousness

There are many who feel that the offenses of lower-class youngsters are more likely to be serious. Ohlin, for example, maintains that middle-class delinquency is "petty" in comparison with lower-class delinquency.[14] The inclination to violate the law, he believes, is more deeply ingrained in the lower-class youngster who therefore possesses a greater potential for the development of a criminal career. The evidence pertinent to this question is limited but that which is available is not entirely supportive of Ohlin's position.

The Myerhoffs, in their observations of middle-class "gangs" in Los Angeles, reported that the violations of these "gangs" were often more "mischievous" than violent.[15] However, violence is not the only dimension of seriousness. Included in these "mischievous" acts was the frequent and regular theft of articles that were by no means small nor inexpensive: radios,

[12] Maynard L. Erickson and LaMar T. Empey, "Court Records, Undetected Delinquency and Decision-Making," *Journal of Criminal Law, Criminology and Police Science* (December, 1963), pp. 456–469; Fred J. Murphy, M. Shirley, and Helen L. Witmer, "The Incidence of Hidden Delinquency," *American Journal of Orthopsychiatry* (October, 1946), pp. 686–696; Gold, op. cit.; Porterfield, op. cit.

[13] Gold found that the police were more likely to record lower-class offenders; see Gold op. cit., p. 38. Empey and Erickson found that low-class adolescents were overrepresented in a training school in proportion to the offenses they reported having committed; see Empey and Erickson, op. cit.

[14] Lloyd E. Ohlin, *The Development of Opportunities for Youth* (New York: Youth Development Center, Syracuse University, 1960), pp. 8–9; and Cloward and Ohlin, op. cit., p. 12.

[15] Howard L. and Barbara G. Myerhoff, "Field Observations of Middle-Class Gangs," *Social Forces* (March, 1964), pp. 328–336. See also Andrew Greely and James Casey, "An Upper-Middle-Class Deviant Gang," *American Catholic Sociological Review* (Spring, 1963), pp. 33–41.

phonographs, car accessories, television sets, all usually taken from employers or personal acquaintances.

Such findings were corroborated by Empey and Erickson in a more systematic enumeration of offenses in a *nonmetropolitan* center.[16] They found that, while the more serious forms of delinquency were less common among all class groups, such violations as grand theft, forgery, breaking and entering, destroying property, and even arson, when they did occur, were more often committed by middle- than lower-class juveniles. This rather surprising finding held true whether the self-reported data came from boys with no official record or boys who were incarcerated in a training school.[17] Middle-class groups in both populations were the ones who rated disproportionately high on these kinds of offenses.

Even with respect to violence, Karacki and Toby found fighting gangs that did not come from economically deprived homes.[18] These gangs placed emphasis on many of the characteristics traditionally associated with lower-class delinquent groups: physical aggression, loyalty to peers, and immediate gratification. Shanley located a similar group of middle- and upper-class boys in the suburbs of Los Angeles who had patterns of police contact which were as extensive and serious as samples of adjudicated delinquents from lower-class neighborhoods.[19] Finally, other analyses suggest that particular patterns of delinquency may be associated as much with differences in place of residence—rural, urban, or type of neighborhood—as with social class position.[20]

In summary, these findings suggest that the inverse relationship between social class and delinquency may be less potent than has been traditionally assumed and that we should search for other determinants;[21] social class by itself may be a poor clue. The behavior of some middle-class groups suggests that we might discover as many differences *within* classes regarding delinquency as we now discover between them. In other words, instead of using a two- or three-celled table to compare lower-, middle-, and upper-class

[16] Empey and Erickson, op. cit., pp. 551–554.

[17] Albert H. Herskovitz, Murray Levene, and George Spivak, "Anti-Social Behavior of Adolescents from Higher Socio-Economic Groups," *Journal of Nervous and Mental Diseases* (November, 1959), pp. 1–9. They found no sharply different patterns between middle- and low-class incarcerated offenders and little variation in the seriousness of their offenses.

[18] Larry Karacki and Jackson Toby, "The Uncommitted Adolescent: Candidates for Gang Socialization," *Sociological Inquiry* (Spring, 1962), pp. 203–215.

[19] Fred J. Shanley, "Middle-Class Delinquency as a Social Problem," paper presented at the Annual Meetings of the Pacific Sociological Association, Salt Lake City, April 1965, p. 2. A recent article in *Life* magazine was also devoted to the extensive drug use and other delinquent patterns of middle-class groups on Sunset Strip in Hollywood. The Strip is also the locale of the heaviest concentration of "gay" (homosexual) hangouts in the city; see *Life* (August 26, 1966), pp. 75–83.

[20] Irving Spergel, *Racketville, Slumtown, Haulburg: An Exploratory Study of Delinquent Subcultures* (Chicago: University of Chicago Press, 1964); and Clark and Wenninger, op. cit.

[21] Identification with particular sets of peers is one that has appeared. See Erickson and Empey, op. cit., pp. 272–281.

groups across the board, we should use four- or six-celled tables to compare the delinquent acts of various groups within, as well as between, classes.[22] More precise distinctions of this type might provide better clues to the nature of delinquency than do gross comparisons between classes.

DIMENSIONS OF GROUP DELINQUENCY

What about the second set of facts which theory must fit—the proposition that delinquency is typically a group phenomenon? The available evidence has a paradoxical quality which illustrates both the complexity of the subject and the meagerness of our information.

There are few findings which question seriously the basic proposition that delinquency is typically a group phenomenon. Most studies, including some which use self-reported data, place the incidence of group delinquency somewhere between 60 and 90 per cent of the total.[23] It may be that with more systematic data this range will be extended, since some offenses—defying parents or running away—are by nature less likely to be group-related than others. However, the group aspects of delinquency seem to be well established with a modal figure of about 75 per cent.

What is not well established is a consensus regarding the nature of delinquent groups—their cohesiveness, their structural qualities, their subcultural characteristics. The most commonly used term to refer to delinquent groups has been the word "gang." The term has been so overworked and is so imprecise that its use in scientific discourse may well be questioned. An examination of evidence relative to the cohesiveness and structural qualities of delinquent groups illustrates the elusiveness of the "gang" and other group concepts.

Group Cohesiveness

Conflicting themes run through the literature regarding cohesiveness. The first theme, exemplified most clearly by Thrasher and the Chicago school, emphasizes the idea that delinquent groups are characterized by *internal cohesion—esprit de corps,* solidarity, cooperative action, shared tradition, and a strong group awareness.[24] Despite the qualifications which Thrasher placed on this theme—and he did qualify it—there is no denying that a traditional perspective has developed emphasizing the romantic quality of delinquent gangs, the free and easy life, the joint commitments of members

[22] Miller, for example, noted differences in theft behavior among three different groups, all *within* the lower class. See Walter B. Miller, "Theft Behavior in City Gangs," *Juvenile Gangs in Context: Theory, Research and Action,* Malcolm W. Klein and Barbara G. Myerhoff, eds. (Englewood Cliffs, N.J.: Prentice-Hall, 1967).

[23] See footnote 2, page 476 for relevant studies. Unpublished data in our possession on self-reported delinquency, both from Utah and California, confirm this figure.

[24] Thrasher, op. cit., pp. 40–46. See also Short's discussion of this theme in his introduction to the abridged edition, passim.

to one another. The key to this theme is its emphasis upon the culture-generating qualities and attractiveness of the peer group.

The second theme, as Bordua notes, is irrationalistic and deterministic in its emphasis. "Gang boys are driven," he notes, "not attracted. Their lives are characterized by desperation rather than fun." [25] Such theories as those of Cohen,[26] Cloward and Ohlin,[27] and Miller [28] emphasize the idea that lower-class children are downgraded in both the child and the adult status hierarchies of our middle-class institutions. They are ill-prepared by family background and cultural heritage to achieve successfully and, as a consequence, their lives are characterized by frustration, negativistic retaliation, alienation, and radical separation from conventional successes and satisfactions. This theme is much less romantic in its emphasis than the first and implies, not internal attraction, but external pressure as the source of gang cohesion.

It is the role of the individual youngster in the social structure, not his role in the street group, that is of primary significance. He is alienated before he enters the group, not because of it. The group is simply the instrument that translates his individual discontent into a collective solution.[29] By implication, the group can do little to remedy his sensitivity to the middle-class measuring rod, to provide him with the material and social satisfactions to which he aspires.

The fundamental question, then, asks what the forces are that hold delinquent groups together. Are they the group rules and loyalties which emerge from gratifying relationships within the group, as the first theme suggests, or are they due to the position of gang boys in the class structure as suggested by the second theme?

First of all, we are confronted with the apparent fact that, if the delinquent group were not rewarding to the individual, it would cease to exist. In this vein, Short and Strodtbeck have observed that when it comes to assuming adult roles—occupation and marriage—". . . the lure of the gang may spell disaster." [30] Even when challenging jobs are obtained for them, when the pay is good or when gang members are married and have children, the lure of the street is not easily forgotten and any inclination to return to it is supported by the gang. The implication, of course, is one of *internal* cohesiveness and attraction: gang membership has much to offer. However, as might be expected, there are other interpretations. . . .

Klein and Crawford argue that *internal* sources of lower-class gang co-

---

[25] David J. Bordua, "Some Comments on Theories of Group Delinquency," *Sociological Inquiry* (Spring, 1962), pp. 245–246; see also David J. Bordua, "A Critique of Sociological Interpretations of Gang Delinquency," *Annals of the American Academy of Political and Social Science* (November, 1961), pp. 120–136.

[26] Cohen, op. cit.

[27] Cloward and Ohlin, op. cit.

[28] Miller, op. cit.

[29] Bordua, op. cit., pp. 252–257.

[30] Short and Strodtbeck, op. cit., pp. 221–234.

hesion are weak.[31] Group goals which might be unifying are minimal, membership stability is low, loyalty is questionable, and even the names of gangs —Gladiators, Vice Lords, Egyptian Kings—are unifying only when external threat is present. When the threat is diminished, cohesion is diminished. It is their feeling that were it not for the external pressures of police and other officials, the threats of rival groups, or the lack of acceptance by parents and employers, many delinquent gangs would have nothing to unify them. By themselves, such gangs do not develop the kinds of group goals and instrumentally oriented activities which are indicative of much organization and cohesion.

Group Cohesion and Delinquent Acts

The commission of delinquent acts seems to illustrate this lack of organization. One of the most striking things about them is not their planned and patterned characteristics but their episodic and highly situational character.[32] One would think that if delinquent groups were highly cohesive or highly structured this would not be the case. Yet, most delinquent acts are more spontaneous than planned and, even though they involve groups, they rarely involve all members of a gang acting together.

Even complex crimes reveal considerable spontaneity and what Matza calls "shared misunderstanding." [33] Thrasher describes three college students who began to phantasize about robbing a post-office.[34] Subsequent interviews with them revealed that none of them wanted to be involved in the actual robbery but the more they talked the deeper they became involved, each hoping, actually believing, that the others would call a halt to this crazy phantasy but each reluctant, on his own, to "chicken out." The result was that, in a state of almost total individual disbelief, they robbed the post-office and found themselves in legal custody.

Careful observation of delinquents reveals countless repetitions of this phenomenon—the wandering kinds of interaction that lead to delinquent acts and the mixed motivations that accompany them. Even in regard to fighting, as Miller points out, "A major objective of gang members is to put themselves in the posture of fighting without actually having to fight." [35]

Group Cohesion and Member Interaction

Observations of delinquent gangs led Short and Strodtbeck, like Klein and Crawford, to depreciate nostalgic references to "that old gang of mine" and

[31] Malcolm W. Klein and Lois Y. Crawford, "Groups, Gangs and Cohesiveness," *Journal of Research in Crime and Delinquency* (January, 1967), p. 63.

[32] Many works allude to this phenomenon. For examples see Thrasher, op. cit.; Short and Strodtbeck, op. cit., Yablonsky, op. cit.

[33] David Matza, *Delinquency and Drift* (New York: John Wiley and Sons, 1964), pp. 35–59.

[34] Thrasher, op. cit., pp. 300–303.

[35] Walter B. Miller, "Violent Crimes in City Gangs," *Annals of the American Academy of Political and Social Science* (March, 1965), p. 110.

to deny the image of the delinquent gang as a carefree and solidary group. They report that such an interpretation may derive more from the projections of middle-class observers than from the realities that dominate street life.[36] They document this interpretation with a considerable amount of data.

They found that, compared with others, gang boys were characterized by a long list of "social disabilities": unsuccessful school adjustment, limited social and technical skills, a low capacity for self-assertion, lower intelligence scores, and also a tendency to hold other gang members in low esteem.[37] Interaction within the gang seemed to be characterized by an omnipresent tone of aggression as a result of these disabilities and the insecurities they engendered.

This account is complemented by Matza's use of the term "sounding," which refers to the incessant plumbing and testing through insult by delinquent boys of one another's status and commitment to delinquency.[38] Miller speaks of the "focal concerns" of lower-class gang culture as toughness, smartness, and excitement.[39] Whatever the terms, it appears that delinquent boys are under constant pressure to protect status and assert masculinity.

While this pressure to project a particular image may not be qualitatively different from many of the highly stylized kinds of interaction found in a host of other status-conscious groups, the point is that such interaction is not characteristic, at least hypothetically, of *primary* groups. Primary groups, ideally, are supposed to provide warmth and support. With the constant "sounding" that goes on in delinquent groups it is questionable whether lower-class gangs are conducive to close friendships.[40]

The picture that is painted suggests that gang members, like inmates in a prison, are held together, not by feelings of loyalty and solidarity, but by forces much less attractive. It is not that structure is lacking but that it is defensive and highly stylized, not supportive. Group members stay together simply because they feel they have more to lose than to gain by any breach in their solidarity. While they may appear to the outsider to be dogmatic, rigid, and unyielding in their loyalty to each other, the sources of this loyalty are not internal but external. Remove the pressure and you remove the cohesion.

Seeming to comment on this very point, Short and Strodtbeck report that they "find the capacity of lower-class gangs to elaborate and enforce norms of reciprocity is very much below what might be required to sustain the group if alternative forms of gratification were available." [41] Similarly, Matza argues that the majority of delinquents are not strongly committed either to delinquent groups or to a criminal career but are "drifters" who are held

[36] Short and Strodtbeck, op. cit., p. 231.
[37] Ibid., Ch. 10 and 12.
[38] Matza, op. cit., pp. 53–55.
[39] Miller, op. cit., p. 519.
[40] Short and Strodtbeck, op. cit., p. 233. See also Lewis Yablonsky, "The Delinquent Gang as a Near-Group," *Social Problems* (Fall, 1959), pp. 108–117.
[41] Short and Strodtbeck, op. cit., p. 280.

together by a kind of pluralistic ignorance.[42] When in the company of others, the boy is inclined to attribute to them a greater commitment to delinquent relationships and values than he has himself.

These points of view indicate the need for more direct investigation of delinquent group cohesiveness *per se* and for the study of middle-class as well as lower-class groups. Our lack of information is so great that we do not have even an adequate baseline from which to begin; that is, we know very little about the cohesiveness and inherent gratifications of adolescent groups in general. Therefore, until we can establish a baseline, it will be difficult either to generalize about delinquent groups or to compare them with other groups. Furthermore, the possible lack of cohesiveness in delinquent groups raises questions regarding the nature of delinquent subculture. If delinquent groups are not cohesive and internally gratifying, can it be expected that delinquents, especially those in the lower class, have either the personal motivation or the organizational skills to promote and maintain a deviant subculture which is in total opposition to prevailing values?

Delinquent Subculture

Such theorists as Cloward and Ohlin have defined the subcultural concept in narrow terms.[43] They see a delinquent subculture as unique and as autonomous. Organization around a specific delinquent activity, they say, distinguishes a delinquent subculture from other subcultures. Such behaviors as truancy, drunkenness, property destruction, or theft are legally delinquent activities but these they would not include as characteristic of a delinquent subculture unless they were the focal activities around which the dominant beliefs and roles of a group were organized.

The narrowness and rigor of their postulates regarding criminal, retreatist, and conflict-oriented subcultures characterize the logical structure of their theory but do these postulates accurately characterize delinquent groups and subculture? Are they this focused? Are they this unique and autonomous?

When Short and his associates set about trying to study these kinds of subcultures, they had extreme difficulty in locating them.[44] They found a number of gangs in which marijuana smoking was rather common and in which there was experimentation with heroin and pills, but it took more than a year of extensive inquiries among police and local adults to locate a clearly drug-oriented group. They never did find a full-blown criminal group. Consequently, they concluded that their failure casts doubt on the generality of the Cloward-Ohlin postulates.[45]

Short, et al., had no difficulty in locating a number of gangs who were well-known for their conflict, toughness, and fighting but one still must

[42] Matza, op. cit., pp. 27–30, 56.
[43] Cloward and Ohlin, op. cit., p. 7.
[44] Short and Strodtbeck, op. cit., pp. 10–13.
[45] Ibid., p. 13.

question what it means to say that the "focal" concern of gangs is conflict. The bulk of even the most delinquent boys' time is spent in nondelinquent activity and their delinquent acts make up a long list of different offenses.[46] How precise can we be, then, in referring to the characteristics of a "conflict" subculture or gang?

In observing "typical," "tough" city gangs over a two-year period, Miller found that assault was *not* the most dominant form of activity.[47] In fact, two thirds of the male gang members who were observed were not known to have engaged in *any* assaultive crimes over the two-year period and 88 per cent did not appear in court on such a charge. Similarly, Klein and his colleagues in Los Angeles have found that less than 10 per cent of the recorded offenses for gang members are assaultive.[48] Instead, the *frequency* with which adolescents commit a long list of different offenses seems to better characterize their commitments to delinquency than their persistent adherence to a particular offense pattern.[49] There seems to be limited empirical support for the idea of autonomous and highly focused delinquent subcultures and somewhat more support for the notion of a ubiquitous, "parent" subculture of delinquency in which there is a "garden-variety" of delinquent acts.[50]

A ubiquitous, but amorphous, subculture would be more consistent with the notion of weak internal bonds in delinquent groups and highly situational delinquent acts than with the idea of internally cohesive groups who participate in planned and highly patterned delinquent activities. Furthermore, if delinquent subculture is not highly focused and autonomous, question is raised regarding its relation to the larger culture.

Subculture: Contraculture or Infraculture?

Most contemporary theory has suggested that lower-class delinquent subculture is *contra*culture [51] in which status is gained by demonstrating opposition to prevailing middle-class standards.[52] Theories of middle-class delinquency suggest that the delinquent group is a collective response to adolescent efforts to establish sexual identity and to deal with frustrations attendant on the transition from childhood to adulthood.[53] But does this mean that a middle-class delinquent group is, like a lower-class gang, the instrument that translates individual discontent into a delinquent *contra*culture?

Matza takes issue with the notion of *contra*culture on any class level and

[46] Short, Introduction in Thrasher, op. cit., pp. xlvii–xlviii.

[47] Miller, op. cit., pp. 105, 111.

[48] Malcolm W. Klein, Youth Studies Center, University of Southern California, Personal Communication, September 1966.

[49] Erickson and Empey, op. cit., pp. 465–469; Gold, op. cit., pp. 27–46.

[50] Albert K. Cohen and James F. Short, Jr., "Research in Delinquent Subcultures," *Journal of Social Issues* (Summer, 1958), pp. 20–36.

[51] J. Milton Yinger, "Contraculture and Subculture," *American Sociological Review* (October, 1960), pp. 625–635.

[52] Cohen, op. cit.; Cloward and Ohlin, op. cit.; Miller, op. cit.

[53] England, op. cit.; Bloch and Niederhoffer, op. cit.

emphasizes a subtle but important distinction. He argues that "there is a subculture of delinquency but it is not a delinquent subculture." [54] American culture, he believes, is not a simple puritanism exemplified by the middle-class. Instead, it is a complex and pluralistic culture in which, among other cultural traditions, there is a "subterranean" tradition—an *infra*culture of delinquency.[55]

This *infra*culture does not represent ignorance of the law nor even general negation of it; instead, it is a complex relationship to law in a symbiotic rather than an oppositional way. It is not a separate set of beliefs which distinguish delinquents from other youth, or youth from adults; it is that part of the overall culture which consists of the personal, more deviant, and less-publicized version of officially endorsed values. The two sets of traditions—conventional and deviant—are held simultaneously by almost everyone in the social system and, while certain groups may be influenced more by one than the other, both determine behavior to a considerable degree.

Daniel Bell's analysis of crime as an American way of life is probably a good illustration of Matza's point.[56] Bell notes that Americans are characterized by an "extremism" in morality, yet they also have an "extraordinary" talent for compromise in politics and a "brawling" economic and social history. These contradictory features form the basis for an intimate and symbiotic relationship between crime and politics, crime and economic growth, and crime and social change, not an oppositional relationship. The tradition of wanting to "get ahead" is no less an ethic than wanting to observe the law.

Crime has been a major means by which a variety of people have achieved the American success ideal and obtained respectability, if not for themselves, for their children. The basic question, therefore, is whether this deviant tradition contributes more than we realize to the behavior of younger as well as older people. Rather than delinquent subculture being uniquely the property of young people, it may have roots in the broader culture.

Empirical investigation of the matter would seem to involve two questions: (1) the extent to which adolescents legitimate official, conventional patterns and (2) the extent to which they simultaneously participate in, or espouse in some way, deviant patterns. With reference to the first question both Kobrin [57] and Gordon *et al.*[58] suggest that adolescents from all strata are inclined to legitimate official patterns. The gang members they studied did not seem to be alienated from the goals of the larger society and ". . . even

---

[54] Matza, op. cit., p. 33; David Matza and Gresham M. Sykes, "Juvenile Delinquency and Subterranean Values," *American Sociological Review* (October, 1961), pp. 712–719.

[55] The idea of *infra*culture was suggested by J. A. Pitt-Rivers, *The People of the Sierra* (Chicago: University of Chicago Press, 1961), who referred to "infrastructure" rather than "infraculture."

[56] Daniel Bell, *The End of Ideology* (Glencoe, Ill.: The Free Press, 1959), pp. 115–136.

[57] Solomon Kobrin, "The Conflict of Values in Delinquency Areas," *American Sociological Review* (October, 1951), pp. 642–661.

[58] Robert A. Gordon, James F. Short, Jr., Desmond F. Cartwright, and Fred L. Strodtbeck, "Values and Gang Delinquency," *American Journal of Sociology* (September, 1963), pp. 109–128, as reproduced in Short and Strodtbeck, op. cit., Ch. 3.

the gang ethic, is not one of 'reaction formation' *against* widely shared conceptions of the 'good' life." Gang, low-class and middle-class boys, Negro and white ". . . *evaluated images representing salient features of the middle-class styles of life equally high."* [59] This finding confirmed that of Gold in Michigan with a much different population [60] and led to the conclusion that ". . . if the finding is valid, three separate theoretical formulations [Cohen, Miller, and Cloward-Ohlin] fail to make sufficient allowance for the meaningfulness of middle-class values to members of gangs." [61] In fact, given the strength of the findings, one wonders whether we are correct in referring to official values as "middle-class" values or whether we should be using some more inclusive term.

The second question, regarding the simultaneous possession of deviant patterns, presents a more confused picture. A curious omission in our conjectures and research has been our failure to examine the extent to which deviant values are widely transmitted to young people. Several elaborate theories hypothesize that all children, including those in the lower class, are conditioned by official, "middle-class" stimuli. They watch television, listen to the radio, go to the movies, read the ads, and attend middle-class dominated schools; as a consequence, they acquire common desires for status, recognition, and achievement. Despite these conjectures, we have not had similar conjectures regarding the possible transmission of deviant patterns.

Kvaraceus and Miller have suggested that middle-class delinquency represents an upward diffusion of lower-class attitudes and practices; [62] but are lower-class patterns all that are diffused? To what extent are children on all class levels conditioned not just by lower-class values but by mass stimuli which emphasize violence, toughness, protest, kicks, and expedience? These are certainly important aspects of our "brawling" American history, a part of our cultural tradition. If we pay too little heed to them then we may be inclined to overemphasize the narrowness and autonomy of delinquent subculture, especially as the sole possession of the lower class. It is seductively easy to overemphasize the uniqueness of problem people and thereby to obscure their similarities to non-problem people. For example, studies of self-reported delinquency reveal that the extent of hidden law violation is widespread,[63] so widespread, indeed, that Murphy, Shirley, and Witmer were led to remark that "even a moderate increase in the amount of attention paid to it by law enforcement authorities could create the semblance of a 'delinquency wave' without there being the slightest change in adolescent behavior." [64] This finding, coupled with the questionable strength of the theory of an inverse relationship between social class and delinquency, sug-

[59] Short and Strodtbeck, op. cit., pp. 271, 59. Italics theirs.
[60] Martin Gold, *Status Forces in Delinquent Boys* (Ann Arbor: University of Michigan, Institute for Social Research, 1963).
[61] Short and Strodtbeck, op. cit., p. 74.
[62] Kvaraceus and Miller, op. cit., pp. 77–79.
[63] Erickson and Empey, op. cit.; Gold, op. cit.
[64] Murphy, Shirley, and Witmer, op. cit.

gests that, unless we are to assume that deviant traditions actually pre-dominate, they must occupy a symbiotic tie of some kind with conformist traditions.

Conventional Values and Deviance

In order to investigate the matter further, several factors should be considered. One important factor is the nature of adult-youth relationships. What perspectives, for example, are transmitted from adults to youth? Is the youthful search for "kicks" or the irresponsible acquisition of wealth and leisure profoundly different from adult desires for the same things or, rather, a projection of them? A double standard for judging adult and youthful behavior is certainly not uncommon and could be far more influential than a double standard distinguishing between the sexes. Personal access to various adult role models, as contrasted to a vague and abstract relationship with them, would likely affect the selection of deviant or conformist behavior. The absence of a strong personal relationship would make the juvenile more dependent upon the images projected by such secondary sources as the movies or television.

A second important factor has to do with the relative valences of delinquent and conformist values for different populations of adolescents. How do they balance? Short and Strodtbeck found that, while conventional prescriptions were generally accepted, subterranean, deviant values were accepted differentially. While gang boys were as willing as lower- and middle-class nongang boys to legitimate official *pre*scriptions, they were not as inclined to support official *pro*scriptions.[65] This particular research failed to explore other important aspects of the issue.

Besides obtaining some indication of the general valences of both deviant and conventional values, we need to explore their valences in various specific contexts. We know, for example, that if changes in group context or social situation occur, both behavior and the espousal of particular values are likely to change also. The citizen who is in favor of racial equality in a general way is often one of the first to sell his home when integration occurs in his neighborhood. Specific considerations alter his behavior. Similarly, the delinquent boy, when placed in the context of having to exercise leadership over his peers in a conventional setting, will often act remarkably like a conventional adult. His actions are surprisingly stereotyped, a response not to norms in general but to norms as they apply in a specific context.

In studying the relative valences of conventional and deviant *pro*scriptions we also need to compare not only lower-class gang boys with others, as Short and Strodtbeck did, but excessively delinquent boys from other classes with their peers as well. We need a better indication of the extent to which deviant values are diffused either throughout the entire class structure or through subgroups on all class levels.

[65] Short and Strodtbeck, op. cit., pp. 59–76.

Finally, we need more careful study of the way official and societal responses to juvenile behavior contribute to definitions of delinquency and delinquent subcultures, either by overemphasizing their uniqueness or by contributing to their development. Becker argues that the process by which some juveniles but not others are labeled may be as crucial in defining the problem as the behavior of the juveniles themselves.[66] For example, as mentioned earlier, there are those who think that the coalescence and persistence of delinquent gangs may be due as much to external pressure from official and other sources as to the internal gratifications and supposedly unique standards of those groups.

The contribution which could be made by a study of official systems—the police, the courts, the correctional agencies—would be clarification of the total *gestalt* to which officials respond: how legal statutes, official policies, and perceptual cues affect the administration of juvenile justice.[67] It seems apparent that official and societal reactions to juveniles are due not entirely to criminalistic behavior but also (1) to acts which, if committed by adults, would not warrant legal action and (2) to a number of "social disabilities" that are popularly associated with deviance: unkempt appearance, inappropriate responses due to lack of interpersonal skills, and educational deficiencies.[68]

These are characteristics which traditionally have been more closely associated with lower- than middle-class juveniles and are characterized in legal terms by truancy, dependency, or incorrigibility. It would be important to learn the extent to which these identifying characteristics, as contrasted to demonstrably delinquent *values*, contribute to the definition of some groups, but not others, as seriously delinquent. Since only a small fraction of their time and attention is devoted to law violation, even among the most seriously delinquent, the meanings which these juveniles assign to themselves are usually far less sinister than the meanings which officials assign to them.

CONCLUSION

It seems apparent that, in order to complete the picture of the total phenomenon, we need a series of related studies which would, first, identify a representative population of adolescents, their class positions, their value-

---

[66] Howard S. Becker, *Outsiders: Studies in the Sociology of Deviance* (Glencoe, Ill.: The Free Press, 1963), Ch. 1.

[67] See Irving Piliavin and Scott Brian, "Police Encounters with Juveniles," *American Journal of Sociology* (September, 1964), pp. 206–215; Joseph D. Lohman, James T. Carey, Joel Goldfarb, and Michael J. Rowe, *The Handling of Juveniles From Offense to Disposition* (Berkeley: University of California, 1965); Nathan Goldman, *The Differential Selection of Juvenile Offenders for Court Appearance* (National Research and Information Center, National Council on Crime and Delinquency, 1963).

[68] For conflicting evidence, see A. W. McEachern and Riva Bouzer, "Factors Related to Disposition in Juvenile Police Contacts," *Juvenile Gangs in Context*, Klein and Myerhoff, eds., op. cit.

beliefs and commitments, various measures of delinquent acts (self-reported and official), their symptoms of disability, and their group affiliations; and, second, follow these adolescents through the institutional paths—educational, economic, or correctional—along which they are routed by officials. Which juveniles are processed legally and on what criteria? In what ways are they the same or different from nonprocessed juveniles in terms of values, class position, group affiliations, actual delinquent acts, and so on.

Given such research we might then be in a better position to know not only what the consequences are for those who are apprehended and processed by legal and correctional institutions but also what the consequences are for those who are *not* processed. This would most certainly apply to middle-class as well as lower-class juveniles. Hopefully, we might gain better insight into the total mosaic composed of delinquent values, actual behavior, and official reaction. Are delinquent values widely shared and is delinquent behavior common? Does legal or semilegal processing contribute to the solidification of delinquent groups? Is there differential treatment of juveniles based not on actual behavioral or value differences but on other identifying characteristics? Information of this type would help to indicate whether delinquent subculture is *contra*culture or *infra*culture.

We are only recently becoming aware of the extent of the symbiotic and mutually supporting characteristics of official and client roles in a long list of social systems; for example, policeman-offender, captor-captive, teacher-pupil, therapist-patient, caseworker-client. These are inextricably tied together by a host of traditional expectations and definitions. Change one and you are likely to change the other. We need to know more clearly the extent to which these definitions and the systems of which they are a part make delinquency and delinquents appear to be what they are, as well as the standards, beliefs, and behavior which may be unique to delinquents. Interactive relations between and among juveniles and official agencies may be as important as the behavior exhibited by juveniles in delimiting delinquency for purposes of both etiological inquiry and social control.

Victor J. Ganzer
Irwin G. Sarason

Variables Associated with Recidivism Among Juvenile Delinquents

Is it possible to predict recidivism (parole violations and recommitment) among previously institutionalized juvenile delinquents? Ganzer and Sarason sought to identify the variables that would be of practical value in identifying recidivists. Two-hundred adolescent boys and girls between eleven and eighteen years of age were studied; half had been returned to a juvenile institution and half had no subsequent record. The findings indicate that female delinquents in general come from more disorganized and socially less adequate families than do males and that "the most promising potential predictors of recidivism were associated with (a) family background factors, (b) age at first offense and commitment, and (c) diagnostic classification."

Instructional Objectives

To compare male and female recidivists and nonrecidivists on variables associated with family-background, socioeconomic status, and family contact with law enforcement agencies.

To compare youth on the basis of such variables as age at first institutional commitment, age at first record of antisocial behavior, pre-institutional delinquent behavior, diagnostic classification, estimates of subsequent adjustment, and intelligence.

To discuss implications of sex differences in delinquent behavior.

To note relationships between recidivism and "primary sociopathic" personality diagnosis.

THIS ARTICLE describes an attempt to determine which of a number of sociological, family background, and personality variables would discriminate between recidivists and nonrecidivists in a population of formerly institutionalized juvenile offenders. The study employed experience table methodology. An experience table is a list of variables yielding a total score

FROM *Journal of Consulting and Clinical Psychology*, XL (1973), pp. 1–5. Copyright 1973 by the American Psychological Association. Reprinted by permission of the authors and the publisher.

which discriminates between groups (e.g., recidivists and nonrecidivists). Hart [1] and Warner [2] pioneered the development of the experience table as a prediction device. The method has been used by Ohlin [3] to distinguish between adults who succeeded or failed on parole, and by Glueck and and Glueck [4] to predict juvenile delinquency.

METHOD

Subjects

The Ss were 100 boys and 100 girls who previously had been committed to Washington juvenile rehabilitation institutions. Half of each group subsequently had been identified as recidivists, and the other half had no further record of recidivism, as of at least 20 months after release from an institution. The age range of the sample was 11 to 18 years, with a mean of 15 years 4 months for males and 14 years 9 months for females. Recidivism was defined as the return to a juvenile institution as either a parole violator or a recommitment, Superior Court conviction with resulting probationary placement, or conviction and incarceration in an adult correctional institution.

Procedure

Thirty-four dependent variables were quantified from institution case files. The variables fell into two groups, background variables (e.g., parents' marital status) and S variables (e.g., IQ). In most case files, the rated information was entered in two or more reports, thus permitting independent verification of accuracy. Case selection was essentially random except that records that did not contain complete information were not used. The interrater reliability in extracting and quantifying data was established for two independent raters' judgments on nine cases (433 judgments, 97.9 per cent agreement).

The present sample did not correspond to base rates for the population proportions for recidivism and sex of Ss. The base rate for recidivism in the Washington juvenile population ranged from 20 per cent to 30 per cent, and the commitment rate for males was approximately three times greater than that for females.

RESULTS AND DISCUSSION

Comparisons were made for males and females and recidivists and nonrecidivists. Numbers of cases falling within various categories were tabulated as the dependent variables.

[1] H. Hart, "Predicting Parole Success," *Journal of Criminal Law and Criminology*, XIV (1923), 405–413.

[2] S. B. Warner, "Factors Determining Parole from the Massachusetts Reformatory," *Journal of Criminal Law and Criminology*, XIV (1923), 172–207.

[3] L. E. Ohlin, *Selection for Parole: A Manual for Parole Prediction* (New York: Russell Sage Foundation, 1951).

[4] S. Glueck, and E. T. Glueck, *Unraveling Juvenile Delinquency* (New York: Commonwealth Fund, 1950).

Background Variables

MARITAL STATUS OF NATURAL PARENTS. Only a slightly greater proportion of recidivists than nonrecidivists came from broken homes. However, females more often came from broken homes than did males, regardless of whether or not they were recidivists ($X^2 = 4.49$, $p < .05$). Monahan [5] has reported similar findings.

SOCIOECONOMIC STATUS. Socioeconomic status was classified according to the two-factor system of Hollingshead and Redlich.[6] Socioeconomic status was not related to recidivism for either sex. However, 85 per cent of the classifiable families fell within the two lowest socioeconomic status categories (i.e., 4 and 5), a finding consistent with data reported by Briggs and Wirt.[7] Also, a greater proportion of Ss classified in the higher socioeconomic status categories (1–3) were males ($X^2 = 7.69$, $p < .01$). Educational level of head of household was not related to recidivism. A greater proportion of males came from families with upper status occupations than did females ($X^2 = 4.95$, $p < .05$). With sexes combined and lower-middle-range socioeconomic status categories 4 and 5 omitted from analyses, a significantly greater proportion of nonrecidivists came from the upper categories 1–3 than did recidivists ($X^2 = 5.28$, $p < .05$).

FAMILY CONTACT WITH LAW ENFORCEMENT AGENCIES. There were no appreciable differences between recidivists and nonrecidivists in family contacts with the police, but strong sex differences were present. A greater number of the families of females (parents and/or siblings) had histories of prior police contact than did the families of males ($X^2 = 8.85$, $p < .01$).

Subject Variables

S's AGE AT FIRST INSTITUTIONAL COMMITMENT. Males who did not become recidivists were significantly older at the time of their first commitment (mean age = 16 years 1 month) than were either the male recidivists (mean age 14 years 7 months; $p < .001$) or female nonrecidivists (mean age = 15 years 2 months; $p < .02$). This latter finding was replicated with independent samples of 50 males and 50 females ($p < .01$). Female nonrecidivists were significantly older at commitment than were female recidivists (mean age = 14 years 6 months; $p < .01$). Male recidivists did not differ from female recidivists in age at first commitment.

AGE AT FIRST RECORD OF ANTISOCIAL BEHAVIOR. The age which maximized the discrimination between recidivists and nonrecidivists differed for the sexes. More female recidivists than nonrecidivists had a history of antisocial behavior (e.g., vandalism, truancy) at age 14 or younger, whereas more non-

[5] T. Monahan, "Family Status and the Delinquent Child," *Social Forces*, XXXV (1957), 250–258.

[6] A. B. Hollingshead and F. C. Redlich, *Social Class and Mental Illness* (New York: Wiley, 1958).

[7] P. F. Briggs and R. D. Wirt, "Prediction," in H. C. Quay, ed., *Juvenile Delinquency* (New York: Van Nostrand, 1965).

recidivists were age 15 or older when first identified ($X^2 = 8.20$, $p < .01$). These data are consistent with those reported for age of first commitment.
PREINSTITUTIONAL DELINQUENT BEHAVIOR. All known delinquent activities were classified into one of four mutually exclusive offense categories: (a) aggressive-personal (e.g., assault, forcible rape), (b) aggressive-property (e.g., arson, vandalism), (c) nonaggressive-personal (e.g., runaway, drug usage), and (d) nonaggressive-property (e.g., larceny, forgery). Each offense in each category was rated on an 11-point scale of increasing severity, adapted from Sellin and Wolfgang.[8] The fourfold classification of type of offense did not differentiate between recidivists and nonrecidivists. A relationship between type of most frequently committed offense and recidivism might have been expected since Gough, Wenk, and Rozynko[9] and Craig and Budd[10] have reported that juvenile male recidivists more frequently committed property offenses (e.g., theft) than did nonrecidivists.

Expected sex differences did emerge regarding aggressive offenses (both personal and property). Eighteen per cent of the males were rated as having committed offenses in this category, whereas no females had done so ($X^2 = 17.50$, $p < .001$). Further analyses of the offense classes of females were not performed because 89 per cent of the cases of female delinquency fell within the nonaggressive-personal category.

Analyses of the most severe offense leading to commitment, and the sum severity (combined frequency and severity) of all preinstitutional offenses, revealed several relationships. A significantly greater proportion of males than females was committed for offenses that received higher severity (i.e., ≥ 4) ratings ($X^2 = 32.08$, $p < .001$). Similarly, males had more severe and chronic histories of preinstitutional delinquent behavior than did females ($X^2 = 10.00$, $p < .01$). The most obvious interpretation of these differences would be that females are less delinquent than males. However, this interpretation must be approached with caution for reasons which are discussed elsewhere in this report. Neither the severity of the committing offense nor the weighted total of all offenses distinguished recidivists from nonrecidivists, but this comparison masks an important sex difference. Female recidivists had less severe histories of delinquent activity prior to first commitment than did female nonrecidivists ($X^2 = 4.85$, $p < .05$).

DIAGNOSTIC CLASSIFICATION. Table 1 shows the diagnostic groups represented in the sample. There were more than twice as many females as males diagnosed as neurotic ($X^2 = 7.08$, $p < .01$). For males, equal numbers of recidivists and nonrecidivists were diagnosed neurotic. For females, however, almost twice as many diagnosed neurotics were nonrecidivists as were recidivists ($X^2 = 3.46$, $p < .10$).

[8] T. Sellin and M. E. Wolfgang, *The Measurement of Delinquency* (New York: Wiley, 1964).

[9] H. G. Gough, E. A. Wenk, and V. V. Rozynko, "Parole Outcome as Predicted from the CPI, the MMPI, and the Base Expectancy Table," *Journal of Abnormal Psychology,* LXX (1965), 432–441.

[10] M. M. Craig and L. A. Budd, "The Juvenile Offender—Recidivism and Companions," *Crime and Delinquency,* XIII (1967), 344–351.

The Ss classified as passive-aggressive personality constituted the largest proportion of the sample for males and the second largest for females. Significantly more males in this category were nonrecidivists than were recidivists ($X^2 = 4.83$, $p < .05$), whereas an opposite, but nonsignificant, trend was found for females.

Table 1   Diagnostic Category Representation of the Sample

Primary Diagnosis	Male n		Female n		Sample %	
	R	N	R	N	MALE	FE-MALE
Neurosis [a]	8	8	12	23	16	35
Passive-aggressive	11	24	16	12	35	28
Passive-dependent	5	2	5	3	7	8
Sociopathic	17	5	8	3	22	11
Schizoid	3	3	6	7	6	13
Psychosis [b]	6	8	3	2	14	5

Note. R = recidivist; N = nonrecidivist.
[a] Includes primary stress reaction.
[b] Includes primary and secondary.

The diagnosis of sociopathic personality (including both antisocial and dyssocial subtypes) demonstrated the strongest relationship to recidivism for both males and females of any diagnostic category. There were significantly more sociopathic recidivists than nonrecidivists ($X^2 = 4.38$, $p < .05$). Sarason and Ganzer [11] also found that a greater proportion of males diagnosed as sociopathic personality subsequently became recidivists than would have been expected from the proportion represented in the sample. The families of four of the five male sociopathic nonrecidivists had no history of disorganization (e.g., divorce, mental illness, police records), whereas 14 of the 17 recidivists came from disorganized families. The difference for recidivists is significant ($p = .002$, binomial test). While the number of sociopathic nonrecidivists is too small to permit firm conclusions, it seems likely that a stable family background is important for the successful post-institutional adjustment of males in this diagnostic category. Other diagnostic groups did not show similar relationships.

Diagnostic groups were compared to determine if differences existed in the type of offenses most frequently committed. For males, the only finding which differentiated recidivists from nonrecidivists was again confined to the category of sociopathic personality. Five of the 17 sociopathic recidivists had committed aggressive personal types of offenses. Not one of the five nonrecidivist sociopaths had been known to have committed aggressive per-

[11] I. G. Sarason and V. J. Ganzer, *Modeling: An Approach to the Rehabilitation of Juvenile Delinquents* (Final Report) (Seattle: University of Washington, Social and Rehabilitation Service, 1971).

sonal offenses ($p = .06$, binomial test). Moreover, seven of the eight socio-pathic boys who had committed a large proportion of aggressive kinds of offenses (personal or property) became recidivists ($p = .07$ binomial test). The only other differences that emerged from these comparisons were associated with the tendencies of neurotic and sociopathic boys to commit different types of delinquent offenses. Neurotic males more frequently committed property offenses, whereas sociopathic boys more frequently committed personal offenses ($X^2 = 10.84$, $p < .01$).

ESTIMATES OF SUBSEQUENT ADJUSTMENT. Estimates were made at case staffing of each S's probable subsequent institutional adjustment and his long-term prognosis. These estimates fell into four categories (good, fair, marginal, or poor). Most estimates of institutional adjustment were in the category of "fair" (70 per cent), which did not discriminate between recidivists and nonrecidivists, and the category was eliminated from further analysis. A greater proportion of nonrecidivists than recidivists was given ratings of "good" institutional adjustment, whereas more recidivists than nonrecidivists received estimates of "marginal" or "poor" adjustment ($X^2 = 6.88$, $p < .01$). The second estimate, long-term prognosis, did not differentiate between groups.

INTELLIGENCE. Estimates of verbal intelligence were based on Wechsler's [12] six-category classification system. Proportions of male and female recidivists and nonrecidivists whose IQs were estimated as "low average" and below did not differ significantly from those with IQs of "high average" and above. An extreme groups comparison revealed that a greater proportion of recidivists than nonrecidivists had IQs in the "dull normal range" and below, whereas more nonrecidivists were judged to be "bright normal" or above ($X^2 = 5.18$, $p < .05$). Similar results were reported by Laulicht [13] but for only the low end (IQs of 60 to 89) of the intelligence continuum. While the present findings are not especially strong, they do offer some support for the inference that if intelligence serves as a basis of reality testing as well as a form of impulse control, then recidivists might be expected to possess lower levels of intellectual abilities.

Conclusion

The data presented reveal a number of variables which, when cross-validated, may be of practical value in predicting recidivism. Several important sex differences were found. Generally, the most promising potential predictors of recidivism were associated with (a) several family background factors, (b) age at first offense and commitment, and (c) diagnostic classification.

The persistent finding that female delinquents came from more disorga-

[12] D. Wechsler, *The Measurement and Appraisal of Adult Intelligence* (4th ed.) (Baltimore, Md.: Williams and Wilkins, 1958).

[13] L. Laulicht, "Problems of Statistical Research: Recidivism and its Correlates," *Journal of Criminal Law, Criminology, and Police Science*, LIV (1963), 163–174.

nized and socially less adequate families than did males has several implications. This greater family disorganization might be causally related to the finding that females were committed at earlier ages and had less chronic and severe histories of preinstitutional delinquent behavior than did males. Socially disorganized families may be more highly "visible" in a community because they tend more frequently to come in contact with the police, the courts, public assistance, and other agencies. Visibility might be related to the earlier detection and commitment of females because they and their families have become known to agencies and possibly labeled as "bad" persons from whom further trouble is to be expected. As a result of these expectations, as well as other differential social and sex-role expectancies, juvenile courts might sooner institutionalize female offenders. If this reasoning is valid, the finding that females were also less severely delinquent (possibly because they were apprehended and institutionalized earlier) and showed different patterns of relationships on diagnostic category and intelligence variables than did males might also be explained.

The potential influence of yet another factor, the differential base rates for male and female commitments, seems significant. Does the fact that only one-third as many females as males reach an institution mean that only the very most severely delinquent girls are represented in the female sample because of a systematic selection factor? The present data on the severity of delinquent offenses suggest that females were less delinquent than males, but it cannot help resolve the question of whether equal commitment rates would change the statistical patterns of offenses and recidivism. If it were true that female commitments represent proportionally more severely delinquent children than do male commitments, it might also be expected that the rate of female recidivism would be higher than the male rate. Just the opposite is in fact true. Unfortunately, the present investigation cannot answer these questions because no relationship was found between severity of delinquent behavior prior to first commitment and recidivism, and further because severity appears confounded with sex differences in age of commitment, types of offenses, and family background variables.

The findings suggest that juveniles diagnosed as primary sociopathic personalities tend more often to become recidivists. While diagnosis of primary neurosis is generally considered to reflect good treatment potential and favorable prognosis, the present data suggest that this is true primarily for females.

Of interest are other variables associated with the diagnosis of primary sociopathic personality for the male sample. While a significant proportion became recidivists, those few who did not appear to have come from intact homes, had not committed offenses of an aggressive nature (especially toward other persons), and had been older (i.e., over age 14) at the time of first coming to the attention of police or school authorities. The opposite relationships were true of the sociopathic recidivists, and a combination of these variables in the direction specified identifies virtually all of them.

Physical and Cognitive Growth During Adolescence: Relationships Between Maturational and Societal Factors

Each of the papers in Part 8 discusses aspects of hereditary and environmental interaction in adolescent development. G. Stanley Hall once declared that "growth upward out of the womb of nature is the one miracle of the world and its direction is the only clue to human destiny." Heredity must be acknowledged as it relates to height and weight, spurt in growth, body proportions, reproduction, physique, and physiological and endocrinological growth. But the effects on physical growth of nutrition, climate, season, and social class must be acknowledged, too. Herbert Spencer, a nineteenth-century forerunner of contemporary theorists of cognitive behavior viewed cognitive development as a confluence of hereditary and environmental factors. He thought that intelligence differentiated itself during development into a hierarchy of cognitive traits—sensory, perceptual, associational, and relational. Cognitive development today is still viewed as progressing through a series of stages, and identifying how children and adolescents differ in mode of functioning has become a major issue in the study of cognition. The five papers in Part 8, which deal with either physical or cognitive development, are grouped together, therefore, because the viewpoints expressed in each are predicated on assumptions about hereditary and environmental interaction.

In the first paper, Tanner observes that while comparable physical changes have been occurring during adolescence for the past five thousand years, the trend in the last century has been toward increased size and earlier maturation. He describes in detail the growth spurt, the developmental order of parts of the body, and the significance of changes in body-size, body-shape, and athletic abilities. In his comprehensive review, Tanner also notes that the timing of the adolescent growth spurt may affect youth's personality development. An early-maturing boy, for example, may dominate in athletics, and adults and peers may offer early-maturing boys and girls tasks and privileges that are ordinarily reserved for older adolescents. Weatherley, in the second paper, concentrates on relationships between rate of physical maturation and personality development. He divided nineteen-year-old boys and girls on the basis of their perceived rate of physical maturation into early, average, and late-maturers and then compared the groups' scores on several personality tests. His data show that early- and average-maturing youth resemble one another in personality attributes relative to late-maturers; hence, to mature at an average age may be as much of an advantage as to mature early. Late-maturing boys were more likely to seek attention and affection, resist leadership roles, and participate in unconventional behavior, suggesting that only the obvious late-maturers are socially handicapped.

The assumption that cognitive growth advances from elementary to complex thought processes is a major cornerstone of psychological theory. Cognitive growth appears to take place in invariant sequences; for purposes of contrast, the child's cognitive developmental status is usually designated as concrete *and the adolescent's, as* abstract. *A child's thinking tends to be bound to symbolic representations of perceptual and functional aspects of reality; an adolescent's thinking, on the other hand, may lead to hypothetical relationships between ideas and novel manipulation of symbols. Among the psychologists who have attempted to explain how children and adolescents acquire conceptual structures, Jean Piaget has emerged the most influential. His voluminous research has been the subject of countless discussions. Piaget not only emphasizes the adolescent's ability to deal with "formal" thought processes, but also explains how the adolescent acquires the capacity to view propositions systematically and to make analyses of the full range of possibilities inherent in a problem or situation. Dulit, in the third paper of Part 8, describes the basic Piagetian principles of cognitive development and contrasts the concrete stage of late childhood with the formal stage of adolescence. Dulit also attempts to substantiate Piaget's interpretations in two formal-stage experiments. Dulit's data reveal that although children in general follow the cognitive pathways Piaget has described, formal-stage thinking emerges in adolescence as a potentiality "only partially attained by most and fully attained only by some." The researcher speculates that development of formal thinking during adolescence reflects actual "demand" for it in everyday life. The fourth paper adds further clarification to the link between stages of cognitive development and the dynamics of personality development. Looft illustrates within Piaget's framework how stages of cognitive development relate to affective experience and behavior. He traces briefly different forms of egocentrism through childhood and adolescence. Looft focuses on the cognitive behavior of adolescents; formal-stage thinking, he says, is attained (a) cognitively, by "the eventual differentiation between one's own preoccupations and those of others" and (b) affectively, as one "gradually recognizes and integrates the feelings of others with his own feelings." Looft also explains "decentering" as a corrective mechanism and suggests how egocentrism may be overcome.*

Creativity is often overlooked in discussions of formal thinking and cognitive maturity. According to Davis, in the fifth paper, an adolescent who reaches the stage of formal operations is capable of thinking consciously of himself or herself "as a more open and creative individual." He defines the characteristics of creative persons and strongly urges that adolescents be taught the significance of human creativeness and allowed first-hand involvement in creative experiences.

Sequence, Tempo, and Individual Variation in the Growth and Development of Boys and Girls Aged Twelve to Sixteen

Tanner surveys the major features of adolescent physical growth. He discusses the (a) adolescent growth spurt in skeletal and muscular dimensions, (b) reproductive system, (c) variability among youth in the timing of pubertal development, (d) development of sex-differentiated morphological characteristics, (e) interaction of physical and social development, and (f) trends toward larger size and earlier maturation during adolescence.

Instructional Objectives
To discuss the physical growth spurt and body changes in size, shape, and tissue composition.
To describe the developmental sequence of body changes associated with the reproductive system.
To discuss variations in pubertal development and the manner in which puberty is initiated.
To discuss relations among physical maturation, intelligence, and social development.
To describe the "secular trend" in adolescence toward larger size and earlier maturation.

FOR THE majority of young persons, the years from twelve to sixteen are the most eventful ones of their lives so far as their growth and development is concerned. Admittedly during fetal life and the first year or two after birth developments occurred still faster, and a sympathetic environment was probably even more crucial, but the subject himself was not the fascinated, charmed, or horrified spectator that watches the developments, or lack of developments, of adolescence. Growth is a very regular and highly regulated process, and from birth onward the growth rate of most bodily tissues decreases steadily, the fall being swift at first and slower from about three

FROM *Daedalus*, © (1971), pp. 907–930. Journal of the American Academy of Arts and Sciences, Boston, Massachusetts, *Twelve to Sixteen: Early Adolescence.* Reprinted by permission of the author and the publisher.

years. Body shape changes gradually since the rate of growth of some parts, such as the arms and legs, is greater than the rate of growth of others, such as the trunk. But the change is a steady one, a smoothly continuous development rather than any passage through a series of separate stages.

Then at puberty, a very considerable alteration in growth rate occurs. There is a swift increase in body size, a change in the shape and body composition, and a rapid development of the gonads, the reproductive organs, and the characters signaling sexual maturity. Some of these changes are common to both sexes, but most are sex-specific. Boys have a great increase in muscle size and strength, together with a series of physiological changes, making them more capable than girls of doing heavy physical work and running faster and longer. The changes specifically adapt the male to his primitive primate role of dominating, fighting, and foraging. Such adolescent changes occur generally in primates, but are more marked in some species than in others. Male, female, and prepubescent gibbons are hard to distinguish when they are together, let alone apart. No such problem arises with gorillas or Rhesus monkeys. Man lies at about the middle of the primate range, both in adolescent size increase and degree of sexual differentiation.

The adolescent changes are brought about by hormones, either secreted for the first time, or secreted in much higher amounts than previously. Each hormone acts on a set of targets or receptors, but these are often not concentrated in a single organ, nor in a single type of tissue. Testosterone, for example, acts on receptors in the cells of the penis, the skin of the face, the cartilages of the shoulder joints, and certain parts of the brain. Whether all these cells respond by virtue of having the same enzyme system, or whether different enzymes are involved at different sites is not yet clear. The systems have developed through natural selection, producing a functional response of obvious biological usefulness in societies of hunter gatherers, but of less certain benefit in the culture of invoice clerk and shop assistant. Evolutionary adaptations of bodily structure usually carry with them an increased proclivity for using those structures in behavior, and there is no reason to suppose this principle suddenly stops short at twentieth-century man. There is no need to take sides in the current debate on the origins of aggression to realize that a major task of any culture is the channeling of this less specifically sexual adolescent energy into creative and playful activity.

The adolescent changes have not altered in the last fifteen years, or the last fifty, or probably the last five thousand. Girls still develop two years earlier than boys; some boys still have completed their whole bodily adolescent development before other boys of the same chronological age have begun theirs. These are perhaps the two major biological facts to be borne in mind when thinking of the adolescent's view of himself in relation to his society. The sequence of the biological events remains the same. But there has been one considerable change; the events occur now at an earlier age than formerly. Forty years ago the average British girl had her first menstrual period (menarche) at about her fifteenth birthday; nowadays it is shortly before her thirteenth. Fifty years ago in Britain social class differences played a considerable part in causing the variation of age of menarche in the population, the less well-off growing up more slowly. Nowadays, age at menarche is almost the same in different classes and most of the variation is due to genetical factors.

In this essay, I shall discuss (1) the growth of the body at adolescence and its changes in size, shape, and tissue composition, (2) sex dimorphism and the development of the reproductive system, (3) the concept of developmental age and the interaction of physical and behavioral advancement, (4) the interaction of genetic and environmental influences on the age of occurrence of puberty and the secular trend toward earlier maturation.

GROWTH OF THE BODY AT ADOLESCENCE

The extent of the adolescent spurt in height is shown in Figure 1. For a year or more the velocity of growth approximately doubles; a boy is likely to be growing again at the rate he last experienced about age two. The peak velocity of height (PHV, a point much used in growth studies) averages about 10.5 centimeters a year (cm/yr) in boys and 9.0 cm/yr in girls (with a standard deviation of about 1.0 cm/yr) but this is the "instantaneous" peak given by a smooth curve drawn through the observations. The velocity over the whole year encompassing the six months before and after the peak is naturally somewhat less. During this year a boy usually grows between 7 and 12 cm and a girl between 6 and 11 cm. Children who have their peak early reach a somewhat higher peak than those who have it late.

The average age at which the peak is reached depends on the nature and circumstances of the group studied more, probably, than does the height of the peak. In moderately well-off British or North American children at present the peak occurs on average at about 14.0 years in boys and 12.0 years in girls. The standard deviations are about 0.9 years in each instance. Though the absolute average ages differ from series to series the two-year sex difference is invariant.

The adolescent spurt is at least partly under different hormonal control from growth in the period before. Probably as a consequence of this the amount of height added during the spurt is to a considerable degree independent of the amount attained prior to it. Most children who have grown steadily up, say, the 30th centile line on a height chart till adolescence end up at the 30th centile as adults, it is true; but a number end as high as the 50th or as low as the 10th, and a very few at the 55th or 5th. The correlation between adult height and height just before the spurt starts is about 0.8. This leaves some 30 per cent of the variability in adult height as due to differences in the magnitude of the adolescent spurt. So some adolescents get a nasty and unavoidable shock; though probably the effects of early and late maturing (see below) almost totally confuse the issue of final height during the years we are considering.

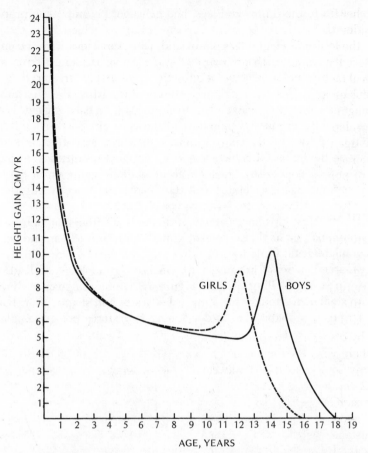

Figure 1. Typical individual velocity curves for supine length or height in boys and girls. These curves represent the velocity of the typical boy and girl at any given instance. (From J. M. Tanner, R. H. Whitehouse, and M. Takaishi, "Standards from Birth to Maturity for Height, Weight-Height Velocity and Weight Velocity; British Children, 1965," Archives of the Diseases of Childhood, 41, [1966], 455–471.)

Practically all skeletal and muscular dimensions take part in the spurt, though not to an equal degree. Most of the spurt in height is due to acceleration of trunk length rather than length of legs. There is a fairly regular order in which the dimensions accelerate; leg length as a rule reaches its peak first, followed by the body breadths, with shoulder width last. Thus a boy stops growing out of his trousers (at least in length) a year before he stops growing out of his jackets. The earliest structures to reach their adult status are the head, hands, and feet. At adolescence, children, particularly girls, sometimes complain of having large hands and feet. They can be reassured that by the time they are fully grown their hands and feet will be a little smaller in proportion to their arms and legs, and considerably smaller in proportion to their trunk.

The spurt in muscle, both of limbs and heart, coincides with the spurt in skeletal growth, for both are caused by the same hormones. Boys' muscle widths reach a peak velocity of growth considerably greater than those reached by girls. But since girls have their spurt earlier, there is actually a period, from about twelve and a half to thirteen and a half, when girls on the average have larger muscles than boys of the same age.

Simultaneously with the spurt in muscle there is a loss of fat in boys, particularly on the limbs. Girls have a velocity curve of fat identical in shape to that of boys; that is to say, their fat accumulation (going on in both sexes from about age six) decelerates. But the decrease in velocity in girls is not sufficiently great to carry the average velocity below zero, that is to give an absolute loss. Most girls have to content themselves with a temporary go-slow in fat accumulation. As the adolescent growth spurt draws to an end, fat tends to accumulate again in both sexes.

The marked increase in muscle size in boys at adolescence leads to an increase in strength, illustrated in Figure 2. Before adolescence, boys and girls are similar in strength for a given body size and shape; after, boys are much stronger, probably due to developing more force per gram of muscle

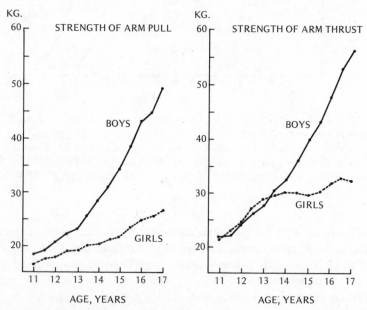

Figure 2.   Strength of arm pull and arm thrust from age 11 to 17. Mixed longitudinal data, 65 to 95 boys and 66 to 93 girls in each age group. (From J. M. Tanner, Growth at Adolescence, 2d ed. [Oxford: Blackwell Scientific Publications, 1962]; data from H. E. Jones, Motor Performance and Growth [Berkeley: University of California Press, 1949].)

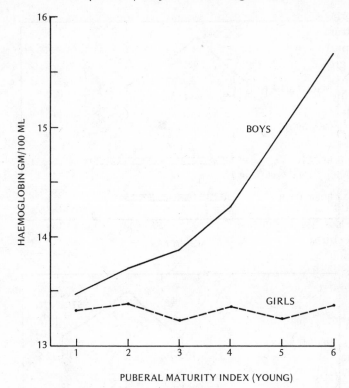

Figure 3. *Blood hemoglobin level in girls and boys according to stage of puberty; cross-sectional data. (From H. B. Young, "Ageing and Adolescence,"* Developmental Medicine and Child Neurology, *5 [1963], 451–460, cited in J. M. Tanner, "Growth and Endocrinology of the Adolescent," in L. Gardner, ed.,* Endocrine and Genetic Disease of Childhood *[Philadelphia and London: Saunders, 1969].)*

as well as absolutely larger muscles. They also develop larger hearts and lungs relative to their size, a higher systolic blood pressure, a lower resting heart rate, a greater capacity for carrying oxygen in the blood, and a greater power for neutralizing the chemical products of muscular exercise such as lactic acid.[1] In short, the male becomes at adolescence more adapted for the tasks of hunting, fighting, and manipulating all sorts of heavy objects, as is necessary in some forms of food-gathering.

The increase in hemoglobin, associated with a parallel increase in the number of red blood cells, is illustrated in Figure 3.[2] The hemoglobin concentration is plotted in relation to the development of secondary sex characters instead of chronological age, to obviate the spread due to early and late

[1] J. M. Tanner, *Growth at Adolescence,* 2d ed. (Oxford: Blackwell Scientific Publications, 1962), p. 168.
[2] H. B. Young, "Ageing and Adolescence," *Developmental Medicine and Child Neurology,* 5 (1963), 451–460.

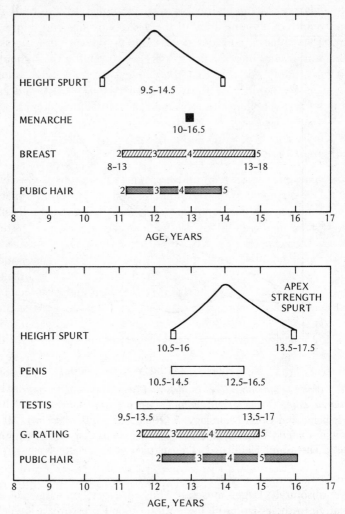

Figure 4. *Diagram of sequence of events at adolescence in boys and girls. The average boy and girl are represented. The range of ages within which each event charted may begin and end is given by the figures placed directly below its start and finish. (From W. A. Marshall and J. M. Tanner, "Variations in the Pattern of Pubertal Changes in Boys,"* Archives of the Diseases of Childhood, 45 [1970], 13.)

maturing. Girls lack the rise in red cells and hemoglobin, which is brought about by the action of testosterone.

It is as a direct result of these anatomical and physiological changes that athletic ability increases so much in boys at adolescence. The popular notion of a boy "outgrowing his strength" at this time has little scientific support. It is true that the peak velocity of strength is reached a year or so later than that of height, so that a short period may exist when the adolescent, having completed his skeletal and probably also muscular growth, still does not have the strength of a young adult of the same body size and shape. But this is a temporary phase; considered absolutely, power, athletic skill, and physical endurance all increase progressively and rapidly throughout adolescence. It is certainly not true that the changes accompanying adolescence enfeeble, even temporarily. If the adolescent becomes weak and easily exhausted it is for psychological reasons and not physiological ones.

SEX DIMORPHISM AND THE DEVELOPMENT OF THE REPRODUCTIVE SYSTEM

The adolescent spurt in skeletal and muscular dimensions is closely related to the rapid development of the reproductive system which takes place at this time. The course of this development is outlined diagrammatically in Figure 4. The solid areas marked "breast" in the girls and "penis" and "testis" in the boys represent the period of accelerated growth of these organs and the horizontal lines and the rating numbers marked "pubic hair" stand for its advent and development.[3] The sequences and timings given represent in each case average values for British boys and girls; the North American average is within two or three months of this. To give an idea of the individual departures from the average, figures for the range of age at which the various events begin and end are inserted under the first and last point of the bars. The acceleration of penis growth, for example, begins on the average at about age twelve and a half, but sometimes as early as ten and a half and sometimes as late as fourteen and a half. The completion of penis development usually occurs at about age fourteen and a half but in some boys is at twelve and a half and in others at sixteen and a half. There are a few boys, it will be noticed, who do not begin their spurts in height or penis development until the earliest maturers have entirely completed theirs. At age thirteen, fourteen, and fifteen there is an enormous variability among any group of boys, who range all the way from practically complete maturity to absolute preadolescence. The same is true of girls aged eleven, twelve, and thirteen.

In Figure 5 three boys are illustrated, all aged exactly 14.75 years and three girls all aged exactly 12.75. All are entirely normal and healthy, yet the first boy could be mistaken easily for a twelve-year-old and the third for a young man of seventeen or eighteen. Manifestly it is ridiculous to consider all three boys or all three girls as equally grown up either physically, or, since much behavior at this age is conditioned by physical status, in their social relations. The statement that a boy is fourteen is in most contexts hopelessly vague; all depends, morphologically, physiologically, and to a considerable extent sociologically too, on whether he is preadolescent, midadolescent, or postadolescent.

The psychological and social importance of this difference in the tempo of development, as it has been called, is very great, particularly in boys. Boys

[3] Details of ratings are in Tanner, *Growth at Adolescence*.

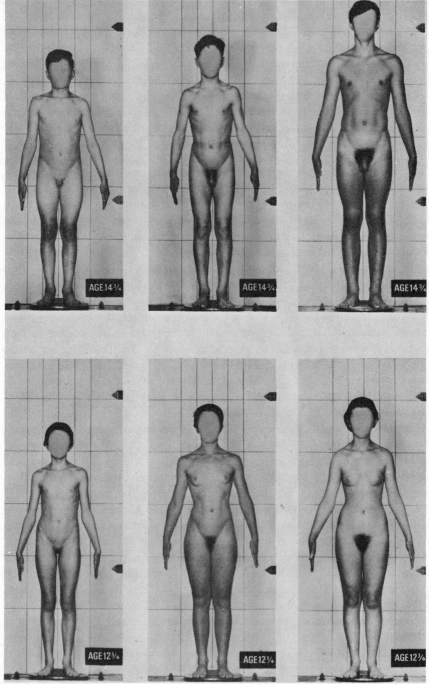

Figure 5.   *Differing degrees of pubertal development at the same chronological age. Upper row three boys all aged 14.75 years. Lower row three girls all aged 12.75 years. (From Tanner, "Growth and Endocrinology of the Adolescent.")*

who are advanced in development are likely to dominate their contemporaries in athletic achievement and sexual interest alike. Conversely the late developer is the one who all too often loses out in the rough and tumble of the adolescent world; and he may begin to wonder whether he will ever develop his body properly or be as well endowed sexually as those others he has seen developing around him. A very important part of the educationist's and the doctor's task at this time is to provide information about growth and its variability to preadolescents and adolescents and to give sympathetic support and reassurance to those who need it.

The *sequence* of events, though not exactly the same for each boy or girl, is much less variable than the age at which the events occur. The first sign of puberty in the boy is usually an acceleration of the growth of the testes and scrotum with reddening and wrinkling of the scrotal skin. Slight growth of pubic hair may begin about the same time, but is usually a trifle later. The spurts in height and penis growth begin on average about a year after the first testicular acceleration. Concomitantly with the growth of the penis, and under the same stimulus, the seminal vesicles and the prostate and bulbo-urethral glands enlarge and develop. The time of the first ejaculation of seminal fluid is to some extent culturally as well as biologically determined, but as a rule is during adolescence, and about a year after the beginning of accelerated penis growth.

Axillary hair appears on the average some two years after the beginning of pubic hair growth—that is, when pubic hair is reaching stage 4. However, there is enough variability and dissociation in these events that a very few children's axillary hair actually appears first. In boys, facial hair begins to grow at about the time the axillary hair appears. There is a definite order in which the hairs of moustache and beard appear; first at the corners of the upper lip, then over all the upper lip, then at the upper part of the cheeks in the mid-line below the lower lip, and finally along the sides and lower border of the chin. The remainder of the body hair appears from about the time of first axillary hair development until a considerable time after puberty. The ultimate amount of body hair an individual develops seems to depend largely on heredity, though whether because of the kinds and amounts of hormones secreted or because of the reactivity of the end-organs is not known.

Breaking of the voice occurs relatively late in adolescence; it is often a gradual process and so not suitable as a criterion of puberty. The change in pitch accompanies enlargement of the larynx and lengthening of the vocal cords, caused by the action of testosterone on the laryngeal cartilages. During the period of breaking, the pitch is variable, and the true adult pitch associated with full growth of the larynx may not be established until late adolescence. In addition to change in pitch, there is also a change in quality or timbre which distinguishes the voice (more particularly the vowel sounds) of both male and female adults from that of children. This is dependent on the enlargement of the resonating spaces above the larynx, due to the rapid growth of the mouth, nose, and maxilla which occurs during adolescence.

In the skin the sebaceous and apocrine sweat glands, particularly of the axillae and genital and anal regions, develop rapidly during puberty and give rise to a characteristic odor; the changes occur in both sexes but are more marked in the male. Enlargement of the pores at the root of the nose and the appearance of comedones and acne, though liable to occur in either sex, are considerably commoner in adolescent boys than girls, since the underlying skin changes are the result of androgenic activity. A roughening of the skin, particularly over the outer aspects of the thighs and upper arms, may be seen in both sexes during adolescence, but again is commoner in boys than girls.

During adolescence the male breast undergoes changes, some temporary and some permanent. The diameter of the areola, which is equal in both sexes before puberty, increases considerably, though less than it does in girls. Representative figures are 12.5 millimeters before puberty, 21.5 millimeters in mature men, and 35.5 millimeters in mature women. In some boys (between a fifth and a third of most groups studied) there is a distinct enlargement of the breast (sometimes unilaterally) about midway through adolescence. This usually regresses again after about one year.

In girls the appearance of the "breast bud" is as a rule the first sign of puberty, though the appearance of pubic hair precedes it in about one in three. The uterus and vagina develop simultaneously with the breast. The labia and clitoris also enlarge. Menarche, the first menstrual period, is a late event in the sequence. It occurs almost invariably after the peak of the height spurt has been passed. Though it marks a definitive and probably mature stage of uterine development, it does not usually signify the attainment of full reproductive function. The early cycles may be more irregular than later ones and are in some girls, but by no means all, accompanied by dysmenorrhea. They are often anovulatory, that is unaccompanied by the shedding of an egg. Thus there is frequently a period of adolescent sterility lasting a year to eighteen months after menarche; but it cannot be relied on in the individual case. Similar considerations may apply to the male, but there is no reliable information about this. On the average, girls grow about 6 cm more after menarche, though gains of up to twice this amount may occur. The gain is practically independent of whether menarche occurs early or late.

NORMAL VARIATIONS IN PUBERTAL DEVELOPMENT

The diagram of Figure 4 must not be allowed to obscure the fact that children vary a great deal both in the rapidity with which they pass through the various stages of puberty and in the closeness with which the various events are linked together. At one extreme one may find a perfectly healthy girl who has not yet menstruated though she has reached adult breast and pubic hair ratings and is already two years past her peak height velocity; at the other a girl who has passed all the stages of puberty within the space of two years.

Details of the limits of what may be considered normal can be found in the articles of Marshall and Tanner.[4]

In girls the interval from the first sign of puberty to complete maturity varies from one and a half to six years. From the moment when the breast bud first appears to menarche averages two and a half years but may be as little as six months or as much as five and a half years. The rapidity with which a child passes through puberty seems to be independent of whether puberty is occurring early or late. There is some independence between breast and pubic hair developments, as one might expect on endocrinological grounds. A few girls reach pubic hair stage 3 (see Figure 4) before any breast development starts; conversely breast stage 3 may be reached before any pubic hair appears. At breast stage 5, however, pubic hair is always present in girls. Menarche usually occurs in breast stage 4 and pubic hair stage 4, but in about 10 per cent of girls occurs in stage 5 for both, and occasionally may occur in stage 2 or even 1 of pubic hair. Menarche invariably occurs after peak height velocity is passed, so the tall girl can be reassured about future growth if her periods have begun.

In boys a similar variability occurs. The genitalia may take any time between two and five years to pass from G2 to G5, and some boys complete the whole process while others have still not gone from G2 to G3. Pubic hair growth in the absence of genital development is very unusual in normal boys, but in a small percentage of boys the genitalia develop as far as stage 4 before the pubic hair starts to grow.

The height spurt occurs relatively later in boys than in girls. Thus there is a difference between the average boy and girl of two years in age of peak height velocity, but of only one year in the first appearance of pubic hair. The PHV occurs in very few boys before genital stage 4, whereas 75 per cent of girls reach PHV before breast stage 4. Indeed in some girls the acceleration in height is the first sign of puberty; this is never so in boys. A small boy whose genitalia are just beginning to develop can be unequivocally reassured that an acceleration in height is soon to take place, but a girl in the corresponding situation may already have had her height spurt.

The basis of some children having loose and some tight linkages between pubertal events is not known. Probably the linkage reflects the degree of integration of various processes in the hypothalamus and the pituitary gland, for breast growth is controlled by one group of hormones, pubic hair growth by another, and the height spurt probably by a third. In rare pathological instances the events may become widely divorced.

---

[4] W. A. Marshall and J. M. Tanner, "Variations in the Pattern of Pubertal Changes in Girls," *Archives of the Diseases of Childhood,* 44 (1969), 291, and "Variations in the Pattern of Pubertal Changes in Boys," *Archives of the Diseases of Childhood,* 45 (1970), 13.

THE DEVELOPMENT OF SEX DIMORPHISM

The differential effects on the growth of bone, muscle, and fat at puberty increase considerably the difference in body composition between the sexes. Boys have a greater increase not only in the length of bones but in the thickness of cortex, and girls have a smaller loss of fat. The most striking dimorphism, however, are the man's greater stature and breadth of shoulders and the woman's wider hips. These are produced chiefly by the changes and timing of puberty but it is important to remember that sex dimorphisms do not arise only at that time. Many appear much earlier. Some, like the external genital difference itself, develop during fetal life. Others develop continuously throughout the whole growth period by a sustained differential growth rate. An example of this is the greater relative length and breadth of the forearm in the male when compared with whole arm length or whole body length.

Part of the sex difference in pelvic shape antedates puberty. Girls at birth already have a wider pelvic outlet. Thus the adaptation for child bearing is present from a very early age. The changes at puberty are concerned more with widening the pelvic inlet and broadening the much more noticeable hips. It seems likely that these changes are more important in attracting the male's attention than in dealing with its ultimate product.

These sex-differentiated morphological characters arising at puberty—to which we can add the corresponding physiological and perhaps psychological ones as well—are secondary sex characters in the straightforward sense that they are caused by sex hormone or sex-differential hormone secretion and serve reproductive activity. The penis is directly concerned in copulation, the mammary gland in lactation. The wide shoulders and muscular power of the male, together with the canine teeth and brow ridges in man's ancestors, developed probably for driving away other males and insuring peace, an adaptation which soon becomes social.

A number of traits persist, perhaps through another mechanism known to the ethologists as ritualization. In the course of evolution a morphological character or a piece of behavior may lose its original function and, becoming further elaborated, complicated, or simplified, may serve as a sign stimulus to other members of the same species, releasing behavior that is in some ways advantageous to the spread or survival of the species. It requires little insight into human erotics to suppose that the shoulders, the hips and buttocks, and the breasts (at least in a number of widespread cultures) serve as releasers of mating behavior. The pubic hair (about whose function the textbooks have always preserved a cautious silence) probably survives as a ritualized stimulus for sexual activity, developed by simplification from the hair remaining in the inguinal and axillary regions for the infant to cling to when still transported, as in present apes and monkeys, under the mother's body. Similar considerations may apply to axillary hair, which is associated with special apocrine glands which themselves only develop at puberty and are related histologically to scent glands in other mammals. The beard, on the other hand, may still be more frightening to other males than enticing to females. At least ritual use in past communities suggests this is the case; but perhaps there are two sorts of beards.

THE INITIATION OF PUBERTY

The manner in which puberty is initiated has a general importance for the clarification of developmental mechanisms. Certain children develop all the changes of puberty, up to and including spermatogenesis and ovulation, at a very early age, either as the result of a brain lesion or as an isolated developmental, sometimes genetic defect. The youngest mother on record was such a case, and gave birth to a full-term healthy infant by Caesarian section at the age of five years, eight months. The existence of precocious puberty and the results of accidental ingestion by small children of male or female sex hormones indicate that breasts, uterus, and penis will respond to hormonal stimulation long before puberty. Evidently an increased end-organ sensitivity plays at most a minor part in pubertal events.

The signal to start the sequence of events is given by the brain, not the pituitary. Just as the brain holds the information on sex, so it holds information on maturity. The pituitary of a newborn rat successfully grafted in place of an adult pituitary begins at once to function in an adult fashion, and does not have to wait till its normal age of maturation has been reached. It is the hypothalamus, not the pituitary, which has to mature before puberty begins.

Maturation, however, does not come out of the blue and at least in rats a little more is known about this mechanism. In these animals small amounts of sex hormones circulate from the time of birth and these appear to inhibit the prepubertal hypothalamus from producing gonadotrophin releasers. At puberty it is supposed that the hypothalamic cells become less sensitive to sex hormone. The small amount of sex hormones circulating then fails to inhibit the hypothalamus and gonadotrophins are released; these stimulate the production of testosterone by the testis or estrogen by the ovary. The level of the sex hormone rises until the same feedback circuit is reestablished, but now at a higher level of gonadotrophins and sex hormones. The sex hormones are now high enough to stimulate the growth of secondary sex characters and support mating behavior.

DEVELOPMENTAL AGE AND THE INTERACTION OF PHYSICAL AND BEHAVIORAL ADVANCEMENT

Children vary greatly in their tempo of growth. The effects are most dramatically seen at adolescence, as illustrated in Figure 5, but they are present at all ages from birth and even before. Girls, for example, do not suddenly become two years ahead of boys at adolescence; on the contrary they are born with slightly more mature skeletons and nervous systems, and gradually increase their developmental lead (in absolute terms) throughout childhood.

Clearly, the concept of *developmental* age, as opposed to *chronological* age, is a very important one. To measure developmental age we need some way of determining the percentage of the child's growth process which has been attained at any time. In retrospective research studies, the per cent of final adult height may be very effectively used; but in the clinic we need something that is immediate in its application. The difficulty about using height, for example, is that different children end up at different heights, so that a tall-for-his-age twelve-year-old may either be a tall adult in the making with average maturational tempo, or an average adult in the making with an accelerated tempo. Precisely the same applies to the child who scores above average on most tests of mental ability.

To measure developmental age we need something which ends up the same for everyone and is applicable throughout the whole period of growth. Many physiological measures meet these criteria, in whole or in part. They range from the number of erupted teeth to the percentage of water in muscle cells. The various developmental "age" scales do not necessarily coincide, and each has its particular use. By far the most generally useful, however, is skeletal maturity or *bone* age. A less important one is dental maturity.

Skeletal maturity is usually measured by taking a radiograph of the hand and wrist (using the same radiation exposure that a child inevitably gets, and to more sensitive areas, by spending a week on vacation in the mountains). The appearances of the developing bones can be rated and formed into a scale; the scale is applicable to boys and girls of all genetic backgrounds, though girls on the average reach any given score at a younger age than boys, and blacks on the average, at least in the first few years after birth, reach a given score younger than do whites. Other areas of the body may be used if required. Skeletal maturity is closely related to the age at which adolescence occurs, that is to maturity measured by secondary sex character development. Thus the range of *chronological* age within which menarche may normally fall is about ten to sixteen and a half, but the corresponding range of *skeletal* age for menarche is only twelve to fourteen and a half. Evidently the physiological processes controlling progression of skeletal development are in most instances closely linked with those which initiate the events of adolescence. Furthermore children tend to be consistently advanced or retarded during their whole growth period, or at any rate after about age three.

Dental maturity partly shares in this general skeletal and bodily maturation. At all ages from six to thirteen children who are advanced skeletally have on the average more erupted teeth than those who are skeletally retarded. Likewise those who have an early adolescence on the average erupt their teeth early. Girls usually have more erupted teeth than boys. But this relationship is not a very close one, and quantitatively speaking, it is the relative independence of teeth and general skeletal development which should be emphasized. There is some general factor of bodily maturity creating a tendency for a child to be advanced or retarded as a whole: in his skeletal ossification, in the percentage attained of his eventual size, in his permanent dentition, doubtless in his physiological reactions, and possibly in the results of his tests of ability. But not too much should be made of this general factor; and especially it should be noted how very limited is the loading, so to speak, of brain growth in it. There is little justification in the facts of physical growth and development for the concept of "organismic age" in which almost wholly disparate measures of developmental maturity are lumped together.

PHYSICAL MATURATION, MENTAL ABILITY AND EMOTIONAL DEVELOPMENT

Clearly the occurrence of tempo differences in human growth has profound implications for educational theory and practice. This would especially be so if advancement in physical growth were linked to any significant degree with advancement in intellectual ability and in emotional maturity.

There is good evidence that in the European and North American school systems children who are physically advanced toward maturity score on the average slightly higher in most tests of mental ability than children of the same age who are physically less mature. The difference is not great, but it is consistent and it occurs at all ages that have been studied—that is, back as far as six and a half years. Similarly the intelligence test score of postmenarcheal girls is higher than the score of premenarcheal girls of the same age.[5] Thus in age-linked examinations physically fast-maturing children have a significantly better chance than slow-maturing.

It is also true that physically large children score higher than small ones, at all ages from six onward. In a random sample of all Scottish eleven-year-old children, for example, comprising 6,440 pupils, the correlation between height and score in the Moray House group test was 0.25 ± 0.01 which leads to an average increase of one and a half points Terman-Merrill I.Q. per inch of stature. A similar correlation was found in London children. The effects can be very significant for individual children. In ten-year-old girls there was nine points difference in I.Q. between those whose height was above the 75th percentile and those whose height was below the 15th. This is two-thirds of the standard deviation of the test score.

It was usually thought that both the relationships between test score and height and between test score and early maturing would disappear in adulthood. If the correlations represented only the effects of co-advancement both of mental ability and physical growth this might be expected to happen. There is no difference in height between early and late maturing boys when both have finished growing. But it is now clear that, curiously, at least part

[5] See references in Tanner, *Growth at Adolescence*, and Tanner, "Galtonian Eugenics and the Study of Growth," *The Eugenics Review*, 58 (1966), 122–135.

of the height I.Q. correlation persists in adults.[6] It is not clear in what proportion genetic and environmental factors are responsible for this.

There is little doubt that being an early or a late maturer may have repercussions on behavior, and that in some children these repercussions may be
considerable. There is little enough solid information on the relation between
emotional and physiological development, but what there is supports the
common sense notion that emotional attitudes are clearly related to physiological events.

The boy's world is one where physical powers bring prestige as well as
success, where the body is very much an instrument of the person. Boys who
are advanced in development, not only at puberty, but before as well, are
more likely than others to be leaders. Indeed, this is reinforced by the fact
that muscular, powerful boys on the average mature earlier than others and
have an early adolescent growth spurt. The athletically-built boy not only
tends to dominate his fellows before puberty, but also by getting an early
start he is in a good position to continue that domination. The unathletic,
lanky boy, unable, perhaps, to hold his own in the preadolescent rough and
tumble, gets still further pushed to the wall at adolescence, as he sees others
shoot up while he remains nearly stationary in growth. Even boys several
years younger now suddenly surpass him in size, athletic skill, and perhaps,
too, in social graces. Figure 6 shows the height curves of two boys, the first
an early-maturing muscular boy, the other a late-maturing lanky one. Though
both boys are of average height at age eleven, and together again at average
height at seventeen, the early maturer is four inches taller during the peak of
adolescence.

At a much deeper level the late developer at adolescence may sometimes
have doubts about whether he will ever develop his body properly and
whether he will be as well endowed sexually as those others he has seen
developing around him. The lack of events of adolescence may act as a
trigger to reverberate fears accumulated deep in the mind during the early
years of life.

It may seem as though the early maturers have things all their own way.
It is indeed true that most studies of the later personalities of children whose
growth history is known do show early maturers as more stable, more sociable, less neurotic, and more successful in society, at least in the United
States.[7] But early maturers have their difficulties also, particularly the girls
in some societies. Though some glory in their new possessions, others are
embarrassed by them. The early maturer, too, has a longer period of frustration of sex drive and of drive toward independence and the establishment of
vocational orientation.

Little can be done to reduce the individual differences in children's tempo

[6] Tanner, "Galtonian Eugenics."
[7] P. H. Mussen and M. C. Jones, "Self-Concepting Motivations and Interpersonal Attitudes of Late- and Early-Maturing Boys," *Child Development,* 28 (1957), 243–256.

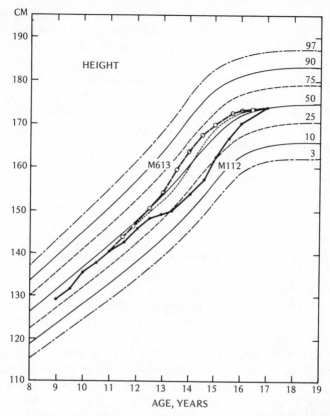

Figure 6. *Height attained of two boys, one with an early and the other with a late adolescent spurt. Note how at age eleven and again at age seventeen the boys are the same height. (From J. M. Tanner* Education and Physical Growth: Implications of the Study of Children's Growth for Educational Theory and Practice *[London: University of London Press, 1961].)*

of growth, for they are biologically rooted and not significantly reducible by any social steps we may take. It, therefore, behooves all teachers, psychologists, and pediatricians to be fully aware of the facts and alert to the individual problems they raise.

TREND TOWARD LARGE SIZE AND EARLIER MATURATION

The rate of maturing and the age at onset of puberty are dependent, naturally, on a complex interaction of genetic and environmental factors. Where the environment is good, most of the variability in age at menarche in a population is due to genetic differences. In France in the 1950s the mean difference between identical twins was two months, while that between nonidentical twin sisters was eight months.[8] In many societies puberty occurs later in the poorly-off, and in most societies investigated children with many siblings grow less fast than children with few.

Recent investigations in Northeast England showed that social class differences are now only those associated with different sizes of family. The median age of menarche for only girls was 13.0 years, for girls with one sibling 13.2, two siblings 13.4, three siblings and over 13.7. For a given number of siblings the social class as indicated by father's occupation was unrelated to menarcheal age.[9] Environment is still clearly a factor in control of menarcheal age, but in England at least occupation is a less effective indication of poor housing, poor expenditure on food, and poor child care than is the number of children in the family.

During the last hundred years there has been a striking tendency for children to become progressively larger at all ages.[10] This is known as the "secular trend." The magnitude of the trend in Europe and America is such that it dwarfs the differences between socioeconomic classes.

The data from Europe and America agree well: from about 1900, or a little earlier, to the present, children in average economic circumstances have increased in height at age five to seven by about 1 to 2 cm each decade, and at ten to fourteen by 2 to 3 cm each decade. Preschool data show that the trend starts directly after birth and may, indeed, be relatively greater from age two to five than subsequently. The trend started, at least in Britain, a considerable time ago, because Roberts, a factory physician, writing in 1876 said that "a factory child of the present day at the age of nine years weighs as much as one of 10 years did in 1833 . . . each age has gained one year in forty years." [11] The trend in Europe is still continuing at the time of writing but there is some evidence to show that in the United States the best-off sections of the population are now growing up at something approaching the fastest possible speed.

During the same period there has been an upward trend in adult height, but to a considerably lower degree. In earlier times final height was not reached till twenty-five years or later, whereas now it is reached in men at eighteen or nineteen. Data exist, however, which enable us to compare fully grown men at different periods. They lead to the conclusion that in Western Europe men increased in adult height little if at all from 1760 to 1830, about 0.3 cm per decade from 1830 to 1880, and about 0.6 cm per decade from 1880 to 1960. The trend is apparently still continuing in Europe, though not in the best-off section of American society.

[8] M. Tisserand-Perrier, "Etude comparative de certains processus de croissance chez les jeuneaux," *Journal de génétique humaine*, 2 (1953), 87–102, as cited in Tanner, *Growth at Adolescence.*

[9] D. F. Roberts, L. M. Rozner, and A. V. Swan, "Age at Menarche, Physique and Environment in Industrial North-East England," *Acta Paediatrica Scandinavica*, 60 (1971), 158–164.

[10] J. M. Tanner, "Earlier Maturation in Man," *Scientific American*, 218 (1968), 21–27.

[11] Tanner, *Growth at Adolescence.*

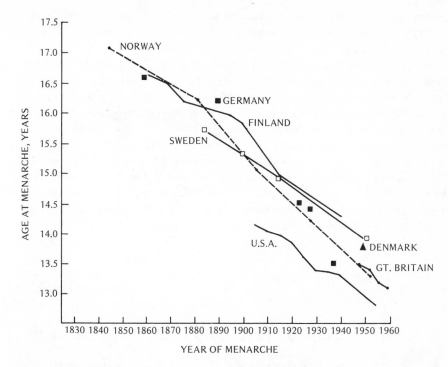

Figure 7. Secular trend in age at menarche, 1830–1960. (Sources of data and method of plotting detailed in Tanner, Growth at Adolescence.*)*

Most of the trend toward greater size in children reflects a more rapid maturation; only a minor part reflects a greater ultimate size. The trend toward earlier maturing is best shown in the statistics on age at menarche. A selection of the best data is illustrated in Figure 7. The trend is between three and four months per decade since 1850 in average sections of Western European populations. Well-off persons show a trend of about half this magnitude, having never been so retarded in menarche as the worse-off.[12]

Most, though not all, of the differences between populations are probably due to nutritional factors, operating during the whole of the growth period, from conception onward. The well-nourished Western populations have median menarcheal ages of about 12.8 to 13.2 years; the latest recorded ages, by contrast, are 18 years in the Highlands of New Guinea, 17 years in Central Africa, and 15.5 years in poorly-off Bantu in the South African Transkei. Well-nourished Africans have a median age of 13.4 (Kampala upper classes) or less, comparable with Europeans. Asians at the same nutritional level as Europeans probably have an earlier menarche, the figure for well-off Chinese in Hong Kong being 12.5 years.

[12] Details on average age of menarche of various populations and the methods for collecting these statistics will be found in Tanner, "Galtonian Eugenics."

The causes of the secular trend are probably multiple. Certainly better nutrition is a major one, and perhaps in particular more protein and calories in early infancy. A lessening of disease may also have contributed. Hot climates used to be cited as a potent cause of early menarche, but it seems now that their effect, if any, is considerably less than that of nutrition. The annual mean world temperature rose from 1850 to about 1940 (when it began to fall again); the polar ice caps have been melting and the glaciers retreating, but on present evidence it seems unlikely that this general warming up has contributed significantly to the earlier menarche of girls.

Some authors have supposed that the increased psychosexual stimulation consequent on modern urban living has contributed, but there is no positive evidence for this. Girls in single-sex schools have menarche at exactly the same age as girls in coeducational schools, but whether this is a fair test of difference in psychosexual stimulation is hard to say.

Donald Weatherley

Self-Perceived Rate of Physical Maturation and Personality in Late Adolescence

The intensity and variability of physical growth during adolescence are such that at any specific age from approximately eleven to eighteen some youth are nearly mature whereas others are relatively immature in respect to their ultimate physical stature. Longitudinal research at the Institute of Human Development, University of California, regarding the effects of early- and late-maturing upon personality dynamics has shown that, for boys, early physical maturation leads to certain advantages, including greater esteem from peers and adults, substantially more athletic prowess, and considerably enhanced heterosexual status. By and large, overall psychological adjustment appears to be more satisfactory in early- rather than late-maturing boys. Research on girls has been more equivocal. Early physical acceleration may cause them to be conspicuously tall and stocky. In contrast to the boys' lot, neither of these attributes is an asset by contemporary standards of feminine pulchritude. Thus the general proposition is widely cited that early-maturing girls are at a disadvantage whereas late-maturing girls are at an advantage. However, contrary to expectations,

FROM *Child Development*, XXXV (1964), 1197–1210. Reprinted by permission of the author and the Society for Research in Child Development.

recent research suggests that the early-maturing girls have "more favorable self-concepts" than those who are late maturing.

In an independent investigation, Weatherley categorizes college students, on the basis of their own reports of their rate of physical maturation, into groups of early, average, and late maturers. The results largely confirm the earlier findings obtained in the Institute studies and help clarify the general assumptions. Late physical maturation represents an apparent handicap to boys' personality development, but average time of maturation is about as advantageous as early maturation. As the earlier studies showed, the effects of rate of maturation on personal adjustment are less salient for girls than for boys; further, in harmony with recent studies, Weatherley suggests both boys and girls benefit from the effects of early physical maturation.

Instructional Objectives

To review the conclusions of earlier investigations regarding relationships between personality development and rate of physical maturation.

To discuss the importance of rate of physical maturation as a variable influencing boys' personality development.

To evaluate the extent to which rate of physical maturation affects girls' personality development.

IT HAS long been recognized that the timing of puberty and of the marked physical changes which herald its onset is subject to wide individual differences. It is relatively recently, however, that attention has been drawn to the differential impact on personal and social adjustment of these individual differences in the rate of physical maturation. This issue has been brought into sharp focus by a recent series of reports stemming from the California Adolescent Growth Study, a project which involved the intensive observation and testing of a group of approximately 180 boys and girls over a seven-year period.[1] These reports were based on comparisons made with a variety of behavioral and personality measures of groups of extremely early and extremely late maturers (the upper and lower 20 per cent of the total Growth Study sample).

Clear-cut results were found for boys. Both trained adult observers and peers described the late-maturing boys' behavior in less favorable terms than that of the early maturers. For example, at age 16 the late maturers were rated by adults as significantly less attractive in physique, less well groomed, less moderate in their behavior, more affected, more tense appearing, and more eager. Peers described the late maturers as more restless, less reserved,

---

[1] H. E. Jones, "The California Adolescent Growth Study," *J. Educ. Res.*, XXXI (1938), 561–567.

less grown-up, and more bossy.[2] In brief, the tense, active, attention-seeking behavior of the late maturers contrasted sharply with the self-assured, well modulated, socially appropriate behavior manifested by the group of early maturers. Moreover, the late maturers were chosen much less frequently than early maturers for positions of leadership in their school and were much less prominent in extracurricular activities.[3]

An analysis of TAT protocols obtained when the boys were 17 years old revealed personality differences consistent with the behavior differences found between early and late maturers. These data indicated that accompanying the late maturers' less adaptive social behaviors were heightened feelings of inadequacy, negative self-conceptions, feelings of rejection and domination, and persistent dependency needs paradoxically coupled with a rebellious quest for autonomy and freedom from restraint.[4]

Finally, a follow-up study [5] provided evidence that the personality differences between the early- and late-maturing boys persisted into adulthood long after physical differences between the groups had disappeared. The male subjects of the Adolescent Growth Study were administered two objective tests of personality (the California Psychological Inventory and the Edwards Personal Preference Schedule) when they had reached an average age of 33. The test results indicated that as adults the late maturers were less capable of conveying a good impression, less self-controlled, less responsible, less dominant, and more inclined to turn to others for help than were the early maturers—a pattern of personality differences quite similar to the pattern that had emerged when the groups were compared in adolescence.

The results of this series of studies on males add up to a consistent picture which makes good theoretical sense. A large, strong stature is a central aspect of the ideal masculine model in our society. Thus, it is reasonable to assume that the early attainment of the physical attributes associated with maturity serves as a social stimulus which evokes from both peers and adults a reaction of respect, acceptance, and the expectation that the individual concerned will be capable of relatively mature social behavior. Such a reaction from others serves to support and reinforce adaptive, "grown-up" actions and contributes to feelings of confidence and security in the early-maturing boys. On the other hand, the late maturer must cope with the developmental demands of the junior high and high school period with the liability of a relatively small, immature appearing physical stature. His appearance is likely to call out in others at least mild reactions of derogation and the expectation

---

[2] M. C. Jones and N. Bayley, "Physical Maturing Among Boys as Related to Behavior," *J. Educ. Psych.*, XLI (1950), 129–148.

[3] M. C. Jones, "A Study of Socialization Patterns at the High School Level," *J. Genet. Psychol.*, XCIII (1958), 87–111.

[4] P. H. Mussen and M. C. Jones, "Self-Conceptions, Motivations, and Interpersonal Attitudes of Late- and Early-Maturing Boys," *Child Developm.*, XXVIII (1957), 243–256.

[5] M. C. Jones, "The Later Careers of Boys Who Were Early- or Late-Maturing," *Child Developm.*, XXVIII (1957), 113–128.

that he is capable of only ineffectual, immature behavior. Such reactions constitute a kind of social environment which is conducive to feelings of inadequacy, insecurity and defensive, "small-boy" behavior. Such behavior once initiated may well be self-sustaining, since it is likely to only intensify the negative environmental reactions which gave rise to it in the first place. This interpretation, fully consistent with the evidence produced by the investigations of the Growth Study workers, implies that the late-maturing boy is likely to be involved in a circular psychosocial process in which reactions of others and his own reactions interact with unhappy consequences for his personal and social adjustment.

Does rate of physical maturation have the same effect on the personal-social development of girls? The early data obtained in the Adolescent Growth Study suggested that it does not—that an effect opposite to that found in boys occurs. H. E. Jones [6] reported that late-maturing girls were rated by adult judges significantly higher than early-maturing girls on a number of socially desirable traits such as sociability, leadership, cheerfulness, poise, and expressiveness. Peers also rated the late maturers in more positive terms than they did the early maturers. Moreover, the late-maturing girls were especially likely to participate in extracurricular activities at high school and hold positions of prestige in school clubs; early-maturing girls played a much less prominent role in school activities.[7]

These findings imply that in contrast to the situation with boys, late physical maturation is an asset and early maturation a liability to the social adjustment of girls. Why should this be true? Mary C. Jones and Mussen [8] offered an explanation which focused upon the likely biosocial consequences of early physical maturation for girls. They pointed out that the early-maturing girl is inclined to acquire a stocky, muscular physique while the late maturer tends toward a slim, slight build, more in keeping with the feminine ideal in our society. Furthermore, the female early maturer is not only slightly out of step in physical development when compared with other girls her age, she is drastically different in physical status from her male peers of similar age, since boys in general lag about two years behind girls in manifesting pubertal growth changes. H. E. Jones [9] also noted that the parents of early-maturing girls might well be unenthusiastic about their daughters' precocious interest in the opposite sex, an interest which is likely to draw them toward social contacts with boys much older than they.

This line of reasoning led Mary C. Jones and Mussen [10] to predict that the personality development of the early-maturing girls in the Adolescent

[6] H. E. Jones, "Adolescence in Our Society," *The Family in a Democratic Society: Anniversary Papers of the Community Service Society of New York* (Columbia University Press, 1949), pp. 70–82.
[7] M. C. Jones, "A Study of Socialization . . .," op. cit.
[8] M. C. Jones and P. H. Mussen, "Self-Conceptions, Motivations, and Interpersonal Attitudes of Early- and Late-Maturing Girls," *Child Developm.*, XXIX (1958), 491–501.
[9] H. E. Jones, "Adolescence in Our Society," op. cit.
[10] Jones and Mussen, op. cit.

Growth Study would reflect the ill effects of an accelerated rate of growth as did their social behavior, investigated earlier. This expectation, however, was not supported by TAT data obtained when the girls were 17 years old. Although the differences found for girls between early and late maturers were not nearly as striking as those found for boys on the TAT, the differences were generally in the same direction for both sexes. The implication of the projective test data was that early-maturing members of both sexes as opposed to late maturers tend to be characterized by more adequate thought processes, a more positive self-conception, and a more relaxed, secure view of themselves and their world.

Thus in the case of girls it is necessary to somehow account for the apparent inconsistency of findings indicating that early maturation leads to less adequate social adjustment in combination with other results indicating that early maturation is associated with a more "healthy" appearing personality picture. It is possible that the personality data were unreliable, that the differences found on the TAT were artifacts of sampling or measurement error; certainly this interpretation is more reasonable than one discounting the behavior rating measures and indices of social participation on similar grounds, as the findings on the latter sets of measures were more clear-cut that the TAT results. On the other hand, it may be as Mary C. Jones and Mussen [11] suggested, that early maturation is a social disadvantage early in the adolescent period, when the behavior ratings were made, but later in adolescence when physical differences due to different rates of maturation are less marked and environmental stress presumably associated with precocious growth is reduced, the early-maturing girls relax and manifest in their personality integration the beneficial effects of their earlier start toward the assumption of an adult status.

It is obvious that additional data bearing on the relation in late adolescence between rate of physical maturation and personality attributes of girls would be helpful in choosing between these alternative explanations of the inconsistent appearing Adolescent Growth Study data. One purpose of the present study was to provide such additional data by assessing the relation between a measure of maturational rate and a variety of personality variables in girls in late adolescence. The design also permitted a between-sex comparison in order to determine whether or not rate of physical maturation had similar implications for the personality development of boys and of girls.

Another purpose of the present study was to assess once again the relation of maturational rate and personality characteristics for a group of males, considered apart from females. Although the California workers' findings for boys were generally clear-cut and consistent, the conclusions they generated rested, in one sense at least, on a quite narrow empirical base (as was also true for the less certain conclusions reached for girls). All the studies reviewed earlier involved the same small group of Ss, all of whom lived in

[11] Ibid.

the Berkeley, California, area. Furthermore, despite the fact that these reports have appeared relatively recently in the literature, all but the one concerning the follow-up study were based on data gathered more than two decades ago; the Growth Study Ss were, at the time the present study was undertaken, close to 40 years old—literally old enough to be the parents of today's adolescents.

It should be noted, however, that the present study was by no means a contemporary replication of earlier research; it differed in several important respects from the California investigations. The Ss in this study were on the average about two years older than were the Ss at the completion of the Adolescent Growth Study. A number of objective personality measures were used in the present study, only one of which (the Edwards Personal Preference Schedule) was used in the California research and then only in the follow-up study.[12] The most noteworthy distinction between the study reported here and the previous research in this area had to do with the nature of the measure of rate of physical maturation. The California studies used an objective skeletal-age index of physical maturation as a basis for identifying early and late maturers. In the present study a simple self-report measure of relative maturational rate was used. Its use involved the assumption that adolescents have a fairly accurate idea of the relative timing of their physical maturation and can reliably report this information.

Obviously, any one or more of the factors mentioned above could be responsible for differences found between results of the present study and the findings of the California series of investigations; such differences might not be easy to interpret. On the other hand, it was felt that if the present study yielded findings with implications convergent with those generated by previous research, especially that dealing with males where prior evidence was most definitive, the generality of the conclusions reached would be strongly supported.

METHOD

The Ss were 234 male and 202 female college students enrolled in the elementary psychology course at the University of Colorado. The mean age of the girls was 19.4 ($SD = 2.6$), the mean age of the boys, 19.9 ($SD = 1.9$).

Early in the semester the MMPI K scale [13] and the Taylor Manifest Anxiety Scale (TMAS) [14] were administered to the Ss in large group sessions. Approximately five weeks later 96 of the boys and 92 of the girls took the Edwards Personal Preference Schedule (EPPS).[15]

[12] M. C. Jones, "The Later Careers . . .," op. cit.
[13] J. C. McKinley, S. R. Hathaway, and P. E. Meehl, "The Minnesota Multiphasic Personality Inventory: VI. The K Scale," *J. Consult. Psychol.*, XII (1948), 20–31.
[14] J. A. Taylor, "A Personality Scale of Manifest Anxiety," *J. Abnorm. Soc. Psychol.*, XLVIII (1953), 285–290.
[15] A. L. Edwards, *Manual for the Edwards Personal Preference Schedule* (Psychological Corp., 1959).

In order to obtain measures reflecting degree of identification with parents and peers, the Ss were asked in the initial testing sessions to give self-ratings of the degree to which they saw themselves as similar to each of the following individuals: their mother, father, same-sex best friend, and opposite-sex best friend. These self-ratings of perceived similarity were obtained for each of the following dimensions: overall personality, intelligence, warmth, orderliness, political views, and religious views. Seven-point rating scales were used, yielding scores which ranged from one (indicating the lowest degree of perceived similarity) to seven (indicating the highest degree of perceived similarity).

Rate of physical maturation was assessed by responses to the following multiple-choice question presented to the Ss during the initial testing sessions: "With regard to your physical maturation, you would say that you matured: (a) quite early, (b) somewhat early, (c) average, (d) somewhat late, (e) quite late." These alternatives were assigned weights from one (quite early) to five (quite late) so that the choice made by each S could be represented as a numerical score. In addition, each S was categorized into one of three groups on the basis of his response to the physical maturation question. Individuals who had chosen either the alternative "quite early" or "somewhat early" were considered early maturers. Those who had chosen the alternative "average," were considered average maturers. Those who had chosen the alternatives "somewhat late" or "quite late" were categorized as late maturers.

Means of these three groups for each of the personality measures were compared by t tests, with boys and girls treated separately. This analysis was considered more suitable than a correlational analysis as a basis for describing relations between maturational rate and personality variables within each sex group because it permitted the identification of nonlinear as well as linear relations in the data.

Table 1   Distribution of Responses to Item Measuring Timing of Physical Maturation

	Males (N = 234)	Females (N = 202)
Very early	11.1%	15.8%
Somewhat early	21.4	21.8
Average	44.9	48.5
Somewhat late	19.6	12.9
Very late	3.0	1.0

RESULTS

In Table 1 are presented the distributions for boys and girls of responses to the item measuring perceived rate of physical maturation. The distributions for both sexes were skewed in a direction indicating that both boys and girls are more likely to see themselves as accelerated in development than retarded. For boys and girls combined, there was a significantly greater number of responses in the "somewhat early" and "very early" categories considered together than in the "somewhat late" and "very late" categories ($X^2 = 21.64$; $df = 1$, $p < .01$). While the skewness appeared slightly more marked in the distribution for girls than for boys, the distributions did not differ significantly from one another ($X^2 = 7.31$, $df = 4$, $p > .10$).

Mean scores obtained by early, average, and late maturers on the personality measures are shown in Table 2. This table includes only results for personality variables on which at least one inter-group comparison revealed a difference significant at the .10 level or less.

In general, the findings for boys were highly consistent with the California Adolescent Growth Study results. The most clear-cut differences found in the present study between early-maturing boys and those who described themselves as late maturers were on the same two EPPS variables—dominance and succorance—on which early- and late-maturing males differed when they were tested as adults in the Growth Study follow-up.[16] In the present study, late maturers as opposed to early maturers scored lower on the dominance scale ($p < .05$) and higher on the succorance scale ($p < .01$). They also differed in the same direction on these variables from the group of average maturers. Thus the late maturers revealed relatively weak tendencies to lead and control others and relatively strong tendencies to seek encouragement, sympathy, and understanding from others—characteristics found previously to be associated with late maturation not only in the follow-up study mentioned above,[17] but in two other investigations done as part of the California Growth Study.[18] It is also noteworthy that low scores on the EPPS dominance scale, and high scores on the succorance scale (i.e., the pattern characteristic of the late maturers) have been shown to be associated with scores on the Minnesota Multiphasic Personality Inventory indicative of maladjustment.[19]

The late-maturing boys also obtained higher EPPS autonomy scores than did the early maturers, a difference which just failed to reach significance at the .05 level. This may at first appear to be a finding inconsistent with the implications of previous research, since the term autonomy is one often included in conceptions of the "ideal" personality. Yet a consideration of the items included in the EPPS autonomy scale (e.g., "to do things that are unconventional," "to criticize those in positions of authority," "to avoid responsibilities and obligations") points up the anti-conventional, at least mildly rebellious trends tapped by this measure. Thus the late maturers'

[16] M. C. Jones, "Later Careers of Boys," op. cit.
[17] Ibid.
[18] Mussen and Jones, op. cit.; P. H. Mussen and M. C. Jones, "The Behavior-Inferred Motivations of Late- and Early-Maturing Boys," *Child Developm.*, XXIX (1958), 61–67.
[19] R. M. Merrill and L. B. Heathers, "The Relation of MMPI to the Edwards Personal Preference Schedule on a College Counseling Center Sample," *J. Consult. Psychol.*, XX (1956), 310–314.

Table 2   Mean Scores on Personality Measures for Early, Average, and Late Maturers

	Early Maturers	Average Maturers	Late Maturers	Early vs. Average	Average vs. Late	Early vs. Late
					Significance of Differences	
Males						
TMAS	6.84 (76)	6.44 (105)	8.09 (53)	ns	< .05	ns
EPPS:						
Achievement	15.40 (30)	17.44 (36)	16.96 (30)	< .10	ns	ns
Autonomy	15.17 (30)	15.69 (36)	17.17 (30)	ns	ns	< .06
Intraception	16.30 (30)	14.03 (36)	13.83 (30)	< .10	ns	< .10
Succorance	9.20 (30)	9.86 (36)	12.27 (30)	ns	< .05	< .01
Dominance	19.13 (30)	18.81 (36)	16.33 (30)	ns	< .10	< .05
Abasement	11.47 (30)	9.56 (36)	12.20 (30)	ns	< .05	ns
Endurance	10.17 (30)	13.42 (36)	10.50 (30)	< .05	< .05	ns
Perceived similarity to:						
Mother's political views	4.46 (76)	4.77 (105)	4.13 (53)	ns	< .05	ns
Mother's religious views	4.63 (76)	4.65 (105)	4.09 (53)	ns	< .10	ns
Father's political views	4.65 (68)	5.12 (100)	4.35 (51)	< .10	< .02	ns
Father's religious views	4.76 (68)	4.94 (100)	4.29 (51)	ns	< .10	ns
Boy friend's warmth	5.11 (76)	5.08 (105)	4.52 (52)	ns	< .05	< .05
Boy friend's political views	4.89 (76)	4.79 (105)	4.31 (52)	ns	< .10	< .05
Boy friend's intelligence	5.41 (76)	5.13 (105)	5.71 (52)	ns	< .05	ns
Females						
TMAS	6.91 (76)	7.46 (98)	9.54 (28)	ns	< .05	< .02
EPPS:						
Exhibition	16.38 (37)	14.96 (45)	17.00 (10)	< .05	< .10	ns
Nurturance	16.05 (37)	16.27 (45)	13.50 (10)	ns	< .10	< .10
Perceived similarity to:						
Mother's religious views	4.43 (76)	5.12 (98)	4.54 (28)	< .05	ns	ns
Father's political views	4.90 (68)	4.96 (92)	5.70 (23)	ns	< .05	< .10
Boy friend's orderliness	4.67 (76)	5.23 (97)	4.39 (28)	< .05	< .05	ns

Note: This table includes only those variables on which at least one between-group comparison was significant at the .10 level or less. The *N* for each cell is given in parentheses.

relatively high autonomy mean score, considered in combination with their high succorance but low dominance scores suggests a prolongation of the typically adolescent independence-dependence conflict in late-maturing boys. The previous research of Mussen and Mary C. Jones [20] led them to a similar conclusion for the group of boys they studied.

If late maturers are in fact caught between competing strivings for dependency and strivings for freedom from restraint we should expect to find in them evidence of less well resolved internal conflict in the form of heightened tension and subjective distress. Two measures used in the present study are most pertinent to this question, and on both the results confirmed expectations. On the TMAS and the EPPS abasement scale late-maturing boys scored higher than average or early maturers, differences which were statistically significant ($p < .05$) in the comparisons between late and average maturers. Scores on the TMAS reflect the degree of tension and

[20] Mussen and Jones, "Self-Conceptions, Motivations . . .," op. cit.

manifest anxiety an individual acknowledges and have been shown to be highly correlated negatively with a measure of self-esteem.[21] The abasement scale items refer to feelings of guilt, inferiority, and depression; there is evidence that high scores on this scale are associated with maladjustment.[22] Of interest here also is the finding of the present study that the late-maturing males tended to score lower than the early maturers ($p < .10$) on the EPPS intraception scale (e.g., "to analyze one's motives and feelings," "to understand how others feel about problems"), suggesting that perhaps because the late maturer is, as indicated above, more likely than individuals maturing earlier to experience negative, presumably unpleasant feelings, he is less likely to develop a "psychological mindedness" in his orientation to himself and others.

On one EPPS variable—the endurance scale—a curvilinear relation with rate of maturation in boys was found; both the late and early maturers evidenced lower scores on the endurance scale (e.g., "to keep at a puzzle or problem until it is solved," "to put in long hours of work without distraction") than did the group of average maturers ($p < .05$). This is not an easy finding to interpret. The appreciable personality differences that set late and early maturers apart, however, suggest that a relative lack of persistence may have a different functional significance for early as opposed to late maturers. It may be, for example, that the late maturer as a corollary of his heightened tension and feelings of inferiority has less conviction that he will be able to succeed at tasks and thus is inclined to give up trying relatively quickly, while the early maturer is inclined to persist less than the average maturer because he is accustomed to success with less effort and seeks alternate routes to his goals when he meets a barrier. It must be recognized, however, that any such interpretation is, at this state in our knowledge, highly speculative.

The data for boys involving ratings of perceived similarity to parents and friends among various dimensions by no means revealed startling differences among the maturation groups (Table 2). Of the 72 comparisons made only 10 differences significant at the .10 level or less were found. Yet it is noteworthy that in eight of these ten instances, late maturers rated themselves less similar to parents or friends than did Ss who matured earlier. This at least suggests that late maturers are more inclined to see themselves as being different from others. A resulting sense of estrangement may contribute to the heightened subjective distress found in the late-maturing boys. This line of reasoning is consistent with the findings of previous studies which have shown that the tendency to view oneself as relatively dissimilar to others in personal characteristics is associated with relatively high anxiety.[23]

In previous research, no difference was found between groups of early-

[21] A. W. Siegman, "Cognitive, Affective, and Psychopathological Correlates of the Taylor Manifest Anxiety Scale," *J. Consult. Psychol.*, XX (1956), 137–141.

[22] Merrill and Heathers, op. cit.

[23] J. E. Chance, "Adjustment and Prediction of Others' Behavior," *J. Consult. Psychol.*, XX (1958), 191–194; J. R. Davitz and D. J. Mason, "Manifest Anxiety and Social Perception," *J. Consult. Psychol.*, XXIV (1960), 554.

and late-maturing boys in degree of achievement motivation.[24] In the present study, boys classified as early maturers tended to obtain lower scores on the EPPS achievement scale (e.g., "to be able to do things better than others") than did the group of average maturers ($p < .10$). This may be a chance result. The high social prestige attained by the early-maturing boys who participated in the Adolescent Growth Study [25] certainly does not lead one to anticipate finding a less strong achievement need in early maturers. Also of pertinence here are data obtained in connection with a study of academic over- and under-achievement in which a number of the male Ss of the present study participated.[26] Thirteen of these Ss were identified as over-achievers (i.e., their academic performance appreciably exceeded that expected on the basis of aptitude scores) and compared in terms of their scores on the measure of perceived rate of maturation with 16 Ss classified as under-achievers (i.e., their academic performance was below that expected on the basis of aptitude scores). The results indicated a tendency for the over-achievers to report an earlier physical maturation than the under-achievers ($p < .10$). This suggestion of a link between academic over-achievement and early physical maturation in males also serves to raise a question concerning the reliability of the findings of a lesser degree of striving for achievement in the early maturers. It is, of course, possible that both findings are valid: early maturers may have less strong achievement needs but because of a more efficient and effective use of their personal resources manifest a relatively higher level of success in the academic as well as the social sphere.

Turning now to the results for girls, it can be seen in Table 2 that many fewer differences were found between the maturation groups than were found for boys. The most clear-cut result was obtained on the TMAS: late-maturing girls scored higher on this measure than either the average ($p < .05$) or early maturers ($p < .02$), indicating a higher level of manifest anxiety associated with late maturation. This finding, in the same direction as TMAS results for boys, is congruent with those data obtained in the Adolescent Growth Study that suggested a less adequate personality integration in late-maturing girls.[27]

Aside from these results on the TMAS, the implications of which appear to be quite meaningful, the infrequent differences among groups that were found on the EPPS and similarity rating measures do not suggest any specific personality pattern associated with either early or late maturation. The relatively few statistically significant differences which occurred in those data may well be the product of chance in view of the large total number of comparisons made. While failure to find definitive differences among groups under study may be due to a number of factors (e.g., in the present

[24] Mussen and Jones, "Self-Conceptions, Motivations . . .," op. cit.; Mussen and Jones, "The Behavior-Inferred Motivations . . .," op. cit.

[25] Jones, "A Study of Socialization . . .," op. cit.; Jones and Bayley, op. cit.

[26] R. S. Wyer, D. Weatherley and G. Terrell, "Social Role, Aggression and Academic Achievement," *J. Abnorm. Soc. Psychol.* (in press).

[27] Jones and Mussen, op. cit.

instance the relatively small number of late-maturing girls who took the EPPS reduced the probability of uncovering real differences on that measure which may exist in the population), it is pertinent to note that the previous research that attempted to trace the personality correlates of late and early maturation also produced much less clear-cut findings with girls than with boys.[28]

DISCUSSION

Whenever a research strategy involves the assessment of relations between a response-inferred independent variable or variables and a response-inferred dependent variable or variables, an important question arises which must be considered before the results can be taken seriously. To what extent is it likely that the relations found between the independent and dependent variables are the artifactual products of a response bias which similarly affects the measures used to define the independent variables on the one hand and the dependent variables on the other? This question is especially pertinent in connection with the present study since the distribution of scores on the measure of self-perceived maturation—the independent variable—was skewed in a direction indicating a greater tendency for Ss to see themselves as maturing relatively early than as maturing relatively late. Frazier and Lisonbee[29] reported a similar nonsymmetrical distribution of self-rated physical maturation in tenth-grade boys and girls.

It is possible that this skewness reflects a defensive inclination on the part of at least some of the Ss to describe themselves in what they regard as more favorable terms—i.e., as being relatively advanced in physical development. Conversely, the identification of oneself as retarded in maturation could stem in part from a response bias toward self-derogation. Certainly the retrospective report of so ambiguous a characteristic as maturational rate is potentially subject to such distortions. If in fact an appreciable portion of the variance in maturation scores is due to differences among individuals in their willingness to describe themselves in unfavorable terms, then serious doubt would be cast upon the validity of the relations found in the present study between the maturation measure and those dependent measures which are also subject to influence by this sort of response bias. While the EPPS was specifically designed to minimize the effect of a bias to respond in either a socially desirable or undesirable direction, the TMAS and the similarity ratings are dependent measures certainly susceptible to such influence.

Fortunately, in the present study data were gathered that made possible an assessment of the degree to which the maturation score involved variance attributable to individual differences in willingness to describe oneself unfavorably. An estimate of each S's defensiveness was obtained by use of the

[28] Ibid.
[29] A. Frazier and L. K. Lisonbee, "Adolescent Concerns with Physique," *Sch. Rev.,* LVIII (1950), 397–405.

MMPI K scale that was administered to all Ss. An individual characteristically inclined to distort his self-description in a derogatory direction should obtain a very low K scale score; a very high K scale score is indicative of a defensive inclination to slant one's self-description in a favorable direction.

In the present study for neither boys nor girls were there found any differences in K scale scores approaching statistical significance when the groups of early, average, and late maturers were compared. When responses to the question concerning physical maturation were converted to numerical scores, the correlations found between these scores and scores on the K scale were essentially zero both for boys ($r = .024$) and for girls ($r = .047$). This finding fails to support an argument that scores on the maturation measure were contaminated by a personality-linked response bias. Thus it is not reasonable to discount the results found in this study as merely the product of a measurement artifact.

In the case of boys, the findings of the present study are clear-cut. They indicate that the late-maturing boy of college age is less likely than his earlier-maturing peers to have satisfactorily resolved the conflicts normally attending the transition from childhood to adulthood. He is more inclined to seek attention and affection from others and less inclined to assume a position of dominance and leadership over others. Yet he is not ready to accept the dictates of authority gracefully; he is inclined, rather, to defy authority and assert unconventional behavior in a rebellious vein. In view of the evidence of these potentially competing forces at work within him, it is not surprising that the late maturer also tends to acknowledge a heightened level of subjective tension and readiness to indulge in guilt-implying self-abasement. Nor is it surprising that he tends to see himself as being different from his peers and parents.

The foregoing portrait of the late-maturing boy is, of course, misleading in that it ignores the obviously large overlap among the groups studied and the obviously appreciable individual differences within the group of late maturers. It does, however, serve to bring into focus a central conclusion to be drawn from the results of the present study: late maturation is associated with less mature appearing, less "healthy" appearing personality characteristics. The high degree of congruence between the results of this study and the results of previous studies which involved quite different procedures, measures, and subjects, underscores the generality and importance of rate of physical maturation as a variable influencing personality development in boys.

A second conclusion which can be drawn from the results of the present study, a conclusion which involves a more precise description of the nature of the relation between rate of maturation and personality in boys, has no precedent in the earlier work done as part of the California Adolescent Growth Study. These earlier investigations used an extreme-groups design in which individuals who were extremely late in maturing were compared with individuals extremely early in maturation; no comparisons were made between either of these groups and a group of individuals whose rate of maturation was average. The inclusion in the present study of the group of average maturers made possible an inference concerning the relative impact upon personality characteristics of early versus late maturation when each extreme group was compared to an average group. As an inspection of Table 2 reveals, many fewer significant differences were found when the group of early-maturing boys was compared with the group of average maturers (of a total of 41 comparisons only 1 reached significance at the .05 level or less) than when late maturers were compared with the average maturers (9 of the 41 comparisons made were significant at the .05 level or less). The early- and average-maturing groups were quite similar to one another in the personality attributes they manifested, while the late maturers were set apart from both of these groups. Thus it is clear that the relations found between rate of physical maturation and the personality characteristics measured were not in general linear ones. The implication is that while late maturation is apparently a handicap to the personality development of boys, early maturation may not be an asset; it appears rather to have an effect on personality development no different from the effect of an average rate of physical maturation.

One of the questions that prompted the present study was whether late physical maturation was a liability or an asset to the personality development of girls. The results for girls, however, were much less striking than those for boys; they do not permit a definitive answer to the question. It is clear, nevertheless, that they offer absolutely no support for the proposition that the effect of rate of physical maturation on the adequacy of personality integration in girls is the reverse of that operating in boys. On the other hand, the fact that on the TMAS the results for girls paralleled those for boys lends limited support to the alternative proposition that late physical maturation has adverse effects on personal adjustment in both sexes in late adolescence. The very slim evidence on which it is based, however, makes it necessary to emphasize the tentative nature of this conclusion.

What is perhaps more noteworthy in the findings for girls is the very fact that they were so much less dramatic than those for boys. Since previous research [30] also produced less definitive results for girls than boys, one is drawn to the conclusion that for girls as opposed to boys rate of physical maturation is a much less influential variable mediating personality development. This is not surprising. In our society the cultural sex-role prescription for males is relatively unambiguous and is one which places a high value upon attributes associated with physical strength and athletic prowess, especially in the adolescent and young adulthood years. As Lynn [31] pointed out, however, the feminine sex-role prescription is much less definite and stereotyped; consequently it is less likely to be closely tied to any specific pattern of physical attributes.

A final word is in order regarding the measure of physical maturation

[30] Jones and Mussen, op. cit.
[31] D. B. Lynn, "A Note on Sex Differences in the Development of Masculine and Feminine Identification," *Psychol. Rev.*, LXVI (1959), 126–135.

used in the present study. An assumption involved in the use of this measure was that individuals are both aware of the relative rate of their physical maturation and are willing to report it with reasonable accuracy. The generally high degree of congruence between the results based on the simple self-report measure used in the present study and previous findings based on an objective skeletal-age measure of physical maturation is evidence bolstering this assumption. The veridicality of such self-ratings cannot be firmly established, of course, without directly comparing the ratings with an objective measure of physical growth. Nevertheless, the present results constitute sufficient indirect evidence of the validity of the self-report measure of physical maturation to encourage the use of a measure of this sort in situations where it is impractical to obtain objective indices of maturational rate.

The present study and those done earlier have clearly established the importance of rate of physical maturation as a variable influencing personality development at least in boys; this variable deserves further study. Especially interesting would be research bearing upon the interaction of the maturation variable and variables such as social class membership, parental child-rearing practices, or peer-group social structure.

Everett Dulit

Adolescent Thinking à la Piaget:
The Formal Stage

An adolescent acquires the capacity to construct "formal" theories of events; relative to a child, an adolescent possesses the ability to analyze what is logically possible in a situation, systematically manipulating variables and expressing himself or herself in terms of proportions and hypotheses. This report, however, reveals that many youth fail to realize their inherent potentiality. Dulit reviews Piagetian premises for distinguishing between childhood and adolescent thought and describes two "formal-stage" experiments in which average and gifted adolescents participated. Dulit's interpretation of his findings both support and qualify a widely held assumption about adolescent thinking; he acknowledges

FROM *Journal of Youth and Adolescence*, I (1972), pp. 281–301. Reprinted by permission of the author and the publisher.

formal-stage thinking to be an ideal outcome of cognitive development, but he sees it as an aspect of maturity "fully attained only by some."

Instructional Objectives

To distinguish between "concrete" and "formal" stages in cognitive development.

To describe functions basic to formal stage thinking—the combinatorial system, the INRC group, and the role of proportionality.

To illustrate proportional and combinatorial logic in two formal-stage experiments.

To discuss whether formal-stage thinking suggests atypical examples of "cognitive maturity" among adolescents.

INTRODUCTION

PIAGET introduces his concept of the formal stage for the first time and most fully in *The Growth of Logical Thinking from Childhood to Adolescence*, published in English by Basic Books in 1958. The formal stage is the final and highest stage in the sequence of stages described and defined by Piaget in what he calls "genetic epistemology," his systematic conception of the development of intelligence from childhood through adolescence.

This paper reports a replication of some selected parts of that work, with gifted and average adolescents, leading to results which mostly support but which significantly qualify some of the central themes of the Piaget-Inhelder point of view. This paper begins with a brief exposition of the formal stage set against the background of the concrete stage which it follows, then reports the experiments and the results, and concludes with a discussion of findings and implications and with some reformulations.

Piaget's genetic epistemology distinguishes four main stages: (1) *the sensorimotor stage*, in the first 2 years of life; (2) *the egocentric or "preoperational" stage* (sometimes treated merely as a transitional stage), roughly covering the years 2 through 5; (3) *the concrete stage* of middle childhood, with gradual onset over the years 5 through 8, gradually giving way in preadolescence and early adolescence to (4) *the formal stage*, characteristic of the years from middle adolescence onward, including adulthood.

The focus in genetic epistemology is on cognition (problem solving, directed thinking) and not on thinking more broadly defined to include motivations, affects, or fantasy. Furthermore, the emphasis throughout is on the study of relatively universal features of cognitive development, with little systematic attention given to the matter of "individual differences"; they are recognized but treated as relatively peripheral matters. Each stage reflects what is essentially an optimal trend within its associated age range.

The Concrete Stage

Thinking in the concrete stage is limited primarily (almost exclusively) to thinking about *things*. (By contrast, in the formal stage thinking is about words, ideas, concepts, hypotheses, propositions, etc., in addition to being about things. In this respect, as is generally the case, the formal stage subsumes the concrete stage hierarchically as a part of itself rather than replacing it altogether.) The fundamental "building blocks" of the concrete stage are the Logic of Class and the Logic of Relations.

The *Logic of Class* refers to the child's capacity to handle problems of classification. The child decides whether something is or is not a member of a given class. (The class boundaries are treated as "given." Thinking at this stage is about things, and the class boundaries are, by and large, *not* treated as "things.")

The *Logic of Relations* refers to the child's capacity to relate things of differing size within the context of graded and ordered series. The child can take things of varying sizes and place them in size place, relating any one to any other one within the context of the series. Furthermore, the child can set one series into correspondence with another series by means of "one to one correspondence," which is a major first step toward the mastery of cause and effect relationships.

The operations of this stage, like all others, function generally outside of awareness. In that sense, they are more commonly latent rather than manifest, although they can be made manifest to some degree under circumstances that call for it.

By and large, the concrete-stage child is limited to thinking about actual concrete situations and things as they are presented to him in the real world. (Fantasy and reverie are for these purposes "something else"; the focus here is on cognition, on thinking as directed problem solving.) To be sure, there is some limited capacity in the concrete stage to think about some abstractions (such as "redness," for example), but the degree is sufficiently limited and the "abstractions" are usually sufficiently close to concrete and perceptual realities as to warrant the generalization that thought about abstractions does not come until the formal stage. (One could point in passing to a relation here with the Vigotsky-type tests of "concrete thinking" in schizophrenia and organic mental syndrome, where the thinking of the patient, like that of the concrete-stage child, is much more "bound" to "the thing itself," as compared with the thinking of the normal adult, who is capable of shifting much more flexibly among different ways of categorizing the very same "things.")

The Formal Stage

The distinguishing characteristics of the formal stage are suggested by the three names that are used interchangeably for this stage: "formal," "propositional," "abstract." "Formal" emphasizes that what "counts" is form and not content, as in formal logic where the focus is on the formal relations between the propositions or as in mathematics where an equation represents a formal relation among the symbols that is essentially independent of the particular realities they represent. "Propositional" emphasizes that, as in formal logic, thinking is cast in terms of "propositions," statements, hypotheses. "Abstract" emphasizes that thinking here is no longer bound by "the thing itself" but deals with attributes abstracted from the thing itself; formal-stage thinking deals with words, thoughts, propositions, concepts, hypotheses, ideas, ideologies, as well as with "things" themselves.

Perhaps the single most important hallmark of the formal stage, according to Piaget, is the reversal of the relation between concrete *reality* (*actuality*) and *possibility*. In the concrete stage, *actuality* is in the foreground. In the formal stage, the relation is reversed and *possibility* comes to the foreground. New possibilities can be derived and are derived from recombinations of the variables inherent in the problem, without regard to whether they were ever previously actualized or experienced. That is perhaps the most crucial new development of the formal stage. What counts in the formal stage is what "could be" and not merely what "is" or "was." Formal-stage thinking is cast in terms of the *full range of possibilities* inherent in the problem or situation at hand. All combinations of all possible values of all the relevant variables are given equal weight in formal-stage thought without regard to whether they are actualized or not. In the actual experiments, the subject commonly "turns away" (sometimes literally) from the setup on the table to deal in thought with some relevant subset of the full matrix of possibilities inherent in the problem and then "turns back" to the actualized situation at hand, which is in that sense treated as "merely the interesting special case at hand."

The fundamental theoretical "building blocks" of the formal stage are the Combinatorial System (sometimes also called the Structured Whole) and the INRC Group of Operations. They are conceptualized as the theoretical foundations of the formal stage, analogous to the Logic of Class and the Logic of Relations for the concrete stage.

The *Combinatorial System* refers to the complete and ordered (organized) matrix of all possible combinations of all possible values of all possible variables inherent in a problem. It can be visualized as an n-dimensional matrix, like the girder framework of a building in three dimensions, with each intersection representing some particular combination of values of the variables. (The Combinatorial System is described here in terms of a *matrix,* which implies variables that take on discrete values. The model can be generalized to cover continuous variables, but for Piaget's purposes the discrete form is most appropriate since application here is primarily to propositions which have only two discrete values, true or false. In principle, one could extend the model to cover "probabilistic logic" with its continuously variable degree of "truth.")

The *INRC Group* is the set of four logical operations that together with the Combinatorial System constitutes the theoretical foundations of the formal stage. The four operations are Identity, Negation, Reciprocity, and Correlativity, each represented by its initial in INRC. They are the operations by means of which one "gets around" within the Combinatorial Matrix, transforming one combination into another and grouping combinations into logically significant groupings. They are a "complete set" (in mathematical terms a Kleinian Viergruppe); i.e., they are all the operators necessary and sufficient to do the job. They have the special relation of "going with" the Combinatorial System, like the relation that the four arithmetical operations (addition, subtraction, multiplication, division) have with the complete system represented by all the arithmetical numbers. They "go together."

The INRC Group can be rigorously defined in terms of mathematical logic, but will be defined here in terms of a concrete example; what is lost in rigor hopefully will be more than made up for in accessibility. *Identity* refers to some initial given operation. *Negation* is a simple direct undoing of that operation. *Reciprocity* is undoing the *effect* of the initial operation by changing some other variable in the system. *Correlativity* refers to negation of the reciprocal change, completing the set. As illustration, if putting weight onto one side of a previously balanced scale is the initial operation, then Negation would be directly removing that weight, Reciprocity would be either shifting the pan or adding weight on the other side to restore the balance, and Correlativity would be the operation undoing that reciprocal change thereby leading to the same effect as was created by the initial operation (with which it thus "correlates").

It should be emphasized that the essential new acquisition in the formal stage, in these terms, is the appearance for the first time, in the context of the INRC Group, of a fully developed form of Reciprocity in an integrated functional relation with Negation. Negation itself is well developed by the end of the concrete stage; well-developed Reciprocity working "easily and interchangeably" with Negation appears in the formal stage.

The Combinatorial System can be illustrated particularly well by utilizing an example which has special theoretical and practical importance: the 16-element matrix formed by two propositions and their negatives. This matrix is the prototype of the Combinatorial System because it is the smallest such matrix one can construct, having only two variables (propositions), each variable having only two values (true or false). Because so much of formal-stage reasoning is concerned with trying to relate just two variables ("all other things being held constant"), this 16-element matrix is also the particular Combinatorial System that recurs most frequently in Piaget's logical analysis of the interview data.

Let P and Q stand for two propositions (statements, hypotheses, assertions). Let $\bar{P}$ and $\bar{Q}$ stand for their negatives. In other words, P stands for "P is true" or "P is present," whereas $\bar{P}$ stands for "P is false" or "P is not present."

The whole Combinatorial Matrix, arrived at by forming all possible combinations of P, $\bar{P}$, Q, and $\bar{Q}$, would look like the following:

PQ   PQ   PQ   PQ

PQ and PQ   PQ and PQ   PQ and PQ   PQ and PQ   PQ and PQ   PQ and PQ

PQ and PQ and PQ   PQ and PQ and PQ   PQ and PQ and PQ   PQ and PQ and PQ

PQ and PQ and PQ and PQ

Zero

Expressing the same things in numbers, where 1, 2, 3, and 4 stand for the first four combinations, it looks like

$$\begin{array}{ccccccc}
 & 1 & 2 & 3 & 4 & & \\
12 & 13 & 14 & 23 & 24 & 34 & \\
 & 123 & 124 & 134 & 234 & & \\
 & & 1234 & & & & \\
 & & 0 & & & &
\end{array}$$

Each of the foregoing represents some particular logical relation between two hypotheses, each of which has a name as follows:

1. PQ — Conjunction
2. PQ — Nonimplication of Q by P
3. PQ — Nonimplication of P by Q
4. PQ — Conjunctive Negation
5. PQ and PQ — Affirmation of P
6. PQ and PQ — Affirmation of Q
7. PQ and PQ — Equivalence
8. PQ and PQ — Reciprocal Exclusion
9. PQ and PQ — Negation of Q
10. PQ and PQ — Negation of P
11. PQ and PQ and PQ — Dysjunction
12. PQ and PQ and PQ — Reciprocal Implication (Q implies P)
13. PQ and PQ and PQ — Implication (P implies Q)
14. PQ and PQ and PQ — Incompatibility (inverse of 1)
15. PQ and PQ and PQ and PQ — Complete Affirmation
16. 0 — Negation

Note that the four pairs given in the first line of the Combinatorial Matrix are routinely generated by subjects in the concrete stage. (For example, a concrete-stage child can routinely generate the four possibilities red long, red short, black long, black short from red or black "times" long or short.) But when dealing with hypotheses, the formal-stage subject goes *beyond* that to generate the *further* combinations, each of which has some logical significance and some potentially necessary role to play in thinking. Here we see illustrated quite explicitly in the matrix itself how the formal stage includes the concrete stage as a part of itself.

Let us look at some of the combinations more closely to illustrate the role they might play when the matrix is used as part of logical thinking: (a) The double combination PQ and PQ corresponds to equivalence or mutual implication. In other words, they go together or not at all. (b) The double combination formed by PQ and P̄Q corresponds to reciprocal exclusion. In other words, if one is true the other is false. If one is present the other is absent. (c) The triple combination of PQ and P̄Q and P̄Q̄ corresponds to the logical implication of Q by P. We can have both present, or neither present, or Q present for some other reason than P. But to say that P implies Q, there must be *no* instance of PQ̄. Where the concrete-stage subject might conclude that "P implies Q" from merely noting many cases of PQ, the formal-stage subject would have a sharp eye out for instances of PQ̄ and would require that there be instances of *everything except PQ̄*.

How does the formal-stage subject use the Combinatorial System and the INRC Group? By feeding data from an "experiment" into it and by reading logical conclusions and guidelines out of it. Combinations within the matrix are guided by the "incoming data" (which combinations do or do not occur in reality? which propositions are true and which are false?), and in turn the grouping guides the search for further data (which facts do I need to decide between these various hypotheses?). Not all of the potentially available matrix need be involved at any one time; only some parts of it may "light up" as relevant and needed. It is this process of working implicitly with combinations within the matrix that is conceptualized as the basis of formal thought.

Note that the Combinatorial System and INRC Group are not expected to be manifest and explicit in the interview material. They are inferred (induced) from the subject's capacity to seek for and to operate with those combinations which are necessary and sufficient to enable him to test hypotheses and to solve problems at the formal level. Thus, in general, they are conceptualized as latent rather than manifest, implicit rather than explicit.

As previously noted, in the concrete stage Actuality dominates while Possibility is limited to little more than re-evocation of previous actualities. In the formal stage, Possibility comes to the fore and Actuality becomes "just one of the many possibilities" all of which are generated by the thought process itself rather than from re-evocation of previous experience. Clearly that provides a cognitive base for the characteristic full flowering in adolescence of an intense commitment to systems of thought and especially to "those things which could be but are not." The valedictory address would be a classic example.

Proportionality is emphasized here because it is central to the Rings Experiment (Piaget and Inhelder, 1958, Chapter 13), which is one of those replicated here. The capacity to handle problems requiring an operational grasp of the concept of Proportionality makes its appearance in the formal stage. Piaget derives this from the INRC Group via the concept of "logical proportions."[1] For a less rigorous argument, note that the numerator and denominator in a ratio (i.e., a proportion) bear a *reciprocal* relation to one another (one can compensate for increase in one by increase in the other).

[1] J. Piaget and B. Inhelder, *The Growth of Logical Thinking from Childhood to Adolescence* (New York: Basic Books, 1958), p. 314.

Reciprocity is a characteristic acquisition of the formal stage. Note also that comparing two ratios (which is fundamental in using ratios for problem solving) amounts to setting up a relation between relations. Insofar as the concrete stage tends to be restricted to thinking about "things," one would expect that operations involving a "relation between relations" would have to await the formal stage.

Summary of the Distinctions Between Concrete- and Formal-Stage Function

The *concrete stage* roughly spans the years of latency, 7 to 11. Concrete thinking is restricted, by and large, to thought about things. The logical foundations of the concrete stage are the Logic of Class (in or out, a member or not a member of a given class) and the Logic of Relations (bigger or smaller, size place). Some central features of the concrete stage, which are treated as derivatives of the Logic of Class and Relations, are Seriation (the capacity to form ordered series) and Correspondence (the capacity to relate two ordered series by means of one to one correspondence). The latter can serve as a means for relating two variables ("the bigger it is, the heavier it is"), which is a precursor of more complex cause and effect relations. Multiple variables at this stage are characteristically handled by means of Logical Multiplication. For the particularly important example of two variables and their negatives, this gives only the four pairs PQ, PQ, PQ, PQ. The dominant form of reversibility at this stage is Negation. Quantitative operations are largely restricted to addition and subtraction.

The *formal stage* has its onset in early adolescence and is regarded as characteristic of the years from middle adolescence on through adulthood, being the "final equilibrium" in cognitive development as formulated by Piaget. The terms "abstract" or "propositional" are also used for the formal stage. Formal-stage thinking is not only about things, but it goes beyond that to be thought about thoughts, including words, ideas, concepts, hypotheses, and, particularly important from the logical point of view, propositions. In general, the formal stage bears a hierarchical relation to the concrete stage, subsuming concrete-stage function as a part of itself rather than simply replacing it. The logical foundations of the formal stage are the Combinatorial System (also referred to as the Structured Whole) and the INRC Group of Operations. The Combinatorial System is the matrix of all possible combinations of all possible values of all possible variables inherent in the problem. The INRC Group of Operations includes the two different forms of reversibility, Negation and Reciprocity, which are integrated for the first time into one system of logical operations. Negation has already been a characteristic of the concrete stage. The new acquisition is Reciprocity in an integrated working relation with Negation. Some central features of the formal stage which are regarded as derivatives of the Combinatorial System and the INRC Group are the capacity to operate with Proportions and access to the schema All Things Held Constant Except the Variable in Question. One also notes for the first time access to the classical operations of formal deductive and inductive logic (e.g., implication, exclusion, equiva-lence, dysjunction). Multiple variables at this stage are composed by means of the Combinatorial System. For the particularly important case of two variables and their negatives, this gives the matrix of 16 elements. That matrix includes as a part of itself the four pairs given by the concrete-stage opera-tion of Logical Multiplication. Each of the 16 combinations corresponds to some particular logical relation between the two variables (propositions) involved. Quantitative operations include multiplication and division, along with addition and subtraction. At another level of description, one notes a reversal of the relation between actuality and possibility. The full range of possibility inherent in a problem comes to the fore and is generated by the thought process itself, while actuality comes to be treated as "just one of the many possibilities."

THE EXPERIMENTS

The Choice of Experiments

The *Growth of Logical Thinking* reports a total of 15 experiments. Of those, the two experiments that were chosen for replication and further study were

1. The Rings Experiment: [2] This experiment seemed to have the advantage of being directly related to the concept of *Proportionality,* which is identified as an acquisition of the formal stage and as a direct derivative of the formal INRC operations.

2. The Liquids Experiment: [3] This experiment is directly related to the concept of the *Combinatorial System,* which, along with the INRC opera-tions, is fundamental to Piaget's conception of the formal stage.

Both experiments seemed free of technical difficulties with the apparatus, unlike some of the others.

The Rings Experiment

Piaget describes this experiment as follows: "Rings of varying diameters are placed between a light source and a screen. The size of their shadows is directly proportional to the diameters and inversely proportional to the distance between them and the light source. Specifically, we ask the subject to find two shadows which cover each other exactly, using two unequal sizes. To do so, he need only place the larger one further from the light, in pro-portion to its size, and there will be compensation between distances and diameters."

Of the relation between this particular experiment and the theory of the formal stage, he says: "the present research raises a question about the formal operational schema relative to proportionality. . . . the proportions we shall study in connection with the projection of shadows are of an essentially geometrical nature."

[2] Ibid., ch. 13: "The Projection of Shadows."
[3] Ibid., ch. 17: "The Combinations of Colored and Colorless Chemical Bodies."

The apparatus consists of a graded series of metal rings, each on a stalk. Piaget and Inhelder used rings 5, 10, 15, 20 cm in diameter. For this study, rings of 8, 13, 17 cm were *added* to make it possible to be more confident that a correct placement of the rings necessarily implied some operational grasp of the principle of Proportionality. It will be noted that the series used by Piaget and Inhelder (5, 10, 15, 20 cm) can be placed correctly on the basis of a simpler schema than the principle of Proportionality, i.e., simply by placing all the rings and the candle at *equal* spacings. Since that schema, which we have dubbed "Equal to or Twice," seemed so very common in our sample, and since so many subjects in the pilot studies seemed to achieve correct placement of the regular series by *that* means without showing any evidence in the interview that they had an operational grasp of the principle of Proportionality, it seemed advantageous to use odd-size rings. For correct placement of such rings, the lesser principle will not suffice. (In theory, one can always use the interview to tell whether correct placement was made on the basis of the principle of Proportionality, but it is not always easy to be sure. With odd-size rings, the correct placement speaks for itself.)

To begin the experiment, the interviewer shows one of the rings to the subject and says: "Here we have a candle, a screen, and a number of rings of different sizes. If we were to light the candle and put one of these rings somewhere here between the candle and the screen like this (setting the stalk upright into one of the holes), the candle would cast a shadow of the ring onto the screen. (If there appears to be any appreciable confusion here, the interviewer demonstrates or lets the subject experiment with one ring.) Now, the question I want to ask is this: If I give you these two rings, do you think you could place them in such a way that the shadow from *this one* (5 cm) and the shadow from *this one* (8 cm) would both be *exactly the same size* on the screen. I mean so that if we could put one shadow right on top of the other it would look as if there was just one shadow. I'd like you to try to figure it out before we light the candle, and then we'll light the candle and see if you've got it right. Please try to think out loud as much as possible because we're mostly interested in trying to find out how people think about these problems as they go along."

From there on, in keeping with "the clinical method," the interviewer is largely guided by the subject and the answer given. In general, the procedure was to encourage subjects to think out loud, to encourage them to proceed when they became discouraged, eventually to shift to the 5, 10, 15, 20 series if they couldn't manage at all with an odd-size ring in the group and then come back to the odd-size rings, and to change to other rings to be sure they had the principle correct if they got it with one pair of rings.

The Liquids Experiment

Piaget describes the rationale for including this experiment as follows: "One may wonder what would happen if we posed a problem that involved combinations directly . . . . The best technique with regard to this matter is to ask subjects to combine chemical substances among themselves." The experiment is intended to elicit quite directly the subject's capacity for generating a complete Combinatorial System.

The apparatus consists of five large bottles, each filled to the same level with fluids that all look like plain water. The bottles are distinguished only by the large numbers, 1 through 5, with which each is labeled. On the table are a number of empty glasses. The experimenter shows the subject a glass full of yellow-colored fluid (or actually prepares it while the subject is present but not looking) and says: "I made this colored fluid from the fluids in those bottles. I didn't use anything else. Do you think you could do the same thing? How would you go about trying?"

The correct combinations are 245 and 1245. Note especially that *no* mere pair will suffice.[4]

In the pilot studies, it was noted that the actual manipulation of the liquids was very time consuming, especially if there was spillage or if subjects lost track of what they had already done and had to retrace their steps. As a consequence, I tried a paper and pencil simulation of the experiment, and eventually converted to it altogether. The work reported here was all done with bottles, glasses, and liquids sketched on paper and the instructions "I used to bring in the actual bottles and glasses and liquids, but if you will just tell me what you would have done, I'll tell you what would have happened." The main advantage was to accelerate the procedure so that we could complete the interview in less than 45 min (the duration of a single school period, and near the upper limit of most subjects' capacity to attend with interest). With actual materials and a carefully nondirective approach, the interviews had frequently taken *considerably* longer.

The question arises about comparison between this "paper and pencil method" and the Piaget-Inhelder method using the actual materials. To be most scrupulous, one could identify this as a "different but related" method assessing the same underlying capacities. But I had the impression that for subjects at or near the formal level, it made virtually no difference, such subjects tending to plan it out in advance anyway. Often they would come up with virtually the same paper and pencil method on their own before I began using it regularly. For subjects who functioned closer to the concrete level, it may have focused their attention somewhat more on the "plan" aspect of the problem. However, that would have tended if anything to have improved their performance, and since my actual results tend if anything to be in the opposite direction (formal functioning *less* common in my subject groups than one might expect from the Piaget-Inhelder reports), I

---

[4] The bottles actually contain (1) plain water, (2) dilute sulfuric acid, (3) sodium thiosulfate solution, (4) hydrogen peroxide, (5) potassium iodine. The peroxide will oxidize the iodine in the presence of acid, releasing iodine, which colors the solution. Thus at least 245 are required. Adding 1 (water) makes no change; 3 excludes the color, the reducing agent functioning as a bleach. *Thus, of all the combinations possible with the five bottles, only 245 and 1245 will give the color reaction.* Any reasonable quantities will suffice, and subjects are so informed if they begin to become concerned about quantitative variations.

am inclined to conclude that there is little or no difference in final results between the two methods and that they are equivalent in the essentials which concern us here.

The main task for the interviewer here was simply to keep the subject motivated without "giving anything away." A half-dozen failures could easily lead to "I give up." Nonspecific encouragement usually sufficed.

It is crucially important to avoid communicating to the subject that he is missing some combinations by asking "Are you sure that's all?" more insistently about an incomplete list than about a complete list. It was evident, on replay of pilot tapes and while training an assistant, that this was an easy pitfall for the interviewer.

After a few questions, most subjects realized that combinations were involved and at least began some attempt at going through the possibilities. Only a few of the younger subjects seemed to think of the task as infinite. A few of the younger subjects became so absorbed in alternate ways of attempting to solve the problem (e.g., smelling the solutions, checking the level of fluids left in the bottles) as to require us to give broad hints that what we wanted them to do was to try to figure out the possible combinations.

The Subject Groups

1. Average Younger Adolescent Group: Age 14. Randomly selected from a large junior high school in a suburban community. Students who were doing failing work in science and math were excluded, to avoid subjects who might be regarded as particularly impaired.

2. Average Older Adolescent Group: Ages 16, 17. Randomly selected from a large high school in a suburban community. Science and math failures also excluded.

3. Gifted Older Adolescent Group: Ages 16, 17. Selected from a high school where the entire student population is highly selected for very superior academic aptitude and performance, especially in the sciences. (This special school draws from a very large metropolitan area. Only very superior students generally apply. There is a competitive entrance exam, and only a fraction of the applicants are accepted. The average IQ is reported to be in the 130 to 140 range.) Some of the early subjects in this group were randomly selected from within the school, but most of the subjects in our group were even more highly selected, being those students with the highest academic ratings in the senior class. The random group was small and the differences between the two subgroups were not great, so the two groups were combined for this report.

4. Average Adult Group: Ages ranged from 20 to 55. What was intended here was simply a "spot check" to test the expectation, based on results with the older adolescents, that it would not be difficult to find "normal adults" who fail to function at the fully formal level. Only a very rough criterion of "normal" was used; individuals were chosen who functioned well at some

"middle level" occupation and who seemed to be of average intelligence or better. The occupations and approximate ages were two secretaries (20, 25), two laboratory research assistants (25, 30), two businessmen (45, 55), two business administrators (30, 35), two housewives (45, 55), one school teacher (40), one plumber (45).

Data Collection and Scoring

While the interview was in progress, an assistant recorded the interview material on a sheet which listed an extensive set of criteria and relevant observables for each experiment, the criteria being drawn directly from the Piaget-Inhelder text. Immediately following the interview, this was reviewed by the interviewer, who then added a brief "ad lib" paragraph setting down immediate impressions, including highlights, idiosyncracies, and an immediate judgment as to cognitive level. Subsequently, these sheets were reviewed, particular points being checked against tape recordings which were made of each interview. Then all data for each subject were reviewed, and a final determination of cognitive level was made on the basis of the criteria given below.

The criterion for "full formal function" (Piaget's stage III) on the Rings Experiment was the capacity to place two rings properly (including at least one of the odd-size rings), to make some verbal statement equivalent to the proportionality principle, and to be able to show some understanding of the connection between the principle and the correct placement. We scored some few subjects IIIA (*almost* full formal function) who failed to get final correct placement but seemed on the verge of it (e.g., seeming to make some "careless mistake" in placement and never recouping it but making a correct statement of the Proportionality principle).

The criterion for "full formal function" (stage III) on the Liquids Experiment was the capacity to generate *all* the combinations by *any* systematic procedure. Duplications and going back to fill in were allowed. A few subjects seemed to have the idea but missed a few combinations (e.g., they might leave out one pair and one trio, seemingly "carelessly"). They were scored as IIIA (almost full formal function) if they missed no more than *one* combination in any group (pairs, trios, quartets).

The Major Findings Summarized

1. No subject in the youngest (14-year-old) group functioned at the fully formal level on *both* problems (Tables 1 and 2). (In the Liquids Experiment, 2 out of 21 subjects did function at the fully formal level.)

2. The most representative figure for the average older adolescent and adult groups would appear to be something like *one-quarter to one-third functioning at the fully formal level* (Tables 1 and 2). (Note that these figures are themselves averages of the distinctly different results for boys and girls, for which see Table 4 and item 5 below.)

Table 1 *Summary of Data*

		Rings Experiment		Liquids Experiment	
		FORMAL LEVEL	NOT FORMAL LEVEL	FORMAL LEVEL	NOT FORMAL LEVEL
Average younger adolescent (N = 21)	Boys	0	10	0	10
	Girls	0	11	2	9
		—	—	—	—
	Total	0	21	2	19
Average older adolescent (N = 40, rings; N = 36, liquids)	Boys	11	8	4	13
	Girls	3	18	2	17
		—	—	—	—
	Total	14	26	6	30
Gifted older adolescent (N = 23, rings; N = 21, liquids)	Boys	12	5	12	4
	Girls	1	5	1	4
		—	—	—	—
	Total	13	10	13	8
Average adult (N = 12)	Men	3	3	2	4
	Women	1	5	1	5
		—	—	—	—
	Total	4	8	3	9

Table 2 *Percentage of Subjects Who Functioned at the Fully Formal Level* [a]

	Rings Experiment	Liquids Experiment
Average younger adolescent	0%	10%
Average older adolescent	35%	17%
Gifted older adolescent	57%	62%
Average adult	33%	25%

[a] Percentages in this table are based on numbers from Table 1.

3. Roughly 60% of the gifted group functioned at the fully formal level. For boys in the group, the percentage of fully formal was 75%, the highest percentage in these study groups.

4. Note that including the "almost formal" subjects with fully formal subjects (in Piagetian terminology: including IIIA with III) leads to no significant change in the broad outline of the results, there being only a modest rise of only some of the percentages (Table 3).

Table 3   *Percentages of Formal Level Obtained Using "Relaxed Criteria"*

	Rings Experiment		Liquids Experiment	
	STANDARD CRITERIA	RELAXED CRITERIA	STANDARD CRITERIA	RELAXED CRITERIA
Average younger adolescent	0	0	10	19
Average older adolescent	35	50	17	28
Gifted older adolescent	57	65	62	62
Adult	33	33	25	25

5. Boys functioned at the fully formal level significantly more frequently than did girls (Table 4). For the three older groups (where the numbers seem large enough to support the generalization), the percentages for boys were from two to four times as great as those for girls.

6. On the Liquids Experiment, it was most unusual for a subject to go on spontaneously once he had hit upon a successful combination (i.e., once he

Table 4   *Percentages of Fully Formal Level, Boys and Girls Compared*

	Rings Experiment			Liquids Experiment		
	BOYS	GIRLS	RATIO	BOYS	GIRLS	RATIO
Average younger adolescent	0	0	–	0	18	–
Average older adolescent	58	14	4	23	10	2
Gifted older adolescent	71	17	4	75	20	4
Adult	50	17	3	33	17	2

had hit 245, which is usually achieved before 1245). That runs somewhat counter to the claim made by Piaget that the formal-stage subject is "not satisfied with a single solution to the problem, does not stop there but looks for others," in a search through *all* the possible combinations. In this study, subjects almost always stopped when they hit on a correct combination and gave every indication that they felt that they were "through." We found it necessary, after a while, to wonder aloud whether there might not be "any other possibilities," after which they usually started up again and generated all the additional combinations they could think of.

7. On the Rings Experiment, we noted the schema we dubbed "Equal to or Twice," which refers to the subject's almost automatic readiness to try a distance which is equal to (or, next best, twice as great as) some other distance which "looks important." The most common example occurred when subjects had to place a third ring after two rings were already correctly placed. The single most common response at that point in the experiment was to try the same spacing again (without regard to the size of the rings) and if that didn't work to say "Maybe twice as far?" Other forms occurred of a similar "pull" toward thinking in terms of distances that are "equal or twice" some prominent or presumably significant distance. The schema seems of importance because (a) it is so common, (b) it seems intermediate between concrete (addition) and formal (the simplest ratio: two to one), (c) it seems to serve as a steppingstone from concrete to formal for some subjects, (d) it is neither specifically identified nor discussed by Piaget and Inhelder in this context (although one *could* relate it to their more general concept of "absolute distances"), (e) it may contribute to an apparent difference in results between the Geneva study and this one, since subjects *can* correctly place the regular series of rings used in the Piaget-Inhelder study on the basis of this simpler principle *without* really being in the formal stage.

CONCLUSIONS AND DISCUSSIONS

1. Fully developed formal-stage thinking seems to be far from commonplace or routine among normal adolescents and adults. Using the definitions and criteria for the formal stage as given by Piaget and Inhelder in *The Growth of Logical Thinking*, the publication in which they first define and describe the formal stage within the context of their systematic conception of the development of intelligence, we find formal-stage thinking to be fully developed in only a modest proportion of the population and only very partially developed in most. In our group of average older adolescents, only 20 to 35% functioned at a fully formal level. The same modest percentages applied to our "spot check" of a small group of average adults.

To get consistently higher percentages, it is necessary to turn to increasingly select groups. The highest percentage in this study was 75% functioning at the fully formal level in a group of scientifically gifted older adolescent boys. (To get higher percentages would require either even more highly select groups or criteria *appreciably* relaxed *below* the standards implied by the Piaget-Inhelder definition of the stage.)

2. In this respect, the formal stage appears to differ appreciably and significantly from the earlier Piagetian stages. Full development appears to be very much the rule at the earlier stages, but it appears to be the exception at this stage. Failure to develop fully at the earlier stages seems highly correlated with major psychopathology or with major cultural difference.[5] Not so for the formal stage, where failure to develop fully appears commonplace among normal adolescents and adults.

3. These results appear to be in conflict with the Piaget-Inhelder publications on the formal stage. Their report leaves the firm impression that formal-stage thinking is the rule in adolescence, since all adolescent protocols included in their report are at the fully formal level and because throughout the book they link "formal stage" with "adolescence." However, a closer look reveals that the difference is more appearance than reality. Nowhere in their book do they make any *explicit* claim that *all* (or even most) adolescents actually do function at the fully formal level, nor do they make any explicit claim that they are reporting *all* cases tested. Personal communication with Dr. Inhelder confirms that *indeed not all cases were reported*. Their orientation was to describe and to formulate for the first time the characteristics of the formal stage. There was no intention to speak to the question of "frequency" or "incidence." Protocols were used simply as illustrations. Adolescents who failed to function at the formal stage were simply not reported. Thus there is no real conflict between the results of this study and the essentials of their basic contribution.

However, their presentation *is* seriously misleading on the matter of "frequency," which may be of peripheral concern within the context of genetic epistemology but is of central import in other contexts, such as in clinical work or in educational psychology. Their presentation *leaves the impression* that full formal-stage thinking is the rule in adolescence. This study shows that it is not.[6]

4. This study makes fully developed formal-stage thinking appear to stand somewhere between the more nearly universal developmental acquisitions (walking, talking, the early Piagetian stages) and the relatively rare special "talents" (highly developed musical, mathematical, graphic, mechanical capacities). It seems neither so common as the former nor so exceptional as the latter, but somewhere in between.

---

[5] J. Bruner, *Studies in Cognitive Growth* (New York: Wiley, 1966), chs. 11, 12, and 13.

[6] Before having the information noted above, that not all cases are reported in the Piaget-Inhelder book, it occurred to me and others that the apparent disparity of results might represent a cross-cultural difference. That interpretation seemed from the outset highly unlikely, since it seemed hard to believe (chauvinism aside) that an *unselected* Swiss group would function at *100%* and a *highly select* American group (scientifically gifted, intellectually oriented, the best from a large metropolitan area) would function at *75% or less*. But with the information that not all cases are reported we have neither the need nor support for any cross-cultural hypotheses.

5. Since formal-stage functioning does *not* appear to be commonplace among normal adolescents, formal-stage thinking is not "characteristic" or "typical" of adolescence in all senses. Adolescence does indeed seem to be the *characteristic age of onset.* Latent formal patterns *may* even impart a characteristic "formal flavor" to adolescent thought in some cases despite the fact that adolescents may lack access to formal patterns adequate to the task of problem solving. But formal-stage thinking does *not* appear to be "characteristic" of adolescence in the sense of being routine, expected, or highly likely. By contrast, the earlier Piagetian stages *are* characteristic or typical at their age ranges in *all* the usual senses of those words. Thus for adolescents the formal stage is more of a *characteristic potentiality* only sometimes becoming an actuality: an intriguing echo of a central feature of the stage itself.

6. The data suggest an overall formulation something like the following: Up through early adolescence, it appears that the development of intelligence can be characterized fairly well as a sequence of stages—sensorimotor, egocentric, concrete—through which virtually every child passes. The model would be that of a single path. Everyone in the "normal population" goes down that path, with only some modest variations in pace and emphasis. Although that model may exclude some refinements, as a first approximation it seems to serve very well to cover the facts.

But from early adolescence onward, that kind of a model will no longer serve at all, *even as a first approximation.* From that age onward, there is no longer any single path down which nearly everyone goes. Even to begin to cover the facts, one must introduce into the model at least some such concept as "dropout rate" or "branching into parallel tracks." One main track would be the formal stage, but only some modest proportion of the normal population would proceed down that royal road to full formal function. Other tracks would represent the development of alternative patterns of thought, those alternative patterns (see below) involving only partial or minimal development of the capacity for formal-stage thought as defined by Piaget.

Such a formulation would be consistent with other work in the study of intelligence (intelligence testing) which shows that a single measure of general intelligence (IQ, G factor) is most serviceable through childhood because in that age range the intercorrelation among the various subtests is high. But by adolescence that *single* measure of intelligence becomes increasingly and seriously inadequate because of decreasing intercorrelation among the various subtests. In other words, there is increasing "specialization" or "branching," with some components of functioning intelligence developing rather independently of others. Full formal-stage functioning can be viewed as one of those components, albeit a centrally significant one.

To treat formal-stage functioning as one among alternatives is not to put it on a par with the alternatives. It seems clear that the formal stage is a natural, logical, and "optimal" extension of the earlier cognitive stages to the next higher and most general logical level. Piaget even more strongly gives the formal stage a very special status, identifying it as the "final equilibrium" beyond which there is no other. The essence of Piaget's exposition on this point is that the logical character of the formal stage, *as theoretically defined,* is complete and general (those words being rather specifically defined within the context of mathematical logic) in such a way as to make it the "highest stage" by definition. I have the impression that his analysis does not do justice to meaningful variations *within* the formal stage as it occurs "in nature," all of which are treated together within one overarching definition of the formal stage as a *ne plus ultra.* While the Piagetian formulation may indeed point to a meaningful quasimathematical *theoretical reality,* it gives too little attention to variations *within* the formal stage as a *functioning psychological reality* (let alone to the fact that *most* people don't even seem to make it fully into that stage at all).

7. As for the alternative "tracks" associated with partial or minimal development of the capacity for formal-stage thinking, I think we saw two of them in our study: (a) Among the groups from the high school for academically superior students, it was common to find subjects who failed to function at a fully formal level but who tried instead to match the problem at hand to some repertoire of "standard problems with their standard solutions." We called them "standard method" types. On a scale of cognitive development, clearly such an approach is inferior to fully developed formal-stage thought. It lacks the power of formal-stage thought for the solution of *new* problems. But from an adaptive point of view such a method of problem solving may serve quite well in "everyday life" if the repertoire of standard methods is at all adequate to the range of problems encountered and if there is adequate "skill" in matching the problems with the methods. Judging from the fact that many of these students ranked at the top of their class in a difficult and selective school, it seems to have served them well enough, judged by that standard in that particular "average expectable environment." (b) Less frequent, and occurring more commonly among subjects in our "average high school," we saw individuals whom we dubbed as "inspirational." They would leap at a solution, or, to put it differently, answers just seemed to leap into their minds. Usually they could say very little by way of explanation. Sometimes they were right. (If so, we scored them as formal, since the Piagetian criteria do not require awareness of the underlying formal mechanisms.) But more commonly they were only right in part and were unable to come up with an adequate solution to the problem. These seemed to be young people who had career ambitions in the arts or letters, who had occasional and partial access to their capacity for formal thought in "inspirational leaps," but who tended to be relatively less successful than the "standard method" subjects at this kind of problem solving, judging from their school performance and their performance in this study. They were probably cultivating other aspects of themselves.

These two types fit nicely with the formulations of Liam Hudson [7] in

[7] L. Hudson, *Contrary Imaginations* (New York: Schocken Books, 1966).

his book *Contrary Imaginations.* Hudson identifies two rather different cognitive styles among bright adolescents which he labels "convergent" (focusing down on one right answer) and "divergent" (freely generating a rich variety of answers). Our standard method type adolescents do seem aptly identified as convergers and our inspirational types as divergers. Using that terminology, optimal formal-stage function might be identified with some optimal balance ("equilibrium") between divergence and convergence, especially since Piaget quite explicitly identifies the Combinatorial Matrix as having the virtue of being the framework within which one can *both* focus down on one crucial combination and/or freely generate all possible relevant combinations. The subjects in our study who did function at the fully formal stage, however, did, in their handling of the problems, seem to manifest a more convergent style (like those only partially formal subjects we dubbed the "standard method" types). They may have been influenced in that direction by the nature of the problems, which tend to call for "a right answer." Or it may well be that the concept of the formal stage itself is much more appropriate and useful as a model for convergent styles of thought, as compared with divergent styles to which it may apply technically but without being a good model for capturing "naturally" crucial features of that style.

8. It seems reasonable to speculate that one reason for the relatively modest incidence of fully developed formal-stage functioning in the normal population, especially by comparison with the earlier stages, is that there is less of a "demand" for it. It is probably correct that the "average expectable environment" for most normal individuals does not make much demand for full formal function. By contrast, the "demand" for concrete-level functioning (conservation of number, conservation of mass and volume, serial ordering, correspondence) is very considerable in modern society, even in "everyday life." Piagetian studies of primitive or agrarian societies have shown that in such societies even adults may not function at the concrete level,[8] (see Bruner, 1966), which would tend to support speculation about some connection between the "demand function" of the society and the degree to which the potential for each stage is actualized. One would draw a parallel here to the "emergence" of childhood as a stage of life in medieval times [9] and to the emergence of "adolescence" and "youth" [10] as increasingly well-defined developmental stages in more "advanced" industrialized affluent societies. The nearly universal "emergence" of the concrete stage in societies like our own and the *still only partial* emergence of the formal stage is a parallel phenomenon on the cognitive level.

9. The markedly greater percentage of boys in our fully formal samples is noteworthy, but this study throws no light whatsoever on reasons for the difference; therefore, beyond recording the fact, it seems appropriate to add nothing but that the finding is consistent with a similar sex difference noted

[8] Bruner, op. cit.
[9] P. Aries, *Centuries of Childhood* (New York: Vintage Books, 1965).
[10] K. Keniston, "A New Stage of Life," *American Scholar,* XXXIX (1970), 631–654.

in virtually all studies of abstract thinking (particularly on mathematical and "scientific" forms) in adolescence. If one accepts the finding (and it seems solid enough), then clearly the next questions are what are the complex interactions here of nature and nurture, of biological givens, of culture-based child-rearing practices, of educational practices, and of psychosexual developmental patterns and influences? On those questions this study throws no light whatsoever.

10. In summary, then, fully developed formal-stage thinking appears to be a kind of "cognitive maturity." It integrates all that has gone before. It is far from being commonplace among adolescents or adults. In that sense, it is more ideal than typical, more potential than actual. It has important quantitative aspects, varying degrees of access for a given individual being common and partial degrees of access being more common in the normal population than either full or zero access. Like most other aspects of psychological maturity, it is a potentiality only partially attained by most and fully attained only by some.

ACKNOWLEDGMENTS

The author wishes to thank Dr. S. Escalona and Professors Piaget and Inhelder for their help and support.

William R. Looft

Egocentrism and Social Interaction in Adolescence

Cognitive structures particular to given levels of development appear to be related to affective experiences. Each adolescent's effort to attain conceptual bases for social interaction apparently also generates forms of egocentrism, which are "negative by-products." Egocentrism produces at each achieved level of thought "a new set of unrealistic, nonobjective representations of the world." In his provocative discussion Looft reveals the characteristics of egocentrism that must be resolved in adolescence before cognitive growth can continue toward formal operational thought.

FROM *Adolescence*, VI (1971), pp. 485–494. Reprinted by permission of the author and the publisher.

He illustrates how "decentering" serves as a corrective mechanism which enables adolescents to achieve sophisticated levels of objectivity, and he suggests that participation in social interaction and productive work hasten the dissolution of egocentrism.

Instructional Objectives
To describe egocentrism as a facet of cognitive development.
To define decentering, a corrective mechanism in egocentric thinking.
To discuss the characteristic forms of adolescent egocentrism.
To discuss social interaction and productive work as major elements of decentering.

EGOCENTRISM has been a central concept in cognitive developmental psychology. In this sense the term does not pertain to selfishness or to an overly keen regard of oneself or even to the frequent use of "I" and "me." The essential meaning of egocentrism is an embeddedness in one's own point of view.

Piaget[1] has placed fundamental emphasis on the egocentrism concept in his theory of intellectual development. In the early stages of ontogenesis, egocentrism characterizes the child's functioning in virtually all spheres of activity. Piaget's voluminous writings contain many discussions of various kinds of functioning which reveal the effects of this pervasive egocentric cast of mind, including the child's primitive conceptions of the physical world (artificialism, animism), representations of objects and space, attitudes about moral-ethical problems, speech, and interpersonal activities which require role-taking ability. Each of the major stages of cognitive development that Piaget has so exhaustively investigated and described possesses its own characteristic form of egocentrism. The infant's activities are characterized by a radical egocentrism—a complete lack of differentiation between himself and his actions and the characteristics of the given situation. The "preoperational" child (2 to 7 years) displays a new form of egocentricity primarily through his speech, for he seems to assume that words carry much more information than they actually do. Thus there exists a lack of differentiation between the child's own viewpoint and those of other persons. The school-age child displays a third form of egocentrism, which is manifested in his inability to differentiate accurately between mental products (resulting from his newly acquired forms of thought) and perceptual givens. When the school child constructs a hypothesis, he naturally assumes this is a product imposed by the external data rather than the result of his own thought. If he is challenged, typically the child will reinterpret that data to be congruent

[1] J. Piaget, *The Psychology of Intelligence* (New York: Harcourt, Brace, 1950); B. Inhelder and J. Piaget, *The Growth of Logical Thinking from Childhood to Adolescence* (New York: Basic Books, 1958).

with his hypothesis, rather than change his initial stance. This transition from one stage of egocentrism to another takes place in a dialectic fashion in that the cognitive structures that free the child from a lower form of egocentrism are the same structures that entangle him in a higher egocentric form. The particular form of egocentrism thus is a negative by-product of any emergent mental system, for it produces a new set of unrealistic, non-objective representations of the world at each newly achieved level of thought.

The principal mechanism that enables the individual to overcome these early forms of egocentrism is the developmental process of *decentering*. This is a corrective process by which attention can be shifted to several aspects of a stimulus array or event; thus initial systematic errors and others arising can be corrected, and reformulation of the previous point of view can take place. Essential to the development of decentering skill is the child's involvement in his social world. In addition to the effects of the maturation of biologically programmed "structures," the child gains cognitive facility because the nature of his interactions with other people also changes. Specifically, it appears that the crucial factor in overcoming childhood egocentrism, particularly after age seven or eight, is the appearance of dissonant information in verbal exchanges with persons around him. In the course of his interactions with children and adults, the child increasingly finds himself forced to reexamine his own percepts and concepts in light of those held by others. Piaget [2] expressed this point most clearly:

> When then gives rise to the need for vertification? Surely it must be the shock of our thought coming into contact with that of others, which produces doubt and the desire to prove. . . . The social need to share the thought of others and to communicate our own with success is at the root of our need for verification. Proof is the outcome of argument. . . . Logical reasoning is an argument which we have with ourselves, and which reproduces internally the features of a real argument.

To summarize, cognitive developmental theory holds that development consists of the passage from an initial state of total egocentricity to a subsequent state of objectivity, or at least the capacity for objective, decentered thought. The individual progressively develops the ability to differentiate among several aspects of an event and between his own and other persons' points of view. Eventually he is able to reflect upon these differences and integrate his reflections into a personal "theory" of the relationship of himself to other things and people in a given event.

THE EGOCENTRIC ADOLESCENT

Adolescence in cognitive developmental theory is marked by the acquisition of formal operational thought. This mode of thinking is characterized by two

---

[2] J. Piaget, *Judgment and Reasoning in the Child* (New York: Harcourt, Brace, 1928), p. 204.

major abilities, which are (a) the ability to think about one's own thinking, and (b) the ability to recognize possibilities as well as actualities. Yet these same higher forms of thought, which were instrumental in eliminating the egocentricity of concrete operational thought, now immerse the individual in new forms of egocentricity. Previous discussions and investigations of the egocentrism phenomenon have been primarily limited to the childhood years. However, Elkind [3] has more recently developed extensive theoretical formulations concerning the nature of egocentric manifestations in adolescence. The remainder of this paper will review these concepts and suggest additional possible considerations related to this issue. (The present author has also extended the egocentrism notion to account for certain behaviors in adulthood and senescence.[4])

Parallel to his ability to conceptualize his own thought, the adolescent now also has the ability to conceptualize the thought of others. According to Elkind,[5] "It is this capacity to take account of other people's thought, however, which is the crux of adolescent egocentrism." Thus, in this theoretical framework, the adolescent fails to differentiate between the events to which his own thought is directed and those about which others are concerned. Certainly the rapid physical and physiological changes occurring within him contribute to his self concern. Psychoanalytically oriented writers have long noted the resurgence of narcissism and self-absorption in the early adolescent period.[6] Furthermore, the adolescent assumes that others are as obsessed with his outward appearance and behavior as he is himself. As opposed to the child's inability to take the other person's point of view, the adolescent "takes the other person's point of view to an extreme degree."[7]

Using the notion of adolescent egocentrism as a conceptual framework, it seems possible to account for many well-documented characteristics of youth in Western cultures. These would include attention-attracting behaviors, the influence of peers, short-lived romantic affairs, and other impermanent interpersonal relations. Elkind [8] has suggested that friendships during this period take on an exploitative nature, for they often appear to be founded on an egocentric need for self-definition and self-interest rather than on a basis of mutuality of concerns and interests.

Adolescent egocentrism assumes two characteristic forms, according to Elkind.[9] The adolescent's *imaginary audience* accounts for his self-consciousness. This is a mental construction based upon the notion that other people are as admiring or critical of him as he is himself. Thus, because he believes

[3] D. Elkind, "Egocentrism in Adolescence," *Child Development*, XXXVIII (1967), 1025–1034.

[4] W. R. Looft, "Egocentrism and Social Interaction Across the Life Span," *Psychological Bulletin*, 1972.

[5] Elkind, op. cit., p. 1029.

[6] P. Blos, *On Adolescence: A Psychoanalytic Interpretation* (New York: The Free Press, 1962); H. S. Sullivan, *The Interpersonal Theory of Psychiatry* (New York: Norton, 1953).

[7] D. Elkind, "Adolescent Cognitive Development," in J. F. Adams, ed., *Understanding Adolescence* (Boston: Allyn and Bacon, 1968), p. 153.

[8] Ibid., pp. 128–158.

[9] Elkind, "Egocentrism in Adolescence," op. cit.

himself to be the focus of attention, the adolescent operates on a stage on which he is the principal actor and all the world is the audience. This audience is "imaginary" because, of course, in actual social situations this is seldom the case. The second form of adolescent egocentrism is the *personal fable*, which is complimentary to the imaginary audience and stems from the adolescent's belief in the uniqueness of his own experiences. "Perhaps because he believes he is of importance to so many people, the imaginary audience, he comes to regard himself, and particularly his feelings, as something special and unique." [10] Elkind has suggested that the belief held by many adolescent girls that unwanted pregnancies happen only to other girls, but could never happen to themselves, is a representative manifestation of the personal-fable notion. Many other examples can be found with the analysis of adolescent autobiographies and diaries. To date these two constructs apparently have not been operationally defined or tested. However, they appear to represent a fruitful area for research. It seems possible that marked differences may exist in the nature of personal fables held by adolescents of different socioeconomic classes, in light of existing evidence indicating differences in aspiration level and other values held by these and other subcultural groups.

These forms of egocentrism do not, in the main, characterize adult thought, which suggests that some mechanism operates to dispel them in later adolescence. In this theoretical framework, it would appear that formal operational thought itself, in conjunction with the individual's interaction in a social world, leads to the dissolution of the adolescent's egocentrism. When the adolescent thinks about his own thoughts, almost as if these thoughts were objects, he becomes able to recognize the difference between his own preoccupations and concerns and the concerns of other people. Social interaction plays a major role in this process. According to Piaget,[11]

> Adolescent social interaction . . . is aimed primarily at discussion. Whether in twosomes or in small coteries, the world is reconstructed in common, and the adolescent loses himself in endless discussion as a means of combating the real world."

Therefore, as the adolescent discusses his personal "theory" with friends, he begins to recognize the weaknesses inherent in it, particularly as he encounters other adolescents with personal theories quite different from his own. He comes to realize that others are more concerned with themselves and their own problems than they are with him and his problems. In this way the adolescent's imaginary audience is gradually dispelled. Elkind [12] has proposed that one's personal fable is overcome by the eventual establishment of intimate relations with another person or persons, thereby effecting

10 Ibid., p. 1031.
11 J. Piaget, *Six Psychological Studies* (New York: Random House, 1967), p. 68.
12 Elkind, "Egocentrism in Adolescence," op. cit.

genuine rather than self-interested interpersonal relations. It seems entirely possible, however, that an individual may continue to entertain personal-fable notions in his fantasy life. That is, through the course of social inter-action the person not only discovers that his personal experiences are not necessarily unique, but he also learns that it is socially undesirable to express such notions of uniqueness to others. Thus, his personal fable may go "underground," but in an altered form; intellectually he now understands the fallacy of his theory of uniqueness, but affectively he continues to derive enjoyment from it in his imaginational life.

Decentering in adolescence is seen to be supported by one other major social factor, that of taking on an occupation.[13] This contention holds that productive work is the element that ultimately combines thought with action and which compels the individual to acquire a perspective more directed toward the future and less tied to the present. "In other words, the job leads thinking away from the dangers of formalism back into reality."[14] As a com-mentary on this aspect of adolescent development, it is well to recognize that socialization pressures, particularly in Western countries, which direct young persons into occupational pursuits and somewhat away from prin-cipally self-oriented concerns are the basic elements which give a society stability and a sense of continuity. However, these are the very pressures and assumptions that appear to be the focal point for attack by contemporary activist elements in the late-adolescent/young-adult population of these same societies. Ironically, Paul Goodman, the social critic and iconoclast who has assumed guru-like importance in the eyes of many young activists, seems to espouse a similar position regarding the importance of taking on a productive role in late adolescence. However, he does make an important distinction regarding the purpose of this activity. "It has been my Calvinistic and Aris-totelian experience that most people cannot organize their lives without productive activity. Of course, this does not necessarily mean paid activity."[15]

To summarize, adolescent egocentrism is thus seen to be overcome on two dimensions. Cognitively, this process occurs as a result of the eventual differentiation between one's own preoccupations and those of others. Affec-tively, this occurs as the individual gradually recognizes and integrates the feelings of others with his own feelings.

Little actual research has been conducted with adolescents that relates to this egocentrism/social-interaction framework. An exception is a study by Rockway[16] which investigated the development of the logical nature of interpersonal judgments in adolescent males. In a task which required sub-jects to predict the behavior of a person in a programmed case history, Rock-way noted an increase in the hypothetico-deductive quality of the boys'

[13] J. Langer, *Theories of Development* (New York: Holt, Rinehart and Winston, 1969).

[14] Inhelder and Piaget, op. cit., p. 346.

[15] H. H. Hart, ed., *Summerhill: For and Against* (New York: Hart, 1970), p. 217.

[16] A. M. Rockway, "Cognitive Factors in Adolescent Person Perception Development," *Developmental Psychology*, I (1969), 630.

social judgments and a decrease in egocentric self-focusing sets. Also discerned was a trend in twelfth graders toward another form of self-focusing judgments, which Rockway labelled "enlightened egocentrism." As opposed to the blanket assumption by younger adolescents that one's own reactions are necessarily relevant data, these older adolescents sometimes focused upon their own past reactions to predict another person's behavior where it appeared reasonable to assume that oneself and others were in some way alike.

It is well to recognize that a factor that may be operative in these researches with adolescents is that of a social desirability response set. When asked to make judgments on or to predict the behavior of another person, an individual who presumably cognizes in a formally operational manner may choose to provide responses that reflect more that person's judgment about the most socially acceptable behavior in that context rather than his truer feelings about the matter. In fact, the very concept of decentering, particularly that form manifested after the acquisition of formal operational thought, implies the corollary ability to recognize the distinction between generally acceptable values in social contexts and those values that an individual might privately hold. Conceivably this tendency to provide socially desirable responses could mask the effects that a researcher is looking for in his studies of egocentrism in subjects beyond childhood.

In closing, it appears that a strong case can be made regarding the influence of egocentrism in the lives of members of the human species, both individually and collectively. The cognitive developmental theorists have demonstrated that a major portion of the developmental energies within the individual is invested into the process of overcoming his egocentric reference system. Perhaps on the larger social scale it can be argued that egocentricity of thought—the illusions caused by the immediate point of view—has been the central problem in the history of human affairs.

Gary A. Davis

Care and Feeding of Creative Adolescents

Adolescents predisposed to react favorably to new and innovative ideas and to engage in imaginative behavior have acquired attitudes essential to creativity. In the following paper, Davis explains the characteristics of adolescent creativity and urges that adolescents be trained in creativity in

FROM Paper prepared especially for this volume.

order to approach their education, interpersonal relationships, and ultimately, their careers from broader, more flexible perspectives. Drawing from the extensive literature dealing with creativity, Davis describes the nature of creative ideas and discusses techniques teachers might employ in actualizing adolescents' creative potential.

Instructional Objectives
To define the characteristics of creativity.
To discuss the nature of creative ideas.
To illustrate techniques designed to assist in the production of new ideas and solutions—invention methods, brainstorming, and creative dramatics.
To note three guidelines for stimulating creativity in the classroom—creative tactics, active involvement, and creative atmosphere.

A FEW years ago, Abraham Maslow distinguished two forms of human creativity. The first, *Special Talent Creativeness*, belongs only to gifted artists, writers, composers, along with outstanding inventors and scientists, all of whom spend their professional lives producing brilliantly creative artifacts. Most probably, only a small fraction of our adolescent population will inherit large doses of special talent creativeness. The second variety of human creativity, however, is not so closely tied to genetically-fixed genius. *Self-Actualizing Creativeness* is the mentally-healthy tendency to be habitually openminded and flexible, to do whatever you do in a self-confident, unique, and creative fashion. Maslow described a poor, uneducated housewife who was ". . . a marvelous cook, mother, wife and homemaker. . . . I learned from her and others like her that a first-rate soup is more creative than a second-rate painting." And, "From a young athlete, I learned that a perfect tackle could be as aesthetic a product as a sonnet and could be approached in the same creative spirit." [1] Although the self-actualizing creative person is likely to live a fully functioning, well-adjusted and enthusiastic life, the special-talent genius need not be happy or emotionally stable. Van Gogh, Wagner, and Byron were Maslow's examples of neurotic genius.

Maslow's distinction between special talent and self-actualized creativity helps clarify the dual problems of understanding and increasing adolescent creative potential. Skeptics who claim creativity cannot be trained are mostly right in regard to special talent creativeness—no amount of educational wizardry will transform Arnold Average into Albert Einstein or Millie Mediocre into Marie Curie. But if we focus on a youth's self-actualizing creativeness, the prognosis is quite exciting. There is very, very much that can be done to guide the adolescent toward habits of thinking and behaving which will add to his self-actualized creative development.

[1] A. H. Maslow, "Creativity in Self-Actualizing People," in G. A. Davis and T. F. Warren, eds., *Psychology of Education: New Looks* (Lexington, Mass.: Heath and Co., 1964).

CREATIVITY AND ADOLESCENT IDENTITY

The significance of adolescence for molding the adult hardly needs documenting. It is these years during which the young person discovers his strengths and limitations, and he formulates the personal goals and philosophies which, all together, build his self-image. To a great degree the adolescent also takes a steering role in forging an acceptable identity: Does he wish to be well-liked? Does he wish to be perceived as a scholar? An athlete? An ethical and honest person? Does he wish to be "in"? Such semiconscious decisions both shape his behavior and firm-up his portrait of himself.

It is sad that one critical feature is usually missing from the adolescent's self-concept, namely his creativeness. Chances are good that the typical adolescent never even thinks about being creative. He probably never hears the word *creativity* except in a passing comment by an art, science, history, or English teacher on the creative accomplishments of a few gifted people.

I have no doubt that the adolescent is fully capable of understanding the nature of problem solving and creative thinking well enough to begin consciously thinking of himself as a more open and creative individual. Indeed, Piaget tells us that the final stage of intellectual growth begins at age eleven or twelve.[2] In this stage of *formal operations* the child can deal with abstract relationships much as can an older adult. My recommendation for increasing the creative potential of the adolescent then, is to make full use of this rational, adult-like mentality. We can teach him, on a verbal-intellectual basis, about the nature and significance of human creativeness; and more important, we can involve him first-hand in creative experiences.

More specifically, we can explain to the adolescent the role of creative ideas both in the history of civilization and in the student's personal life. Where would humanity be without discoveries and inventions in science and technology, in medicine, in the literary and graphic arts, and in law and government? What other spheres of civilization benefit from new ideas? Can new ideas ever damage the quality of life? We can illuminate the personality of the creative person—the attitudes, motivations, and thinking habits which lead him to be more flexible, original, and open to new ideas and experiences. Can these characteristics be learned? What is the role of education and training in preparing the creative business person, artists, or scientist? Can formal schooling stifle creative thinking? We can discuss the nature of ideas and where they come from. Is it possible to think of something totally new? Or are new ideas mainly combinations, modifications, and extensions of what the thinker already knows? Most critically, we must provide active experience in "being creative." Nothing is more critical for cultivating creative potential than practice in behaving creatively. My own experiences with sixth-,

---

[2] D. Tuddenham, "Jean Piaget and the World of the Child," in Davis and Warren, op. cit.

seventh-, and eighth-grade students show that, with training, many students do become more creativity conscious and more willing to respond in an original and flexible manner.[3]

The following sections sketch briefly a few ideas for increasing a youth's understanding and awareness of creative thinking, and for engaging him in creative activities. If an adolescent can grasp these concepts, and if he becomes personally involved in creating, it is very possible that he will consciously adopt a more creative identity, and a more self-actualized life style.

THE CREATIVE PERSON

The creative or self-actualized person necessarily must be a unique individual. Still, there exists a constellation of attitudes, values, interests, and motivations which regularly characterize the creative individual and, in fact, predisposes him to behave flexibly and creatively. All of these important traits can be meaningfully explained to adolescents.

The student can learn, for example, that a creative person is likely to be more independent and self-confident than the average. His confidence allows him to take risks and to make mistakes, as all innovators must. A particularly important characteristic of the creatively productive individual is his high level of energy and enthusiasm. This energy usually takes the form of strong curiosity, high need for novelty, and a keen attraction to new ventures. He will, in fact, score high on a test of *sensation seeking*, which asks if he would like to take up skiing, flying, mountain climbing, or parachute jumping, and asks if he enjoys flashy modern art, exploring new cities, and spending unplanned vacations tent-camping instead of at Holiday Inns.[4] The high energy level of the creative person also accounts for his tremendous involvement with and commitment to his work. He may become totally engrossed in seemingly trivial projects; or he may work intensely on a project for much of the night.

Directly relevant to the adolescent's understanding of creativity is the fact that the creative individual consciously considers himself unconventional and original in many aspects of his life—and of course, he is. By habit he will search for new ideas and creative problem solutions, and he will be open to the innovativeness of others.

[3] G. A. Davis, "Training Creativity in Adolescence: A Discussion of Strategy," in R. E. Grinder, ed., *Studies in Adolescence* II (New York: Macmillan, 1969), pp. 538–545; G. A. Davis, S. E. Houtman, T. F. Warren, and W. E. Roweton, "A Program for Training Creative Thinking: I. Preliminary Field Test," *Technical Report No. 104*, Wisconsin Research and Development Center for Cognitive Learning, University of Wisconsin, 1969.

[4] G. A. Davis, "Attitude and Personality Measures of Creative Potential," presented in a symposium entitled, "Psychological Processes in Creative Thinking and Problem Solving," American Educational Research Association, New Orleans, La., March 1973; G. A. Davis, J. M. Peterson, and F. H. Farley, "Attitudes, Motivation, Sensation Seeking, and Belief in ESP as Predictors of Real Creative Behavior," *Journal of Creative Behavior*, VIII (1974).

Also critical, the creative individual is able to maintain a child-like playfulness, which gives him considerable mental freedom in creating and exploring new possibilities. As Barron noted, "In the creative adult, the child remains fully alive."[5] The playfulness of the creative person accounts in part for his above-average sense of humor, if not keen wit.

The above traits create a person with noticeably different interests and spare-time activities. In fact, by the time the creative youth reaches college, he is likely to have accumulated a noteworthy history of creating. He may have been active in art, in writing, or in school science projects. Whether or not he is particularly adept at these, he probably can claim a variety of unusual hobbies and handicrafts, legitimate outlets for his creative drives.

Nature of Creative Ideas

Apart from class discussions of traits and habits of creative people, students can learn about the composition and source of creative ideas and about the process of creating. We naturally cannot explain the source of every creative inspiration. "Peanuts" cartoonist Charles Schultz, for example, claims that some ideas mysteriously come from "things that go bump in the night." But most creative ideas that the teacher or student can point to will be either (a) a combination of previously unrelated ideas, or (b) a modification of an existing idea or object. The printing press, for example, was invented by combining wooden printing blocks with a grape-squashing wine press. *Close-Up* toothpaste is a combination of toothpaste and mouthwash. *Phase III* soap is a combination of soap plus cleansing cream. The new shock-absorbing auto bumpers are combinations of, well, shock absorbers and auto bumpers. New clothing fashions invariably are modifications and combinations of existing patterns, materials, and styles. Even such a creative genius as the late Pablo Picasso produced ideas from recognizable sources—he borrowed African designs and he used a harlequin theme many times. Even his most abstract works involved mentally dismembering his subject, then reconstructing it in a different pattern. The source of painter Gaugin's ideas is quite straightforward, the Polynesian people and villages inspired virtually all of his paintings.

In music old tunes often are modified to create an innovative "new" melody. In the 1930s Chopin's Polonaise was reborn as "'Til the End of Time." An old melody entitled "Wild Horses" from my own 1940 piano lesson book was modified in the mid-1950s to become a hit tune with the same name. Beethoven's Ninth Symphony has appeared in at least three rock forms in the past 15 years. The Indian sitar music of Ravi Shankar became popular in the mid-1960s, and the Beatles soon began producing popular tunes with a distinct Middle-East flavor. In 1973 the symphonic music from the movie "2001" was given a rock beat and sold a million copies.

Jokes—or humor in general—also demonstrate combining and modifying

[5] F. Barron, *Creative Person and Creative Process* (New York: Holt, Rinehart, and Winston, 1969), p. 193.

in producing surprising new idea combinations. What weighs 50 tons, is green and swims? Moby Pickle, of course. Did you hear about the old-time comedian who was brought to trial? The judge threw the pie at him. Phyllis Diller claims to be only half interested in women's lib—she burned one cup. Is it true that teasing bears can be a grizzly experience? All jokes may be considered creative—they are surprising new combinations of ideas, or else they include an unexpected change in meaning.

One also may look at the process of creation. Usually, ideas for any problem solving or creative purpose are found by freely playing with problem elements—by pushing, twisting, extending or modifying until—aha!—something fits. Whether decorating a room, fixing a bicycle, writing a theme, or inventing a better mouse-trap, most creating takes place by the uniquely human ability to look at something familiar and imagine something original.

Many artists and other creators experience two distinct stages in creating. First is the sudden original inspiration, followed by a longer period of elaboration and refinement of the idea. The artist might discover (as one did) that old Sylvania flash cubes create an intriguing artistic effect. After this sudden discovery, the idea would be carefully developed to create a number of striking art pieces.

In problem solving the sudden "Aha!" experience sometimes occurs after an incubation period, during which the thinker mostly ignores the problem. As Edison noted, the solution might politely present itself and say, "Here I am." At other times, the problem is solved by sheer trial-and-error effort—different ideas and solutions are tested until the difficulty is resolved.

Invention Methods

Once the student is acquainted with the nature of a creative idea and the dynamics of creating, he can understand some techniques used in professional problem solving to produce new ideas and problem solutions. We must note, however, that these "forced" thinking procedures normally would be used to supplement one's "intuitive" idea finding. When the individual thinker hits a blank wall, then the deliberate thinking techniques may be used to produce still further ideas.

Some problem-solving techniques, which are taught in most professional problem-solving courses, are described in more detail elsewhere.[6] Briefly, the *attribute listing* (or *part-changing*) method of Crawford suggests that a product may be improved by listing important characteristics of that product, then thinking of ways to modify or improve each characteristic.[7] For example, one exercise in the workbook *Thinking Creatively* lists such attributes of

---

[6] G. A. Davis, *Psychology of Problem Solving: Theory and Practice* (New York: Basic Books, 1973); G. A. Davis and J. A. Scott, eds., *Training Creative Thinking* (New York: Holt, Rinehart, and Winston, 1971).

[7] R. P. Crawford, "Techniques of Creative Thinking," in Davis and Scott, op. cit., pp. 52–57.

breakfast cereals as size, shape, color, and flavor.[8] The student problem solver can invent countless new Munchies and Soggies by thinking of new flavors, new shapes and sizes, and new colors. He may even add a few new attributes to be modified—such as noise, soakability, or consumer age group. The attribute listing procedure is called the *substitution method* when used in design engineering. Last year's refrigerator may become immediately obsolete by listing and modifying such attributes as color or color pattern, capacity, arrangement of doors, shelf-design, materials, and so on. Anyone can use this method, even children, and the strategy may be applied to virtually any task needing new ideas.

The *checklist* procedure involves using a prepared idea list as a source of inspiration. Some lists suggest ideas directly, as when we use the Yellow Pages, a catalog, or a thesaurus to provide ideas for such problems as: Who can fix my English bicycle? What can I buy little Ignatius for his birthday? What is a synonym for *discuss?* One sixth-grade class studying *Thinking Creatively* used a library book as a checklist of ideas for decorating their classroom in an oriental mode. A teacher wanting ideas for stimulating creative thinking might consult one of Smith's books, which contain lists of suggestions for teaching creativity in language arts, creative arts, social sciences, math, and science.[9]

Other idea lists have been designed to stimulate ideas for many kinds of problems. The most well-known of these is Osborn's "73 Idea Spurring Questions." [10] For example:

What can we add or subtract?
Change meaning, color, motion, sound, shape?
Other material? Other process?
Interchange components?
Combine units? Combine purposes?
Does past offer a parallel?
Etc.

Such questions would suggest ideas for a wide variety of problems. My experience with Osborn-type lists in adult creativity workshops indicates that the checklist method is more suited to thoughtful individual thinking than to fast-moving group sessions. With five or ten active thinkers spewing forth new ideas and perspectives, members rarely needed to refer to their idea checklists for further suggestions.

[8] G. A. Davis and S. E. Houtman, "Thinking Creatively: A Guide to Training Imagination," Wisconsin Research and Development Center for Cognitive Learning, University of Wisconsin, 1968.
[9] J. A. Smith, *Setting Conditions for Creative Teaching in the Elementary School* (Boston, Mass.: Allyn and Bacon, 1966). Others in this series are entitled *Creative Teaching of the Language Arts (Reading and Literature; Creative Arts; Social Studies; Mathematics; Science) in the Elementary School*, also published by Allyn and Bacon.
[10] A. F. Osborn, *Applied Imagination* (New York: Charles Scribner's Sons, 1963); Davis, *Psychology of Problem Solving*, op. cit., Ch. 8.

The *synectic* methods emphasize analogical thinking, looking usually to natural biological systems for new ideas.[11] After posing a problem, teachers would encourage students to ask how animals, insects, or even plants have solved similar problems. Ideas for such a problem as "How can we conserve energy?" might be found by looking at animal conservation practices: animals store and consume only what is needed; they do not waste or destroy; they do not use dishwashers or two-ton automobiles; they make superb use of body heat; they have no need of neon signs or spot-lights on public buildings; and traveling is limited to necessary migrations. Synectics founder W. J. J. Gordon originally devised his analogical thinking procedures for use in invention design and in solving engineering problems. More recently, he and his colleagues at Synectics Education Systems have prepared idea-stimulating workbooks for the schools, still stressing empathetic and metaphorical thinking, for example, in science, social studies, language arts and vocation training.[12]

Brainstorming

One of the easiest and best methods for involving students of any age in creative thinking is classroom brainstorming. The main rule for brainstorming is the *deferred judgment* principle: do not evaluate or criticize, simply because these judicial functions interfere with the mind's creative functions. Alex Osborn, the originator of brainstorming, also recommends that ideas be wild, since it is easier to make a wild idea workable than to think of the novel viewpoint in the first place. Topics for brainstorming can be local problems of grounds sanitation, traffic safety, pollution, or flooding. Imaginary problems (What would happen if the sun never went down? If all rulers and leaders were women?); or problems related to the subject matter of a course (What would have happened if Germany had won World War II? How many different ways can we learn about history? What good is mathematics?). A courageous teacher who asks, "How can school be made more interesting or enjoyable?" will get some good answers. Brainstorming will provide a free creative atmosphere and will give students practice stretching their minds. Teachers, as well as professional brainstorm leaders, however, must insure that the thinking is not dominated by the few most outspoken group members.

Creative Dramatics

Another worthwhile experience is creative dramatics. Unlike children's theater, the point of creative dramatics is not to create actors. Rather, the

---

[11] W. J. J. Gordon, *Synectics* (New York: Harper and Row, 1961); T. Alexander, "Invention by the Madness Method," in Davis and Scott, op. cit., pp. 1–13; G. M. Prince, "The Operational Mechanisms of Synectics," in David and Scott, op. cit., pp. 30–42.

[12] W. J. J. Gordon, *The Metaphorical Way of Learning and Knowing* (Cambridge, Mass.: Porpoise Books, 1971); for lists of materials, write to Synectics Education Systems, 121 Brattle Street, Cambridge, Mass. 02138.

goal is to develop each individual as a more complete, whole person. For example, creative dramatics helps the student become more self-confident in speaking and moving in front of his peers. His sensory and body awareness is sharpened and his ability to empathize is strengthened. His imagination is stretched as he is asked to interpret roles and generate ideas. He also will come to feel more open, spontaneous, and especially happy.

There are several varieties of creative dramatics activities.[13] For example, with *movement exercises* students (any age) might walk like wooden soldiers, robots, or rag dolls, perhaps through fields of imaginary jello, flypaper, or peanut butter. Students themselves can invent giant people machines—a typewriter, an ice cream machine, a people machine that makes people— with each person play-acting a moving part, a noise, or both. For fostering *sensory awareness,* students might lie prone with eyes shut, listening to sounds that are near, then sounds that are far. Smaller groups, again with eyes shut, can pass around different scents, comparing memories stimulated by, e.g., a sniff of vanilla extract, Vicks Vaporub, or Evening in Paris. To encourage *empathy* and to experience feelings of trust and dependence, students may try the Blind Walk exercise, where a blindfolded person is led by a sighted partner—under tables, dashing a few steps, identifying objects and meeting people by touch.

If a creative dramatics class extends over a period of weeks the teacher no doubt would initiate *pantomime* and *playmaking,* both of which may take infinite forms. With pantomime, small groups might become the Three Stooges hanging wallpaper, holding up a bank, or building a birdhouse for vultures, or they might act out a more sober event, such as hiding slaves from Confederate searchers. For clowning or more serious pantomime, music usually helps the atmosphere. How could giants invade the school without *Hall of the Mountain King* in the background? In playmaking, teacher and students discuss details of a plot, practice movements and emotions, and always improvise their lines. The plot might be taken from history, mythology, or fictional literature, or the students can make up their own short plot.[14]

FINAL COMMENTS

A few years ago I suggested three guidelines for stimulating creativity in the classroom.[15] First, one must use *creative tactics*—imaginative methods and materials. Traditional methods are suited for imparting facts and concepts in science and history, or for teaching conceptual skills of reading and math. Different strategies are needed for strengthening flexibility, open-mindedness

[13] For an overview of creative dramatics, see G. A. Davis, "Let's Be an Ice Cream Machine," *Journal of Creative Behavior,* VII (1973), 37–48.

[14] For further direction on creative dramatics, especially pantomime and playmaking, see B. Way, *Development Through Drama* (London, England: Longman, 1967); G. B. Siks, *Children's Literature for Dramatization: An Anthology* (New York: Harper and Row, 1964).

[15] G. A. Davis, "Teaching for Creativity: Some Guiding Lights," *Journal of Research and Development in Education,* IV (No. 3, 1971), 29–34.

and other creative attitudes; for teaching conscious techniques for producing new idea combinations; and for reinforcing the use of the students' innate creative abilities. With creative tactics, the teacher or the training materials can serve as a model of what being creative is like. Second, *active involvement* in actually creating—learning by doing—is essential in teaching for creativity. The student must become actively engaged in finding solutions, trying ideas, stretching imaginations, and "feeling creative." Finally, the *creative atmosphere* is a necessary third component. Receptiveness and encouragement are as critical for classroom creativity as for professional problem-solving groups. Indeed, if the student does not feel free to create in art, science, writing, or classroom problem solving, he simply won't.

It is interesting that school administrators regularly list "stimulating problem solving and creative skills" as high priority educational goals. Yet when we lift the lid and look into the junior or senior high school we find that these skills are not being developed. At least not much more now than in decades past. It is possible, however, to heighten Maslow's self-actualized creativeness and to add the concept of *creative person* to a student's growing identity. Many methods and materials are available to aid the interested teacher. The *Journal of Creative Behavior* continually publishes articles pertaining to classroom creativity, along with lists of training materials, games, workbooks, courses, texts, films, and other resources.[16] Torrance, who has contributed greatly to creative education, has produced workbooks, the *Sounds and Images* imagination-prodding phonograph record, and several textbooks, most of which are engineered for animating adolescent imaginations.[17]

One new publisher, D.O.K., Inc., specializes in low cost creativity workbooks.[18] One of their programs, particularly dear to my heart, is the *Saturday Subway Ride*. Developed especially for adolescents, the *Saturday Subway Ride* is a highly creative piece of writing that illustrates creativity in action. The program emphasizes creative attitudes, creative thinking techniques (such as those previously described), and provides exercises to strengthen creative abilities. A few lines from the introduction will give the flavor of *Saturday Subway Ride:*

Let me tell you about last Saturday.
I took a ride on a new super subway that travels a fast circle from Kansas City to Pittsburgh to Dublin to Tokyo to Santa Monica and back.
What's wrong?

[16] *The Journal of Creative Behavior* is published by the Creative Education Foundation, 1300 Elmwood Avenue, Buffalo, New York 14222.
[17] R. E. Myers and E. P. Torrance, *Invitations to Speaking and Writing Creatively* (Boston, Mass.: Ginn and Co., 1965); R. E. Myers and E. P. Torrance, *Plots, Puzzles, and Ploys* (Boston, Mass.: Ginn and Co., 1966); B. F. Cunnington and E. P. Torrance, *Sounds and Images* (Boston, Mass.: Ginn and Co., 1965); E. P. Torrance, *Encouraging Creativity in the Classroom* (Dubuque, Iowa: W. C. Brown Co., 1970); E. P. Torrance and R. E. Myers, *Creative Learning and Teaching* (New York: Dodd, Mead, and Co., 1970).
[18] D. O. K. Publishers, 771 E. DeLavan Avenue, Buffalo, New York 14215.

You say there's no such subway, and you're about to close the book and stare out the window.

Well, maybe you're wrong. Maybe I zipped around the world on an underground thought, a daydream, a nightdream, or a superfastspecialfivecity idea.

You say my subway ride is just a wild idea and pretty silly.

Well, what about flying? People said that men flying around in machines was a wild idea and pretty silly. Then the Wright brothers took off and ZIP!

A wild idea is something that people find hard to accept because it's new and sounds strange and looks funny and maybe it's light green suede and smells of paprika. Anyway, it's something people haven't seen before, and that makes them afraid.

That's what this book is all about—learning to stretch your mind, learning to reach out for big, new, different, and even wild ideas.

Ideas are good anywhere, anytime, in any climate, and even underwater.

There remains a great need for creative awareness to be more systematically built into the identity of the adolescent. We have the means to stimulate Maslow's self-actualizing creativeness. The pressing need is for self-actualized teachers committed to adolescent creative development.

Index

R